NATURE CONSERVATION LAW
(THIRD EDITION)

NATURE CONSERVATION LAW

Third Edition

COLIN T. REID

Professor of Environmental Law
University of Dundee

W. GREEN

 THOMSON REUTERS

First edition   1994
Second edition   2002

Published in 2009 by
Thomson Reuters (Legal) Limited
(Registered in England and Wales,
Company No 1679046.
Registered office and address for service
100 Avenue Road, Swiss Cottage,
London, NW3 3PF) trading as W. Green

Typeset by YHT Ltd, London
Printed and bound in Great Britain by MPG Books Ltd, Bodmin, Cornwall

No natural forests were destroyed to make this product; only
farmed timber was used and re-planted.

A catalogue record for this title is available
from the British Library

ISBN 978-0-414-01695-8

Thomson Reuters and the Thomson Reuters logo are
trademarks of Thomson Reuters.

© 2009 Thomson Reuters (Legal) Limited

PREFACE

The aim, scope and structure of this book remain the same as in the previous editions, explained more fully in the Preface to the First Edition. Two key points made in that Preface must be re-emphasised. First, although the book is entitled *Nature Conservation Law*, no such sharply defined area of law exists. There is an increasing volume of law specifically dedicated to nature conservation, and this forms the core of the book, but many other areas of law will affect the survival of species and habitats and these too must be given some consideration.

Secondly, this is a book about *Nature Conservation Law*, not conservation policy or practice. It deals with the legal rules penalising certain conduct and establishing public authorities and their powers to intervene in the ways in which individuals treat wildlife and the land and waters that support it. Within the legal framework, it is the ways in which policies are shaped, powers are exercised and money spent that will decide how far-reaching and effective any conservation measures are in practice. Studying the law alone will give an incomplete, and indeed sometimes misleading, view of how nature conservation in Great Britain operates, especially since the law often gives wide discretion to authorities and individuals. Yet it is the law that sets the boundaries on what authorities are permitted or required to do and on what individuals can be forced to do or abstain from doing, so that an awareness of these limits is an essential part of any study and understanding of nature conservation in practice. This book tries to explain that legal framework, not to offer a complete guide to conservation theory, administration, policy or practice.

Since the Second Edition was completed in 2002, a lot has happened in terms of the law on conservation. From the reader's point of view perhaps the most notable developments are the substantial changes to the law needed to remedy the many failings in the implementation of the Habitats and Species Directive identified by the European Court of Justice in 2005 and the complete rewriting of much of the law in Scotland by the Nature Conservation (Scotland) Act 2004. That Act and related changes not only provided a wholly new scheme for Sites of Special Scientific Interest in Scotland but extended the protection given to much wildlife by punishing acts done recklessly as well as intentionally. The belated implementation of the provisions of the Environmental Liability Directive on "biodiversity damage" introduce a further new dimension to the law.

From the author's point of view the biggest change has been the deepening impact of devolution. At the time of the First Edition, the decision was taken to confine the book geographically to the law in Great Britain, i.e. Scotland, England and Wales. Despite some differences, largely in background matters such as local government, enough of the law in Scotland, England and Wales was the same or similar for these jurisdictions to be discussed together, whereas Northern Ireland had distinct legislation and administrative structures on most issues. Since then there has been increasing divergence within Great Britain. This affects the core elements of this book, most notably the substantially different changes made to what were once the common rules in the Wildlife and Countryside Act 1981 and the Conservation (Natural Habitats, etc.) Regulations 1994. Yet the impact is as great in the more peripheral matters discussed here, where there is often separate, if not always different, legislation and policy that has to be hunted down and checked with the aim of avoiding general statements that are misleading for any individual country. I hope that although my Scottish origins do show through occasionally I have accurately reflected the position throughout Great Britain, albeit at the price of making some passages more awkward to read. I apologise to my Northern Ireland friends for continuing to omit coverage of the law there, even though the extent to which different rules would have to be dealt with is now no greater than is the case for many matters within Great Britain.

One further comment must be made about the state of the legislation considered here. The 1981 Act and the 1994 Regulations are the central sources of the law, yet they are in a state that makes them incredibly difficult to use. Each exists in two quite different forms, for Scotland and for England and Wales, that are the result of a complicated history of "cut and paste" amendments rather than coherent reformulations of the law. Although the experienced user and those with access to the commercial databases of legislation can find their way to the correct version of the law, it is still not easy to work with; to anyone else finding out what the law says must be virtually impossible. The single most useful step to improve the understanding and application of the law would be consolidation of the main legislation in each jurisdiction, ideally with proper integration of the rules in the 1981 Act and the 1994 Regulations.

The bulk of the law described here is statutory. Although I hope that major amendments have been noted, I have not mentioned every minor adjustment to the legislation, e.g. when public authorities have been renamed or restructured, and all references should be read as referring to the legislation as amended. For the sake of brevity, the following abbreviations have been used for legislation that is frequently mentioned:

CA 1968	Countryside Act 1968
CNHR 1994	Conservation (Natural Habitats, etc.) Regulations 1994 (SI 1994/2716)
CNHAR 2007	Conservation (Natural Habitats, etc.) (Amendment) Regulations 2007 (SI 2007/1843)
CNHASR 2004	Conservation (Natural Habitats, etc.) Amendment (Scotland) Regulations 2004 (SSI 2004/475)
CNHSAR 2007	Conservation (Natural Habitats, etc.) Amendment (Scotland) Regulations 2007 (SSI 2007/80)
CRWA 2000	Countryside and Rights of Way Act 2000
CSA 1967	Countryside (Scotland) Act 1967
EA 1995	Environment Act 1995
EPA 1990	Environmental Protection Act 1990
NERCA 2006	Natural Environment and Rural Communities Act 2006
NHSA 1991	Natural Heritage (Scotland) Act 1991
NPACA 1949	National Parks and Access to the Countryside Act 1949
NPSA 2000	National Parks (Scotland) Act 2000
TCPA 1990	Town and Country Planning Act 1990
TCPSA 1997	Town and Country Planning (Scotland) Act 1997
WCA 1981	Wildlife and Countryside Act 1981

Throughout the book there are references to the websites of the statutory conservation bodies, government departments, international organisations and others. These provide invaluable, if at times overwhelming, sources of information but can also be a great source of frustration as the structure, format and addresses of websites change and as material is rearranged, updated or archived in unexpected and unexplained ways, or is left untouched despite major developments taking place. All the links were confirmed in late spring 2009, but that is no guarantee that they are still working by the time the book leaves the publisher, far less is actually read.

I have endeavoured to state the law as at the end of March 2009, but it has been possible to take account of some later developments and to note substantial legislative amendments which are not yet in force.

ACKNOWLEDGEMENTS

So many people have been of assistance in preparing this book, that it is impossible to mention all of them by name, or even by category. Among the groups who have given me great assistance are: academic colleagues in the School of Law at Dundee University who have read and commented on parts of my work and answered daft questions as I strayed beyond my competence, as well as listening to my ranting as the frustration of chasing minor legislative developments through obscure amendments across three jurisdictions had got the better of me; colleagues at the Dundee Law School on the secretarial and technical side who have enabled me to get this and other work done with some efficiency; academic colleagues elsewhere, whose works and comments have been so useful; undergraduate and postgraduate students whose understanding, or lack of it, has helped to clarify my ideas or expression; library staff at Dundee University and elsewhere who have helped to track down materials of assorted kinds; and the staff of many government departments and public bodies who have been unfailingly helpful, even when faced with the most obscure and technical questions. I am most grateful to you all.

Special thanks go to Sarah McLaren who in the summer of 2008 acted as my research assistant under the vacation scholarship scheme of the Carnegie Trust for the Universities of Scotland. As well as providing general help in updating several sections of the book she produced the first draft of the revised section 8.4 on Agriculture (although subsequent developments have demanded significant changes) and became the expert on the general licences issued to permit action to be taken against protected wildlife.

To the publishers, I am grateful for their forbearance over the extended schedule for producing the text and for their work in preparing the Tables and Index and producing the book. In advance, I thank anyone who points out things that I may have missed or misunderstood in preparing this text; such comments will be received with gratitude, not resentment. Finally my thanks go to my family for their assorted help and forbearance and especially to my wife Anne for her assistance on scientific matters and in so many other ways.

Colin T. Reid
Dundee
April 2009

CONTENTS

TABLE OF CASES

TABLE OF EUROPEAN CASES

TABLE OF UK STATUTES AND SCOTTISH ACTS OF PARLIAMENT

UK Statutes

Acts of Scottish Parliament

TABLE OF UK AND SCOTTISH STATUTORY INSTRUMENTS

UK Statutory Instruments

Scottish Statutory Instruments

TABLE OF EUROPEAN AND OTHER MATERIALS

Decisions

International Conventions

1. INTRODUCTION

HISTORY AND DEVELOPMENT

Although the law has concerned itself with the natural world from the **1.1.1**
earliest times, nature conservation law in its present form is a modern
development. Inspired first by Victorian reactions against cruelty and bla-
tantly destructive over-exploitation, the law has developed in keeping with
changing perceptions of environmental issues and of the value of wild plants
and creatures. The conservation of wild plants and animals is now widely
recognised as a desirable policy objective, and the protection and
enhancement of biodiversity feature in many policy statements. To some
this conclusion is justified by moral or religious arguments, to others by
aesthetic considerations. Justifications also exist from a utilitarian view-
point, accepting the desirability of preserving resources for future generations and of maintaining genetic diversity in order to provide the basis for
future developments of benefit to mankind. Whatever the justification,[1]
nature conservation is now accepted as a legitimate concern of the state and
the law reflects this.

However, nature conservation is not the only concern of the state, nor is it **1.1.2**
necessarily high in the list of priorities. The claims of nature conservation
will often have to compete against those of many other interests, such as
economic development, agricultural production and the protection of
individual rights. Much of the law in this area has accordingly been shaped
by the need to balance a concern for nature conservation with the other
demands on the state, an exercise which is frequently left to the wide discretion of public bodies to be exercised in individual cases. In many situations, therefore, nature conservation may be forced to take a back seat, but
in past decades it has been given increasing official recognition, and measures exist to ensure that those who are taking decisions do have to include
the protection of habitats, plants and animals as one of the factors to be
taken into account.

The policy in the early law was quite different. There were laws which **1.1.3**
addressed humankind's dealings with the natural world, but the sole aim
was to serve immediate human interests. The law provided for the exploitation of plants and animals as valuable natural resources and for protection
against the damage which uncontrolled nature could cause to human
interests. In both Scotland and England many laws were made and the
legislation of the Scottish Parliament can serve to illustrate the sort of
measures which were adopted.[2] Although the frequent repetition of many
provisions suggests that the law was not always rigidly observed or

---

[1] House of Commons Environment, Transport & Regional Affairs Committee, *UK Biodiversity*, 20th Report of 1999–2000, HC Paper No.441 (Session 1999–2000), para.8.
[2] C.T. Reid, "Environmental Legislation of the Scottish Parliament" in H. McQueen (ed.),
Miscellany VI (Stair Society, forthcoming).

enforced—a situation not unknown today in many areas of environmental law—this legislation does reveal the attitudes and legal responses to issues involving wildlife. Several broad categories of laws can be identified.

1.1.4　　One major category is provided by the laws aimed at the destruction of pests. Legislation was directed against rooks, crows, and other birds which destroyed corn,[3] and against birds of prey,[4] wolves[5] and foxes.[6] Landowners were instructed to destroy the nests of rooks on pain of forfeiting any tree wherein they were nesting,[7] to destroy the nests and eggs of "foulys of reif",[8] and to destroy birds of prey by all means possible.[9] Organised wolf hunts were to be held[10] and there was a bounty on the head of foxes.[11] In relation to wolves at least, these measures proved successful. Local rules also existed to further these aims, e.g. for some years in Shetland all tenants, ministers, gentlemen and bailies had to produce at the annual head court the heads of weasels, crows, ravens or eagles, or their eggs, or else pay a fine, the number of items required (and the fine) increasing with status of the person (one for a tenant, six for a bailie),[12] while the slayers of eagles were entitled to a reward.[13] Measures also existed against farmers who allowed their crops to be infested with "guld", the corn marigold.[14]

1.1.5　　A second group of laws sought to protect animals that were a valuable resource to the community. Wild fowl were not to be slain at moulting time when they could not fly, and their eggs and nests were protected.[15] Hares were not to be killed "in time of snow",[16] and for a period herons were given special protection, those who kept their nests and prevented others from killing them being entitled to the King's thanks.[17] Salmon, which were a major economic resource, were the subject of much legislation, regulating the size of cruives,[18] setting the close times and seasons,[19] prohibiting the taking of fish at mills,[20] and requiring the removal of obstructions and traps.[21] The law also protected[22] and encouraged[23] rabbit warrens and

---

[3] e.g. RPS 1458/333 (*A.P.S.* ii, 51, c.32).

[4] e.g. RPS 1458/333 (*A.P.S.* ii, 51, c.32).

[5] RPS 1428/3/6 (*A.P.S.* ii, 15, c.5); RPS 1458/3/36 (*A.P.S.* ii, 51, c.35).

[6] RPS 1458/3/36 (*A.P.S.* ii, 51, c.35).

[7] RPS 1424/21 (*A.P.S.* ii, 6, c.20).

[8] RPS 1458/3/32 (*A.P.S.* ii, 51, c.31).

[9] RPS 1458/3/33 (*A.P.S.* ii, 51, c.32).

[10] RPS 1428/3/6 (*A.P.S.* ii, 15, c.5); RPS 1458/3/36 (*A.P.S.* ii, 51, c.35).

[11] RPS 1458/3/36 (*A.P.S.* ii, 51, c.35).

[12] G. Donaldson (ed.), *Court Book of Shetland 1615–1629* (Lerwick: Shetland Library, 1992), pp.160 and 167.

[13] G. Donaldson (ed.), *Court Book of Shetland 1615–1629* (1992), p.165.

[14] Frag. Coll. 11–12 (*A.P.S.* i, 750).

[15] RPS 1458/3/32 (*A.P.S.* ii, 51, c.31).

[16] RPS 1401/2/14 (*A.P.S.* i, 576), RPS 1458/3/37 (*A.P.S.* ii, 52, c.36).

[17] RPS A1493/5/20 (*A.P.S.* ii, 235, c.19).

[18] e.g. RPS 1318/13 (*A.P.S.* i, 469, c.11), RPS 1424/11 (*A.P.S.* ii, 5, c.12), RPS 1478/6/84 (*A.P.S.* ii, 119, c.6).

[19] e.g. RPS 1425/3/13 (*A.P.S.* ii, 7, c.12), RPS 1669/10/131 (*A.P.S.* vii, 655, c.114).

[20] e.g. RPS 1469/27 (*A.P.S.* ii, 96, c.13); RPS 1490/2/21 (*A.P.S.* ii, 221, c.15).

[21] e.g. RPS 1478/6/84 (*A.P.S.* ii, 119, c.6).

[22] e.g. RPS 1425/3/11 (*A.P.S.* ii, 7, c.10).

[23] e.g. RPS A1504/3/119 (*A.P.S.* ii, 243, c.21).

dovecotes, whose inhabitants were not treated as wild animals, and which were a valuable source of fresh meat to their owners, although presumably less welcome to those who were farming the surrounding land.[24]

Such measures existed, of course, not for the benefit of the species con- **1.1.6** cerned, but to ensure that there were adequate numbers for continuing exploitation, and particularly for hunting. Hunting played a very important part in the lives of the monarch, the nobility and their followers,[25] and produced a wealth of legislation. The special laws for the forests,[26] in essence hunting reserves, served to protect them and their game for their noble owners, and incidentally from being converted to agricultural use or denuded for timber. More general provisions prohibited hunting on other lands,[27] restricted the killing of particular game to particular classes of society,[28] while the shooting of deer, other beasts and wild fowl was prohibited.[29]

A final category of legislation can be identified, often overlapping with the **1.1.7** above, namely laws which recognise and try to limit the harm which man was doing to the bounty of the natural world. Several of the acts relating to hunting comment on the dearth of game compared to its past abundance and for this reason impose temporary restrictions,[30] while the harvesting of solan geese (gannets) on the Bass Rock was regulated because of over-exploitation, especially as those who were interested only in the feathers were destroying the value of the birds as meat.[31] Other laws were a response to the fact that "the wood of Scotland is utterly destroyed",[32] requiring that woods, trees and broom be planted[33] and that all fencing be done by living hedges, not dry sticks.[34] In order to prevent erosion, especially in the wake of the disaster at Culbin where moving sandhills covered a village, the pulling of shrubs and vegetation on sand dunes was prohibited.[35]

This considerable legal heritage in both jurisdictions has had a significant **1.1.8** influence on the law relating to game and fishing, and its spirit lives on in some pest control measures. However, as far as the modern law of nature conservation is concerned, a new start was made in relation to birds in Victorian times, and it is only within recent decades that legal protection has been extended to animals, especially reptiles, insects, other invertebrates,

---

[24] Because of the "great inconveniences" being caused, in 1617 dovecotes were restricted to one per landowner and only where substantial surrounding land was owned (RPS 1617/5/33: *A.P.S.* iv, 548, c.19).

[25] "[I]n time of peace in all time bygone the said pastimes of hunting and hawking were the only means and instruments to keep the whole lieges bodies from not becoming altogether effeminate" (RPS 1600/11/47 (*A.P.S.* iv, 236, c.34)).

[26] For a detailed study of this topic and an edited version of the forest laws see J.M. Gilbert, *Hunting and Hunting Reserves in Medieval Scotland* (Edinburgh: John Donald, 1979).

[27] RPS A1474/5/15 (*A.P.S.* ii, 107, c.15).

[28] e.g. RPS A1552/2/15 (*A.P.S.* ii, 486, c.15), permitting only gentlemen and nobles using hawks to kill certain wild fowl.

[29] e.g. RPS A1567/12/16 (*A.P.S.* iii, 26, c.17).

[30] e.g. RPS A1552/2/15 (*A.P.S.* ii, 486, c.15), RPS 1469/27 (*A.P.S.* ii, 96, c.13) (salmon).

[31] RPS 1592/4/167 (*A.P.S.* iii, 614, c.140).

[32] RPS 1504/3/33 (*A.P.S.* ii, 242, c.15).

[33] e.g. RPS 1458/3/28 (*A.P.S.* ii, 51, c.27).

[34] RPS 1458/3/31 (*A.P.S.* ii, 51, c.30).

[35] RPS 1695/5/189 (*A.P.S.* ix, 452, c.54).

and non-commercial fish, and that broad protection has been given to wild plants.[36]

1.1.9 The modern legislation has its origin in two facets of nineteenth-century society. In the first place, there was the movement against cruelty to animals. The Society for the Prevention of Cruelty to Animals was founded in the 1820s (becoming the RSPCA in 1840) and in the following decades the concerns of its members and of those who shared their views expanded. The protection of wildlife, especially birds, was added to the struggles against the ill-treatment of horses and other domesticated animals and against bear-baiting, cock-fighting, etc. In addition to the more general provisions, specific measures were promoted to prevent particular manifestations of cruelty to wildlife, e.g. the banning of the use of pole-traps[37] and hooks[38] to catch birds.

1.1.10 The second factor which prompted legislation was an awareness of the gross over-exploitation of wildlife which was taking place.[39] The huge numbers of birds killed by shooting parties, the use of birds essentially as moving targets without any part of the carcase being collected or used, and the widespread use of feathers in the fashion trade[40] were all aspects of this mistreatment of a natural resource, aside from the cruelty involved in many cases.

1.1.11 More ironically, particular damage was done by the growing public interest in the natural world, as those with leisure to indulge their interest devoted their energies not simply to observing nature, but to amassing large collections of eggs and other specimens. Inevitably, the collectors were most interested in the rarest specimens and were prepared to pay for them, so that the damaging consequences of this hobby were concentrated on the species least able to bear the pressure.[41] The greater accessibility of the countryside through the spread of railways and later the motor car allowed more people to become involved in collecting, and the efforts of collectors had a very

---

[36] On the development of the modern law see generally, D. Stamp, *Nature Conservation in Britain* (London: Collins, 1969); J. Sheail, *Nature in Trust* (Glasgow: Blackie, 1976); D.E. Allen, *The Naturalist in Britain – A Social History* (London: Allen Lane, 1976); D. Evans, *A History of Nature Conservation in Britain*, 2nd edn (London: Routledge, 1997); J. Sheail, *Nature Conservation in Britain – The Formative Years* (London: Stationery Office, 1998).

[37] Wild Birds Protection Act 1904.

[38] Wild Birds Protection Act 1908.

[39] The ambivalent attitudes in the nineteenth century can be detected in many sources. In Jules Verne's *Twenty Thousand Leagues under the Sea* (1870) the author fears that "barbarous and inconsiderate greed" will lead to the disappearance of the last whale from the ocean (Part II, Ch.12) but at the same time comments on an enormous heap of oysters, saying that "this mine was inexhaustible, for Nature's creative power is far beyond man's instinct of destruction" (Part II, Ch.2).

[40] This prompted particular attention, and the "Fur, Fin and Feather" movement was effective in persuading many women to refrain from wearing the feathers of birds not killed for food; generally the animal welfare and nature conservation movement was one where women became deeply involved in political activities.

[41] "If a vulture is foolish enough to perch on rocks in Cork Harbour, as one did in 1843, it must expect to be shot and placed in a museum. It is far better, in the cause of science, that the three rustic buntings which landed on our shores should be captured and identified than that their lives should be spared." H. Russell, "The Protection of Wild Birds", *The Nineteenth Century*, Vol.42 (1897) 614 at 616 (thanks to Dr K. Last for this reference).

damaging effect on some species of birds, insects and plants, many of which were already suffering as a result of changes in land use and agriculture.

A number of societies with concern for nature conservation were formed, **1.1.12** e.g. the Selborne Society for the Protection of Birds, Plants and Pleasant Places, founded in 1885, and these, and those who shared their views, attempted to educate the public and to secure a measure of legal protection for birds, animals and plants. Slowly they made progress, and it is probably true to say that now it is only in a few cases (e.g. orchids and some birds of prey) that animals and plants in Britain are severely threatened by deliberate collecting or hunting as opposed to the incidental results of man's other activities.

It is birds which were the first recipients of protection under the modern **1.1.13** law, and which have been the subject of most legislation. Prompted particularly by the mass slaughter of sea-birds at Flamborough Head, as sport and to provide plumage for the fashion trade, the Sea Birds Preservation Act 1869 was passed, imposing a close season during the breeding months for over 30 kinds[42] of sea bird. A further 79 kinds of bird were similarly protected by the Wild Birds Protection Act 1872, the close season being extended by the Wild Fowl Preservation Act 1876. These early measures were replaced by the more general Wild Birds Protection Act 1880. It is interesting to note that at this stage the legislation already displayed many of the features of the current law: a schedule to list species given additional protection, offences based on the possession of dead birds with the onus on the accused to show their lawful origin, ministerial powers to vary the close seasons, powers to grant exemptions for all or some birds in particular areas, and provisions to assist in the enforcement of the law.

During the decades following the 1880 Act many amendments, extensions **1.1.14** and refinements of the law were made before the law was again consolidated and reformed by the Protection of Birds Act 1954. In the intervening period there had been 14 statutes concerned with protecting birds, some general, some relating to particular species: the Wild Birds Protection Acts 1881, 1894, 1896, 1902, 1904 and 1908, the Sand Grouse Protection Act 1888, the Wild Birds Protection (St. Kilda) Act 1904, the Captive Birds Shooting (Prohibition) Act 1921, the Protection of Birds Acts 1925 and 1933, the Protection of Lapwings Act 1928, the Quail Protection Act 1937, and the Wild Birds (Ducks and Geese) Protection Act 1939. All of these were repealed by the 1954 Act, following which two further statutes were enacted, the Protection of Birds Act 1954 (Amendment) Act 1964 and the Protection of Birds Act 1967.

The basis of the current law is the Wildlife and Countryside Act 1981, **1.1.15** which replaced the earlier legislation on the protection of wild birds, as well as that dealing with most other animals and plants and aspects of habitat conservation. Prompted by the need to implement the European Community's Directive on the conservation of wild birds[43] and by the United Kingdom's acceptance of the Bern Convention on the Conservation of

---

[42] The birds were identified by common names, which meant that there was some uncertainty as to exactly which species were protected, with considerable overlap in the list as names might apply to more than one species (e.g. gull), and more than one name for a species was included (e.g. puffin and sea parrot).

[43] Directive 79/409/EEC; see paras 7.4.6–7.4.17, below.

European Wildlife and Natural Habitats,[44] as well as by more general pressure to do more for conservation, the 1981 Act recast the law on nature conservation in Britain. Its passage proved to be a battleground between conservationists and those with competing interests, with well over 2,000 amendments being proposed, and conservation and the environment firmly becoming issues of political importance. The 1981 Act has now itself been subject to very significant amendment.

1.1.16 While the protection of birds was dealt with by fairly far-reaching legislation as early as the 1880s, the protection of other animals has been more fragmented, and generally more recent. There had long been rules on game and fishing, which in regulating the exploitation of many species did contain an element of conservation, but the first statute primarily motivated by such concern was probably the Grey Seals (Protection) Act 1914.[45] This imposed a close season for the taking of such seals to coincide with the breeding period during which mothers and pups were on shore and particularly vulnerable to hunting parties. The 1914 Act was replaced by the Grey Seals (Protection) Act 1932, which in turn was replaced by the Conservation of Seals Act 1970, which extended protection to the common seal.[46]

1.1.17 As far as the conservation of other animals was concerned, it was only badgers that attracted specific protective legislation, through the Badgers Act 1973,[47] while deer were made the subject of comprehensive provisions dealing with both their conservation and exploitation, in the Deer (Scotland) Act 1959 and the Deer Act 1963.[48] It was with the Conservation of Wild Creatures and Wild Plants Act 1975 that protection was extended to other species, species less likely to have a place in the public's affections (two bats, a lizard, a snake, a toad and a butterfly). As in so many areas, the law here was transformed and greatly extended by the Wildlife and Countryside Act 1981, with subsequent amendments to its Schedules conferring protection on an increasing number of cold-blooded creatures and invertebrates.

1.1.18 The fate of birds and other animals overseas was also not wholly neglected. The Importation of Plumage (Prohibition) Act 1921 restricted the import of all feathers except those of the eider and ostrich. The Animals (Restriction of Importation) Act 1964 made similar provisions regarding some animals, alive or dead, but the law was wholly reshaped and greatly extended (covering plants as well as animals) by the Endangered Species (Import and Export) Act 1976, enacted largely to implement the Convention of International Trade in Endangered Species.[49]

1.1.19 Although the threat to wild plants from over-collecting[50] as well as changes in land use was well known from the middle of the nineteenth century, no general provisions were enacted until the 1970s. A major concern was the conflict between any conservation measures and the rights of

---

[44] See paras 7.5.15–7.5.21, below.

[45] This was also the earliest to use the scientific name to assist in identifying the species concerned.

[46] See paras 3.4.32–3.4.37, below.

[47] Replaced by the Protection of Badgers Act 1992; see paras 3.4.22–3.4.30, below.

[48] See now the Deer (Scotland) Act 1996 and Deer Act 1991; see paras 4.2.16–4.2.29, below.

[49] See paras 7.3.6–7.3.22, below.

[50] Most notably, perhaps, the widespread devastation of ferns during the "fern fever" which raged from the 1840s to the 1870s; see D.E. Allen, *The Victorian Fern Craze – A History of Pteridomania* (London: Hutchison, 1969), esp. pp.54–55.

landowners to do as they wish on their own land, and to their own property since unlike wild animals, plants, being an accretion to the ground, are owned by the owner of the land.[51] Although byelaws prohibiting the picking or uprooting of plants were adopted by many counties, the Conservation of Wild Creatures and Wild Plants Act 1975 was the first national measure to prohibit (subject to a number of exceptions, particularly for landowners) the uprooting of plants, with 21 species being given further protection against being picked. Again, this is an area where the Wildlife and Countryside Act 1981 greatly changed the legal position, with protection being extended to many more species. As with the provisions on animals, the amendments since 1981 have granted protection to many more species which are not so widely appreciated by the public, e.g. mosses and liverworts.

While these measures designed to protect particular species from direct **1.1.20** harm were being introduced, measures were also being taken to protect habitat. Individuals and local and national societies had been active for years in protecting nature at locations throughout the country, and in persuading public bodies and other landowners to manage their land with at least some regard for the wild animals and plants which it supported. After many years of work by interested groups and a number of influential reports,[52] legislation in 1949 finally created a number of official designations.

The National Parks and Access to the Countryside Act 1949 provided for **1.1.21** the creation (in England and Wales only) of National Parks, where landscape and nature conservation were to be combined with the provision of access and facilities to allow public enjoyment of the countryside,[53] and of Areas of Outstanding Natural Beauty, areas where the planning system should have particular regard to natural beauty.[54] Nature reserves were given statutory recognition, at national and local level,[55] and the Act also created the system of Sites of Special Scientific Interest,[56] although in this first incarnation the designation served merely as a source of information for public bodies, without the owner or occupier of the site being even notified. Subsequent legislation provided for other designations, e.g. sanctuary orders under the Protection of Birds Act 1954. Again it was the Wildlife and Countryside Act 1981 that reformed this area of the law, with major changes to the system for SSSIs[57] and the creation of Nature Conservation Orders,[58] marine nature reserves[59] and protection for limestone pavement.[60]

Since the 1981 Act there has been much more widespread official recog- **1.1.22** nition of nature conservation and of the value of biodiversity. The ways in which biodiversity is treated are more fully considered in the next section,

---

[51] See paras 6.1.2–6.1.5, below.

[52] See generally J. Sheail, *Nature in Trust* (1976), Chs 5–6; J. Sheail, *Nature Conservation in Britain – The Formative Years* (1998), Ch.1; D. Evans, *A History of Nature Conservation in Britain*, 2nd edn (1997), Ch.4.

[53] See section 5.9, below.

[54] See paras 5.10.1–5.10.8, below; legislation in Scotland was passed for National Scenic Areas in 1986 (see paras 5.10.9–5.10.11, below) and for National Parks in 2000 (see paras 5.9.24–5.9.37, below).

[55] See section 5.3, below.

[56] See section 5.5, below.

[57] See section 5.5, below.

[58] Now limited to Scotland; see section 5.6, below.

[59] See section 5.4, below.

[60] See section 5.7, below.

but the policy shift has gradually been reflected in more substantive changes in the law. As well as the institutional reforms discussed below there have been major legal developments affecting both species and habitat conservation.

1.1.23   The most important of these has been the adoption by the EC of the Habitats and Species Directive in 1992[61] and its implementation in Great Britain by the Habitats (Nature Conservation, etc.) Regulations 1994.[62] This measure not only required stricter protection for certain listed species, but imposed a requirement on Member States to ensure that habitat was adequately protected. This required the introduction of significantly stricter legal controls over the European sites qualifying for such protection, such that damaging operations could not simply be delayed (as was the maximum restriction for SSSIs at the time) but actually prohibited indefinitely.[63] From the beginning, though, it was noted that the 1994 Regulations did not fully implement the Directive and eventually infraction proceedings were taken before the European Court of Justice.[64] In 2005 the United Kingdom was held to be in breach of EC law on several grounds and this decision has led to substantial amendments being made to the Regulations in 2007 seeking to ensure that they do give full effect to the Directive,[65] followed by further amendments when the Commission threatened further action over the inadequacy of these remedial steps.[66]

1.1.24   A second major development has been the reaction to concerns that the Wildlife and Countryside Act 1981 was not adequate to ensure protection for habitat and wildlife. Despite the fact that it was largely doing its job in relation to the specific threats which it was designed to prevent,[67] it had not stopped the continuing loss of habitat through gradual deterioration or other causes outwith its scope and had not proved as effective as it might in enforcing the law (e.g. the absence of a power to impose custodial sentences meant that there was little deterrent against impecunious egg-thieves).[68] At the same time, the rush to re-designate sites during the 1980s in order to invoke the greater protection under the 1981 Act led in places to resentment over the role and approach of what were perceived as "outsiders" who arrived suddenly in an area and on the basis of supposed scientific data but no local knowledge started telling established land managers what they could and could not do on land that local people had managed for years in a

---

[61] Directive 92/43/EEC; see paras 7.4.18–7.4.42, below.

[62] SI 1994/2716.

[63] See section 5.2, below.

[64] *Commission v UK* (C-6/04) [2005] E.C.R. I-5261; C.T. Reid and M. Woods, "Implementing EC Conservation Law" (2006) 18 J.E.L. 135.

[65] Conservation (Natural Habitats, etc.) Amendment (Scotland) Regulations 2007 (SSI 2007/80); Conservation (Natural Habitats, etc.) Amendment (No.2) (Scotland) Regulations 2007 (SSI 2007/349); Offshore Marine Conservation (Natural Habitats, etc.) Regulations 2007 (SI 2007/1842); Conservation (Natural Habitats, etc.) (Amendment) Regulations 2007 (SI 2007/1843); see para.7.4.42 below.

[66] Conservation (Natural Habitats, etc.) Amendment (No.2) (Scotland) Regulations 2008 (SSI 2008/425); Conservation (Natural Habitats, etc.) (Amendment) (England and Wales) Regulations 2009 (SI 2009/6); Offshore Marine Conservation (Natural Habitats, etc.) (Amendment) Regulations 2009 (SI 2009/7).

[67] K. Last, "Habitat Protection: Has the Wildlife and Countryside Act 1981 Made a Difference?" (1999) 11 J.E.L. 15.

[68] *Forsyth v Cardle*, 1994 S.C.C.R. 769.

way that had actually preserved its value for biodiversity. In 1998 separate consultation papers proposed different approaches to reform of the SSSI system in Scotland and in England and Wales.[69] In England and Wales this led to legislation in the Countryside and Rights of Way Act 2000, strengthening aspects of the SSSI system[70] and amending the 1981 Act in other significant ways.[71] In Scotland, legislative activity initially centred on bringing to fruition a separate initiative to establish the first National Parks in Scotland,[72] but the SSSI system and other aspects of conservation law were reformed under the Nature Conservation (Scotland) Act 2004.[73]

A third development has been the strengthening of the laws on species **1.1.25** protection hinted at above. As well as introducing the biodiversity duties on public authorities discussed in the next section, the legislation this century has made a large number of adjustments to the laws to extend the protection offered to animals and plants, to reduce the exceptions and defences that allowed harmful acts to continue and to assist the enforcement of the law. These changes have been achieved in a single step in Scotland through the Nature Conservation (Scotland) Act 2004 and in two steps south of the border through the Countryside and Rights of Way Act 2000 and the Natural Environment and Rural Communities Act 2006. In all cases, unfortunately, the changes have taken the form of separate amendments to the 1981 Act, adopting the "cut and paste" approach rather than replacing whole provisions. This means that the 1981 Act now exists in two different versions, one for each side of the border, and that the law currently in force is a complex jigsaw of the 1981 Act and its many amendments. Consolidated versions of the law, ideally incorporating the 1994 Regulations (which themselves are in urgent need of consolidation following the amendments in 2007) would be a great boon to all users of the law.

At the same time as these formal changes have been taking shape, the **1.1.26** operation of the legal structures has been assisted by a generally more sympathetic policy background. A concern for sustainable development[74] and for biodiversity[75] now should suffuse policy across all areas of activity and thus at least mitigate the extent to which economic and development policies promote activities harmful to wildlife. As a specific example, with a variety of pressures moving agricultural and forestry policy away from the simple objective of maximising production and with financial difficulties facing many farmers,[76] it has been possible for grant-aided conservation measures to be seen as a worthwhile option for land managers seeking a reliable economic return, as opposed to something that inevitably obstructs the profitable use of the land. On the other hand, new tensions are arising, notably in relation to the promotion of renewable energy developments as a

---

[69] *People and Nature: A New Approach to SSSI Designations in Scotland* (Scottish Office, 1998); *Sites of Special Scientific Interest: Better Protection and Management* (DETR, 1998).

[70] See paras 5.5.5–5.5.29, below.

[71] In contrast to the battles at the time of the 1981 Act, the wildlife provisions of the Countryside and Wildlife Bill produced very little debate or opposition, although the access provisions gave rise to much controversy and debate, threatening the passage of the Bill.

[72] National Parks (Scotland) Act 2000; see paras 5.9.24–5.9.37, below.

[73] See paras 5.5.29–5.5.48, below. Consultation on a further Wildlife and Natural Environment Bill began in June 2009.

[74] See section 2.2, below.

[75] See section 1.2, below.

[76] See sections 6.4 and 8.4, below.

response to climate change, e.g. the development of wind farms on valuable natural habitats.[77]

1.1.27   In relation to the institutional arrangements for nature conservation, again the story is one of prolonged activity, with varying degrees of official involvement, by societies and interested individuals leading to several reports and committee investigations before formal action was taken.[78] The Nature Conservancy was established by royal charter in 1949. It derived its powers from the National Parks and Access to the Countryside Act 1949 and had as its main tasks the provision of scientific advice to the government, the establishment and maintenance of nature reserves, and the organisation of scientific research. Its links with the Natural Environment Research Council[79] were redrawn by the Science and Technology Act 1965, before it was given a full statutory basis and a new name, the Nature Conservancy Council, by the Nature Conservancy Council Act 1973. During the 1960s all public bodies were placed under a general duty to have regard to the desirability of conserving the natural beauty of the countryside, which includes its flora and fauna.[80]

1.1.28   The Environmental Protection Act 1990 and the Natural Heritage (Scotland) Act 1991 radically changed the institutional structure, dividing the Nature Conservancy Council on a geographical basis and creating new bodies: Scottish Natural Heritage, English Nature (now Natural England)[81] and the Countryside Council for Wales as well as the Joint Nature Conservancy Council as a vehicle for certain functions on a joint geographical basis. A further feature of the reform was the merging in Scotland and Wales of the tasks acquired from the Nature Conservancy Council with those of the Countryside Commissions.[82] In England a later but wider merger of functions has taken place.[83]

1.1.29   The Countryside Commission for Scotland had been created by the Countryside (Scotland) Act 1967, with broadly defined functions (but little direct power) with regard to the provision, development and improvement of facilities for enjoying the countryside and to the conservation and enhancement of its natural beauty and amenity. For England and Wales, the starting point was the National Parks Commission established under the 1949 Act, and it was by the Countryside Act 1968 that this body's functions were extended, with broad functions similar to those of the Scottish Commission being added to its more specific role in the National Parks. Under the Environmental Protection Act 1990 the Countryside Commission was restricted to functions in England and became the Countryside Agency, following the addition of further functions related to rural development.

---

[77] e.g. the refusal of consent in April 2008 for a major wind farm on Lewis—decision letter at *http://www.scotland.gov.uk/Resource/Doc/917/0059358.doc* [Accessed May 3, 2009]. The conflict can also arise in relation to proposals for hydro-electric schemes: A.L. Pillai, C.T. Reid and A.R. Black, "Reconciling Renewable Energy and the Local Impacts of Hydro-electric Development" (2005) 7 Env. L. Rev. 110.

[78] See J. Sheail, *Nature in Trust* (1976), Ch.8; J. Sheail, *Nature Conservation in Britain – The Formative Years* (1998), Ch.2.

[79] See para.2.7.21, below, and J. Sheail, *Nature Conservation in Britain – The Formative Years* (1998), Ch.7.

[80] Countryside (Scotland) Act 1967 s.66; Countryside Act 1968 s.11; see para.2.2.6, below.

[81] See paras.2.6.20–2.6.23, below.

[82] See section 2.6, below.

[83] See para.2.6.20, below.

The Countryside Agency has now been merged with English Nature to form Natural England, achieving the integration introduced in Scotland and Wales over 15 years earlier.[84]

The geographical divide at agency level was followed by the more fun- **1.1.30** damental constitutional transformation brought about by devolution, which transferred most responsibility for nature conservation issues to the Scottish Parliament and Government, and some functions to the National Assembly for Wales.[85] Even before these measures took effect, there were some signs of divergence between Scotland on the one hand and England and Wales on the other. The legislation creating SNH had also created for Scotland only an Advisory Committee on SSSIs, the policy proposals on reforms to the SSSI system took significantly different approaches, and the proposals for National Parks in Scotland developed a model different from that in Eng- land and Wales.[86] Since devolution came into force in 1999, nature con- servation law has diverged considerably between the jurisdictions, with a number of substantial differences as well as the need to consult separate legislation to find the current law. Although the need to comply with EC law is a constraint on how far the various systems can diverge, the simple fact that legislation is made separately, e.g. to respond to the European Court's finding that the Habitats and Species Directives was not properly imple- mented,[87] means that it is increasingly difficult to talk of the law across Great Britain rather than in its constituent parts.[88]

This brief account has recorded merely the stages in the development of **1.1.31** the law, and is in no way a history of nature conservation in Britain. Any such history would emphasise the massive contribution made by committed individuals and societies of various kinds, a commitment to practical con- servation work, to the promotion of the ideas of nature conservation and to the development of appropriate structures and policies for public bodies. It is to these unofficial efforts, rather than to the law, that the main credit must go for the conservation of as much of our natural heritage as has survived to this day.[89]

BIODIVERSITY

The history described so far has largely omitted the key term which has **1.2.1** dominated policy discussion of nature conservation over the last two dec- ades: "biodiversity". This dominance is largely attributable to the Con- vention on Biological Diversity[90] signed at the "Earth Summit" in Rio in 1992, where the concept was introduced to a global audience, alongside that

---

[84] Natural Environment and Rural Communities Act 2006; see para.2.6.20, below.

[85] See section 2.3, below.

[86] Although the National Parks (Scotland) Act 2000 was passed by the Scottish Parliament, the proposals on which it is based pre-date the implementation of the devolution arrangements.

[87] See fnn.65 and 66, above.

[88] See paras 2.3.4–2.3.6 and 2.3.10, below.

[89] See D. Stamp, *Nature Conservation in Britain* (1969); J. Sheail, *Nature in Trust* (1976); D.E. Allen, *The Naturalist in Britain – A Social History* (1976); D. Evans, *A History of Nature Conservation in Britain*, 2nd edn (1997); J. Sheail, *Nature Conservation in Britain – The For- mative Years* (1998).

[90] See paras 7.5.22–7.5.24, below, and *http://www.cbd.int* [Accessed May 3, 2009].

of sustainable development. Both of these terms have been eagerly seized by governments and others, partly as elements of a new and fashionable rhetoric as states try to show that they are environmentally aware, partly because the reporting and strategy-forming requirements of the Rio Conventions lead to the use of the terms in structuring responses to the international agreements, but also because of the convenience of the terms in encapsulating important ideas.

1.2.2   Whereas part of the attraction of the term "sustainable development" may lie in its lack of precise definition,[91] "biodiversity" does have a clearer, if broad, meaning. The definition given in the Convention on Biological Diversity is that:

> "*'Biological diversity*' means the variability among living organisms from all sources including, *inter alia*, terrestrial, marine and other aquatic ecosystems and the ecological complexes of which they are part; this includes diversity within species, between species and of ecosystems."[92]

The power of the definition is that it covers several different but interconnected forms of diversity, all of which must be considered if the natural heritage of the earth is to be passed down to future generations. Diversity between species, the presence of a number of distinct sorts of plant or animal, is perhaps the simplest aspect of this and is what drives the concern to prevent the extinction of endangered plants and animals. Diversity within species reflects the extent of genetic variation between species, and the fact that local populations may have traits different from those in other areas, traits that may prove essential to the long-term survival or value of the species (e.g. disease resistance, adaptation to climate variations) and in some cases may eventually lead to differentiation as a separate species. Diversity of ecosystems is the basis for the conservation of different habitat types, whilst diversity within ecosystems is often a measure of the health and undisturbed nature of a habitat. Nature conservation must take account of all of these aspects of our biological heritage.[93]

1.2.3   Each of these can be measured and therefore provide useful ways of assessing and monitoring the varied natural environment,[94] but there are dangers in allowing what may appear to be clear statistical measures to dominate policy to the exclusion of a more rounded picture. There is often no simple answer on whether or not a group of similar organisms represent one "species" or several, and taxonomic debates (and fashions)[95] ebb and

---

[91] See paras 2.2.2–2.2.5, below.

[92] Convention on Biological Diversity (1992) art.2.

[93] "Too much of biodiversity policy is based on ignorance or prejudice or single-minded enthusiasm for a single species, and has often little understanding of the naturally evolving world." House of Commons Environment, Transport and Regional Affairs Committee, *UK Biodiversity*, 20th Report of 1999–2000, HC Paper No.441 (Session 1999–2000), para.12.

[94] As one example see *Scotland's Biodiversity Indicators* (Scottish Government, 2007).

[95] Arguments between "lumpers" (who are reluctant to acknowledge some minor differences as justifying separate recognition at species level) and "splitters" (who are more willing to assert the existence of separate species) can run on for decades, with a consequent to-ing and fro-ing of classification of species, sub-species, varieties and geographical races.

flow, quite apart from the issue of hybrids. Views on such issues, and that of diversity within species, are of course being fundamentally changed by developments in DNA techniques, which are revealing that we know a lot less about biological diversity than we thought we did. In relation to habitats, the number of species recorded for a site may often be a guide to the health of the ecosystem, but this clearly does not apply in extreme environments and may not by itself capture the significance of a site in view of the dynamic nature of populations, land use patterns and climate, quite apart from being dependent on the quality of the original recording process.[96] Biological diversity is, though, a very useful concept that deserves its place at the heart of policy and practice.

One requirement of the Convention on Biological Diversity is the devel- **1.2.4** opment of "national strategies, plans or programme for the conservation and sustainable use of biological diversity".[97] The UK's response was to produce in 1994 *Biodiversity: the UK Action Plan*[98] which set a framework within which more specific plans were developed, in the form of Species and Habitat Action Plans and Local Biodiversity Action Plans. The UK Biodiversity Steering Group published its report in 1995[99] which contained the first set of species and habitat plans. Since then the work has continued with the UK Biodiversity Partnership Standing Committee[100] as the co-ordinating body, producing in 2007 a new document *Conserving Biodiversity – The UK Approach*.[101] Biodiversity strategies have been produced for each country individually,[102] and there is also an Action Plan at EU level.[103]

The detailed work of producing species and habitat action plans has also **1.2.5** continued, each setting out detailed proposals for improving the conservation status of the species or habitat concerned, identifying the actions required, the key bodies who can take the lead in implementing the plans and seeking "champions" to assist in providing the resources for such

---

[96] Particularly for invertebrates and lower plants, the number of recorded species is often an indication more of the level of recording effort than of the number of species actually present. A detailed study over 15 years has recorded 1,782 species of animal and 42 species of plant in one suburban garden in Leicester (J. Owen, *The Ecology of a Garden: The first fifteen years* (Cambridge: CUP, 1991)), whilst much shorter and less intensive study of a garden in Dundee has led to the recording of 52 species of hoverflies, 6 bumblebees and 162 moths (data from Anne Reid).

[97] Convention on Biological Diversity (1992) art.6.

[98] *Biodiversity: the UK Action Plan* (Cm.2428). A European Community Biodiversity Strategy was also produced in the 1990s (COM (1998) 42 final).

[99] *Biodiversity: The UK Steering Group Report* (1995) and see Government Response, Cm.3260, (1996).

[100] Its members are: Countryside Council for Wales; DEFRA; Department of Environment, Northern Ireland; Joint Nature Conservation Committee; Natural England; Northern Ireland Biodiversity Group; Scottish Government; Scottish Natural Heritage; Welsh Assembly Government; Wildlife and Countryside Link. See *http://www.ukbap.org.uk* [Accessed May 3, 2009].

[101] Published by DEFRA on behalf of the Steering Group.

[102] *Working with the grain of nature – A biodiversity strategy for England* (2002), *Scotland's Biodiversity: It's in Your Hands – A strategy for the conservation and enhancement of biodiversity in Scotland* (2004), *Wales Biodiversity Framework – Making the connections for biodiversity action in Wales* (2008).

[103] *Halting the loss of biodiversity by 2010 – and beyond: Sustaining ecosystem services for human well-being* (COM (2006) 216 final).

implementation.[104] Almost 180 Local Biodiversity Action Plans have also been produced by local partnerships involving the conservation bodies, local authorities, non-governmental organisations and other interests. These consider the needs of biodiversity at a local level and seek to guide policy, land use and management decisions by the public and private sector. None of these species, habitat or local plans, however, has any direct statutory status although they are closely linked to the biodiversity duties discussed below.

1.2.6   One exception is under the Greater London Authority Act 1999, where the duties of the Mayor include the preparation of a "state of the environment report" for London, to include information on biodiversity,[105] and the preparation of the London Biodiversity Action Plan.[106] This Plan must contain information on the ecology, wildlife and habitat of Greater London, proposals for conserving and promoting biodiversity and commitments to this end made by other bodies and it must take into account any biodiversity plans made by London borough councils. However, unlike the waste management and air quality strategies that also have to be produced, there is no explicit obligation on local authorities within London to have regard to this plan in their own actions.[107] Outside London, though, the status of Local Biodiversity Action Plans is based on policy alone or comes indirectly through the more general biodiversity and other duties.[108]

1.2.7   At first, all of the activity on biodiversity at policy level had only a limited effect on the law itself, with the existing wildlife and planning provisions forming the background against which the more specific plans were to be put into effect. References to protecting or enhancing biodiversity appeared frequently in the preambles to EC legislation, but initially the term made only rare and insignificant appearances in domestic law. Land management to support and enhance biodiversity has been a feature of several grant schemes,[109] biodiversity appears in several places in the legislation on zoos,[110] and as an issue to be covered in environmental assessments[111] whilst the "effect on biodiversity" is one of the adverse environmental effects of road

---

[104] There are 1,150 priority species and 65 priority habitats covered by plans. Full details and progress reports on the species, habitat and local plans are available at the UK Biodiversity website at *http://www.ukbap.org.uk* [Accessed May 3, 2009] and at the national websites at: *http://www.biodiversityscotland.gov.uk/*; *http://www.biodiversitywales.org.uk/* and *http://www.ukbap.org.uk/EBG/default.asp* [All Accessed May 3, 2009].

[105] Greater London Authority Act 1999 s.351.

[106] Greater London Authority Act 1999 s.352.

[107] cf. Greater London Authority Act 1999 ss.355 and 364.

[108] e.g. as an element in preparing the community strategies required by s.4 of the Local Government Act 2000 (as amended by Sustainable Communities Act 2007 s.7(1)).

[109] e.g. Environmentally Sensitive Areas (Stage III) Designation Order 2000 (SI 2000/3051) Sch.2 Pt 3; Environmentally Sensitive Areas (Stage IV) Designation Order 2000 (SI 2000/3052) Pt 3 of the various Schedules; Rural Stewardship Scheme (Scotland) Regulations 2001 (SSI 2001/300) Sch.2 para.30; Rural Development Contracts (Rural Priorities) (Scotland) Regulations 2008 (SSI 2008/100) Sch.2; Land Management Contracts (Menu Scheme) (Scotland) Regulations 2005 (SSI 2005/225) Sch.1 paras 10 and 16.

[110] Zoo Licensing Act 1981 (as amended) ss.1A (promoting public education and awareness in relation to the conservation of biodiversity), 14 (considerations in exempting zoos from some requirements), 13 and 16E (considerations on closure of a zoo).

[111] Environmental Assessment of Plans and Programmes Regulations 2004 (SI 2004/1633) Sch.2 para.6; Environmental Assessment of Plans and Programmes (Wales) Regulations 2004 (SI 2004/1656) Sch.2 para.6.

traffic to be taken into account in setting targets for traffic reduction.[112] Biodiversity is also mentioned as one of the areas of competence for Acts of the Welsh Assembly.[113] More significantly, though, biodiversity has been given great prominence through the imposition of general "biodiversity duties" on public authorities.

A general duty with regard to biodiversity was first introduced in England **1.2.8** and Wales by virtue of the Countryside and Rights of Way Act 2000,[114] now replaced under the Natural Environment and Rural Communities Act 2006, whilst in Scotland a more strongly phrased duty was created under the Nature Conservation (Scotland) Act 2004. The Scottish duty requires every public body and office-holder[115] to further the conservation of biodiversity in the exercise of their functions, so far as is consistent with the proper exercise of those functions.[116] In doing so they must have regard to the Scottish Biodiversity Strategy and the Convention on Biological Diversity.[117] The Scottish Ministers must designate and publish one or more strategies for this purpose as well as lists of species and habitats of principal importance for the conservation of biodiversity. These lists must be reviewed from time to time and every three years the Ministers must report to the Scottish Parliament on the implementation of the Strategy.[118] Details of the Strategy and lists are available at the Biodiversity Scotland website.[119]

In England and Wales a duty applies to every public authority[120] but it is **1.2.9** only "to have regard to", rather than "to further", the purpose of conserving biodiversity[121] in the exercise of their functions, so far as is consistent with their proper exercise,[122] and there is no equivalent of the Scottish requirement on the government to produce reports on how this duty is being implemented. Further obligations, though, are imposed in some cases. Firstly, Ministers, government departments and the National Assembly for Wales must in particular have regard to the Convention on Biological Diversity in complying with this duty. More significantly, the Secretary of State and the National Assembly for Wales must, after consulting the relevant statutory conservation bodies, publish a list of living organisms and habitats they consider to be of principal importance for conserving biodiversity; these lists are available on the websites of DEFRA[123] and the Wales Biodiversity Partnership.[124] The Secretary of State and Assembly must then

---

[112] Road Traffic Reduction (National Targets) Act 1998 s.2.

[113] Government of Wales Act 2006 Sch.7 Pt 1 para.6; see paras 2.3.7–2.3.10, below.

[114] CRWA 2000 s.74.

[115] "Public body or office-holder" is given a broad definition, including statutory undertakers; NCSA 2004 s.58.

[116] NCSA 2004 s.1.

[117] The Act expressly refers to the Convention as amended from time to time and to any UN convention that replaces it; NCSA 2004 s.1(2).

[118] NCSA 2004 s.2.

[119] Available at *http://www.biodiversityscotland.gov.uk/* [Accessed May 3, 2009]. There are 1,915 species and 265 habitats on the lists.

[120] Again a broad definition including statutory undertakers is given: NERCA 2006 s.40(4)–(5).

[121] "Conserv[ing] biodiversity" includes restoring or enhancing a population or habitat.

[122] NERCA 2006 s.40.

[123] At *http://www.defra.gov.uk/wildlife-countryside/biodiversity/action-uk/legislation.htm* [Accessed May 3, 2009]. There are 943 species and 56 habitats on the lists for England.

[124] Available at *http://www.biodiversitywales.org.uk/* [Accessed May 3, 2009]. There are 541 species and 55 habitats on the Welsh lists.

take such steps as appear reasonably practicable to further the conservation of the listed species and habitats and promote the taking of such steps by others.[125]

1.2.10   Since these duties may be more aspirational than operational, as discussed more fully below,[126] the precise differences between the two jurisdictions may not be of great significance in practice. Nevertheless the Scottish obligation does seek to require a much wider range of bodies not merely to consider but to further conservation and does include a reporting requirement, whilst the one for England and Wales seeks to force the Secretary of State and the Assembly to take some specific action. At the very least such duties ensure that biodiversity is an issue that cannot simply be ignored as irrelevant to the legal functions of public bodies and thereby opens the door for arguments and pressure to be applied whenever nature is seen to be suffering or opportunities for enhancement being missed.[127]

1.2.11   As well as being a key concept in policy debate, biodiversity is therefore making its mark in the legal framework for conservation. With its emphasis on diversity within species and within habitats, it may help to shift attention away from an undue concentration on a few endangered species and outstanding sites towards the wider needs of flora and fauna.[128] Nevertheless, it is still the specific measures dealing with such issues which do most of the work in terms of the conservation of biodiversity through the law.

NATURE CONSERVATION AND THE GENERAL LAW

1.3.1   The law on nature conservation is a statutory creation, operating against the background provided by the general civil and criminal law. An outline of this legal background is necessary so that the need for and form of the statutory intervention can be appreciated. In particular the law relating to the ownership of wild animals, of plants and of land must be considered, as a significant factor in shaping the law on nature conservation has been the potential conflict between the private property rights of individuals and the public interest in securing conservation.

Ownership

1.3.2   As far as plants are concerned, the law is simple; all plants growing in the ground belong to the owner of the land. This is the case regardless of whether the plant occurs naturally or has been deliberately planted.[129]

---

[125] NERCA 2006 ss.41 and 42.

[126] See paras 2.2.12–2.2.15, below, where the impact of a wider range of general duties in relation to nature is discussed.

[127] On the need for an ecosystem approach that pervades all areas of policy and progress towards the government's target of halting biodiversity loss by 2010, see *Halting Biodiversity Loss*, 13th Report of 2007–08 of House of Commons Environmental Audit Committee, HC Paper No.743 (Session 2007–08).

[128] "Designated conservation sites have an important role in protecting biodiversity. ... However, the main reservoir for biodiversity is the 'wider countryside', outwith these protected sites, and it is here that biodiversity action is likely to produce the greatest gains." *Action for Scotland's Biodiversity* (Scottish Biodiversity Group, 2000), p.9.

[129] Some crops can be treated differently where there are various interests in the land (*Boskabelle Ltd v Laird*, 2006 S.L.T. 1079); see para.6.1.3, below.

Subject to the rights of anyone else with an interest in the land, the land-owner has the right to nurture or destroy the plant as he thinks fit, and statutory intervention has been necessary to restrict this freedom for a number of purposes, e.g. weed control, nature conservation and forestry. The legal position and its consequences are discussed more fully in Chapter 6.[130]

The law relating to animals is more complicated. Apart from a handful of **1.3.3** special rules relating to specific animals (such as the Crown's rights in swans,[131] sturgeon and whales[132]), the starting point of the law, which essentially follows Roman Law on this topic, is a distinction between wild animals (animals *ferae naturae*) and domestic ones (animals *mansuetae* or *domitae naturae*). The latter, such as dogs, horses, sheep and cattle are treated in the same way as all other moveable property, being fully owned throughout their lives and subject to the standard rules for lost or abandoned property. Wild animals are treated differently. While in the wild, they are deemed to be ownerless, *res nullius*, and become the subject of property only when seized and actually taken into possession.[133] The categorisation of an animal is a matter of law, and although generally straightforward may be uncertain in some cases, e.g. where domesticated animals become feral[134] or in relation to fish.[135]

In order for an animal *ferae naturae* to become the property of someone, **1.3.4** it must be taken. This can be achieved by killing it or by taking it into captivity, e.g. putting it in a cage or restricting it within a park or enclosure.[136] Setting traps does not by itself create any property rights in the target animals.[137] A hunter who wounds an animal will be recognised as having rights over it so long as he continues to give chase, but once the chase is abandoned the animal is once again *res nullius* and free to become the property of the first person to seize it. In relation to some species, ownership is also recognised where the animal may be free to roam, but consistently returns to the owner's premises, displaying what is known as an *animus revertendi*. This applies, for example, to pigeons returning to a dovecote[138] and bees returning to a hive,[139] but is thought unlikely to extend to the habit of salmon returning to their spawning grounds.[140]

The principle that property is acquired by the person who takes such **1.3.5** animals is subject to a qualification in England and Wales. It is accepted

---

[130] Paras 6.1.2–6.1.5, below.

[131] In England and Wales only; *Case of Swans* (1592) 7 Co. Rep. 15b.

[132] Stair, II, i, 5; Blackstone, *Commentaries* (1783) i, 223.

[133] Stair, II, i, 33; Erskine, II, i, 10; Blackstone, *Commentaries* (1783) ii, 389–395.

[134] *Falkland Islands Co v R* (1863) 2 Moo. P.C. N.S. 266 (status of sheep and cattle found wild in the Falkland Islands after being introduced by earlier settlers).

[135] In *Valentine v Kennedy*, 1985 S.C.C.R. 89 at 91 it was doubted that any fish, even non-indigenous ones specially reared, could be properly regarded as "tamed" and therefore other than *ferae naturae*; see also, on the status of snails, A.P. Herbert's *Cowfat v Wheedle*, reprinted in many collections including *Uncommon Law* (1982).

[136] Stair, II, i, 33; Blackstone, *Commentaries* (1783) ii, 389–392.

[137] *Cresswell v DPP* [2006] EWHC 3379 Admin.

[138] *Hamps v Darby* [1948] 2 K.B. 311.

[139] *Kearry v Pattinson* [1939] 1 K.B. 471.

[140] This is an obstacle to the potential development of a "salmon ranching" industry, whereby salmon are reared to be released into the open sea then harvested by their "owner" on their return to fresh water to spawn; see W. Howarth, *The Law of Aquaculture* (1990), Ch.17.

that once killed and taken wild animals cease to be *res nullius* and become the subject of property, but as the courts have not been willing to recognise that a poacher could gain ownership by his unlawful acts, property has been held to vest in the owner of the land.[141] In Scotland, however, the courts have been willing to follow the logic of the basic principle, so that property is acquired even by a poacher taking animals unlawfully, contrary to the game rights of the owner of the land concerned.[142] In such circumstances the landowner may be entitled to claim compensation from the poacher, but has no right to restitution of the animals taken.

1.3.6   The English approach has perhaps been influenced by the tendency there to describe the owner of game rights over land as having a qualified property right in the game there, a right perfected on the taking of the game.[143] This is arguably a misleading way of expressing the position as although a landowner may have the power to control any hunting on his land, and have the exclusive right to take the game, he does not have any true property rights in the animals unless and until he physically takes them. Those who take game without any right to it may commit a wrong against the person who is entitled to take the game,[144] but it is not truly an interference with his property in the game. Similarly misleading are references to a form of property in young animals and fledglings not yet able to fly.[145]

1.3.7   Ownership generally is lost once a wild animal ceases to be held in captivity (or to have an *animus revertendi*), but is retained so long as the owner is in pursuit.[146] In *Kearry v Pattinson*,[147] a case involving bees swarming away from a hive, the English court considered the old statements that the owner retained his rights in animals escaping from captivity provided that he had the animals in sight and the power to pursue them. It was emphasised that the owner's rights lasted only as long as he had the lawful power to pursue the creatures, so that once the animals entered the land of another where their owner could not enter except as a trespasser, then they were no longer his property. In England and Wales, once an animal *ferae naturae* has ceased to be the property of someone, it reverts to its former status as *res nullius*, capable of being acquired by the first person to capture it again.[148] In Scotland the same rule, taken from Roman Law, applies and is a departure from the more general rule of feudal origin that property which has once been owned does not become *res nullius* once abandoned by its owner but reverts to the Crown, a rule which applies to animals not *ferae naturae*.[149]

1.3.8   The legal position on the ownership of wild animals has several consequences for the criminal and civil law. As far as the criminal law is

---

[141] *Blades v Higgs* (1865) H.L.C. 621.

[142] Erskine, II, i, 10; *Leith v Leith* (1862) 24 D. 1059 (Lord Curriehill at 1077–1078); *Scott v Everitt* (1853) 15 D. 288 (in the absence of a statutory entitlement police have no right to seize unlawfully taken game).

[143] See, e.g. *Case of Swans* (1592) 7 Co. Rep 15b at 17b.

[144] The right to take game may be separated from the ownership or occupation of the land; see paras 4.2.6–4.2.8, below.

[145] On the difficulties of applying the language and concepts of property to wild animals, see the Australian case *Yanner v Eaton* [1999] HCA 53.

[146] Stair, II, i, 33; Blackstone, *Commentaries* (1783) ii, 393.

[147] *Kearry v Pattinson* [1939] 1 K.B. 471.

[148] *Hamps v Darby* [1948] 2 K.B. 311.

[149] Erskine, II, i, 10; D.L. Carey Miller with D. Irvine, *Corporeal Moveables in Scots Law*, 2nd edn (Edinburgh: W. Green, 2005), para.2.02; cf. *Valentine v Kennedy*, 1985 S.C.C.R. 89 at 91.

concerned, the basic position that wild animals (unless in captivity) are not the property of anyone, means that they cannot be stolen at common law. In Scotland, therefore, it has been held that if a charge of theft is based on the taking of an animal *ferae naturae*, the charge must set out how the animal ceased to be *res nullius* and came to be somebody's property.[150] The same would apply to a charge of malicious mischief or vandalism.[151] It is also specifically provided by the Theft Act 1607[152] that a person who takes bees is guilty of theft[153] and the taking of oysters and mussels from marked beds is also theft.[154] In *Valentine v Kennedy*[155] four men were held guilty of stealing trout which had escaped from a reservoir into surrounding burns, but the fish in question were rainbow trout which are not indigenous and which the men knew must have come from the reservoir. The sheriff commented that if the fish in question had been native brown trout a charge of theft would have been unlikely to succeed as it was unlikely that it could have been proved that the trout came from the reservoir and were not simply wild.

In England and Wales the position is governed by statute. Section 4(4) of **1.3.9** the Theft Act 1968 states that wild animals, tamed or untamed, are to be regarded as property for the purposes of the Act. However, it continues to provide that although wild animals which are tamed or ordinarily kept in captivity may be stolen, a charge of theft of a wild animal or its carcase will otherwise be possible only where the animal has been reduced into possession by or on behalf of another person and the possession has not since been lost or abandoned, or where another person is in the course of reducing the animal into possession. A similar provision governs the position for criminal damage.[156] These provisions in essence repeat the common law rules on ownership, including recognition of the traditional rules of the chase. A specific offence penalises the taking or destruction of fish from a private fishery, the offence being treated as less serious if committed by means of angling during daylight.[157]

The civil law is also affected. As wild animals do not form the property of **1.3.10** anyone, and do not in themselves have any other recognition in the law, they fall outwith the law's protection. In the absence of statutory provisions, killing or destroying wild animals is not in itself a wrong against anyone, as no legally recognised personal or property rights are affected. The destructive conduct may involve a trespass or breach of other rights which

---

[150] *Wilson v Dykes* (1872) 10 M. 444.

[151] Criminal Justice (Scotland) Act 1980 s.78.

[152] As amended by Statute Law Revision (Scotland) Act 1964 Schs 1–2 and Salmon and Freshwater Fisheries (Consolidation) (Scotland) Act 2003 Sch.4 Pt 2.

[153] The same used to apply to taking fish from a stank (see Lord Rodger of Earlsferry, "Stealing Fish" in R.F. Hunter (ed.), *Justice and Crime – Essays in Honour of the Rt. Hon. Lord Emslie* (Edinburgh: T&T Clark, 1993)), but this provision has been replaced by an offence of fishing without permission in a stank or loch where the fishing rights are owned by one person (Salmon and Freshwater Fisheries (Consolidation) (Scotland) Act 2003 s.11 and Sch.4).

[154] Oyster Fisheries (Scotland) Act 1840 s.1; Mussel Fisheries (Scotland) Act 1847 s.1.

[155] *Valentine v Kennedy*, 1985 S.C.C.R. 89.

[156] Criminal Damage Act 1971 s.10(1); a news report in the *The Times* of August 19, 1993 notes that a man was convicted under this Act after injuring some swans, which, exceptionally, are the property of the Queen at all times (*Case of Swans* (1592) 7 Co. Rep. 15b); this enabled a custodial sentence to be imposed, at a time when this was not available for the offences under the WCA 1981 that might otherwise have been the basis for prosecution.

[157] Larceny Act 1861 s.24, preserved by Theft Act 1968 s.32 and Sch.1 para.1; *Environment Agency v Russell* Unreported (1997) 9 E.L.M. 19.

the law will acknowledge, but any action must be based on the breach of those rights, and no legal value can be attached to the wild animals. This may affect the likelihood of obtaining a remedy, as the effect on wild animals of the unwanted conduct should be disregarded and wild animals, not being the property of anyone, have no legally recognised value.[158]

1.3.11   It follows that the standard civil law is of little use in securing the direct protection of wild animals. It can be invoked only when some legally recognised rights are also affected, e.g. a landowner may be able to take action if a trespass or nuisance is involved, or the holder of game or fishing rights may be able to intervene. However, conservation groups and individuals who have an interest in preserving wildlife, but no legal rights at stake, lack the standing to do anything.[159]

1.3.12   The law's failure to accord any value to wildlife may also have indirect consequences. Policies of land management and investment which protect and encourage wild plants and animals at the expense of maximising financial returns will be regarded as producing no legally recognised return. For someone dealing with his own property this is of no consequence, but much property is held by trustees who are under a duty to do their best for the beneficiaries. The duty of the trustees is to obtain the best return, regardless of moral, social and political considerations,[160] especially where property is expressly held for investment purposes, as is the case with considerable areas of land. Environmentally friendly management of land and recourse to "green investments" may well produce a satisfactory return. However, unless the power to be influenced by such matters is expressly included in the trust, trustees may be acting in breach of their duties if they allow a concern for nature conservation to stand in the way of obtaining any appropriate financial returns from the property which they hold, regardless of the value which they or others see in the conservation of nature.[161] On the other hand, the creation of a trust whose express purposes include the protection of wildlife on particular land will put the trustees in a stronger position to take action against anything which threatens this objective.

Land ownership

1.3.13   Under the general law it is the owners of a piece of land who enjoy the power to determine what happens on that land and therefore the extent to which plants and animals are conserved there. The owners of the land own the plants growing on it, they control who can enter the land[162] and they decide the way in which the land is to be used. As far as nature conservation is concerned, this is a mixed blessing. If the owners are keen to protect wild plants and animals, they are in the position to ensure that this takes place by

---

[158] A landowner might be able to create a value entitled to legal protection, e.g. by charging visitors to observe wild animals on his land.

[159] See section 1.4, below.

[160] *Martin v Edinburgh District Council*, 1988 S.L.T. 329; *Cowan v Scargill* [1985] Ch. 270; *Harries v Church Commissioners for England* [1992] 1 W.L.R. 1241.

[161] The same issue may arise in other circumstances, e.g. in *Williams v Schellenberg*, 1988 G.W.D. 29-1254 one *pro indiviso* proprietor of land argued that her interest had been damaged by the proprietor in occupation encouraging the designation of the land as an SSSI, thereby restricting its management and reducing its value.

[162] Subject to the public rights of access provided under the Land Reform (Scotland) Act 2003 Pt 1 and CRWA 2000 Pt 1; see paras 1.3.23–1.3.25, below.

managing the land to preserve and enhance habitats, prohibiting activities which are likely to cause damage or disturbance, eliminating threats to the natural flora and fauna and excluding unwelcome visitors. On the other hand, if landowners do not wish to conserve nature, any measures requiring them to do so will amount to an infringement of their right to do as they wish with their own property,[163] and any enduring restrictions may affect the value of property considerably.

It follows that if an individual or conservation body wishes to conserve **1.3.14** nature in a particular area, the best approach is to acquire the land, or a sufficient interest in the land, in order to ensure that appropriate steps are taken.[164] If an interest in the land cannot be acquired, it may be sufficient to enter an agreement with the landowner which obliges him to act, or refrain from acting, in particular ways. Difficulties arise, however, in trying to ensure the long-term protection of sites and in ensuring that the successors of the parties to the initial deal continue the conservation measures. The law on land-ownership and related matters in Scotland is very different from that in England and Wales, and in both jurisdictions is a subject of some complexity. What follows is merely a brief indication of some of the issues and possibilities which arise.

As far as ownership of the land is concerned, if one wishes to secure the **1.3.15** land for more than the lifetime of one individual, or to protect against an individual owner's change of mind, the solution lies in the complexities of the law on trusts, charities and associations. Land may be acquired by a conservation body in its own right if it is an incorporated association and therefore enjoys its own legal personality. Otherwise, the land must be vested in trustees, either for an association, or subject to a trust the objectives of which include the conservation of nature. Such a trust can avoid the legal restrictions on private trusts, in Scotland by being a public trust and in England and Wales by seeking charitable status. In the 1920s a trust to create a specific form of sanctuary for wild animals was held not to constitute a valid charitable trust as it had no benefit to the community,[165] but "the advancement of environmental protection or improvement" is now expressly recognised as a charitable purpose.[166]

If outright ownership is not possible or desired, land may be taken on a **1.3.16** lease, the terms of which allow the land to be managed in a way compatible with nature conservation. This is a common device as landowners may be reluctant to part with their land permanently, but be prepared to allow the land to be used for conservation purposes for a fixed term, at the end of which the owners will be free to reconsider how they wish the land to be used.

A simple agreement between the owner of the land and some other party **1.3.17** to the effect that the owner will do or not do certain things in order to conserve or enhance the nature conservation value of the land is also possible, and can be framed so as to be legally enforceable. However, such an

---

[163] See paras 1.5.9–1.5.11, below.

[164] Many National Nature Reserves are not owned by the conservation bodies but leased or simply subject to management agreements.

[165] *Re Grove-Grady* [1929] 1 Ch. 557; cf. *Re Verrall* [1916] 1 Ch. 100, confirming as charitable the purposes of the National Trust.

[166] Charities and Trustee Investment (Scotland) Act 2005 s.7(1)(m); Charities Act 2006 s.2(2)(i).

agreement suffers from the severe drawback that it will be a personal agreement, which binds only the original parties. Therefore if the owner dies or sells the land to another, the agreement is at an end. In relation to such "management agreements" entered by many official bodies, this problem is solved by statutory provisions which ensure that such agreements, once registered, do run with the land, binding successors to the original contracting owner.[167]

1.3.18 Without statutory intervention, it is unlikely that similar management agreements between private parties can practically be prolonged and protected in such a way. In England and Wales agreements limiting the use of land, restrictive covenants, can run with the land, binding successors to the owner who initially agreed to the limitations, but this is possible only where the covenant is for the benefit of some land held by the other party to the agreement or his successors, and where the covenant has been registered. Moreover, it is only the holder of the benefited land who can enforce the covenant.

1.3.19 An agreement not to use or develop a site in certain ways may in some circumstances be regarded as benefiting other land, but for this to be a useful conservation device, the conservation body or whoever made the initial agreement with the landowner must have done so in a capacity as owner of that benefited land, and only if it continues to be the owner of the benefited land (or the succeeding owner shares its views on this point) will the covenant be enforced. In practice, this requires a fairly unlikely combination of circumstances. Similar requirements that there be land which benefits from an obligation before it can be recognised as running with the burdened land prevent the development of "conservation easements", a concept which has developed across the US.[168]

1.3.20 In Scotland the rights of the feudal superior that enabled the creation and enforcement of enduring restrictions and conditions on the use of land, regardless of whether neighbouring land was held, were abolished as part of the wholesale reform of land law in Scotland.[169] In general, therefore any conditions that can be imposed will face the same limitations as in England and Wales in that they will run with the land only if imposed for the benefit of some adjoining land and be enforceable only by those with an interest in such land.[170]

1.3.21 However, special provision is made for "conservation burdens", conditions imposed for the benefit of one of the prescribed "conservation bodies" or the Scottish Ministers and designed to preserve or protect the special characteristics of the land, including its flora and fauna.[171] Once the burden has been registered, the conservation body or the Ministers can enforce the conditions even though they have no interest in related land and the right to enforce the burden can subsequently be assigned between conservation bodies and the Ministers. The approved conservation bodies are designated

---

[167] e.g. NPACA 1949 s.16.

[168] See E. Byers and K. Marchetti Ponte, *The Conservation Easement Handbook*, 2nd edn (Washington DC: Land Trust Alliance & Trust for Public Land, 2005); Uniform Conservation Easement Act drafted by the National Conference of Commissioners on Uniform State Laws (1981).

[169] Abolition of Feudal Tenure (Scotland) Act 2000.

[170] Title Conditions (Scotland) Act 2003.

[171] Title Conditions (Scotland) Act 2000 ss.38–42.

by the Ministers and include SNH, the National Trust for Scotland, Plantlife, the Scottish Wildlife Trust and the Woodland Trust.[172] So long as they acted promptly, it was possible for conservation bodies or the Ministers to convert any rights to enforce conditions that they held on the basis of their role as feudal superiors into rights under a conservation burden.[173]

Even if it does prove possible for an agreement to run with the land as **1.3.22** described above, in both jurisdictions parties can apply to the relevant Lands Tribunal to be discharged from their obligations under the agreement. The Tribunals have the power to modify or discharge the obligations if in Scotland they are found to be unreasonable,[174] or in England and Wales if they are found to be obsolete or to be impeding a reasonable use of land, or if the proposed modification or discharge causes no injury to the beneficiary of the covenant.[175] It is clear therefore that resort must be had to statutory provisions if effective steps are to be taken to control the way in which land is managed so as to further nature conservation.

Public Rights of Access

One of the most basic rights of the landowner, to control who can and **1.3.23** cannot enter the land, has been significantly affected by recent legislation conferring public rights of access to the countryside. It may therefore no longer be possible for a landowner to protect certain habitat from disturbance by the simple means of excluding all visitors. The statutory access rights do, however, recognise the need to ensure that the exercise of these rights does not lead to damage to the natural heritage.[176]

In England and Wales, the public right of access under the Countryside **1.3.24** and Rights of Way Act 2000 is to "access land" as shown in the conclusive maps drawn up for this purpose by Natural England and CCW.[177] The areas covered are essentially open land which is mountain, moor, heath or down or land dedicated for this purpose, although within these areas there are many exceptions. Any members of the public can enter and remain on access land for the purposes of open-air recreation provided that they comply with the restrictions on this right, which include prohibitions on: intentionally or recklessly either taking, killing, injuring or disturbing any animal, bird or fish, or damaging or destroying any eggs or nest; intentionally removing, damaging or destroying any plant, shrub, tree or root or any part of one; engaging in any operation connected with hunting, shooting, fishing, snaring or trapping or having such equipment.[178] The access rights therefore do not cover any conduct that will consciously prejudice wildlife. To protect nesting birds, dogs must be kept on a short lead (no more than 2 metres)

---

[172] Title Conditions (Scotland) Act 2003 (Conservation Bodies) Order 2003 (SSI 2003/453) as amended.

[173] Abolition of Feudal Tenure (Scotland) Act 2000 s.27.

[174] Title Conditions (Scotland) Act 2003 Pt 9.

[175] Law of Property Act 1925 s.84, as amended by Law of Property Act 1969 s.28.

[176] For further information see the relevant web-pages operated by Natural England (*http://www.countrysideaccess.gov.uk/content/view/full/75*), CCW (*http://www.ccw.gov.uk/enjoying-the-country.aspx*) and SNH (*http://www.outdooraccess-scotland.com/default.asp*) [All Accessed May 4, 2009].

[177] CRWA 2000 s.1.

[178] CRWA 2000 s.2 and Sch.2.

between March 1 and July 31.[179] More specifically, one of the grounds on which the relevant body[180] can issue directions restricting or excluding access rights is for the purpose of conserving flora, fauna or geological or phy- siographical features.[181]

1.3.25 In Scotland the right of responsible access under the Land Reform (Scotland) Act 2003 applies to most land that has not been developed or is not being used for crops[182] and understanding the natural heritage is expressly stated as one of the reasons why people can enter and stay on the land.[183] Responsible access does not include access for hunting, shooting or fishing, nor with a dog not under proper control[184] and more generally is to be judged with regard to the provisions of the statutory Scottish Outdoor Access Code,[185] a distinct section of which is devoted to "Care for your environment" and gives guidance on avoiding disturbance to wildlife. The conservation and enhancement of the natural heritage is one of the purposes for which the local authority can make byelaws prohibiting, restricting or regulating access rights.[186] Additionally, SNH has the power to put up notices designed to protect the natural heritage by warning of the adverse impacts of behaviour,[187] and disregard of such warnings is again to be taken into account in determining if access rights are being exercised responsibly.[188]

Other Rights

1.3.26 Certain rights relating to wild animals may be held by someone other than the owner of the land concerned. The rights to take fish and game are incidents of the ownership of land, but can be separated from the land and granted to others.[189] In Scotland the right to take salmon is exceptionally a separate tenement, belonging to the Crown as part of the *regalia minora* unless granted to others, but generally the extent of any separation will depend on the terms of the particular grant by the owner of the land. The issue is complicated as the nature of the grant will depend on its terms—it may be viewed as a form of lease or merely as a personal licence granted by the landowner—and is to some extent affected by statute, especially in relation to agricultural land.[190] The provisions relating to game or fishing

---

[179] CRWA 2000 Sch.2 paras 4 and 6.

[180] NE, CCW or the Forestry Commissioners; CRWA 2000 s.21.

[181] CRWA 2000 s.26(3).

[182] The excluded land is set out in the Land Reform (Scotland) Act 2003 s.6 and further land can be excluded by the local authority (Land Reform (Scotland) Act 2003 s.11). The extent of the exclusion for land adjacent to a house "to enable persons living there to have reasonable measures of privacy in that house ... and to ensure that their enjoyment of that house ... is not unreasonably disturbed" (Land Reform (Scotland) Act 2003s.6(1)) has been explored in high-profile cases: *Gloag v Perth and Kinross Council*, 2007 S.C.L.R. 530; *Snowie v Stirling Council*, 2008 S.L.T. (Sh. Ct) 61.

[183] Land Reform (Scotland) Act 2003 s.1.

[184] Land Reform (Scotland) Act 2003 s.9.

[185] Land Reform (Scotland) Act 2003 s.2; the Code is governed by s.10.

[186] Land Reform (Scotland) Act 2003 s.12.

[187] Land Reform (Scotland) Act 2003 s.29.

[188] Land Reform (Scotland) Act 2003 s.2.

[189] See generally W.M. Gordon, *Scottish Land Law*, 2nd edn (Edinburgh: W. Green, 1999), Chs 8 and 9; C. Parkes & J. Thornley, *Fair Game: The Law of Country Sports and the Protection of Wildlife*, new revised edn (London: Pelham Books, 1997), Chs 3 and 12.

[190] e.g. the rights of a tenant to kill ground game (Ground Game Act 1880 s.3); see paras 4.2.6–4.2.8.

may also form part of a broader agreement and be affected by its character, e.g. it is common for landowners to reserve game and fishing rights when leasing land.

From a nature conservation point of view the separation of game and **1.3.27** fishing rights has significance in two ways. In the first place, if the wildlife of a site is to be protected, it may be necessary not only to ensure that suitable arrangements are made with the parties who own and occupy the land, but also to ascertain who holds the game and fishing rights and to make arrangements with them. Otherwise the measures undertaken to conserve nature may be undermined by the exercise of these separate rights over the land.

Secondly, game and fishing rights may be used as a means of furthering **1.3.28** conservation. In order to protect the species concerned, such rights may be acquired by those with an interest in conservation and then not exercised, thereby producing a de facto ban on shooting and fishing on the land, subject to statutory rights and pest control measures.[191] Short of such a policy, the existence of separate rights ensures that there is some party other than the owner of the land with an interest in its management. As measures to encourage a large and sustainable harvest of game and fish may also be of benefit to other wildlife,[192] particularly in preserving land in a comparatively natural state, free from intensive agriculture, the protection and enhancement of game rights may in itself be beneficial for nature conservation. It must be recognised though, that the protection of game can also lead to measures highly detrimental to some wild species, e.g. the unlawful destruction of birds of prey.

Legal Standing

The general position on the ownership of wild plants and animals has a **1.4.1** further consequence of major significance for the law on nature conservation. This relates to the legal standing of those wishing to protect the interests of wild plants and animals, or rather to their general lack of standing. The courts will only entertain actions from parties with a legally recognised interest in the subject of the litigation, therefore the issue of standing is of crucial importance to the extent to which those concerned for nature conservation can invoke the courts' assistance to further their aims and prevent damaging activities taking place.

What qualifies a person as having legal standing depends on the nature of **1.4.2** the action being raised, but generally the courts insist on some direct connection with the matter in dispute. It is not enough that a person is interested in an issue, in the way that a person may be interested in sport or the arts as their leisure pursuit; the law requires the person to have some legal interest in the subject matter. In relation to judicial review a slightly more

---

[191] A similar policy has been adopted in relation to salmon in Scotland, with the acquisition and dismantling of coastal netting stations in order to increase the stocks entering the rivers to breed.

[192] But not always, e.g. the large numbers of deer in parts of Scotland, allegedly encouraged by shooting interests, can do a lot of damage by overgrazing and preventing natural regeneration of woodland.

relaxed standard may be imposed, but the courts will still look for some real connection with the issue and will firmly shut their doors to anyone who appears to be interfering in something which is not properly his or her business.

1.4.3   Many of the provisions designed to protect wildlife do so by creating criminal offences. The extent to which nature conservation groups or concerned individuals can ensure that alleged offenders are brought to justice varies. In Scotland the position is that proceedings are instigated by the public prosecutors in all but the most exceptional circumstances. As any private prosecutors will have to show that they have been personally wronged by the alleged crime,[193] there appears no likelihood of private prosecution in the case of offences created to protect wild plants and animals or habitat.

1.4.4   In England and Wales the position is different, and although most prosecutions are handled by the public authorities, especially now the Crown Prosecution Service, prosecutions may be brought by private individuals, even where they have not themselves been the victim of the alleged crime. This means that action can be taken to invoke the criminal law, and prosecutions have been successfully brought by individuals, usually with the support of some organisation, e.g. cases relating to birds raised by officers of the Royal Society for the Protection of Birds.[194] However, as it is only the police or other authorised officers who enjoy the various statutory powers of search, etc. which may well be necessary in order to obtain the requisite evidence, co-operation with the public authorities is useful. Throughout Great Britain many police forces now have designated "wildlife" or "nature conservation" officers in an effort to make the work of the police in this field more effective.

1.4.5   In the civil law, the position in both jurisdictions is essentially the same. If there is an agreement of some sort with terms designed to promote nature conservation, in all but a handful of cases it is only the parties to that agreement who have the standing to enforce it.[195] Therefore, unless they are parties to the original agreement, there is no scope for conservation groups or the like to take action to ensure that a landowner keeps to the terms of a management agreement, or that the parties to a lease abide by terms designed to protect natural features.[196]

1.4.6   For actions in delict or tort, the pursuers/claimants must be able to show that they have suffered some legal wrong. As animals in the wild are not owned by anyone, nobody suffers a wrong if they are harmed, so that no recourse can be had to the courts. Plants are the property of the owners of the land, so that they alone are in a position to respond to damage done to them. Actions may be possible if the damaging conduct can be shown to

---

[193] *McBain v Crichton*, 1961 J.C. 25.

[194] For a discussion of trends in, and factors influencing the use of, private prosecutions see D.Carney, "Environmental interest groups and private prosecutions: a critical analysis" (2007) 19 E.L.M. 291.

[195] It may be possible to give effect to a clear intention to give a third party some rights under an agreement if the contract is drafted so as to invoke the general rules on third party rights provided in Scots law by the *jus quaesitum tertio* and in England and Wales under the Contracts (Rights of Third Parties) Act 1999.

[196] Agreements which run with the land, binding successors to the original parties, are discussed at paras 1.3.17–1.3.22, above.

cause harm to the pursuers' domestic animals, and in *Mull Shellfish Ltd v Golden Sea Produce Ltd*[197] the pursuers were allowed to seek damages for harm caused to free-floating mussel larvae that would have settled on the equipment maintained for the commercial rearing and cultivation of mussels. Damage to an interest in the land concerned, or in other land affected, will also create title to sue.[198] Nevertheless, the class of potential pursuers is small and firmly excludes conservation groups which may have a deep concern for, and interest in, the well-being of the species being affected, but no patrimonial interest which is being harmed.

There is potential for European Community law to be argued as a source **1.4.7** of rights providing a basis for action. The crucial question is whether the relevant legislation is regarded as creating individual rights which can be enforced through the courts. In some cases this is clear, especially in relation to procedural rights, such as the opportunities for public participation under the Environmental Assessment Directive.[199] In relation to substantive rights the position is less certain, as shown in *Bowden v Southwest-Services Ltd*,[200] where it was held that the Bathing Water and Urban Waste Water Directives[201] did not have such a direct impact on the interests of fisherman to support a case, whereas it was at least arguable that the Shellfish Directive[202] did create individual rights for mollusc fishermen which could form the basis of a claim for damages where harm resulted from a failure to implement its terms properly. Since any EC measures directly protecting wildlife are unlikely to be regarded as creating individual rights, it is in such procedural or indirect contexts that access to the courts may be provided. Actions based on the European Convention on Human Rights are available only to those who qualify as "victims", as interpreted by the European Court of Human Rights, but this may be possible for those who are the victims of unfair decision-making procedures or whose property is affected.[203]

A rare example where those with wider environmental concerns are spe- **1.4.8** cifically recognised is under the Environmental Liability Directive.[204] The power to take action in relation to biodiversity damage lies in the hands of the public authorities, but certain others are entitled to notify the authorities of instances of damage and request them to take action. If the information is plausible, the relevant authority must then consider the circumstances, consulting with the person responsible for the incident, and then either take action under the Directive or refuse the request, giving reasons for this decision (which will be subject to judicial review). The right to request action in this way is open to those with a sufficient interest in environmental decision making relating to the damage, which includes "any non-governmental organisation promoting environmental protection".[205]

---

[197] *Mull Shellfish Ltd v Golden Sea Produce Ltd*, 1992 S.L.T. 703.

[198] This would include game or fishing rights, which might form the basis for an action where harm is caused to the natural environment.

[199] e.g. *R. v Durham County Council, ex p. Huddleston* [2000] 2 C.M.L.R. 313; [2000] Env. L.R. 488.

[200] *Bowden v Southwest-Services Ltd* [1999] 3 C.M.L.R. 180; [1999] Env. L.R. 438.

[201] Directives 76/160/EEC and 91/271/EEC.

[202] Directive 79/923/EEC.

[203] Human Rights Act 1998 s.7; see para.1.5.4, below.

[204] Directive 2004/35/EC; see section 5.12, below, for a full account of this Directive that the UK has been shamefully late to implement.

[205] Directive 2004/35/EC arts 12 and 13.

1.4.9   Most nature conservation law at some stage involves public authorities, either the statutory conservation bodies or central or local government in the exercise of their planning and other powers. As statutory bodies they must keep within the limits of their statutory powers and properly fulfil their responsibilities and follow the prescribed procedures for their action. In most cases considerable discretion is conferred on the authorities, but their conduct will usually be subject to judicial scrutiny,[206] and the courts will be prepared to intervene if they are found to be acting ultra vires, i.e. illegally, irrationally or in breach of procedural propriety.[207] In both Scotland and England special procedures exist for parties challenging the conduct of public authorities by means of judicial review,[208] and a fundamental element of both is that the court will only consider a case at the instance of someone with sufficient standing.[209] A similar point arises under many statutory schemes where rights of appeal or challenge are restricted to "persons aggrieved".

1.4.10   The general approach is that only a person with some direct connection with the issue will be recognised as having sufficient standing to invoke the court's powers of judicial review. Regrettably, though, it is not possible to provide a simple, reliable statement of when a party will have standing. Apart from difficulties in assessing the extent to which recent decisions mark a significant shift in the law and in taking account of differences between jurisdictions, the issue is clouded by the fact that even where there may be room for argument, the legal standing of a party is often not challenged. Moreover, parties may be connected with a case in more than one way, so that it is difficult to identify precisely what features of their connection establish their title and interest to sue. The differing fates of local residents challenging quarry developments in *R. v North Somerset Council, ex p. Garnett* and *R. v Somerset County Council, ex p. Dixon*[210] reveal that the extent of connection with a case required before the courts will recognise standing can vary.

1.4.11   In Scotland the courts view the issue of title and interest to sue as a preliminary matter, to be determined before the substance of the case is considered,[211] and the two elements of the test may be treated separately, so that a party who is viewed as having title to sue, may fail on the basis that in the particular circumstances he has no sufficient interest.[212] No comprehensive definitions exist, but as far as title is concerned reference is

---

[206] Either under statutory procedures allowing reference to the court, e.g. in relation to planning (TCPA 1990 Pt XII; TCPSA 1997 Pt XI) or by means of judicial review.

[207] *Council of Civil Service Unions v Minister for the Civil Service* [1985] A.C. 374.

[208] In Scotland Chapter 58 of the Rules of the Court of Session, introduced by Act of Sederunt (Rules of the Court of Session 1994) 1994 (SI 1994/1443); in England and Wales, Supreme Court Act 1981 s.31, Part 54 of the Civil Procedure Rules 1998, as added by the Civil Procedure (Amendment No.4) Rules 2000 (SI 2000/2092).

[209] Similarly, decisions of EC institutions can be challenged under art.230 of the EC Treaty only by Member States or those with a "direct and individual concern" in the matter; see *Stichtung Greenpeace Council (Greenpeace International) v Commission* (C-321/95P) [1998] E.C.R. I-1651. Despite attempts to encourage a more relaxed approach, this requirement has been given a narrow interpretation by the European Court of Justice, e.g. *Unión de Pequeños Agricultores v Council* (C-50/00P) [2002] E.C.R. I-6677.

[210] Both reported in full at (1998) 10 J.E.L. 161, with commentary by J. Alder.

[211] *Scottish Old People's Welfare Council, Petitioners*, 1987 S.L.T. 179; in some cases, though, it is accepted that the issue of standing may not be separable from a consideration of the merits, *Gordon v Kirkcaldy District Council*, 1989 S.L.T. 507.

[212] As in *Scottish Old People's Welfare Council, Petitioners*, above.

frequently made to Lord Dunedin's comment in *D. & J. Nicol v Dundee Harbour Trustees*[213] that to have title a person:

"[M]ust be a party (using the word in its widest sense) to some legal relation which gives him some right which the person against whom he raises the action either infringes or denies".

This idea has been given a broad interpretation and in *Wilson v Independent Broadcasting Authority*[214] it has been held that where a public body owes a duty to the public, individual members of the public may have title to sue.[215]

However, even if person qualifies as having title to raise an issue, the court **1.4.12** must also be satisfied that he has an interest to do so. This requires that the particular issue is of some real concern to the party, and not an academic issue or merely something which he is raising as a matter of general public spirited concern.[216] Such interest, though, need not be a formal legal or property interest, e.g. in *Kincardine and Deeside District Council v Forestry Commissioners*[217] it was held that a local authority had interest on the basis of its "reasonable concern with a major project in their area which may affect the economy or amenity of the area generally".

In England and Wales, procedural reforms to the process of judicial **1.4.13** review in 1977 swept away a number of restrictive rules on locus standi and replaced them with the general test that the applicant must demonstrate "a sufficient interest in the matter to which the application relates".[218] This test has generally been given a fairly liberal interpretation, and been viewed as an issue which has to be considered as part of the broader consideration of the factual and legal circumstances of the case, not as a preliminary issue.[219] Some interest over and above that of the ordinary citizen has to be shown. If this is not possible, a party who does not have locus standi can attempt to persuade the Attorney General to instigate proceedings by way of a relator action, although the likelihood of success is small.[220]

The most significant development in recent years has been the courts' **1.4.14** increasing willingness to grant standing to campaigning groups. Decisions allowing Greenpeace to challenge the commissioning of a nuclear reprocessing unit at Sellafield and the World Development Movement to challenge financial support for a dam in Malaysia appear to establish that standing can be granted to such bodies.[221] Important features in these

---

[213] *D. & J. Nicol v Dundee Harbour Trustees*, 1915 S.C. (HL) 7 at 12–13.

[214] *Wilson v Independent Broadcasting Authority*, 1979 S.L.T. 279.

[215] In contrast it has been held that members of the public have no standing to challenge immigration decisions; *Rape Crisis Centre v Secretary of State for the Home Department*, 2000 S.C. 527.

[216] *Scottish Old People's Welfare Council, Petitioners*, 1987 S.L.T. 179.

[217] *Kincardine and Deeside District Council v Forestry Commissioners*, 1991 S.C.L.R. 729 at 734.

[218] Supreme Court Act 1981 s.31(3).

[219] *R. v Inland Revenue Commissioners, ex p. National Federation of Self-employed and Small Businesses Ltd* [1982] A.C. 617.

[220] H.W.R. Wade and C.F. Forsyth, *Administrative Law*, 9th edn (Oxford: OUP, 2004), pp.579–587.

[221] *R. v Inspectorate of Pollution, ex p. Greenpeace Ltd (No.2)* [1994] 4 All E.R. 329; *R. v Secretary of State for Foreign & Commonwealth Affairs, ex p. World Development Movement Ltd* [1995] 1 W.L.R. 386.

decisions were the advantages of a single action from an organised group, as opposed to many individual cases, and the importance of maintaining the rule of law where there may be no individual with a stronger right to sue. These cases represent a marked change of attitude from that shown in the *Rose Theatre* case[222] at the start of the 1990s, but do seem to represent the current generally accepted view, so much so that in one recent case raised by Greenpeace the judge stated that its legal standing to bring proceedings was "well established".[223] It is not yet clear how far this shift in the law will be reflected in Scotland, where there is no authoritative decision in a directly relevant field. In significant recent cases involving conservation issues, the standing of the Worldwide Fund for Nature and the Royal Society for the Protection of Birds has not been challenged,[224] and the cases in other areas where organisations have been refused standing can be distinguished, either because of the potential presence of individuals with a stronger interest[225] or because of the very different context of the dispute.[226]

1.4.15   In relation to more narrowly focused groups, e.g. residents' groups, the courts look at the substance of the party's interest in the matter, and the particular legal form of the party is not of crucial importance. Therefore if individuals would have title to sue in the particular circumstances, the fact that they have banded together to form an incorporated association which is in law a different person, is of no significance, and the association will enjoy standing to the extent that the individuals would personally.[227] However the capacity of unincorporated associations in England and Wales to become parties to legal action remains uncertain.[228]

1.4.16   Organisations or individuals can seek to strengthen their standing by ensuring that they take the opportunity to build a connection with any site in dispute and to participate in any formal procedures leading up to the decision they may wish to contest. In relation to planning decisions, the simplest way to become involved is through making representations in response to the initial application or at a public inquiry or other appeal proceedings, as it is well established that objectors have a clear right to ensure that proceedings have been conducted lawfully. Such involvement can transform someone from a concerned bystander, but a bystander

---

[222] *R. v Secretary of State for the Environment, ex p. Rose Theatre Trust Co* [1990] 1 Q.B. 504.

[223] *R. v Secretary of State for Trade and Industry, ex p. Greenpeace (No.2)* [2000] Env. L.R. 221 at 224; [2000] 2 C.M.L.R. 94 at 97 (Maurice Kay J).

[224] *WWF UK v Secretary of State for Scotland* [1999] 1 C.M.L.R. 1021; [1999] Env. L.R. 632; *RSPB v Secretary of State for Scotland*, 2000 S.L.T. 1272.

[225] *Scottish Old People's Welfare Council, Petitioners*, 1987 S.L.T. 179.

[226] *The Rape Crisis Centre v Secretary of State for the Home Department*, 2001 S.L.T. 389.

[227] *Scottish Old People's Welfare Council, Petitioners*, 1987 S.L.T. 179 at 185; *R. v Hammersmith and Fulham London Borough Council, ex p. People Before Profit Ltd* (1982) 80 LGR 322, at p.333, *R. v Secretary of State for the Environment, ex p. Rose Theatre Trust Co* [1990] 1 Q.B. 504, at 521; *Residents Against Waste Site Ltd v Lancashire County Council* [2007] EWHC 2558 Admin; [2008] Env. L.R. 27.

[228] Discussed in Law Commission, *Administrative Law: Judicial Review and Statutory Appeals* (Law Com., No.226, 1993–94 HC 669) at pp.51–52; *R. v Traffic Commissioners, ex p. "Brake"* [1996] COD 248.

nonetheless, into a legally interested party.[229] For example, in *Patmor Ltd v City of Edinburgh District Licensing Board*[230] it was held that the holders of a gaming licence had no title in that capacity to challenge the grant of a licence to another company for similar premises in the area, despite their obvious concern as rival traders to limit competition, but did have title in their capacity as objectors to the new application, having formally taken advantage of the opportunity to submit representations when the application was advertised. A failure to take an earlier opportunity to raise arguments may also lead to the court refusing to entertain them on the basis of acquiescence or estoppel.[231]

Problems of standing can often be avoided in practice but there are two **1.4.17** other features of judicial review that must be considered if cases are to be brought to court. The first is the need to act promptly.[232] In England and Wales the ability to refuse cases on the basis of "undue delay" takes statutory form,[233] and the maximum period allowed is three months from the contested decision.[234] This period is, however, the maximum, and action may be required well before it expires.[235] In Scotland the law is based on the doctrine of *mora* and acquiescence, with no fixed time periods but rather an assessment of whether the delay indicates acquiescence or would result in prejudice to others if the action were allowed to go ahead.[236] Especially where the decision to be challenged comes at the end of a protracted process, or the factual situation entails the interaction between different statutory procedures, there can be great difficulty in ascertaining exactly when "the clock starts running" for the purposes of determining whether action has been taken promptly.[237] It

---

[229] Despite the recent changes noted above, a court faced with the same circumstances as in *R. v Poole Borough Council, ex p. Beebee* (1991) 3 J.E.L. 293, might still view the failure of the Worldwide Fund for Nature to make representations in response to the initial planning application to be fatal to its standing, in contrast to the long history of involvement with the site by the British Herpetological Society (survey work, financial input to the site, planning authority's express provision for an opportunity to relocate lizards).

[230] *Patmor Ltd v City of Edinburgh District Licensing Board*, 1987 S.L.T. 492 (affirmed 1988 S.L.T. 850).

[231] *WWF UK v Secretary of State for Scotland* [1999] 1 C.M.L.R. 1021; [1999] Env. L.R. 632.

[232] C.T. Reid, "Environmental Citizenship and the Courts" (2000) 3 Env. L. Rev. 177 at pp.183–186; D. Carney, "The timing rules in judicial review and the practical difficulties they cause environmental interest groups: the need for reform" (2006) 8 Env. L. Rev. 278.

[233] Supreme Court Act 1981 s.31(6).

[234] Civil Procedure Rules 1998 r.54.5, as added by Civil Procedure (Amendment No.4) Rules 2000 (SI 2000/2092).

[235] e.g. *R. v Secretary of State for Trade and Industry, ex p. Greenpeace (No.1)* [1998] Env. L.R. 415; *R. v Ceridigion County Council, ex p. McKeown* [1998] 2 P.L.R. 1; G. Roots and R. Walton, "Promptness and Delay in Judicial Review – an update on the continuing saga" [2001] J.P.L. 1360.

[236] *Swan v Secretary of State for Scotland*, 1998 S.C. 479, noted at (1999) 11 J.E.L. 184; *R (Burkett) v Hammersmith and Fulham London Borough Council* [2002] UKHL 23, [2002] 1 W.L.R. 1593 at [59]–[66] (Lord Hope); *Scottish Water v Scottish Ministers*, 2004 S.L.T. 495.

[237] See, for example, *R. v Secretary of State for Trade and Industry, ex p. Greenpeace (No.1)* [1998] Env. L.R. 415 and *R. v Secretary of State for Trade and Industry, ex p. Greenpeace (No.2)* [2000] Env. L.R. 221, [2000] 2 C.M.L.R. 94; the initial licensing process took over 16 months, and then the need to await the outcome of the first case added a further dimension to the problem of determining when the basis for action had crystallised.

is clear though, in England and Wales at least,[238] hat the vital date is the date of the formal award of any permission, etc. although starting an action before then will be possible in relation to crucial flaws earlier in the process.[239]

1.4.18　　A second feature is the practical one of cost.[240] The legal and other costs of taking an action, and in particular the liability to pay the other side's costs in the event of defeat, present a major obstacle to many parties who might consider seeking judicial review.[241] In recent years, though the courts have shown increased willingness to contemplate protective costs orders, limiting a party's potential liability, where actions are of general public importance.[242] In relation to interim relief, though, e.g. halting development of a site while the legality of the authorisation for it is challenged, a major obstacle is provided by the usual requirement to provide cross-undertakings in damages (paying compensation for losses arising from the delay if the legal challenge fails).[243] As in the *Lappel Bank* case,[244] this can mean that ultimate success in the courts is of limited practical value if damaging operations have taken place in the meantime.

HUMAN RIGHTS

1.5.1　　The legal background in the United Kingdom was transformed as a result of legislation in 1998 which also merits brief discussion. The impact of the Acts of Parliament giving effect to devolution is discussed in the following Chapter,[245] but at this stage something has to be said about the new status of human rights. The Human Rights Act 1998, which came fully into force in October 2000, provides that it is unlawful for any "public authority" to act in a way that is incompatible with an individual's Convention rights; these are set out in Schedule 1 to the Act which in effect reproduces most of the content of the European Convention on Human Rights. Some key points of the legal framework and then the potential for specific rights to affect nature conservation law will be mentioned. Under the devolution arrangements any

---

[238] A different view was taken in the Court of Session in *Simson v Aberdeenshire Council* [2007] CSIH 10; 2007 S.C. 366, a case in which remarkably no reference was made to the decision of the House of Lords in *Burkett* (all the more remarkable because of Lord Hope's substantial comments there on the position in Scots law—[59]–[66]).

[239] *R. (Burkett) v Hammersmith and Fulham London Borough Council* [2002] UKHL 23; [2002] 1 W.L.R. 1593; *R. (Catt) v Brighton and Hove City Council* [2007] EWCA Civ 298; [2007] Env. L.R. 32.

[240] Brooke L.J., "David Hall Memorial Lecture: Environmental Justice: the cost barrier" (2006) 18 J.E.L. 341.

[241] So much so that it can be argued that the cost of litigation means that the UK is failing to meet its obligation under the Aarhus Convention to provide access to review procedures that are "not prohibitively expensive"; Convention on Access to Information, Public Participation in Decision-Making and Access to Justice in Environmental Matters (UNECE, 1998), art.9(4).

[242] *R. (Corner House Research) v Secretary of State for Trade and Industry* [2005] EWCA Civ 192; [2005] 1 W.L.R. 2600; *McArthur v Lord Advocate*, 2006 S.L.T. 170.

[243] M. Beloff, "How Green is Judicial Review?" (2004) 16 E.L.M. 175 at 180–181.

[244] *R. v Secretary of State for the Environment, ex p. RSPB* (C-44/95) [1996] E.C.R. I-3805.

[245] See section 2.3, below.

action incompatible with Convention rights is also outwith the powers of the devolved authorities in Scotland and Wales and can be declared invalid by the procedures in the devolution legislation.[246]

The "public authorities" which must not act in a way incompatible with **1.5.2** Convention rights are defined to include courts and tribunals and other persons or bodies with at least some functions "of a public nature".[247] It is clear that Ministers are public authorities, as are local authorities, National Park authorities, the statutory conservation bodies, arguably the National Trusts and potentially bodies such as the RSPB to the extent that certain of their activities, such as managing an officially declared National Nature Reserve,[248] can be classed as "public". Action that is incompatible with Convention rights is unlawful and may in some circumstances give rise to a claim for damages where such an award is necessary to ensure "just satisfaction" for the recipient, taking all the circumstances into account; in many cases judicial review resulting in the quashing of the offending decision is likely to be the appropriate remedy.[249] If recourse to the British courts does not provide a satisfactory solution, it remains possible to raise a case before the European Court of Human Rights in Strasbourg, arguing that the United Kingdom has acted in breach of the Convention, although this is a lengthy process.

Where it is argued that the effect of legislation is incompatible with **1.5.3** Convention rights, the first duty of the courts is to "read and give effect to" legislation in a way that is compatible with Convention rights,[250] giving the courts more than the usual room for manoeuvre in finding a meaning that meets the requirements of the Convention. If legislation cannot be read in a way that is compatible, then subordinate legislation, including any legislation from the Scottish Parliament and the National Assembly for Wales, can be declared to be invalid. However there is no power to override an Act of the Westminster Parliament or Order in Council made under the Royal Prerogative, and in these cases the most that the courts can do is issue a declaration of incompatibility, drawing the attention of Parliament and the government to the situation.[251] Remedial action to bring matters into line with Convention rights is expected but not legally required, thereby conserving the idea of parliamentary sovereignty and the powers of Parliament to have the final say. The position of Convention rights is thus very different from that of rights under EC law, which must be protected by the courts even though this involves overriding the terms of an Act of Parliament.[252]

1.5.4 Recourse to the courts is available only to those who claim to be **1.5.4**

---

[246] Scotland Act 1998 ss.29(2) and 57(2); Government of Wales Act 2006 ss.81 and 94; the provisions relating to devolved administrations took effect before the Human Rights Act 1998 came into force and in Scotland generated a large volume of litigation, mainly in relation to criminal procedure.

[247] Human Rights Act 1998 s.6; acts "of a private nature" of those bodies which have some public functions fall outwith the scope of the requirement.

[248] WCA 1981 s.35; see para.5.3.9, below.

[249] Human Rights Act 1998 s.8; *Watkins v Secretary of State for the Home Department* [2006] UKHL 17; [2006] 2 A.C. 395.

[250] Human Rights Act 1998 s.3.

[251] Human Rights Act 1998 s.4; measures of the Church Assembly and the General Synod of the Church of England are similarly protected.

[252] e.g. *R. v Secretary of State for Transport, ex p. Factortame Ltd (No.2)* [1991] 1 A.C. 603.

"victims" of an infringement of their rights.[253] Although the Convention refers in its title to "human rights", and some of the rights protected are clearly limited to human beings,[254] it has long been accepted that many of the rights are also enjoyed by "legal" as well as "natural" persons, so that companies and some associations can also seek recourse if their rights or freedoms are unduly restricted. The test for being a victim is essentially that one has been directly affected by the breach of rights, but although there is some generosity for family members or where a class of people are affected,[255] the test does impose a stricter standard than that adopted in some judicial review cases permitting public interest groups access to the courts.[256] It is, of course, fundamental to the whole enterprise that it is human rights that are protected and therefore the Convention offers very little to those seeking to protect wildlife. Indeed the European Court of Human Rights has explicitly stated that the Convention is not designed to provide general protection to the environment and that interference with the conditions of animal life on neighbouring land is not an attack on any person's rights, unless their own well-being is affected.[257]

1.5.5   In relation to nature conservation law therefore the argument is likely to be that aspects of the restrictions imposed for the benefit of nature conservation infringe the rights of those subject to controls.[258] The two articles that have given rise to argument are article 6, the right to a fair trial, and article 1 of Protocol 1, protection of property. The first of these, article 6, provides that "in the determination of his civil rights and obligations ... everyone is entitled to a fair and public hearing within a reasonable time by an independent and impartial tribunal", and the application of this provision to statutory decision-making and appeal mechanisms has generated much argument, including cases from the United Kingdom before the European Court of Human Rights, long before the 1998 Act was enacted. The fundamental issue in this area has been whether decision-making procedures, especially for designating Sites of Special Scientific Interest or under the town and country planning system, offer decisions made by "an independent and impartial tribunal" when either there is no external appeal from the initial administrative decision-maker or such appeals are to the Minister.[259] This leads on to the question of whether the potential for subsequent recourse to the courts (either under statutory procedures or by judicial review) is sufficient to ensure that the process as a whole meets the standards set in the Convention.

1.5.6   This issue has arisen in several cases, initially in the planning system.

---

[253] Human Rights Act 1998 s.7.

[254] e.g. the right to marry (art.12).

[255] e.g. *Open Door Counselling and Dublin Well Women v Ireland* (1992) 15 E.H.R.R. 244.

[256] In *R. (Vetterlein) v Hampshire County Council* [2001] EWHC 560 Admin; [2002] Env. L.R. 8 it was held that "generalised environmental concerns" are not enough to entitle an individual to invoke Convention rights as the basis of a claim.

[257] *Kyrtatos v Greece* (2005) 40 E.H.R.R. 16 at [52]–[53]; see also *R. (Vetterlien) v Hampshire County Council* [2001] EWHC 560 Admin; [2002] Env. L.R. 8 at [61].

[258] See generally C. Rodgers, "Protecting Sites of Special Scientific Interest: The Human Rights Dimension" [2005] J.P.L. 997.

[259] The potential for Ministers to call in decisions for their personal attention means that this criticism applies even where in practice appeals are delegated to inspectors or reporters.

Before the 1998 Act, the European Court of Human Rights held in *Bryan v United Kingdom*[260] that the recourse to the courts did mean that the planning process as a whole was sufficiently impartial, but at first instance the Court of Session in *County Properties Ltd v Scottish Ministers*[261] and the English High Court in *R. v Secretary of State for Environment, Transport & the Regions, ex p. Holding & Barnes Plc*[262] held that planning procedures[263] did involve an infringement of rights under article 6. The English case was then referred to the House of Lords[264] where it was decided that the appeal procedures did in fact live up to the standards demanded by the Convention, a decision followed by the Inner House in Scotland.[265] The system of appeals to ministers and their delegates, with recourse to judicial review for those aggrieved, could therefore be maintained. A subsequent case in a different area[266] has shown that the availability of judicial review will not be enough by itself to guarantee that a process lives up to the Convention's standards—the nature of the decision, the degree to which the initial decision-maker may have an interest in the outcome and the procedural safeguards in place at the initial stages are all relevant—but the parallel with planning is much more apt for decisions under the nature conservation regimes.

Like the planning system, the procedures for designating Sites of Special **1.5.7** Scientific Interest have also withstood challenges before the English courts that they are not compliant with article 6, most notably in *R. (Aggregate Industries UK Ltd) v English Nature*.[267] Especially in view of the strengthened impact of the designation under the reforms in 2000,[268] it has been accepted that designation by itself does affect "civil rights and obligations" so as to invoke article 6. [269] The fact that English Nature notifies and then confirms the designations itself, without any appeal to an external body[270] means that there is a lack of formal impartiality and independence at that stage, but in view of the procedural safeguards in the process, the nature of the decision (one of policy not of fact) and the availability of judicial review, the procedure as a whole was held to meet the standard set in article 6.[271]

Slightly apart from this line of litigation but also related to article 6 is **1.5.8**

---

[260] *Bryan v United Kingdom* (1996) 21 E.H.R.R. 342; followed by the European Court in *Chapman v United Kingdom* (2001) 33 E.H.R.R. 18.

[261] *County Properties Ltd v Scottish Ministers*, 2000 S.C. 430.

[262] *R v Secretary of State for Environment, Transport & the Regions, ex p. Holding & Barnes Plc* [2001] J.P.L. 291; [2001] P.L.R. 58 (known as the *Alconbury* case, after one of other cases in this joined action).

[263] Decisions affecting individual properties but not the making of a development plan—*R (Aggregate Industries UK Ltd) v English Nature* [2002] EWHC 908; [2003] Env. L.R. 3 at [71]–[72].

[264] *R. v Secretary of State for Environment, Transport & the Regions, ex p. Holding & Barnes Plc* [2001] UKHL 23; [2003] 2 A.C. 295.

[265] *County Properties v Scottish Ministers*, 2002 S.C. 79.

[266] *Tsfayo v United Kingdom* (2009) 48 E.H.R.R. 18, concerning housing and council tax benefit.

[267] *R. (Aggregate Industries UK Ltd) v English Nature* [2002] EWHC 908 Admin; [2003] Env. L.R. 3; see para.5.5.9, below.

[268] See paras 5.5.12–5.5.16, below.

[269] *R. (Aggregate Industries UK Ltd) v English Nature* [2002] EWHC 908; [2003] Env. L.R. 3; *R. (Boyd) v English Nature* [2003] EWHC 1105 Admin.

[270] In Scotland, the potential of a reference to the Advisory Committee adds a more external element, but the decision still rests with the conservation body itself; see para.5.5.32, below.

[271] *R. (Aggregate Industries UK Ltd) v English Nature* [2002] EWHC 908; [2003] Env. L.R. 3.

Lafarge Redland Aggregates v Scottish Ministers,[272] where it was held that there was insufficient appearance of impartiality when the Ministers in determining a planning application referred the question of whether the area concerned should be proposed as a Special Area of Conservation[273] to Scottish Natural Heritage, which had been among the main objectors to the application. Taken at its extreme, this decision seems to render it impossible for the statutory conservation bodies to fulfil their function of providing advice to ministers and at the same time to play any active part in any procedures where ministers may have to make decisions affecting legal rights. Such a conclusion would call for a wide reassessment of the many roles of these bodies,[274] but there is no indication at present that this analysis will be followed. In this case the court also held that article 6 had been breached on another ground, namely the inordinate delay in determining the planning application,[275] which had denied the applicants their right to a decision within a reasonable time, an outcome that may be welcome even though its precise legal basis may not be wholly clear.

1.5.9   In contrast to the procedural nature of the concerns under article 6, the second main issue raises substantive matters. Article 1 of Protocol 1 follows the pattern of most of the substantive articles of the Convention, with a broad statement of the right "to the peaceful enjoyment of ... possessions" followed by a qualification which permits a person to be deprived of his property "in the public interest and subject to conditions provided for by law." Issues under this article can arise in relation to nature conservation measures authorising compulsory purchase of land or restricting the owners' rights to do as they wish with their property. Case law from the European Court of Human Rights shows that property rights can legitimately be restricted in pursuit of environmental objectives, and that whether there has been a breach of the Convention will depend on the individual circumstances, with the decision resting on ideas such as a fair balance of interests and whether the interference with the individual's rights can be justified as a proportionate measure to achieve a permissible public goal.[276]

1.5.10   Such arguments have been discussed in two cases. In *R. (Fisher) v English Nature*[277] the potential for nature conservation measures to offend against the rights of the landowner was recognised, but on the facts it was held that there was no basis for arguing that the SSSI designation in question had a disproportionate impact on the landowner which English Nature had failed to take into account. The issue was more fully explored in *R. (Trailer & Marina (Leven) Ltd) v Secretary of State for the Environment, Food and Rural Affairs*[278] where it was argued that the amendments to the SSSI regime introduced in 2000 resulted in a significant reduction in the profit-earning capacity and hence in the value of land designated as an SSSI and that in the

---

[272] *Lafarge Redland Aggregates v Scottish Ministers*, 2000 S.L.T. 1361.

[273] See section 5.2, below.

[274] See para.2.6.9, below.

[275] Over five years after the end of the public inquiry (that itself came after lengthy proceedings), no decision had been made.

[276] e.g. *Fredin v Sweden* (1991) 13 E.H.R.R. 784; *Tre Traktörer AB v Sweden* (1989) 13 E.H.R.R. 309; *Matos e Silva Lda v Portugal* (1997) 24 E.H.R.R. 573.

[277] *R. (Fisher) v English Nature* [2004] EWCA Civ 663; [2005] 1 W.L.R. 147.

[278] *R. (Trailer & Marina (Leven) Ltd) v Secretary of State for the Environment, Food and Rural Affairs* [2004] EWCA Civ 1580; [2005] 1 W.L.R. 1267.

absence of compensation this amounted to a breach of article 1 of Protocol 1. After studying the case-law from the European Court of Human Rights, the court said that not every restriction of property requires compensation:

> "[P]rovided the state could properly take the view that the benefit to the community outweighs the detriment to the individual, a fair balance will be struck, without any requirement to compensate the individual".

However in other circumstances compensation would be required.[279] Examining the detailed statutory provisions and their effect, it was held that they did not:

> "[C]ome anywhere near the hypothetical category of a measure which is so manifestly disproportionate that it offends against the first sentence of article 1 of the First Protocol."[280]

The central scheme for restricting the rights of landowners for the purposes of nature conservation is therefore not incompatible with the Convention.

Since many of the conservation measures discussed below do have the **1.5.11** effect of restricting property rights, there may be scope for further challenges, but if decisions are taken with due regard for the competing public and private interests, if fair procedures are followed and appropriate appeal mechanisms operate promptly and if proper compensation is available in the event of compulsory acquisition, these should meet the standards of the Convention.

Other cases affecting property have given rise to arguments under article 8 **1.5.12** of the Convention, the right to respect for one's home and private life, where again the legitimacy of action on environmental grounds has been recognised, provided that there is an appropriate balance between the public interest being promoted and the private rights of individuals.[281] The right to life (article 2) has been raised where health is at risk from pollution or other dangers,[282] but this is unlikely to be an issue in relation to nature conservation, and the invocation of other rights will require a significant degree of legal ingenuity. The ban on hunting with dogs was also unsuccessfully challenged on the basis that it improperly infringed the rights of those affected.[283]

After the initial concern that decision-making procedures would need to **1.5.13** be radically overhauled, it seems that overall the Human Rights Act 1998 may not have much effect on the final results of the law with respect to nature conservation. Nevertheless it does provide a new discipline requiring

---

[279] *R. (Trailer & Marina (Leven) Ltd) v Secretary of State for the Environment, Food and Rural Affairs* at [58].

[280] *R. (Trailer & Marina (Leven) Ltd) v Secretary of State for the Environment, Food and Rural Affairs* at [71].

[281] e.g. *Powell and Rayner v United Kingdom* (1990) 12 E.H.R.R. 355; *Buckley v United Kingdom* (1996) 23 E.H.R.R. 101; *Chapman v United Kingdom* (2001) 33 E.H.R.R. 18; *Hatton v United Kingdom* (2003) E.H.R.R. 28.

[282] e.g. *Lopez Ostra v Spain* (1995) 20 E.H.R.R. 277; *Budayeva v Russia*, March 20, 2008, European Court of Human Rights.

[283] *Whaley v Lord Advocate* [2007] UKHL 107; 2008 S.C. (HL) 107; *R. (Countryside Alliance) v Attorney General* [2007] UKHL 52; [2008] 1 A.C. 719.

decision-makers to ensure that in taking decisions for conservation purposes due regard is paid to the personal and property rights of individuals and companies who are affected by those decisions.

LEGAL APPROACHES

1.6.1 Over the last 60 years, there has been significant evolution in the legal approaches to providing protection for wild plants and animals. Since the general legal background offers few opportunities for furthering conservation beyond the initiatives of private individuals on their own land, the development of nature conservation has depended on action by Parliament and government. The legislation enacted and the legal, economic and other tools used to give effect to policies aiming at conservation have changed considerably. Although the criminal law has always been used to control actions directly harmful to particular species, until the 1990s habitat protection rested almost entirely on the voluntary principle, with the emphasis on persuasion rather than direct regulation. Now significant direct controls are in place, but accompanied by an emphasis on conservation as a process that requires not just the prevention of harmful acts but also the positive management of land and other resources, in a partnership between private owners and the conservation authorities.

1.6.2 A detailed analysis (legal, historical, social, economic and political) of the approaches and techniques adopted, and those which have been rejected, would be a fascinating and lengthy study, especially when comparisons are drawn over time, with other areas of policy, e.g. agriculture and planning, and with the situation in other countries.[284] In the context of this book, however, it must suffice to look briefly at the voluntary principle that for so long dominated this area and to identify some key elements in the mechanisms discussed in the following Chapters that confer some protection on wild creatures and plants. These are:

- general conservation duties;
- the use of the criminal law;
- sanctions;
- enforcement powers;
- the acquisition of property rights;
- the imposition of notification requirements of various sorts;
- the use of agreements to provide long-term conservation;
- the use of management plans and schemes;
- financial incentives and penalties; and
- the innovation of liability for biodiversity damage.

Underlying all of this is a shift from a wholly voluntary approach to one that still favours voluntary measures but promotes these against a background where meaningful sanctions are available not only against those who clearly damage but also against those who fail to maintain the conservation interest of their land.

---

[284] See, for example, L. Fromond, J. Similä and L. Suvantola, "Regulatory Innovations for Biodiversity Protection in Private Forests – Towards Sustainability" (2009) 21 J.E.L. 1.

From Voluntary Principle to Partnership

The structure of the law on nature conservation was until fairly recently **1.6.3**
completely dominated by reliance on the voluntary principle. The legal
structures were based on persuasion, not compulsion. This was in marked
contrast to other areas of law, so that whereas the controls imposed under
the modern town and country planning system have always clearly prohibited activities that were considered undesirable, the nature conservation
measures essentially offered protection only if the landowner agreed to
accept restrictions, usually in exchange for compensation. A range of social,
political and technical arguments can explain this disparity, but two key
points can be identified. First, nature conservation was not viewed as
important enough to justify direct interference with private rights.[285] Secondly, there was a view that the land was best cared for through the stewardship of its existing owners, not through rules and regulations.

Reliance on the voluntary principle has had its strong supporters and **1.6.4**
critics. Supporters argue that the best guardians of the countryside and its
valuable habitat are those who own it and live and work there. Successful
conservation requires the continuing commitment of those on the ground,
and this is best achieved by obtaining the willing co-operation of those
involved. Any attempt to order them to manage their land in a particular
way would in many cases be met with at best resentful compliance with the
mere letter of the law, whereas proper conservation measures depend on a
thorough acceptance of the objectives being pursued, so that the whole
management of the land and of the activities on it takes account of the
natural heritage. Even if it were possible to specify everything necessary to
ensure appropriate management, the problems of monitoring and enforcement on a long-term basis mean that laws imposed on unwilling landowners
would not prove a success. The need for continuing management of the land
in appropriate ways provides a valid distinction with the planning system.
For this reason, it is argued, nature conservation is better served by offering
assistance and encouragement so that landowners become willing partners
in the conservation enterprise, not reluctant servants.

The voluntary approach also emphasises the importance of education. **1.6.5**
The law cannot hope to deal with all of the matters of significance for
biodiversity, nor to regulate all the sites that contribute to the overall health
and richness of the environment, therefore a general raising of awareness of
the value and requirements of conservation is what is called for. Through
the operation of the statutory designations and consultation requirements,
and through the provision of advice and information, people can be made
aware of how they can protect and promote biodiversity, and in many cases
do so without prejudicing any of their other interests. In the long-term this
gentle encouragement to a change in attitudes will provide a more secure
basis for nature conservation than will any specific legal measures which are
subject to repeal or amendment to suit the political exigencies of the day.

On the other hand, a negative assessment of the voluntary approach is to **1.6.6**
say that it gives far too much weight to private interests at the expense of the

---

[285] A view held particularly by some of those with political influence: see, e.g. the debates in
the House of Lords during the passage of the Natural Heritage (Scotland) Bill, especially on
January 23, 1991; *Hansard*, HL Vol.525, cols 173–185.

public interest in nature conservation. The rights of landowners to do as
they please with their property are given undue protection,[286] and landowners (often already of considerable wealth) could receive large payments
in order to do nothing. Conservation is seen as a public objective, yet the
state uses bribery at the taxpayers' expense, not the power of the law, to
promote it. Moreover the voluntary system that was adopted was open to
abuse, as payments for maintaining the land in its desired condition could be
triggered by proposals which were at best speculative and which the landowner never really intended to carry through. The overall approach left
unsympathetic landowners free to ruin even the most valuable of sites, and
put all habitat protection at the mercy of the willingness of landowners to
co-operate and of the resources available to the conservation bodies for
compensation payments. The relentless history of habitat destruction over
past decades by itself condemns the voluntary approach on its own as an
inadequate way of achieving meaningful conservation.

1.6.7   Whatever one's assessment, it should be recognised that in the past the
voluntary principle had to operate against a generally unsympathetic
background, in which environmental concerns were a low priority for
government and for individuals. With changes in official and public attitudes[287] and an official commitment to sustainability, that background has
changed markedly since the early 1980s, and there is the potential for the
voluntary principle really to come into its own, supported at last by adequate funding and by complementary policies in agriculture, forestry and
other areas which have a major effect on the countryside. The past failures
can to some extent be attributed to the fact that the principle was never
given the opportunity to work properly.

1.6.8   The voluntary approach has, however, been abandoned as the sole basis
for conservation measures. The need to guarantee the protection of sites in
order to meet the requirements of the Habitats and Species Directive meant
that total reliance on voluntary measures was no longer tenable and growing
public concern for conservation and awareness of the failings of the previous
law have led to the stronger measures introduced for this century.[288] These
do include prohibitions and a degree of compulsion at odds with a wholly
voluntary approach,[289] but to a considerable extent they remain in the
background. The foreground emphasis is still on co-operation and on a
partnership between public bodies and private interests. Thus the mechanisms for European Sites and the reformed system of SSSIs still give prominence to management agreements as the key means of securing the

---

[286] Compare the restrictive approach to interpreting statutory provisions which interfere with
property rights suggested in *North Uist Fisheries Ltd v Secretary of State for Scotland*, 1992
S.L.T. 333 with the recognition of conservation measures as a valid reason for limiting landowners' rights to enjoy their property in *R. (Trailer & Marina (Leven) Ltd) v Secretary of State
for the Environment, Food and Rural Affairs* [2004] EWCA Civ 1580; [2005] 1 W.L.R. 1267 (see
para.1.5.10, above).

[287] It is interesting to speculate whether the educational and persuasive impact of the
voluntary approach itself contributed to this change, or whether the change was slowed by the
fact that the voluntary approach appeared to give conservation a low priority in competition
with other public goals.

[288] See para.1.1.24, above.

[289] The extent of the increase in the legal powers of the conservation bodies is shown by the
fact that appeal mechanisms have had to be introduced to review their actions, where none were
needed before; see paras 5.5.16 and 5.5.36, below.

protection of sites, and management schemes for SSSIs in England and Wales[290] do not by themselves impose direct obligations.

Establishing an effective partnership is undoubtedly made easier by the presence of the stronger measures "in the shadows", and also by the more sympathetic background created by the gradual changes in agricultural policy.[291] Both of these encourage landowners to co-operate with the conservation bodies and to see conservation-related measures as a sensible and indeed desirable part of their management of the land. It is thus possible to gain many of the advantages of the voluntary approach, whilst ensuring that its one great flaw is cured by the presence of compulsion as a measure of last resort. **1.6.9**

A further element in securing partnership is the increased emphasis on positive management of sites. Attention has shifted from merely trying to prevent specific activities that damage sites to endeavouring to protect them from gradual deterioration and to enhance their conservation value. The increased attention paid to management statements, plans and schemes[292] is part of a wider move towards looking at the enhancement of areas and the financial mechanisms are reflecting this. A criticism of the older management agreements was that too often they rewarded those who had proposed damaging changes to their sites but did nothing for those who willingly cared for the wildlife on their land. Money was spent on stopping things happening rather than actually furthering conservation. Over the last 20 years there has been a significant change away from compensatory payments to positive payments for the active management and enhancement of the land.[293] The new attitude was boldly stated in the *Guidelines on Management Agreement Payments and Other Related Matters* issued in February 2001[294]: **1.6.10**

> "Ministers expect that management agreements on SSSIs will be used to facilitate their positive management. ... Ministers are not prepared for public money to be paid out simply to prevent new operations which could destroy or damage these national assets."

We are still in the early days of transition, from a "toothless" system[295] that was totally dependent on the voluntary principle with almost nothing to support it if agreement could not be reached, to one where significant legal powers do exist to take the steps necessary to preserve and enhance the natural heritage, but voluntary partnership is the preferred means of achieving significant gains. The "mould was broken" by the implementation of the Habitats and Species Directive which introduced compulsion in place **1.6.11**

---

[290] See para.5.5.18, below.

[291] See paras 8.4.3–8.4.12, below.

[292] See paras 1.6.31–1.6.32, below.

[293] Even before the reforms under the CRWA 2000 took effect, compensatory agreements accounted for only four per cent of the land covered by management agreements in England (English Nature, *Annual Report for 2000–2001*, p.9).

[294] DETR, 2001, para.1.2; technically this applied to England only but the same approach was taken throughout Great Britain: "The continuing and future use of Management Agreements as a positive tool forms the backbone of [our strategy]" (SNH, *Natural Care Strategy*, 2001).

[295] Lord Mustill in *Southern Water Authority v Nature Conservancy Council* [1992] 1 W.L.R. 775 at 778.

of a wholly voluntary approach and this breakthrough has been followed by the reforms this century. Already it must seem remarkable to those studying this area for the first time that the old, voluntary system was seen as the appropriate way to deal with the manifold threats to biodiversity in this country.

1.6.12   Whatever the overall approach, the law employs a combination of mechanisms to achieve its end. The rest of this section comments briefly on some of the key devices used in the protection of both species and habitats, and in doing so reveals how the law has been changing and some impending developments.

General Conservation Duties

1.6.13   A feature of nature conservation law is the prevalence of general duties placed on public bodies and statutory undertakers to have regard to or to further biodiversity, sustainable development, natural beauty or other general interests. These are discussed in more detail elsewhere.[296] The significance of such duties may lie more in their aspirational and symbolic role than in the scope for enforcing them directly, but they are not without value. Against a legal background which traditionally has recognised only a narrow range of interests, primarily human health and property rights, they make it clear that conservation is a legitimate concern that can shape decisions. Without such statutory recognition, conservation interests could in many circumstances be wholly ignored, and indeed in some circumstances might have to be ignored, so that such obligations do have an important role in shaping the context within which individual conflicts of interests and priorities must be resolved.

Criminal Law

1.6.14   The criminal law is used to mark out forms of conduct which are considered to be unacceptable in society. As well as the direct penalties and deterrent, the use of the criminal courts and the stigma of conviction should bring home to offenders, and the public generally, the fact that such actions are regarded as unacceptable. The law has been used to create a number of offences prohibiting the killing, injuring or other harm to wild animals and plants.[297]

1.6.15   There are good reasons for utilising laws which render harm to wild animals and plants criminal. In the first place the most obvious thing which we can do to protect wildlife is to refrain from killing, injuring or disturbing it, and making such conduct a crime is the most direct legal way of trying to prevent it. Secondly, from the legal point of view, such laws are comparatively simple. The undesirable conduct is defined, any necessary exceptions are stated, and then the operation of the law is left to the general system of law enforcement, with no need for special administrative arrangements. Thirdly, such laws are useful in terms of publicity and education, as they should be readily comprehensible, although public awareness of the law is not necessarily high, and there may be problems in relation to provisions

---

[296] See sections 1.2, above, and 2.2, below.
[297] e.g. the intentional killing of most wild birds; see Ch.3, below.

designed to protect particular species which may not be widely recognised in the field.

However, there are factors which may reduce the effectiveness of this **1.6.16** approach to conservation legislation. By requiring the express prohibition of the undesirable conduct, there is a risk that some forms of harm, or some species in need of protection, will be omitted. The presence of gaps and possible loopholes may undermine the law, and it may be difficult to persuade the legislators to make the effort to enact the necessary amendments promptly. In the second place, criminal offences are likely to be directed against obvious and direct harm, so that the gradual deterioration of habitats and the harmful consequences incidental to other legitimate activities are likely to escape sanction. Thirdly, given the nature of the acts and their locations, the commission of criminal offences that focus exclusively on the doing of harmful acts may be hard to prove in court. This problem is eased, though, by the central measures prohibiting direct harm against wildlife being supported by ones on possession and sale of specimens or equipment so that the law can catch more than just the instant when harm is done.[298] Similarly, what would otherwise be a very heavy burden on the prosecution in proving that acts were done with criminal intent is avoided by the use of strict liability. This enables criminal liability to be imposed without the need to prove that the prohibited act was done intentionally, recklessly, negligently or knowingly, but does carry the risk of trivialising the offences in some eyes since they are not seen as truly criminal.[299] Another heavy burden for the prosecution is also avoided on occasions by placing the onus on the accused to establish that they fall within any exceptions to an offence.

The criminal law is also used in another way, as the final sanction to **1.6.17** secure compliance with a number of essentially administrative schemes, e.g. in relation to the planning system.[300] In this context the use of the criminal law shares the features of its use in many other regulatory schemes, especially the general perception that the offences involved are not "real crimes". This means that the offences are given a low priority at all stages in the administration of justice, and that the consequences of conviction, in terms of penalty and stigma, are often minimal.[301]

Sanctions

The effectiveness of the law is weakened if there are no meaningful sanctions **1.6.18** against those who ignore its provisions. The criminal law is undermined by the courts imposing only low penalties on offenders, penalties which are trivial in proportion to the economic gain which has been achieved by ignoring the law and the irreparable nature of the harm done. The penalties available were originally limited to fines but crimes against wildlife sometimes attracted substantial penalties, remarkably so in view of the derisory fines that are too often imposed for offences in other areas of environmental law. Judges had on occasion expressed their view that in fact imprisonment

---

[298] See para.3.2.5, below.

[299] K. Hawkins, *Environment and Enforcement* (Oxford: Clarendon Press, 1984), pp.202–207.

[300] See section 8.2, below.

[301] J. Rowan-Robinson, P. Watchman and C. Barker, *Crime and Regulation: A Study of the Enforcement of Regulatory Codes* (Edinburgh: T&T Clark, 1990).

would have been the appropriate sentence and heavier penalties, including custodial sentences, have been provided under the Countryside and Rights of Way Act 2000 and the Nature Conservation (Scotland) Act 2004 and have been used. The use of forfeiture powers can also make a penalty more meaningful.[302]

1.6.19   A further substantial sanction that can be available is the imposition of a restoration order.[303] In addition to imposing a penalty, offenders can be required to restore any natural feature affected by their offence to its former state. Failure to comply with such an order is itself an offence and entitles the conservation body to undertake the restoration itself and recover the costs from the offender. Not only does this seek to repair the damage to the natural world, but also compliance may involve more substantial costs and a longer term commitment than simply paying the fine determined by the court. The loss of financial subsidies may also be a significant sanction in the event of failing to live up to environmental expectations.[304]

1.6.20   New options in relation to sanctions may be available under the Regulatory Enforcement and Sanctions Act 2008.[305] Under Part 3 of this Act orders can be made giving regulatory bodies a new range of powers to deal with breaches of the law. Where such an order has been made, the regulatory body can itself, without having to go to court, impose a fixed monetary penalty or a "discretionary requirement", requiring payment of a financial penalty determined in accordance with guidelines and/or action to ensure that there is no recurrence of the offence and/or that restoration takes place. Another possibility is accepting an "enforcement undertaking" whereby the "offender" agrees to take measures to prevent recurrence of the offence and to restore the position. Where a fixed penalty has been imposed or the offender is complying with the other measures, no criminal prosecution can be started. These new measures give regulatory bodies, such as the statutory conservation bodies, the potential to operate a wider range of sanctions themselves, without relying on the courts, and Natural England is known to be interested in being able to use these powers.[306] There are, however, concerns that such measures may go too far in removing from those subject to penalties the procedural safeguards built in to the criminal justice system to ensure a fair trail.[307]

---

[302] e.g. WCA 1981 s.21(6) which says that the court must order the forfeiture of any specimen that was the subject of the offence and may order the forfeiture of any vehicle, animal or other thing used in committing the offence. There is also interest being shown in using in an environmental context the general legislation on recovering the proceeds of crime; see "£1.2 million seized from illegal landfill operator" (2008) 397 ENDS Report 59.

[303] e.g. WCA 1981 s.31; NCSA 2004 s.40.

[304] See para.1.6.35, below.

[305] The background to this Act lies in Prof. Macrory's report, *Regulatory Justice: Making Sanctions Effective* (Better Regulation Executive, 2006). The Act has limited application in Scotland.

[306] "Civil Sanctions for Offences against Nature" (2008) 405 ENDS Report 34.

[307] These procedural safeguards are guaranteed under art.6 of the European Convention on Human Rights and apply on the basis of the nature of the process involved, not its label (criminal/civil/administrative): *Öztürk v Germany* (1984) 6 E.H.R.R. 406.

Enforcement Powers

If legal protection of wildlife is to be successful, as well as there being well- **1.6.21**
constructed laws supported by appropriate sanctions, there must be effective
powers to enable compliance to be monitored in practice. Nature conservation offences present particular difficulties in detection, investigation
and preparation for court since there may be problems in identifying the
species which are given special protection or proving the origin of particular
specimens, whilst by their very nature many of the offences are going to be
committed in remote places away from the eyes of witnesses. In Scotland
some recognition is given to these latter difficulties by the relaxation in some
instances of the rules on corroboration, allowing the evidence of one witness
to suffice for conviction.[308]

The ability to enforce the law is considerably enhanced by the powers **1.6.22**
given to the police and wildlife inspectors. These powers, primarily found in
the Wildlife and Countryside Act 1981 but greatly augmented this century,[309] give wildlife inspectors authorised by the Minister wide powers of
entry to land and premises to carry out inspections and powers to take
samples, including having a veterinary surgeon take blood from living
creatures. The police also enjoy wide powers of stop, search and seizure,[310]
and many forces now have wildlife crime officers dedicated to work in this
area, frequently involving close liaison with statutory and voluntary conservation bodies.[311] The powers available to official bodies are important not
just to take action in connection with suspected offences but to enable other
aspects of the law to operate effectively, e.g. habitat protection laws are
enhanced by the powers of entry and inspection enjoyed in relation to the
designation and monitoring of SSSIs and other sites.[312] Through these
means the authorities can gather the information and evidence needed to
ensure that the law can actually be implemented and enforced effectively.

Property Rights

Turning to more positive measures, an obvious mechanism in seeking to **1.6.23**
protect habitat is to make use of the rights that the general law confers on
owners of land. The landowner's rights to control what happens on the land
and who has access to it[313] provide a strong and simple way of ensuring that
the land is managed in a particular way, and making use of the normal rules
of property law has the advantage that there is no need for any special rules
or procedures. The large-scale acquisition of land and its transfer to

---

[308] e.g. Deer (Scotland) Act 1996 s.23(5); WCA 1981 s.19A, added by Prisoners and Criminal
Proceedings (Scotland) Act 1993 s.36.

[309] In Scotland WCA 1981 ss.19, 19ZC and 19ZD, as amended and added by NCSA 2004
Sch.6 paras 16–17; in England and Wales WCA 1981 ss.18A–19XB, as amended and added by
NERCA 2006 Sch.5 paras 1–3; see paras 3.2.6–3.2.9, below.

[310] WCA 1981 s.19; NCSA 2004 s.43.

[311] Although it is recognised that there remains room for improvement, e.g. HM Inspectorate
of Constabulary for Scotland and the Inspectorate of Prosecution in Scotland: *Natural Justice:
A Joint Thematic Inspection of the Arrangements in Scotland for Preventing, Investigating and
Prosecuting Wildlife Crime* (2008), available at: *http://www.scotland.gov.uk/Publications/2008/
04/03143616/0* [Accessed May 4, 2009].

[312] WCA 1981 s.50, repealed for Scotland by NCSA 2004 Sch.7 para.4; NCSA 2004 s.44.

[313] Subject to the public rights of responsible access noted above; see paras 1.3.23–1.3.25,
above.

stewards who can be guaranteed to secure its management for long-term conservation would therefore be an option for securing the future of the country's natural heritage.

1.6.24   This approach is used on some occasions,[314] but most designated habitat has not been taken under the direct control of the state in any form. The potential for greater use of ownership is available, with assorted powers of compulsory purchase where this is considered necessary,[315] but both the cost of compensating owners and a reluctance to use compulsory powers in this area have limited its deployment. There may, though, be more pressure to make greater use of these powers if arrangements to encourage the positive management of sites in private ownership do not in fact secure them from deterioration[316] or do not succeed in achieving the enhancement of degraded habitats that is desired.

Notification

1.6.25   Notification procedures have played a central part in conservation measures, and have worked in two directions. First the conservation authorities have notified those dealing with land of the fact that it is of special value, so that those taking decisions about its management and use are aware of its conservation value and the harm that might be done. Secondly those dealing with the land have been required to notify the conservation authorities when they are planning to carry out activities that might affect it, so that there is an opportunity for conservation measures to be agreed or imposed.

1.6.26   The first form of notification occurs throughout the habitat protection structures. The starting point of all these measures is the designation of particular sites so that the areas of special value are identified and people alerted to the need to have special consideration.[317] Under the original version of Sites of Special Scientific Interest only the planning authorities were notified of the designation, so that only a narrow range of decisions in relation to the land were affected, but under the more recent legislation notification is made not only to the owners and occupiers responsible for day-to-day management but also to a range of statutory undertakers who may be carrying out operations affecting the land, and in Scotland more widely.[318] Letting people know of the value of the land does not by itself guarantee any protection, but does avoid damage occurring through ignorance alone and should ensure that conservation issues are at least included in the list of factors influencing management decisions, even if they are given little or no weight. Awareness of the potential for harm may by itself be enough to lead sympathetic occupiers to change their plans, or at least to adapt them to accommodate conservation concerns. In a wider context this approach is manifested in the whole system of environmental

---

[314] Essentially this has been the case only for National Nature Reserves.

[315] e.g. in relation to European Sites, National Nature Reserves, or where management arrangements for an SSSI cannot be achieved or are broken (see paras 5.2.23, 5.3.4, 5.5.21 and 5.5.38, below).

[316] Especially in relation to European Sites; see para.5.2.23, below.

[317] Although there are also more direct legal consequences, the listing of species as qualifying for enhanced protection also fulfils this notification role; see para.3.2.4, below.

[318] See section 5.5, below.

impact assessment,[319] which does not by itself prevent any environmentally harmful developments taking place, but does try to ensure that decision-makers do at least take account of the environmental costs of a proposal as they consider whether or not to give consent.

A further dimension to this aspect of notification is the growing interest in **1.6.27** designations as accolades, "which have the potential to generate local pride in the quality of the natural heritage", and which might be "encouraged and publicised with a view to promoting tourism and other local economic development".[320] The designation by itself can thus provide a focus for interest, education and enthusiasm, as well as adding an official "quality mark" which can be useful to anyone using the quality of the natural heritage of an area as a resource in attracting visitors or business of various sorts. Long-term conservation will only be achieved in a culture where nature is valued, and simply telling people of the value of what is around them has an important part to play in generating such a culture.

The second form of notification, from the occupier to the conservation **1.6.28** authorities, was at the heart of the arrangements for SSSIs introduced by the Wildlife and Countryside Act 1981 and remains important.[321] Although stronger powers may now lie in the background, the occupiers are not prohibited from carrying out certain activities, but must inform the statutory conservation body before doing so. This notification serves two purposes. The first is to make the occupiers realise that they are doing something potentially harmful to the site, reinforcing the impact of the designation, and the second, more important, is to give the body the opportunity to consider invoking any further conservation measures. Again, therefore, the notification requirements by themselves do not secure the protection of the site, but they provide the trigger for dialogue between occupiers and the conservation bodies and for invoking the range of conservation options available. This puts the onus on the effectiveness of those further options, and in the past these were limited to the negotiation of a management agreement, but initially for European Sites[322] and now under the new regime for SSSIs[323] it is generally possible for the notification to be followed by a prohibition. Notification requirements alone, therefore, do not provide protection, but do have a part to play in informing, educating and encouraging the desired behaviour.

Agreements

The dominant mechanism for habitat protection over the last few decades **1.6.29** has been the management agreement.[324] Until the stronger powers were introduced for European sites and under the new SSSI regimes, any meaningful and long-term controls on the use of land were the product of agreement rather than imposition.[325] This manifestation of the voluntary

---

[319] See section 8.3, below.
[320] *Natural Heritage Designations Review* (Scottish Office, 1996), p.46.
[321] See section 5.5, below.
[322] See section 5.2, below.
[323] See section 5.5, below.
[324] See generally C. Rodgers and J. Bishop, *Management Agreements for Promoting Nature Conservation* (London: RICS, 1998); A. Ross and J. Rowan-Robinson, "Behind Closed Doors: The use of agreements in the UK to protect the environment" (1999) 1 Env. L. Rev. 82.
[325] See paras 5.1.7–5.1.8, below.

principle allowed the requirements of each site to be individually addressed, although the transaction costs involved in negotiating individual agreements have increasingly led to the use of standard schemes operating over shorter periods.[326] Over the years a very large number of agreements have been made[327] and they have taken different forms over the years, from the long-term nature reserve agreements made when reserves were established, through the compensatory agreements offered to prevent damaging operations being carried out on an SSSI to the positive agreements that are now being made to provide for the positive management and enhancement of sites.

1.6.30   The use of agreements encapsulates the voluntary principle and has been the focus of the arguments for and against that approach. Their current role is changing in two ways. First, the powers that now enable the conservation authorities to take stronger action to secure conservation aims mean that the agreements are free to place more emphasis on positive action. Secondly, the changes in agricultural policy mean that conservation agreements can increasingly combine with or even be integrated into, as opposed to competing against, at least some of the support schemes for agriculture.[328] When they had to serve not only as an incentive but also as almost the only way of offering protection to threatened sites, agreements could be seen as a very weak mechanism, doomed to fail in the face of an unwilling landowner. Now they are not the only means of preventing harm occurring and are thus free to fulfil the role that they are best equipped for—a positive role in enabling measures to be taken beyond the bare minimum, and benefiting all parties affected and showing a positive return for the public money spent.

Management Plans

1.6.31 As noted above, the emphasis on taking positive steps to conserve and enhance habitat, as opposed to seeking merely to prevent specific damage being done, has led to greater attention being paid to management plans and schemes. This manifests itself in several ways. The most notable recent development has come in relation to SSSIs where the designation of a site must be accompanied by a management statement setting out views on the management of the land, similar statements must be produced for existing sites, and mandatory management schemes or land management orders can be made.[329] But this is just part of a wider feature. European Sites, National Parks and Areas of Outstanding Natural Beauty all require plans to guide their management and to co-ordinate the activities of the different public authorities and private interests concerned.[330] To these specific plans must be added the biodiversity plans developed for particular species, habitats and local areas,[331] and the role of various plans as the basis for management agreements.[332]

---

[326] *Natural Care Strategy* (SNH, 2001), p.8.

[327] There were 1,308 agreements in force in Scotland at the end of February 2009, covering 611,819 hectares and at a cost of £3,667,223 (data from SNHi, the "Interactive Facts and Figures" section on the SNH website: *http://www.snh.org.uk* [Accessed May 4, 2009]).

[328] See section 8.4, below.

[329] See paras 5.5.5, 5.5.18, 5.5.30 and 5.5.38, below.

[330] See paras 5.2.36, 5.9.14, 5.9.32 and 5.10.7, below.

[331] See para.1.2.5, above.

[332] e.g. *Natural Care Strategy* (SNH, 2001), p.8.

Such plans are not an innovation, but increasingly they are enjoying **1.6.32** statutory status or some means of ensuring their implementation. Their enhanced role, and the opportunities for consultation and participation as they are developed, are part of the wider move towards a more positive approach, based on a partnership for management, not prohibition. The details of what is done in practice may come to depend more and more on such plans and less on any formal legal provision.

Financial Incentives

Closely connected to the role of agreements and the development of a **1.6.33** partnership approach is the availability of financial support. Payments to landowners have been central to site protection for many years, with a shift over time away from compensatory payments, aimed at encouraging abstinence from damaging but potentially profitable development of the land, to positive payments for work done to maintain or enhance its conservation value. The integration of conservation concerns into financial schemes operated for other purposes, notably agriculture and forestry, has given conservation policy some powerful tools to influence behaviour across the countryside as a whole, not just on designated sites.[333]

Changes to grant schemes can by themselves produce big changes in **1.6.34** behaviour without the law being changed or any more coercive measures being applied, as shown by the many changes in forestry since the late 1980s.[334] So long as the basic legal provision authorising payments is wide enough, the details of grant schemes can be adjusted to reflect developing policy without requiring the time and resources for legislative change, but this flexibility can be a weakness as well as a strength, as shown by the recent abandonment of the agricultural set-aside scheme which had benefitted many farmland species.[335]

A new dimension in the role of financial incentives has been shown in **1.6.35** recent developments in Scotland. In 2008 an estate owner in Angus was required to repay £107,650 of the agricultural subsidies paid to him following the discovery of illegal pesticides connected with the poisoning of birds of prey.[336] This dramatic example of the cross-compliance rules,[337] whereby specified elements of good conservation practice are a requirement of receiving payments, illustrates the power of this mechanism but is also controversial. In comparison to fines imposed by a criminal court, this very substantial financial consequence has been imposed without any formal hearing or procedure, is based on the civil standard of proof rather than the

---

[333] The incorporation of SNH's Natural Care programme and other schemes within the Scottish Rural Development Programme is a further element of integration; see *http://www.snh.org.uk/about/lmc.asp* [Accessed May 4, 2009].

[334] The changes took place before the legislative steps to introduce environmental impact assessments and consent procedures for planting, measures which in any event apply only in comparatively few cases: C.T. Reid, "Forestry, the Law and the Environment" in C. Rodgers (ed.), *Nature Conservation and Countryside Law* (Cardiff: University of Wales Press, 1996) and paras 6.4.6–6.4.10, below.

[335] See para.8.4.12, below.

[336] (2008) 405 ENDS Report 53.

[337] See para.8.4.8, below.

criminal one,[338] and the appeal route is through internal review, review by an external panel and finally to the Scottish Land Court.[339] The withdrawal of subsidies as a sanction, determined by procedures such as this rather than through a criminal prosecution, is in line with the wider interest in civil penalties and a broader range of non-criminal enforcement tools, but raises the same concerns about procedural justice.[340]

Liability

1.6.36 A quite different legal approach is being introduced as a result of the EC Directive on Environmental Liability,[341] which the United Kingdom has been appallingly late in implementing.[342] This Directive, discussed more fully below,[343] in essence makes those whose activities threaten or cause environmental damage responsible for taking preventive or remedial action. The innovation is that in this approach, unlike standard liability regimes in delict or tort, the focus is not on personal injury or harm to property rights but on damage to the environment itself, including damage to protected species and natural habitats (often referred to as "biodiversity damage"). Those responsible for any "occupational activity"[344] can be held liabile for biodiversity damage where they are at fault or negligent, and for the operators of certain industrial activities,[345] a test of strict liability is applied, both for biodiversity damage and also for damage to water and land. Ensuring that operators meet their responsibilities is in the hands of public authorities.

1.6.37 The details of the various tests for what constitutes "damage", as well as the exceptions and defences, mean that the Directive's provisions may apply in very few cases, and their effectiveness remains to be tested. Nevertheless, the Directive makes an important first step in applying the "polluter pays" principle in respect of damage to biodiversity and doing so in a way which puts an emphasis on preventing harm and considers the appropriate remedial steps with the short- and long-term interests of the species or habitats affected in mind. Although still limited to designated sites and species, rather than benefitting wildlife as a whole, the Directive's basic approach of making those who cause the harm directly responsible for putting things right is a marked departure from most of the other legal regimes where restoration can only be ordered as part of a sanction rather than being at the centre of the regime.[346]

---

[338] Balance of probabilities, not beyond reasonable doubt; Written Answer by Environment Minister in Scottish Parliament (October 21, 2008; S3W-5481).

[339] Agricultural Subsidies (Appeals) (Scotland) Regulations 2004 (SSI 2004/381).

[340] See para.1.6.20, above; indeed penalties under the Regulatory Enforcement and Sanctions Act 2008 can be imposed only where the regulator is satisfied beyond reasonable doubt that the offence has been committed (ss.39(2) and 42(2)).

[341] Directive 2004/35/EC.

[342] The implementation date was April 30, 2007 and the first implementing regulations, for England and offshore areas, came into force on March 1, 2009; Environmental Damage (Prevention and Remediation) Regulations 2009 (SI 2009/153).

[343] See section 5.12, below.

[344] Essentially any economic activity in the private or public sector.

[345] Essentially those already subject to regulation under EC law.

[346] See para.1.6.19, above.

Goals

The elements discussed here and others can be combined in different ways to **1.6.38** produce detailed schemes reflecting different balances of interests and priorities. Within such schemes the law frequently allows wide discretion to official bodies, and even where overt discretion is not created, the availability, or lack, of resources will inevitably affect considerably the way in which the law is administered. The legal framework may thus operate in different ways according to the different priorities of different bodies at any given time. Moreover, the increasing use of plans and grant schemes enables significant shifts in policy direction to take place without any need to change the law itself. The crucial factor is whether there is the real political will to give priority to nature conservation, a priority which inevitably means that other interests must in some cases suffer. The law has recently changed to offer greater assistance to the protection of biodiversity. If the rhetoric of sustainability is carried through into practice, and environmental considerations are truly integrated with other policies, then even without further changes to the law, the impact of nature conservation measures may be considerably increased.

Given our limited knowledge of the natural world and its complex **1.6.39** interactions, a further issue will be how precautionary an approach we are willing to take.[347] In *North Uist Fisheries Ltd v Secretary of State for Scotland*,[348] the view was taken that legislation referring to operations "likely to destroy or damage" the valuable features of a site[349] should be read as referring to operations which would probably cause damage, not just those which might possibly have that result. By contrast, in the *Waddenzee* case[350] the European Court of Justice took the view that only where there was no scientific doubt as to this fact could one proceed on the basis that a project would have no adverse effect on a site. The former view is in keeping with the traditional approach of giving a strict interpretation to measures imposing restrictions on property rights and leading to potential criminal liability; the latter is in accordance with the precautionary principle enshrined in many policy statements[351] and EC law.[352] What balance should be struck between these different approaches?

In deciding on the future of nature conservation law, attention will **1.6.40** inevitably turn back to the big question of why we are conserving nature. The law at present to some extent contains both ecocentric and anthropocentric ideas—the former through the duty to designate sites when they meet

[347] For an introduction to this issue and the vast literature on this topic see S. Bell and D. McGillivray, *Environmental Law*, 7th edn (Oxford: OUP, 2008), pp.63–71 and 77.
[348] *North Uist Fisheries Ltd v Secretary of State for Scotland*, 1992 S.L.T. 333; reported with commentary at (1992) 4 J.E.L. 241.
[349] WCA 1981 s.29(3). The relevant provisions have been repealed for England and Wales and wholly replaced for Scotland; see section 5.6, below.
[350] *Landelijke Vereniging tot Behoud van de Waddenzee, Nederlandse Vereniging tot Bescherming van Vogels v Staatssecretaris van Landbouw, Natuurbeheer en Visserij* (C-127/02) [2004] E.C.R. I-7405, in the context of the Habitats and Species Directive (see paras 5.2.26 and 7.4.29, below).
[351] e.g. *One Future – Different Paths: The UK's shared framework for sustainable development* (HM Government et al., 2005), p.8.
[352] EC Treaty art.174(2); see para.2.9.4, below.

certain scientific criteria,[353] and the latter by permitting designated sites to the destroyed where social and economic interests justify this.[354] These differing approaches can coexist to some extent, but inevitably conflicts will arise. Even within each approach, there are difficulties, exacerbated by the impact of climate change on the natural and human worlds. If an ecocentric approach is taken, what is the ultimate goal, given that many habitats are to a great extent artificial, the creation not of natural processes but of human intervention?[355] How are renewable energy projects seeking to limit long-term climate change to be balanced against the immediate loss of habitat? From a purely anthropocentric point of view, how does one balance, say, arguments of amenity against the demand for houses in the countryside, or the interests of farmers against those of other groups? The scope for differing views of what the law should be trying to do will ensure that debate will continue over its application and development.

MARINE CONSERVATION

1.7.1 The legal approaches described above are based on the conservation of biodiversity on land, where the ownership of land is central to its management. Conservation at sea poses a range of different problems, both legally and in practice. The variety and distribution of marine life is much less well known than on land and while some species are sedentary, many other species are much less tied to specific locations. The marine environment is subject to threats from many sources, some fairly obvious, e.g. excessive fishing or pollution from a wrecked oil tanker, and some much less so, e.g. the cumulative effects of diffuse pollution flowing into the sea. Monitoring and enforcement of any laws at sea is difficult and further complicated by the rules governing jurisdiction over foreign ships and the extent to which national and international law recognises "public" rights of navigation and fishing, as well as the difficulties when a problem originates in one state and spreads to waters controlled by another.

1.7.2 In terms of exercising control over marine areas, there are fundamental issues of jurisdiction to be dealt with—which laws and authorities control which areas of sea? For present purposes (and what follows is a considerable over-simplification) it is possible to identify four areas around the United Kingdom, based on a combination of domestic and international law.[356]

---

[353] This applies to the European designations and SSSIs; see sections 5.2 and 5.5, below.

[354] Through the structured decision-making in relation to projects affecting European Sites and the powers of the conservation bodies and planning authorities to consent to damaging activities on SSSIs; see sections 5.2 and 5.5, below.

[355] The reintroduction of extinct species raises questions about what environment we are trying to create, or recreate, since if one goes back far enough all of Great Britain should just be covered in ice.

[356] See generally, R.R. Churchill and V. Lowe, *The Law of the Sea*, 3rd edn, (Manchester: Manchester Univeristy Press, 1999).

Nearest the shore, the areas that are periodically covered by the tide can be treated in the same way as the land for most purposes. The area between high and low tide[357] is legally the foreshore and owned by the Crown unless it has been transferred to private ownership. The law that applies on land applies to this area as well, so that powers of planning authorities still apply[358] and terrestrial conservation designations can include this area.[359]

The second and third areas can be treated together. The second is **1.7.3** "internal waters". These are the waters inside the baselines from which the territorial sea is measured. The low-water mark is the normal baseline for such measurements but in accordance with international law it is replaced by straight lines across the mouths of certain firths and bays and in areas heavily fringed by islands or where there is a heavily indented coast. The United Kingdom has declared such straight baselines along the length of the west coast of Scotland, with all the waters east of the Outer Hebrides being internal waters.[360] The third area is the territorial sea, an area of 12 nautical miles from the coast or any straight baselines.[361] In both of these areas the United Kingdom, as coastal state, enjoys full jurisdiction and for areas adjacent to Scotland it is the devolved government that has power in relation to devolved matters in this area.[362]

The fourth area is "offshore waters" which are the areas beyond the **1.7.4** territorial sea. The outer limits of these are determined separately for different purposes, such as the boundary of British fishery limits and all the areas designated under the Continental Shelf Act 1964.[363] Usually these limits will coincide[364] and can extend up to 200 nautical miles from the baseline for the territorial sea but in most directions from the United Kingdom the limit is less, in accordance with the international boundaries agreed with neighbouring states. Within this area the United Kingdom has more limited jurisdiction, controlling certain activities, e.g. fishing and mineral exploitation, but without British law having full effect. As a general rule, it is the law of the state where a ship is registered that governs what happens on the ship once it is beyond territorial waters. Where there are powers in this area they lie with the UK authorities, except that sea fishing

---

[357] In Scotland, based on mean spring tides, in England and Wales based on mean tides; on a gently shelving shore the different definitions can produce very different results in practice; D.J. McGlashan, R.W. Duck and C.T. Reid, "Defining the foreshore: geomorphology and British laws" (2005) 62 *Estuarine and Coastal Shelf Science* 183-192. In parts of Orkney and Shetland separate rules based on udal law apply, with no foreshore and the land extending to the furthest ebb of the sea; D.J. McGlashan, "Udal Law and Coastal Land Ownership" (2002) J.R. 251.

[358] *Argyll & Bute District Council v Secretary of State for Scotland*, 1976 S.C. 248.

[359] *Burnet v Barclay*, 1955 S.L.T. 282.

[360] Territorial Waters Order in Council 1964, amended by Territorial Sea (Amendment) Order 1998 (SI 1998/2564).

[361] Territorial Sea Act 1987; a "nautical mile" is defined in s.1(7) of the 1987 Act as an international nautical mile of 1,852 metres.

[362] Following the definition of "Scotland" in the Scotland Act 1998 s.126. The Welsh Assembly government exercises limited powers in relation to areas off Wales.

[363] Marine Nature Conservation (Natural Habitats, etc.) Regulations 2007 (SI 2007/1842) reg.2.

[364] Where there is a geological continuation of the continental shelf beyond 200 miles, jurisdiction for related purposes may extend with it.

in areas adjacent to Scotland[365] and boats registered in Scotland fall under the control of the Scottish Government.[366]

1.7.5   The lower visibility of marine biodiversity, the practical difficulties and the jurisdictional jigsaw have combined to make marine conservation the "poor relation" as conservation law has developed.[367] Where legal measures exist they have been little used[368] and even a clear decision of the English courts that the failure to extend the Habitats and Species Directive offshore was in breach of EC law produced only a partial response.[369] It took further infraction proceedings before the European Court of Justice before full implementation took place.[370] Marine conservation continues to lag significantly behind the conservation of terrestrial sites.

1.7.6   Things are changing, however, and although progress may be slow it is being made. This is partly the result of awareness of the need to do more to protect marine biodiversity (spurred on by an increasingly high-profile public campaign reflecting the mounting frustration felt by conservation groups about the absence of adequate measures for the marine environment). At the same time there has been a recognition of the need to tidy up the current fragmented and partial legal regulation of activities at and beyond the shore, the defects in which have been highlighted in the face of increasing pressure on the marine environment as a result of renewable energy developments. Considerable progress towards comprehensive legislation including a strong role for conservation interests has been made, with the Marine and Coastal Access Bill introduced to the UK Parliament at the end of 2008,[371] and the Marine (Scotland) Bill 2009 introduced at Holyrood in April 2009.[372] Difficult problems are being resolved, not least over devolved responsibilities,[373] and the likelihood is that new legislation making significant changes to the law will be in place before too long. In the meantime, local initiatives are also making some progress, e.g. the "Community Marine Conservation Area" in Lamlash Bay, Arran, given effect under the inshore fishing legislation.[374] Such developments are taking place in the shadow of the European Union's Marine Strategy, with legislation

---

[365] "The Scottish zone" as defined by Scotland Act 1998 s.126 and the Scottish Adjacent Waters Boundaries Order 1999 (SI 1999/1126).

[366] Scotland Act 1998 Sch.5 Pt II C6.

[367] House of Commons Environment, Transport and Regional Affairs Committee, *UK Biodiversity*, 20th Report of 1999–2000, HC Paper No.441 (Session 1999–2000), paras 53–54.

[368] e.g. the very limited creation of Marine Nature Reserves; see para.5.4.7, below.

[369] *R. v Secretary of State for Trade and Industry, ex p. Greenpeace Ltd* [2000] 2 C.M.L.R. 94, [2000] Env. L.R. 221, leading to the Offshore Petroleum Activities (Conservation of Habitats) Regulations 2001 (SI 2001/1754).

[370] *Commission v United Kingdom* (C-6/04) [2005] E.C.R. I-5261, leading to the Offshore Marine Conservation (Natural Habitats, etc.) Regulations 2007 (SI 2007/1842) and the Offshore Marine Conservation (Natural Habitats, etc.) (Amendment) Regulations 2009 (SI 2009/7).

[371] T. Mosedale, "The Marine Bill – rights and duties with respect to marine nature conservation" (2008) 20 E.L.M. 251.

[372] Note also the creation of Marine Scotland, combining the functions of several Scottish Government bodies; see *http://www.scotland.gov.uk/About/Directorates/Wealthier-and-Fairer/marine-scotland* [Accessed June 17, 2009].

[373] Powers beyond the territorial seas are being devolved to the Scottish authorities in relation to planning and conservation (Cabinet Office press release CAB/113/08, November 27, 2008).

[374] Inshore Fishing (Prohibition on Fishing) (Lamlash Bay) (Scotland) Order 2008 (SSI 2008/317), made under the Inshore Fishing (Scotland) Act 1984.

requiring the preparation of marine strategies with the goal of securing good environmental status in the marine environment by 2020.[375]

---

[375] Directive 2008/56/EC.

2. THE AUTHORITIES RESPONSIBLE FOR NATURE CONSERVATION

2.1.1 Responsibility for matters affecting nature conservation is spread among a range of official bodies. Various departments of central government and the devolved administrations are involved, as are local government and the European Community. The most direct responsibility is borne by a group of public bodies which enjoy a degree of independence from government while in practical terms a major role is played by charitable organisations. The fragmentation of responsibility is exacerbated by the different structures which exist in the different jurisdictions in Great Britain, and by the effects of devolution.

2.1.2 In view of the many activities which can have an impact on the environment some division of responsibilities is inevitable. However, although it is sensible for there to be bodies dealing with all aspects of agriculture, of river quality, etc. such division can mean that the interests of nature conservation are pushed into the background. Because it is not the central concern of such bodies, conservation can be seen as a marginal issue, primarily the responsibility of others, and consequently not as something to be given any priority when policies are formulated or powers exercised. In this way, the approach to the countryside and the environment becomes fragmented and unnecessary conflicts and disputes can arise. What is required is an integrated approach, with co-operation between the various bodies so that complementary decisions are taken and conservation concerns are taken into consideration (whether or not they are fully accepted) from the earliest stage of formulating policy. Without such integration one can have the absurd situation of one official body offering grants to people to do things in the interests of agriculture or forestry while another official body offers payments in order to stop them in the interests of nature conservation.[1]

2.1.3 Mechanisms for co-operation between the various authorities exist at different levels. The activities of the conservation bodies can to some extent be kept in line with other aspects of official policy by the power to issue ministerial directions and by requirements for ministerial consent before certain powers are exercised. The conservation authorities are also placed under a duty to have regard to more than just the interests of nature conservation in carrying out their functions. On the other hand, authorities whose main responsibilities lie elsewhere are bound to pay heed to the concerns of conservation both by similar "balancing obligations" and by more particular duties, especially by requirements that the statutory conservation bodies be consulted either before particular powers are exercised or on the general management of certain issues. However the advice which is proffered need not be followed and in view of an authority's prime

---

[1] This was the position in *Cameron v Nature Conservancy Council*, 1991 S.L.T. (Lands Tr.) 85 but since then major steps have been taken to ensure that the legal and financial measures in both areas work towards the same, rather than conflicting, goals.

responsibilities it may be quite proper for it to place other interests before those of nature conservation.

Significant moves have been made toward greater integration in recent **2.1.4** decades. At the institutional level, the divide between the bodies responsible for landscape and natural beauty and those concerned with nature conservation has ended, initially in Scotland and Wales with the creation of Scottish Natural Heritage and the Countryside Council for Wales, and more recently in England.[2] Such mergers allow for a broader approach to be taken to issues affecting particular areas, but it must also be recognised that real conflicts remain to be resolved before an integrated policy can emerge. These conflicts can exist not only between the traditionally contrasted goals of economic development and conservation of the natural environment but also between objectives that are often grouped together as part of the broad environmental agenda, e.g. between the interests of nature conservation and those of public access to the countryside or of promoting renewable energy.[3] Nonetheless, the slow but now very real increase in the weight of environmental considerations within agricultural policy is one manifestation that progress is being made towards increased integration, as is the incorporation of various grant schemes, previously run by SNH and the Forestry Commission, within the Scottish Rural Development Programme.[4] At a more administrative level, the SEARS initiative in Scotland aims to provide rural land managers with a "one door" approach for their dealings with a range of public bodies, providing a single point of contact for information and coordinating inspections and visits that may now serve several purposes.[5] Within conservation policy itself, the promotion of an ecosystem approach is a further sign of greater integration.[6]

More generally, the government's commitments on environmental mat- **2.1.5** ters have frequently referred to the need to integrate environmental and other policies "to ensure ... that we are not undoing in one area what we are trying to do in another."[7] The sustainable development strategy produced in 1999 expressly referred to the "building of concern for wildlife into other policies",[8] but although the rhetoric of such an integrated approach has been common for some time, the practical results are not always as obvious. The inquiry into UK Biodiversity by the House of Commons Environment Committee in 2000 found a lack of integration and a limited commitment to

---

[2] See section 2.6, below.

[3] A.L. Pillai, C.T. Reid and A.R. Black, "Reconciling Renewable Energy and the Local Impacts of Hydro-electric Development" (2005) 7 Env. L. Rev. 110.

[4] See section 8.4, below.

[5] Scotland's Environmental and Rural Services, a partnership involving Animal Health, Cairngorms National Park Authority, Crofters Commission, Deer Commission for Scotland, Forestry Commission Scotland, Loch Lomond and the Trossachs National Park Authority, Scottish Environment Protection Agency (SEPA), Scottish Government Rural Payments and Inspections Directorate and Scottish Natural Heritage; see *http://www.sears.scotland.gov.uk* [Accessed May 5, 2009].

[6] *Halting Biodiversity Loss: Government Response to the Thirteenth Report of Session 2007– 08 of the Environmental Audit Committee*, HC Paper No.239 (Session 2008–2009).

[7] *This Common Inheritance: Britain's Environmental Strategy*, Cm.1200 (1990), para.1.6.

[8] *A Better Quality of Life: A strategy for sustainable development for the UK*, Cm.4345 (1999), para.8.57.

biodiversity in some departments, and called for more efforts to promote biodiversity, and monitor progress, across all aspects of government.[9] Since then, the development of Biodiversity Strategies, supported by legal duties,[10] has served to highlight many of the elements that must work together to achieve meaningful progress, and integration continues to be a key theme in sustainable development strategies and policies.[11]

2.1.6   Whatever the formal policy and institutional structure, much will always depend on the attitudes and approaches of the people involved. A simple awareness of environmental concerns on the part of those responsible for branches of government and other activities will do much to prevent needless damage and conflict being caused. Constructive informal dialogue can achieve more in practice than the most carefully designed structure operating without goodwill or mutual understanding.[12]

SUSTAINABLE DEVELOPMENT AND BALANCING OBLIGATIONS

2.2.1   Before considering the authorities which have specific responsibilities for nature conservation, something should be said about two more general features of many public bodies. The fact that public authorities are under duties to further or have regard to biodiversity has already been discussed, but there are other general obligations that must also be considered. The first area for consideration is the increasing imposition[13] of duties in relation to sustainable development, which should include at least some attention to biodiversity and conservation. The second is the presence of more precise balancing obligations which require public authorities to have some regard to the environment in the exercise of their functions. The impact of such duties must then be considered.

---

[9] House of Commons Environment, Transport and Regional Affairs Committee, *UK Biodiversity*, 20th Report of 1999–2000, HC Paper No.441 (Session 1999–2000), paras 104–107.

[10] See paras 1.2.7–1.2.9, above.

[11] e.g. the policies for "mainstreaming sustainable development" in *Choosing our Future: Scotland's Sustainable Development Strategy* (Scottish Executive, 2005) Ch.14, and *Securing the Future: The UK Government Sustainable Development Strategy*, Cm.6467 (2005) esp. Ch.7 and Foreword by the Prime Minister (p.3): "We are increasingly aware of the need to make care of the environment an integral part of policy making from the start, rather than dealing with the consequences of neglect down the line."

[12] cf. Alexander Pope, *An Essay on Man*, (1734) Epistle iii. 1.303:
    "For Forms of Government let fools contest;
    Whate'er is best administer'd is best."

[13] Between 1999 and 2005 almost 5% of UK statutes and 11% of Scottish statutes included references to sustainable development; A. Ross, "Why Legislate for Sustainable Development? An Examination of Sustainable Development Provisions in UK and Scottish Statutes" (2008) 20 J.E.L. 35 at p.37.

Sustainable Development

Since the early 1990s, sustainable development has been accepted as a **2.2.2** national policy goal,[14] and whatever the arguments over exactly what the term means,[15] it is clear that regard for biodiversity and nature conservation falls within its scope. The presence of obligations to have regard to or to further sustainable development therefore means that authorities must at least consider the impact of their activities on the natural environment. As noted by Ross in her analysis of legislative provisions,[16] there are various forms in which sustainable development makes an appearance in legislation.[17]

Sustainable development can be included as a general aim or purpose of a **2.2.3** statutory body or regime. For example, development planning functions must be exercised "with the objective of contributing to the achievement of sustainable development",[18] the aims of the National Parks in Scotland include promoting sustainable use of natural resources and sustainable economic and social development of the local communities,[19] the principal aim of the Environment Agency includes "contribut[ing] towards attaining the objective of achieving sustainable development"[20] and the purposes of Regional Development Agencies include "contribut[ing] to the achievement of sustainable development in the United Kingdom".[21] The slight variations in the form of words apparent in these few examples are typical of the legislation here.

The provisions can take the form of a more direct duty, but in such cases **2.2.4** this is usually either very weakly phrased or subject to a qualification. Thus, in Scotland, the Scottish Further and Higher Education Funding Council is obliged to "have regard to the desirability of the achieving of sustainable development"[22] while the water legislation places the much more robust duty on authorities to "act in the way best calculated to contribute to the achievement of sustainable development", but only "so far as is consistent with the purposes of the relevant enactment or designated function in question."[23] Other formulations include obliging an authority to act "in the way which it considers best calculated to contribute to the achievement of

---

[14] *Sustainable Development – The UK Strategy*, Cm.2426 (1994); *A Better Quality of Life: A strategy for sustainable development for the UK*, Cm.4345 (1999); *Securing the Future: Delivering the UK Sustainable Development Strategy*, Cm.6467 (2005).

[15] "It is a pity that the issue which everyone on the planet will have to tackle at some point has acquired this impenetrable title. It is even more problematic that no definition exists which can be understood by everyone and built into their lives." *Down to Earth – A Scottish Perspective on Sustainable Development* (Scottish Office, 1999), p.4. See also para.2.6.13, below.

[16] A. Ross, "Why Legislate for Sustainable Development? An Examination of Sustainable Development Provisions in UK and Scottish Statutes" (2008) 20 J.E.L. 35.

[17] The very first reference was not to sustainable development but the requirement of SHN to have regard to the desirability of securing that action was taken "in a manner which is sustainable"; Natural Heritage (Scotland) Act 1991 s.1(1) (see para.2.6.13, below).

[18] Planning and Compulsory Purchase Act 2004 s.39(2); TCPSA 1997 s.3E (added by Planning etc. (Scotland) Act 2006 s.2).

[19] National Parks (Scotland) Act 2000 s.1; see para.5.9.25, below.

[20] Environment Act 1995 s.4. For SEPA the equivalent provision is more indirect, requiring the Minister to give SEPA guidance towards the same objective to which SEPA must have regard (Environment Act 1995 s.31).

[21] Regional Development Agencies Act 1998 s.4(1).

[22] Further and Higher Education (Scotland) Act 2005 s.20.

[23] Water Environment and Water Services (Scotland) Act 2003 s.2(4).

sustainable development",[24] giving plenty of scope for discretion and for conflicting factors to be taken into account.

2.2.5 Any such obligation is strengthened by the presence of clear procedural obligations. The strongest, perhaps, is on the Welsh Ministers who must make and publish a sustainable development scheme and report annually on how the proposals in it have been implemented.[25] Local authorities in England and Wales similarly have to prepare sustainable community strategies for promoting the economic, social and environmental well-being of their area and contributing to the achievement of sustainable development in the UK.[26] This obligation is supported by a general background power to do things likely to achieve the promotion or improvement of the environmental well-being of their area.[27] More generally, the aim of achieving sustainable development is bolstered by the processes of environmental impact assessment for projects, strategic environmental assessment of policies[28] and sustainability appraisals.[29] One rare instance where judgments on sustainable development do play a more direct role is in relation to the "community right to buy" under the Land Reform (Scotland) Act 2003, where compatibility with the achievement of sustainable development is a criterion in recognising a community body, registering its interest in particular land and allowing it to exercise its right to buy it.[30]

Balancing Obligations

2.2.6 Before sustainable development and biodiversity[31] attracted legislative attention, many other "balancing obligations", duties to have regard to various considerations relevant to nature conservation, were imposed on a range of public authorities.[32] One of the most general requires that in the exercise of their statutory functions relating to land, every minister, government department and public body is obliged to have regard to the desirability of conserving the natural heritage (in Scotland)[33] or the natural beauty and amenity of the countryside (in England and Wales).[34]

2.2.7 In addition to the very general terms of these provisions, some obligation with respect to the countryside or conservation can be imposed on specific bodies or in relation to specific tasks. Particular obligations to have regard

---

[24] e.g. Greater London Authority Act 1999 s.30(5); Railways Act 1993 s.4, amended by Transport Act 2000 s.224.

[25] Government of Wales Act 2006 s.79.

[26] Local Government Act 2000 s.4, amended by Sustainable Communities Act 2007 s.7.

[27] Local Government Act 2000 s.2.

[28] See section 8.3, below.

[29] Required for Regional Spatial Strategies in England and Wales; Planning and Compulsory Purchase Act 2004 s.5(4).

[30] Land Reform (Scotland) Act 2003 ss.34, 38 and 51.

[31] See paras 1.2.8–1.2.9, above.

[32] See generally C.T Reid and I.R. Roberts, "Nature Conservation Duties: More appearance than substance" (2005) 17 E.L.M. 162. The first such provision was the duty on the North of Scotland Hydro-Electricity Board in the exercise of its functions to "have regard to the desirability of preserving the beauty of the scenery and ... of avoiding as far as possible injury to fisheries and to the stock of fish in any waters"; Hydro-Electricity Development (Scotland) Act 1943 s.9(1).

[33] CSA 1967 s.66, amended by NHSA 1991 Sch.10 para.4(7); for the meaning of "natural heritage" see para.2.6.12, below.

[34] CA 1968 s.11; conserving natural beauty includes conserving flora, fauna and geological and physiographical features (CA 1968 s.49(4)).

to the purposes for which land has become subject to various conservation designations are features of many regulatory schemes and are discussed in the context of each designation in Chapter 5 below.[35] Almost invariably, though, such duties are expressed to be subject to the proper exercise of the primary statutory functions of the bodies involved and provided that an authority can produce some justification for its conduct based on these functions and some evidence that the environmental impact was not wholly ignored, it is unlikely that a court would be willing to hold that an authority was in breach of such a broadly phrased duty.

One general formulation which is used is to require the authority in question to seek a balance between various interests, including those of conservation. The interests listed may be irreconcilable in many situations, but such an obligation does at least ensure that some thought is given to the matters specified. Thus, "so far as may be consistent with the proper discharge of [their] functions", under the Forestry Acts 1967–1979, the Forestry Commissioners must "endeavour to achieve a reasonable balance between" the development and maintenance of forestry and timber production and the conservation and enhancement of natural beauty and the conservation of flora, fauna and geological or physiographical features of special interest.[36] The agriculture ministers must seek a balance between the promotion and maintenance of a stable and efficient agricultural industry, the economic and social interests of rural areas, the conservation and enhancement of the natural beauty and amenity of the countryside[37] and its features of archaeological interest, and the promotion of the enjoyment of the countryside by the public.[38] Similarly, in discharging their functions under the Sea Fisheries Acts, ministers and local fisheries committees are obliged, so far as consistent with the proper and efficient exercise of those functions, to have regard to the conservation of marine flora and fauna and to endeavour to achieve a reasonable balance between conservation and their other concerns.[39] **2.2.8**

In some cases there is a fuller statement of the environmental responsibilities of new public bodies, although the effect of such provisions is often merely to emphasise their existence rather than to confer any greater legal weight. The formulations vary, even within the same statute. Without prejudice to their general function of furthering the improvement of the environment,[40] Scottish Enterprise is obliged merely to "have regard to ... the desirability of safeguarding the environment",[41] whereas for Highlands and Islands Enterprise the duty is more fully expressed as being to: **2.2.9**

---

[35] e.g. National Parks in England & Wales (NAPCA 1949 s.11A, added by EA 1995 s.62); Areas of Outstanding Natural Beauty (CRWA 2000 s.85); National Parks in Scotland (National Parks (Scotland) Act 2000 s.14); SSSIs (WCA 1981 s.28G, added by CRWA 2000 Sch.9; NCSA 2004 s.12).

[36] Forestry Act 1967 s.1(3A), added by Wildlife and Countryside (Amendment) Act 1985 s.4.

[37] Expressly stated to include the conservation of flora and fauna and geological and physiographical features.

[38] Agriculture Act 1986 s.17; there is also a provision enabling them to provide services for the benefit of such conservation and enhancement (Agriculture Act 1986 s.1).

[39] Sea Fisheries (Wildlife Conservation) Act 1992 s.1.

[40] Enterprise and New Towns (Scotland) Act 1990 s.1.

[41] Enterprise and New Towns (Scotland) Act 1990 s.4(4).

"[H]ave regard to the desirability of safeguarding—

(a) the natural beauty of the countryside in;
(b) the flora and fauna of; and
(c) the geological and geomorphological[42] features of special interest of,

the Highlands and Islands."[43]

The fuller terms of the latter provision may result in environmental considerations appearing more significant, but it is unlikely that there is any difference in legal terms to the place of such issues in the authorities' deliberations.

2.2.10　　More positive obligations are imposed on the authorities concerned with water resources and drainage in England and Wales.[44] One function of the Environment Agency in England and Wales is "to such extent as it considers desirable, generally to promote the conservation of ... flora and fauna which are dependent on an aquatic environment" and the conservation of the natural beauty and amenity of waters and associated land.[45] Ministers, the Agency, internal drainage boards, and water and sewerage undertakers are all obliged not merely to have regard to the desirability of conservation, but (so far as is consistent with the relevant statutory functions) to exercise their powers so as to further the conservation and enhancement of natural beauty and the conservation of flora, fauna and geological or physiographical features of special interest, and to take into account the effect of their conduct on the beauty, wildlife and features of any affected area.[46] Such a formulation may somewhat increase the weight of environmental considerations, but as always the prime statutory functions of the authorities take priority.

2.2.11　　As well as being attached to the general functions of particular authorities, balancing obligations appear in relation to a range of specific tasks. The general obligations on the regulatory bodies for gas and electricity to have regard to the effect on the environment of gas transmission through pipelines[47] and of the generation, transmission and supply of electricity[48] are supplemented by more specific duties. The desirability of preserving natural beauty and conserving flora, fauna and geological and physiographical features must be taken into account at all stages in the preparation and approval of proposals for new pipelines,[49] and for the underground storage

---

[42] There is probably no practical significance in the use of "geomorphological" in place of the more usual "physiographical".

[43] Enterprise and New Towns (Scotland) Act 1990 s.5(3).

[44] See para.2.7.19, below.

[45] Environment Act 1995 s.6.

[46] Water Industry Act 1991 s.3(2); Water Resources Act 1991 s.16(1); Land Drainage Act 1991 s.61A, added by Land Drainage Act 1994 s.1; the same applies to the British Waterways Board under s.22 of the British Waterways Act 1995 (a private Act of Parliament).

[47] Gas Act 1986 s.4AA(5), added by Utilities Act 2000 s.9; contributing to the achievement of sustainable development was also added to this provision and the one in the following note by the Energy Act 2004 s.83.

[48] Electricity Act 1989 s.3A(5), added by Utilities Act 2000 s.13.

[49] Pipe-lines Act 1962 s.43.

of gas,[50] while for electricity generating stations and transmission lines,[51] there is the further requirement that the proposals include measures to mitigate any adverse effects on the environment. Housing authorities must bear in mind the effect of their proposals on the beauty of the landscape or countryside.[52] The Cardiff Bay Development Corporation must have regard to the desirability of developing and conserving flora and fauna,[53] and in the interests of conservation additional conditions can be imposed on works otherwise automatically authorised under the Electronic Communications Code[54] or approved for the Channel Tunnel.[55] The Coal Authority in dealing with its property must take into account the effect of proposals on the natural beauty, flora and fauna of the area and have regard to the desirability of preserving and conserving these.[56]

Impact

The general obligations discussed in this section, and the biodiversity duties discussed earlier[57] show official recognition of the desirability of conservation, but not in a particularly strong way. That recognition is nevertheless of some value in itself. Virtually all public authorities are the creatures of statute, and their powers and functions are defined by the legislation which creates them. It is only if legislation requires or permits them to do so that they are able to shape their policy and conduct with regard to the concerns of nature conservation. Without some such provision, authorities acting in the interests of conservation might well be found to be acting ultra vires and unlawfully by allowing an irrelevant consideration to influence the exercise of their statutory functions.[58] The presence of such provisions is therefore vital if nature conservation is not to be ignored and is to be integrated into the policies and actions of bodies across the public sector. **2.2.12**

Even where a duty is apparently strongly phrased in terms of an obligation to further conservation, direct enforcement in the courts is however unlikely.[59] Such duties confer no rights on anyone who might then be in a position to enforce them, and given the complexity of the real world it will often be arguable which of the options open to a decision-making body are actually the ones that further biodiversity, and even more so sustainable **2.2.13**

---

[50] Gas Act 1965 s.4(4).

[51] Electricity Act 1989 Sch.9 paras 1 and 3.

[52] Housing Act 1985 s.607; Housing (Scotland) Act 1987 s.6(1).

[53] Cardiff Bay Barrage Act 1993 s.14; it is not clear exactly what "developing" flora and fauna means.

[54] Communications Act 2003 s.109(2).

[55] Channel Tunnel Act 1987 Sch.3 para.2.

[56] Coal Industry Act 1994 s.3(7); see also s.53.

[57] See paras 1.2.8–1.2.9, above.

[58] *Associated Provincial Picture Houses Ltd v Wednesbury Corporation* [1948] 1 K.B. 223. See for example the controversy over whether the gas industry regulator was legally entitled to provide funds for the Energy Saving Trust; (1994) 231 ENDS Report 31.

[59] See generally S. Hendry, "Worth the paper that it's written on? An analysis of statutory duty in modern environmental law" [2005] J.P.L. 1145; C.T. Reid and I.R. Roberts, "Nature Conservation Duties: More appearance than substance" (2005) 17 E.L.M. 162, pp.166–168; A. Ross, "Why Legislate for Sustainable Development? An Examination of Sustainable Development Provisions in UK and Scottish Statutes" (2008) 20 J.E.L. 35, pp.60–65.

development, given the lack of precision in such terms.[60] In practice therefore the strongest duties may be not those that require authorities to further
biodiversity or conservation, but those that add some reporting mechanism
to support the duty, however phrased. The requirements on the Scottish
Government to report on the implementation of their biodiversity strategy[61]
and on the Welsh Ministers of their sustainable development scheme[62] will
ensure at least some scrutiny of progress and means of accountability, albeit
political rather than legal.[63]

2.2.14   In any event, most of the duties are also very weakly phrased and impose
no obligation to act in the interests of conservation or sustainability—
merely to have regard to such matters. Moreover, they also expressly give
priority to the main statutory functions of the bodies concerned, functions
which may call for works and activities with serious adverse effects on the
natural environment. Such provisions may not offer much by way of support for conservation. However, they do achieve something by ensuring that
conservation is always a relevant consideration which cannot be wholly
ignored when decisions are being taken. The authorities cannot claim that
they are not allowed to respond to the interests of nature conservation and
cannot shut their eyes to the environmental impact of their activities nor
their ears to the arguments of those pressing for conservation to be taken
into account. There is also a remote possibility of a legal challenge to the
validity of any action which is clearly damaging to the natural heritage and
cannot be supported by any other considerations. Moreover, the fact that
natural beauty and heritage must be borne in mind adds weight to the voices
of conservation groups and others in pressing their arguments on the
authorities in question, albeit that no legal standing is conferred. Other
considerations may in practice override those of the countryside in individual circumstances, but authorities cannot completely ignore the impact of
their activities on wildlife and natural habitats.

2.2.15   In most instances, therefore, the presence of conservation duties is more
symbolic than significant. There may be little likelihood of an authority ever
being found to be in breach of such obligations, but their presence does give
some legal weight to the interests of biodiversity, conservation and sustainability. The symbolic function is, however, considerably weakened by
the fact that the one authority may be subject to such a jumble of overlapping provisions. Local authorities, for example, are subject to duties with
regard to biodiversity, conserving natural heritage or beauty, sustainable
development and best value. The cumulative effect may be to blur rather
than to strengthen any message.

---

[60] See *Friends of the Earth v Secretary of State for Business Enterprise and Regulatory Reform*
[2008] EWHC 2518 Admin, considering the government's duties in relation to its fuel poverty
strategy.

[61] See para.1.2.8, above.

[62] See para.2.2.5, above.

[63] "Parliament has become fond of imposing duties of a kind which, since they are of a
general and indefinite character, are perhaps best to be considered as political duties rather than
as legal duties which a court could enforce." H. Wade and C. Forsyth, *Administrative Law*, 9th
edn (2004), p.589. "[T]he juxtaposition of policy and legal duty in this Act poses difficulties in
the task of statutory construction", McCombe J. in *Friends of the Earth v Secretary of State for
Business Enterprise and Regulatory Reform* [2008] EWHC 2518 Admin at [14].

DEVOLUTION

The implementation in 1999 of the devolution arrangements for Scotland **2.3.1** and Wales, with the latter significantly altered in 2007, has had a major impact on the way in which powers relating to nature conservation are distributed throughout Great Britain. The position is now much more complicated than before, and care must be taken in ascertaining where governmental power now rests. One obvious consequence is that the many statutory provisions conferring powers or functions on "the Secretary of State" can no longer be taken at face value, since the devolution arrangements may well have transferred the tasks to the Scottish or Welsh Ministers. There is a marked difference between Scotland and Wales both in the mechanisms by which powers have been transferred and the scope of the powers actually divided. The transfer of power to the Scottish Parliament and Ministers extends to all matters not expressly reserved for Westminster and Whitehall, and the Parliament has the power to make primary legislation. In contrast, powers have been transferred to Wales only in relation to the matters expressly specified and the legislative powers are restricted to the making of subordinate legislation.

Scotland

The Scotland Act 1998 created both the Scottish Parliament and the Scot- **2.3.2** tish Executive[64] with wide powers. Full legislative and ministerial[65] powers are transferred to these new authorities except in the area of reserved matters,[66] but it is expressly provided that the UK Parliament retains the power to legislate on any subject.[67] Nature conservation and most of the other matters covered in this book, e.g. agriculture, planning and the environment generally, clearly fall within the scope of devolved matters, so that responsibility for these now lies with the Scottish authorities.[68] Nevertheless, some of the reservations may be significant either by preventing the use of certain mechanisms to achieve policy objectives,[69] or by retaining at Westminster control of policy areas with an indirect impact on conservation.[70] The scope of the Scottish Ministers' powers is actually wider than that of the Scottish Parliament since by the process of executive

---

[64] Since 2007 the term "Scottish Government" has been widely adopted but the statutory term is "Scottish Executive".

[65] Where previously power lay with the Secretary of State, it now lies with "the Scottish Ministers".

[66] The reserved matters are set out in Sch.5 to the 1998 Act, with further restrictions stated in Sch.4.

[67] Scotland Act 1998 s.28(7).

[68] See generally G. Little, "Scottish Devolution and Environmental Law" (2000) 12 J.E.L. 155; C.T. Reid, 'Devolution and the Environment' in A. Ross (ed.), *Environment and Regulation (Hume Papers on Public Policy)* (Edinburgh: Edinburgh University Press, 2000).

[69] e.g. the reservation of tax matters prevents the creation of new taxes or tax reliefs to further policy goals; Scotland Act 1998 Sch.5 Head A.

[70] e.g. most energy matters and many transport ones are reserved; Scotland Act 1998 Sch.5 Heads D and E.

devolution it is possible for powers reserved to the UK government to be delegated to the Scottish Ministers in relation to their exercise in Scotland.[71]

2.3.3 Special provision is made for a number of public authorities whose functions straddle the border and whose activities include both reserved and devolved matters.[72] The "cross-border public authorities" designated under the Act, must report to both the UK and Scottish Parliaments, and although ministerial powers are not devolved, the relevant UK minister can act in some matters only in consultation with the Scottish Ministers. More detailed provision can be made for individual bodies. The list of cross-border public authorities includes the Joint Nature Conservation Committee,[73] the Forestry Commission[74] and the Royal Commission on Environmental Pollution.[75] Special provision is also made for the border rivers.[76]

2.3.4 Important restrictions on the powers of the Scottish Parliament and Executive relate to EC law and international obligations. Within the range of devolved maters, the primary responsibility to ensure compliance with EC law rests on the Scottish authorities, and it is beyond the competence of the Parliament to legislate, or the Ministers to act, in a way which is incompatible with EC law.[77] However, it is expressly stated that the UK government can still exercise powers to implement EC law in Scotland.[78] This reflects the position that it is the United Kingdom that is the Member State of the EC and therefore the United Kingdom government that is entitled to a seat in the Council when decisions are made but is also responsible before the European Court of Justice for contraventions of EC law.[79] Thus in relation to such matters as compliance with EC Directives, it is expected that the Scottish authorities will ensure that all of the necessary measures are in place[80] but any measures incompatible with the EC

---

[71] Scotland Act 1998 s.63; see, e.g. the Scotland Act 1998 (Transfer of Functions to Scottish Ministers) Order 1999 (SI 1999/1750). To assist this process there is provision for the division of functions not previously exercised separately in Scotland; Scotland Act 1998 s.106; see, e.g. the Scotland Act 1998 (Modification of Functions) Order 1999 (SI 1999/1756).

[72] Scotland Act 1998 ss.88–90.

[73] See paras 2.6.24–2.6.28, below.

[74] See paras 2.7.5–2.7.10, below.

[75] Scotland Act 1998 (Cross-border Public Authorities) (Specification) Order 1999 (SI 1999/1319), as amended on several occasions.

[76] Under the Scotland Act 1998 (Border Rivers) Order 1999 (SI 1999/1746) and the Scotland Act 1998 (River Tweed) Order 2006 (SI 2006/2913), detailed arrangements are made, enabling the Scottish Ministers to exercise some powers over the Tweed in England and the Environment Agency over the border Esk in Scotland; although not a cross-border body, the Environment Agency is required to submit its annual report to the Scottish Ministers for laying before the Parliament.

[77] Scotland Act 1998 ss.29(2) and 57(2).

[78] Scotland Act 1998 s.57(1); see A. Ross, H. Nash and C.T. Reid, "The Implementation of EU Environmental Law in Scotland" (2009) 13 Edin. L.R. 224.

[79] It is no defence for the national government of a Member State to say that the matter is a responsibility of another tier of government; e.g. *Commission v Belgium* (Cases 227–230/85) [1988] E.C.R. 1; *Commission v Italy* (Case C-33/90) [1991] E.C.R. I-5987.

[80] If there are any financial penalties or costs imposed on the UK as a result of a failure to implement or enforce EC law (see section 2.9 below), responsibility for meeting these will lie with the administration responsible for the failure, so that the Scottish budget will bear the cost of a failure in Scotland on a devolved matter (*Memorandum of Understanding and supplementary agreements between the United Kingdom Government, Scottish Ministers and the Cabinet of the National Assembly for Wales*, Cm.5240 (2001), para.20).

obligations can be challenged in the courts and held to be invalid, and Whitehall can intervene directly if it is thought that EC law is being breached. The extent to which different parts of the United Kingdom can legitimately implement EC measures in different ways has been referred to the European Court of Justice in a case concerning agricultural support.[81] The Concordats between the London and devolved governments endeavour to establish arrangements for co-operation and consultation between the different administrations,[82] but the Scottish authorities have no formal involvement in British dealings with the EC, which remain wholly in the hands of the UK government.

In relation to international obligations, the restrictions on the Scottish **2.3.5** Parliament and Executive are enforced through political rather than judicial intervention. The Secretary of State, a member of the UK government, can intervene to prevent a Bill being presented for Royal Assent if he or she has reasonable grounds to believe that it would be incompatible with international obligations,[83] and on the same grounds can intervene to require the Scottish Ministers to take, or to desist from taking, any action, including making any delegated legislation or proposing any Bill.[84] The new Scottish authorities are therefore constrained to ensure that the United Kingdom's international obligations are properly respected in Scotland.[85] Again, since foreign affairs are a reserved matter, there is no formal role for the Scottish Parliament or Ministers in the negotiation of these obligations.

One important consequence of the devolution of power to legislate is not **2.3.6** only that new legislation can be made separately for the two jurisdictions but that pre-devolution legislation can be amended separately for Scotland and for other parts of the UK. There have always been examples of legislation being adjusted in this way, but this has become a very notable feature of the law on nature conservation. The key provisions on species protection remain within the Wildlife and Countryside Act 1981 but this Act now exists in two significantly different versions, one for England and Wales incorporating the major changes made by the Countryside and Rights of Way Act 2000 and the Natural Environment and Rural Communities Act 2006, and the other for Scotland, incorporating the changes made separately by the Nature Conservation (Scotland) Act 2004. Similarly, the Conservation (Natural Habitats etc.) Regulations 1994[86] have been amended differently in the two jurisdictions. On some points the two versions are separate but parallel, but on other issues there are differences of substance, and in any

---

[81] *R. (Horvath) v Sec. of State for the Environment, Food and Rural Affairs* (C-428/07) [2007] EWCA Civ 620.

[82] *Memorandum of Understanding and supplementary agreements between the United Kingdom Government, Scottish Ministers and the Cabinet of the National Assembly for Wales*, Cm.5240 (2001); the main Memorandum is supported by an Agreement on the Joint Ministerial Committee and Concordats on among other topics Co-ordination of European Union Policy Issues.

[83] Scotland Act 1998 s.35.

[84] Scotland Act 1998 s.58.

[85] Where international or EC law sets targets or quotas, there is express power for these to be divided between the parts of the United Kingdom; Scotland Act 1998 s.106.

[86] SI 1994/2716.

event the different legislative time schedules can mean that provisions achieving the same thing are made and take effect at quite different times.[87]

Wales

2.3.7 The transfer of power to Wales has been much more limited, and the arrangements made by the Government of Wales Act 1998 were significantly altered by those in the Government of Wales Act 2006. The National Assembly for Wales has no power to make primary legislation, although the potential for this in future is now provided under the 2006 Act,[88] but Welsh Ministers and the Assembly can make some subordinate legislation. Under the 1998 Act, all of the powers transferred, ministerial as well as legislative, went to the National Assembly for Wales, although in practice many ministerial functions were delegated to committees or to the Assembly First Secretary and his or her fellow Assembly Secretaries.[89] The 2006 Act now establishes the Welsh Assembly Government and the majority of ministerial powers have been transferred from the Assembly to the Welsh Ministers.[90] There is no direct equivalent of the cross-border authorities in Scotland, but the Assembly's general power to call for witnesses and documents on matters relevant to the exercise of the Welsh Ministers' functions will allow it to exercise some scrutiny.[91]

2.3.8　　In contrast to the Scottish arrangements, the areas of competence devolved to Wales are specifically listed, often by listing the enactments under which ministerial powers can be exercised.[92] These include many statutes falling within the scope of this book. In many cases it is only certain powers under an Act that are transferred, either by specifying the individual sections or sub-sections where power is passed, or by making exceptions when powers under an Act are transferred as a whole.[93] The position is further complicated by the fact that in some instances the powers are transferred only to the extent that they had previously been passed to the Secretary of State for Wales from other Ministers under earlier

---

[87] e.g. following the decision of the European Court of Justice in *Commission v United Kingdom* (C-6/04) [2005] E.C.R. I-9017, the Scottish changes to CNHR 1994 came into effect in February and June 2007, whereas the equivalent measure for England and Wales, and some provisions applying in Scotland, took effect in August 2007; Conservation (Natural Habitats etc.) Amendment (Scotland) Regulations 2007 (SSI 2007/80); Conservation (Natural Habitats etc.) Amendment (No.2) (Scotland) Regulations 2007 (SSI 2007/349); Conservation (Natural Habitats etc.) Amendment Regulations 2007 (SI 2007/1843).

[88] Matters relating to the environment, including biodiversity and nature conservation, can fall within the extended powers of the Assembly to legislate by means of Assembly Measures and Acts of the Assembly (the latter powers require a referendum before being brought into force); Government of Wales Act 2006 Pts 3 and 4.

[89] As authorised by Government of Wales Act 1998 s.62.

[90] Government of Wales Act 2006 s.45 and Sch.11 para.30; some powers remain with the Assembly (Government of Wales Act 2006 para.31).

[91] Government of Wales Act 2006 s.37.

[92] Specified in the National Assembly for Wales (Transfer of Functions) Orders: there were two in 1999 (SI 1999/672 and SI 1999/2787) and about one a year since then.

[93] As examples, ministerial powers under the whole of the Conservation of Seals Act 1970 is transferred, except for the power under s.1(2) (specification of permitted firearms and ammunition; see para.3.4.33, below), whereas for long and complex pieces of legislation such as the Water Resources Act 1991, there is a detailed list of specific provisions where power is transferred; National Assembly for Wales (Transfer of Functions) Order 1999 (SI 1999/672) Sch.1.

arrangements for administrative devolution[94]; this is especially prevalent in the area of agriculture and fisheries. In a number of further cases powers can be exercised concurrently by the Welsh and UK Ministers or remain in the hands of the United Kingdom government but can be exercised only after consulting, or with the agreement of, the Assembly.[95] There are similar provisions to those described above for Scotland to restrain the Assembly from acting in breach of EC or international obligations.[96]

Given the very detailed nature of these transfer arrangements, any gen- **2.3.9** eralisation as to the scope of devolution to Wales is difficult. Many significant powers in relation to nature conservation are transferred to the Welsh Ministers,[97] e.g. most powers under the Conservation (Natural Habitats, Etc.) Regulations 1994[98] and under the legislation for specific animals,[99] while others may be exercised concurrently by Welsh and UK ministers, e.g. the granting of licences under section 16 of the Wildlife and Countryside Act 1981. The position in relation to agriculture and fisheries, water, and town and country planning requires section by section analysis of the particular legislation and the Transfer of Power Orders before the full picture emerges.

So far devolution to Wales has produced little difference in substance in **2.3.10** the areas of law dealt with in this book, although the fact that some Welsh legislation parallel to that being introduced for England is not made at the same time means that there are transitional periods when substantive differences do exist. In other areas of policy, however, there are significant differences, and the regulations implementing the Environmental Liability Directive diverge on the treatment of harm arising as a result of genetically modified organisms.[100]

Treatment in this Book

The complex distribution of power that results from these devolution **2.3.11** arrangements creates problems for authors writing about the exercise of ministerial powers in more than one jurisdiction (and England and Wales can no longer be treated as a single, undifferentiated jurisdiction).[101] Technically the correct approach is to specify in each case which of the range of

---

[94] e.g. Transfer of Functions (Wales) Order 1969 (SI 1969/388); Transfer of Functions (Wales) (No.1) Order 1978 (SI 1978/272).

[95] e.g. both the Welsh Ministers and the Secretary of State have concurrent powers to grant licences under Part I of the Wildlife and Countryside Act 1981 (s.16) and the Welsh authorities must be consulted on the charging schemes for various environmental licences (Environment Act 1995 ss.41 and 42); National Assembly for Wales (Transfer of Functions) Order 1999 (SI 1999/672) Schs 1 and 2.

[96] Government of Wales Act 2006 ss.80–82, 94 and 108.

[97] As authorised by Government of Wales Act 1998 s.62.

[98] SI 1994/2716; there is no transfer of the powers under regs 71–78 (electricity and pipelines).

[99] e.g. all of the powers under the Protection of Badgers Act 1992, most of those under the Conservation of Seals Act 1970 and some under the Deer Act 1991 have been transferred.

[100] The qualification in reg.19(4) of the Environmental Damage (Prevention and Remediation) (Wales) Regulations 2009 (SI 2009/995) does not appear in the English provisions (Environmental Damage (Prevention and Remediation) Regulations 2009 (SI 2009/153); see para.5.12.5, below.

[101] Indeed, whereas formerly it made good sense to approach the subject of this book on the basis of a distinction between the broadly shared law in Great Britain and the quite different provisions in Northern Ireland, the extent to which there is now separate legislation in each of the jurisdictions within Great Britain calls into question the future of this approach.

options applies, from Secretary of State throughout Great Britain, to Secretary of State in England, Scottish Ministers in Scotland and Welsh Ministers or National Assembly in Wales, noting the big difference in the scope of the competences devolved to Scotland and to Wales and the variations such as concurrent powers, consultative arrangements and Scottish Ministers acting under executive devolution. But that approach rapidly produces an almost unreadable text and tends to obscure rather than assist any account of the substantive provisions. Throughout this book, therefore, the term "the Minister" is used as a short-hand phrase for the holder of powers that before 1999 lay in the hands of one of the Secretaries of State. In almost all cases in practice for England this will be the Secretary of State, for Scotland it will be the Scottish Ministers (but with the possibility of intervention from London especially in relation to implementing EC law), and for Wales either the Secretary of State or the Welsh Ministers.

CENTRAL GOVERNMENT

2.4.1 Although most of the detailed administration of nature conservation lies in the hands of specialist bodies, especially the statutory conservation bodies, central government is deeply involved in the making of overall policy and retains many significant powers to control or influence the way in which the law operates in practice. This applies as much to the Scottish Government and the Welsh Assembly Government within their areas of competence as to the Westminster government. The strength of the government's commitment to nature conservation will determine its place (usually fairly low) in relation to conflicting concerns, such as promoting economic development or expanding the motorway system, and to competing claims for public funds. It is too early to say whether the biodiversity obligations introduced this decade have had much real impact in moving conservation up the list of government priorities.[102] The policy lead given by central government will be crucial in determining where the balance between various interests is to be struck, especially as so much of the law relies on discretionary powers. More fundamentally, central government is responsible for providing the funds for the various conservation bodies and for promoting the legislation under which they operate.

2.4.2   In addition to functions within the domestic system, the central authorities are responsible for handling conservation issues at European and international levels. It is the Westminster government, in the name of the Crown, which signs and ratifies international treaties. It is the Westminster government whose representatives on the Council of Ministers of the European Community negotiate and agree to European legislation, and it is the Westminster government which is ultimately responsible for ensuring that Community law is properly implemented and observed in this country.[103] The fact that the government may ultimately have to answer before the European Court of Justice for the state of our law gives central government an added incentive to keep a close eye on what is happening, even where the

---

[102] See section 2.2, above.
[103] See para.2.3.4, above.

prime responsibility lies with the devolved administrations, and even more when it may initially rest with local authorities or other public bodies.

Within government, responsibility is divided between a number of **2.4.3** departments, and now between Westminster and the devolved administrations as discussed above, the devolved administrations similarly dividing responsibilities between departments. Whatever the practical arrangements, the formal approach has been for statutes to confer powers simply on "the Secretary of State", which means that any of Her Majesty's Principal Secretaries of State can lawfully exercise the power.[104] In relation to any legislation that pre-dates the devolution arrangements, any such reference to the Secretary of State must now be read in the light of the transfer of powers to the Scottish and Welsh Ministers. The statutory language used after devolution became effective tends to reflect the new arrangements expressly.

The role of government ministers is often hidden behind the more obvious **2.4.4** and direct official powers lying in the hands of the conservation and other public bodies. However, although lying in the background, the power of central government should not be underestimated, especially in relation to the conservation bodies. This power comes in various forms. In the first place, it is the government which appoints the members of the boards of these bodies,[105] and in so doing can obviously influence the general approach which is likely to be taken by them. Secondly, as the finances which are to be available to these bodies are also determined by the government,[106] some control can be exercised over how much the agencies are actually able to achieve in carrying out their functions, e.g. the extent to which funds are available will obviously have a direct effect on the number, scale and nature of management agreements which can be offered to landowners.[107] There is also the possibility of direct involvement through the power of government to issue to the agencies directions which must be obeyed.[108]

In addition to these general powers over the statutory conservation bodies **2.4.5** and other agencies, the government exercises controls over their activities in other ways. The making of grants and loans by such bodies is usually subject to government approval,[109] as is the exercise of any power of compulsory purchase.[110] Byelaws have to be confirmed by the Minister,[111] and Ministers play a key role in some of the significant designations of land for conservation purposes.[112]

In other areas, such as agriculture and town and country planning, the **2.4.6** role of government ministers is more direct. Regulations made by the Ministers govern most aspects of agriculture, and the grant schemes which play such an important role in shaping the industry and in the management

---

[104] Interpretation Act 1978 Sch.1; *Agee v Lord Advocate*, 1977 S.L.T. (Notes) 54.

[105] e.g. NHSA 1991 Sch.1 para.3.

[106] e.g. NHSA 1991 s.8.

[107] An issue highlighted after the decision in *Cameron v Nature Conservancy Council*, 1991 S.L.T. (Lands Tr.) 85.

[108] e.g. NHSA 1991 s.11.

[109] e.g. NHSA 1991 s.9.

[110] e.g. NPACA 1949 s.103(1), substituted by Nature Conservancy Council Act 1973 Sch.1 para.2 and amended by EPA 1990 Sch.9 para.1.

[111] e.g. NPACA 1949 s.106.

[112] e.g. proposing European Sites; CNHR 1994 reg.7.

of the countryside[113] are created and administered by central government (within European Community guidelines). In the planning system, the Ministers make the detailed rules which exempt certain forms of development from the need for permission,[114] have a major role in development planning,[115] decide appeals[116] and can call in individual applications for their own determination.[117] The number of references throughout this book to "the Minister" is itself testament to the extent of direct power enjoyed by ministers in matters relevant for conservation.[118]

2.4.7   Central government, including the Scottish Government and Welsh Assembly Government, is thus deeply involved in the handling of nature conservation.[119] From the framing of the fundamental pieces of legislation to the determination of individual applications for grants or planning permission, the government can affect the whole form and direction of the law and policy throughout the country, a position strengthened by its control over the membership and finances of the public bodies established outside government to play the leading part in conservation matters. In practice governments have not generally exercised their powers so as to interfere with the detailed workings of the conservation bodies, but the extent of power and influence which lies in the hands of central government must always be remembered.

LOCAL AUTHORITIES

2.5.1 The range of powers and responsibilities exercised by local authorities means that they are heavily involved in matters affecting nature conservation. The variety of structural arrangements throughout Great Britain renders it increasingly difficult to describe the formal distribution of power and functions briefly but accurately. What follows favours brevity over comprehensive detail. The basic structure is that in Scotland and Wales there is a single tier of local government,[120] whereas in England there are both unitary and two-tier arrangements,[121] with a separate structure in London involving the London boroughs and the new institutions created by

---

[113] e.g. see the list of grant schemes at *http://www.scotland.gov.uk/Topics/Agriculture/grants/A-Z/Intro* [Accessed May 5, 2009].

[114] TCPSA 1997 s.30; TCPA 1990 s.59.

[115] See section 8.2, below.

[116] TCPSA 1997 s.47; TCPA 1990 s.79.

[117] TCPSA 1997 s.46; TCPA 1990 s.77.

[118] As discussed at para.2.3.11 above, for the purposes of this book the term "the Minister" includes those to whom ministerial power has been devolved.

[119] Further information is available from the Scottish Government at *http://www.scotland.gov.uk*, the Welsh Assembly Government at *http://www.wales.gov.uk*, the Department for Environment, Food and Rural Affairs at *http://www.defra.gov.uk* and the Department for Communities and Local Government at *http://www.communities.gov.uk* [All Accessed May 5, 2009].

[120] Local Government etc. (Scotland) Act 1994; Local Government (Wales) Act 1994.

[121] Metropolitan District Councils are single-tier authorities, whereas in other areas there is either a unitary authority or a divide between County and District Councils; Local Government Acts 1972, 1985 and 1992; Local Government and Public Involvement in Health Act 2007. Following significant changes introduced on April 1, 2009, unitary authorities cover about 60% of England. For a number of purposes relevant to this book, the Isles of Scilly are treated as if they formed a separate county.

the Greater London Authority Act 1999. In all cases the creation of joint boards to carry out particular tasks (e.g. police and fire services in Scotland) and other co-operative arrangements of various sorts further complicate the position in practice.

The wide discretion and broad powers enjoyed by local authorities mean **2.5.2** that there is much that an authority can do to further the interests of nature conservation if it is so minded. Within authorities, though, the demands of nature conservation must compete with the many other demands placed on local government and it is not surprising if authorities at times view economic development as more important than nature conservation when it comes to determining land use, and education, housing and social services as more deserving when it comes to the allocation of resources.

The balance is, however, affected by a number of broad legal duties. In **2.5.3** addition to the duties in relation to conserving biodiversity that apply to all public authorities,[122] further obligations on local authorities require them to pay heed to environmental considerations. In England and Wales there is a duty to prepare a sustainable community strategy promoting or improving the environmental, as well as social and economic, well-being of the area and contributing to sustainable development,[123] supported by the introduction of a new background power for authorities to do things considered likely to promote the environmental well-being of their area.[124] The express requirement to consider environmental issues as a whole, as opposed to a fragmented approach with particular planning, public health, pollution control and nuisance responsibilities considered separately, may promote a greater awareness of the potential for measures promoting biodiversity to play a part in enhancing overall amenity and the quality of life. There is no equivalent strategy required in Scotland and the general power to advance well-being offers no definition of the term or its components,[125] potentially leaving scope for argument over how far measures that promote biodiversity but not human amenity can be taken as contributing to the well-being of an area. On the other hand, the obligation on local authorities in Scotland to pursue best value does include a requirement that this is done in a way that contributes to sustainable development,[126] reference to which is absent in the broadly equivalent provision for England and Wales.[127] More significantly, the extension of strategic environmental assessment to all policies and strategies of local authorities in Scotland will mean that their attention is drawn to the environmental consequences of their activities,[128] which in conjunction with the stronger phrasing of the biodiversity duty should give biodiversity some greater priority.

Perhaps the most obvious part played by local authorities is in the **2.5.4** operation of the system of town and country planning. As this subject is well covered in more specialised works, it is not the intention to deal with it in

---

[122] NCSA 2004 s.1; NERCA 2006 s.40; see section 1.2, above. There are also the further duties to have regard to the desirability of conserving the natural heritage or natural beauty and amenity; para.2.2.6, above

[123] Local Government Act 2000 s.4, amended by Sustainable Communities Act 2007 s.7.

[124] Local Government Act 2000 s.2.

[125] Local Government in Scotland Act 2003 s.20.

[126] Local Government in Scotland Act 2003 s.1.

[127] Local Government Act 1999 s.3.

[128] Environmental Assessment (Scotland) Act 2005 s.4; see section 8.3, below.

any detail in this book.[129] At present it is enough to note that as planning authorities,[130] local authorities are engaged in development planning for their areas[131] and for the approval of the individual applications for permission to carry out building, engineering or mining operations or to change the use of any land.[132] Within the scope of these powers, which exclude most agricultural and forestry matters,[133] the authorities have considerable control over changes in the use of land and thus on the sort of habitat which will be available within their areas, a control emphasised by the fact that a grant of planning permission can authorise activities in an SSSI, however damaging to its value as natural habitat.[134]

2.5.5   Direct powers over the countryside are also enjoyed by local authorities. Local nature reserves can be created,[135] public access can be arranged through agreements or orders,[136] and management agreements can be made for the preservation and enhancement of the natural beauty of the countryside and the promotion of its enjoyment by the public.[137] Country parks (and in Scotland, regional parks) can be created[138] and there is a variety of powers to make byelaws[139] and appoint rangers or wardens[140] for areas where an authority has intervened in some way. The law also allows authorities more general powers which may be of relevance, e.g. in Scotland local authorities may undertake works for the preservation and enhancement of natural beauty[141] and to further well-being,[142] whilst in England and Wales there is the general power to act for the benefit of environmental well-being.[143]

2.5.6   An authority's other functions will also have an effect on habitat and nature conservation. Local authorities act as coast protection authorities,[144]

---

[129] See section 8.2, below.

[130] Planning functions are generally divided between the two tiers of local government where these exist (TCPA 1990 s.1) and National Park Authorities also act as planning authorities (see section 5.9, below).

[131] TCPSA 1997 Pt II, as significantly amended by the Planning etc. (Scotland) Act 2006; Planning and Compulsory Purchase Act 2004 Pts 1, 2 and 6.

[132] TCPSA 1997 Pt III; Planning and Compulsory Purchase Act 2004 Pt III.

[133] TCPSA 1997 s.26(2)(e); Planning and Compulsory Purchase Act 2004 s.55(2)(e).

[134] In Scotland NCSA 2004 s.17(1); in England and Wales WCA 1981 s.28P(4), added by CRWA 2000 Sch.9; see section 5.5, below.

[135] NPACA 1949 s.21; see para.5.3.10, below.

[136] CSA 1967 Pt II (this power is now shared with SNH; NHSA 1991 s.13); NPACA 1949 Pt V.

[137] CSA 1967 s.49A(2), added by Countryside (Scotland) Act 1981 s.9, amended by NHSA 1991 Sch.10 para.4; WCA 1981 s.39.

[138] CSA 1967 ss.48 and 48A, added by Countryside (Scotland) Act 1981 s.8; CA 1968 s.7.

[139] e.g. for country parks and areas covered by access agreements: NPACA 1949 s.90; CSA 1967 s.54; CA 1968 s.41. Wider powers to make byelaws are conferred under the access to the countryside provisions in England and Wales by the CRWA 2000 s.17 and in Scotland by the Land Reform (Scotland) Act 2003 s.12.

[140] NPACA 1949 s.92; CSA 1967 s.65, amended by Countryside (Scotland) Act 1981 Sch.1 para.4. Again further powers are conferred under the new access legislation (CRWA 2000 s.18 and Land Reform (Scotland) Act 2003 s.24).

[141] Local Government (Development and Finance) (Scotland) Act 1964 s.2, amended by CSA 1967 s.52.

[142] Local Government in Scotland Act 2003 s.20 (see para.2.5.3, above).

[143] Local Government Act 2000 s.2.

[144] Coast Protection Act 1949 s.1, amended by Local Government Act 1972 Sch.30, Local Government etc. (Scotland) Act 1994 Sch.13 para.32; in Scotland local authorities are also responsible for flood prevention (Flood Prevention (Scotland) Act 1961 s.1, amended and applied by Local Government etc. (Scotland) Act 1994 Sch.13 para.56; see also Flood Risk Management (Scotland) Act 2009).

and as roads and highways authorities,[145] in all of which capacities works with significant environmental impact can be undertaken or authorised. Involvement in aspects of public health[146] and pollution control[147] gives authorities a role in environmental issues. The responsibility for providing recreational facilities[148] could also be invoked to justify support for facilities for bird-watching, etc. whilst the way in which an authority treats the land under its direct control (schools, offices and cemeteries) will also be of importance in terms of habitat at a local level. On occasions this may in itself become a controversial issue, as in *R. v Somerset County Council, ex p. Fewings*[149] where it was held that the council had acted unlawfully in exercising its management powers over land in order to give effect to the councillors' ethical view that hunting was wrong, as opposed to acting after a broader consideration of what was to the benefit of its area.[150] As with central government, throughout this book the multitude of references to local authorities in their many capacities illustrates the range of powers which they enjoy and which are of importance for nature conservation.

STATUTORY CONSERVATION BODIES

The past two decades have seen considerable change in the statutory bodies **2.6.1** given direct responsibility for conserving our natural heritage. Until 1991 responsibility for nature conservation and other countryside matters was divided along functional lines. There was a single body, the Nature Conservancy Council (NCC),[151] responsible for nature conservation throughout Great Britain, whilst separate bodies, the Countryside Commissions,[152] were responsible for the natural beauty of the countryside and promoting its enjoyment by the public. As the task of preserving the natural beauty of the countryside was expressly declared to include the conservation of its flora and fauna and its geological or physiographical features of special interest,[153] this division was somewhat artificial, but the NCC and the Commissions developed their own clear areas of activity.

---

[145] Roads (Scotland) Act 1984 s.151; Highways Act 1980 s.1.

[146] Public Health (Scotland) Act 1897 s.12, as amended by Local Government (Scotland) Act 1994 Sch.13 para.9; to be replaced by Public Health etc. (Scotland) Act 2008; Public Health Act 1936 s.1, amended by Local Government Act 1972 Sch.14 para.1; Local Government (Wales) Act 1994 Sch.9 para.3.

[147] Local authorities have significant roles in relation to contaminated land, statutory nuisance, and in England and Wales integrated pollution prevention and control; EPA 1990 Pts IIA, added by EA 1995 s.57, and III, as extended to Scotland by EA 1995 s.107 and Sch.17; and Environmental Permitting (England and Wales) Regulations 2007 (SI 2007/3538) reg.32.

[148] Local Government and Planning (Scotland) Act 1982 ss.14–18; Local Government (Miscellaneous Provisions) Act 1976 s.19.

[149] *R. v Somerset County Council, ex p. Fewings* [1995] 1 W.L.R. 1035; see also *R. v Sefton Metropolitan District Council, ex p. British Association of Shooting and Conservation Ltd* [2001] Env. L.R. 10.

[150] Local Government Act 1972 s.120.

[151] Established in its final form by the Nature Conservancy Council Act 1973.

[152] The Countryside Commission for Scotland, established under CSA 1967, and the Countryside Commission, which operated in England and Wales and was created by CA 1968 as successor to the National Parks Commission created by NPACA 1949.

[153] CSA 1967 s.78(2); CA 1968 s.49(4).

2.6.2   This structure has been transformed and the division is now on a geographical basis. In the early 1990s, new bodies were created in Scotland and in Wales, Scottish Natural Heritage[154] and the Countryside Council for Wales,[155] which exercise the functions of both the NCC and the Countryside Commissions. Only in England did a functional division remain, but now an even wider integration has been achieved there. The functions derived from the NCC were initially exercised by English Nature,[156] whilst the Countryside Commission (no longer extending to Wales)[157] continued to operate until 1999 when it was revised and renamed as the Countryside Agency, acquiring functions from the Development Commission that was abolished as part of the wider reform of the development agencies in England.[158] In 2006 both English Nature and the Countryside Agency were incorporated into the new body Natural England,[159] with just a few functions passed to the newly created Commission for Rural Communities,[160] namely promoting both awareness of the social and economic needs of people in rural areas and communities and the meeting of these needs in ways that contribute to sustainable development.[161] Scottish Natural Heritage (SNH), the Countryside Council for Wales (CCW) and Natural England (NE) do not have a formal collective title, and are generally referred to here as the statutory conservation bodies.[162]

2.6.3   The aim of creating single bodies in Scotland and Wales was to provide the opportunity for an integrated approach to be taken to all conservation and countryside matters, and to recognise the fact that the issues and pressures affecting conservation in those countries are different from those in much of England.[163] In Scotland further elements were the desire to

---

[154] NHSA 1991 Pt I; for one year a separate Nature Conservancy Council for Scotland was in existence (EPA 1990 s.128) before the 1991 Act created SNH as the integrated body.

[155] EPA 1990 ss.128 and 130.

[156] Originally established as the Nature Conservancy Council for England (EPA 1990 s.128) but with statutory recognition granted in 2000 for the shorter title that had been in use since the body's creation (CRWA 2000 s.73).

[157] EPA 1990 s.130 and Sch.8.

[158] Regional Development Agencies Act 1998 ss.34–35; Development Commission (Transfer of Functions and Miscellaneous Provisions) Order 1999 (SI 1999/416). The Development Commission, often referred to as the Rural Development Commission, was created by the Miscellaneous Financial Provisions Act 1983.

[159] NERCA 2006 ss.1–16 and 26–30.

[160] NERCA 2006 ss.17–30.

[161] NERCA 2006 s.18.

[162] The term "conservation bodies" has been used in legislation (e.g. CRWA 2000 s.74; NERCA 2006 s.32), as has the term "nature conservation bodies" (e.g. CNHR 1994 reg.4) but neither is ideal, since they could easily be seen as including the charitable and unofficial bodies which play an important part in practical conservation and in policy debates. "Statutory conservation bodies" is rather clumsy (and might be read as including the National Trusts in view of their unusual statutory position (see para.2.8.4, below) or the bodies concerned with the conservation of cultural, as opposed to natural, heritage), but reduces the risk of confusion with "conservation boards" created in relation to Areas of Outstanding Natural Beauty (see paras 2.7.3–2.7.4, below) while the alternative of "conservation agencies" risks giving the false impression that the bodies are "Next Steps agencies" operating within the departmental structure of government rather than separate, non-departmental statutory corporations (T. Daintith and A. Page, *The Executive in the Constitution* (Oxford: OUP, 1999), pp.37–50).

[163] On the background to the changes see S. Tromans, *The Environmental Protection Act 1990* (London: Sweet & Maxwell, 1991), pp.43.226–43.228; F. Reynolds and W.R. Sheate, "Reorganization of the Conservation Authorities" in W. Howarth and C.P. Rodgers (eds), *Agriculture, Conservation and Land Use* (Cardiff: University of Wales Press, 1992).

transfer the conservation body to the ambit of the Scottish Office[164] and the hope that a new body could establish better relations with local communities than had been the case with the NCC which had become involved in a number of very public controversies over land use during the 1980s.[165] The arguments for integration, however, were not seen as convincing enough in 1990 for a similar merger to be carried out in England. The position there changed after the Haskins Review[166] in 2003 "[revealed] a picture of bureaucratic complexity and customer confusion in rural delivery arrangements"[167] and was very critical of the fragmented delivery arrangements for the government's sustainable land management policies, leading to the creation of Natural England in 2006.

The splitting of the NCC attracted much criticism as being likely to **2.6.4** weaken the scientific base of the conservation authorities and as being an unhelpful fragmentation of responsibility when many issues required study and action at a British level,[168] to say nothing of the practical difficulties caused by dividing responsibility for such areas as the Solway Firth and Bristol Channel. The legislation was hotly debated, and the establishment of the Joint Nature Conservation Committee (JNCC)[169] did little to quieten the concern being expressed that the splitting of the NCC could only weaken the voice of nature conservation on important matters. In view of the vast range of conflicting factors that have influenced the weight given to conservation arguments during the past decade and a half, it is difficult to judge how much impact the structural change has had by itself, while the subsequent moves towards devolution would in any event have demanded a geographical division of the main conservation responsibilities. The reconstitution of the JNCC in 2006,[170] now including full involvement from Northern Ireland, confirms the pattern of separate bodies within the UK coming together through the JNCC when combined action is required.

The structural changes in the administration of nature conservation did **2.6.5** not by themselves affect the substantive rules to be applied. The conservation bodies initially operated by means of the same provisions as governed the powers and functions of the NCC, and the law at first remained the same throughout Great Britain, subject to the one major exception that some changes to the law in Scotland on Sites of Special Scientific Interest (SSSIs) were made at the time of the structural division.[171] Since devolution more significant divergence has occurred, partly the result of policy differences that had emerged during the 1990s[172] and partly detailed differences that are the almost inevitable consequence of different legislatures operating on

---

[164] All aspects of the NCC's work were under the supervision of the Department of the Environment.

[165] e.g. over the Flow Country in Sutherland and the management of geese on Islay.

[166] C. Haskins, *Rural Delivery Review: A report on the delivery of government policies in rural England* (DEFRA, 2003).

[167] C. Haskins, *Rural Delivery Review: A report on the delivery of government policies in rural England* (DEFRA, 2003), para.1.2.

[168] As ever, Northern Ireland is treated separately and is regarded as a special case, although in this instance its geographical separation might in fact justify a different approach in any event.

[169] EPA 1990 s.128(4); see paras 2.6.24–2.6.28, below.

[170] NERCA 2006 Sch.4.

[171] The establishment of the Advisory Committee; see para.5.5.32, below.

[172] See para.5.5.3, below.

different timescales.[173] At an administrative level, though, the councils can still to some extent be discussed together since they share many features.[174] The following paragraphs describe the common features of the bodies, before examining the special aspects of each in turn and the role of the Joint Committee.

2.6.6   A final preliminary point is to consider the meaning of "conservation" itself, a term used widely in defining the purpose and functions of these bodies.[175] The issue arose in *Boggis v English Nature*[176] where the designation of an area of eroding cliffs as an SSSI was challenged by landowners whose homes would be lost as the erosion progressed. One argument was that the designation, based on the geological value of the eroding fossil-rich cliff, was not a legitimate act of conservation since it involved the cliff and its fossils being washed into the sea; conservation involves keeping things from harm whereas here the relevant features were being lost. It was held, though, that conservation can include not only keeping things as they are but also allowing natural processes to take their course. Acting to ensure the continuing exposure and erosion of the cliffs was a legitimate exercise of powers to further conservation.

Common Features

2.6.7   Each body has about a dozen members,[177] all of whom are appointed by the relevant Minister[178] and on terms determined by him[179]; members may be removed in the event of bankruptcy, prolonged absence from the body's business (unless permission has been granted) or other causes rendering them unfit or unable to continue.[180] For SNH the Minister is bound to have regard to the desirability of ensuring so far as practicable that there are

---

[173] e.g. s.1(3A) was added to WCA 1981 for England in July 2004, for Wales in August 2004 and in slightly different form for Scotland in October 2004: Wildlife and Countryside Act 1981 (England and Wales) (Amendment) Regulations 2004 (SI 2004/1487) reg.3; Wildlife and Countryside Act 1981 (Amendment) (Wales) Regulations 2004 (SI 2004/1733) Sch.1 para.1; NCSA 2004 Sch.6 para.2.

[174] Tracing the exact legal position is not straightforward since what were once common provisions in EPA 1990 have been fragmented by the establishment of SNH and the changes to English Nature and then to Natural England, leaving the 1990 Act applying to CCW alone (a change noted in the amendments made by NERCA 2006 Sch.11 paras 117–127).

[175] e.g. EPA 1990 s.131 (the provision relevant to the case below).

[176] *Boggis v English Nature* [2008] EWHC 2954 Admin; [2009] Env. L.R. 20; press reports suggested that both parties intended to appeal from this first-instance judgment whilst the judge urged further efforts to negotiate on the one practical issue dividing the parties.

[177] Between 8 and 12 for CCW and SNH, and between 9 and 15 for NE (EPA 1990 s.128(2), as substituted by NERCA 2006 Sch.11 para.117; NHSA 1991 Sch.1 para.3; NERCA 2006 Sch.1 para.3); the number of members can be varied by ministerial order (EPA 1990 s.128(3) (as substituted); NHSA 1991 Sch.1 para.8; NERCA 2006 Sch.1 para.3(4)).

[178] EPA 1990 s.128(2) (as substituted); NHSA 1991 Sch.1 para.3; NERCA 2006 Sch.1 para.3; membership of one of the bodies is a disqualification from being an MP (for SNH, House of Commons Disqualification Act 1975 Sch.1 Pt II, amended by NHSA 1991 Sch.10 para.8; for CCW House of Commons Disqualification Act 1975 Sch.1 Pt III, amended by EPA 1990 Sch.6 para.24 (members in receipt of remuneration only); and for NE House of Commons Disqualification Act 1975 Sch.1 Pt II, amended by NERCA 2006 Sch.11 para.60).

[179] EPA 1990 Sch.6 para.4; NHSA 1991 Sch.1 para.7; NERCA 2006 Sch.1 para.5.

[180] EPA 1990 Sch.6 para.6; NHSA Sch.1 para.9; NERCA 2006 Sch.1 para.7; the English and Welsh provisions refer to six consecutive months' absence, the Scottish ones to three months' as well as including a power to dismiss members who are "unsuitable" as well as unable or unfit to continue in office.

among the members persons of knowledge or experience of SNH's principal areas of activity,[181] and to satisfy himself that the members have no financial or other interest likely to be prejudicial to their performance in office[182]; for NE the requirement is to have regard to the desirability of appointing members who have experience of, and have shown capacity in, matters relevant to its functions.[183] In all cases a chairman and deputy chairman are appointed by the Minister[184] while the chief officer is appointed by the council with the Minister's approval.[185] Each body has control of its own procedure[186] and can appoint committees including outside members.[187]

Although independent of government departments, the conservation **2.6.8** bodies remain under a degree of central supervision. Annual reports and accounts must be prepared and are subject to scrutiny by the relevant Parliament and auditing body.[188] As well as being able to influence the bodies through the appointment of their members, the Minister has the power to give the bodies directions of a general or specific character with regard to the discharge of their functions.[189] More significantly, the funds made available to the bodies are determined by the Minister[190] and for CCW and SNH the grants and loans made by these bodies are also subject to authorisation (specifically or by means of a general authorisation) by those exercising devolved ministerial power.[191] The conservation bodies also fall within the jurisdiction of the relevant Ombudsman.[192] Although these powers have not in fact been used to interfere with the workings of the conservation bodies, or the NCC before them, it must be noted that the independence of the bodies could be undermined by the existence of such provisions.[193]

The conservation bodies are given a range of general functions and **2.6.9**

---

[181] NHSA 1991 Sch.1 para.4.

[182] NHSA 1991 Sch.1 para.5; for this purpose the Minister can request information from members and potential members (NHSA 1991 para.6).

[183] NERCA 2006 Sch.1 para.3(3).

[184] EPA 1990 Sch.6 para.4; NHSA 1991 Sch.1 para.10; NERCA 2006 Sch.1 para.4 (here there is a power, rather than a duty, to appoint a deputy).

[185] EPA 1990 Sch.6 para.8; NHSA 1991 Sch.1 para.12; NERCA 2006 Sch.1 para.13.

[186] EPA 1990 Sch.6 para.12; NHSA 1991 Sch.1 para.15; NERCA 2006 Sch.1 para.17.

[187] EPA 1990 Sch.6 para.14; NHSA 1991 Sch.1 para.16; NERCA 2006 Sch.1 paras 19–20. For example SNH used this power to establish three Area Boards to maintain closer contacts with local communities, replaced in 2007 by the Local Adviser Forum.

[188] NPACA 1949 s.3; EPA 1990 Sch.6 paras 19–21, NHSA 1991 s.10; NERCA 2006 Sch.1 paras 23–25.

[189] EPA 1990 s.131(4); NHSA 1991 s.11; NERCA 2006 s.15; there are limitations on the scope of directions in relation to the exercise of many conservation functions by SNH and to the functions that NE exercises through the JNCC.

[190] EPA 1990 s.129; NHSA 1991 s.8; NERCA 2006 s.14.

[191] EPA 1990 s.134; NHSA 1991 s.9; there is no general requirement for ministerial approval in the equivalent provisions for NE (NERCA 2006 s.6).

[192] Parliamentary Commissioner Act 1967 Sch.2, amended by NERCA 2006 Sch.11 para.39; Scottish Public Services Ombudsman Act 2002 Sch.2; Public Services Ombudsman (Wales) Act 2005 Sch.3.

[193] The extent to which such powers entitle ministers to intervene in the affairs of non-departmental bodies was the focus of heated political debate in the aftermath of the failure of the Scottish Qualifications Authority to deliver accurate and timeous exam results in the summer of 2000; see *Scottish Parliament Official Report*, vol.8, cols 142–144 (September 7, 2000). The issue is also relevant to whether the bodies can provide a fair hearing before an independent tribunal to satisfy art.6 of the European Convention on Human Rights; see paras 1.5.6–1.5.8, above.

powers to enable them to carry out their responsibilities for nature conservation.[194] All of their functions must be exercised so as to secure compliance with the requirements of the Habitats and Species Directive.[195] These functions include the provision of advice to government ministers on the development and implementation of policies for nature conservation, the provision of advice to any persons about nature conservation, the dissemination of relevant knowledge, and the commissioning and support (financial or other) of research.[196] The general powers enable the conservation bodies to initiate and carry out research themselves, to accept and apply gifts and contributions for the achievement of their purposes, to hold land, to make charges for their services and to do all other things incidental or conducive to their functions.[197] These provisions are wide enough to allow the bodies to operate freely without continually checking the limits of their legal powers and are in addition to the specific measures contained in the detailed provisions on nature conservation.

2.6.10   The substantive provisions are discussed in detail below, but in summary, the statutory conservation bodies are responsible for the designation of nature reserves and the making of byelaws and management agreements for them, for the designation of SSSIs, the approval of activities within them and the making of management agreements for them, and for the licensing of activities relating to protected species. The bodies are also involved as consultees in many official procedures and are charged with the provision of advice to government at all levels on matters relating to nature conservation, from the formulation of policy to the desirability of particular acts and the protection of individual species. For all of these tasks a major research effort is necessary.

Scottish Natural Heritage

2.6.11 Scottish Natural Heritage (SNH)[198] was created by the Natural Heritage (Scotland) Act 1991, as the successor to both the Nature Conservancy Council for Scotland and the Countryside Commission for Scotland. Its general aims reflect those of its two predecessors, being:

> "(a) to secure the conservation and enhancement of; and
> (b) to foster understanding and facilitate the enjoyment of, the natural heritage of Scotland."[199]

SNH is thus charged with the responsibility both for conservation and for recreation and amenity, a combination which offers the opportunity for an

---

[194] In provisions that now survive for CCW only, this is defined for this purpose as "the conservation of flora, fauna or geological or physiographical features"; EPA 1990 s.131(6).

[195] CNHR 1994 reg.3(2).

[196] EPA 1990 s.132(1), amended by NERCA 2006 Sch.11 para.121; NHSA 1991 s.2(1); NERCA 2006 ss.4–10 and 13.

[197] EPA 1990 s.132(2) (as amended); NHSA 1991 s.2(1) and (2); NERCA 2006 ss.3, 11 and 13: the Scottish legislation expressly includes reference to the power to form partnerships and companies, whilst the English provisions require ministerial approval to form companies (s.13(2)).

[198] Information about SNH can be found on its web-site at *http://www.snh.org.uk* [Accessed May 6, 2009].

[199] NHSA 1991 s.1(1).

integrated approach to be taken on many countryside and environmental issues. However, much closer coordination with the authorities responsible for agriculture, forestry and other rural land uses is necessary before a truly integrated approach is possible, while the present dual objectives of SNH may lead to internal conflicts in areas where recreational pressure may damage fragile environments.[200]

The legislation creating SNH contains two novelties. First, the concept of **2.6.12** the "natural heritage" of Scotland is introduced. This is defined as including the flora and fauna of Scotland, its geological and physiographical features, and its natural beauty and amenity,[201] thereby combining and replacing the somewhat ungainly terms which have been used in previous conservation and countryside legislation.

The second novelty is the first statutory reference to the concept of sus- **2.6.13** tainability, noted above.[202] As part of its general aims, SNH is required to have regard to the desirability of ensuring that anything done in relation to the natural heritage of Scotland "is undertaken in a manner which is sustainable."[203] The exact meaning and impact of this provision are far from clear, especially as no definition is provided of "sustainable". The most that was offered in the parliamentary debates was the quotation of very broad principles taken from a document prepared by the International Union for the Conservation of Nature.[204] The introduction of this concept can be viewed as either a strengthening or a weakening of the commitment to conservation. A strengthening may result from the test of sustainability being applied to all activities which in any way affect the natural heritage, assessing their acceptability in terms of their long-term impact on the natural environment. On the other hand the commitment to conservation could be weakened either if the social and economic aspects of the concept are given prominence over biodiversity issues, or if questions as to the sustainability of any new development divert attention from the more fundamental issue of whether any development at all should be allowed to interfere with the status quo. Whatever one's approach, and despite the term's appearance in many other statutory provisions since 1991, sustainability remains more of a political, economic and ethical principle than a legal standard by which conduct can be judged. In view of the lack of definition and the fact that SNH is merely required "to have regard to" the desirability of securing sustainability, arguments over the meaning and effect of this provision are likely to take place at the policy rather than the legal level, and this provision has not been the focus of legal argument.

In addition to having regard to the desirability of ensuring sustainability, **2.6.14** SNH is required to pay heed to a number of other considerations, balancing the concerns of conservation with a range of other interests.[205] As with all such balancing obligations, the precise weight to be given to any

---

[200] Issues such as the development of the Cairngorm funicular railway brought out this clear potential for conflict; see *WWF-UK Ltd v Secretary of State for Scotland* [1999] 1 C.M.L.R. 1021; [1999] Env. L.R. 632.
[201] NHSA 1991 s.1(3).
[202] See para.2.2.2, above.
[203] NHSA 1991 s.1(1).
[204] A draft of *Caring for Our World – A Strategy for Sustainability*; HC 1990–1991, First Scottish Standing Committee C, col.55.
[205] NHSA 1991 s.3(1).

consideration is left to the discretion of SNH in each instance, but the various factors must at least be borne in mind and will obviously exert some influence on the making of policy and determination of particular cases. In keeping with SNH's main responsibilities actual or possible ecological and other environmental changes to the natural heritage of Scotland must be considered,[206] and it is also to have regard to aspects of what is sometimes called the "cultural heritage", namely the need to conserve sites and landscapes of archaeological and historical interest. Such conservationist concerns are balanced by the duty to consider the needs of agriculture, fisheries and forestry and the need for social and economic development. There is also a duty to consider the interests of owners and occupiers of land and of local communities. These latter needs and interests will obviously conflict at times with those of nature conservation (and of promoting recreation), but any successful conservation policy must pay heed to the concerns of the people who often feel themselves as being the most endangered species in the remote areas valued for their natural features. The emphasis given to working closely with local communities is reflected in the arrangements for SSSIs[207] and National Parks[208] in Scotland.

2.6.15   From the Nature Conservancy Council for Scotland, SNH inherited the detailed nature conservation functions described later in this book as well as a role as official consultee on many planning and related matters.[209] From the Countryside Commission for Scotland, it inherited a range of advisory functions and concern for the promotion of public recreation in the countryside. SNH's latter role has been enhanced by the power for SNH itself to enter access agreements and to make access orders to provide public access to areas of the countryside for recreational purposes[210]; previously the Countryside Commission for Scotland had been restricted to an advisory role, with the relevant legal powers being exclusively in the hands of planning authorities.

2.6.16   The powers which the Countryside Commission for Scotland enjoyed have been retained and broadened in scope, both geographically, as they are no longer restricted to "the countryside",[211] and in terms of their use, as they can now be exercised in connection with the full range of SNH's functions, not merely those inherited from the Commission. There is a general power to enter management agreements[212] and a power to undertake and promote development schemes designed to enhance or conserve or to foster understanding or enjoyment of the natural heritage.[213] Such schemes must involve the application of new techniques and methods or serve to illustrate the appropriateness of such schemes to particular areas,[214] and wide powers,

---

[206] This is the only consideration to be taken into account in the exercise of functions relating to the Joint Nature Conservation Committee (NHSA 1991 s.3(2)).

[207] See para.5.5.31, below.

[208] See paras 5.9.28–5.9.29, below.

[209] Detailed amendments to the relevant legislation to take account of this transfer of functions to SNH are made by EPA 1990 Sch.9 and NHSA 1991 Sch.2.

[210] NHSA 1991 s.13 and Sch.3, amending Pt II of CSA 1967.

[211] The Commission was restricted to operating in "the countryside" as defined by CSA 1967 s.2.

[212] CSA 1967 s.49A, added by Countryside (Scotland) Act 1981 s.9 and amended by NHSA 1991 Sch.10 para.4.

[213] NHSA 1991 s.5(1).

[214] NHSA 1991 s.5(2).

including that of compulsory purchase of land, are provided to allow such schemes to be carried out.[215] From both predecessors SNH acquired the power to make or propose byelaws for areas where it is exercising various powers[216] and the ability to offer grants, loans and other forms of assistance to those furthering its objectives.[217]

Countryside Council for Wales

In Wales the structural change was achieved in a single step when the **2.6.17** Countryside Council for Wales (CCW)[218] was created by the Environmental Protection Act 1990[219] and it remains in being largely unaltered. Like SNH it is charged with the tasks previously carried out by separate conservation and countryside bodies. Responsibility for nature conservation in Wales and the relevant statutory powers and functions were transferred to CCW from the Nature Conservancy Council,[220] while it was provided that in Wales CCW is to exercise the functions of the Countryside Commission, which had previously operated in both England and Wales.[221] Thus, the 1990 Act created for Wales a single body which should be able to offer a more integrated approach to countryside and conservation issues than was previously the case, a process repeated for Scotland in 1991 and for England in 2006.

The conservation functions and powers of CCW are the same as those of **2.6.18** the other statutory conservation bodies,[222] and the countryside functions and powers are the same as those enjoyed by the Countryside Commission.[223] The latter powers are to be exercised for dual purposes.[224] First, CCW is to act for the conservation and enhancement of natural beauty in Wales[225] and of the natural beauty and amenity of the countryside in Wales, both in areas designated as National Parks and Areas of Outstanding Natural Beauty and elsewhere.[226] Secondly, CCW is to encourage the provision and improvement of facilities for the enjoyment of the Welsh

---

[215] NHSA 1991 s.5(3)–(11); any compulsory purchase of land must be approved by the Minister and is subject to special parliamentary procedure.

[216] e.g. for nature reserves (NPACA 1949 s.2) and for areas covered by access arrangements (CSA 1967 s.54(4), amended by NHSA 1991 Sch.10 para.4).

[217] Now governed by NHSA 1991 s.9.

[218] The name *Cyngor Cefn Gwlad Cymru* can also be used, by virtue of the Alternative Names in Welsh Order 1994 (SI 1994/2889). Information about CCW can be found on its website at *http://www.ccw.gov.uk* [Accessed May 6, 2009].

[219] EPA 1990 ss.128 and 130; the relevant provisions in EPA 1990 originally governed all three conservation bodies but have now been amended to refer clearly to CCW alone (NERCA 2006 Sch.11 paras 117–127). The role of CCW is also asserted in NPACA 1949 s.1, as amended, most recently by NERCA 2006.

[220] The detailed amendments necessary to achieve this are contained in EPA 1990 Sch.9.

[221] EPA 1990 s.130; the detailed amendments necessary are contained in EPA 1990 Sch.8, in particular substituting a new s.1 and adding ss.4A, 50A and 86A to NPACA 1949.

[222] And in the exercise of these CCW must take appropriate account of actual or possible ecological changes; EPA 1990 s.131(2).

[223] The additional powers in England transferred from the Development Commission to what was the Countryside Agency and is now Natural England do not extend to Wales.

[224] EPA 1990 s.130(2).

[225] The conservation of natural beauty includes the conservation of flora and fauna and geological and physiographical features; EPA 1990 s.130(3).

[226] Earlier legislation had suggested that efforts should be concentrated on the designated areas by stating that the conservation and enhancement of natural beauty were to be sought "particularly" in the designated areas; NPACA 1949 s.1 as originally enacted.

countryside and of opportunities for open-air recreation and the study of nature. At the same time CCW is required to have regard to the social and economic interests of rural areas in Wales,[227] but there are no more detailed balancing obligations to mirror those imposed on SNH.[228] The National Assembly of Wales has the power to adjust the functions of CCW, but only so as to give it additional functions.[229]

2.6.19 The powers acquired from the Countryside Commission are largely advisory and supportive,[230] rather than offering scope for the implementation of major independent initiatives. Areas where CCW does play a major "executive" role are in the designation of National Parks and Areas of Outstanding Natural Beauty,[231] and in the implementation of the public rights of access to the countryside introduced by the Countryside and Rights of Way Act 2000, with responsibility for drawing up the definitive maps of open country over which access rights may be exercised[232] and on issues relating to the exclusion or restriction of access.[233] Information and publicity can be provided about the countryside and for the benefit of visitors to it,[234] and a more direct role can be taken in relation to experimental schemes demonstrating the application of new techniques or approaches.[235] In other areas, particularly the promotion of public access by means of access and public path agreements and orders,[236] CCW can make initiatives and offer advice, but ultimately depends on planning authorities and others to implement its ideas.[237] CCW is further charged with the task of advising government at all levels on countryside matters, acting on its own initiative as well as in response to formal requests,[238] and is a consultee in many official procedures.

Natural England

2.6.20 The integration of conservation and countryside responsibilities which took place in Scotland and Wales did not take place in England during the 1990s, so that after the division of the NCC and the transfer to CCW of countryside functions in Wales, England was left with two bodies, defined by both functional and geographical limits. Until 2006, English Nature exercised responsibility for nature conservation, as successor to the NCC.[239]

---

[227] EPA 1990 s.130(2).
[228] See para.2.6.14, above.
[229] Government of Wales Act 1998 s.28 and Sch.4 Pt III.
[230] CA 1968 s.2.
[231] See sections 5.9 and 5.10, below.
[232] CRWA 2000 ss.4–11.
[233] CRWA 2000 ss.21–33.
[234] CA 1968 s.2(8).
[235] CA 1968 s.4 (partly substituted by WCA 1981 s.40).
[236] NPACA 1949 Pt V.
[237] As well as advice it can provide practical help in the form of specially skilled staff; CA 1968 s.2(5).
[238] CA 1968 s.2(4).
[239] This body's statutory name was originally the Nature Conservancy Council for England (EPA 1990 s.128) but it operated under the name English Nature and this change of name was given statutory recognition (CRWA 2000 s.73 and Sch.8).

Meanwhile, the Countryside Commission continued to perform its functions in relation to the countryside and recreation,[240] but limited to activities in England.[241] In 1999, when Regional Development Agencies were created for England, the functions of the Development Commission[242] were transferred to the Countryside Commission, which was renamed the Countryside Agency.[243] The final integration of these functions with those relating to nature conservation took part in 2006, following the Haskins Review which was deeply critical of the fragmented nature of the way in which the government's policies relating to sustainable land management were delivered. The integrated body, called Natural England (NE), was created by the Natural Environment and Rural Communities Act 2006.[244]

The general purpose of NE is stated to be: **2.6.21**

> "[T]o ensure that the natural environment is conserved, enhanced and managed for the benefit of present and future generations, thereby contributing to sustainable development."[245]

This general purpose shows how the language of sustainable development has flowed into statutory provisions,[246] but more traditional language is used in describing a number of elements included within this purpose. These are:

> "(a) promoting nature conservation and protecting biodiversity,
> (b) conserving and enhancing the landscape,
> (c) securing the provision and improvement of facilities for the study, understanding, and enjoyment of the natural environment,
> (d) promoting access to the countryside and open spaces and encouraging open-air recreation, and
> (e) contributing in other ways to social and economic well-being through management of the natural environment."[247]

The first of these asserts the conservation role taken over from English Nature (with the modern addition of a reference to biodiversity), the next three derive from the Countryside Commission's functions, and the final one is a further example of promoting sustainable development, with its social

---

[240] The origins of the Countryside Commission lay with the National Parks Commission established in 1949 (NAPCA 1949 s.1) which was transformed when the Countryside Act 1968 gave it responsibility for the countryside in general and the new name (CA 1968 ss.1–2). The Commission's constitution was restructured by the Wildlife and Countryside Act 1981 Sch.13.

[241] EPA 1990 s.130.

[242] The Development Commission was widely known as the Rural Development Commission and was created by the Miscellaneous Financial Provisions Act 1983 as a successor to the Development Commissioners under the Development and Road Improvement Funds Act 1909. It was formally dissolved by the Development Commission (Dissolution) Order 2000 (SI 2000/1505).

[243] Development Commission (Transfer of Functions and Miscellaneous Provisions) Order 1999 (SI 1999/416).

[244] Further information about Natural England can be found on its website at *http://www.naturalengland.org.uk* [Accessed May 6, 2009].

[245] NERCA 2006 s.2(1).

[246] See section 2.2, above.

[247] NERCA 2006 s.2(2).

element emphasised by the further provision that this goal may in particular be carried out by working with local communities.[248]

2.6.22   In addition to the specific functions conferred by existing legislation, Natural England is given a wide advisory role. It can offer advice on any issue relating to its general purpose. In particular it must provide advice if requested to do so by any public authority, and in these circumstances it is entitled to be informed whether and why such advice has been rejected.[249] Financial or practical assistance can be given to others[250] and Natural England can itself carry out or assist proposals furthering its general purpose.[251] It can carry out experimental schemes developing, testing or applying methods, concepts or techniques that further its general purpose,[252] carry out or assist publications or other provision of information[253] and provide consultancy and training services,[254] being able to charge for its advice or assistance.[255] It is also expressly authorised to bring criminal prosecutions.[256] Natural England also enjoys a broad power to make management agreements in relation to any land in order to further its purposes[257]; this all-encompassing power will avoid the need to examine the older legislation to ensure that any agreements are covered by the narrower and more fragmented specific powers that its predecessors enjoyed.

2.6.23   In practice the most significant functions of NE are governed by the detailed conservation and countryside legislation that was in operation before it was created. Thus NE takes over all of the functions on English Nature in relation to the conservation of species and habitats under the Wildlife and Countryside Act 1981 and the Conservation (Natural Habitats etc.) Regulations 1994, and the roles of the Countryside Agency in relation to National Parks and Areas of Outstanding Natural Beauty and to the public right of access to the countryside.[258]

Joint Nature Conservation Committee

2.6.24   In order to counter some of the disadvantages of splitting the NCC in 1990, the Joint Nature Conservation Committee (JNCC) was established.[259] This body has now been reconstituted under the Natural Environment and Rural Communities Act 2006,[260] the most significant changes being to give the

---

[248] NERCA 2006 s.2(3).

[249] NERCA 2006 s.4.

[250] NERCA 2006 s.6.

[251] NERCA 2006 s.5.

[252] NERCA 2006 s.8.

[253] NERCA 2006 s.9.

[254] NERCA 2006 s.10.

[255] NERCA 2006 s.11.

[256] NERCA 2006 s.12; a prosecutor authorised by NE before the magistrates' court need not be a barrister or solicitor; see para.1.4.4, above.

[257] NERCA 2006 s.7.

[258] See paras 2.6.18–2.6.19, above.

[259] EPA 1990 s.128(4). Information about the JNCC can be found on its website at *http://www.jncc.gov.uk* [Accessed May 6, 2009].

[260] Some of the more detailed changes had initially been made by the Regulatory Reform (Joint Nature Conservation Council) Order 2005 (SI 2005/634).

Committee a stronger independent existence and the full incorporation of Northern Ireland matters so that it operates fully on a United Kingdom basis.[261] The Committee is comprised of 14 members, being a chairman and five members appointed by the Secretary of State,[262] the chairman or deputy chairman and one other member (chosen by the body itself) from each of SNH, CCW, NE and the Council for Nature Conservation and the Countryside from Northern Ireland.[263] The Secretary of State's appointees are not to be members of any of the statutory conservation bodies,[264] but are required to be people appearing to have experience in or scientific knowledge of nature conservation, chosen after consultation with the chairman of the Committee and such persons with scientific knowledge of nature conservation as the Secretary of State considers appropriate.[265] The JNCC has been designated as a cross-border public authority under the Scotland Act 1998.[266]

The Committee has control of its own procedure[267] and is obliged to **2.6.25** produce an annual report to the Minister, who must lay it before both Westminster and Holyrood Parliaments, and to each of the statutory conservation bodies.[268] These bodies and the relevant Northern Ireland department must provide the Committee with the financial resources for the proper discharge of its functions,[269] and the Secretary of State can make grants to the Committee directly.[270] The Committee, with ministerial approval, can employ people[271] and form a company for certain purposes,[272] and it can delegate any of its functions to its members or employees, to such a company or to any of the statutory conservation bodies.[273] It must comply with any direction given by the Secretary of State, but this ministerial power cannot be exercised in relation to the Committee's specific task of listing protected species.[274] A broad range of incidental powers are given to the Committee and the statutory conservation bodies to further the functions of the Committee,[275] and the statutory conservation bodies are authorised to

---

[261] Previously representatives from Northern Ireland attended in a non-voting capacity and the Committee's functions were expressed in terms of Great Britain rather than the United Kingdom; EPA 1990 ss.128 and 133 and Sch.7 (as originally enacted).

[262] The Secretary of State must consult the devolved administrations before making these appointments (NERCA 2006 Sch.4 para.3(2)).

[263] NERCA 2006 Sch.4 para.1.

[264] NERCA 2006 Sch.4 para.2.

[265] NERCA 2006 Sch.4 para.3.

[266] Scotland Act 1998 (Cross-border Public Authorities) (Specification) Order 1999 (SI 1999/1319). This entails obligations on the Secretary of State to consult the Scottish Ministers, a requirement for the Committee to report to the Scottish as well as the Westminster Parliament (Scotland Act 1998 s.88); the JNCC also falls under the jurisdiction of both the Parliamentary Commissioner for Administration and the Scottish Public Services Ombudsman (Parliamentary Commissioner for Administration Act 1967 Sch.2; Scottish Public Services Ombudsman Act 2002 Sch.2).

[267] NERCA 2006 Sch.4 para.16.

[268] NERCA 2006 Sch.7 para.10.

[269] NERCA 2006 Sch.4 para.14.

[270] NERCA 2006 Sch.4 para.18.

[271] NERCA 2006 Sch.4 para.10.

[272] NERCA 2006 Sch.4 para.13; the company must be one limited by guarantee and the main purposes are to provide support services and holding land.

[273] NERCA 2006 Sch.4 para.17.

[274] NERCA 2006 s.38.

[275] NERCA 2006 s.37.

give advice and information to each other and the Committee in relation to its functions.[276]

2.6.26   The functions conferred by the 2006 Act are shared by the statutory conservation bodies and the Committee, but some can be discharged only through the Committee. The functions to be discharged through the Committee relate to matters at an international level or which affect the United Kingdom as whole, thereby seeking to ensure that after the splitting of the NCC there continues to be consistency and coherence on matters of more than local interest. In particular it is useful for there to be a single body providing advice and information on dealings outside the United Kingdom, a matter of growing importance as the government becomes involved in more European Community and international measures, which increasingly contain obligations for regular monitoring and reporting. In all cases the functions are conferred for the purposes of nature conservation and fostering the understanding of this, and must be exercised with regard to actual or possible ecological changes and the desirability of contributing to sustainable development.[277]

2.6.27   The functions to be exercised through the Committee[278] are, first, the provision of advice to the Whitehall and devolved governments on policies for or affecting nature conservation in the United Kingdom as a whole or outside the United Kingdom,[279] and, secondly, the provision of advice and dissemination of knowledge to anyone about the same matters. A matter qualifies if it arises throughout the United Kingdom and raises issues common to England, Scotland, Wales and Northern Ireland,[280] or arises in one or more constituent parts and affects the interests of the United Kingdom as a whole. A third special function for the Committee is the establishment of common standards throughout the United Kingdom for the monitoring of and research into nature conservation and the analysis of the resulting information. The Committee is also empowered to commission or support research relevant to these functions and to give advice or information to any of the statutory conservation bodies.[281] Most particularly, the Committee is further charged[282] with the periodic review of and making of recommendations for change to the lists of wild plants and animals given protection by virtue of Schedules 5 and 8 of the Wildlife and Countryside Act 1981.[283]

2.6.28   As recognised by the 2006 Act, the Committee has established a strong and independent role for itself since it came into being. It is much more than just a joint committee and is really an important body in its own right, linking the work of the statutory conservation bodies with the wider developments in the science, law and policy of nature conservation.

---

[276] NERCA 2006 s.37.

[277] NERCA 2006 s.33.

[278] NERCA 2006 s.34.

[279] The JNCC is involved in conservation matters for British territories overseas.

[280] e.g. the JNCC acts as the scientific authority in relation to trade in endangered species; see para.7.3.20, below.

[281] NERCA 2006 s.35.

[282] NERCA 2006 s.36; relevant research can also be commissioned and supported.

[283] WCA 1981 ss.22(3) and 24(1), amended by EPA 1990 Sch.9 para.11; see paras 3.4.2 and 6.2.4, below.

OTHER PUBLIC BODIES

National Park Authorities and Conservation Boards

In the National Parks, a range of powers are exercised by the National Park **2.7.1**
Authorities, with notable differences in the detailed arrangements for
Scotland and for England and Wales.[284] These bodies enjoy many of the
powers of local authorities and their general task is to further the purposes
for which the National Parks are created. In England and Wales these are to
conserve and enhance the natural beauty, wildlife and cultural heritage of
the area and to promote opportunities for the understanding and enjoyment
of its special qualities.[285] In Scotland these are to conserve and enhance the
natural and cultural heritage of the area, promote sustainable use of its
natural resources, promote the understanding and enjoyment of the area
and to promote sustainable economic and social development of the area's
communities.[286] In both cases the conservation and enhancement duty is to
take priority in the event of a conflict between these purposes.[287]

The park authorities are comprised of members nominated by the local **2.7.2**
authorities for the area affected and those appointed by the Minister, but in
Scotland a number of members are also directly elected.[288] The powers
enjoyed by the authorities in England and Wales are different from those in
Scotland, where the order designating each park can specify the precise
range of powers conferred on the authority. Central to their functions is the
preparation of a park plan, which in Scotland enjoys statutory status.[289] The
National Parks are discussed in more detail in section 5.9, below.

Despite their rather general title, conservation boards are in fact very **2.7.3**
limited in extent and in their geographical application. These bodies are
created under the Countryside and Rights of Way Act 2000 and are able to
acquire some powers from local authorities in order to conserve and
enhance the natural beauty of an Area of Outstanding Natural Beauty
(AONB) and to increase the public's understanding and enjoyment of the
area's special qualities.[290] Each board is constituted individually by a ministerial order, with members who are local authority and parish council
nominees and ministerial appointees.[291]

The order creating a conservation board can transfer to it any of the **2.7.4**
functions of local authorities relating to the AONB, or arrange for these to
be exercisable concurrently by the board and authorities. Significantly,
though, the key planning functions of the local authority cannot be transferred or shared in this way.[292] One specific task for the boards is to prepare
and publish a management plan for their area.[293] The role of conservation
boards and the impact of Areas of Outstanding Natural Beauty are discussed more fully in section 5.10, below.

---

[284] See section 5.9, below.
[285] NPACA 1949 s.5(1), as amended by EA 1995 s.61; see para.5.9.5, below.
[286] NPSA 2000 s.1; see para.5.9.25, below.
[287] NPACA 1949 s.11A, added by EA 1995 s.62); NPSA 2000 s.9(6).
[288] See paras 5.9.11 and 5.9.28–5.9.30, below.
[289] See paras 5.9.14 and 5.9.32–5.9.33, below.
[290] CRWA 2000 s.87(1); in case of conflict, the former purpose is to take priority.
[291] CRWA 2000 Sch.13; see para.5.10.5, below.
[292] CRWA 2000 s.86.
[293] CRWA 2000 s.89; see paras 5.10.5–5.10.7, below.

Forestry

2.7.5 In view of the large areas affected and the dramatic impact on wildlife habitat caused by the planting or felling of trees on a large scale, the actions of the Forestry Commission can be of considerable significance for nature conservation. The Commission fulfils a dual role, being responsible for the management of the large areas of productive woodland still in public ownership, and for encouraging and regulating the development of private forestry.[294] To cope with these potentially conflicting functions, the management of woodland and plantations is mostly entrusted to Forest Enterprise agencies operating within the Commission,[295] whilst the Commission now exercises its policy and regulatory functions on a fully devolved basis.[296] In the past the Commission itself was active in the establishment of new plantations, but since the 1980s the main responsibility for extending afforestation has lain with the private sector, guided by the Commission's supervisory powers.

2.7.6 The Commission comprises a Chairman and up to 10 Commissioners, appointed by the Crown, and including at least three with knowledge and experience of forestry, one with relevant scientific attainments and one with experience of the timber trade.[297] The Commission is subject to fairly standard provisions on preparing annual reports and accounts,[298] and is subject to ministerial direction.[299] The formal structures for its operation have been significantly affected by devolution, and within the statutory framework of a Commission with responsibilities throughout Great Britain[300] there are now separate bodies for Scotland, England and Wales. In relation to Scotland, forestry is a devolved matter, and the Commission has been designated as a cross-border public authority under the Scotland Act 1998,[301] which means that it reports to the Scottish Parliament as well as to Westminster.[302] The Forestry Act 1967 has been subjected to many amendments to reflect the division of functions and responsibilities arising

---

[294] Information about the Forestry Commission can be found on its website at *http://www.forestry.gov.uk* [Accessed May 6, 2009] and for each country at *http://www.forestry.gov.uk/website/fchomepages.nsf/hp/Scotland*, */England* and */Wales* [All Accessed May 6, 2009].

[295] In 2003, following devolution, separate agencies were created for Scotland and England (Forest Enterprise Scotland and Forest Enterprise England) and initially for Wales, but in 2004 Forest Enterprise Wales was wound up with its functions resumed by the Commission in Wales.

[296] There is a further agency within the Commission, Forest Research, whose role is to provide research, surveys and related services to the forest industry and advice to support forestry policy.

[297] Forestry Act 1967 s.2, amended by Forestry Act 1981 s.5.

[298] See especially Forestry Act 1967 s.45 for Scotland, Government of Wales Act 1998 Sch.7 for Wales and the Government Resources and Accounts Act 2000.

[299] Forestry Act 1967 s.1(4).

[300] Some adjustments to the Commission's incidental powers in England and Wales only are made by the Regulatory Reform (Forestry) Order 2006 (SI 2006/780).

[301] Scotland Act 1998 (Cross-border Public Authorities) (Specification) Order 1999 (SI 1999/1319).

[302] Scotland Act 1998 ss.88–90 (see para.2.3.3, above); Forestry Act 1967 s.45, as amended by the Scotland Act 1998 (Cross-Border Public Authorities) (Adaptation of Functions etc.) Order 1999 (SI 1999/1747) Sch.12 para.4(36).

from devolution.[303] In relation to Wales, the funding of the Commission's functions in Wales is now a responsibility of the Welsh authorities,[304] and more detailed arrangements have been made to transfer ministerial powers to the Welsh Ministers[305] and for the separate exercise of the Commission's functions in Wales.[306]

The Commission's duty is to promote the interests of forestry, the **2.7.7** development of afforestation and the production and supply of timber and other forest products,[307] but this is now tempered by an obligation to endeavour to achieve a reasonable balance between these aims and the conservation and enhancement of natural beauty and the conservation of flora and fauna and geological and physiographical features of special interest.[308] This obligation reflected a growing appreciation within the Commission of environmental matters, and there has been a very significant shift in policies during the last two decades, although as trees grow only slowly, the effects of this will not be apparent for some time.[309] Forestry policy today is aimed at achieving a range of benefits, including maintenance and enhancement of biodiversity.[310]

The Forestry Commission's control over private forestry is achieved in **2.7.8** two ways, discussed more fully in Chapter 6.[311] As far as felling is concerned, there is a full statutory scheme which imposes a requirement for a felling licence to be obtained before any significant felling is carried out. For planting, formal approval is necessary only in those situations where an environmental impact assessment is required,[312] but control is exercised through grant schemes operating in an economic context which means that no major planting will be economically viable without grant support.[313] These grant schemes now take into account considerations of habitat diversity, environmental protection and amenity as well as commercial timber production. These arrangements mean that the Commission will be involved in considering the desirability of any major forestry activities and is in a position to ensure that conservation matters are at least taken into

---

[303] Scotland Act 1998 (Cross-Border Public Authorities) (Adaptation of Functions etc.) Order 1999 (SI 1999/1747) Sch.12; Scotland Act 1998 (Cross-Border Public Authorities) (Forestry Commissioners) Order 2000 (SI 2000/746); property issues arising from devolution are dealt with by the Transfer of Property etc. (Scottish Ministers) Order 1999 (SI 1999/1104) art.4.

[304] Government of Wales Act 1998 s.105, as amended by the Government of Wales Act 2006 Sch.10 para.44.

[305] National Assembly for Wales (Transfer of Functions) Order 1999 (SI 1999/672) Sch.1.

[306] Government of Wales Act 1998 Sch.7, as amended by the Government of Wales Act 2006 Sch.10 para.55.

[307] Forestry Act 1967 s.1(2). The Climate Change (Scotland) Bill introduced in 2008 contains provisions to allow the functions of the Commission in Scotland to be altered in relation to climate change and especially to contribute to compliance with the ministerial duties to reduce Scotland's net greenhouse gas emissions (s.47 of the Bill as introduced).

[308] Forestry Act 1967 s.1(3A), added by Wildlife and Countryside (Amendment) Act 1985 s.4.

[309] See C.T. Reid, "The Changing Pattern of Environmental Regulation: British Forestry and the Environmental Agenda" (1997) 9 J.E.L. 23.

[310] See, e.g. *Sustainable Forestry: the UK Programme*, Cm.2429 (1994); Forestry Commission: *Woodlands for Wales* (2001); *The Scottish Forestry Strategy* (2006); *A Strategy for England's Trees, Woods and Forests* (2007).

[311] See section 6.4, below.

[312] Environmental Impact Assessment (Forestry) (Scotland) Regulations 1999 (SSI 1999/43); Environmental Impact Assessment (Forestry) (England and Wales) Regulations 1999 (SI 1999/2228); see paras 6.4.19–6.4.23, below.

[313] See paras 6.4.8–6.4.10, below.

account. To the extent that its functions involve authorising certain activities affecting a Site of Special Scientific Interest in Scotland, it must consult SNH before doing so.[314]

2.7.9 Some cases involving disputes arising from the exercise of the Commission's powers may be referred to the relevant Regional Advisory Committee. The composition of these committees is governed partly by convention and partly by statute. In keeping with the shift away from timber production as the sole aim of forestry policy, the relevant provisions were amended in 1991, increasing the membership from 9 to 12 to allow for a greater representation of environmental interests after criticism that there was an inherent bias in favour of forestry developments in the Committees.[315] By law, at least four of the members must be appointed after consultations with organisations representing the interests of owners of woodlands and timber merchants and with organisations concerned with the study and promotion of forestry.[316] In practice these were joined by an independent chairman and one person representing each of agricultural, planning, trade union and environmental interests. Although there is no legal prescription, the government has undertaken that the three additional members will be chosen to reflect environmental interests, one of them concerned with public access and recreation.[317] There are thus four members with environmental interests to balance the four with forestry ones. The aim of the proceedings is one of conciliation, to resolve the problem and to find a solution acceptable to all parties. In the event of failure, a report is prepared for the Forestry Commission to make the final decision. Although there is no formal appeal, a dissatisfied applicant can make representations to the appropriate Forestry Minister, who may ask the Commission to reconsider its decision. Only a few cases are referred to the Committees,[318] but by the very nature of the procedure, they are the most controversial ones.

2.7.10 The Commission encourages visitors to parts of its land and has the power to provide facilities for them,[319] including in Scotland the express power to appoint rangers.[320] There is also a power to make byelaws to regulate the conduct of those on land managed by the Commission,[321] and byelaws have been made prohibiting the lighting of fires, any form of damage to trees and plants, the wilful disturbance of animals and their lairs of all sorts and the catching of butterflies, moths and dragonflies (one of the few legislative measures to make special mention of insects of any sort).[322] In other words, visitors must ensure that the natural environment in the

---

[314] This is a consequence of designation as a "relevant regulatory authority" for the purposes of NCSA 2004 s.15 (see para.5.5.45, below); Nature Conservation (Designation of Relevant Regulatory Authorities) (Scotland) Order 2004 (SSI 2004/474).

[315] Forestry Act 1967 s.38, amended by Forestry Act 1991 s.1.

[316] Forestry Act 1967 s.38(3).

[317] Statements by the Earl of Lindsay during debate in the House of Lords, June 11, 1991, House of Lords Official Report, Vol.529, cols 1073–1078.

[318] Even at a time when forestry proposals were generating a lot of controversy, between 1984 and 1990 only 113 cases were referred to the Committees from 28,598 grant applications and 11,712 applications for felling licences (Forestry Commission: *Woodland Grant Scheme Applicant's Pack* (1991), Grants and Procedures, p.12).

[319] CSA 1967 s.58; CA 1968 s.23.

[320] CSA 1967 s.65, amended by Countryside (Scotland) Act 1981 Sch.1 para.4.

[321] Forestry Act 1967 s.46.

[322] Forestry Commission Byelaws 1982 (SI 1982/648).

woodland is disturbed as little as possible by their presence, so that on Forestry Commission land the general laws protecting plants and animals are considerably strengthened. In Scotland, following a review prompted by section 30 of the Land Reform (Scotland) Act 2003,[323] these byelaws were repealed in 2007[324] on the basis that some provisions were contrary to the access provisions in the 2003 Act and the Scottish Outdoor Access Code and that other matters were either dealt with by other provisions or were unnecessary.

Crown Estate Commission

The Crown Estate Commissioners are responsible for administering the **2.7.11** rights of the Crown in areas of land where the Crown retains a major interest,[325] most notably the foreshore and seabed.[326] Any activity, e.g. fish farming, which involves the positioning of structures on or over the seabed will require their permission. The Commissioners are appointed by the Crown,[327] are subject to ministerial direction[328] and report annually to Her Majesty and the UK Parliament.[329] Regulations can be made to control the conduct of the public granted access to Crown land.[330] The general duty of the Commissioners is, while maintaining the Crown Estate as an estate in land, to maintain and enhance its value and the return obtained from it, but with due regard to the requirements of good management.[331] No specific environmental duty is placed on the Commissioners, but they are bound by the general balancing duties applicable to all public bodies,[332] and have committed themselves to "the highest standards of environmental stewardship" in all their activities.[333] Other than the requirement for environmental impact assessment of certain marine fish farming developments,[334] there are no other legal restrictions specifically imposed on the Commissioners for environmental or conservation grounds, and they enjoy a wide immunity from legal challenge to the exercise of their powers.[335] It is anomalous at least for significant regulatory powers to remain in the hands

---

[323] This required a review of all byelaws relating to access to land for inconsistencies with the public access rights provided in the new Act.

[324] Forestry Commission Byelaws 1982 Revocation (Scotland) Byelaws 2007 (SSI 2007/66).

[325] Crown Estates Act 1961 s.1; information about the Crown Estate can be found at the website at *http://www.thecrownestate.co.uk* [Accessed May 6, 2009].

[326] See generally M.E. Deans, "The Crown Estate Commissioners – Their Role and Responsibilities in respect of the Foreshore and Sea-bed around Scotland" (1986) 4 *Journal of Energy and Natural Resources Law* 166.

[327] Crown Estates Act 1961 Sch.1 para.1.

[328] Crown Estates Act 1961 s.1(4).

[329] Crown Estates Act 1961 s.2.

[330] Crown Estates Act 1961 s.6.

[331] Crown Estates Act 1961 s.1(3).

[332] CSA 1967 s.66; CA 1968 s.11; NCSA 2004 s.1; NERCA 2006 s.40; see section 2.2, above.

[333] Crown Estate Environmental Policy (2003). The Crown Estate Biodiversity Action Plan (2009) is available at *http://www.thecrownestate.co.uk/biodiversity_action_plan.pdf* [Accessed May 6, 2009].

[334] Environmental Impact Assessment (Fish Farming in Marine Waters) Regulations 1999 (SI 1999/367), as amended by the Environmental Impact Assessment (Scotland) Regulations 2006 (SSI 2006/614) paras 8–9 and the Town and Country Planning (Marine Fish Farming) (Scotland) Order 2007 (SSI 2007/268); see para.8.3.7, below.

[335] Crown Estates Act 1961 s.1(5); see *Walford v Crown Estates Commissioners*, 1988 S.L.T. 377.

of a body so far removed from the normal structures of political, public and legal accountability, but significant reforms will be made by the marine legislation currently in train.[336]

Deer Commission for Scotland

2.7.12 In Scotland, the Deer Commission for Scotland has general responsibility for the conservation, control and sustainable management of deer, including their welfare.[337] The Commission is the successor to the Red Deer Commission, which was initially limited to concern for red deer but subsequently extended to other species.[338] The Commission is appointed by the Scottish Ministers and comprises a chairman and between 9 and 12 members selected as being appropriate to represent the interests of persons or organisations concerned with deer management, agriculture, forestry and the natural heritage. Nominations can be made by representative organisations and at least one-third of the members must have knowledge and experience of deer management.[339] Local panels can be established to carry out the Commission's tasks in particular localities.[340] An annual report must be presented to the Ministers.[341]

2.7.13 The Commission advises both the Ministers[342] and landowners, collaborates with scientific investigations and supports or carries out its own research into matters affecting deer in Scotland.[343] It has power to deal with marauding deer and to introduce wider deer control schemes,[344] and can provide services and equipment to those involved in the control of deer.[345] It is one of the authorities designated under the Nature Conservation (Scotland) Act 2004 and is therefore required to consult SNH before authorising certain activities in a Site of Special Scientific Interest.[346] Authority from the Commission acts as an exemption from the normal requirements for game licences to kill deer.[347] The details of the Commission's powers are discussed in relation to the law on deer generally.[348]

2.7.14 In early 2008 the Scottish Government announced plans to merge the Commission with SNH because of their shared focus on the natural environment. Following a consultation exercise, provisions transferring the

---

[336] See para.1.7.6, above.

[337] Deer (Scotland) Act 1996 s.1; information about the Commission can be found on its website at *http://www.dcs.gov.uk* [Accessed May 6, 2009].

[338] Deer (Scotland) Act 1959, almost every section of which was amended by the Deer (Amendment) (Scotland) Act 1982.

[339] Deer (Scotland) Act 1996 s.1; if nominations are made by relevant bodies, the members reflecting the interests of deer managers must be selected from these (s.1(6)(c)).

[340] Deer (Scotland) Act 1996 s.4.

[341] Deer (Scotland) Act 1996 s.2(3).

[342] Deer (Scotland) Act 1996 s.2(1).

[343] Deer (Scotland) Act 1996 s.3.

[344] Deer (Scotland) Act 1996 ss.6–10.

[345] Deer (Scotland) Act 1996 s.12.

[346] NCSA 2004 s.15; Nature Conservation (Designation of Relevant Regulatory Authorities) (Scotland) Order 2004 (SSI 2004/474).

[347] NCSA 2004 s.38.

[348] See paras 4.2.17–4.2.23, below.

Commission's functions to SNH were contained in the Public Services Reform (Scotland) Bill introduced in May 2009.[349]

Scottish Environment Protection Agency and Environment Agency

The Scottish Environment Protection Agency (SEPA) and the Environment **2.7.15** Agency were established by the Environment Act 1995 in order to create single bodies which would exercise a wide range of pollution control and related functions in Scotland and in England and Wales. SEPA took over the functions of Her Majesty's Industrial Pollution Inspectorate, river purification boards, many functions of local authorities, e.g. in relation to waste, and some powers of the Secretary of State. The Environment Agency similarly took over the functions of Her Majesty's Inspectorate of Pollution, the National Rivers Authority (much broader than those of the river purification boards) and some functions of local authorities (a narrower range than in Scotland) and the Secretary of State.[350] Both bodies are statutory corporations similar in form and status to the statutory conservation bodies.

The provisions establishing the Environment Agency state that its prin- **2.7.16** cipal aim is to protect and enhance the environment, taken as a whole, so as to make a contribution towards the objective of achieving sustainable development; guidance towards this end can be given by the Minister.[351] SEPA does have such an express general aim, but it too is subject to ministerial guidance as to the contribution it can make towards achieving sustainable development.[352] Both bodies are subject to broad duties to have regard to the desirability of conserving or enhancing the natural heritage (SEPA) or natural beauty, flora, fauna and geological and physiographical features (Environment Agency).[353] In particular, both agencies are under a duty, to the extent that they consider desirable, to promote the conservation of flora and fauna dependent on an aquatic environment and the conservation and enhancement of natural beauty.[354] Further duties apply in England and Wales where the activities or operations carried out or authorised by the agencies might affect certain areas designated for their conservation value,[355] whilst SEPA must consult SNH before approving certain activities in Sites of Special Scientific Interest.[356]

Through their pollution control functions, especially with regard to water, **2.7.17** and with the wider aquatic powers of the Environment Agency, both of these bodies may have a significant influence on nature conservation issues. The impact on biodiversity is a relevant factor in deciding on pollution permits of various kinds and measures to achieve improvements to water

[349] *Report on the proposed merger between Deer Commission Scotland (DCS) & Scottish Natural Heritage (SNH)* (Scottish Government, 2008); Public Services Reform (Scotland) Bill s.1 and Sch.1 (as first introduced).

[350] EA 1995 ss.2 and 21. Information about SEPA and the Environment Agency can be found on their websites at *http://www.sepa.org.uk* and *http://www.environment-agency.gov.uk* [Both Accessed May 6, 2009].

[351] EA 1995 s.4.

[352] EA 1995 s.31.

[353] EA 1995 ss.7 and 32.

[354] EA 1995 ss.6 and 34(2).

[355] EA 1995 s.8; see para.5.5.23, below.

[356] NCSA 2004 s.15; Nature Conservation (Designation of Relevant Regulatory Authorities) (Scotland) Order 2004 (SSI 2004/474).

and atmospheric quality and precautions to prevent spillages and discharges benefit flora and fauna as much as humans.

Water

2.7.18 As noted above, authorities with responsibility for rivers and other aspects of the aquatic environment can also play a significant part in nature conservation. The link is emphasised by the Water Framework Directive,[357] which places the ecological quality of water at the centre of the legal regime[358] and is bringing about a transformation of water law throughout the country, especially in Scotland. The requirements of the Directive in terms of river basin management planning and the more direct controls on activities affecting the water environment are gradually being implemented, and the Ministers and other authorities are obliged to exercise their functions so as to ensure compliance with it.[359] This is not the place for a detailed examination of the relevant law in all its complexity; all that the following paragraphs aim to do is to identify which authorities have responsibility for the major activities in this field.[360]

2.7.19 In England and Wales the water industry was restructured in 1989,[361] but the National Rivers Authority created at that time to safeguard and manage water resources[362] has since been subsumed within the Environment Agency. The Agency can impose restrictions on the abstraction or impounding of water,[363] setting a minimum acceptable flow for specific waters,[364] and imposing further restrictions in the event of drought.[365] It is responsible for issuing consents where activities are likely to lead to the entry (direct or indirect) of polluting matter into waters and for other pollution control measures,[366] and for the general supervision of flood defence.[367] The Agency has some responsibilities for fisheries[368] and may have navigation functions

---

[357] Directive 2000/60/EC.

[358] The first purpose of the Directive is to protect and enhance aquatic ecosystems; Directive 2000/60/EC art.1(a).

[359] Water Environment and Water Services (Scotland) Act 2003 s.2(1); Water Environment (Water Framework Directive) (England and Wales) Regulations 2003 (SI 2003/3242) reg.3.

[360] See S. Hendry, "Water Resources and Water Pollution", Title 6 in F. McManus (ed.), *Environmental Law* in Scotland (Edinburgh: W. Green, 2007); *Stair Memorial Encyclopaedia of the Laws of Scotland* (Edinburgh: LexisNexis / Law Society of Scotland, 1989), Vol.25, "Water and Water Rights", "Water Supply" and *Reissue*, "Environment", paras 352–511; W. Howarth and D. McGillivray, *Water Pollution and Water Quality Law* (Crayford: Shaw & Sons, 2001), W. Howarth, *Wisdom's Law of Watercourses*, 5th edn (Crayford: Shaw & Sons, 1992); W. Howarth, *Flood Defence Law* (Crayford: Shaw & Sons, 2002); J.H. Bates, *Water and Drainage Law* (London: Sweet & Maxwell), (looseleaf). See further section 8.6, below.

[361] The restructuring was carried out by the Water Act 1989, but the relevant legislation was consolidated in the Water Industry Act 1991, the Water Resources Act 1991, the Statutory Water Companies Act 1991, the Land Drainage Act 1991 and the Water Consolidation (Consequential Provisions) Act 1991. Significant later changes include revision of the rules on abstraction by the Water Act 2003 and the introduction of river basin management planning by the Water Environment (Water Framework Directive) (England and Wales) Regulations 2003 (SI 2003/3242).

[362] Water Resources Act 1991 s.1.

[363] Water Resources Act 1991 Pt II c.II, as significantly amended by the Water Act 2003.

[364] Water Resources Act 1991 Pt II c.I.

[365] Water Resources Act 1991 Pt II c.III.

[366] Water Resources Act 1991 Pt III.

[367] Water Resources Act 1991 Pt IV.

[368] Water Resources Act 1991 Pt V.

transferred to it from existing navigation and harbour authorities.[369] Land drainage is also under the supervision of the Agency,[370] although in most circumstances immediate responsibility lies with the internal drainage boards comprised of elected and appointed members under the Land Drainage Act 1991[371]; subsequent legislation has added duties to further the conservation of natural beauty, flora, fauna and geological and physio-graphical features in the exercise of drainage powers, with more precise obligations on designated sites.[372] All of these responsibilities can obviously have a major impact on the survival and quality of the habitat necessary for communities of aquatic plants and animals.

In Scotland much of the law has been fundamentally transformed by the **2.7.20** Water Environment and Water Services (Scotland) Act 2003, enacted to implement the Water Framework Directive. This process has been con-tinued by subsequent regulations, in particular the Water Environment (Controlled Activities) (Scotland) Regulations 2005[373] which introduced new controls on abstraction and engineering works affecting watercourses and restructured the rules on discharges and pollution control. On its creation SEPA inherited all of the functions of the river purification authorities with respect to pollution control and flood warning systems,[374] whilst three new water authorities were created to take over water supply and sewerage functions as part of the wider restructuring of local government in the mid-1990s[375]; these authorities have since been merged to form Scottish Water.[376] SEPA's general duty with regard to water is noted above, while the Scottish Ministers and Scottish Water have general duties to promote the con-servation and effective use of water resources.[377] Scottish Water must act in the way best calculated to contribute to the achievement of sustainable development[378] and the Ministers and Scottish Water in exercising their functions must act to further the conservation of flora, fauna and geological or physiographical features of special interest.[379] Scottish Water has further duties with regard to certain designated sites.[380] Scottish Water is responsible for the maintenance of water supplies, e.g. it is this body that can initiate the procedure for drought orders.[381] SEPA is responsible for controls on the

---

[369] Water Resources Act 1991 s.2 and Sch.2.

[370] Land Drainage Act 1991 s.7.

[371] Land Drainage Act 1991 s.1 and Schs 1 and 2.

[372] Land Drainage Act 1991 ss.61A and 61C, added by Land Drainage Act 1994 s.1; the duties are essentially the same those that apply generally to the Environment Agency.

[373] SSI 2005/348.

[374] EA 1995 s.21.

[375] Local Government etc. (Scotland) Act 1994 Pt II.

[376] Created by the Water Industry (Scotland) Act 2002 Pt 3.

[377] Water (Scotland) Act 1980 s.1, as substituted by Local Government etc. (Scotland) Act 1994 s.65(1) and amended by Water Industry (Scotland) Act 2002 Sch.6 para.2.

[378] Water Industry (Scotland) Act 2002 s.51.

[379] Water Industry (Scotland) Act 2002 s.53(3).

[380] Water Industry (Scotland) Act 2002 s.54, as amended by NCSA 2004 Sch.7 para.13.

[381] NHSA 1991 Pt III, as amended by Local Government etc. (Scotland) Act 1994 Sch.13 para.170 and Water Industry (Scotland) Act 2002 Sch.7 para.22.

abstraction and impoundment of water.[382] Flood prevention is a matter primarily for local authorities,[383] but SEPA has a role in flood warning and risk assessment.[384] Statutory control of land drainage is primarily in ministerial hands,[385] while matters affecting fisheries are dealt with by the Ministers, proprietors and district salmon fishery boards.[386] Responsibility for the aquatic environment is thus much more fragmented in Scotland, and the activities of a range of authorities can affect the habitat for aquatic life.

Natural Environment Research Council

2.7.21 The Natural Environment Research Council plays a major role in research relevant to nature conservation.[387] Established under royal charter and the Science and Technology Act 1965, its statutory functions are to carry out research in earth sciences and ecology, to facilitate, encourage and support such research by other institutions and people, and to disseminate knowledge and provide advice on these subjects.[388] It has no legal powers to intervene directly for the benefit of nature conservation, although it is represented on some other bodies which do have direct powers and must be consulted in some circumstances. However the research which it carries out in its own institutes and supports elsewhere is of major significance, and it is the parent body for, among others, the British Antarctic Survey, the British Geological Survey and the Centre for Ecology and Hydrology.[389]

Non-Governmental Bodies

2.8.1 Non-governmental bodies have played a major part in the development of concern for nature conservation and in the achievement of practical measures to this end. A large number of charitable bodies have been active in this field, providing a voice for those concerned for nature and actively seeking ways of conserving threatened habitat and species. Much can be achieved by small groups and even individuals in relation to particular sites, and apparently insignificant tasks such as the recording of the distribution and preferred habitat of species in an area provide essential information on biodiversity, creating the scientific base on which major decisions can be founded. The contribution made by such voluntary efforts to nature conservation in Britain is immense.

2.8.2   There is a large number of ways in which such activities can be organised, and few raise any legal issues specific to this area. The general law of trusts,

---

[382] Water Environment and Water Services (Scotland) Act 2003 s.20 and Water Environment (Controlled Activities) (Scotland) Regulations 2005 (SSI 2005/348).

[383] Flood Prevention (Scotland) Act 1961, as amended, most notably by Flood Prevention and Land Drainage (Scotland) Act 1997. Significant changes to the law will be made under the Flood Risk Management (Scotland) Act 2009.

[384] Agriculture Act 1970 s.92, as amended by EA 1995 Sch.22 para.14; EA 1995 s.25.

[385] Land Drainage (Scotland) Acts 1930 and 1958.

[386] Constituted under the Salmon and Freshwater Fisheries (Consolidation) (Scotland) Act 2003.

[387] Information about NERC can be found on its website at *http://www.nerc.ac.uk* [Accessed May 6, 2009].

[388] Science and Technology Act 1965 s.1(3).

[389] See J. Sheail, *Natural Environment Research Council: A History* (Swindon: NERC, 1992).

charities and unincorporated associations must however be borne in mind, especially if an organisation wishes to acquire an interest in land or to enter other formal legal relationships in order to secure its aims. "The advancement of environmental protection or improvement" is expressly recognised as a charitable purpose under the new charities legislation both in Scotland and in England and Wales.[390] Careful attention to the legal formalities is essential if any effective long-term arrangements are to be made. Disputes during the 1990s over the acceptability of hunting over National Trust land served to emphasise the significance of the land management decisions of such bodies and the extent and means by which they are or are not accountable to members and others.[391]

A number of charities, most notably the Royal Society for the Protection of Birds, do own and manage significant areas of land as nature reserves and this is one place where the law does come into contact with the activities of such voluntary bodies. Land which is being managed as a nature reserve by any body approved by a statutory conservation body and which that statutory body considers to be of national importance can be declared by it to be a National Nature Reserve[392]; this means that the statutory body can make byelaws for the protection of the reserve in the same way as it can for those which it manages itself.[393] This power provides a means by which the voluntary efforts in this field can be integrated with the official ones and offers official recognition of the efforts made by the voluntary bodies to support those of the public conservation bodies.

2.8.3

National Trusts

The National Trusts occupy a position halfway between official and private organisations, in that although they are in no way governmental bodies, they do enjoy some statutory recognition. The National Trust was incorporated under a private Act of Parliament in 1907,[394] and the National Trust for Scotland likewise in 1935,[395] and their constitutions are embodied in statute. Both have among their purposes:

2.8.4

> "[T]he permanent preservation for the benefit of the nation of lands ... of beauty or historic interest and ... the preservation (so far as practicable) of their natural aspect and features and animal and plant life",[396]

---

[390] Charities and Trustee Investment (Scotland) Act 2005 s.7(2)(m); Charities Act 2006 s.2(2)(i).

[391] *Ex p. Scott* [1998] 1 W.L.R. 226, deciding that the National Trust was not directly subject to judicial review and that the Charity Commissioners would have to authorise any legal proceedings; see below for the special status of the National Trusts. The legal position of charities in Scotland is very different.

[392] WCA 1981 s.35.

[393] NPACA 1949 s.20; see section 5.3, below.

[394] National Trust Act 1907; see also National Trust Charity Scheme Confirmation Act 1919 and National Trust Acts 1937, 1939, 1953 and 1971, and Charities (National Trust for Places of Historic Interest or Natural Beauty) Order 1994 (SI 1994/2181).

[395] National Trust for Scotland Order Confirmation Act 1935; see also National Trust for Scotland Order Confirmation Acts 1938, 1947, 1952, 1961 and 1973.

[396] National Trust Act 1907 s.4(1); National Trust for Scotland Order Confirmation Act 1935 Sch. s.4.

so that nature conservation does fall within the purposes for which the Trusts can act.

2.8.5 Certain land which is held by the Trusts is declared to be inalienable,[397] so that there is a guarantee that it will continue to be used in accordance with the Trusts' purposes. Such land is accorded special treatment in other legislation, e.g. special procedures are required for its compulsory purchase.[398] On land in which they have an interest, the Trusts have the power to make byelaws, including ones to prevent any damage or disturbance to plants or animals,[399] and in England and Wales the power[400] to make and enforce restrictive covenants even though no adjacent land is held may allow something akin to a management agreement.[401] As the Trusts are significant landowners, particularly in areas of scenic beauty, considerable benefits for nature conservation can arise from these provisions.

European Community

2.9.1 Although the European Community had been active on environmental issues for many years previously, it was only in 1987 that it was given express competence to act in this field. The impact of the Community is felt through its legislation on environmental topics and also through the influence of its policies in other areas, particularly agriculture, which play a major part in shaping the way in which individuals and businesses act within the UK.[402] The European dimension is now an integral part of the law on nature conservation; while the substantive rules are described where relevant in other Chapters below, this section offers a brief outline of the basic framework of Community involvement in conservation matters.[403]

2.9.2 The powers and competence of the Community[404] depend upon the treaties which create it, and at first there was no reference in these to environmental matters. However, this did not prevent the Community from taking an interest in such issues and in addition to environmental

---

[397] National Trust Act 1907 s.21; National Trust for Scotland Order Confirmation Act 1935 Sch. s.22.

[398] Acquisition of Land (Authorisation Procedure) (Scotland) Act 1947 s.1(2); Acquisition of Land Act 1981 s.18.

[399] National Trust Act 1971 s.24; National Trust for Scotland Order Confirmation Act 1935 Sch. s.33.

[400] National Trust Act 1937 s.8.

[401] See paras 1.3.18–1.3.19, above.

[402] C.T. Reid, "Nature Conservation Law" in J. Holder (ed.), *The Impact of EC Environmental Law in the United Kingdom* (Chichester: John Wiley, 1997).

[403] There is a large literature on EC environmental law, including: L. Krämer, *EC Environmental Law*, 6th edn (London: Sweet & Maxwell, 2007); M. Lee, *EU Environmental Law – challenges, change and decision-making* (Oxford: Hart, 2005); R. Macrory (ed.), *Reflections on 30 Years of EU Environmental Law – a high level of protection?* (Groningen: Europa, 2005).

[404] Although often the terms are used as if interchangeable, there is a significant legal difference between the European Union and the European Community. The former term covers the full range of co-operation arrangements between the 27 Member States, including areas such as foreign affairs, whereas the latter refers to the formal structure of institutions, legislation and decision-making processes which have legal force in the Member States within the areas of competence specified in the EC Treaty.

considerations affecting its activities in other areas, a range of specifically environmental measures[405] were produced under the authority of two general provisions of the EEC Treaty as it stood at that time: article 100 which provided for the approximation (or harmonisation) of laws affecting the establishment or functioning of the common market, and article 235 which allowed measures to be taken where necessary for the attainment of the Community's objectives and where the Treaty had not specifically provided the necessary powers. These were not an altogether satisfactory basis for Community activity in this field and when the treaties were amended by the Single European Act which took effect in 1987, a new title was added conferring on the Community powers relating to the environment.[406] Subsequent amendments to the Treaty have strengthened the position of environmental law.

The Treaty, in its current form as agreed at Nice in 2001,[407] makes it clear **2.9.3** that environmental matters are important to the Community and contains specific environmental provisions. Promoting "a high level of protection and improvement of the quality of the environment" is one of the Community's express tasks[408] and "environmental protection requirements must be integrated into the definition and implementation" of the Community's other policies and activities.[409] This last point is particularly important given the environmental impact of policies in other areas, such as agriculture and fisheries, and even the extent to which free trade requirements can stand in the way of national environmental policies.

The specific environmental provisions in Title XIX call on the Commu- **2.9.4** nity to take action to contribute to the objectives of preserving, protecting and improving the environment, protecting human health, the prudent and rational utilisation of natural resources, and promoting measures at international level.[410] Community action should aim at a high level of protection, taking into account the diversity within the Community, and be based on the precautionary principle and the principles that preventive action should be taken, that environmental damage should be rectified at source and that the polluter should pay.[411] Regard must be had to scientific and technical data, environmental conditions in the different regions of the Community, potential costs and benefits of any action or lack of action, and the economic and social development of the Community, including the balanced development of its regions.[412] A variety of decision-making procedures are prescribed for different topics, including the involvement of the European

---

[405] e.g. the Directive on the Conservation of Wild Birds (79/409/EEC) made in 1979; see section 7.4, below.

[406] Title VII of the EEC Treaty (arts 130r–130t), added by art.25 of the Single European Act; for a detailed account of these provisions see L. Krämer, *EEC Treaty and Environmental Protection* (London: Sweet & Maxwell, 1990).

[407] The article numbers given here refer to the consolidated version of the Treaty approved following the Treaty of Amsterdam (1997) and subsequently amended by the Treaty of Nice (2001) and subsequent accession treaties. It is not yet clear when, or if, the further rewriting of the Treaties under the Treaty of Lisbon (2007) will come into force.

[408] EC Treaty art.2.

[409] EC Treaty art.6; this must be done "in particular with a view to promoting sustainable development".

[410] EC Treaty art.174(1).

[411] EC Treaty art.174(2).

[412] EC Treaty art.174(3).

Parliament and consultation with the Economic and Social Committee and the Committee of the Regions, and on some matters there is scope for majority voting in the Council of Ministers.[413] Member States remain free to adopt more stringent protective measures for themselves, provided that these are compatible with the Treaty, e.g. that they do not impose an undue restriction on free trade.[414] Environmental policy has been laid down in broad terms in a series of Environmental Action Programmes, and nature and biodiversity form one of the priority areas in the current Sixth Programme that covers the period until 2012.[415]

2.9.5   Legislation from the Community comes in the form of Regulations and Directives. Regulations automatically become part of the domestic law of the Member States and must be followed by individuals and enforced by the authorities in the same way as other laws within the national legal system. Directives are addressed to the Member States which are required to take whatever measures are necessary to ensure that the objectives set out in Directive are achieved within their own national legal systems within the period specified in the Directive. Therefore where the national law does not already provide for the requirements of the Directive, new national legislation should be introduced, and in the UK this can be achieved by delegated legislation under the European Communities Act 1972.[416] Any implementing measures are to be interpreted so far as possible to ensure that the terms of the Directive are in fact completely satisfied.[417]

2.9.6   If a Directive has not been fully or properly implemented, the European Commission (frequently acting on the basis of a complaint from an individual) can take steps to ensure that the defaulting state does fulfil its obligation to give effect to the Directive.[418] This process can lead ultimately to an action before the European Court of Justice, with fines being imposed on a Member State that fails to respond to a judgement against it.[419] Such actions have been necessary on many occasions to enforce the implementation of Directives on environmental topics,[420] and the first three cases of fines being imposed were all in environmental cases.[421] A Directive which

---

[413] EC Treaty art.175; this was the only environmental provision amended by the Treaty of Nice.

[414] EC Treaty art.176; see, for example, *Ditlev Bluhme* (C-67/97) [1998] E.C.R. I-8033, where it was argued (unsuccessfully) that measures banning the keeping of other kinds of bees in order to protect a local subspecies on a remote Danish island did not fall within the permitted grounds for infringing the principle of the free movement of goods. See further paras 7.3.25–7.3.28.

[415] Decision 1600/2002/EC.

[416] European Communities Act 1972 s.2(2); to give one example, it was under this authority that the Conservation (Natural Habitats etc.) Regulations 1994 were made to implement the Habitats and Species Directive; see para.1.1.23, above. Note that UK ministers can exercise this power even on devolved matters: Scotland Act 1998 s.57, Government of Wales Act 2006 ss.59 and 80.

[417] *Litster v Forth Dry Dock and Engineering Co Ltd*, 1989 S.L.T. 540; [1990] 1 A.C. 546.

[418] See generally M. Hedemann-Robinson, *Enforcement of European Union Environmental Law: Legal Issues and Challenges* (Abingdon: Routledge-Cavendish, 2007).

[419] EC Treaty arts 226 and 228. Within the UK this fine will be met by the administration responsible for the failure properly to implement or enforce the law, so a fine resulting from a failure in Scotland on a devolved matter will have to be met from the Scottish budget (*Memorandum of Understanding* (see para.2.3.4, above), para.20).

[420] e.g. in relation to the United Kingdom's failure to implement properly many aspects of the Habitats and Species Directive; *Commission v United Kingdom* (C-6/04) [2005] E.C.R. I-9017.

[421] *Commission v Greece* (C-387/97) [2000] E.C.R. I-5047; *Commission v Spain* (C-278/01) [2003] E.C.R. I-14141; *Commission v France* (C-304/02) [2005] E.C.R. I-6263.

has not been implemented by the due date may also have direct effect.[422] This means that individuals in their dealings with a branch of defaulting state[423] (but not against other individuals)[424] can rely on its terms as if they had been implemented in national law, provided that the relevant provisions are sufficiently precise and unconditional for it to be clear exactly what the legal position would have been had the Directive been properly implemented.[425] An individual who has suffered harm as a direct result of a Member State failing to implement a Directive may also be entitled to claim compensation from that state.[426]

The failure to observe the terms of a Directive may further be used as a ground of challenge to the validity of decisions or actions taken by Member States. Although it may not be possible to invoke direct effect as described above, the European Court of Justice has emphasised that national courts are required to ensure that states fulfil their obligation to give effect to Directives and held that this imposes a constraint on the lawful extent of their discretion that can be enforced by individuals taking action in the national courts.[427] **2.9.7**

It is thus important to know what is provided in Community Law, both as a guide to the proper interpretation of domestic law implementing its terms and as a source of law which may supplement or override[428] domestic provisions. Although some of the measures on the protection of particular species are precise enough to be given direct effect, much of the legislation on nature conservation contains too great an element of discretion on the part of the Member State to be given direct effect,[429] and it is unlikely that any individual will be able to demonstrate a sufficiently direct loss to benefit from the potential for compensation. Nevertheless, the terms of the **2.9.8**

---

[422] *Van Duyn v Home Office* (41/74) [1974] E.C.R. 1337; *Pubblico Ministero v Ratti* (148/78) [1979] E.C.R. 1629.

[423] This covers all public authorities and other bodies given powers or responsibilities over and above those of private individuals and companies; *Foster v British Gas Plc* (C-188/89) [1990] E.C.R. 1-3313; [1991] 1 Q.B. 405.

[424] *Marshall v Southampton and South West Hampshire Area Health Authority (Teaching)* (152/84) [1986] E.C.R. 723, [1986] Q.B. 401; *Faccini Dori v Recreb srl* (C-91/92) [1994] E.C.R. I-3325; this can apply even though the practical consequences are felt indirectly by other individuals, as in *R. (Wells) v Secretary of State for Transport, Local Government and the Regions* (C-201/02) [2004] E.C.R. I-723.

[425] *Becker v Finanzamt Munster-Innenstadt* (8/81) [1982] E.C.R. 53.

[426] *Francovich, Bonifaci and Others v Italy* (C-6/90, C-9/90) [1991] E.C.R. I-5357; *Brasserie du Pêcheur SA v Germany, R. v Secretary of State for Transport, ex p. Factortame Ltd (No.4)* (C-46/93, C-48/93) [1996] E.C.R. I-1029.

[427] *Aannemersbedrijf P.K. Kraaijeveld BV e.a. v Gedeputeerde Staten van Zuid-Holland* (C-72/95) [1996] E.C.R. I-5403; *WWF v Autonome Provinz Bozen* (C-435/97) [1999] E.C.R. I-5613; *Landelijke Vereniging tot Behoud van de Waddenzee, Nederlandse Vereniging tot Bescherming van Vogels v Staatssecretaris van Landbouw, Natuurbeheer en Visserij* (C-127/02) [2004] E.C.R. I-7405.

[428] *R. v Secretary of State for Transport, ex p. Factortame Ltd (No.2)* [1991] 1 A.C. 603.

[429] See, e.g. comments on the Birds Directive in *Kincardine and Deeside District Council v Forestry Commissioners*, 1992 S.L.T. 1180 at 1187; more general discussions include L. Krämer, "The Implementation of Community Environmental Directives within Member States: Some Implications of the Direct Effect Doctrine" (1991) 3 J.E.L. 39; C. Hilson, "Community Rights in Environmental Law: Rhetoric or Reality?" in J. Holder (ed.), *The Impact of EC Environmental Law in the United Kingdom* (Chichester: John Wiley, 1997); M. Hedemann-Robinson, *Enforcement of European Union Environmental Law: Legal Issues and Challenges* (2007), Ch.6. See also para.1.4.7, above.

Directives must be followed by the Member States and individuals can rely on the terms of Directives in seeking to establish that a state is acting outwith its powers. The detailed discussion of EC measures throughout the following Chapters show many cases where Member States have been found to be acting unlawfully through a failure to comply fully with Directives.

2.9.9   Community law has had a major impact on all aspects of environmental law in Great Britain. As far as nature conservation is concerned, the need to comply with the Birds Directive was one of the factors which led to the Wildlife and Countryside Act 1981, whilst the implementation of the Habitats and Species Directive called for very significant changes to the law, greatly strengthening the protection given to designated sites,[430] a process reinforced by the threat of financial penalties in the event of a failure to remedy the many ways in which the implementation of that Directive has been held to fall short.[431] The increased protection for European sites in turn influenced the more recent changes to the law for nationally designated sites, whilst the EC initiatives on environmental impact assessment, nitrate pollution of water and many other topics have also changed the legal rules and approach in this country. It may be rare for Community law to be given direct effect so as to override the domestic legislation on a topic, but the threat of enforcement action before the European Court of Justice and the publicity which even the consideration of the issue by the Commission can attract, mean that Community law acts as a fundamental consideration in the development and operation of the law in Great Britain.

---

[430] See para.1.1.23, above.
[431] *Commission v United Kingdom* (C-6/04) [2005] E.C.R. I-9017.

3. PROTECTION OF WILD ANIMALS

The most straightforward legal approach to protecting wildlife is to enact **3.1.1** laws punishing people who cause it direct harm.[1] Most of the early legislation designed to preserve game and other species considered to be of value took this form, and similar laws continue to play a major role in nature conservation, although increasingly supported by measures to protect the habitat necessary for the continued survival of the protected species. The long-term decline of some species is the direct result of man's deliberate conduct in exterminating them, for food, fur and feathers, for sport or display, or to prevent harm to more valued species. Putting an end to such direct assaults is an obvious and essential first step in seeking to protect wildlife.

Such laws can be relatively simple. Certain actions directed towards **3.1.2** certain specified animals are prohibited; the law affects everybody and is of general application. The straightforward nature of such measures means that they can be simple to understand, with real benefits in terms of publicity and education. Although detracting from the simplicity of the law, a further advantage of structuring the law on the basis of prohibiting direct harm to wildlife is that the particular threats to each species can be specifically addressed. Some creatures are in need of more protection than others; some are the special victims of particular conduct. In other cases a degree of exploitation may be tolerated whilst protection is also required in some situations. Enacting a separate law for each species would achieve the maximum of individual attention, but this would be quite unacceptable in terms of the legislative time and effort required, to say nothing of producing an unworkably fragmented system. To reduce this problem, species can be grouped into a handful of categories, and different regimes designed for each category, offering different levels of protection whilst leaving the law in a relatively manageable state.

Aside from the risk of excessive fragmentation, three factors may reduce **3.1.3** the effectiveness of this very direct approach to conservation legislation, quite apart from the fact that simply preventing direct harm will not by itself be sufficient to secure the long-term survival of any species. By requiring the express prohibition of the undesired conduct, there is a risk that some forms of harm, or some species in need of protection, will be omitted, or will come to be appreciated only after the law is in place. In particular, conduct that causes very real, but indirect, harm to the survival of a species may escape. The presence of gaps and possible loopholes may undermine the law, and it may be difficult to persuade the legislators to make the effort to enact the necessary amendments promptly. In the second place, such legislation is likely to favour the large and "cuddly" animals. More tends to be known

---

[1] See generally K. Last, "The Protection of Species" in J. Rowan-Robinson and D. McKenzie-Skene, *Countryside Law in Scotland* (Edinburgh: T&T Clark, 2000); K. Cook, *Wildlife Law: Conservation and Biodiversity* (London: Cameron May, 2004), Part II.

about such animals,[2] they are more in the public's eye, and elected legislators are more likely to act on behalf of those creatures which enjoy public sympathy than those whose importance or value is not widely appreciated.[3] Thus there is in Britain special legislation for badgers and seals, but no Woodlice Act is readily conceivable, however endangered or ecologically vital some species of woodlice may be in the wild.

3.1.4 The third feature which besets specific legislation is that of identifying the creatures and plants to which protection is given. A law which makes it a criminal offence to disturb certain species will only work if potential offenders can identify those species and moderate their conduct accordingly. How many people can tell the difference between the reed warbler and the strictly protected marsh warbler,[4] between the black-headed gull and the protected little and Mediterranean gulls? This is a problem which is even more severe in relation to the law on plants and invertebrates. The good intentions of such legislation may be undermined by a lack of public knowledge which makes a nonsense of the attempt to categorise species carefully. At a more detailed level the problems of hybridisation and arguments over taxonomy and classification can undermine even the attempt to specify clearly individual species.

3.1.5 The law relating to wildlife is, however, not concerned only with its protection. It is also concerned to permit and regulate the exploitation of wild creatures through various forms of hunting, and to secure the destruction of those creatures viewed as pests. There are thus provisions imposing requirements to destroy damaging species, regulating who can hunt for animals and controlling the means which can be used to kill or take animals and birds. Any attempt to present an overall picture of the law regulating the harm which can be done to wildlife must therefore bring together provisions from these somewhat different areas. It may seem odd in a book on nature conservation to discuss laws designed to allow, or even require, the destruction of wildlife, but such measures play an essential part in the overall legal background for conservation, and even the law on hunting plays a part in conservation by imposing a degree of regulation as opposed to allowing a destructive or indiscriminate free-for-all. Moreover, such measures may be used to achieve incidental benefits for wildlife generally, e.g. by acquiring but not exercising the right to hunt game, interested parties can offer some protection to animals and birds in a particular area.

3.1.6 The law remains fragmented, and this Chapter and the next endeavour to integrate the various threads of the law, presenting a picture based on the eventual legal results, rather than the structure of the legislation. The arrangement which follows draws a general distinction between measures which have as their primary objective the conservation of wildlife, those which seek primarily to regulate the exploitation of particular species, those which restrict the means by which creatures can be killed or caught, and those which require the destruction of species. This distinction is artificial,

---

[2] This applies particularly in relation to marine species.

[3] See, for example, the leader in *The Times* (January 4, 1991) and subsequent letters (January 12, 1991) when adders were first given statutory protection.

[4] A leading field guide to birds described the marsh warbler as "Very hard to tell from Reed and Blyth's Reed [Warblers], except by song, though adults more olive-brown with whiter throat and pinker legs"; H. Heinzel et al., *The Birds of Britain and Europe*, 5th edn (London: Harper Collins, 1995), p.282.

since the law in most cases contains elements of all four functions, but it does offer a rough framework on which to structure what would otherwise be a compilation of isolated pieces of legislation in either chronological or some arbitrary order. A degree of repetition has been inevitable in the attempt to present as coherent a guide as possible to this jumble of law.

Overview, Legal Framework and Enforcement

Unfortunately, the law on species protection within Great Britain has **3.2.1** become very fragmented. The Wildlife and Countryside Act 1981 provided a coherent and comparatively straightforward statement of the law in this area but in addition to minor amendments over the years it has since been partly overwhelmed by two significant developments. The first of these is the Conservation (Natural Habitats etc.) Regulations 1994,[5] introduced to ensure protection for the species and habitats singled out in the EC Habitats and Species Directive.[6] In relation to species protection, the Regulations created a separate set of rules which largely overlapped with those contained in the 1981 Act, and applied to some of the same species, but with marginal differences which ensured that great care had to be taken in studying the detail of the law. The position here has been simplified recently to avoid the overlaps in relation to particular species by removing those protected under the 1994 Regulations from the lists of those given special protection under the 1981 Act.[7]

The second development is the separate reforms carried out for Scotland **3.2.2** by the Nature Conservation (Scotland) Act 2004 and for England and Wales by the Countryside and Rights of Way Act 2000[8] and subsequently the Natural Environment and Rural Communities Act 2006. In addition to more substantial changes to habitat protection, these measures have changed several features of the law on species protection, e.g. extending the crimes of disturbing certain birds or animals to cover actions taken recklessly as well as intentionally.[9] In each case, though, the approach has been to achieve this by way of amendments and additions to the 1981 Act, so that there are now two very different versions of the Act in force. In both jurisdictions there is a pressing need to consolidate the law to produce a coherent and understandable set of rules.[10] Before looking at the detailed rules on protecting birds and animals, some general points can be made about the legal framework.

---

[5] SI 1994/2716.

[6] Directive 92/43/EEC.

[7] See paras 3.4.7 and 6.2.5, below.

[8] J. Lowther, "Wildlife Offences with Added Bite: Evaluating Recent Amendments to the Wildlife and Countryside Act 1981" (2001) 13 E.L.M. 249.

[9] WCA 1981 ss.1(5) and 9(4), amended by CRWA 2000 Sch.12 para.1, CNHAR 2007 reg.7(4) and NCSA 2004 Sch.6 paras 5 and 8; see paras 3.3.6 and 3.4.3, below.

[10] Environment and Rural Development Committee of the Scottish Parliament, *Stage 1 Report on the Nature Conservation (Scotland) Bill*, SP Paper No.66 (7th Report, 2003), paras 16–18. In Scotland, consultation began in June 2009 on a further Wildlife and Natural Environment Bill.

Wildlife and Countryside Act 1981

3.2.3 The Wildlife and Countryside Act 1981, in its two amended versions, remains the single most important statute relating to the protection of wildlife and creates a large number of offences relating to the killing and taking of birds, other animals and plants. These provisions, contained in Part I of the Act, will be considered in detail below,[11] but some structural features of the Act and other aspects of general application can usefully be considered at this stage.

Schedules

3.2.4 The Act relies heavily on the use of Schedules to identify categories of species which are to enjoy differing levels of protection under the Act. In this way the needs of many species can be catered for without the Act becoming too fragmented or even more complex. This approach also has the advantage that whilst the basic provisions are contained in parliamentary legislation, their detailed application is determined by the content of the Schedules, which can be more easily amended. The Minister is given wide powers to alter the various Schedules, and many of the other details of the legislation, by means of Statutory Instruments,[12] in most cases subject to only the negative resolution procedure at the parliamentary stage.[13] This enables the law to retain some flexibility and to respond to changing pressures or scientific appreciation of the status of particular species. There is an obligation on the conservation bodies, acting jointly through the JNCC, to review the schedules of protected animals and plants every five years.[14]

Possession and Sale

3.2.5 The central provisions in Part I of the Act outlawing the killing and taking of animals, birds and their eggs are backed up by a number of other provisions to overcome the difficulty of proving all of the elements of such offences. When a dead eagle, an osprey's egg or an otter's pelt is discovered, it may be impossible for anyone but the persons involved to know exactly when and in what circumstances it was killed or taken. The difficulties of providing legal proof of deliberate killing, etc. are so great that most offenders would probably escape were it not for the supporting provisions which exist. It is therefore made an offence simply to possess wild birds and animals, and to sell them or engage in related activities and this approach has been extended to cover the possession of pesticides with certain prescribed ingredients.[15] Strict liability is employed but mitigated by a number of defences, but the onus is placed on the accused to show that their conduct has been innocent, a reflection both of the fact that they alone are likely to be in a position to provide evidence on such matters, and of the policy that

---

[11] See section 6.2, below, in relation to plants.

[12] WCA 1981 s.22.

[13] WCA 1981 s.26; there must be express parliamentary approval for amendments to the provisions on the methods of killing or taking birds or animals (s.26(3)).

[14] WCA 1981 s.24(1), amended by EPA 1995 Sch.9 para.11 and NERCA 2006 Sch.11 para.75.

[15] WCA 1981 s.15A, added by NCSA 2004 Sch.6 para.14; NERCA 2006 s.43.

those who wish to keep wild animals or birds (alive or dead) or birds' eggs should do so at their own risk.[16]

Enforcement

The enforcement of the law is assisted by a range of powers granted to the **3.2.6** police and to wildlife inspectors and by some special rules in relation to criminal procedure. Under section 19 of the Act,[17] a police officer who reasonably suspects that a person is committing or has committed an offence under Part I of the Act and reasonably suspects that evidence of the commission of the offence may be found, is authorised without warrant to stop and search the person, and to search or examine anything which the suspect is using or has in his possession. There is also a power to seize and detain anything which may be evidence of the commission of an offence; it has been held that this power is of general application, and is not restricted to circumstances where there has been a search under the previous provisions.[18] An arrest without warrant is also possible.[19] In order to exercise these powers, a power of entry to land other than a dwelling house is given where the suspicion is that an offence is currently being committed. Warrants are available from justices of the peace[20] to authorise entry and search in relation to all the wildlife crime offences under Part I of the Act.[21]

As well as these powers enjoyed by the police, a range of powers to assist **3.2.7** in the enforcement of the law are enjoyed by "wildlife inspectors".[22] These are individuals who have been authorised in writing by the Minister to exercise the powers set out in the Act. In Scotland the powers are to enter and inspect premises in relation to offences involving the selling of protected species, compliance with the provisions on keeping wild birds, offences in relation to the introduction or sale of non-native species and to verify statements made in relation to any relevant registration or licence.[23] Inspectors must also be allowed to inspect any specimen, including live wild birds or other animals, plants and derivatives from plants, birds and animals. Obstructing or impersonating an inspector is a crime, as is failing to

---

[16] See *Kirkland v Robinson* [1987] Crim. L.R. 643.

[17] WCA 1981 s.19, amended for Scotland by Criminal Justice (Scotland) Act 2003 Sch.3 para.4 and NCSA 2004 Sch.6 para.16; for England and Wales by Police and Criminal Evidence Act 1984 Sch.6 para.25 and Sch.7 Pt I, CRWA 2000 Sch.12 para.7, Serious Organised Crime and Police Act 2005 Sch.7(4) para.56 and NERCA 2006 Sch.5 para.2.

[18] *Whitelaw v Haining*, 1992 S.L.T. 956.

[19] WCA 1981 s.19(1)(c) for Scotland; for England and Wales this provision has been repealed by the Police and Criminal Evidence Act 1984 Sch.7, but the general power of arrest under s.25 of that Act is available. In *Morrison v O'Donnell*, 2001 S.C.C.R. 272, it was held to be unlawful to detain a suspect and search him at a police station, although the power of stop and search could have been used at the place where the suspect was found.

[20] Expressly including sheriffs in Scotland.

[21] WCA 1981 s.19(3).

[22] In Scotland, WCA 1981 s.19ZC, added by NCSA 2004 Sch.6 para.17; in England and Wales, WCA 1981 s.18A, added by NERCA 2006 Sch.5 para.1 (the provisions described here replace those initially introduced under CRWA 2000 (WCA 1981 ss.19ZA and 19ZB, now repealed).

[23] Respectively, offences under ss.6, 9(5) and 13(2), offences under s.7, offences under ss.14 and 14A and registration under s.7(1) and certain licences under s.16, all of WCA 1981; WCA 1981 s.19ZC. The power to enter dwellings is restricted to where the occupier holds or has applied for a licence or registration and cannot be used with respect to ss.14 or 14A.

give assistance reasonably requested from the person in possession or control of a live bird or animal for the purpose of examining the creature.

3.2.8   In England and Wales, the powers of the wildlife inspectors are structured differently and extend to the enforcement of other legislation. For this purpose the offences under the 1981 Act are divided into Group 1 and Group 2 offences. The Group 2 offences are the same as those covered in the Scottish legislation and the powers similarly extend to allow entry to dwellings in relation to licences and registrations.[24] The Group 1 offences include the main provisions protecting wild birds, animals and plants, restricting the methods by which they can be taken and imposing controls on the sale of non-native species,[25] and the powers in relation to these Group 1 offences are also available in relation to offences under the Destructive Imported Animals Act 1932, the Conservation of Seals Act 1970, the Deer Act 1991 and the Protection of Badgers Act 1992.[26] The crucial difference between the Group 1 and Group 2 powers is that for the Group 1 offences the power to enter premises does not extend to any dwelling.[27] Obstructing or impersonating a wildlife inspector or failing to give assistance reasonably requested is an offence.[28]

3.2.9   The powers of inspectors and police officers extend to requiring the taking of samples of blood or tissue in order to determine the identity or ancestry of a sample, an essential prerequisite of applying the expanding range of DNA and other techniques that enable the origins of live or dead animals, plants or creatures to be traced.[29] There are slight differences in wording between the Scottish and the Group 1 and Group 2 provisions,[30] but in essence samples can be taken from live birds, animals or plants only where the person concerned is satisfied on reasonable grounds that no lasting harm will be done by taking the sample. Samples from live birds or animals may be taken only by a veterinary surgeon, and the person having control of a live creature must give such assistance as is reasonably required to enable a sample to be taken. The powers of entry granted to police officers and inspectors are extended to enable them to be accompanied by a vet for the purpose of taking a sample. Again, obstruction and refusing reasonable assistance are offences.

3.2.10   In keeping with much modern legislation, there is an express provision that where a crime is committed by a company or other body corporate, there can also be personal liability for any director, manager or the like through whose consent, connivance or neglect the crime is committed.[31] Attempts to commit crimes under the species protection provisions of the Act are expressly declared to be crimes in themselves, and possession for the

[24] WCA 1981 s.18D.
[25] WCA 1981 s.18B(2), referring to ss.1, 5, 9(1), (2) and (4), 11, 13(1) and 14ZA.
[26] See respectively paras 7.2.10, 3.4.32–3.4.37, 4.2.24–4.2.29 and 3.4.22–3.4.31, below.
[27] WCA 1981 s.18B.
[28] WCA 1981 s.19XB.
[29] WCA 1981 s.19ZB.
[30] In Scotland, WCA 1981 s.19ZD; in England and Wales WCA 1981 s.19XA for police constables, and for wildlife inspectors, s.18C for Group 1 offences, s.18E for Group 2 offences, s.18F for restrictions in relation to live specimens and s.19XB for obstructing inspectors.
[31] WCA 1981 s.69; in the Regulations dealing with European protected species, the equivalent provision is expressly extended to apply to partnerships in Scotland with personal liability for any partner who is responsible in this way (CNHR 1994 reg.106(2)).

purposes of committing an offence of items capable of being used to that end is also a crime in its own right.[32]

In Scotland, the standard rules on corroboration are relaxed in relation to **3.2.11** charges of taking or destroying birds' eggs, enabling convictions to be obtained on the evidence of a single witness.[33] The time limits for summary proceedings are that they may be started within six months of the prosecutor having evidence to warrant proceedings but no later than two years after the offence in England and Wales[34] or three years in Scotland.[35] Natural England has the power to institute criminal proceedings itself,[36] whereas in Scotland cases must be referred to the Crown Office and Procurator Fiscal Service, which does now have a network of specialist prosecutors for wildlife crimes.

Sanctions

The 1981 Act as originally enacted did not allow for penalties other than **3.2.12** fines in relation to the wildlife protection offences. This led to repeated criticism, and to difficulties in the courts when dealing with those who committed serious offences but had only limited resources.[37] The reforms this century have changed this, introducing powers of imprisonment for up to two years and unlimited fines for some offences.[38] Where more than one bird, nest, egg, animal, plant, etc. is concerned, the maximum fine can be calculated as if there was a separate offence in relation to each item.[39] The sanctions on conviction are strengthened by the fact that the court can order the forfeiture of any items taken in breach of the Act or of vehicles, animals (e.g. dogs) or other things used to commit the crime.[40]

Licences

A further general feature of the 1981 Act is the possibility for exemptions to **3.2.13** be granted from many of the Act's provisions, over and above the general defences which exist. Licences which authorise conduct which would otherwise be an offence may be obtained for a variety of reasons, from Ministers or the statutory conservation bodies.[41] These licences may be

---

[32] WCA 1981 s.18; the possession of certain pesticides is itself an offence (WCA 1981 s.15A, added by NCSA 2004 Sch.6 para.14; NERCA 2006 s.43).

[33] WCA 1981 s.19A, added by Prisoners and Criminal Proceedings (Scotland) Act 1993 s.36.

[34] WCA 1981 s.20.

[35] WCA 1981 s.20, amended by NCSA 2004 Sch.6 para.18.

[36] NERCA 2006 s.12.

[37] *Seiga v Walkingshaw*, 1994 S.C.C.R. 146; *Forsyth v Cardle*, 1994 S.C.C.R. 769.

[38] WCA 1981 s.21, as amended for Scotland by NCSA 2004 Sch.6 para.19 and for England and Wales by CRWA 2000 Sch.12 para.10, and NERCA 2006 Sch.5 para.5 and Sch.11 para.73.

[39] WCA 1981 s.21(5).

[40] WCA 1981 s.21(6). In *RSPCA v Munur* [2008] EWHC 199 Admin, following a conviction for keeping birds in inadequate cages (contrary to WCA 1981 s.8; see para.3.3.21) forfeiture of both birds and cages was ordered, despite an argument that it was only the cages that gave rise to the offence.

[41] WCA 1981 s.16. Such licences clearly provide a defence to a charge under the 1981 Act, but where more than one person has an interest in the land concerned, there is scope for argument over the precise nature of the rights conferred by them. In *Re Wildfowl Trust (Holdings) Ltd* Unreported January 19, 1994, Outer House, the landlord and tenant disputed whether a licence issued to the tenant to kill geese fell within the terms of the lease creating an exception for "conjunct rights conferred upon the tenant by statute" and therefore allowed the tenant to shoot the geese despite the landlords' reservation of exclusive hunting rights; the issue was never authoritatively resolved and the decision on whether to grant an interim interdict was resolved on the balance of convenience in favour of allowing the tenant to shoot.

conditional, may be general or specific, may be personal or in favour of a class of people and will be of fixed duration.[42] For certain licences it is a requirement that there should be no other satisfactory solution before the licence can be granted, and certain licences relating to birds are expressly limited to those granted on a selective basis in respect of small numbers of birds. The purposes for which licences can be granted appear in Appendix C below.[43] The possibility of obtaining a licence must always be borne in mind when the prohibitions in the Act are being considered, and the scope and availability of licences can considerably alter the effect of the law in practice.[44]

3.2.14   General licences are issued separately for England, Scotland and Wales, in most cases to the same effect, but they are organised differently and there are many differences of detail which may be significant. The licences are subject to conditions and in some cases to recording and reporting requirements. Since the licences are of limited duration and not published in any standard form, finding out exactly what one is permitted to do in any part of the country at any particular time is far from as straightforward as it should be. In recent years, though, the position has improved with most licences being available on the internet[45] and a Scottish consultation on amendments to the licences making the process more transparent.[46]

"Authorised Persons"

3.2.15 One definition of general application can also be conveniently discussed here. In several places the Act declares that it is permissible for an "authorised person" to do acts which are otherwise criminal. For these purposes an authorised person is defined as: the owner or occupier of the land where the action takes place or someone authorised by him, a person authorised in writing by the local authority for the area,[47] or in England and Wales a person authorised in writing by the Environment Agency, a water undertaker or a sewerage undertaker. In relation to birds, authorisation in writing can also be provided by the statutory conservation bodies, a district salmon fishery board in Scotland or a local fisheries committee in England

---

[42] WCA 1981 s.16(5); licences authorising the killing of birds or animals must specify the area and method of killing and have a maximum validity of two years (s.16(6)).

[43] The division of responsibility between the Minister and the conservation body varies across Great Britain, e.g. English Nature has been authorised to exercise a wide range of ministerial powers by virtue of an agreement with the Secretary of State under NERCA 2006 s.78.

[44] e.g. in relation to pest species of birds; see paras 3.3.10–3.3.15, below. Under the Wildlife and Countryside Act 1981, English Nature/Natural England issued over 1,000 licences relating to birds in 2005 and in 2007 over 50 licences relating to animals, plus over 1,000 under the Protection of Badgers Act 1992; information taken from *http://www.naturalengland.org.uk/ conservation/wildlife-management-licensing/statistics.htm* [Accessed May 8, 2009] (November 2008).

[45] For Scotland at *http://www.scotland.gov.uk/Topics/Environment/Wildlife-Habitats/16330/ general-licences*; for England at *http://www.naturalengland.org.uk/conservation/wildlife-management-licensing/genlicences.htm*; at the time of writing the Welsh licences were not available on the Welsh Assembly Government website although CCW did display those it issued at *http://www.ccw.gov.uk/landscape-wildlife/habitats-species/species-protection/licensing/ general-licences.aspx* [All Accessed May 8, 2009].

[46] *Consultation on Amendments to the Scottish Executive General Licences Under the Wildlife and Countryside Act 1981* (Scottish Executive, January 2007).

[47] Where there are not unitary authorities, both authorities have this power.

and Wales.[48] Many of the general licences issued under the Act also permit "authorised persons" to do particular things, but the licences give their own, sometimes much narrower, definitions of who is an "authorised person" for the purposes of the particular licence.

Taking

A final point to mention in passing is that although in some contexts **3.2.16** references to the taking of animals includes references to their taking by killing (especially in the context of the taking of game), in the legal context "taking" appears to mean only their capture.[49] This contrasts with the position in the US where the legislation protecting endangered species prohibits their "taking" and gives this term the wide definition of "harass, harm, pursue, hunt, shoot, wound, kill, trap, capture or collect",[50] which has been interpreted as extending to cover "significant habitat modification or degradation where it actually kills or injures wildlife by significantly impairing essential behavioural patterns, including breeding, feeding or sheltering".[51] Capturing animals (whether to kill them or to keep them) in theory poses different problems from direct killing in terms of legal control, but since in almost all cases the taking of animals is regulated along with their killing, it is possible to deal with both together. For England and Wales, the Conservation (Natural Habitats, Etc.) Regulations 1994 have been amended to replace some references to "taking" animals with references to "capturing" them.[52]

Conservation (Natural Habitats, etc.) Regulations 1994[53]

The simplicity of having virtually all of the key laws on species protection in **3.2.17** one place was lost when the decision was taken to implement the Habitats and Species Directive by means of separate legislation, as opposed to integrating its provisions with those of the 1981 Act. This was very much in keeping with the policy at the time of adopting the "copy-out" approach to implementing EC Directives, simply transposing their provisions more or less directly into UK law as opposed to ensuring that the terms of the Directive were met by amending or adding to existing provisions.[54] Where there is a complete copy-out, this approach has the advantage of simplicity for the legislator, as well as guaranteeing that there has been complete legal implementation of the measure in a way that is transparent to the Brussels authorities, without argument over whether the adjustments to existing law do in fact fully implement all the provisions of the Directive. On the other hand, for the user of the law, the result is complexity and confusion, as two

---

[48] WCA 1981 s.27, as amended on various occasions, notably by Water Act 1989 Sch.25 para.66.

[49] The legislation consistently uses separate words for killing and taking; cf. *Wells v Hardy* [1964] 2 Q.B. 447, catching and returning fish is not "taking" for the Larceny Act 1861.

[50] Endangered Species Act 1973 (US) s.3.

[51] Interior Department regulations approved by the Supreme Court in *Babbitt v Sweet Home Chapter of Communities for a Great Oregon* 515 US 687 (1995).

[52] CNHR 1994 reg.41 as amended by CNHAR 2007 reg.5(15).

[53] SI 1994/2716.

[54] L. Ramsey, "Copy Out Technique: More of a 'Cop Out' than a Solution?" (1996) 17 Stat. L.R. 218.

largely overlapping sets of law have to be examined, taking careful note of where there are differences in the details of the law, and even worse, trying to work out whether minor differences in wording actually signify a difference in meaning.

3.2.18   In this instance there were two problems with the implementation of the Directive through the Conservation (Natural Habitats, etc.) Regulations 1994. In the first place, the Regulations did not accurately transpose the Directive. A number of significant failings had been identified from an early stage but it was only after a formal finding to this effect in the case of *Commission v United Kingdom*[55] that remedial action was taken.[56] Again, sadly, the changes have taken the form of detailed amendments to the existing legislation rather than presenting a clear version of the law. What has been gained by removing the overlap noted below has been lost through more "cut-and-paste" amendments, which for Scotland appear in three sets of regulations made within five months of each other[57] and a further set made less than 18 months later.

3.2.19   The second problem was that the effect was to leave some species subject to two overlapping sets of law. The provisions in the Regulations are largely parallel to those in the Act, but there were some differences in the scope of the protection, e.g. extending the offence of destroying breeding sites to cover non-intentional activity, some differences in the scope of permissible exceptions and some places where there are differences in phrasing which probably do not represent differences in substance, e.g. is "deliberately" killing an animal (the offence under the Regulations) any different from "intentionally" doing so (the offence under the Act)? This overlap has been resolved by removing the European protected species covered by the Regulations from the scope of the Act,[58] so that none are now covered by two sets of rules, although it remains the case that there are two sets of rules to be applied, depending on the species concerned.

3.2.20   The species protection measures in the Directive are of similar structure to those in the 1981 Act, prohibiting the deliberate killing or taking of protected species, disturbance to breeding and resting sites, possession or sale of the creatures or derivatives and restrictions on the methods of killing or taking where such is permissible at all. Licences can be granted to authorise conduct normally prohibited.[59] The Regulations also have their own provisions on attempts, possessing items with intent to commit crimes,

---

[55] *Commission v United Kingdom* (C-6/04) [2005] E.C.R. I-9017; see C.T. Reid and M. Woods, "Implementing EC Conservation Law" (2006) 18 J.E.L. 135.

[56] Conservation (Natural Habitats, etc.) Amendment (Scotland) Regulations 2007 (SSI 2007/80); Conservation (Natural Habitats, etc.) Amendment (No.2) (Scotland) Regulations 2007 (SSI 2007/349); Conservation (Natural Habitats, etc.) (Amendment) Regulations 2007 (SI 2007/1843); followed by Conservation (Natural Habitats, etc.) Amendment (No.2) (Scotland) Regulations 2008 (SSI 2008/425); for other parts of Great Britain the 2007 Regulations (SI 2007/1843) have been followed by Conservation (Natural Habitats, etc.) (Amendment) (England and Wales) Regulations 2009 (SI 2009/6) and Offshore Marine Conservation (Natural Habitats, etc.) (Amendment) Regulations 2009 (SI 2009/7).

[57] Although most of CNHAR 2007 applies only to England and Wales some provisions do apply to Scotland.

[58] CNHSAR 2007 regs 28–29; CNHAR 2007 reg.7(7)–(8).

[59] CNHR 1994 regs 44–46A; almost 700 licences were issued by English Nature in 2005, over 500 of these in relation to bats; *http://www.naturalengland.org.uk/conservation/wildlife-management-licensing/statistics.htm* [Accessed May 8, 2009] (November 2008).

corporate liability, forfeiture and powers of search and seizure.[60] For Scotland it is also provided that regulations made under the European Communities Act 1972 in order to implement the Habitats and Species Directive can impose higher penalties than are normally permitted by this route.[61]

BIRDS AND EGGS

3.3.1 The main legislation concerning birds is to be found in Part I of the Wildlife and Countryside Act 1981 which replaced the previous legislation protecting birds. The starting point for the law is the simple statement in section 1(1) that it is an offence for any person intentionally to kill, injure or take any wild bird, in Scotland extended to anyone who recklessly does so as well.[62] However, in order to meet the requirements of different species, birds are divided into various categories: some are covered simply by the general law, some given added protection, others are given protection during a close season only and pest species are in practice deprived of the general protection granted to others. In all cases it must be remembered that licences may be granted allowing exemptions from the various prohibitions in the 1981 Act, but the methods by which birds can be killed or taken are always controlled.[63] Legal protection for birds is also granted by the provisions of the European Community's Birds Directive, which requires Member States to establish a general system of protection for all species naturally occurring in the wild state, seeking to maintain their populations at (or restore them to) a level corresponding to ecological, scientific and cultural requirements, taking account of economic and recreational requirements.[64] The Birds Directive is discussed further in Chapter 7. Separate rules apply to game birds.[65]

The General Position

3.3.2 It is an offence for any person intentionally to do any of the following: to kill, injure or take any wild bird; to take, damage or destroy or otherwise interfere with the nest of a wild bird while it is in use or being built; or to take or destroy the egg of any wild bird.[66] In Scotland this offence extends to those who act recklessly as well as intentionally and to those who knowingly cause or permit the prohibited acts, as well as covering or obstructing a nest or preventing any bird from using it.[67] A "wild bird" is defined as being any bird of a species ordinarily resident in, or a visitor to, Great Britain in a wild state, other than poultry or game birds, and anything calculated to prevent the hatching of an egg is included within the meaning of "destroying eggs".[68]

---

[60] CNHR 1994 regs 100–101, 103 and 106.
[61] WCA 1981 s.26A, added by NCSA 2004 Sch.6 para.22.
[62] WCA 1981 s.1(1), as amended by NCSA 2004 Sch.1 para.2.
[63] See paras 4.4.18–4.4.20, below.
[64] Directive 79/409/EEC arts 1 and 5; see section 7.4, below.
[65] See section 4.2, below.
[66] WCA 1981 s.1(1).
[67] WCA 1981 s.1, as amended by NCSA 2004 Sch.6 para.2.
[68] WCA 1981 s.27, as amended by NCSA 2004 Sch.6 para.23 and Wildlife and Countryside Act 1981(England and Wales) (Amendment) Regulations 2004 (SI 2004/1487) reg.4.

The offence does not apply to birds shown[69] to have been bred in captivity.[70] It is not altogether clear whether the intention applies only to the killing, etc. or extends to require knowledge that the bird was "wild" for the purposes of the Act. In relation to the taking or destruction of eggs, the law of corroboration is relaxed in Scotland so that a person may be convicted on the evidence of one witness.[71]

3.3.3   Several defences are provided to limit the scope of this general prohibition. A person's taking of disabled birds in order to tend and release them is excluded, as is the mercy killing of seriously disabled birds with no reasonable chance of recovery, provided in both cases that the original injury was not the result of that person's unlawful act.[72] A more general defence excludes acts which are the incidental result of a lawful operation. In England and Wales this requires simply that the result could not reasonably have been avoided,[73] whereas in Scotland the defence applies only in the stricter conditions that the person involved must have either taken reasonable precautions to avoid the harm or did not, and could not reasonably, foresee the harmful incidental result and must have taken the reasonably practicable steps to minimise the damage or disturbance as soon as the consequences became apparent.[74] In each of these cases the onus is on the accused to show that they fall within the terms of the defence.

3.3.4   Further allowances are made for authorised persons.[75] They are allowed a defence if they can show that their action was necessary for the purpose of preserving public health, public safety or air safety, for preventing the spread of disease, or for preventing serious damage to livestock, crops, fruit, growing timber or fisheries.[76] However, this defence is available only where the authorised person can show that there is no other satisfactory solution, and provided that the Minister is informed and that it was not apparent in advance that the action was necessary, so as to allow for a licence to be sought.[77] A more specific exemption allows the gathering for human consumption of gannets on Sula Sgeir, gulls' eggs, and in England and Wales (before April 15th each year) of lapwings' eggs, provided that this is done in accordance with a licence from the Minister.[78]

---

[69] In *Hughes v DPP* [2003] EWHC 2470 Admin it was said obiter that the onus is on the defendant to show on the balance of probabilities that that a bird has been bred in captivity (at [17]).

[70] WCA 1981 s.1(6); to be bred in captivity a bird's parents must have been lawfully in captivity when the egg was laid (WCA 1981 s.27(2)), but in England and Wales a bird bred in captivity is to be regarded as wild if it has been released as part of a re-population or re-introduction programme (WCA 1981 s.1(6) and (6A), added by NERCA 2006 s.48).

[71] WCA 1981 s.19A, added by Prisoners and Criminal Proceedings (Scotland) Act 1993 s.36.

[72] WCA 1981 s.4(2)(a) and (b).

[73] WCA 1981 s.4(2)(c).

[74] WCA 1981 s.4(2) and (2A), amended by NCSA 2004 Sch.6 para.5.

[75] See para.3.2.15, above.

[76] WCA 1981 s.4(3).

[77] WCA 1981 s.4(4)–(6), added by Wildlife and Countryside Act 1981 (Amendment) Regulations 1995 (SI 1995/2825) reg.2.

[78] WCA 1981 s.16(2), amended by NCSA 2004 Sch.6 para.15; no general licences to this effect were issued in 2008 or 2009.

Further exceptions are created by the general licences issued by Minis- **3.3.5**
ters,[79] e.g. permission to remove abandoned eggs from nest boxes between
August 1st and January 31st, provided that the eggs are not kept,[80] and to
take mallard eggs before March 31st for incubation to assist birds unlikely
to withstand adverse weather conditions,[81] while individual licences can be
issued to deal with particular situations. No offence is committed[82] if the
action in question is required by ministers in the exercise of their powers
relating to agricultural pest control,[83] or is done under the Animal Health
Act 1981 or an order made under it.[84] As noted above, the definition of
"wild bird" means that poultry (domestic fowls, geese, ducks, guinea fowls,
pigeons, quails and turkeys) and game birds (pheasant, partridge, grouse
(moor game), black (heath) game and ptarmigan) fall outside the range of
this protection,[85] as do birds shown to have been bred in captivity.[86]

Protected Birds

A number of birds listed in Schedule 1 to the 1981 Act enjoy enhanced **3.3.6**
protection. Almost 100 species are listed.[87] The general position is modified
in three ways in relation to such birds. First, in addition to the offences
mentioned above, it is an offence intentionally or recklessly to disturb any
wild bird included in Schedule 1 whilst it is building a nest or is at or near its
nest containing eggs or young, or intentionally or recklessly to disturb the
dependent young of such a bird.[88] Over-zealous photographers and birdwatchers may be in danger of falling foul of this provision. Secondly, some
of the defences noted above do not apply in relation to Schedule 1 birds. The
exemption for acts done under the Animal Health Act 1981 is restricted to
acts done in pursuance of orders made under sections 21 and 22 of that Act
(wildlife destruction orders),[89] and none of the further defences available to
authorised persons apply.[90] In the case of three species of bird which are
listed in Schedule 1 but may be hunted,[91] the special rules apply only during
the close season[92]; the birds concerned are goldeneye, pintail and (in parts of
northwest Scotland only) greylag geese. Thirdly, in Scotland any intentional
or reckless disturbance of a listed bird during a lek is also an offence.[93]

The nests of a few species enjoy further protection as a consequence of the **3.3.7**

---

[79] See paras 3.2.13–3.2.14, above.
[80] Licences SGGL 7/2009, WML Gen-L14 (12/08); the equivalent licence for Wales is not readily accessible.
[81] Licences SGGL 11/2009, WML Gen-L15 (12/08); the equivalent licence for Wales is not readily accessible.
[82] WCA 1981, s.4(1).
[83] Agriculture Act 1947 s.98; Agriculture (Scotland) Act 1948 s.39; see para.4.5.2, below.
[84] See para.4.5.11, below.
[85] WCA 1981 s.27.
[86] WCA 1981 s.1(6).
[87] See Appendix A.
[88] WCA 1981 s.1(5), amended by CRWA 2000 Sch.12 para.1 and NCSA 2004 Sch.12 para.5.
[89] WCA 1981 s.4(1); see para.4.5.11, below.
[90] WCA 1981 s.4(3).
[91] WCA 1981 Sch.1 Pt II; see Appendix A.
[92] WCA 1981 s.1(7); the close season is February 21–August 31 for areas below high-water mark, and February 1–August 31 for other areas (WCA 1981 s.2(4)); see Appendix B.
[93] WCA 1981 s.1(5A), added by NCSA 2004 Sch.12 para.2; a lek is an assembly for breeding displays, as practised by black grouse, capercaillie and some other species.

birds being listed in Schedule A1 (Scotland) or ZA1 (England and Wales) to the 1981 Act. In relation to these birds it is an offence intentionally (or in Scotland additionally recklessly) to take, damage or destroy (or in Scotland additionally interfere with) any habitually used nest at any time of the year, not only while it is being built or in use.[94] The Scottish list is limited to just one species, the white-tailed eagle, whereas the list for England and Wales also includes the golden eagle and osprey. In Scotland the white-tailed eagle is also protected from any intentional or reckless harassment at any time.[95]

3.3.8   Birds listed in Annex I of the Birds Directive[96] are also entitled to "special conservation measures concerning their habitat", primarily the designation and care of Special Protection Areas, and these are discussed with other habitat protection measures in Chapter 5. The interaction of domestic and EC law may be significant, as in *RSPB v Secretary of State for Scotland*,[97] where it was accepted that the fairly broad power under the Wildlife and Countryside Act 1981 to grant licences to kill wild geese was in law constrained by the narrower tests set in the Birds Directive.

Birds which may be Hunted

3.3.9 Game birds are excluded from the scope of most of the 1981 Act and the general position described above is modified in order to allow the hunting of a number of other species of birds, listed in Part I of Schedule 2 to the Act.[98] The Birds Directive similarly permits the hunting of some species, listed in Annex II.[99] No offence is committed by killing or taking such birds outside the close season, or by injuring them in the attempt to kill them,[100] although certain methods are prohibited in relation to all birds,[101] and it remains an offence to injure such a bird deliberately, except in the course of trying to kill it. The various close seasons are defined in the Act[102] and hunting is not permitted in Scotland on Sundays or on Christmas Day, nor on Sundays in any area of England and Wales prescribed by the Minister.[103] The Minister has the power to make orders varying the close seasons.[104] After consulting a representative of shooting interests he may also make orders offering to any birds listed in Part II of Schedule 1 or Part I of Schedule 2 special protection for a period of up to 14 days at a time. These orders, intended for periods of exceptionally severe weather or other temporary crises for the birds, operate so as to apply the rules for the close season during the period of special

---

[94] WCA 1981 s.1(1)(ba), added for Scotland by NSCA Sch.12 para.2, and WCA 1981 s.1(1)(aa), added for England and Wales by NERCA 2006 s.47(2).

[95] WCA 1981 s.1(5B) and Sch.1A, added by NCSA 2004 Sch.6 paras 2 and 25.

[96] Directive 79/409/EEC.

[97] *RSPB v Secretary of State for Scotland*, 2000 S.L.T. 22 (OH) and 1272; see para.3.3.12, below.

[98] See Appendix A; the three species listed in Pt II of Sch.1 and thereby enjoying enhanced protection during the close season also appear in Pt I of Sch.2.

[99] Birds Directive art.7.

[100] WCA 1981 s.2(1); see Appendix B for a table of close seasons for the birds covered here and for game birds.

[101] See paras 4.4.18–4.4.20, below.

[102] WCA 1981 s.2(4).

[103] WCA 1981 s.2(3). The Wild Birds (Sundays) Orders made under s.2 of the Protection of Birds Act 1954 presumably continue in effect in prescribing such areas; SI 1955/1286, SI 1956/1310, SI 1957/429 and SI 1963/1700.

[104] WCA 1981 s.2(5).

protection, and may affect all or only part of the country.[105] In England and Wales, some of these birds enjoy further protection in that it is an offence for anyone to take or destroy their eggs unless authorised by the person with the right to kill game on the land in question.[106]

Pests and Licences

The statutory provisions originally contained a considerable relaxation of **3.3.10** the general protection for wild birds to allow authorised persons to deal with birds widely regarded as pests. The birds were listed in Part II of Schedule 2 and no offence was committed by an authorised person who killed or took such a bird, destroyed, damaged or took its nest or destroyed or took its eggs.[107] However this legislative exception for pest species was considered to fall foul of the terms of the Birds Directive[108] which imposes a prohibition on the killing and taking of all wild birds[109] and permits derogations only where certain criteria are met.[110] Accordingly, all of the species were removed from Part II of Schedule 2 and in its place a number of licences have been issued by the Minister under section 16 of the 1981 Act.[111] The general licences permit authorised persons to kill or take the listed species or their eggs for a variety of purposes,[112] provided that they are satisfied that appropriate non-lethal methods are ineffective or impracticable. The licences are annual but apply to all authorised persons as defined in the licences,[113] so that there is no need for individual applications to be made. The change of form, from statutory exception to general licences, does not have any real impact on the practical effect of the law, but makes it even harder for anyone to find out exactly what they are or are not permitted to do (and therefore whether or not they are committing a crime), and removes the details of the law from any direct parliamentary scrutiny.

The purposes for which the Birds Directive allows derogations from the **3.3.11** general protection for birds cover action in the interests of public health and safety, including air safety, to prevent serious damage to crops, livestock, forests and water, to protect flora and fauna, for research and repopulation and to permit the limited keeping and "other judicious use" of small numbers of birds.[114] The grounds for granting licences under section 16 of the 1981 Act largely match these, but it can be argued that the general defence for actions which are the incidental results of lawful actions permits harm to birds in too wide a range of circumstances.

Other requirements in the Directive are met within the terms of individual **3.3.12** licences. The requirement that there should be no other satisfactory solution

---

[105] WCA 1981 s.2(6).

[106] Game Act 1831 s.24, applying to game and "any swan, wild duck, teal and widgeon."

[107] WCA 1981 s.2(2).

[108] Directive 79/409/EEC; see para.7.4.10, below.

[109] Directive 79/409/EEC art.5.

[110] Directive 79/409/EEC art.9.

[111] See paras 3.2.13–3.2.14, above.

[112] Even if this limitation does not appear on the face of the licence, the licences cover only action taken for one of the specified statutory purposes and do not permit the general killing of the pest species; *RSPCA v Cundey* [2001] EWHC 906 Admin; [2002] Env. L.R. 17.

[113] See para.3.2.15, above.

[114] Directive 79/409/EEC art.9(1); "judicious use" can include hunting (*Ligue pour la protection des oiseaux v Premier ministre* (C-182/02) [2003] E.C.R. I-12, 105). See Appendix C.

before a derogation is made[115] is incorporated in relevant licences requiring that the authorised person must be satisfied that appropriate non-lethal methods of control are either ineffective or inappropriate. In *RSPB v Secretary of State for Scotland* [116] it was argued that the provision of compensation to farmers for damage done to their crops by geese provided an alternative to allowing some geese to be shot, but it was held that the alternatives to be considered must be ones that actually prevent the harm arising.[117] The licences also specify the means that may be used for killing or capturing the birds[118] and there are some reporting requirements that allow the monitoring necessary to ensure that the consequences of the derogations are not incompatible with the Directive.[119]

3.3.13   It is the detail of each licence that determines what is or is not lawful, and to emphasise the extent of the differences within Great Britain, the most general licence will be considered in detail.[120] Each jurisdiction issues a licence[121] to permit the killing and taking of birds to prevent serious damage to livestock, foodstuffs for livestock, crops, vegetables and fruit; the English and Welsh licences also include the protection of growing timber, fisheries or inland waters, not covered by any Scottish licence, and the prevention of the spread of disease, covered by a different licence in Scotland.[122] A core of species is covered by all the licences—crow, collared dove, greater black-backed gull, herring gull, jackdaw, magpie, feral pigeon, rook and wood-pigeon[123]; in England and Wales the list also includes the jay and the lesser black-backed gull; in Scotland and Wales it includes the house sparrow and starling; in England it includes the greater Canada goose; in Scotland it includes the hooded crow. The methods that can be used vary slightly, e.g. in Scotland including targeted falconry, and the range of species that can be used as decoys in cage traps, is specified (differently) for Scotland and for England but not for Wales. In Scotland alone there is in relation to the herring gull, house sparrow and starling a requirement to provide to the Scottish Government a report on the monthly number of birds or eggs killed, taken or destroyed and the specific reasons, methods and locations. It is therefore vital to check the precise terms of the relevant licence since there are substantial differences in what is permitted in the different parts of Great Britain.

3.3.14   Further general licences are issued for the conservation of wild birds,[124] the preservation of public health and public safety[125] and air safety.[126]

---

[115] Directive 79/409/EEC art.9(1).

[116] *RSPB v Secretary of State for Scotland*, 2000 S.L.T. 22 (OH); this point was not argued in the Inner House (2000 S.L.T. 1272).

[117] See also *Ligue Royale Belge pour la Protection des Oiseaux ASBL v Région Wallonne* (C-10/96) [1996] I-E.C.R. 6775.

[118] Directive 79/409/EEC art.9(2).

[119] Directive 79/409/EEC art.9(4).

[120] Although the licences are issued annually the terms usually remain unchanged.

[121] SGGL 2/2009; WML Gen-L05 (12/08); the Welsh licence in the form that the author was supplied with did not have a reference number (although others do).

[122] SGGL 3/2009.

[123] There are variations in the form of the English names used and in the order of listing.

[124] SGGL 1/2009, WML Gen-L08 (12/08); the equivalent Welsh licences are not readily accessible.

[125] SGGL 3/2009, WML Gen-L07 (12/08).

[126] SGGL 4/2009, WML Gen-L06 (12/08).

Individual licences may be granted in relation to more localised problems,[127] e.g. in relation to geese damaging agricultural crops[128] or cormorants damaging fisheries, and in England a general licence authorises the killing of ruddy ducks.[129]

In relation to protected species within Special Protected Areas, any **3.3.15** licensing decision must take account of the fact that the basis for derogation is even more restricted in that there is an obligation to prevent any disturbance affecting the birds, so far as these are significant having regard to the objectives of the relevant provision.[130] The shooting of geese under the licence granted in *RSPB v Secretary of State for Scotland*[131] clearly would be a disturbance, and it was held that the "significance" had to determined looking at the impact both locally and on the wider position of the species, bearing in mind the objectives of the relevant article, as amended by the Habitats and Species Directive.

Possession

In view of the difficulty of proving that someone has intentionally or **3.3.16** recklessly killed a wild bird, and in order to suppress the demand for birds and their eggs, the 1981 Act renders their possession unlawful. It is a criminal offence to possess any live or dead wild bird or anything derived from one, or to possess the egg of any wild bird or part of an egg.[132] Unlike the earlier legislation,[133] the offences are not limited to birds which have been recently killed or taken, and a stuffed and mounted bird continues to be a "dead wild bird" the possession of which may be a criminal offence.[134] Subject to the exceptions noted below, these are offences of strict liability, as decided in *Kirkland v Robinson*.[135] In deciding that the law did impose strict liability the court was influenced by the contrast with the other offences created by the same section, e.g. killing birds, which expressly required intentional conduct, by the presence of statutory defences to mitigate the potential harshness of strict liability, and by the importance of environmental protection. It was right that those who chose to possess wild birds should do so at their own risk.

The offence of possession is widely drawn, rendering it unlawful for any **3.3.17** persons to have in their possession or control any live or dead wild bird, any part of one or anything derived from such a bird or any egg (whole or part) of a wild bird.[136] Those in possession of the bird or egg can establish a

---

[127] See Appendix C for the purposes for which a licence can be granted. According to press reports citing RSPB Scotland, during 1999 in Scotland 22 licences to kill robins were issued.

[128] As in *RSPB v Secretary of State for Scotland*, 2000 S.L.T. 1272; see below.

[129] WML Gen-L29 (12/08); the attempt to eliminate this American species to prevent hybridising the European white-headed duck has proved controversial.

[130] See para.7.4.28, below.

[131] *RSPB v Secretary of State for Scotland*, 2000 S.L.T. 1272.

[132] WCA 1981 s.1(2).

[133] Protection of Birds Act 1954 s.1.

[134] *Robinson v Everett* [1988] Crim. L.R. 699.

[135] *Kirkland v Robinson* [1987] Crim. L.R. 643.

[136] WCA 1981 s.1(2); the reference to derivatives has led to general licences being issued in England authorising the retention of blood and tissue samples obtained as part of forensic investigations into offences under the Act (WML Gen-L12 (12/08)).

defence if they can show that the bird or egg had not been killed or taken (in other words had come under their control by natural means), or had been killed or taken otherwise than in contravention of the 1981 Act or its predecessors[137] (in other words was the product of lawful activity or had been taken before 1954). A defence is also available if it can be shown that the bird or egg had at some stage been sold otherwise than in contravention of the 1981 Act or its predecessors. A defence also exists that essentially covers items that have been brought in to the country lawfully, but the details vary between Scottish provisions and those for England and Wales.[138] The offences do not apply in relation to any bird shown to have been bred in captivity.[139]

Keeping

3.3.18   The keeping of certain live wild birds is covered by the general possession offence described above, but a number of other provisions exist to regulate the keeping of birds, and the conditions in which they are kept. In practice the application of these rules is significantly affected by a number of general licences relating to the keeping of birds issued by the Minister under the powers in section 16 of the Act. In addition to the licences on the keeping of certain species, general licences authorise veterinary surgeons and certain others to keep wild birds for treatment and rehabilitation.[140] For many species a person with a bird in his possession or control must ensure that the bird is registered and ringed or marked in accordance with regulations made by the Minister.[141] The species to which this provision may apply are listed in Schedule 4 to the 1981 Act.[142]

3.3.19   The law here is severe on persistent offenders. Regardless of whether the bird is registered and ringed, it is an offence for a bird listed in Schedule 4 to be kept by any person who has been convicted within recent years of certain offences. The offences are those under the 1981 Act and certain others, which in England and Wales are divided into two categories, some with a

---

[137] Protection of Birds Acts 1954–1967.

[138] WCA 1981 s.1(3) and (3A), as amended by NCSA 2004 Sch.6 para.2; Wildlife and Countryside Act 1981 (England and Wales) (Amendment) Regulations 2004 (SI 2004/1487) reg.3; Wildlife and Countryside Act 1981 (Wales) (Amendment) Regulations 2004 (SI 2004/1733) reg.3 and Sch.

[139] WCA 1981 s.1(6).

[140] Licences SGGL 5/2009 and SGGL 6/2009, WML Gen-L09 (12/08) and WML Gen-L10 (12/08). Licences in England also permit the keeping of birds by some official bodies without registration, pending legal proceedings (WML Gen-L11). The equivalent Welsh licences are not readily accessible.

[141] WCA 1981 s.7(1); Wildlife and Countryside (Registration and Ringing of Certain Captive Birds) Regulations 1982 (SI 1982/1221) (amended by Wildlife and Countryside (Registration and Ringing of Certain Captive Birds) (Amendment) Regulations 1991and 1994 (SI 1991/478 and SI 1994/1151) and Wildlife and Countryside (Registration and Ringing of Certain Captive Birds) (England) (Amendment) Regulations 2004 and 2008 (SI 2004/640 and SI 2008/2357)). In Wales, the 1982 Regulations were replaced by the Wildlife and Countryside (Registration, Ringing and Marking of Certain Captive Birds) (Wales) Regulations 2003 (SI 2003/3235). Provision for a fee to be charged for registration was added by the Birds (Registration Charges) Act 1997.

[142] See Appendix A.

five-year and others with a three-year ban, with a five-year ban applying for all those listed for Scotland.[143] It is also an offence for anybody knowingly to dispose or offer to dispose of a Schedule 4 bird to anyone falling within these categories of past offenders.[144] Powers of entry are provided to inspect premises where birds covered by Schedule 4 are being kept, and obstruction of such inspectors is an offence.[145]

3.3.20 It is an offence to cause or permit certain birds to be shown for the purposes of competitions or at premises where a competition is taking place.[146] This prohibition applies to any live wild bird, or bird which has a wild bird as a parent, other than the species listed in Part I of Schedule 3 and ringed or marked in accordance with regulations made by the Minister.[147] Licences cover the showing of certain captive-bred wild birds.[148]

3.3.21 In order to prevent unnecessary suffering, the general rule is laid down that if birds are kept it must be in a cage or other receptacle which is large enough to allow the bird to stretch its wings freely.[149] This rule applies to all birds, not just wild birds, with the exceptions of poultry, birds in the course of conveyance, birds undergoing examination or treatment by a veterinary practitioner, and birds being shown at a public exhibition or competition provided that the bird is not confined in the smaller cage for more than 72 hours.[150] It is also a crime for anyone to promote, take part in or organise an event in which captive birds are liberated for the purpose of being shot immediately after they have been freed.[151] The owners and occupiers of land used for this purpose are likewise liable.

Sale

3.3.22 The sale of birds and their eggs is also strictly controlled. The provisions on sale are expressed so as to cover not merely the sale of birds or eggs, a requirement which may be difficult to prove and prevent early intervention by the authorities, but also offering or exposing for sale, possessing or transporting for the purpose of sale, and publishing or causing to be published an advertisement likely to be understood as meaning that a person does or intends to buy or sell.[152] In this way all activities relating to a sale should be covered and there should be little if any room for defences based on technicalities or a failure to prove that a formal legal sale has taken place.

---

[143] WCA 1981 s.7(3) and (3A), as amended for Scotland by Criminal Justice (Scotland) Act 2003 Sch.3 paras 1–2, NCSA 2004 Sch.6 para.7 and for England and Wales by CRWA 2000 Sch.12 para.4, NERCA 2006 ss.47 and 49. Spent convictions under the Rehabilitation of Offenders Act 1974 are to disregarded (WCA 1981 s.7(5)).

[144] WCA 1981 s.7(4), as amended.

[145] In Scotland these powers can be exercised by those authorised by the Minister (WCA 1981 s.7(6) and (7)); in England and Wales the specific provision is now replaced by the wider powers of wildlife inspectors (CRWA 2000 Sch.16 Pt 4; see paras 3.2.7–3.2.19, above).

[146] WCA 1981 s.6(3).

[147] WCA 1981 s.6(5); Wildlife and Countryside (Ringing of Certain Birds) Regulations 1982 (SI 1982/1220).

[148] e.g. SGGL 9/2009, WML Gen-L16 (12/08) and WML Gen-L17 (12/08).

[149] WCA 1981 s.8(1).

[150] WCA 1981 s.8(2).

[151] WCA 1981 s.8(3).

[152] WCA 1981 s.6(1) and (2).

3.3.23   There is a complete prohibition on the sale of the eggs of wild birds or of live wild birds other than those listed in Part I of Schedule 3,[153] and only then provided that they have been bred in captivity and are ringed or marked in accordance with regulations made by the Minister.[154] For dead wild birds and things derived from them, the prohibition extends to all species apart from those listed in Parts II and III of Schedule 3.[155] For dead birds listed in Part III of the Schedule sale is permitted only during the shooting season, from September 1 to February 28.[156] The 1981 Act contained a scheme limiting sales to registered dealers,[157] but this remains in operation only in Scotland.[158] Registration for the purposes of selling dead birds is not available to anyone within five years of being convicted of offences under the 1981 Act or other offences of ill-treatment.[159] The Minister may authorise people to enter and inspect premises where a registered person keeps wild birds, and obstruction of such inspectors is an offence.[160] Again, the application of these rules in practice is affected by a number of general licences issued under section 16 of the Act.[161] The sale of game birds has been subject to separate licensing requirements, now repealed for England and Wales.[162]

Offshore

3.3.24 In order to give effect to the Birds Directive outside territorial waters, the Offshore Marine Conservation (Natural Habitats, etc.) Regulations 2007[163] introduce broad measures protecting wild birds, mostly without the distinctions created by the various Schedules and Annexes that affect the terrestrial provisions. It is an offence deliberately to capture, injure or kill any wild bird, to take, damage or destroy the nest of any wild bird while it is in use or being built or to take or destroy an egg of such a bird.[164] In relation to fishing activities this offence is modified in that for actions in the course of

---

[153] WCA 1981 s.6(1); see Appendix A. The Birds Directive (art.6) similarly allows the sale of some species, listed in Annex III.

[154] WCA 1981 s.6(5); Wildlife and Countryside (Ringing of Certain Birds) Regulations 1982 (SI 1982/1220).

[155] WCA 1981 s.6(2).

[156] WCA 1981 s.6(6).

[157] WCA 1981 s.6(2); Wildlife and Countryside (Registration to Sell, etc., Certain Dead Wild Birds) Regulations 1982 (SI 1982/1219), amended by Wildlife and Countryside (Registration to Sell, etc., Certain Dead Wild Birds) (Amendment) Regulations 1991 (SI 1991/479). A fee may be charged for registration under the Birds (Registration Charges) Act 1997.

[158] Relevant provisions repealed for England and Wales by CRWA 2000 Sch.16.

[159] WCA 1981 s.6(8), amended by Criminal Justice (Scotland) Act 2003 Sch.3 para.2; spent convictions under the Rehabilitation of Offenders Act 1974 are to be disregarded.

[160] WCA 1981 s.6(9) and (10); in England and Wales now replaced by the wider powers of wildlife inspectors (see para.3.2.16, above).

[161] e.g. authorising the sale of captive-bred birds (with a list of exclusions) (SGGL 8/2009, WML Gen-L24 (12/08)) and of feathers and other derivatives of several species of wildfowl, provided that documentary evidence establishes that they were bred in captivity or lawfully killed or taken (SGGL 13/2009, WML Gen-L21 (12/08)); again the Welsh equivalents are not readily accessible.

[162] See para.4.2.9, below.

[163] SI 2007/1842, amended by the Offshore Marine Conservation (Natural Habitats, etc.) (Amendment) Regulations 2009 (SI 2009/7).

[164] Offshore Marine Conservation (Natural Habitats, etc.) Regulations 2007 (SI 2007/1842) reg.34(1).

sea fishing a person does not "deliberately" kill, etc. a bird merely because he was aware that his actions would have that result,[165] provided that they were not aimed at causing that result and reasonable steps were taken to comply with relevant EC law.[166] Keeping wild birds (alive or dead) or their eggs is also an offence.[167] Defences cover the tending and release of disabled birds (unless disabled by that person's unlawful act), mercy killing, actions in the course of investigating connected offences and keeping lawfully taken individuals or specimens.[168] Any indiscriminate means of capturing or killing birds is banned, as are those capable of causing the local disappearance of any species as well as pursuing birds in any mechanically propelled vehicle and a number of other listed methods.[169]

Licences authorising prohibited conduct can be granted by the Minister **3.3.25** for the purposes of: public health or safety or air safety; preventing serious damage to fisheries; educational purposes; protecting flora and fauna; and for re-populating or reintroducing into an area species of wild birds.[170] The capture, keeping or judicious use of birds can be licensed for other purposes where the Minister is satisfied that there is no other satisfactory solution and the activity relates to a small number of birds under strictly supervised conditions.[171]

Unless licensed, the sale, offer or exposure for sale or possession or **3.3.26** transport for sale activities of any live or dead wild bird, items derived from it or its eggs is an offence. This does not apply to lawfully obtained specimens of birds listed in Annex III/1 of the Birds Directive.[172] There is a presumption that once a specimen is shown to be or come from a bird referred to in article 1 of the Birds Directive, the bird was a wild bird unless the contrary is shown.[173]

ANIMALS

The law relating to other animals is more fragmented than that concerned **3.4.1** with birds. In addition to the provisions of the Wildlife and Countryside Act 1981, amended separately for England and Wales and for Scotland, there are a number of European protected species qualifying for protection under the Conservation (Natural Habitats, etc.) Regulations 1994, again as multiply amended. Older legislation dealing with pests and game must also be considered, and there are a sizeable number of provisions which relate to individual species, e.g. the Protection of Badgers Act 1992. The law on animals generally is blighted by the proliferation of different legislative definitions of "animal", sometimes referring to domestic animals only and

---

[165] Normally this would fall within the meaning of "intentionally", the more usual word in criminal law; *R. v Woollin* [1999] A.C. 82.
[166] Offshore Marine Conservation (Natural Habitats, etc.) Regulations 2007 reg.34(4) and (5).
[167] Offshore Marine Conservation (Natural Habitats, etc.) Regulations 2007 reg.34(2).
[168] Offshore Marine Conservation (Natural Habitats, etc.) Regulations 2007 reg.35.
[169] Offshore Marine Conservation (Natural Habitats, etc.) Regulations 2007 reg.36; the list is similar but not identical to those in WCA 1981 s.5(1) and Annex IV of the Birds directive.
[170] Offshore Marine Conservation (Natural Habitats, etc.) Regulations 2007 reg.49(1).
[171] Offshore Marine Conservation (Natural Habitats, etc.) Regulations 2007 reg.49(2) and (3), expressly referring to the restrictions in art.9(1)(c) of the Birds Directive.
[172] See para.3.3.23, above.
[173] Offshore Marine Conservation (Natural Habitats, etc.) Regulations 2007 reg.37.

frequently defying any scientific classification. In every case where a statute refers to "animals" it is wise to check that the animal which one has in mind is in the particular circumstances an animal for the purposes of the provision in question.

Protected Animals

3.4.2 Under the Wildlife and Countryside Act 1981, a number of animals are given protection similar to that given to those birds listed in Schedule 1 to the Act. The protected animals are listed in Schedule 5[174] and it is an offence for any person intentionally, to kill, injure or take a wild animal of those species. [175] In Scotland doing so recklessly is also an offence[176] and those who knowingly cause or permit an act prohibited by these provisions and those discussed immediately below are also guilty.[177] It is an offence to have in one's possession or control any such animal, whether alive or dead, or anything derived from one.[178] As is the case with birds, it is a defence to show that the animal was not killed or taken, or was not killed or taken in contravention of the 1981 Act or its predecessor (the Conservation of Wild Creatures and Wild Plants Act 1975) or had been sold without contravening those provisions; again the provisions differ between Scotland and England and Wales.[179]

3.4.3 It is a further offence for anyone intentionally or recklessly, to damage, destroy or obstruct access to any place a wild animal included in Schedule 5 uses for shelter or protection, or intentionally to disturb an animal while using such a place,[180] but this offence does not apply to anything done within a dwelling-house.[181] The sale, offer for sale, etc. or advertising of protected animals is also prohibited.[182] In any proceedings a particular animal is generally presumed to be wild unless the contrary is shown.[183] A number of species are listed in Schedule 5 but only in relation to certain aspects of the protection described here, e.g. it is only the rules on sale that apply to several butterfly species.[184]

3.4.4 The above provisions do not apply in certain circumstances. It is not an offence for a person to take a disabled animal for the purpose of treating it and releasing it, nor to kill an animal so severely disabled as to have no reasonable chance of recovery, provided in both cases that it was not that person's unlawful act which caused the disability.[185] More generally, no

---

[174] See Appendix A.

[175] WCA 1981 s.9(1).

[176] WCA 1981 s.9(1) as amended by NCSA 2004 Sch.6 para.8.

[177] WCA 1981 s.9(5A), added by NCSA 2004 Sch.6 para.8.

[178] WCA 1981 s.9(2).

[179] WCA 1981 s.9(3) and (3A), as amended by NCSA 2004 Sch.6 para.8.

[180] WCA 1981 s.9(4), amended for Scotland by NCSA 2004 Sch.6 para.8 and replaced for England and Wales by CNHAR 2007 (SI 2007/1843) reg.7(4).

[181] WCA 1981 s.10(2); the restriction of this exception (s.10(5)) to the living area of a dwelling-house in relation to bats now has no effect; see para.3.4.21, below.

[182] WCA 1981 s.9(5). In England and Wales a general licence authorises the sale outside the breeding seasons of adult specimens of common frogs, common toads and smooth and palmate newts, provided that they were not taken from the wild during the breeding season and excluding newts taken from certain counties (WML Gen-L26 (12/08)).

[183] WCA 1981 s.9(6); the presumption applies to offences under subss.(1), (2) and (5)(a).

[184] See Appendix A for details.

[185] WCA 1981 s.10(3)(a) and (b).

offence is committed where the otherwise unlawful conduct towards the animal is the incidental result of a lawful operation and could not reasonably have been avoided, e.g. the disturbance entailed in lawful agricultural or forestry operations.[186] In Scotland this defence is limited to apply only in relation to animals bred and lawfully held in captivity or where the person involved either took reasonable precautions to avoid the harm or did not, and could not reasonably, foresee the harmful incidental result and took the reasonably practicable steps to minimise the damage or disturbance as soon as the consequences became apparent.[187] No offence is committed by actions done under a ministerial requirement relating to agricultural pest control[188] or under the Animal Health Act 1981.[189]

A further defence is available to "authorised persons",[190] who are allowed **3.4.5** to kill or injure animals where it can shown that the action was necessary to prevent serious damage to livestock, food for livestock, crops, fruit, growing timber or other forms of property or fisheries.[191] This defence is not available if the need for the action became apparent beforehand, unless an application has been made for a licence to authorise the conduct and that application is still being considered,[192] and additionally in Scotland the defence can only be relied on where the Minister has been notified as soon as practicable after the action is taken.[193] As with the rest of Part I of the 1981 Act, licences may be obtained authorising actions which would otherwise constitute offences.[194]

A lesser degree of protection is granted to the animals listed in Schedule 6 **3.4.6** to the 1981 Act.[195] Their protection is limited to a prohibition on the use of certain methods of killing or taking them[196]; certain other methods are prohibited in relation to all species.[197] These include the use of the following devices in killing or taking the listed animals,[198] or their setting (for whatever purpose) in circumstances calculated to cause bodily injury to such animals[199]: traps or snares; electrical devices for killing or stunning; poisonous, poisoned or stupefying substances; or nets.[200] A limited defence is available in relation to the setting of the prohibited devices in that no offence is committed if the accused can show that the article was set for the purpose of

---

[186] WCA 1981 s.10(3)(c).

[187] WCA 1981 s.10(3)(c) and (3A), as added by NCSA 2004 Sch.6 para.9.

[188] Agriculture Act 1947 s.98; Agriculture (Scotland) Act 1948 s.39; see para.4.5.2, below.

[189] WCA 1981 s.10(1); see para.4.5.11, below.

[190] See para.3.2.15, above.

[191] WCA 1981 s.10(4).

[192] WCA 1981 s.10(6); if the application is granted, the licence will authorise the action taken, if refused, the action is unlawful.

[193] WCA 1981 s.10(6A), added by NCSA 2004 Sch.6 para.9.

[194] WCA 1981 s.16; see paras 3.2.13–3.2.14, above and Appendix C. There are no general licences for animals other than birds in Scotland but in England licences include ones to trap and kill edible dormice to prevent serious damage to crops, fruit and timber, to sell dead red squirrels and pine martens (intended for but not legally limited to taxidermy specimens) and for ringing and marking schemes for shrews (WML Gen-L027 (12/08); WML Gen-L028 (12/08);WML Gen-L01 (12/08)).

[195] See Appendix A.

[196] WCA 1981 s.11(2).

[197] See section 4.4, below for the general law on methods of killing and taking animals.

[198] WCA 1981 s.11(2)(b).

[199] WCA 1981 s.11(2)(a).

[200] The setting of nets is not itself prohibited.

the lawful killing of animals in the interests of public health, agriculture, forestry, fisheries or nature conservation, and all reasonable precautions were taken to prevent injury to the animals protected under Schedule 6.[201] Also prohibited is the use of: automatic or semi-automatic weapons; devices for illuminating a target; sighting devices for night shooting; artificial lights; mirrors or dazzling devices; gas or smoke; sound recordings employed as decoys; and mechanically propelled vehicles used in immediate pursuit of animals, for the purpose of driving, killing or taking them.[202] A person who knowingly causes or permits the acts rendered unlawful by these provisions is also guilty of an offence,[203] so that a landowner who deliberately does nothing to stop his gamekeeper offending may himself be prosecuted. Ministers may amend the list of prohibited methods in order to comply with international obligations,[204] and in Scotland can provide criteria for ascertaining whether methods and their use fall within or outwith the prohibition.[205]

European Protected Species

3.4.7 Additional protection is given to those species that qualify as European protected species by virtue of their inclusion in the Habitats and Species Directive, implemented by the Conservation (Natural Habitats, etc.) Regulations 1994. In the past this protection was additional to that provided by the 1981 Act, creating confusion where the two overlapped since, although the two provisions are largely parallel, there are differences between them, in substance as well as wording. Now all of the European protected species, which include fish as well as mammals, reptiles, amphibians and one butterfly,[206] have been removed from Schedule 5 to the 1981 Act for most purposes so that it is just the 1994 Regulations that govern their protection.[207] In England and Wales, though, they remain covered by Schedule 5 for the purposes of the rules on sale and some of the rules on disturbing and obstructing resting places.[208]

3.4.8 The species protection measures in the 1994 Regulations were among those considered by the European Court of Justice in *Commission v United Kingdom*[209] and found to provide inadequate implementation of the Habitats and Species Directive. The Regulations fell short of full implementation in relation to monitoring and surveillance, the detailed rules on the sale of specimens and most significantly through the presence of defences for actions that were the incidental results of lawful operations[210] or taken by

---

[201] WCA 1981 s.11(6) and (7), added by Wildlife and Countryside (Amendment) Act 1991 s.2.

[202] WCA 1981 s.11(2)(c)–(e).

[203] WCA 1981 s.11(2)(d), added by Wildlife and Countryside (Amendment) Act 1991 s.2.

[204] WCA 1981 s.11(4).

[205] WCA 1981 s.11(4A), added by NCSA 2004 Sch.6 para.10.

[206] See Appendix A.

[207] The removal was achieved by CNHAR 2007 reg.7(7) and CNHASR 2007 reg.29.

[208] WCA 1981 Sch.5 as amended by CHNAR 2007 reg.7(7), retaining species in that Schedule for the purposes of s.9(4)(b) and (c) and (5) only; see para.3.4.3, above.

[209] *Commission v United Kingdom* (C-6/04) [2005] E.C.R. I-9017; C.T. Reid and M. Woods, "Implementing EC Conservation Law" (2006) 18 J.E.L. 135, esp. pp.155–157.

[210] The relationship between this now repealed provision and operations authorised under planning law was discussed in *R. (Newsum) v Welsh Assembly Government* [2004] EWCA Civ 1565; [2005] Env. L.R. 16.

authorised persons to prevent serious damage to livestock, crops, fruit, timber or fisheries, providing a much wider derogation from the protective measures than the Directive permits. Separate amending legislation in 2007 for Scotland[211] and for England and Wales,[212] in turn amended in late 2008 and early 2009, has produced versions of the 1994 Regulations that have too many detailed differences for them to be sensibly discussed together and an account of each follows.

In essence, for European protected species as listed in Schedule 2 to the **3.4.9** Regulations[213] (e.g. otters, wild cats, bats, dormice, great crested newts, turtles and cetaceans[214]), deliberately (and in Scotland recklessly) killing, capturing or disturbing any individual or taking their eggs is an offence. This list offers more protection than the 1981 Act in that it extends to deliberate disturbance of the animals in all circumstances, not just while using a place of rest or shelter.[215] The protection for breeding and resting places is also more extensive and the defences are much more restricted than under the 1981 Act, and now also includes protection through the application of the Environmental Liability Directive.[216] In practical terms, the most significant point following the recent changes is that developers and land managers whose activities may disturb relevant species (bats and great crested newts are perhaps the most frequently encountered) can only proceed if they have met the strict criteria and been granted a licence, rather than relying on the former, unduly broad, general defences.[217] The potential for these provisions to have an effect beyond direct criminal charges was shown in *R. v Cornwall County Council, ex p. Hardy*,[218] where planning permission for a landfill site was quashed because the environmental information considered during the environmental impact assessment of the proposal had not properly investigated the likelihood of disturbance to the roosting sites of bats. It is also an offence to keep, sell, offer for sale or exchange any of the protected species, alive or dead, or anything derived from them.

The Scottish provision makes it an offence deliberately or recklessly to do **3.4.10** the following[219]:

- capture, injure or kill a wild animal of a European protected species;
- harass an individual or group of such wild animals;

---

[211] CNHASR 2007. The Regulations for England and Wales also contain some provisions that apply to Scotland.

[212] CNHAR 2007; these contain some provisions that apply in Scotland.

[213] Schedule 2 lists those species specified in Annex IV(a) of the Habitats and Species Directive whose natural range includes any part of Great Britain; CNHR 1994 reg.38.

[214] See paras 3.4.38–3.4.40, below for the rules on whales and dolphins.

[215] Disturbance presumably includes causing injury to the animals, which is expressly covered by s.9 of the 1981 Act but not mentioned in the Regulations.

[216] Directive 2004/35/EC; see section 5.12, below.

[217] A. Ogley, "Taking Care of Protected Species – Meeting the Duty of 'Strict Protection' in England and Wales" [2008] J.P.L. 1547. Concern that the level of protection was excessive and standing in the way of useful activities led in June 2008 to the proposal under the "Ten-minute Rule" of the Protection of Bats and Newts Bill which would have allowed disturbance of bats and newts for various purposes (*Hansard*, HC Vol.478 col.155).

[218] *R. v Cornwall County Council, ex p. Hardy* [2001] Env. L.R. 25.

[219] CNHR 1994 reg.39(1) as replaced by CNHASR 2007 reg.10 and amended by Conservation (Natural Habitats, etc.) Amendment (No.2) (Scotland) Regulations 2008 (SSI 2008/425) reg.4.

- disturb it while it is rearing or caring for its young or occupying a structure or place used for shelter or protection[220];
- damage or destroy its breeding site or resting place or obstruct access to such a place or otherwise deny the animal use of it;
- take or destroy its eggs;
- disturb it while occupying its place of shelter or protection, rearing or caring for its young or migrating or hibernating;
- disturb it in a manner or in circumstances likely to significantly affect the local distribution or abundance of the species or to impair its ability to survive, breed or reproduce or otherwise care for its young.[221]

It is also a crime to possess or control, transport,[222] sell or exchange or offer to sell or exchange a live or dead specimen of, or anything derived from, any of the species listed in Annex IV(a) of the Habitats and Species Directive which has been taken from the wild.[223] It is also an offence to knowingly cause or permit any of the unlawful acts mentioned above.[224]

3.4.11   These offences do not apply to animals shown to be bred and lawfully held in captivity.[225] Defences also apply where an animal has been disabled (other than by the defendant's own act) and is taken or held for humane killing and disposal (other than by sale or exchange)[226] or for tending and releasing it,[227] provided that there was no satisfactory alternative to what was done and that the action is not detrimental to the maintenance of the population at a favourable conservation status in its natural range.[228] In relation to the possession and sale offences, it is a defence if it can be shown that the animal in question was lawfully taken from the wild,[229] unless it is a European protected species[230] being sold or exchanged or held for this purpose.[231] To be lawfully taken from the wild an animal must be taken without contravention of the local law; for specimens taken within the EU this defence does not cover actions after June 10, 1994[232] or the later date when the state became a member.[233] Certain local populations of animals are excluded from the possession and sale offences.[234] This is a much more

---

[220] It is not clear how this latter element and similar provisions would be applied to aquatic species.

[221] Any deliberate or reckless disturbance of a dolphin, porpoise or whale is an offence: CNHR 1994 reg.39(2) (see para.3.4.38, below).

[222] The possession, control and transport offences apply only to actions after May 1, 2007.

[223] CNHR 1994 reg.39(3), as amended.

[224] CNHR 1994 reg.39(10).

[225] CNHR 1994 reg.40(3).

[226] For this to apply the animal must be "seriously disabled" and have no reasonable chance of recovery; CNHR 1994 reg.40(1).

[227] CNHR 1994 reg.40(2).

[228] CNHR 1994 reg.40(4) inserted by Conservation (Natural Habitats, etc.) Amendment (No.2) (Scotland) Regulations 2008 (SSI 2008/425) reg.5.

[229] CNHR 1994 reg.39(6).

[230] Three other species (a moth, a butterfly and a lizard) are treated the same way in Scotland (reg.39(6)) but not in England and Wales.

[231] CNHR 1994 reg.39(7).

[232] The implementation date for the Directive.

[233] CNHR 1994 reg.39(8).

[234] CNHR 1994 reg.39(9) and Sch.2A; these include some non-naturally occurring populations.

restricted list of defences than applied prior to the amendments in 2007, and for any conduct beyond these a licence must be obtained, as described below, in order for actions to be lawful.

In England and Wales, there are a number of differences, mostly in the **3.4.12** phrasing of the law but with some substantive effects, most notably that the basic offences of killing and disturbing are limited to deliberate, not deliberate or reckless, conduct. It is an offence[235] deliberately to capture, injure or kill a wild animal of a European protected species, to take or destroy their eggs or to damage or destroy their breeding site or resting place.[236] It is also an offence[237] deliberately to disturb such animals in a way likely significantly to affect the local population or abundance or the ability of any significant group to survive, breed or rear or nurture their young.[238] It is also an offence to possess or control, transport, sell or exchange or offer to sell or exchange a live or dead specimen of, or anything derived from, any of the species listed in Annex IV(a) of the Habitats and Species Directive which has been taken from the wild.[239]

The defences for the tending or humane killing of disabled animals apply **3.4.13** in the same way as in Scotland[240] and the defences in relation to the possession and sale are virtually identical.[241] An additional defence exists, though, to provide that those who cause harm while involved in legitimate sea fishing operations are not to be taken as having acted deliberately even though they were aware that their action might cause such harm, so long as they did not intend that result.[242] In England and Wales further express provision is made for action taken to further the enforcement of the Regulations and related legislation, covering both possession and any injury involved in taking samples.[243] Again, licences can be obtained for actions not covered by this restricted list of defences.

In both jurisdictions licences to permit actions that are prohibited can be **3.4.14** obtained but are subject to strict restrictions.[244] Licences are normally available only for certain purposes, but licences for other purposes can be granted allowing the taking under strictly supervised conditions, on a selective basis and to a limited extent of limited numbers of specimens. Ministers can grant licences only after seeking and receiving advice from the

---

[235] CNHR reg.39(1), as amended by CNHAR 2007 reg.5(13).

[236] The Scottish regulations extend to obstructing or denying access to such sites; see para.3.4.10, above.

[237] CNHR 1994 reg.39(1) and (1A) amended by Conservation (Natural Habitats, etc.) (Amendment) (England and Wales) Regulations 2009 (SI 2009/6) reg.7.

[238] Guidance on the application of these offences to particular species or activities may be published by the Minister or the statutory conservation bodies and must be taken into account by the courts; CNHR reg.39(12) and (13) as amended by Conservation (Natural Habitats, etc.) (Amendment) (England and Wales) Regulations 2009 (SI 2009/6) reg.7.

[239] CNHR 1994 reg.39(2), as amended.

[240] CNHR 1994 reg.40(1)–(2) as amended by CNHAR 2007 reg.5(14) and Conservation (Natural Habitats, etc.) (Amendment) (England and Wales) Regulations 2009 (SI 2009/6) reg.8.

[241] CNHR 1994 reg.39(5)–(8).

[242] CNHR 1994 reg.39(14)–(16); under the general criminal law a person is held to have intentionally caused a result which is foreseen as a virtually certain consequence of their conduct, even though it was not the purpose of the action; *R. v Woollin* [1999] A.C. 82.

[243] CNHR 1994 reg.40(3)–(5).

[244] CNHR 1994 reg.44, as amended by CNHASR 2007 reg.15 and CNHAR 2007 reg.5(18).

statutory conservation bodies about when licences of that nature should be granted.[245] The purposes listed include scientific research, conservation, protection of property, crops, livestock and fisheries from serious damage, preserving public health or safety, preventing the spread of disease and:

> "[O]ther imperative reasons of overriding public interest including those of a social or economic nature and beneficial consequences of primary importance for the environment".

In all cases, though, a licence can be granted only where the relevant authority is satisfied that there is no satisfactory alternative and that the action authorised will not be detrimental to the maintenance of the population of the species concerned at a favourable conservation status in their natural range. This places a considerable hurdle in the way of those seeking a licence. Licences can be granted to individuals or to a class of persons and the licence must specify the species affected, the maximum number of specimens that can be taken and the methods to be used.[246] Breach of a licence condition is an offence,[247] as is making a false statement for the purposes of obtaining a licence.[248]

3.4.15   By limiting the exceptions, the recent amendments have cured many of the defects in the Regulations identified by the European Court of Justice,[249] and a further gap has been filled by the introduction of rules for the surveillance of habitats and species and for monitoring of the incidental capture and killing of certain species. In response to the European Commission's view that these new rules were not a wholly adequate response, further amendments were made to give them greater specificity and to emphasise their mandatory nature. Arrangements must be made for surveillance of the conservation status of the protected habitats and species[250] and for the monitoring of the incidental capture and killing of all the species listed in Annex IVA of the Habitats and Species Directive,[251] leading to further research or conservation measures to ensure that there is no significant negative impact on the species.[252]

3.4.16   There is also a further group of species, listed in Schedule 3 to the 1994

---

[245] In Scotland, CNHR 1994 reg.44(5), as amended by CNHASR 2007 reg.15; in England and Wales CNHR 1994 regs 44(5)–(6), as amended by Conservation (Natural Habitats, etc.) (Amendment) (England and Wales) Regulations 2009 (SI 2009/6) reg.11.

[246] CNHR 1994 reg.45.

[247] CNHR 1994 reg.46A, added by CNHASR 2007 reg.17 and CNHAR 2007 reg.5(21).

[248] CNHR 1994 reg.46.

[249] Although there are still some loose ends, e.g. the legal status of items whose sale was lawful under UK law by virtue of part of the original Regulations that were held not to be in accordance with EC law.

[250] CNHR 1994 reg.37A, in Scotland added by CNHSAR 2007 reg.9, amended by Conservation (Natural Habitats, etc.) Amendment (No.2) (Scotland) Regulations 2008 (SSI 2008/425) reg.3; in England and Wales, added by CNHAR 2007 reg.5(12), amended by Conservation (Natural Habitats, etc.) (Amendment) (England and Wales) Regulations 2009 (SI 2009/6) reg.5.

[251] Not just of those that are listed as European protected species.

[252] In Scotland, CNHR 1994 reg.41A, added by CHHASR 2007 reg.13, amended by Conservation (Natural Habitats, etc.) Amendment (No.2) (Scotland) Regulations 2008 (SSI 2008/425) reg.6; in England and Wales CNHR 1994 regs.41A and 41B, added by CNHAR 2007 reg.5(16), amended by Conservation (Natural Habitats, etc.) Amendment (England and Wales) Regulations 2009 (SI 2009/6) regs 9–10, which make express provision covering devolution to Wales.

Regulations (being those in Annex V of the Habitats and Species Directive whose natural range includes Great Britain).[253] These enjoy limited protection by virtue of restrictions on the ways in which they can be killed or taken or captured[254]; the same restrictions apply when any of the species listed in Schedule 2 may be taken or killed.[255] For the mammals listed (mountain hare, pine marten, polecat and several types of seals), the prohibited means are: live decoys that are blind or mutilated; tape recorders; electrical devices capable of killing or stunning; mirrors; devices for dazzling or for illuminating targets; night sights; explosives; non-selective nets or traps; crossbows; poison; gassing or smoking out; and automatic and semi-automatic weapons. For the fish (including Atlantic salmon whilst in fresh water), the prohibition is on poison and explosives. In all cases the use of any means which is indiscriminate and capable of causing the local disappearance of, or serious disturbance to, a population is prohibited, as is the use of aircraft and moving motor vehicles.

Provisions essentially the same as the English ones apply offshore, prohibiting the deliberate capture, killing or injuring of any of the species listed in Annex IVA of the Habitats and Species Directive, deliberate damage or destruction of their breeding sites or resting places and significant deliberate disturbance, as well as prohibiting the keeping, transporting, selling or exchanging of live or dead specimens or items derived from them.[256] The means by which European protected species (as listed in Schedule 1)[257] and those species listed in Schedule 3[258] can be killed or taken are also restricted as discussed above.[259] Incidental killing and capture of all Annex IV species must be monitored and action taken to ensure that there is not a significant negative impact on the species.[260] Furthermore, the conservation status of species of Community interest[261] must be kept under surveillance and steps taken to ensure that the exploitation of any species listed in Annex V to the Habitats and Species Directive, e.g. all seals and shad, is compatible with the species being maintained at a favourable conservation status.[262] **3.4.17**

---

[253] See Appendix A.

[254] For England and Wales the word "taking" was replaced with "capturing" by CNHAR 2007 reg.5(15).

[255] CNHR 1994 reg.41, as amended by CNHAR 2007 reg.15(5) and CNHASR 2007 reg.12 (curing defects identified in *Commission v United Kingdom* (C-6/04), para.3.4.8, above).

[256] Offshore Marine Conservation (Natural Habitats etc.) Regulations 2007 (SI 2007/1842) regs 39–40, amended by Offshore Marine Conservation (Natural Habitats, etc.) Regulations 2009 (SI 2009/7) regs 4–5.

[257] All cetaceans, common sturgeon and five species of marine turtle; Offshore Marine Conservation (Natural Habitats, etc.) Regulations 2007 Sch.1.

[258] All seals, the allis and twaite shad and all sturgeon (except the common sturgeon which is in Sch.1).

[259] Offshore Marine Conservation (Natural Habitats, etc.) Regulations 2007 reg.41.

[260] Offshore Marine Conservation (Natural Habitats, etc.) Regulations 2007 regs 46 and 47, amended by Offshore Marine Conservation (Natural Habitats, etc.) (Amendment) Regulations 2009 (SI 2009/7) regs 8 and 9.

[261] Listed in Annexes II, IV and V of the Habitats and Species Directive.

[262] Offshore Marine Conservation (Natural Habitats, etc.) Regulations 2007 regs 44–45, amended by Offshore Marine Conservation (Natural Habitats, etc.) (Amendment) Regulations 2009 (SI 2009/7) regs 6–7; express provision is made for consultation with the devolved authorities on these matters.

Cruelty

3.4.18 Laws against cruelty to animals have been in existence for a long time[263] but although new laws have recently been introduced, they still fall short of offering protection to all wild animals.[264] The main cruelty offences in the Animal Health and Welfare (Scotland) Act 2006 and the Animal Welfare Act 2006 apply only for the benefit of "protected animals", excluding most wildlife. Protected animals are those of a kind normally domesticated in the British Islands, or those under a person's control on a permanent or temporary basis or those not living in a wild state,[265] but "animal" is restricted to vertebrates (other than man) although with a provision for invertebrates to be included by regulations, provided that there is scientific evidence to show that they can experience pain and suffering.[266] The main offence is causing unnecessary suffering when it is known or ought reasonably to be known that this is a consequence of the act in question.[267] In England and Wales this offence extends to include suffering resulting from a failure to act,[268] whereas in Scotland that offence,[269] and in both jurisdictions the further offence of permitting another person to cause suffering, can be committed only by the "person responsible" for an animal,[270] namely its owner (at all times) or the person in charge of it or the person with actual care and control of someone under the age of 16 who is responsible for it.[271] Statutory guidance is given on the factors to consider in determining if suffering is "unnecessary"[272] and in England and Wales it is expressly provided that the offences do not cover anything done in the normal course of fishing.[273]

3.4.19 Wild animals falling outwith the 2006 provisions will also get protection, so long as they are mammals. Under the Wild Mammals (Protection) Act 1996 it is an offence for any person to mutilate, kick, beat, impale, stab, burn, stone, crush, drown, drag or asphyxiate any wild mammal with intent to inflict unnecessary suffering.[274] "Wild mammals" are defined as any that are not "protected animals" under the 2006 legislation, so that there is no

---

[263] Since the Cruel Treatment of Cattle Act 1822 in England and Wales and the Cruelty to Animals (Scotland) Act 1850 in Scotland.

[264] See generally M. Radford, *Animal Welfare Law in Britain: Regulation and Responsibility* (Oxford: OUP, 2001), esp. Chs 8–10; A. Stevenson, "Animals and the Scope of Anti-Cruelty Legislation" (1997) J.R. 12; S. Harrop, "The Dynamics of Wild Animal Welfare Law" (1997) 9 J.E.L. 287.

[265] This is a broader category than the domestic and captive animals that were covered by the previous legislation, viz. the Protection of Animals Act 1911 and Protection of Animals (Scotland) Act 1912.

[266] Animal Health and Welfare (Scotland) Act 2006 ss.16–17; Animal Welfare Act 2006 ss.1–2.

[267] Animal Health and Welfare (Scotland) Act 2006 s.19(1); Animal Welfare Act 2006 s.4(1).

[268] Animal Welfare Act 2006 s.4(1).

[269] Animal Health and Welfare (Scotland) Act 2006 s.19(2).

[270] Animal Health and Welfare (Scotland) Act 2006 s.19(3); Animal Welfare Act 2006 s.4(2).

[271] Animal Health and Welfare (Scotland) Act 2006 s.17; Animal Welfare Act 2006 s.2.

[272] Animal Health and Welfare (Scotland) Act 2006 s.19(4); Animal Welfare Act 2006 s.4(3).

[273] Animal Welfare Act 2006 s.59.

[274] Wild Mammals Act 1996 s.1; on a strict interpretation any other method of causing suffering will fall outwith the scope of this offence, and note that the intent to cause suffering must be shown.

opportunity for cases to fall into a gap between the two sets of rules.[275] There are exceptions to the general prohibition to allow for mercy killing, the swift and humane killing of mammals injured in lawful hunting or pest control activities, acts that are authorised by any statute and the results of any lawful hunting by trap, snare, bird or dog[276] or of the lawful use of poisons.[277] The law therefore does prohibit deliberate cruelty to mammals, but other forms of animal remain unprotected, although for birds, reasonable protection is offered by the wide provisions of the Wildlife and Countryside Act 1981, which penalise any intentional, and in Scotland reckless, injuring of birds.[278]

For instances outside these provisions, there is no direct legal protection **3.4.20** against cruel treatment, unless the animals have been included in one of the statutory lists of protected species or the case falls within the various prohibitions on cruel and indiscriminate means of hunting and killing. Nevertheless, inventive prosecutors can sometimes find a way to intervene. For example, before the recent changes to the law, criminal damage was used in the case of swans as a result of their peculiar status as property of the Queen,[279] and breach of the peace in Scotland when the use of a hedgehog as a football in a public place was held to meet the requirements of conduct likely to cause alarm, upset or annoyance or to provoke a disturbance of the peace.[280]

Bats

Bats are given full protection as European protected species[281] and the **3.4.21** changes that were made in 2007 to the 1994 Habitats Regulations have removed the need for the special provisions on bats that used to apply.[282] The exemption that used to permit some action to be taken against protected species within a dwelling house[283] was restricted in relation to bats to actions taken within the living area of such a house (thereby excluding any

---

[275] Wild Mammals Act 1996 s.3, amended by Animal Health and Welfare (Scotland) Act 2006 (Consequential Provisions) Order 2006 (SSI 2006/536) Sch.1 para.12; Animal Welfare Act 2006 Sch.3 para.13.

[276] The question of whether hunting with dogs should be prohibited on grounds of cruelty was, of course, a key issue in the debates leading to the anti-hunting legislation at the Westminster and Holyrood Parliaments; see para.4.4.17, below.

[277] Wild Mammals (Protection) Act 1996 s.2.

[278] See para.3.3.2, above.

[279] News report in *The Times*, August 19, 1993.

[280] News report *The Scotsman*, October 10, 1993; in England similar facts were expressly held to fall outwith the scope of the Protection of Animals Act 1911 because the hedgehog could not be held to be in captivity (*Hudnott v Campbell*, *The Times*, June 27, 1986—thanks to Mike Radford for this reference). These cases would now be covered by statute either because the animal is under sufficient control for the 2006 Acts to apply or through the application of the 1996 Act. In Scotland, see also *Dempster v Ruxton*, 1999 G.W.D. 1-24, where breach of the peace was used in relation to beating a fox to death.

[281] See *R. v Cornwall County Council, ex p. Hardy* [2001] Env. L.R. 25 (para.3.4.9, above) and *Re All Saints, Hough on the Hill*, *The Times*, January 31, 2002 in relation to consideration for the presence of bats in granting a faculty for installing floodlighting at a church.

[282] Bats are also protected by virtue of the Agreement on the Conservation of Populations of European Bats (EUROBATS) under which 30 states have agreed to take measures to further the conservation of bats; see the website of the EUROBATS Secretariat at *http://www.eurobats.org* [Accessed May 8, 2009].

[283] CNHR 1994 reg.40(2) and (3)(c), offering defences to reg.39.

loft or outbuilding, which are likely sites for roosting places) or taken after the relevant conservation body had been notified.[284] This special provision has now been repealed[285] and although the equivalent survives in the text of the 1981 Act,[286] it no longer has effect since bats have been removed from the list of protected species under that Act to avoid duplication with the 1994 Regulations.[287] A general licence in England permits the temporary possession and transport of dead bats for the purposes of the surveillance programme for bat rabies.[288]

Badgers

3.4.22 The badger is protected against being killed or taken by certain means under Schedule 6 to the Wildlife and Countryside Act 1981,[289] but receives more general protection under the Protection of Badgers Act 1992.[290] The structure and provisions of the 1992 Act are broadly similar to those for protected species under the 1981 Act, with generally-worded prohibitions on killing and taking being supported by provisions on possession and sale, and qualified by a number of defences, but the scope and, in particular, the wording of the two Acts differ so that where badgers are involved the precise wording of the 1992 Act must be carefully studied. Amendments have also introduced minor differences between the 1992 Act as it applies in Scotland and in England and Wales.[291]

3.4.23   It is an offence wilfully to kill, injure or take a badger, or to attempt to do so, otherwise than as permitted under the Act.[292] Moreover, the onus of proof is reversed in relation to this offence, in that where someone is charged with attempting to kill, injure or take a badger, and there is evidence from which it can reasonably be concluded that he was involved in such an attempt, he is presumed to have been so involved unless the contrary is shown.[293] It is also an offence[294] cruelly to ill-treat a badger, to use any badger tongs in the course of killing or taking a badger or attempting to do so, to use against badgers any firearm other than one of the specified size and power,[295] or to dig for badgers. In relation to digging for badgers, the onus of proof is again reversed, with evidence from which it could reasonably be concluded that a person was digging for a badger giving rise to a presumption that he was so doing unless the contrary is shown.[296]

---

[284] CNHR 1994 reg.40(4).
[285] CNHASR 2007 reg.11;CNHAR 2007 reg.5(14).
[286] WCA 1981 s.10(5).
[287] CNHASR 2007 reg.28; CNHAR 2007 reg.7(7).
[288] WML Gen-L04 (08/07); this licence is valid until 2032.
[289] See para.3.4.6, above.
[290] Consolidating the Badgers Act 1973, which had been amended on several occasions, the Badgers Act 1991 and the Badgers (Further Protection) Act 1991.
[291] The amendments for Scotland that are noted in this section were all made by NCSA 2004 Sch.6 para.26.
[292] Protection of Badgers Act 1992 s.1(1).
[293] Protection of Badgers Act 1992 s.1(2) (England and Wales) and s.11A (Scotland).
[294] Protection of Badgers Act 1992 s.2(1).
[295] A smooth bore weapon of not less than 20 bore or a rifle using ammunition having a muzzle energy of not less than 160 footpounds and a bullet weighing not less than 38 grains; Protection of Badgers Act 1992 s.2(1)(d).
[296] Protection of Badgers Act 1992 s.2(2).

These prohibitions designed to protect badgers are subject to a number of **3.4.24** exceptions.[297] They do not apply to a person taking or attempting to take a badger in order to tend it when it has been disabled otherwise than by his own act, nor to the killing or attempted killing of a badger appearing to be so seriously injured or in such a condition that killing it would be an act of mercy; for Scotland these provisions have been slightly amended to refer to badgers injured other than by the accused's *unlawful* act and tended with a view to release when no longer disabled and to badgers appearing so seriously disabled that there is no reasonable chance of recovery. The unavoidable killing or injuring of a badger as an incidental result of a lawful action and conduct authorised under the Animals (Scientific Procedures) Act 1986 are also exempt. Killing a badger, taking one or injuring one while attempting to kill or take it is not an offence if the accused can show that his conduct was necessary for the purpose of preventing serious damage to land, crops, poultry or other forms of property.[298] However, the benefit of this provision is not available if the need for such action became apparent beforehand unless an application for a licence authorising the action has been made and is still under consideration.[299]

In order to back up these offences, it is further provided that it is an **3.4.25** offence to have in one's possession or control a dead badger, or any part of one or anything derived from one.[300] This is an offence of strict liability, but specific defences are provided if it can be shown that the badger had not been killed or had been killed otherwise than in contravention of the Act or the Badgers Act 1973, or that the badger or other article had at some stage been sold in circumstances such that the purchaser had no reason to believe that the badger had been killed in contravention of the Acts.[301] A person commits a crime by selling or offering for sale a live badger, or by having one in his possession or under his control,[302] unless he has possession or control of it in the course of his business as a carrier, or unless it was disabled otherwise than by his own act and is being kept to be tended.[303] Ringing or otherwise marking a badger is also an offence unless a licence is obtained.[304]

Protection is extended to badger setts, defined for the purposes of the Act **3.4.26** as "any structure or place which displays signs indicating current use by a badger."[305] It is an offence intentionally or recklessly to interfere with a badger sett by damaging or destroying it, by obstructing access to it, by causing a dog to enter it or by disturbing a badger in occupation; in Scotland it is also an offence knowingly to cause or permit such acts.[306] In

---

[297] Protection of Badgers Act 1992 s.6, as amended.
[298] Protection of Badgers Act 1992 s.7(1).
[299] Protection of Badgers Act 1992 s.7(2).
[300] Protection of Badgers Act 1992 s.1(3).
[301] Protection of Badgers Act 1992 s.1(4).
[302] Protection of Badgers Act 1992 s.4.
[303] Protection of Badgers Act 1992 s.9; again reworded for Scotland as s.6 has been.
[304] Protection of Badgers Act 1992 s.5.
[305] Protection of Badgers Act 1992 s.14.
[306] Protection of Badgers Act 1992 s.3; the Scottish provision extends liability compared to the position in England, but compared to many other instances is limited by the requirement for knowledge in relation to both causing and permitting, whereas the more usual formula in many areas of environmental law is "to cause or knowingly permit".

Green v DPP[307] it was held that the ground above a badger sett did not fall within the scope of this offence, so that digging above a sett but without destabilising or damaging the tunnels or chambers was not in itself an offence.[308] A defence is provided for action necessary to prevent serious damage to land, crops, poultry or other forms of property,[309] provided that if the need for such action was known in advance a licence had been applied for and is still under consideration.[310] It is a defence that the conduct was the incidental result of a lawful operation and could not reasonably have been avoided,[311] but this does not apply to interference in the form of causing a dog to enter the sett or the destruction of the sett. It follows that a licence is required for the destruction of a sett, even if this is merely incidental to some lawful operation, e.g. development authorised by planning permission.[312] Further exceptions for actions connected with hunting foxes with hounds have been repealed as a consequence of the banning of such hunting.[313]

3.4.27 Licences authorising conduct prohibited under the Act are available from the statutory conservation bodies and the agriculture ministers. The bodies can grant licences in relation to any action taken for scientific or educational purposes, for the purpose of the conservation of badgers, for the purpose of zoological gardens, or for marking badgers. The bodies can also grant licences permitting interference with badger setts for the purposes of development authorised under the town and country planning legislation, for preserving scheduled ancient monuments[314] or carrying out archaeological investigations of them, and for investigations into any offence or for gathering evidence for any court proceedings.[315] Both the bodies and the Minister can grant licences to interfere with setts for the purpose of controlling foxes in order to protect livestock, game or wild life.[316]

3.4.28 The agriculture ministers can grant licences for the killing or taking of badgers in order to prevent the spread of disease[317] or to prevent serious damage to land, crops, poultry or other forms of property. Licences for interference with badger setts can be granted for the same purposes and for any agricultural or forestry operation or for drainage works.[318] The Minister must consult the appropriate conservation body on the exercise of his

---

[307] *Green v DPP* [2001] Env. L.R. 15.

[308] B. Martin, "Protecting badger setts after the *Green* case" [2003] J.P.L. 1098.

[309] Protection of Badgers Act 1992 s.8(1).

[310] Protection of Badgers Act 1992 s.8(2) applying s.7(2).

[311] Protection of Badgers Act 1992 s.8(3).

[312] Natural England granted 644 licences in 2005; data from the "Licensing Statistics" pages within the Wildlife Management and Licensing section of Natural England's website at *http://www.naturalengland.org.uk* [Accessed May 8, 2009].

[313] Protection of Badgers Act 1992 s.8(4)–(9), repealed by Protection of Wild Mammals (Scotland) Act 2002 para.5 of the Schedule and Hunting Act 2004 Sch.3 para.1.

[314] Under the Ancient Monuments and Archaeological Areas Act 1979.

[315] Protection of Badgers Act 1992 s.10(1).

[316] Protection of Badgers Act 1992 s.10(3).

[317] On the controversial issue of badgers and the spread of bovine tuberculosis, see the House of Commons Environment, Food and Rural Affairs Committee, *Badgers and Cattle TB: The final report of the Independent Scientific Group on Bovine TB*, 4th Report of 2007–08, HC Paper No.130 (Session 2007–2008), the statement and discussion in the Welsh Assembly on April 8, 2008 on the TB Eradication Programme which calls for some culling (Record of proceedings, p.53), and the press release from DEFRA against badger culling in England (*Plans for vaccines to fight Bovine TB*: ref.213/08 of July 7, 2008).

[318] Protection of Badgers Act 1992 s.10(2).

functions under this provision and must not grant a licence unless he has received the body's general advice of the circumstances in which such licences should be granted.[319] In Scotland this provision is restricted to licences granted for the protection of land and property[320]; in England and Wales it extends to licences granted for any of the above purposes except for preventing the spread of disease.[321]

3.4.29 Licences can be revoked at any time by the authority which granted them,[322] but are not to be unreasonably withheld or revoked.[323] Action authorised under a licence cannot constitute an offence under the general restrictions on the placing of poison,[324] but failure to adhere to the conditions in a licence is itself an offence, regardless of any other liability.[325]

3.4.30 A number of provisions exist to assist in the enforcement of the law protecting badgers. Anyone found on any land committing an offence of killing, injuring or taking a badger or in possession of a dead badger can be required to leave the land by the owner or occupier (or their servants), or by a constable and required to give his full name and address. Wilful refusal to comply with these requirements is an offence.[326] The police are also given powers to stop and search suspected offenders, to arrest them and to seize anything which may be evidence of the commission of an offence.[327] The power of seizure extends to articles liable to forfeit under the further provisions which state that on conviction the court shall order the forfeiture of any badger or skin which was the subject of the offence and may order the forfeiture of any weapon or item used in the commission of the offence.[328] Further provisions authorise the destruction or disposal of any dog used in committing an offence and the disqualification of the offender from having custody of a dog[329] and extend the normal period for commencing summary prosecutions.[330] Further adjustments to the law in Scotland allow some offences to be punished with imprisonment,[331] and provide for the personal liability of directors, managers and partners where an offence is committed by a company, partnership or unincorporated association.[332]

3.4.31 The law has also had a role in relation to badgers in a different way. In *R. v Cresswell*,[333] opponents of badger culling took direct action against traps set as part of a DEFRA programme investigating methods of controlling bovine tuberculosis.[334] The accused were convicted of criminal

---

[319] Protection of Badgers Act 1992 s.10(6).
[320] Protection of Badgers Act 1992 s.10(7).
[321] Protection of Badgers Act 1992 s.10(6).
[322] Protection of Badgers Act 1992 s.10(8).
[323] Protection of Badgers Act 1992 s.10(9).
[324] Protection of Badgers Act 1992 s.10(10), referring to Protection of Animals Act 1911 s.8, and Protection of Animals (Scotland) Act 1912 s.7; see para.4.4.3, below.
[325] Protection of Badgers Act 1992 s.10(8).
[326] Protection of Badgers Act 1992 s.1(5).
[327] Protection of Badgers Act 1992 s.11; there are different versions for Scotland and for England and Wales.
[328] Protection of Badgers Act 1992 s.12(4).
[329] Protection of Badgers Act 1992 s.13.
[330] Protection of Badgers Act 1992 s.12ZA, added by NERCA 2006 Sch.6 para.6, and s.12A.
[331] Protection of Badgers Act 1992 s.12(1A).
[332] Protection of Badgers Act 1992 s.12B.
[333] *R. v Cresswell* [2006] EWHC 3379 (Admin).
[334] See the press release from DEFRA against badger culling in England (*Plans for vaccines to fight Bovine TB*: ref.213/08 of July 7, 2008).

damage under the Criminal Damage Act 1971 being unable to bring their actions within the defences of acting to protect property (seeking to protect the badgers attracted to the traps could not be considered since they were not the property of DEFRA until they were actually caught) or to prevent crime (Crown immunity meant that DEFRA's actions were not illegal).

Seals

3.4.32 The Conservation of Seals Act 1970 offers legal protection to seals in a number of ways.[335] As usual, though, there are a number of exceptions and the possibility of licences being granted to authorise for certain purposes action which is normally prohibited.

3.4.33 In the first place, there is a prohibition on the use of poison of any sort for killing or taking seals, and it is an offence to use firearms other than those of prescribed power to kill, injure or take a seal.[336] The possession of poison or prohibited firearms or ammunition with intent to kill or take a seal is itself an offence.[337] The rules restricting the means of killing do not apply to a person's mercy killing of a seal so seriously disabled that it has no reasonable chance of recovery, provided that it was not his own act that disabled it in the first place.[338] Seals are further protected under Schedule 3 to both the Conservation (Natural Habitats, etc.) Regulations 1994[339] and to the Offshore Marine Conservation (Natural Habitats, etc.) Regulations 2007[340] which protect them from all indiscriminate methods by which they can be killed or captured and from methods that can seriously disturb local populations.[341] These measures follow the listing of seals in Annex V of the Habitats and Species Directive, which additionally means that their conservation status must be kept under review and any exploitation is compatible with their being maintained at a favourable conservation status.[342]

3.4.34 A close season is laid down for both species of seal found in British waters and it is an offence wilfully to kill, injure or take a seal during the close seasons. For grey seals the close season is September 1–December 31, for common seals June 1–August 31.[343] The effect of these close seasons can be extended by orders made by the Minister where it appears necessary for the proper conservation of seals. Such orders can apply to specific areas and to either or both species,[344] and in practice greatly extend the protection offered to seals. Currently there is a prohibition on killing, injuring or taking

---

[335] See generally D. McGillivray, "Seal Conservation Legislation in the UK – Past, Present, Future" (1995) Int. J. of Marine and Coastal Law 19.

[336] Conservation of Seals Act 1970 s.1; the permitted firearms are rifles using ammunition of muzzle energy of not less than 600 footpounds and bullets weighing not less than 45 grains; the Minister can amend this prescription by statutory instrument (Conservation of Seals Act 1970 s.1(2)).

[337] Conservation of Seals Act 1970 s.8(2).

[338] Conservation of Seals Act 1970 s.9(2).

[339] SI 1994/2716.

[340] SI 2007/1842.

[341] CNHR 1994 reg.41, amended by CNHAR 2007 reg.5(15) and CNHASR 2007 reg.12; Offshore Marine Conservation (Natural Habitats, etc.) Regulations 2007 reg.41; see para.3.4.16, above.

[342] Habitats and Species Directive arts 11 and 14(1); see paras 7.4.37–7.4.40, below.

[343] Conservation of Seals Act 1970 s.2.

[344] Conservation of Seals Act 1970 s.3. This power has been used to impose far-reaching temporary restrictions during epidemics of phocine distemper affecting seal populations.

either species of seal on the North Sea coast of England[345] and in the Moray Firth[346] and common seals around Orkney and Shetland and on part of the east coast of Scotland.[347]

A number of defences are available. No offence is committed by the **3.4.35** taking of a disabled seal in order to tend it (provided that the tender did not cause the injury), by a mercy killing, by the unavoidable killing or injuring of a seal as an incidental result of a lawful action, or by the killing or injuring of a seal in order to prevent damage to a fishing net or tackle, or to fish which are in a net.[348] This last defence is available only to the person in possession of the equipment or someone acting at his request and only when the seal is in the vicinity of the fishing net or tackle, but there is no definition of "vicinity" and this was a key factor in the acquittal of a fisherman charged with killing seals allegedly some distance from his nets, a decision that provoked considerable criticism from conservation groups.[349] It does not allow those seeking to reduce competition for fish stocks to kill seals which are not immediately threatening fishery operations. The operation of this defence in relation to fish farms is controversial, although the Scottish Government has stated its view that it cannot be used by those operating fish farms, since the nets and cages at a fish farm are not "fishing nets or tackle".[350]

Licences may be granted by the Minister for a number of purposes **3.4.36** authorising the killing or taking of seals,[351] but in no case can the use of strychnine be authorised,[352] nor any other method that contravenes the restrictions on the use of indiscriminate methods in the Habitats and Species Directive.[353] The licences can be granted for scientific or educational purposes, for the purposes of a zoo or other collection, for the prevention of damage to fisheries,[354] for the reduction of a population surplus of seals either for management purposes or to use them as a resource, or for the protection of flora or fauna in nature reserves, marine nature reserves, SSSIs and in Scotland land protected by a Nature Conservation or Land

---

[345] Conservation of Seals (England) Order 1999 (SI 1999/3052).

[346] Conservation of Seals (Scotland) Order 2004 (SSI 2004/283).

[347] The area covered is from Garron Point to Torness Point (just north of Stonehaven to south of Dunbar); Conservation of Seals (Scotland) Order 2007 (SSI 2007/126).

[348] Conservation of Seals Act 1970 s.9.

[349] See *Dundee Courier*, August 4, 2007.

[350] See Legislative Matrix on the Management of Scottish Seal Populations, available at *http://www.scotland.gov.uk/Topics/Environment/Wildlife-Habitats/19887/22437* [Accessed May 8, 2009]; see also W. Howarth, *The Law of Aquaculture* (Oxford: Fishing News Books, 1990), pp.149–152.

[351] Conservation of Seals Act 1970 s.10, amended by WCA 1981 Sch.7 para.7.

[352] Conservation of Seals Act 1970 s.10(1).

[353] Conservation of Seals Act 1970 s.10(4A) and (6), added by CNHAR 2007 reg.6(62) and CNHASR 2007 reg.26. These amendments follow the conclusion of the European Court of Justice that the relationship between the limits on methods in the 1970 Act and 1994 Regulations implementing the Directive contained an element of legal uncertainty amounting to incorrect transposition of art.15 of the Directive; *Commission v UK* (C-6/04) [2005] E.C.R. I-9017, [99]–[105].

[354] The Scottish Government takes the view that fish farms do not qualify as "fisheries" for the is purpose; see Legislative Matrix on the Management of Scottish Seal Populations, available at *http://www.scotland.gov.uk/Topics/Environment/Wildlife-Habitats/19887/22437* [Accessed May 8, 2009].

Management Order.[355] Before granting licences, the Minister is to consult with the Natural Environment Research Council, and he must have the consent of the relevant statutory conservation body before granting a licence for the areas listed above.[356] Contravening the conditions in a licence is itself an offence, regardless of other liabilities.[357]

3.4.37   In order to assist in the enforcement of the Act and to allow any authorised culling to take place, there are provisions for powers of entry,[358] for powers of arrest, search and seizure,[359] for the forfeiture of unlawfully taken seals or sealskin and of firearms, etc. used in committing offences,[360] and provisions regulating the jurisdiction of courts where offences are committed on the coast or at sea.[361] The Natural Environment Research Council is to provide the Minister with scientific advice on the management of seal populations.[362]

Whales and other Cetaceans

3.4.38 All species of whales, dolphins and porpoises are given protection as European protected species[363] and it is also an offence deliberately or recklessly to disturb any such creature.[364] With a view to preventing such disturbance arising from the growing interest in whale-watching, in Scotland SNH is obliged to prepare and issue the Scottish Marine Wildlife Watching Code.[365]

3.4.39   Hunting whales and related species has been banned around Britain for a long time and the catching of all species of cetacean, or their treatment once caught, is prohibited within the coastal waters of the United Kingdom.[366] In Scotland it is also an offence to drive ashore any of the smaller types of whale commonly known as bottlenose or pilot whales.[367] Wider legislative controls on whaling remain in place[368] and any British ship involved in the catching or treatment of whales or any factory treating whales or producing whale oil must have a licence from the Minister, and no such licences are currently in force. However, the Minister may issue permits granting exemptions from these provisions for scientific or other exceptional purposes.[369]

---

[355] Conservation of Seals Act 1970 s.10(4), amended by CRWA 2000 Sch.16 Pt III and NCSA 2004 Sch.7 para.3.

[356] Conservation of Seals Act 1970 s.10(3).

[357] Conservation of Seals Act 1970 s.10(2).

[358] Conservation of Seals Act 1970 s.11.

[359] Conservation of Seals Act 1970 s.4, amended for England and Wales by the Police and Criminal Evidence Act 1984 Sch.7 Pt I.

[360] Conservation of Seals Act 1970 s.6.

[361] Conservation of Seals Act 1970 s.7; the Act also extends the standard period for initiating a prosecution in England and Wales (Conservation of Seals Act 1970 s.5(3)–(6), added by NERCA 2006 Sch.6 para.2).

[362] Conservation of Seals Act 1970 s.13.

[363] See paras 3.4.7–3.4.17, above.

[364] In Scotland under CNHR 1994 reg.39, as substituted by CNHASR 2007 reg.10; in England and Wales under WCA 1981 s.9(4A), added by CRWA 2000 Sch.5 para.12, amended by CNHAR 2007 reg.7(7).

[365] NCSA 2004 s.51. The Code is available at *http://www.marinecode.org* [Accessed May 8, 2009], as well as *A Guide to Best Practice for Watching Marine Wildlife*.

[366] Whaling Industry (Regulation) Act 1934 ss.1 and 2 (amended by the Fisheries Act 1981 s.35).

[367] Fisheries Act 1981 s.36.

[368] Fisheries Act 1981 s.4.

[369] Fisheries Act 1981 s.7.

Around Britain a more immediate threat is posed by the incidental effects **3.4.40** of fishing activity directed at other species and this is now subject to express controls.[370] Certain fishing operations are lawful only if active acoustic deterrent devices are used, the use of certain driftnets was banned from the beginning of 2008 and a system of on-board observers established.[371] More specific control measures have been called for and following the refusal of the UK's request for measures at an EC level in relation to the risks posed by pair trawling for bass in the Western Channel, more local measures[372] were introduced and survived a legal challenge arguing that they were unreasonable since as a result of displacing fishing activity they might increase rather than decrease the risk.[373]

Fish

Fish do not have the same place in the public's affection as seals and whales **3.4.41** and the hunting of fish is still widely accepted as a legitimate pastime, as well as a commercial activity. The protection of fish has thus attracted considerably less attention than that devoted to marine mammals, but the law has not ignored fish. Fish can benefit directly from the more general legislation on nature conservation, and a few species of fish are protected under Schedule 5 to the Wildlife and Countryside Act 1981.[374] The sturgeon is a European protected species under the 1994 Regulations,[375] while several species are listed in Schedule 3 to those Regulations and therefore benefit from the express prohibition on the use of poison and explosives,[376] although these are already outlawed by more general fisheries measures. The basking shark is given additional protection by the introduction of a specific provision making it an offence intentionally or recklessly to disturb, or in Scotland disturb or harass, individuals.[377]

Nonetheless, the majority of legislation dealing with fish is designed to **3.4.42** regulate the exploitation of fish stocks and is discussed in Chapter 4. The law on fishing, as well as trying to regulate the catching of certain species so as protect future stocks, can have incidental benefits for the conservation of aquatic fauna. The restrictions on when and how fishing can take place serve to provide some protection for fish and aquatic animals generally. In particular, the prohibitions on the use of indiscriminate and destructive methods of fishing, such as electric devices and poison, will obviously benefit all

---

[370] In addition, surveillance of incidental killing is required as a result of cetaceans' status as European protected species and addressing the bycatch of small cetaceans is required under ASCOBANS; see para.7.5.28.

[371] EC Regulation 812/2004, amended by Reg.809/2007 art.2; enforced through the Incidental Catches of Cetaceans in Fisheries (England) Order 2005 (SI 2005/17) and Prevention and Monitoring of Cetacean Bycatch (Scotland) Order 2005 (SSI 2005/330); there appears to be no equivalent enforcement measure for Wales.

[372] Within the 12-mile limit, where the Common Fisheries Policy allows the coastal state to impose controls.

[373] South-west Territorial Waters (Prohibition of Pair Trawling) Order 2004 (SI 2004/3397); *Greenpeace Ltd v Secretary of State for the Environment, Food and Rural Affairs* [2005] EWHC 2144 (Admin); [2006] Env. L.R. 19.

[374] See para.3.4.2, above.

[375] See paras 3.4.7–3.4.17, above.

[376] See para.3.4.16, above.

[377] WCA 1981 s.9(4A), added by CRWA 2000 Sch.12 para.5 and NCSA 2004 Sch.6 para.8.

forms of aquatic life.[378] Moreover, the value of waters for fishing can provide a strong incentive for their retention in an unpolluted state, to the benefit of animal and plant life generally.[379]

---

[378] See paras 4.3.10–4.3.16, below.
[379] e.g. the effect of the Shellfish Waters Directive (79/923/EEC).

4. EXPLOITATION AND DESTRUCTION OF WILDLIFE

Animals and birds have been hunted for food since the beginning of human **4.1.1**
existence, and more recently for sport.[1] It was in order to protect wildlife for
such purposes that the first laws affecting them were made, and the law
regulating hunting and fishing continues to play a major role in controlling
what can be done to wildlife. It therefore deserves to be considered in a book
on nature conservation. An account of the full complexities of the law in this
field, especially in relation to administration and detailed control of fishing,
inland and marine, would take this book beyond reasonable size, and what
follows is a brief guide, with an emphasis on those parts of the law which
may have most impact on nature conservation. Fuller accounts exist of the
law on game and inland fisheries, but unfortunately it is much harder to
keep track of the ever-changing mass of legislation, national and European,
on offshore fishing.[2]

Although the law dealt with in this Chapter is designed to allow the killing **4.1.2**
and taking of wildlife, it may be of considerable benefit to nature conservation. It was in order to preserve deer for royal hunting that areas of
forest were shut off from agricultural or commercial forestry use, with
lasting benefits to many forms of plant and animal life. The law stipulating
close seasons, etc. seeks at least to ensure that the species concerned are not
exterminated, albeit with a view only to their future exploitation, and other
controls may serve to limit the likelihood of harm afflicting species other
then the intended targets. On a more practical level, the economic potential
of shooting rights, etc. may help to prevent areas of "natural" countryside
being destroyed by other forms of exploitation. Moreover, the offences
created to punish those hunting particular species by unauthorised means, in
unauthorised places or at unauthorised times may also offer a means of
taking action against those engaged in activities which are harmful to other
species, e.g. the likelihood of game being caught might allow the game laws
to be invoked against those using nets to catch wildlife, even though game
was not their intended target. By acquiring, but then not exercising, game
rights over land those interested in nature conservation may be able to
achieve a degree of protection for some species in the area, otherwise possible only at the expense of acquiring the land itself.

The legal provisions requiring the destruction of animals are not so likely **4.1.3**
to produce such incidental benefits. Some pest control measures may be of
benefit to other species, but generally the significance of the law lies not in
any potential benefits for nature conservation, but in the ways in which it
can conflict with and even override other measures adopted to further
conservation, e.g. requiring the destruction of wild animals even within
nature reserves.

This Chapter is organised in an attempt to bring some order to a very **4.1.4**

---

[1] "More recent" is a comparative term, for example it is in the latter context that hunting
laws were proposed by Plato in *The Laws* 7.827.
[2] See paras 4.3.14–4.3.16, below.

fragmented area of law. First the law on hunting, shooting and fishing is considered for its effect in regulating who is permitted to kill or take wildlife and in what circumstances. Then the various provisions affecting the methods which can be used for killing and catching animals are considered. Finally the law requiring or permitting the destruction of wildlife is examined.

HUNTING AND SHOOTING

Game Laws

4.2.1　Although the broad objectives and basic structure of the law of game are the same in Scotland and in England and Wales, there are many differences of considerable importance,[3] including the recent abolition of game licences in England and Wales.[4] The law is further complicated by the existence of a number of overlapping provisions. One initial problem common to both jurisdictions is the absence of clear and consistent definitions of what is meant by "game".

The Meaning of "Game"

4.2.2　There is no single definition of "game" in either Scotland or England and Wales. Different statutes provide their own definitions, definitions which themselves give rise to doubts since they usually state that game "includes" the species which are listed rather than offering a complete definition.[5] In both jurisdictions it is clear that the term "ground game" refers to hares and rabbits only,[6] but the broader position is less clear. As a common core, though, it can be said that the following will be regarded as game in virtually all circumstances: hares, pheasants, partridges, grouse, heath or moor game and black game.[7]

4.2.3　　The position in Scotland is particularly complex. The Game (Scotland) Act 1772 contains provisions affecting hares, partridges, pheasants, muir fowl, tarmagans (ptarmigan), heath fowl and snipe.[8] The Night Poaching Act 1828 defines "game" as including the species listed in the core definition given above, with the addition of bustards,[9] and also applies to rabbits.[10] The Game (Scotland) Act 1832 applies to game, woodcock, snipe, wild ducks and conies (rabbits); no definition of "game" is given, but that in the

---

[3] See generally, S. Scott Robinson, *The Law of Game, Salmon and Freshwater Fishing in Scotland* (Edinburgh: Butterworths / Law Society of Scotland, 1990); W. Gordon, *Scottish Land Law*, 2nd edn (Edinburgh: W. Green, 1999), Ch.9; A. Nicol, "Hunting and Shooting" in J. Rowan-Robinson and D. McKenzie Skene (eds), *Countryside Law in Scotland* (Edinburgh: T&T Clark, 2000); C. Parkes and J. Thornley, *Fair Game: The Law of Country Sports and the Protection of Wildlife* (New Revised edn) (London: Pelham Books, 1997).

[4] See para.4.2.7, below; major reform of the game laws in Scotland is proposed in the consultation on a Wildlife and Natural Environment Bill launched in June 2009.

[5] For a discussion of the definition in relation to an indenture of land, see *Inglewood Investment Co Ltd v Forestry Commission* [1988] 1 W.L.R. 959.

[6] Ground Game Act 1880 s.8.

[7] Heath, moor and black game are terms covering the red and black grouse and ptarmigan.

[8] Game (Scotland) Act 1772 ss.1 and 3.

[9] Night Poaching Act 1828 s.13.

[10] Night Poaching Act 1828 s.1.

1828 Act is generally accepted to apply here.[11] It has also been held that capercaillie are game for the purposes of the 1832 Act, but it is now a protected species.[12] The Game Licences Act 1860 requires a licence for hunting game (again the 1828 definition is accepted in the absence of a definition in the Act),[13] woodcock, snipe, rabbits and deer.[14] For the Poaching Prevention Act 1862, game includes the species in the core definition above, the eggs of the birds listed there, woodcock, snipe and rabbits.[15] Only deer, pheasants, partridges, grouse and black game qualify as game for the purpose of compensating agricultural tenants for damage caused by game[16]; the control of rabbits and hares lies within the hands of the tenants.[17]

In England and Wales, the core definition noted above is the one which **4.2.4** appears in the Game Act 1831.[18] The Night Poaching Act 1828 includes bustards within the definition,[19] and the Poaching Prevention Act 1862 applies to the core species and to rabbits, woodcock, snipe and the eggs of the birds in the core definition.[20] The Game Licences Act 1860 required a licence for the hunting of game (undefined, but probably the core definition with the inclusion of bustards as in the 1828 Act) and of deer, rabbits, woodcock and snipe.[21]

Game birds are excluded from the provisions of Part I of the Wildlife and **4.2.5** Countryside Act 1981 which give protection to wild birds, and are defined for that purpose as pheasant, partridge, grouse (or moor game), black (or heath) game or ptarmigan.[22] The other species of wildfowl (ducks and geese) which are hunted do fall within the 1981 Act and their hunting is regulated by the provisions there.[23]

---

[11] Scott-Robinson, *The Law of Game, Salmon and Freshwater Fishing in Scotland* (1990), p.9; deer were originally included in the 1832 Act but removed by the Deer (Scotland) Act 1959 Sch.3.

[12] *Colquhoun's Trs v Lee*, 1957 S.L.T. (Sh. Ct) 50; the status of the capercaillie is complicated by the fact that it became extinct in Britain during the second half of the eighteenth century, but it was reintroduced to Scotland from Sweden in 1837. The legal status of the capercaillie changed when it was given protection under WCA 1981 Sch.1 by the Wildlife and Countryside Act 1981 (Amendment) (Scotland) Regulations 2001 (SSI 2001/337).

[13] Scott Robinson, *The Law of Game, Salmon and Freshwater Fishing in Scotland* (1990), p.14.

[14] Game Licences Act 1860 ss.2 and 4.

[15] Poaching Prevention Act 1862 s.1.

[16] Agricultural Holdings (Scotland) Act 1991 s.53; the equivalent English legislation no longer refers to "damage from game" but to "damage from wild animals or birds the right to kill and take which is vested in the landlord or anyone (other than the tenant himself) claiming under the landlord" (Agricultural Holdings Act 1986 s.20).

[17] Ground Game Act 1880; see para.4.2.8, below.

[18] Game Act 1831 s.2.

[19] Night Poaching Act 1828 s.13.

[20] Poaching Prevention Act 1862 s.1.

[21] Game Licences Act 1860 ss.2 and 4. The 1860 Act has been repealed for England and Wales by the Regulatory Reform (Game) Order 2007 (SI 2007/2007) art.3.

[22] WCA 1981 s.27.

[23] See para.4.2.15, below.

Killing and Taking Game

4.2.6 The right to take and kill game is one of the incidents of the ownership of land. The animals and birds themselves are *res nullius*, capable of appropriation by anyone who can take them, but no one has the right to enter land to take game in the absence of permission from the owner. This position at common law is backed up by a large number of statutory provisions creating offences relating to trespass in pursuit of game. The right to take game may, however, be severed from other rights in the land and is frequently the subject of a separate lease or is reserved, for his own use or for separate leasing, when the proprietor allows a tenant to occupy the land.[24] The particular extent of the rights granted or reserved, and other matters relating to the management of the land, will depend on the terms of individual agreements.[25] Where land is held by a public authority, statutory controls may constrain the wide discretion the landowner normally has over the exercise of game rights.[26]

4.2.7 The holder of the right to take game is entitled to access to the land to exercise his right, and can authorise other people to exercise the right with him or in his stead. Until August 2007 those involved in killing or taking game, deer, woodcock and snipe throughout Great Britain required a game licence under the Game Licences Act 1860,[27] but this requirement now applies in Scotland only.[28] A number of exceptions exist including: the taking of woodcock by nets or springes; the hunting of hares with hounds[29]; the taking of rabbits on enclosed land by or with the permission of the proprietor or tenant; and the taking or killing of deer in enclosed lands by or with the permission of the owner or occupier.[30] No licence is required for the killing of hares by the owner or occupier of the land,[31] and the law also provides that members of the Royal Family and gamekeepers appointed by the Queen are exempt from the licensing requirements.[32] When someone is discovered doing acts requiring a licence, the licence must be displayed on request from an HMRC officer, gamekeeper, owner or occupier of the land or the holder of a game licence.[33] A licence is valid for any part of the country unless it has been taken out solely in a person's capacity as a gamekeeper.[34]

---

[24] In Scotland game rights can in some circumstances form a separate tenement; Abolition of Feudal Tenure etc. (Scotland) Act 2000 s.65A, added by Title Conditions (Scotland) Act 2003 s.114(5).

[25] See, e.g. *Re Wildfowl Trust (Holdings) Ltd* Unreported January 19, 1994, Outer House, on the relationship between the game rights reserved in a lease, the tenant's statutory rights and licences granted under the Wildlife and Countryside Act 1981.

[26] *R. v Somerset County Council, ex p. Fewings* [1995] 1 W.L.R. 1037; *R. v Sefton Metropolitan Borough Council, ex p. British Association of Shooting and Conservation Ltd* [2001] Env. L.R. 10.

[27] Game Licences Act 1860 s.4 (amended by Protection of Birds Act 1954 Sch.6).

[28] Game Licences Act 1860 ss.2 and 4. The 1860 Act has been repealed for England and Wales by the Regulatory Reform (Game) Order 2007 (SI 2007/2007) art.3.

[29] Hunting with dogs is now subject to separate controls under the Protection of Wild Mammals (Scotland) Act 2002 and the Hunting Act 2004.

[30] Game Licenses Act 1860 s.5; for deer see paras 4.2.16–4.2.29, below.

[31] Game Licenses Act 1860 s.5; this exception applies to those authorised under the provisions the Hares (Scotland) Act 1848 s.1.

[32] Game Licenses Act 1860 s.5.

[33] Game Licenses Act 1860 s.10.

[34] Game Licenses Act 1860 s.18.

The occupier of land does however have the right to take and kill ground **4.2.8** game (i.e. rabbits and hares) on his land.[35] This right is inseparable from the occupation of the land but may be exercised only by the occupier and those authorised by him in writing. Only the occupier and one other person (who must fall within certain categories) are allowed to use firearms. Even in Scotland, no game licence is required for the exercise of this right.[36]

The licensing requirements in the sale of game have also been repealed in **4.2.9** England and Wales but continue in Scotland, where a dealer in game must obtain both a licence from the local authority[37] and an excise licence.[38] The specific hygiene provisions that used to apply to game[39] have now been incorporated into the more general legislation.[40]

Close Seasons and Methods of Taking

The taking and killing of game is prohibited during the close seasons. A **4.2.10** table showing the open seasons for game appears below.[41] In England the taking or killing of game on Sundays and on Christmas Day is prohibited[42] but no such legal prohibition applies to game in Scotland.[43] There is no close season on the killing of rabbits and hares, although rights under the Ground Game Act 1880 may be exercised on open moorland and unenclosed land in England and Wales only between September 1–March 31, with the use of firearms permitted only between December 11–March 31 unless all interested parties agree to waive this further restriction.[44] In Scotland such rights may be exercised all year, but the use of firearms is not permitted in April, May or June.[45] The close seasons do not apply in Scotland to the taking of pheasants and partridges for breeding purposes.[46] The means by which it is permissible to kill and take game are dealt with later.[47]

Close seasons also apply to the sale of game, but again these have been **4.2.11** affected by the recent changes in England and Wales. It is now in Scotland only that game birds cannot lawfully be bought or sold 10 days after the start of their close seasons.[48] Throughout Great Britain the sale of indigenous hares is prohibited in the months of March, April, May, June and July.[49]

---

[35] Ground Game Act 1880 s.1.

[36] Ground Game Act 1880 s.4.

[37] Game Act 1831 s.18, extended to apply to Scotland by Game Licences Act 1860 s.13.

[38] Game Licences Act 1860 s.14.

[39] Wild Game Meat (Hygiene and Inspection) Regulations 1995 (SI 1995/2148), repealed by the Food Hygiene (England) Regulations 2005 (SI 2005/2059), Food Hygiene (Wales) Regulations 2005 (SI 2005/3292) and the Food Hygiene (Scotland) Regulations 2005 (SSI 2005/505).

[40] Food Hygiene (England) Regulations 2006 (SI 2006/14); Food Hygiene (Wales) Regulations 2006 (SI 2006/31); Food Hygiene (Scotland) Regulations 2006 (SSI 2006/3).

[41] See Appendix B.

[42] Game Act 1831 s.3.

[43] See Parkes and Thornley, *Fair Game: The Law of Country Sports and the Protection of Wildlife* (New Revised edn) (1997), p.58; cf. the position for wildfowl, para.4.2.15, below.

[44] Ground Game Act 1880 s.1(2); Ground Game Act 1906 ss.1 and 2.

[45] Ground Game Act 1880 s.1(2) (amended by Agriculture (Scotland) Act 1948 s.48).

[46] Game (Scotland) Act 1772 s.2.

[47] See section 4.4, below.

[48] Game Act 1831 s.4 (amended by Game Act 1970 s.1).

[49] Hares Preservation Act 1892 s.2.

Poaching

4.2.12 It is a criminal offence unlawfully to take or kill game or rabbits at night,[50] to enter land with any gun, net or other instrument in pursuit of game at night,[51] or trespass in pursuit of game, woodcock, snipe or rabbits during the day.[52] Greater penalties are incurred if at night there are three or more offenders or they are armed,[53] and by day if there are five or more offenders or (in Scotland only) if the offender has a blackened or otherwise disguised face.[54] These provisions do not apply to those hunting with hounds for hares, foxes or (in England and Wales only) deer,[55] although such hunting is now subject to other restrictions.[56] In England and Wales it is also an offence for a person without the right to take game, to remove or destroy the eggs of any game bird, swan, wild duck, teal or widgeon.[57]

Enforcement

4.2.13 Any person found trespassing in pursuit of game[58] can be required by the person holding the game rights, the occupier of the land or their servants to give his name and address and to leave the land. If he fails to comply with such a request he can be apprehended by the same people; at night he can be apprehended immediately, without preliminaries.[59] Any game found on such a suspected offender can be seized,[60] and any assault on those exercising such powers is an offence.[61] In Scotland the onus of proving any permission, licence, etc. lies on the accused.[62]

Wildfowl

4.2.14 Wild ducks and geese generally fall outwith the scope of the game legislation, although wild ducks are included in the scope of some provisions. In Scotland it is an offence to trespass during the day in pursuit of wild ducks,[63] and in England and Wales it is an offence for someone with no game rights on the land to remove or destroy their eggs.[64] Snipe and woodcock are similarly covered by some of the provisions on game discussed above. No game licence is required to shoot wildfowl. Landowners may restrict access to their land, and although it appears that in Scotland the foreshore can be

---

[50] Night Poaching Act 1828 s.1, extended to apply to roads and highways by Night Poaching Act 1844 s.1.

[51] Night Poaching Act 1828 s.1.

[52] Game Act 1831 s.30; Game (Scotland) Act 1832 s.1.

[53] Night Poaching Act 1828 s.9.

[54] Game Act 1831 s.30; Game (Scotland) Act 1832 s.1.

[55] Game Act 1831 s.35; Game (Scotland) Act 1832 s.4.

[56] Protection of Wild Mammals (Scotland) Act 2002; Hunting Act 2004.

[57] Game Act 1831 s.24; see also para.3.3.9, above.

[58] The statutory rights of access to land (see paras 1.3.23–1.3.25, above) expressly exclude access for hunting; CRWA 2000 s.2(1) and Sch.2 para.1(f) and (j); Land Reform (Scotland) Act 2003 s.9.

[59] Game Act 1831 s.31; Game (Scotland) Act 1832 s.2; Night Poaching Act 1828 s.2.

[60] Game Act 1831 s.36; Game (Scotland) Act 1832 s.5.

[61] Game Act 1831 s.32; Game (Scotland) Act 1832 s.6.

[62] Game (Scotland) Act 1832 s.12.

[63] Game (Scotland) Act 1832 s.1.

[64] Game Act 1831 s.24.

used by the public for shooting wildfowl,[65] in England and Wales restrictions imposed from a number of sources limit any such use.[66]

Wild ducks, wild geese, snipe, woodcock and other birds which do not **4.2.15** count as "game" do, however, fall within the provisions of Part I of the Wildlife and Countryside Act 1981. This imposes a general prohibition on any intentional (or in Scotland, reckless) killing or taking of wild birds, except for those species listed in Part I of Schedule 2 to the Act.[67] These species (including snipe, woodcock, and several ducks and geese) may be killed or taken except during the close seasons, on Sundays and Christmas Day in Scotland, and on Sundays in areas of England and Wales prescribed by the Secretary of State.[68] Shooting can also be suspended during prolonged periods of severe winter weather.[69] The means by which these and all other sorts of wild bird may be killed or taken are also regulated.[70]

Deer

The law concerning deer offers these animals protection at some times of the **4.2.16** year and in some circumstances, regulates their hunting, controls the means by which they can be killed or taken and provides for their destruction as pests.[71] As the law is found in modern legislation providing more or less comprehensive codes, it is sensible to examine all aspects of the law together. The law in Scotland is somewhat different from that in England and Wales. During the 1990s the legislation in each jurisdiction was consolidated, but although the overall effect of the two sets of legislation is broadly similar, the existence of the Deer Commission in Scotland, the abolition of game licences in England and Wales and the many detailed differences mean that the two jurisdictions have to be treated separately. One point that does apply throughout Great Britain is that is it an offence to release to the wild any muntjac, or sika deer (or hybrids with sika ancestry), while in relation to many Scottish islands the prohibition extends to the release of any deer of the genus *Cervus* (covering red deer as well as sika) and hybrids.[72]

---

[65] *Hope v Bennewith* (1904) 6 F. 1004.

[66] See Parkes and Thornley, *Fair Game: The Law of Country Sports and the Protection of Wildlife* (New Revised edn) (1997), pp.222–224.

[67] The Birds Directive also permits the hunting of some species of ducks and geese provided that this is in accordance with national laws; art.7 and Annex II.

[68] WCA 1981 ss.1 and 2; see paras 3.3.2–3.3.8, above.

[69] See the JNCC guidance on this at *http://www.jncc.gov.uk/page-2894* [Accessed May 9, 2009].

[70] See paras 4.4.18–4.4.20, below.

[71] See generally C. Parkes and J. Thornley, *Fair Game: The Law of Country Sports and the Protection of Wildlife* (New Revised edn) (1997), Ch.11 and *Deer: Law and Liabilities* (2008).

[72] WCA 1981 s.14 and Sch.9 (see paras 7.2.3–7.2.4, below) as applied by Wildlife and Countyside Act 1981 (Variation of Schedule 9) Order 1997 (SI 1997/226) (for muntjac) and Wildlife and Countryside Act 1981 (Variation of Schedule 9) Order 1999 (SI 1999/1002) (for sika and red deer).

Scotland

4.2.17 The relevant legislation in Scotland is the Deer (Scotland) Act 1996.[73] The control and conservation of deer is supervised by the Deer Commission for Scotland, which has a significantly wider remit than its predecessor, the Red Deer Commission.[74] As the change of name suggests, the Commission is now responsible for more species of deer in Scotland, namely red, sika, roe and fallow and hybrids of these species,[75] while its concerns have been extended to include measures to protect the natural heritage.[76] The Commission may impose control schemes and grant authority for its own staff or others to kill deer in certain circumstances. Generally though, as with game, the right to take or kill deer is a right enjoyed by the owners of the land or those to whom they have transferred this right. A game licence is required to take or kill deer,[77] except where the deer are killed or taken on enclosed land by or with the permission of the owner or occupier,[78] or through the actions of those authorised or required to take action by the Deer Commission.[79] Licences are also required for dealing in venison.[80]

4.2.18 There are close seasons for four species of deer in Scotland, set out in Appendix B, and during the close season it is an offence to take or wilfully to kill or injure any deer.[81] This prohibition does not apply to farmed deer which are enclosed and properly marked,[82] nor to action required or authorised by the Deer Commission in relation to deer causing damage.[83] Also excluded is action taken by the occupier of agricultural land or enclosed woodland or others authorised by him[84] where deer are found on arable land or enclosed grassland or woodland and where the occupier has reasonable cause to believe that serious damage will be caused to crops, pasture, trees, or animal or human foodstuffs unless the deer are killed.[85] Licences granted for scientific purposes by the Commission can also authorise conduct normally prohibited during the close season.[86] It is also

---

[73] Replacing the Deer (Scotland) Act 1959, as amended, primarily by the Deer (Amendment) (Scotland) Acts 1967, 1982 and 1996. The 1996 Act has escaped amendment except to allow certain applications, notices, etc. to be in electronic format; Electronic Communications (Scotland) Order 2006 (SSI 2006/367) art.3.

[74] See paras 2.7.12–2.7.14, above. Provisions to merge the Deer Commission and SNH were included in the Public Services Reform (Scotland) Bill introduced in May 2009.

[75] Deer (Scotland) Act 1996 ss.1 and 45(1).

[76] See para.2.6.12, above; "natural heritage" is widely defined to include flora and fauna, geological and physiographical features and the natural beauty and amenity of the countryside (Deer (Scotland) Act 1996 s.45).

[77] Game Licences Act 1860 s.4.

[78] Game Licences Act 1860 s.5.

[79] Deer (Scotland) Act 1996 s.38.

[80] Deer (Scotland) Act 1996 ss.33–36.

[81] Deer (Scotland) Act 1996 s.5.

[82] Deer (Scotland) Act 1996 s.43.

[83] Deer (Scotland) Act 1996 s.14.

[84] Only certain categories of person can be authorised without the approval of the Deer Commission.

[85] Deer (Scotland) Act 1996 s.26.

[86] Deer (Scotland) Act 1996 s.5(7).

lawful to do acts in order to prevent suffering by injured or diseased deer or by a calf or fawn deprived of its mother.[87]

The only lawful method of taking, killing or injuring a deer is by shooting with a firearm.[88] The permitted categories of firearms and ammunition are prescribed in Regulations made by the Minister, which also prohibit the use of certain forms of sights, and allow him to grant special exemptions.[89] The use of shotguns is permitted in the case of action against deer causing serious damage to crops, etc. but only with the specified forms of ammunition. Taking, killing or injuring a deer at night is unlawful, unless the Deer Commission has authorised the occupier of agricultural land or woodland, or his nominee, where this is necessary to prevent serious damage to crops, pasture, foodstuffs or woodland and no other reasonable control measures would be adequate.[90] The discharge of any firearm or missile at a deer from any moving vehicle is prohibited,[91] as is the use of aircraft to transport live deer unless the animal is inside the aircraft[92] or the operation is approved by a veterinary practitioner.[93] Also prohibited is the use of vehicles to drive deer on unenclosed land with a view to killing or injuring the deer, or to taking them alive.[94] The wilful injury of any deer with a firearm is an offence.[95] **4.2.19**

As noted above, the law is relaxed in relation to the close seasons in order to allow occupiers to take action to control deer which are causing serious damage to agriculture or forestry, and is similarly relaxed to allow for control measures authorised by the Deer Commission.[96] The Commission can authorise the killing of deer where it is satisfied that they are causing serious damage to woodland or agricultural production, causing injury to livestock (e.g. by serious overgrazing of pasture or competition for supplementary feeding) or constitute an actual or potential to public safety, and further that the killing of the deer is necessary to resolve the problem and that none of the Commission's others powers is adequate to deal with the situation.[97] Any competent person can be authorised to kill the deer, the authorisation lasting for 28 days, and where the power is exercised the landowner must be notified and people likely to be on the land warned. Where the deer are coming from particular land, the person with the right to kill deer there must first be requested to take the necessary action, and authorisation for others to act can only be given once he has proved unable or unwilling to satisfy the request. These powers can also be exercised where **4.2.20**

---

[87] Deer (Scotland) Act 1996 s.25; unlike the "mercy killing" provisions in the Wildlife and Countryside Act 1981 and in relation to seals and badgers, this is not qualified to deny the benefit of the exception to a person who caused the suffering in the first place, although such an initial act is likely to be an offence unprotected by the exception.

[88] Deer (Scotland) Act 1996 s.17(3).

[89] Deer (Scotland) Act 1996 ss.17(4) and 21; Deer (Firearms) (Scotland) Order 1985 (SI 1985/1168) (see Appendix B).

[90] Deer (Scotland) Act 1996 s.18.

[91] Deer (Scotland) Act 1996 s.20(1)(a); "vehicle" includes any aircraft, hovercraft or boat (s.45(1)).

[92] So that deer cannot be carried in a sling or net under a helicopter.

[93] Deer (Scotland) Act 1996 s.20(1)(b) and (2).

[94] Deer (Scotland) Act 1996 s.19.

[95] Deer (Scotland) Act 1996 s.21(5).

[96] Deer (Scotland) Act 1996 s.10.

[97] Where action is required for public safety and killing the deer might by itself constitute such a danger, the authorisation can be for the taking and removal of the deer from the land in question; Deer (Scotland) Act 1996 s.10(5).

the Commission is satisfied that serious damage is being caused to the natural heritage either on enclosed land or on unenclosed land where the damage is the result of the presence of a significantly higher density of deer population than is usual in all the circumstances.[98]

4.2.21   More general control measures can be introduced by means of a control scheme for the reduction in numbers, or total exclusion, of deer in a locality where they are causing or are likely to cause, damage or have become an actual or potential danger to public safety.[99] The relevant forms of harm are damage to woodland, to agricultural production, to livestock, including by serious overgrazing, or to the natural heritage, covering both direct and indirect damage and harm to actual or proposed alterations or enhancements of the natural heritage.[100] The Deer Commission is to form a preliminary view on the necessary measures and consult with the owners and occupiers of the land affected. If all parties agree on the steps to be taken, who is to take them, the time limit for action and any other matters necessary for the agreement to work, a control agreement is drawn up by the Commission and takes effect.[101]

4.2.22   Where it is not possible to reach a control agreement or an agreement is not being carried out, the Commission can impose a control scheme, but only in a more restricted range of circumstances.[102] There must be actual and serious damage or the deer must be a danger to public safety, and a scheme cannot be imposed where the agreement was proposed for the purpose of altering or enhancing the natural heritage. The scheme sets out the area affected, the number and mix of deer to be killed or removed and the steps to be taken by different owners and occupiers, but cannot impose an obligation on owners or occupiers to construct any fence. Control schemes have to be confirmed by the Minister before taking effect. Wilful failure to comply with a requirement imposed by a scheme is a criminal offence, as is obstruction of those acting in execution of a scheme or arrangement.[103] In the event of any failure to comply with a scheme, the Commission must itself carry out any requirements of the scheme which it is satisfied are still necessary, recovering the cost through the sale of the deer killed and any sum still outstanding from the owner or occupier.[104]

4.2.23   The enforcement of the law relating to deer is assisted by a number of provisions. It is an offence for anyone who has no right to do so to take, kill or injure deer or to remove a deer carcase,[105] and where more than one person are acting together the penalties for this and the other offences noted above relating to killing or taking deer at unlawful times or by unlawful means are increased.[106] Trespassing in pursuit of deer is not itself an offence,

---

[98] Deer (Scotland) Act 1996 s.11.

[99] Deer (Scotland) Act 1996 s.7.

[100] Thus if large numbers of deer were likely to impede the proposed natural regeneration of an area of native woodland, action could be taken at an early stage.

[101] Details of the five areas covered by such agreements and the action taken under them are given in the Deer Commission for Scotland's *Annual Report 2006-07*.

[102] Deer (Scotland) Act 1996 s.8.

[103] Deer (Scotland) Act 1996 s.13.

[104] Deer (Scotland) Act 1996 ss.8(8) and 9.

[105] Deer (Scotland) Act 1996 s.17; the provision about removing carcases is necessary because it has been held that the "taking" of deer entails their killing or capture, not just the acquisition of a carcase; *Miln v Maher*, 1979 J.C. 58.

[106] Deer (Scotland) Act 1996 s.22.

but it is likely that a firearms offence will be involved.[107] The possession of deer in circumstances where there are reasonable grounds for suspecting that it has been unlawfully taken is an offence, as is the possession of firearms unlawful for this purpose.[108] Powers of arrest, search and seizure are conferred,[109] and for some offences a single witness suffices for conviction.[110] Those authorised by the Deer Commission enjoy wide powers of entry to land to control deer causing damage, to take a census of deer and to determine whether a control agreement or scheme is required.[111]

England and Wales

The legislation for England and Wales was consolidated in the Deer Act 1991.[112] As in Scotland, the right to take deer lies primarily with the owner of the land, but this right can be transferred separately and occupiers and others are given some rights in relation to deer causing damage. **4.2.24**

For the four main species of deer close seasons are specified, different from those in Scotland.[113] It is an offence to take or intentionally to kill any deer during the close season,[114] except for action taken to prevent the suffering of diseased or injured deer[115] or of a young deer actually or about to be deprived of a female on which it is dependent.[116] Also exempt is action to meet the requirements of an order for agricultural pest control,[117] or where a person falling within certain limited categories acts to prevent damage by deer on cultivated land, pasture or enclosed woodland.[118] The close season does not apply to deer farms where the deer are clearly marked and kept on enclosed land.[119] The Countryside Council for Wales and Natural England can grant licences authorising the taking or killing of deer during the close season or at night[120] for the purposes of preserving public health or public safety or conserving the natural heritage[121] and additionally for actions at night to prevent serious damage to property. The body must be satisfied that the risk being posed is serious, that there is no satisfactory alternative to what is being authorised, that the applicant has permission to enter the land **4.2.25**

---

[107] *Ferguson v Macphail*, 1987 S.C.C.R. 52.

[108] Deer (Scotland) Act 1996 s.23.

[109] Deer (Scotland) Act 1996 ss.27–28.

[110] Deer (Scotland) Act 1996 s.23(5).

[111] Deer (Scotland) Act 1996 s.15.

[112] The 1991 Act replaced the Deer Act 1963, as amended by the Wildlife and Countryside Act 1981, the Deer Act 1987 and the Deer Act 1980, and has now been amended in several places by the Regulatory Reform (Deer) Order 2007 (SI 2007/2183) (the 2007 Order).

[113] Deer Act 1991 s.2 and Sch.1; see Appendix 2.

[114] Deer Act 1991 s.2(1).

[115] Deer Act 1991 s.6(2), (4) and (4A).

[116] Deer Act 1991 s.6(2A), added by the 2007 Order art.3(2); this never applies if the female is the victim of unlawful killing by the person concerned and pre-emptive action is permitted only in the case of the female's position being affected by disease or lawful killing or taking.

[117] Deer Act 1991 s.6(1), referring to action required under s.98 of the Agriculture Act 1948; see para.4.5.2 below.

[118] Deer Act 1991 s.7; see para.4.2.28, below.

[119] Deer Act 1991 s.2(3).

[120] Normally prohibited; see para.4.2.27, below.

[121] The same definition as in Scotland ("natural heritage" is widely defined to include flora and fauna, geological and physiographical features and the natural beauty and amenity of the countryside (Deer (Scotland) Act 1996 s.45)); Deer Act 1991 s.8(6), added by the 2007 Order art.4.

in question for this purpose and that the action will not compromise the long-term ability of red, roe or fallow deer to maintain their population.[122] The statutory conservation bodies can also grant licences for removing live deer from one area to another or the taking of live deer for scientific or educational purposes.[123]

4.2.26   It is an offence to set any trap or snare or to lay any poison in positions likely to cause bodily injury to deer, or to use these methods or a net to take or kill deer.[124] Also prohibited is the use of any firearm other than those permitted by the Minister (different from those allowed in Scotland),[125] any arrow, spear or similar missile or any drugged or poisoned missile.[126] Motor vehicles cannot be used to drive deer or for the discharge of any firearm or missile, unless in relation to enclosed land where deer are normally kept and with the occupier's written permission.[127] The hunting of deer with hounds was deeply controversial, entering the legal sphere through litigation over the power of a public authority or charity to ban this activity on their land. In *R. v Somerset County Council, ex p. Fewings*[128] it was held that the decision on moral grounds to ban hunting from the council's land did not fall within the council's limited statutory power to manage the land for certain purposes, whilst in *ex p. Scott*[129] a challenge to a similar decision by the National Trust fell on procedural grounds. The use of dogs for hunting is now controlled by the Hunting Act 2004, limiting the exercise to a maximum of two dogs used to flush out animals that are to be shot.[130]

4.2.27   It is also an offence to take or wilfully kill deer at night,[131] except in the case of deer taken in accordance with requirements for agricultural pest control,[132] or under an authorisation from Natural England or the Countryside Council for Wales.[133] Action taken to relieve the suffering of diseased or injured deer is exempt from the prohibitions on night shooting and the use of traps and nets, and a wider range of firearms can be used.[134] The use of nets, traps and devices to project these can be authorised by the conservation bodies in relation to live deer for scientific and educational purposes or for the purpose of removing deer from one area to another.[135]

4.2.28   The control of deer as pests can be undertaken under the more general rules on pest control under section 98 of the Agriculture Act 1948 by which the agriculture ministers can make pest control orders requiring measures to combat deer and other pests.[136] More generally and as noted above, the law

---

[122] Deer Act 1991 s.8(3A)–(3H), added by the 2007 Order art.4.

[123] Deer Act 1991 s.8(1)–(2).

[124] Deer Act 1991 s.4(1).

[125] Specified in Deer Act 1991 Sch.2; there are further specifications for guns used for slaughtering (Deer Act 1991 s.8(5)–(6), as amended by the 2007 Order art.3).

[126] Deer Act 1991 s.4(2).

[127] Deer Act 1991 s.4(4) and (5), as amended by the 2007 Order art.2; shooting is permitted from a stationary vehicle with the engine turned off.

[128] *R. v Somerset County Council, ex p. Fewings* [1995] 1 W.L.R. 1037.

[129] *Ex p. Scott* [1998] 1 W.L.R. 226.

[130] See para.4.4.17, below.

[131] Deer Act 1991 s.3.

[132] Deer Act 1991 s.6(1).

[133] See para.4.2.25, above.

[134] Deer Act 1991 s.6(3)–(4A).

[135] Deer Act 1991 s.8(1)–(2).

[136] See para.4.5.2, below.

on the close seasons and night shooting are relaxed to allow action to be taken against deer causing damage.[137] The relaxation is available only to the occupier of the land,[138] members of his household or staff authorised by him and the person who has the right to kill deer on the land (if different from the occupier),[139] and covers the shooting of deer with prescribed firearms[140] on cultivated land, pasture or enclosed woodland.[141] It applies where it can be shown that there is reasonable cause to suspect deer of the same species of causing damage to crops, vegetables, fruit, growing timber or other forms of property, that it is likely that further serious damage will be caused, and that the killing is necessary to prevent such damage.[142] This provision may, however, be restricted by the Minister in relation to particular species or particular areas.[143] The statutory conservation bodies can also authorise action for the purposes of public health or safety or the conservation of the natural heritage.[144]

Trespass in search or pursuit of deer with the intention of killing or **4.2.29** injuring it is an offence, as is any intentional taking, killing or injuring of deer, pursuit of deer or removal of carcases without the consent of the owner, occupier or other lawful authority.[145] An authorised person may require a person suspected of committing these offences to give his name and address and to quit the land,[146] and more general powers of search and seizure are provided to assist in the enforcement of the Acts.[147]

FISHING

Fish and fishing are the subject of considerable legal attention. Although a **4.3.1** few fish are among the protected species under the Wildlife and Countryside Act 1981 and the Conservation (Natural Habitats, etc.) Regulations 1994, most of the law is not expressly conservationist in intention. Nevertheless, the measures designed to protect stocks from over-exploitation and to protect private fishing rights do operate to the benefit of aquatic species generally and are the main way (other than pollution controls[148]) in which the law intervenes with the aquatic environment. Moreover, as with game rights, the economic value of fishing rights can provide a strong incentive for their owners to take steps to protect the quality of waters and limit disturbance to the benefit of wildlife more generally. The following paragraphs offer an outline of the law on issues which are most likely to have

---

[137] Deer Act 1991 s.7.

[138] i.e. the occupier of the land on which the shooting takes place; *Traill v Buckingham* [1972] 1 W.L.R. 459.

[139] Deer Act 1991 s.7(4).

[140] For this purpose including shotguns using specified ammunition; Deer Act 1991 s.7(2); see Appendix B.

[141] Deer Act 1991 s.7(1).

[142] Deer Act 1991 s.7(3).

[143] Deer Act 1991 s.7(5).

[144] Deer Act 1991 s.8; see para.4.2.25, above.

[145] Deer Act 1991 s.1(1) and (2); belief that one has consent or other lawful authority, or that consent would be given were the circumstances known, is a defence (s.1(3)).

[146] Deer Act 1991 s.1(4).

[147] Deer Act 1991 s.12.

[148] See sections 8.5 and 8.6, below.

consequences for nature conservation. The extent to which fish that have been caught are returned to the water alive is very important for conservation purposes, but relies on voluntary schemes rather than legal controls.

4.3.2   Inland fishing is burdened with considerable legal controls, with significant differences between Scotland[149] and England and Wales.[150] On the border, special regimes apply to the Tweed and to the Solway, Esk and Sark; in some cases the Tweed is dealt with as a Scottish river throughout its length[151] and the Esk as an English one.[152] As with taking and killing game, the right to catch fish is largely an incident of the ownership of land, but can be sold and leased separately. In addition to any restrictions imposed by proprietors, the law lays down some general rules relating to closed times and means of fishing, but to some extent the details of the regulation of fisheries is left to the byelaws of the administrative bodies vested with powers in this area. In England and Wales a key role is played by the Environment Agency[153] which as well as gaining some powers from ministers,[154] inherited this function from the National Rivers Authority which had in turn inherited it from the water authorities abolished by the Water Act 1989.[155] Fish farms and other waters where fish are kept in captivity and artificially reared are exempt from many of the provisions noted below.[156]

4.3.3   In Scotland, the law concerning salmon fishing is different from that for other sorts of fish. The right to catch salmon originally lay with the Crown as part of the *regalia minora* (except in Orkney and Shetland where udal law provided differently), but in very many instances the right has been granted to others. Salmon fishings can constitute a separate heritable tenement which can be held independently of any proprietorial rights in the land affected.[157] In relation to other fish, the general rule is that in rivers which are tidal and in tidal lochs the right to catch fish is enjoyed by the public at large.[158] In other waters fishing rights lie with the riparian proprietors, but may be expressly transferred to others, although not as a separate holding.

---

[149] The fragmented legislation in Scotland (16 Acts dating from 1607 to 2001) was consolidated by the Salmon and Freshwater Fisheries (Consolidation) (Scotland) Act 2003, but this has since been amended by the Aquaculture and Fisheries (Scotland) Act 2007.

[150] See generally, S. Scott Robinson, *The Law of Game, Salmon and Freshwater Fishing in Scotland* (Edinburgh: Butterworths / Law Society of Edinburgh, 1990); W.M. Gordon, *Scottish Land Law*, 2nd edn (Edinburgh: W. Green, 1999), Ch.8; C. Hardie, "Fishing" in J. Rowan-Robinson and D. Mackenzie-Skene (eds), *Countryside Law in Scotland* (Edinburgh: T&T Clark, 2000); W. Howarth, *Freshwater Fishery Law* (London: Financial Training, 1987); R.I. Millichamp, *A Guide to Angling Law* (London: Shaw & Sons, 1990); C. Parkes and J. Thornley, *Fair Game* (New Rev. edn) (London: Pelham Books, 1997), Ch.12; P. Carty and S. Payne, *Angling and the Law* (London: Merlin Unwin, 1998).

[151] The detailed legislation for the Tweed is contained in the Scotland Act 1998 (River Tweed) Order 2006 (SI 2006/2913) and the Tweed Regulation Order 2007 (SSI 2007/19).

[152] e.g. EA 1995 s.6(7); Scotland Act 1998 (Border Rivers) Order 1999 (SI 1999/1746).

[153] EA 1995 s.6(6) and Sch.15; see generally *http://www.environment-agency.gov.uk/subjects/fish/* [Accessed May 9, 2009].

[154] EA 1995 Sch.15 paras 7–16.

[155] Water Act 1989 s.141 and Sch.17; see now Water Resources Act 1991 Pt V.

[156] See generally W. Howarth, *The Law of Aquaculture* (Oxford: Fishing News Books, 1990).

[157] This position was unaffected by the Abolition of Feudal Tenure etc. (Scotland) Act 2000; see Scottish Law Commission, *Report on the Abolition of the Feudal System* (Scot Law Com. No.168, 1999), paras 7.14–7.18.

[158] Scottish Law Commission, *Discussion Paper on Law of the Foreshore and Seabed* (Scot Law Com. D.P. No.113, 2001), pp.17–19.

In England and Wales, the right to fish for salmon is not treated separately. The general distinction between public and private fisheries exists, but the Environment Agency operates a licensing scheme to regulate fishing for salmon, trout, freshwater fish and eels.[159] In both jurisdictions the rights of the public may be considerably curtailed in practical terms by the absence of any means of access to the waters where fishing may be permissible.[160]

In Scotland, the proprietors of salmon fisheries in a district may form a **4.3.4** district salmon fishery board, now regulated by Part 3 of the Salmon and Freshwater Fisheries (Consolidation) (Scotland) Act 2003. Such boards may do such acts, execute such works and incur such expenditure as appears expedient for the protection and improvement of fisheries in their district, for the increase of salmon and the stocking of waters with salmon.[161] Ministerial powers to make regulations to conserve salmon have recently been introduced.[162] For other sorts of fish[163] where there can be a significant increase in the availability of fishing, the Minister can make Protection Orders regulating and imposing controls and charges on fishing in specified areas and authorising wardens to exercise enforcement powers.[164] In England and Wales, in addition to operating the licensing scheme, the Environment Agency is responsible for maintaining, improving and developing fisheries for salmon, trout and other species,[165] whilst the Minister may make general regulations for fisheries in any area.[166]

In addition to the restrictions on fishing times and methods described in **4.3.5** the following paragraphs, in Scotland it is an offence to fish for or take any unseasonable or unclean salmon (i.e. one which has spawned or is on the eve of spawning)[167] unless it is taken by accident and returned to the water with the least possible injury.[168] It is also unlawful knowingly to take any smolt or fry (i.e. young salmon before their migration to the sea), or to obstruct the passage of smolt or fry or the passage of mature salmon to spawning grounds during the annual close time, or to injure any spawn or spawning bed or shallow where spawn might be.[169] These prohibitions do not extend to action taken for the propagation of salmon or other scientific purposes, nor to the incidental results of the cleaning of any dam or lade or exercise of property rights over the bed of a watercourse.[170] It is also lawful for a district

---

[159] Salmon and Freshwater Fisheries Act 1975 s.25. Licences are also needed to fish for eels in Scotland (see para.4.3.5, below).

[160] The statutory rights of access (see paras 1.3.23–1.3.25, above) expressly exclude access for fishing; CRWA 2000 s.2(1) and Sch.2 para.1(f) and (j); Land Reform (Scotland) Act 2003 s.9.

[161] Salmon and Freshwater Fisheries (Consolidation) (Scotland) Act 2003 s.45. The boards can raise money by means of an assessment on the fisheries in the district (Salmon and Freshwater Fisheries (Consolidation) (Scotland) Act 2003 s.44).

[162] Salmon and Freshwater Fisheries (Consolidation) (Scotland) Act 2003 s.38 and Sch.1 paras 7–15.

[163] On the meaning of "freshwater fish" see Salmon and Freshwater Fisheries (Consolidation) (Scotland) Act 2003 s.69(1) and *McLeod v Keith*, 1997 S.C.C.R. 475.

[164] Salmon and Freshwater Fisheries (Consolidation) (Scotland) Act 2003 ss.48 and 49.

[165] EA 1995 s.6(6).

[166] Water Resources Act 1991 s.115.

[167] *Brady v Barbour (No.2)*, 1995 S.L.T. 920.

[168] Salmon and Freshwater Fisheries (Consolidation) (Scotland) Act 2003 s.18.

[169] Salmon and Freshwater Fisheries (Consolidation) (Scotland) Act 2003 s.23; the predecessor of this provision was used to prevent an attempt to raft down a salmon river which might have disturbed shallows used by spawning salmon.

[170] Salmon and Freshwater Fisheries (Consolidation) (Scotland) Act 2003 s.23.

salmon fishery board to take measures to prevent salmon reaching beds where from the nature of the stream their spawn might be destroyed.[171] Fixed engines (i.e. fixed nets or traps of any sort) are prohibited in inland waters,[172] and the construction and use of dams, sluices and gratings is also controlled.[173] A licence is needed to fish for or take eels in Scotland.[174]

4.3.6   In England and Wales the intentional killing or taking of any immature or unclean (i.e. about to spawn or not yet recovered from spawning) fish is an offence.[175] It is also an offence wilfully to disturb any spawn or spawning fish or any bed, bank or shallow where spawn or spawning fish might be, except in the exercise of a legal right to extract material (e.g. gravel) from the waters or in cases authorised by the Environment Agency for the purposes of artificial propagation, scientific activities or the development of private fisheries.[176] Fish passes in English and Welsh waters containing salmon or migratory trout are controlled by the Environment Agency, which can require their construction and maintenance when dams are being built or altered, or itself build fish passes.[177] The wilful alteration or injury to a fish pass, and any act obstructing the use of one or scaring, hindering or preventing fish from using it is an offence, as is a failure on the part of the owner or occupier to comply with a notice from the Agency to restore a fish pass which has fallen into disrepair.[178] The law also regulates the use of sluices and provides for gratings to be installed and maintained to protect fish from being caught in mill races, etc.[179] Fixed engines (i.e. any form of fixed net or trap for catching fish) and fishing weirs and mill dams are also prohibited unless expressly authorised.[180]

4.3.7   In both jurisdictions, fishing is prohibited during the close times and there are also requirements relating to the removal of nets and other equipment during the close times to reduce the likelihood of their being improperly used.[181] In Scotland there is in relation to salmon a weekly close time, from

---

[171] Salmon and Freshwater Fisheries (Consolidation) (Scotland) Act 2003 s.23.

[172] Salmon and Freshwater Fisheries (Consolidation) (Scotland) Act 2003 ss.1 and 25. A handful of long-standing cruives may remain in legitimate use as well as some fixed engines and haaf nets in the Solway; see Salmon and Freshwater Fisheries (Consolidation) (Scotland) Act 2003 ss.1 and 25, *Salar Properties (UK) Ltd v Annandale and Eskdale District Council, The Times,* March 19, 1992 and Scott Robinson, *The Law of Game, Salmon and Freshwater Fishing in Scotland* (1990), p.102.

[173] Salmon (Fish Passes and Screens) (Scotland) Regulations 1994 (SI 1994/2524); *Heritage Fisheries Ltd v Duke of Roxburghe,* 2000 S.L.T. 800.

[174] The Freshwater Fish Conservation (Prohibition on Fishing for Eels) (Scotland) Regulations 2008 (SSI 2008/419), applying to the species *Anguilla anguilla.*

[175] Salmon and Freshwater Fisheries Act 1975 s.2(2) and (3); see *Pyle v Welsh Water Authority* Unreported, noted in Howarth, *Freshwater Fishery Law* (1987), p.36.

[176] Salmon and Freshwater Fisheries Act 1975 s.2(4) and (5); *National Rivers Authority v Jones* Unreported, *The Times,* March 10, 1992.

[177] Salmon and Freshwater Fisheries Act 1975 ss.9–11, amended by EA 1995 Sch.15 paras 10–12.

[178] Salmon and Freshwater Fisheries Act 1975 s.12.

[179] Salmon and Freshwater Fisheries Act 1975 ss. 13, 14 (as substituted by EA 1995 Sch.15 para.13) and 15.

[180] Salmon and Freshwater Fisheries Act 1975 ss.6–8. Byelaws regarded as threatening the extinction of haaf netting on the Solway are the subject of dispute and possible legal challenge against the Environment Agency; see *http://haafnet.co.uk/home* [Accessed May 9, 2009].

[181] e.g. Salmon and Freshwater Fisheries (Consolidation) (Scotland) Act 2003 s.15.

6pm on Friday until 6am on Monday, during which it is illegal to fish by nets, whilst fishing by rod and line is unlawful on a Sunday.[182] There is also an annual close time of at least 168 days during which fishing is prohibited, although for fishing by rod and line a shorter period may be prescribed.[183] Each district or part of a district may have a different period set and there are considerable variations throughout Scotland. For trout the close season runs October 7–March 14.[184] Annual close seasons for other freshwater fish and weekly close times can be specific by ministerial order.[185]

In England and Wales the close time can be set by local byelaws made by **4.3.8** the Environment Agency, but in accordance with minimum times provided by statute, which also specifies the dates and times to be applied in the absence of local rules.[186] For salmon there must be an annual close time of at least 153 days for nets, etc.[187] and 92 days for rod and line[188] and a weekly close time of 42 hours.[189] For trout the minimum close times are 181 and 153 days[190] with a 42-hour weekly close time as for salmon. For other freshwater fish and rainbow trout the close time can be dispensed with by byelaws, which has been done for most stillwater and canals, but otherwise extends for at least 93 days.[191] The close season for catching salmon and trout by putt and putcher (a form of fixed trap) is set at 242 days.[192]

The law also restricts the possession and sale of fish during the close **4.3.9** seasons and provides wide enforcement powers to allow for the search and seizure of unlawfully taken fish and equipment used. Provisions exist for the introduction of a scheme for licensing salmon dealers.[193]

Only a limited number of methods are permissible in the catching of fish, **4.3.10** with further limitations applying to protected species under the Wildlife and Countryside Act 1981 and the Conservation (Natural Habitats, etc.) Regulations 1994.[194] In addition to the prohibition of the use of poison discussed more fully below,[195] there are prohibitions in both jurisdictions on the use of explosive or electrical devices.[196] In relation to these and the other activities

---

[182] Salmon and Freshwater Fisheries (Consolidation) (Scotland) Act 2003 s.13 and Salmon (Weekly Close Time) (Scotland) Regulations 1988 (SI 1988/390).

[183] Salmon and Freshwater Fisheries (Consolidation) (Scotland) Act 2003 s.37.

[184] Salmon and Freshwater Fisheries (Consolidation) (Scotland) Act 2003 s.17.

[185] Salmon and Freshwater Fisheries (Consolidation) (Scotland) Act 2003 ss.17A–17B, added by Aquaculture and Fisheries (Scotland) Act 2006 s.22.

[186] Salmon and Freshwater Fisheries Act 1975 s.19 and Sch.1; see the details on the Environment Agency's website *http://www.environment-agency.gov.uk/homeandleisure/recreation/fishing/31465.aspx* [Accessed May 9, 2009].

[187] Aug. 31–Feb. 1.

[188] Oct. 31–Feb. 1.

[189] 6am Saturday–6am Monday.

[190] Aug. 31 and Sep. 30 until Mar. 1.

[191] Mar. 14–June 16.

[192] Aug. 31–May 1.

[193] Salmon Act 1986 s.31; Salmon and Freshwater Fisheries (Consolidation) (Scotland) Act 2003 s.65.

[194] See paras 3.4.2–3.4.17, above.

[195] See paras 4.4.10–4.4.11, below.

[196] Salmon and Freshwater Fisheries Act 1975 s.5; Salmon and Freshwater Fisheries (Consolidation) (Scotland) Act 2003 s.5.

mentioned below, authorisation for their use can be given for scientific purposes or the development of fisheries or the conservation of living things by the district salmon fishery board (in some cases only) or the Minister in Scotland,[197] or by the Environment Agency in England and Wales.[198] In relation to salmon in Scotland, authorisation may also be granted for the purpose of conserving any creature or other living thing.[199]

4.3.11   The only lawful methods of taking salmon in Scotland are by rod and line or by net and coble in relation to inland waters, with bag nets, fly nets or other stake nets being permissible in the other waters of a salmon fishery district.[200] There are specific definitions of what is meant by "rod and line",[201] and the Ministers can make regulations specifying for particular areas certain forms of bait and lure that are prohibited[202] and defining what is meant by the various means of netting.[203] For other fish in inland waters the only permitted method of catching fish is by rod and line, except that where all the proprietors agree nets may be used in a loch or pond and that the proprietor or occupier may catch fish other than trout or salmon with nets or traps.[204] These rules do not prevent the use of a gaff or landing net in conjunction with rod and line,[205] but pike gags and knotted or metallic keepnets are banned.[206] Contravening these provisions is an offence, and the penalties are increased if two or more offenders are involved.[207] The taking of salmon leaping at or trying to ascend falls or going through a fish pass is also an offence.[208]

4.3.12   In England and Wales, the approach of the legislation is to ban the unlawful methods of fishing rather than to specify the lawful ones. The prohibited methods include the use of firearms, wires, spears and lights, and

[197] Salmon and Freshwater Fisheries (Consolidation) (Scotland) Act 2003 ss.27–28.

[198] Salmon and Freshwater Fisheries Act 1975 s.5(2).

[199] Salmon and Freshwater Fisheries (Consolidation) (Scotland) Act 2003 s.27(1)(a)(iii).

[200] Salmon and Freshwater Fisheries (Consolidation) (Scotland) Act 2003 s.1. A handful of long-standing cruives may remain in legitimate use as well as some fixed engines and haaf nets in the Solway; see Salmon and Freshwater Fisheries (Consolidation) (Scotland) Act 2003 ss.1 and 25, *Salar Properties (UK) Ltd v Annandale and Eskdale District Council, The Times,* March 19, 1992 and Scott Robinson, *The Law of Game, Salmon and Freshwater Fishing in Scotland* (1990), p.102. The boards' waters extend seaward five kilometres from the mean low-water springs (Salmon and Freshwater Fisheries (Consolidation) (Scotland) Act 2003 s.34(1)).

[201] Salmon and Freshwater Fisheries (Consolidation) (Scotland) Act 2003 ss.3A and 4, as amended by the Aquaculture and Fisheries (Scotland) Act 2007 s.20; the definition for "salmonids" is stricter, permitting a single rod per person as opposed to the four permitted for other fish, but the limit of four per boat applies in all cases.

[202] Salmon and Freshwater Fisheries (Consolidation) (Scotland) Act 2003 s.33

[203] Salmon and Freshwater Fisheries (Consolidation) (Scotland) Act 2003 s.31(4); Salmon (Definition of Methods of Net Fishing and Construction of Nets) (Scotland) Regulations 1992 (SI 1992/1974); Salmon (Definition of Methods of Net Fishing and Construction of Nets) (Scotland) (Amendment) Regulations 1993 and 1994 (SI 1993/257 and SI 1994/111).

[204] Salmon and Freshwater Fisheries (Consolidation) (Scotland) Act 2003 s.2; and see para.4.3.5 above.

[205] Salmon and Freshwater Fisheries (Consolidation) (Scotland) Act 2003 s.3.

[206] Salmon and Freshwater Fisheries (Consolidation) (Scotland) Act 2003 s.5A (added by Aquaculture and Fisheries (Scotland) Act 2007 s.21).

[207] Salmon and Freshwater Fisheries (Consolidation) (Scotland) Act 2003 s.7.

[208] Salmon and Freshwater Fisheries (Consolidation) (Scotland) Act 2003 s.10.

the use of stones or missiles to facilitate the catching of fish.[209] Also prohibited is the use of fish roe[210] and in relation to salmon or migratory trout the use of nets which stretch across more than three-quarters of the width of a stream or have too small a mesh.[211] Fixed engines, fishing weirs, mills and dams are also prohibited unless containing the requisite gaps, etc. to allow the passage of fish and protect the flow of water and being authorised expressly by the Environment Agency, by general authorisation from the Minister or through being lawfully in use in 1861 by ancient right.[212] Bye-laws add to the range of prohibited methods and equipment, e.g. banning certain sizes of lead weights.[213]

At sea, there is a general public right to fish in tidal waters, but fishing **4.3.13** activity is strictly controlled by many different rules, arising both from the salmon legislation and the rules on marine fishing. One species which has attracted special attention is the basking shark, which as well as being a protected species under Schedule 5 to the Wildlife and Countryside Act 1981[214] now benefits from provisions making any intentional or reckless disturbance an offence.[215]

For marine fishing generally, the law is mostly of recent origin and is **4.3.14** designed to protect stocks from the depredations of fishing fleets which have become extremely, perhaps excessively, efficient, whilst at the same time balancing competing economic and social interests within states and between a large number of states within and outwith the European Community.[216] Regulations emerge in shoals from Brussels and national governments to regulate the total allowable catches and the allocation and the use of national quotas, banning the fishing for particular species in particular places by boats from particular countries at particular times, as well as controlling the types of fishing gear, vessels and methods of fishing which are permitted, the number of days during which fishermen can be at sea and the buying and selling of fish when landed, as well as providing decommissioning schemes and other ways of reducing the overall fishing effort.[217]

At national level there are wide powers for ministers to make orders **4.3.15**

---

[209] Salmon and Freshwater Fisheries Act 1975 s.1; possession of such implements with the intention of using them to catch fish is itself an offence, but gaffs used as an auxiliary to rod and line are permitted. Contrary to the inventive argument for the defence in *Alton v Parker* (1891) 30 LR IR 87, the prohibition on using an "otter" or "otter lath" applies to the use of certain floating devices, not to the use of trained live otters to catch fish.

[210] Salmon and Freshwater Fisheries Act 1975 s.2.

[211] Salmon and Freshwater Fisheries Act 1975 s.3; landing nets used as an auxiliary to rod and line are permitted.

[212] Salmon and Freshwater Fisheries Act 1975 ss.6–8; see *Gray v Blamey* [1991] 1 All E.R. 1; *Mott v Environment Agency*, *The Times*, January 25, 1999; *R. v National Rivers Authority, ex p. Haughey* [1997] Env. L.R. 14.

[213] See details on the Environment Agency's website at *http://www.environment-agency.gov.uk/homeandleisure/recreation/fishing/31471.aspx* [Accessed May 9, 2009].

[214] Wildlife and Countryside Act 1981 (Variation of Schedules 5 and 8) Order 1998 (SI 1998/878).

[215] WCA 1981 s.9(4A), added for England and Wales by CRWA 2000 Sch.12 para.5 and for Scotland by NCSA 2004 Sch.6 para.8; the Scottish provision covers harassment as well as disturbance.

[216] General information on the Common Fisheries Policy of the EC can be found at *http://ec.europa.eu/fisheries/cfp_en.htm* [Accessed May 9, 2009]. See R.R. Churchill and D. Owen, *EU Common Fisheries Policy: Law and Practice* (Oxford: OUP).

[217] The Scottish Fisheries Protection Agency listed almost 100 pieces of UK legislation alone in its *Annual Report and Accounts 2003-04*, Annex D.

regulating the minimum sizes of fish which can be caught and landed, the types of fishing gear permissible, and the areas and seasons in which fishing can take place, while there are licensing arrangements for fishing boats and registration for those buying and selling fish when first landed. In the exercise of these powers ministers must have regard to the conservation of marine flora and fauna and seek a reasonable balance between conservation and their other concerns under the fisheries legislation.[218]

4.3.16　　All of these measures, by controlling the volume, nature and location of fishing activity, have considerable significance for the conservation of marine species, albeit with the traditional aim of ensuring continued exploitation rather than seeking to conserve the environment. The details of this very rapidly changing mass of legislation lie beyond the scope of this work,[219] but those concerned with nature conservation should be aware of the existence of this legal structure which offers potential (and missed opportunities) for furthering conservationist aims and controlling the destructive side-effects for other species of certain forms of fishing gear or techniques.[220] Indeed some measures have been expressly adopted in order to benefit wider conservation interests, e.g. restrictions on fishing for sand eels in the North Sea in order to conserve the food supply for the many seabirds that nest on the east coast of Britain.[221] More specifically the first "Community Marine Conservation Area" has been created in Lamlash Bay, Arran, a "no take zone" established using the inshore fishing legislation.[222] All use of explosives, poisonous or stupefying substances or electrical current for catching marine species (including crustaceans and molluscs) is banned, and it is unlawful to sell specimens caught using any form of projectile.[223]

4.3.17　　The taking of shellfish is also surrounded by legislation, supported by special measures to protect water quality in designated shellfish waters.[224] Private fisheries can be established for oysters, mussels, cockles, clams, scallops and queens and within these the holders of the right to take shellfish can regulate fishing.[225] Private fisheries for oysters and mussels are also

---

[218] Sea Fisheries (Wildlife Conservation) Act 1992 s.1.

[219] For an account of the legal regime, see the entries on "Fisheries", *Stair Memorial Encyclopaedia of The Laws of Scotland* (1990), Vol.11, and *Halsbury's Laws of England*, 4th edn (re-issue) (London: LexisNexis, 2007, Vol.1(2)), and especially the relevant Supplements. The websites of the relevant government departments and of the Sea Fish Industry Authority—*http://www.seafish.org/* [Accessed May 9, 2009]—offer useful information.

[220] See para.3.4.40, above.

[221] Regulation (EC) 850/98 art.29a, as added by Regulation (EC) 1298/2000.

[222] Inshore Fishing (Prohibition on Fishing) (Lamlash Bay) (Scotland) Order 2008 (SSI 2008/317), made under the Inshore Fishing (Scotland) Act 1984.

[223] Regulation (EC) 850/98 art.31; see also Salmon and Freshwater Fisheries (Consolidation) (Scotland) Act 2003 s.5 and Salmon and Freshwater Fisheries Act 1975 s.5, as amended by Fishery Limits Act 1976 Sch.2 para.20.

[224] The Shellfish Waters Directive 79/923/EEC, implemented mainly through the Surface Waters (Shellfish) Classification Regulations 1997 (SI 1997/1332) and the Surface Waters (Shellfish) Classification (Scotland) Regulations 1997 (SI 1997/2470); it has been held that a breach of this Directive may create a right to compensation for shellfish fishermen who are adversely affected (*Bowden v Southwest-Services Ltd* [1999] 3 C.M.L.R. 180; [1999] Env. L.R. 438).

[225] Sea Fisheries (Shellfish) Act 1967 ss.1–3, amended by Sea Fisheries Act 1968 s.15, extended by Shellfish (Specification of Molluscs) Regulations 1987 (SI 1987/218), Shellfish (Specification of Crustaceans) Regulations 2001 (SI 2001/1381) and Shellfish (Specification of Molluscs and Crustaceans) (Scotland) Regulations 1999 (SSI 1999/139).

protected in Scotland by older legislation prohibiting others from dredging or otherwise disturbing or taking shellfish from such beds.[226] In addition to controls on fishing gear and making provision for the minimum permissible size of creatures to be caught,[227] general rules lay down close seasons for the sale of indigenous oysters[228] and ban the possession or sale of lobsters carrying spawn or edible crabs which are carrying spawn or have just cast their shells,[229] and many local restrictions also apply.

On a related issue, it has been held that in England and Wales there is a **4.3.18** public right to dig for bait (usually worms) on the foreshore, as an ancillary to the public right of fishing there.[230] It was stressed however, that this right is just an ancillary one and that no taking of bait for commercial purposes would be legitimate.

METHODS OF KILLING AND TAKING

The means by which wild creatures can be caught and killed is the subject of **4.4.1** considerable legislation which prohibits or controls the use of poison and traps as well as the use of certain aids to taking animals. For some protected species[231] there are further limits on the means by which they can be killed or captured and the risk of harm to such species may have the effect of producing restrictions that apply more generally.[232] More detailed rules apply to specific species, e.g. badgers, seals and deer where there are strict controls on the sort of firearms and ammunition which can be used in hunting them.[233] Byelaws can add to the prohibitions in many situations.

Poison

The use of poisons is controlled in various ways. Pesticides and their use are **4.4.2** controlled generally by Part III of the Food and Environment Protection Act 1985[234] and the regulations made under it,[235] largely implementing EC measures on this topic.[236] The basic conditions for the supply, storage and

---

[226] Oyster Fisheries (Scotland) Act 1840; Mussel Fisheries (Scotland) Act 1847.

[227] Sea Fish (Conservation) Act 1967 s.1; orders have been made in relation to lobsters, edible crabs and spider crabs.

[228] Sea Fisheries (Shellfish) Act 1967 s.16.

[229] Sea Fisheries (Shellfish) Act 1967 s.17; this does not apply if it can be shown that the crabs are for use as bait.

[230] *Anderson v Alnwick District Council* [1993] 1 W.L.R. 1156; the same has been decided for Northern Ireland (*Adair v National Trust for Places of Historic Interest and Scenic Beauty* [1998] NI 33).

[231] See paras 3.4.6 and 3.4.16, above.

[232] See the discussion on whether snares should be banned throughout Scotland because of the risk to otters, a European protected species which is to be protected from all indiscriminate means of killing or capture; *Consultation on Snaring in Scotland* (Scottish Executive Environment Group, 2006) pp.4–6, considering the impact of *Commission v Spain* (C-221/04) [2006] E.C.R. I-4515.

[233] See paras 3.4.23, 3.4.33, 4.2.19 and 4.2.26, above.

[234] As amended by the Pesticides Act 1998.

[235] Control of Pesticides Regulations 1986 (SI 1986/1510); Plant Protection Products Regulations 2005 (SI 2005/1435); Plant Protection Products (Scotland) Regulations 2005 (SSI 2005/331); Pesticides (Maximum Residue Levels) (England and Wales) Regulations 2008 (SI 2008/2570); Pesticides (Maximum Residue Levels) (Scotland) Regulations 2008 (SSI 2008/342).

[236] Notably Directive 91/414/EEC and Regulation (EC) 396/2005.

use of pesticides require that all reasonable precautions are taken to protect the health of human beings, creatures and plants and to safeguard the environment, in particular avoiding the pollution of water,[237] while notification must be given to various authorities before any aerial applications, including notice to the statutory conservation bodies of any spraying within 1,500 metres of a National, Local or Marine Nature Reserve or an SSSI.[238] The absence of similar precautions in relation to people in the vicinity of spraying operations was noted in *Downs v Secretary of State for the Environment, Food and Rural Affairs*, where the relevant rules were held not to provide the level of protection required by EC law.[239] The possession of certain pesticides is itself an offence unless it can be shown that they were to be used for certain lawful purposes.[240] The release of many poisonous substances is controlled by the laws regulating pollution. The discharge and deposit of waste in liquid, gas or solid form are all controlled, with licences or other forms of approval being required for a large range of activities.[241] These provisions should offer a degree of protection against the risks that poisonous substances pose to wildlife.

Animals

4.4.3 For the more specific legislation, perhaps the most convenient starting point is offered by the general provisions in section 8 of the Protection of Animals Act 1911[242] and section 7 of the Protection of Animals (Scotland) Act 1912.[243] These sections make it an offence knowingly to place, or cause to be placed, on any land or in any building any poison or any fluid or edible matter (other than sown seed or grain) which has been rendered poisonous. This general prohibition on the laying of poison is however qualified by the existence of a defence if the poison is placed in order to destroy vermin in the interests of public health, agriculture or the protection of other animals or for manuring the land, provided that all reasonable precautions are taken to

---

[237] Control of Pesticides Regulations 1986 Sch.2 para.2 and Sch.3 para.2, as substituted by Control of Pesticides (Amendment) Regulations 1997 (SI 1997/188) Sch.1.

[238] Control of Pesticides Regulations 1986 Sch.4, as substituted by Control of Pesticides (Amendment) Regulations 1997 (SI 1997/188) Sch.1.

[239] *Downs v Secretary of State for the Environment, Food and Rural Affairs* [2008] EWHC 2666 (Admin); overturned by Court of Appeal [2009] EWCA Civ 664.

[240] In Scotland, WCA 1981 s.15A, added by NCSA 2004 Sch.6 para.14; in England and Wales NERCA 2006 s.43 where the purpose of prescribing banned pesticides is expressly to protect wild birds or animals from harm.

[241] See generally, M. Poustie, "Environment" in *The Laws of Scotland: Stair Memorial Encyclopaedia* (2007 reissue); S. Bell and D. McGillivray, *Environmental Law*, 7th edn (2008).

[242] As amended by the Protection of Animals (Amendment) Act 1927 s.1.

[243] These are among the very few provisions of these Acts to survive when they were largely replaced by legislation in 2006, which contains separate provisions on the administration of poison to "protected animals": Animal Health and Welfare (Scotland) Act 2006 s.22 and Animal Welfare Act 2006 s.7. "Protected animals" are essentially domesticated and captive animals; see para.3.4.18.

protect dogs, cats, fowls and other domestic animals.[244] In *Walkingshaw v McClymont*,[245] the sheriff doubted whether there could ever be adequate precautions to satisfy this legal test when the aim of the exercise was to leave poisoned meat in the open countryside where a fox could get access to it. These sections also prohibit the sale of any seed or grain which has been rendered poisonous, except for their bona fide use in agriculture.

The use of a particular poison can be prohibited or restricted by the **4.4.4** Minister if he or she is satisfied that it cannot be used for destroying animals, or particular kinds of animals, without causing undue suffering and that there are suitable alternative methods for destroying them which are adequate.[246] Only mammals count as "animals" for the purposes of this provision.[247] The effect of the regulations is to take the use of such poisons outwith the scope of the defences provided in section 8 of the Protection of Animals Act 1911 and section 7 of the Protection of Animals (Scotland) Act 1912, so that their use is a criminal offence. This power has been exercised so as to prohibit the use of phosphorous and red squill in all cases and the use of strychnine for all mammals except moles.[248] The sale and storage of poisons generally is controlled under the Poisons Act 1972 and the Poisons Rules[249] made under it.

Just as the use of a poison can be expressly taken outwith the scope of the **4.4.5** defences in the 1911 and 1912 Acts, the use of poisons can be expressly brought within their scope. This can be achieved by ministerial approvals under the Food and Environment Protection Act 1985.[250] More specifically, the use of particular poisons against grey squirrels and coypus can be authorised by the agriculture ministers in particular circumstances[251]; regulations have been made in the exercise of this power to permit the use of warfarin in destroying grey squirrels throughout England and Wales.[252]

The use of poison against rabbits and hares used to be prohibited **4.4.6** throughout Great Britain under section 6 of the Ground Game Act 1880. For Scotland this provision has been repealed,[253] but it would appear that the prohibition on using poison to kill hares, contained in the Hares (Scotland) Act 1848,[254] remains in force. In England and Wales, the relevant

---

[244] The wording of the two provisions differs slightly: the Scottish provision refers simply to the destruction of "vermin" (in *Walkingshaw v McClymont* (below) held to include foxes), whereas the English one refers to "insects and other invertebrates, rats, mice, or other small ground vermin"; the Scottish provision refers to precautions to "prevent access" to the poison by dogs, etc. whereas the English one refers to precautions to "prevent injury" by the poison and includes wild birds within the categories entitled to protection.

[245] *Walkingshaw v McClymont*, 1996 S.L.T. (Sh. Ct) 107.

[246] Animals (Cruel Poisons) Act 1962 s.2.

[247] Animals (Cruel Poisons) Act 1962 s.3.

[248] Animals (Cruel Poisons) Regulations 1963 (SI 1963/1278); phosphorous is elementary yellow phosphorous and red squill is any powder or extract made from the plant *Urginea maritima* (L.) Baker (the sea squill).

[249] Primarily the Poisons Rules 1982 (SI 1982/218), as amended.

[250] Food and Environment Protection Act 1985 s.16(14).

[251] Agriculture (Miscellaneous Provisions) Act 1972 s.19.

[252] Grey Squirrels (Warfarin) Order 1973 SI 1973/744; the laying of warfarin inside buildings is authorised throughout England and Wales, and its use outdoors in specified areas.

[253] Agriculture (Scotland) Act 1948 Sch.10.

[254] Hares (Scotland) Act 1848 s.4.

part of section 6 of the 1880 Act has also ceased to have effect,[255] and the older legislation relating to hares has been repealed.[256] It is expressly stated that it is not an offence under the Protection of Animals Act 1911 to use poisonous gas in rabbit holes[257] or in other burrows, etc. for the purpose of killing rodents of all sorts, foxes and moles under the agricultural pest control provisions of section 98 of the Agricultural Act 1947.[258] A similar provision allows the use of poisonous gas in agricultural pest control in Scotland.[259] It is an offence knowingly to use or to permit the use of a rabbit infected with myxomatosis to spread the disease to unaffected rabbits.[260]

4.4.7   In relation to other particular species, the use of poison will not be an offence under the 1911 and 1912 Acts if its use falls within the scope of a licence granted by the statutory conservation bodies under the Protection of Badgers Act 1992 for scientific or educational purposes, or for the conservation of badgers.[261] The use of poison to kill seals is an offence,[262] as is its use against deer.[263] The use of poison is prohibited in relation to those species given protection under Schedule 6 to the Wildlife and Countryside Act 1981,[264] and under the Habitats and Species Directives.[265]

Birds

4.4.8 In addition to benefiting from the general restrictions on the use of poisons described above, the use of poisonous, poisoned or stupefying substances to kill or take wild birds is expressly prohibited.[266] The offence lies in setting such substances in such a place that they are calculated to cause bodily injury to any wild bird, even though birds may not be the intended victims. For the purpose of this provision, game birds are included within the definition of "wild birds".[267] Those who knowingly cause or permit such action are also guilty, but there is a defence for the setting of substances to kill or take in the interests of public health, agriculture, forestry, fisheries or nature conservation any wild animals which can lawfully be killed or taken in that way. This defence applies, however, only where all reasonable precautions

---

[255] Prevention of Damage by Rabbits Act 1939 s.5(2); this repeal did not however extend to Greater London.

[256] Hares Act 1848 s.5, repealed by Regulatory Reform (Game) Order 2007 (SI 2007/2007).

[257] Prevention of Damage by Rabbits Act 1939 s.4.

[258] See para.4.5.2, below.

[259] Agriculture (Scotland) Act 1948 s.49.

[260] Pests Act 1954 s.12.

[261] Protection of Badgers Act 1992 s.10(10); see para.3.4.27, above.

[262] Conservation of Seals Act 1970 s.1(1); licences may be granted to allow the use of poisons other than strychnine (s.10(1)) but will be restricted by the ban on using any indiscriminate methods that arises from the seals' status as European protected species; see para.3.4.16, above.

[263] In England and Wales this is expressly provided in s.4 of the Deer Act 1991, whereas in Scotland it is included in the general prohibition on using any method other than shooting with a firearm to kill deer (Deer (Scotland) Act 1996 s.17(3)); see paras 4.2.19 and 4.2.26, above.

[264] WCA 1981 s.11(2), amended by Wildlife and Countryside (Amendment) Act 1991 s.2; see para.3.4.6, above.

[265] Directive 92/43/EEC Annex VI; CNHR 1994 Sch.3; see para.3.4.16, above and para.7.4.40, below.

[266] WCA 1981 s.5(1), amended by Wildlife and Countryside (Amendment) Act 1991 s.1; see also the Birds Directive art.8 and Annex IV.

[267] WCA 1981 s.27(1).

have been taken to prevent injury to wild birds.[268] It has been held that this provision creates three separate offences, of using poisonous, using poisoned and using stupefying substances, and a charge of using a poisoned substance failed when it was held that the substance in question was properly described as a narcotic and hence stupefying, not poisoned, substance.[269]

Further measures seek to protect wild birds from the risks of being poi- **4.4.9** soned when lead weights or shot used by fishermen and hunters are ingested and worn down in their craw. The supply, but not the use, of lead weights for fishing is prohibited,[270] and the use of lead shot on or over certain areas is banned. In Scotland this ban applies to all wetlands, specifically defined on the basis of an adjusted version of the definition in the Ramsar Convention,[271] and in England and Wales the ban applies to all shooting below the high water mark, at certain listed SSSIs and for moorhens, coots and all species of ducks and geese.[272]

Fish

The use of poison against fish is strictly prohibited and using poison to catch **4.4.10** any marine organism is prohibited by EC law.[273] In Scotland it is an offence to put poison or any noxious substance in or near water with the aim of taking fish,[274] and it is also unlawful to possess poison for this purpose.[275] Permission can be granted by the Minister for the use of poison for scientific purposes or to protect or develop stocks of fish, or (in relation to salmon only) to conserve any creature or other living thing.[276]

In England and Wales the same offence exists,[277] as does a broader offence **4.4.11** of causing or knowingly permitting to be put into waters which contain fish any matter which causes the water to become poisonous or injurious to fish, their spawn, spawning grounds or food.[278] The very broad terms of that offence are qualified so as not to apply to actions authorised by law (e.g. licensed discharges of waste) provided that the best practicable means within reasonable costs are used to prevent the matter causing injury.[279] Prosecutions may be raised only by the Environment Agency or a person certified by the Minister as having a material interest in the waters affected, a provision

---

[268] WCA 1981 s.5(4) and (4A), added by Wildlife and Countryside (Amendment) Act 1991 s.1.

[269] *Robinson v Hughes* [1987] Crim. L.R. 644.

[270] Control of Pollution (Anglers' Lead Weights) Regulations 1986 (SI 1986/1992), amended by Control of Pollution (Anglers' Lead Weights) (Amendment) Regulations 1993 (SI 1993/49); very large (over 28.35 grams) and very small (under 0.06 grams) weights are excluded. See also Environment Agency byelaws (para.4.3.12, above).

[271] Environmental Protection (Restriction on Use of Lead Shot) (Scotland) (No.2) Regulations 2004 (SSI 2004/358); the definition is in reg.3.

[272] Environmental Protection (Restriction on Use of Lead Shot) (England) Regulations 1999 (SI 1999/2170), amended by Environmental Protection (Restriction on Use of Lead Shot) (England) (Amendment) Regulations 2002 and 2003 (SI 2002/2102 and SI 2003/2512); Environmental Protection (Restriction on Use of Lead Shot) (Wales) Regulations 2002 (SI 2002/1730).

[273] Regulation (EC) 850/98 art.31.

[274] Salmon and Freshwater Fisheries (Consolidation) (Scotland) Act 2003 s.5.

[275] Salmon and Freshwater Fisheries (Consolidation) (Scotland) Act 2003 s.9.

[276] Salmon and Freshwater Fisheries (Consolidation) (Scotland) Act 2003 ss. 27 and 28.

[277] Salmon and Freshwater Fisheries Act 1975 s.5.

[278] Salmon and Freshwater Fisheries Act 1975 s.4.

[279] Salmon and Freshwater Fisheries Act 1975 s.4(2).

which limits the scope for environmental groups to utilise this provision to act against any pollution of waters.[280] The Agency, acting with ministerial approval, may authorise the use of noxious substances for scientific purposes or in order to improve stocks of fish.[281]

Traps and Other Methods

Animals

4.4.12 The law controls both the sort of traps which can be used in catching animals and how they can be used. It is an offence to use or knowingly to permit the use of any spring trap other than one approved under regulations made by the Minister and used in circumstances covered by its approval.[282] The approval for a trap may be general or subject to conditions as to the circumstances of its use or the animals against which it is used, and the Minister may also grant licences authorising the experimental use of traps. The prohibition of the use of spring traps does not extend to those specified in regulations as being adapted solely for the destruction of rats, mice or other small ground vermin.[283] It is also an offence to sell or expose for sale any spring trap with a view to its use other than in accordance with the formal approvals, or to possess any spring trap for a purpose which is unlawful.[284]

4.4.13 Where a spring trap is used against hares or rabbits, it must be placed in a rabbit hole, and it is an offence to use or knowingly permit its use elsewhere.[285] Somewhat surprisingly, the meaning of "in a rabbit hole" has been the subject of decisions of the appellate courts.[286] The use of traps in accordance with a licence from the agriculture minister is outside this prohibition, and a licence to this effect may be embodied in a rabbit clearance order[287] or a notice served for the purpose of agricultural pest control.[288] In England and Wales, where spring traps are used against hares and rabbits, the traps must be inspected at least once a day.[289]

4.4.14 It is an offence to place any self-locking snare so as to cause injury to any wild animal coming into contact with it, or to use a self-locking snare in any way in order to kill or take a wild animal.[290] In Scotland the prohibition

---

[280] Salmon and Freshwater Fisheries Act 1975 s.4(3).

[281] Salmon and Freshwater Fisheries Act 1975 s.5.

[282] Agriculture (Scotland) Act 1948 s.50, substituted by Pests Act 1954 s.10; Pests Act 1954 s.8; Small Ground Vermin Traps Order 1958 (SI 1958/24).

[283] The current regulations are the Spring Traps Approval Order 1995 (SI 1995/2427), amended by Spring Traps Approval (Variation) (England) Order 2007 (SI 2007/2708), and the Spring Traps Approval (Scotland) Order 1996 (SI 1996/2202).

[284] Agriculture (Scotland) Act 1948; Pests Act 1954 s.8.

[285] Agriculture (Scotland) Act 1948 s.50A, added by Pests Act 1954 s.10; Pests Act 1954 s.9.

[286] *Brown v Thompson* (1882) 9 R. 1183 and *Fraser v Lawson* (1882) 10 R. 396, both considering the equivalent provision in the Ground Game Act 1880 s.6.

[287] Pests Act 1954 s.1; see para.4.5.5, below.

[288] Agriculture Act 1947 s.98; Agriculture (Scotland) Act 1948 s.39; see para.4.5.2, below.

[289] Protection of Animals Act 1911 s.10. The equivalent provision in Scotland (Protection of Animals (Scotland) Act 1912 s.9) was repealed by the Animal Health and Welfare (Scotland) Act 2006 but animal welfare considerations can presumably be dealt with by the fact that the cruelty provisions in the 2006 Act extend to all animals "under the control of man on a ... temporary basis" (s.17(1)) and will therefore apply to a trapped animal.

[290] WCA 1981 s.11(1), amended by Wildlife and Countryside (Amendment) Act 1991 s.2 and further for Scotland by NCSA 2004 Sch.6 para.10.

extends to any snare calculated to cause unnecessary suffering and there is a specific requirement to inspect any snare at intervals of no longer than 24 hours and to release or remove any animal (alive or dead) found caught. Further rules in Scotland prohibit the sale of self-locking or other specified snares and, subject to a defence of having a reasonable excuse, make it an offence either to possess or to set such snares on land without the authorisation of the owner or occupier. Using a snare otherwise than in accordance with any ministerial order, or knowingly causing or permitting others to do so, is also an offence.[291]

The use of snares has been the subject of further recent debate in Scotland, with the strongly contrasting views of land managers and animal welfare groups being joined by concerns that the risk of snares catching otters might render them unlawful as an indiscriminate means of killing or capturing this European protected species.[292] In response to the Scottish Government's announcement in February 2008 that snares would not be banned but subjected to further restrictions, animal welfare groups used the public petition process in the Scottish Parliament to call for a complete ban on the manufacture, sale, possession and use of all snares.[293] Legislative proposals are contained in the consultation paper on a Wildlife and Natural Environment Bill issued in June 2009. **4.4.15**

A number of other means of taking animals is also prohibited. The use of leg-hold traps is prohibited throughout the European Community.[294] Also prohibited is the use of any live mammal or bird as a decoy, any bow or crossbow, or explosive other than ammunition for a firearm.[295] A person who knowingly causes or permits the use of such methods is also guilty of an offence. A wider range of devices are prohibited in relation to those animals given enhanced protection under Schedule 6 to the Wildlife and Countryside Act 1981, and similarly for certain species (both protected ones and those which may be hunted) under the Conservation (Natural Habitats, etc.) Regulations 1994.[296] There is further legislation relating to badgers, deer and seals.[297] **4.4.16**

Hunting with dogs is also restricted. After many years of heated debate, legislation was eventually passed both for Scotland, the Wild Mammals (Scotland) Act 2002, and for England and Wales, the Hunting Act 2004, and has survived challenges on the basis that it infringed human rights[298] or was improperly made.[299] **4.4.17**

---

[291] WCA 1981 s.11, as amended by NCSA 2004 Sch.6 para.10.

[292] *Consultation on Snaring in Scotland* (Scottish Executive Environment Group, 2006), pp.4–6, considering the impact of *Commission v Spain* (C-221/04) [2006] E.C.R. I-4515.

[293] PE1124, discussed in the Public Petitions Committee on March 4, 2008 (Official Record cols 572 ff.), September 9, 2008 (cols 1043 ff.) and January 13, 2009 (cols 1391 ff.).

[294] Regulation (EEC) 3254/91 art.2.

[295] WCA 1981 s.11(1) (amended by Wildlife and Countryside (Amendment) Act 1991 s.2 and further for Scotland by NCSA 2004 Sch.6 para.10).

[296] CNHR 1994 reg.41 and Sch.3.

[297] See section 3.4, above.

[298] *Adams v Scottish Ministers*, 2004 S.C. 665; *Whaley v Lord Advocate* [2007] UKHL 53; 2008 S.C. (HL) 107; *R. (Countryside Alliance) v Attorney General* [2007] UKHL 52; [2008] 1 A.C. 719.

[299] *R. (Jackson) v Attorney General* [2005] UKHL 56; [2006] 1 A.C. 262.

Birds

4.4.18 The use of a large number of methods of killing and taking wild birds, which for this purpose includes game birds, is prohibited under the Wildlife and Countryside Act 1981, the list of prohibitions being subject to alteration by an order of the Minister.[300] Such orders can only be made after a draft of the order has been approved by both Houses of Parliament,[301] and changes can be made to the rules affecting firearms only in order to comply with Britain's international obligations.[302]

4.4.19   It is an offence to use any of the following[303]:

  (a) a springe, trap, gin, snare, hook and line;
  (b) an electrical device for killing, stupefying or frightening;
  (c) a poisonous, poisoned or stupefying substance[304];
  (d) a baited board or bird lime or any similar substance;
  (e) a bow or crossbow;
  (f) an explosive other than ammunition for a firearm;
  (g) an automatic or semi-automatic[305] weapon or shot-gun with a barrel or more than 1.75 inches at the muzzle;
  (h) a device for illuminating a target, any form of artificial lighting, any mirror or dazzling device or any sighting device for night shooting[306];
  (i) a gas or smoke;
  (j) a chemical wetting agent;
  (k) a decoy in the form of a sound recording or any live bird or animal which is in any way tethered, secured or maimed[307]; or
  (l) a mechanically propelled vehicle in immediate pursuit of a bird.

In relation to items (a)–(c), the offence depends on the offending article being of such a nature and being so placed that it is calculated to cause injury to any wild bird coming into contact with it; in relation to the others what is covered is the use of the banned method for killing or taking a wild bird.[308] The offences extend to those who knowingly cause or permit the prohibited actions. It is also an offence to be involved in any way with an event where captive birds are liberated for the purpose of being shot immediately after their release.[309]

4.4.20   The ban on the use of nets or traps does not extend to their use by an authorised person in order to catch pest species which may be listed in Part

---

[300] WCA 1981 s.5(2).

[301] WCA 1981 s.26(3).

[302] WCA 1981 s.5(3).

[303] WCA 1981 s.5(1), amended by Wildlife and Countryside (Amendment) Act 1991 s.1; see also art.8 and Annex IV of the Birds Directive.

[304] See para.4.4.8, above.

[305] General licences permit the use of semi-automatic weapons against pest species in certain circumstances (WML Gen-L05 (12/08), SGGL 02/2009).

[306] General licences permit the use of lights for night-shooting of feral pigeons (WML Gen-L05 (12/08), SGGL 2/2009).

[307] In *Holden v Lancaster Justices*, *The Times*, October 10, 1998, it was held that birds with clipped wing feathers were not "maimed" for the purposes of this provision. Larsen traps that use live decoys are permitted in some circumstances; see para.4.4.20, below.

[308] WCA 1981 s.5(1).

[309] WCA 1981 s.8(3).

II of Schedule 2 to the Act, and their use is permitted in the licences which have in effect replaced Part II of Schedule 2.[310] Larsen traps and other cage traps which also make use of a live decoy are authorised, subject to conditions, including limitations on the birds which may be used as decoys (primarily crows and magpies) and killed or kept if caught.[311] In *R. (RSPCA) v Shinton*[312] it was held that the user of a Larsen trap was guilty of causing unnecessary suffering to the magpie that was injured while being used as a decoy[313] but that, except possibly where the user was aware of this yet still persisted, it was not appropriate to argue that the use of the trap fell outside the authorisation granted by the licence on the basis that such trapping could never achieve the specified objective in the circumstances. Nets and traps may also be used to capture game birds when it is shown that the taking of the bird is solely for breeding purposes, and also legitimate is the use of nets in a duck decoy which was in use in 1954, immediately before the passing of the Protection of Birds Act 1954. These exceptions, however, do not permit the use of nets for taking birds in flight, nor the use of any net propelled otherwise than by hand.[314] In relation to the offences of setting articles such that they are likely to cause injury, a defence is available if it can be shown that they were positioned for the lawful killing of any wild animal in the interests of public health, agriculture, forestry, fisheries or nature conservation, and that all reasonable precautions were taken to prevent injury to wild birds.[315]

Fish

Only a limited number of methods are permissible in the catching of fish. **4.4.21** These have been discussed above.[316]

DESTRUCTION OF WILDLIFE

The control of pests has been a concern of the law for centuries, and until **4.5.1** comparatively recently the total extermination of many species would have been regarded as a legitimate aim. Today, although the law does to a considerable extent provide protection to wildlife, regard must also be had to the law regulating its destruction, as such measures can have a significant effect on what can and cannot be done to kill or capture wild animals. The controls on the use of poison and many of the other matters already considered serve to regulate the means by which many pest control operations can be carried out, and in several places exceptions to the law have been noted, whereby the occupiers of land and other limited classes of people are permitted, for the purposes of protecting human, animal and plant health and of protecting property, to take steps normally forbidden by measures enacted to further the interests of nature conservation. There also exists a

---

[310] See paras 3.3.10–3.3.15, above.
[311] e.g. Licences WML Gen-L05 (12/08), Gen-L06 (12/08) and SGGL 1/2009 and 2/2009.
[312] *R. (RSPCA) v Shinton* [2002] EWHC 1696 (Admin).
[313] Under the Protection of Animals Act 1911 s.1 (now replaced; see para.3.4.18, above).
[314] WCA 1981 s.5(5).
[315] WCA 1981 s.5(4A), added by Wildlife and Countryside (Amendment) Act 1991 s.1.
[316] See section 4.3, above.

fragmented mass of provisions specifically directed at the control of pests. Most of these are rarely, if ever, invoked, but they could require action directly contrary to the interests of nature conservation.

4.5.2   One major power is that of the agriculture ministers to serve notices requiring steps to be taken to take or destroy pests.[317] This power can be exercised where it appears expedient for preventing damage to crops, pasture, animal or human foodstuffs, livestock, trees, hedges, banks or works on land and can require action against rabbits, hares, other rodents, foxes, moles, wild birds (other than those enjoying special protection)[318] and (in England and Wales) deer.[319] The notice is to be served on the person who is entitled to take the specified action, who will usually be the owner or the occupier of the land but may be someone different if game and shooting rights are held separately. The specified measures may not include any killing which is otherwise prohibited by law, with the exception of the killing of game which may be required during the close season.[320] A notice under these provisions may also call for the destruction or reduction of breeding places or cover for rabbits, or for steps to limit their movement.[321]

4.5.3   There is no right of appeal against such a notice, and failure to comply with one within the specified time is an offence.[322] Moreover, in the event of a failure to comply, the Minister may arrange for the necessary steps to be taken and recover the expenses incurred.[323] Powers of entry and inspection are provided to assist the Minister in the exercise of the functions under these provisions.[324] The Minister may also provide (at a reasonable charge) services and equipment to assist in compliance with a notice,[325] and anyone who has incurred costs in complying can apply to have these shared on a just and equitable basis with others who have an interest in the land.[326]

4.5.4   The Forestry Commissioners also enjoy the power to take action to control pests.[327] The Commissioners may act where they are satisfied that

---

[317] Agriculture Act 1947 s.98, amended by Pests Act 1954 s.2 and Sch., Protection of Birds Act 1954 Sch.3 para.1 and Agriculture Act 1958 Sch.3; Agriculture (Scotland) Act 1948 s.39, amended by Pests Act 1954 s.2 and Sch. and WCA 1981 s.72(4). Predator control can also be an element of the management of land which is supported under schemes such as the Rural Priorities of the Scottish Rural Development Programme.

[318] The Scottish Act has been amended to refer to WCA 1981 Sch.1 whereas the English one appears still to refer to the Protection of Birds Act 1954, repealed by WCA 1981; however the provisions of WCA 1981 s.4, setting the limits on the defences available to those acting in accordance with notices as described here ensures that the law is in fact the same (see para.3.3.5, above).

[319] Fallow, red, roe and sika deer (and hybrids) are removed from the scope of this provision in Scotland by s.42A of the Agriculture (Scotland) Act 1948, added by Deer (Amendment) (Scotland) Act 1996 Sch.1 para.2 and amended by the Deer (Scotland) Act 1996 Sch.4 para.1. This means that if muntjac deer become a problem in Scotland, action against them could still be taken under these provisions.

[320] As specified in the Game (Scotland) Act 1772 and the Game Act 1831 s.3; see para.4.2.10, above.

[321] Agriculture Act 1947 s.98(7); Agriculture (Scotland) Act 1948 s.39(5), both added by Pests Act 1954 s.2.

[322] Agriculture Act 1947 s.100(1); Agriculture (Scotland) Act 1948 s.41(1).

[323] Agriculture Act 1947 s.100(2); Agriculture (Scotland) Act 1948 s.41(2).

[324] Agriculture Act 1947 s.106; Agriculture (Scotland) Act 1948 s.82.

[325] Agriculture Act 1947 s.101; Agriculture (Scotland) Act 1948 s.42.

[326] Applications are to the county court in England and Wales (Agriculture Act 1947 s.100(5)) and to the Land Court in Scotland (Agriculture (Scotland) Act 1948 s.41(4)).

[327] Forestry Act 1967 s.7.

trees are being or are likely to be damaged by rabbits, hares or vermin (including squirrels)[328] owing to the failure of an occupier of land to take adequate steps to destroy the animals or prevent their causing damage. The owner and occupier of the land must be given an opportunity to take the requisite action before the Commissioners take steps themselves, but the costs of such steps can be recovered by the Commissioners from the occupier.

In addition to the measures requiring the clearance of land offering them **4.5.5** cover,[329] further attention is given to rabbits. Rabbit clearance areas may be designated by the agriculture ministers after consultation with local representatives of farmers, landowners, other farm and forestry interests and after local publicity for the proposal.[330] Within these areas, the occupiers of land have an obligation to take the necessary steps to kill or take wild rabbits, or where destruction is not reasonably practicable, to prevent their causing damage.[331] The existence of a rabbit clearance order does not entitle the occupier of the land to any right to kill rabbits with firearms additional to that conferred by the Ground Game Act 1880,[332] but authorisation for the additional use of firearms can be given by the Minister where such measures are necessary and the person entitled to grant authorisation has unreasonably withheld it.[333] All of England and Wales is designated as a rabbit clearance area, except for the City of London, the Isles of Scilly and Skokholm Island,[334] and all of Scotland is similarly designated apart from Jura and the Outer Hebrides.[335]

Rats and mice come under the responsibility of local authorities by virtue **4.5.6** of the Prevention of Damage by Pests Act 1949.[336] The authorities are under a duty to keep their areas free from rats and mice, and in particular should inspect their areas for such creatures, destroy them on their own land and enforce the duties placed on the occupiers of land by the 1949 Act.[337] Occupiers of land other than agricultural land[338] must forthwith notify the authority when it comes to their knowledge that rats or mice are resorting to or living on their land in significant numbers.[339] If the authority considers it

---

[328] The red squirrel is protected under Sch.5 to the Wildlife and Countryside Act 1981, and no exemption is allowed for action against protected animals under these forestry provisions, in contrast to the exceptions allowed for agricultural pest control (WCA 1981 s.10(1)); see para.3.4.4, above.

[329] See para.4.5.2, above.

[330] Pests Act 1954 s.1.

[331] Pests Act 1954 s.1(2).

[332] See para.4.2.8, above.

[333] Pests Act 1954 s.1(3)–(5).

[334] Rabbit Clearance Order No.148 (1972).

[335] Designation has been by means of 33 Orders, mostly made in 1955 and 1956 with the latest in 1960.

[336] In England, district councils where there are two-tiers of local government; Prevention of Damage by Pests Act 1949 s.1. The legislation has been much amended to cope with the changes in local government structure since 1949 and provision has been made to transfer this function to other relevant bodies, e.g. urban development corporations (Local Government, Planning and Land Act 1980 s.159) and housing action trusts in England and Wales (Housing Act 1988 s.68(1)).

[337] Prevention of Damage by Pests Act 1949 s.2.

[338] In Scotland other categories of land can also be exempted by order (Prevention of Damage by Pests Act 1949 s.3(2)); the equivalent English provision was repealed by the Statute Law (Repeals) Act 2004 Sch.1 Pt 13.

[339] Prevention of Damage by Pests Act 1949 s.3.

necessary, notices[340] may be served requiring the occupier to take reasonable steps as specified to destroy rats and mice on their land.[341] There is a right of appeal against notices and failure to comply is an offence. In the event of non-compliance the council can arrange for the steps to be taken and recover the costs involved, and the council can similarly take action itself and recover the costs if this is the expedient way of allowing land occupied by different people to be dealt with as a single unit.[342] Further measures can be taken or required in the event of disease.[343]

4.5.7   In order to ensure the destruction of rats and mice escaping from hay stacks in Scotland, regulations may impose special requirements on those involved in the threshing or dismantling of stacks.[344] The regulations affect all stacks of grain, beans, peas, tares or mashlum and require such measures as the placing of fences round the stack before it is dismantled and the taking of all practicable steps to destroy any rats or mice escaping.[345] The equivalent regulations dealing with hay ricks in England and Wales were repealed in 1978 and the provision authorising them in 2004.[346]

4.5.8   The provisions on the control of deer which are causing damage have already been discussed.[347] The measures to control non-indigenous pests such as mink are discussed below.[348]

4.5.9   As far as birds are concerned, the general provisions on agricultural pest control apply to them as much as to earth-bound pests, and the protection given to wild birds is relaxed in order to allow action to be taken against the main pest species. Although the Wildlife and Countryside Act 1981 provides for authorised persons[349] to be permitted to kill or take species listed in Part II of Schedule 2 to the Act, and to destroy, damage or take their eggs or nests,[350] no species are now listed in that Part of the Schedule and the authority for such action now rests in licences granted under the Act.[351] Where action is required by ministers in the exercise of their powers of

---

[340] The notice must require sufficiently specific steps for the occupiers to know what is required of them (*Perry v Garner* [1953] 1 Q.B. 335), but there is no specific statutory form required, provided that the content of the notice and the authority of its source are clear (*Albon v Railtrack Plc* [1998] CLY 2295, reported as *Basildon District Council v Railtrack Plc* at [1998] E.H.L.R. 83).

[341] Prevention of Damage by Pests Act 1949 ss.4–6.

[342] Prevention of Damage by Pests Act 1949 s.5. In *Leeds City Council v Spencer, The Times*, May 24, 1999; [1999] E.H.L.R. 394 a claim was successfully resisted when the problem had been caused by the council's failure to carry out its own obligations under the waste legislation.

[343] e.g. Public Health (Infectious Diseases) Regulations 1988 (SI 1988/1546) reg.11; Foot-and-Mouth Disease (Scotland) Order 2006 (SSI 2006/44) Sch.2 para.12.

[344] Prevention of Damage by Pests Act 1949 s.8.

[345] Prevention of Damage by Pests (Threshing and Dismantling of Stacks) (Scotland) Regulations 1950 (SI 1950/980), rendered metric by the Prevention of Damage by Pests (Threshing and Dismantling of Stacks) (Scotland) Amendment Regulations 1976 (SI 1976/1236).

[346] Prevention of Damage by Pests (Threshing and Dismantling of Ricks) (Revocation) Regulations 1978 (SI 1978/1614); Statute Law (Repeals) Act 2004 Sch.1 Pt 13.

[347] See paras 4.2.20–4.2.23 and 4.2.28, above.

[348] See para.7.2.10, below.

[349] See para.3.2.15, above.

[350] WCA 1981 s.2(2).

[351] See paras 3.3.10–3.3.15, above.

agricultural pest control[352] or animal health,[353] the death or injury of birds or damage to their eggs is not an offence.[354] If there were to be a serious outbreak of "avian influenza" there might be calls for significant measures against wild populations known or suspected to be harbouring the disease.

In England and Wales, there is a further power for local authorities to **4.5.10** take steps for abating or mitigating nuisance, annoyance or damage caused by the congregation in built-up areas of house doves, pigeons, starlings or sparrows.[355] Reasonable precautions must be taken to ensure that the seizure and destruction of birds is carried out humanely, and the provision does not authorise action contrary to the terms of the 1981 Act.[356] In London, action can be required to prevent nuisance to pedestrians using a highway as a result of birds habitually nesting, roosting or alighting on adjacent buildings or structures. The measures that the borough council can require of the owner and occupier include fitting baffles, nets and wires and laying gel to prevent the birds landing, but again no action contrary to the Wildlife and Countryside Act 1981 is authorised.[357] As a further measure to discourage pigeons, a byelaw prohibits feeding them in Trafalgar Square.[358]

The legislation on animal health also provides for the destruction of **4.5.11** wildlife. The agriculture ministers have the power to declare infected areas within which wide powers may be exercised.[359] If an area has been declared as being infected with rabies, provision can be made for the destruction of foxes and other wild animals in the area by persons authorised by the Minister.[360] In relation to other diseases, the destruction of any species of wild mammal or bird may be authorised if the Minister is satisfied that a disease existing among the wild members of a species is being transmitted to other animals,[361] and that the destruction of such wild creatures is necessary to eliminate or substantially reduce the incidence of the disease.[362] Orders made under this provision may authorise the use of methods for destroying animals which are otherwise unlawful, but only if such methods are the most appropriate in the light of all relevant circumstances, including the need to avoid unnecessary suffering.[363] The statutory conservation bodies must be consulted before such orders can be made.[364] In nature reserves managed by these bodies seven days' notice must be given before any exercise of the powers of entry to enforce and carry out the required steps, and as far as

---

[352] See para.4.5.2, above.

[353] Under ss.21 or 22 of the Animal Health Act 1981; the same applies for other action taken under the Animal Health Act 1981 except in relation to those species given enhanced protection under Sch.1 to the 1981 Act (and Sch.ZA1 in England and Wales).

[354] WCA 1981 s.4(1).

[355] Public Health Act 1961 s.74.

[356] The species in question are all covered by the licences granted under the 1981 Act.

[357] London Local Authorities Act 2004 (c.i) s.9.

[358] See Mayor of London's press release at *http://www.london.gov.uk/view_press_release.jsp? releaseid=2032* and *http://news.bbc.co.uk/1/hi/england/london/6986166.stm* [Both Accessed May 9, 2009].

[359] Animal Health Act 1981 s.17, amended by Animal Health and Welfare Act 1984 s.4.

[360] Animal Health Act 1981 ss.19 and 20.

[361] The animals which are protected by the Act are cattle, sheep, goats, other ruminating animals and swine, but the Minister can extend this definition to cover any other mammals (except man) and four-footed creatures (Animal Health Act 1981 s.87).

[362] Animal Health Act 1981 s.21.

[363] Animal Health Act 1981 s.21(4).

[364] Animal Health Act 1981 s.21(3).

possible action in such reserves is to be taken with regard to minimising the harm to the flora, fauna and other features of such reserves.[365] The recent foot and mouth disease outbreaks have emphasised the extent of the legal powers available under the animal health provisions but the relevant orders have not required the destruction of wildlife other than rats, mice and rodents within affected premises.[366] The appropriateness (on scientific and ethical levels) of culling badgers as a means of controlling bovine TB continues to be controversial.[367]

4.5.12 The health legislation relating to bees[368] does not authorise the destruction of any animals in the wild, although action can be required to destroy bee pests within premises or vehicles.[369] The Minister has the power to take steps to eliminate pests affecting shellfish from waters other than those covered by private fisheries,[370] and the wider diseases of fish legislation does on occasions allow the Minister to require the removal of fish from certain waters (including by methods otherwise unlawful where this is most expedient).[371] In Scotland barriers can be established to limit the movement of fish to prevent the spread of or assist the treatment of the parasite *Gyrodactylus salaris*,[372] and the Contingency Plan for dealing with such infection contemplates the killing of all fish in certain waters as the appropriate response in some circumstances.[373]

---

[365] Animal Health Act 1981 s.22(7).

[366] Foot-and-Mouth Disease (Scotland) Order 2006 (SSI 2006/44) arts 39–40 and Sch.2 para.12; Foot-and-Mouth Disease (Wales) Order 2006 (SI 2006/179) arts 40–41 and Sch.2 para.12; Foot-and-Mouth Disease (England) Order 2006 (SI 2006/182) arts 40–41 and Sch.1 para.12.

[367] A useful snapshot of the complex and long-running debate is found in *Public Consultation on Controlling the Spread of Bovine Tuberculosis in Cattle in High Incidence Areas in England: Badger Culling – A Report on the Citizens' Panels* (DEFRA, 2006) available at *http://www.defra.gov.uk/animalh/tb/pdf/citizens-panels.pdf* [Accessed May 9, 2009]; see para.3.4.28, above.

[368] Bees Act 1980 and the orders noted below.

[369] Bee Diseases and Pests Control (England) Order 2006 (SI 2006/342) art.8(3); Bee Diseases and Pests Control (Wales) Order 2006 (SI 2006/1710) art.8(3); Bee Diseases and Pests Control (Scotland) Order 2007 (SSI 2006/506) art.8(3).

[370] Sea Fisheries (Shellfish) Act 1967 s.15.

[371] Diseases of Fish Act 1937 s.2B, added by Diseases of Fish Act 1983 s.2.

[372] Diseases of Fish Act 1937 s.5A, added by Aquaculture and Fisheries (Scotland) Act 2007 s.15; the power extends to the compulsory purchase of land where appropriate for this purpose.

[373] *Gyrodactylus salaris* Contingency Plan, 3rd edn (Scottish Government, April 2008); Appendix 1 gives an account of the many pieces of legislation relevant to control measures.

5. CONSERVATION OF HABITAT

By itself, the law protecting individual creatures can never secure their **5.1.1**
survival. Without suitable habitat offering food and shelter, no animal can
survive and it is the loss of habitat, rather than any form of direct attack,
which poses the greatest threat to most species today. The protection of
habitat is equally vital to any attempt to conserve wild plants.[1] If the law is
going to seek the conservation of wildlife, it must therefore take steps to
ensure the continued existence of the range and expanse of habitat necessary
for this. In some countries this can be achieved by setting aside large areas of
land for the exclusive use of wildlife, but in heavily populated islands such as
Great Britain this approach is not possible. Moreover abandoning the land
to nature would in any event prove futile in many areas, since virtually all of
Britain's "natural" countryside is in fact the product of centuries of man's
involvement with the land and some degree of continuing management is
required if it is to survive in its present diversity. The conservation of habitat
has instead been addressed by the creation of a large number of different
designations of land, each with its own objectives, procedures and legal
consequences.[2]

The piecemeal development of the law has resulted in there being about a **5.1.2**
dozen different legal regimes governing areas of land which have been
identified as requiring protection in some form on account of their environmental quality. These regimes reflect different objectives: Areas of Outstanding Natural Beauty and National Scenic Areas are identified solely for
their landscape, National Parks in England were created to serve the twin
purposes of protecting landscape and providing opportunities for recreation, National Nature Reserves aim solely at the conservation and study of
nature, while other designations such as Environmentally Sensitive Areas
have come and gone as part of the response to reduce agricultural overproduction.[3] The effects of each designation vary in the extent to which the
owner or occupier of land is restricted, the emphasis placed on voluntary
agreements, the circumstances in which compensation is available and the
restrictions placed on visitors to the land. The same piece of land can be
subject to many designations.[4] The fragmented structure of the law, exacerbated by the number of different public authorities involved, inevitably

---

[1] The emphasis in conservation is increasingly towards an "ecosystems approach" away
from the past concentration on "headline" species and even specific sites. See Environmental
Audit Committee, *Halting Biodiversity Loss*, Thirteenth Report of 2007–2008, HC Paper
No.743 (Session 2007–2008), paras 18–22 and Government Response, HC Paper No.239
(Session 2008–2009).

[2] See J. Rowan-Robinson, C. Philp and M. de la Torre, "The Protection of Habitats" in J.
Rowan-Robinson and D. McKenzie-Skene (eds), *Countryside Law in Scotland* (Edinburgh:
T&T Clark, 2000); K. Cook, *Wildlife law: Conservation and Biodiversity* (London: Cameron
May, 2004), Part I.

[3] This scheme has now closed although some continuing commitments may remain in force;
see section 5.9 of the previous edition. Nitrate Vulnerable Zones, created to protect water
quality, are discussed at paras 8.4.19–8.4.22, below.

[4] *R. (Fisher) v English Nature* [2004] EWCA Civ 663; [2005] 1 W.L.R. 147 at [132].

leads to confusion and at times exaggerated fears on the part of residents and landowners as to the effects of designation.

5.1.3 Historically, the trend has been towards stricter controls. When SSSIs were first introduced in 1949,[5] the landowner was not even informed and the designation served simply to inform the planning authority of the value of the area. The Wildlife and Countryside Act 1981[6] strengthened the regime by requiring the owner or occupier to give notice before carrying out certain potentially damaging operations, but contained no direct power to prevent these. Subsequently, the regime for European Sites,[7] did introduce provisions allowing damaging operations to be prohibited. Now a wider range of controls, requiring the positive management of land as opposed to merely prohibiting activities, has been introduced for SSSIs.[8] There has thus been a great strengthening of the degree of control exercised over the owners and occupiers of land, albeit accompanied by great emphasis on a partnership approach and assistance for landowners taking positive steps to maintain and enhance the conservation value of their land. This trend has been the product of greater public and political willingness to accept environmental objectives, including nature conservation, as a legitimate reason for restricting the freedom of landowners to do as they wish with their land, coupled with appreciation of the failure of the previous regimes to cope adequately with the varied threats to important habitats and to biodiversity.

5.1.4 Throughout, though, there is a danger that by concentrating attention and effort on the designated sites, the health of the wider countryside (and urban habitats) is ignored. There is a risk that the efforts for designated sites are seen as being a complete response to the need to take action to conserve biodiversity, overlooking the harm being done in other areas. Biodiversity cannot be secured by the conservation of a range of designated sites, however extensive, if the surrounding landscape has been become a "no-go area" for wildlife. Ensuring that the whole of the country offers supportive habitats for species of many sorts is harder than looking after a few designated sites, but ultimately more valuable.

5.1.5 The starting-point for all designations is that while some protection is offered to all land through the operation of the general law—planning controls, pollution controls, nuisance, etc.—particular areas can be identified which are so valuable or so sensitive that further measures are justified in order to protect them. The first task therefore is to establish the criteria for identifying those sites which are to benefit from enhanced protection and procedures for their designation. Then an appropriate legal regime must be adopted to offer the desired level of protection. The following are the most commonly used legal devices.[9]

---

[5] NPACA 1949 s.23.

[6] WCA 1981 s.28 (as originally enacted).

[7] CNHR 1994 Pt II.

[8] WCA 1981 ss.28–28R, as substituted by CRWA 2000 Sch.9; NCSA 2004 Pt II.

[9] See also paras 1.6.23–1.6.35, above; K. Last, "Mechanisms for Environmental Regulation – A Study of Habitat Conservation" in A. Ross (ed.), *Environment and Regulation* (Hume Papers on Public Policy Vol.8, No.1) (2000).

Ownership

Taking the land into the ownership of a body dedicated to nature con- **5.1.6**
servation is probably the strongest way of securing that it will be managed in
the interests of conservation. The owner is in the best position to ensure that
damaging activities are avoided, to exclude visitors who might cause disturbance[10] and to undertake any positive action required to maintain or
enhance the value of the area as habitat for wildlife. Although there is
provision for land being acquired, compulsorily in some circumstances, the
acquisition of land by public authorities has not been a major element in the
approach to conservation. The cost of large-scale acquisitions, respect for
property rights and a confidence in the ability of landowners to treat their
land with respect have combined to limit the area of land taken over by the
state. Outside the statutory schemes, several non-governmental bodies, such
as the National Trusts, the Royal Society for the Protection of Birds and the
John Muir Trust, have become significant landowners in sensitive areas of
the country, extending beyond any formal designations the area of land
managed in the interests of conservation.

Management Agreements

In place of the state acquiring land directly, the preference has been to allow **5.1.7**
existing owners and occupiers to retain their interest in the land, but to
encourage them to use their land in ways which respect the needs of wildlife.
In many situations reliance is placed on management agreements, whereby
those with an interest in land agree with public authorities to deal with the
land in a particular way in exchange for compensation which covers any
expense incurred or (in increasingly rare circumstances) profits foregone.[11]
Such agreements can include both negative and positive obligations on the
part of the occupier, prohibiting certain forms of harmful activity and
requiring certain beneficial ones, and they can run with the land, binding the
successors to those who entered the agreements.

It is hoped that since such agreements are voluntarily entered and offer **5.1.8**
compensation for the restrictions imposed on the land there should be more
willing, and hence more effective, compliance with the agreed measures than
if they were imposed by law, while a system of individual agreements allows
all the particular needs and problems of each site to be taken into account in
a way impossible if general legislation were employed. Critics, however,
pointed out that this system of "buying off" landowners was not only
unduly expensive, but also enabled unscrupulous landowners, by threatening to develop their land, to blackmail the authorities into paying out large
sums, regardless of how speculative the proposed development might be.
This has led to increasing emphasis on the positive aspects of these
arrangements—paying for the active management of the land with conservation in mind rather than offering compensation to desist from causing

---

[10] Subject to public rights of access; see paras 1.3.23–1.3.25, above.
[11] C. Rodgers and J. Bishop, *Management Agreements for Promoting Nature Conservation* (London: RICS, 1998).

harm.[12] The costs of negotiating individual agreements has also led to a greater reliance on focused schemes that offer standard payments in exchange for standard management requirements. The incorporation of environmental elements within agricultural and rural development grant schemes is also significant.[13]

Byelaws

5.1.9 Where legal restrictions are required, particularly to regulate the conduct of visitors to the land as opposed to that of those with a legal interest in it, recourse is frequently had to byelaws. Again this allows the particular needs of each site to be taken into account and the restrictions to be shaped accordingly. Moreover, the consultation and confirmation procedures associated with the making of byelaws allow there to be some check on what is being done in the name of nature conservation. However, there can be difficulties in ensuring that byelaws are brought to the notice of the public, and visitors to a site often will not know that they have crossed into a special area, far less that they are now bound by an additional set of legal rules or what these control.

Planning controls

5.1.10 Throughout Great Britain, the town and country planning system offers a degree of control over many forms of development which could damage the value of an area as far as wildlife is concerned. One way of providing enhanced protection to those areas identified as being of particular value is to ensure that this value is properly respected in the operation of the planning system, which can be strengthened by the addition of further controls for particular areas.[14] Thus, development plans will reflect the status and objectives of the various designated areas, environmental impact assessments (or at the very least consultation with the conservation bodies) may be required when particular proposals are being considered, and express permission may be required for certain minor forms of development which are normally permitted without the need for individual application or consideration. However, two drawbacks of reliance on the planning system must be noted. In the first place, planning controls are operated by local authorities and central government departments which have responsibilities beyond nature conservation, in particular a concern for the economic well-being of their areas, and there may be conflicts between the interests of conservation and other policy objectives. Secondly, planning controls do not extend to most activities in agriculture and forestry, so that many things which can be done on or to the land and which damage its value as a habitat for wildlife fall outwith the scope of planning controls.[15]

---

[12] "Ministers expect that management agreements on SSSIs will be used to facilitate their positive management ... Ministers are not prepared for public money to be paid out simply to prevent new operations which could destroy or damage these national assets." *Guidelines on Management Agreement Payments and Other Related Matters* (DETR, 2001), para.1.2.

[13] See paras 8.4.6–8.4.12, below.

[14] See section 8.2, below.

[15] Extending planning controls to agricultural, forestry, sporting and conservation-related developments was suggested for Scotland in Land Reform Policy Group, *Recommendations for Action* (Scottish Office, 1996), p.35, but this idea was not pursued.

Notifications

A further technique is used to avoid the imposition of too great a burden of **5.1.11** legal restrictions. Where certain activities may be harmful, what the law provides is not that the activity is prohibited nor that it requires some form of official approval, but rather that the appropriate official body must simply be notified of the proposed activity before it takes place. Such notification enables the authority, where it considers it appropriate, to invoke any of the other control mechanisms which may be available in the circumstances. In this way it should be possible for steps to be taken where necessary to prevent damage occurring, whilst avoiding both the blanket imposition of restrictions which may often be inappropriate or unnecessary, and the formality, delay and bureaucracy of a system of licences, permissions or approvals. The efficacy of such an approach is, however, dependent on both adequate knowledge of and compliance with the notification requirement, and the availability of and willingness to use[16] suitable tools to ensure that damage can in fact be avoided in those cases where it is considered necessary to intervene.

Management Plans

The management plans and statements created for designated areas are **5.1.12** acquiring more significance as a result of the increasing emphasis on a positive approach to conservation issues based on partnership between a range of public bodies and landowners. In some cases, such as National Parks[17] and Areas of Outstanding Natural Beauty[18] in England and Wales, there is no specific obligation on others to take these plans into account, although obviously they are very relevant to any general obligation to have regard to the objectives of the designated area. In other cases, though, the plans are given significant status, e.g. for National Parks in Scotland there is a duty on public authorities to have regard to the Park Plans.[19] Site management plans (Scotland) and management statements (England and Wales) are now an integral part of the SSSI regime and land management orders (Scotland) and management schemes (England and Wales) can be introduced, and action taken against occupiers who fail to comply.[20] The Habitats and Species Directive also establishes a role for management plans.[21] The focus thus shifts from prohibiting a few specified activities to endeavouring to give effect to a wider management plan, which is given some direct legal standing, with potential for further measures to ensure implementation if necessary.

The techniques listed above appear in various forms throughout the legal **5.1.13** regimes for the various designated areas, often in combination and with additional devices not mentioned here. More generally, the fact of

---

[16] In Scotland prior to 1998 only six cases of unlawful operations on SSSIs were reported by SNH and its predecessors to the procurator fiscal, and none was prosecuted (A. Osborne, LL.M. dissertation at Aberdeen University).

[17] See para.5.9.14, below.

[18] See para.5.10.7, below.

[19] See paras 5.9.32–5.9.33, below; planning authorities are required to pay "special attention" to the desirability of exercising their powers consistently with the Plan.

[20] See paras 5.5.18–5.5.20 and 5.5.39–5.5.41, below.

[21] Directive 92/43/EEC art.6(1).

designation should alert people to the value of a site and may influence their treatment of it, e.g. a public authority subject to a duty to have regard to the conservation of the countryside, biological diversity, etc.[22] should consider the consequences of their action for nature conservation before doing anything which affects a designated site.[23] As with so much of the law affecting nature conservation, the fragmented form of the law means that any general comments are of limited practical value, and the detailed rules for each of the designations must now be considered. This fragmentation is exacerbated by differences within Great Britain, so that the rules for Sites of Special Scientific Interest are now significantly different in Scotland from those in England and Wales,[24] whilst the National Parks north and south of the border are very different creatures.[25] The various designations are not exclusive, and it is common for the same piece of land to be covered by a number of different legal regimes, in particular as a Site of Special Scientific Interest and as part of a broader conservation or landscape area.

5.1.14   The rest of this Chapter deals with all of the designations given statutory recognition but many others exist, with varying degrees of official recognition. In England and Wales stretches of Heritage Coast have been identified, and in Scotland there are Preferred Coastal Conservation Zones. There is an inventory, originally compiled by the Nature Conservancy Council, of Ancient and Semi-natural Woodlands which are worthy of particular care, while the Forestry Commission designates some of its land as Forest Parks. At the international level there are a number of Biosphere Reserves, designated under UNESCO's Man and the Biosphere Programme, and Biogenetic Reserves under a Council of Europe programme. There are also many other local or more specialised designations. In all cases, however, if these designations are to have any legal impact on the way in which the land is treated, the sites must also be included in one of the statutory designations described below.

5.1.15   Two designations covered in the previous edition of this book are not discussed here. The scheme for Environmentally Sensitive Areas[26] is no longer open to new applications, although some existing arrangements may still have some time to run. From being the focus of this exceptional scheme the objective of encouraging environmentally friendly farming has now become part of the core of agricultural and rural support mechanisms.[27] Natural Heritage Areas have been abolished without ever making it off the legislative page into practice. As noted in the previous edition,[28] after being introduced for Scotland in 1991[29] this designation was overtaken by the establishment of National Parks and the relevant provisions were repealed

---

[22] See section 2.2, above.

[23] Land which has been designated may also be eligible for an exemption from inheritance tax in certain circumstances; Inheritance Tax Act (née Capital Transfer Tax Act) 1984 ss.30–31.

[24] Some of these differences, such as the existence of the Advisory Committee in Scotland (see para.5.5.32, below), pre-date devolution and the more substantial divergence introduced by the Countryside and Rights of Way Act 2000 and Natural Environment and Rural Communities Act 2006 on the one hand and the Nature Conservation (Scotland) Act 2004 on the other.

[25] See section 5.9, below.

[26] Section 5.9 of the previous edition.

[27] See section 8.4, below.

[28] Section 5.10 of the previous edition.

[29] NHSA 1991 s.6.

in 2004 without any such Area ever being created.[30] The table below indicates the extent of the main current designations.

The Chapter ends (section 5.12) with a brief account of the Environmental Liability Directive which takes a different approach to protecting habitat by applying the polluter pays principle to impose obligations to take preventive or remedial action when environmental damage is threatened or occurs. **5.1.16**

---

[30] NCSA 2004 Sch.7 para.8.

Protected Areas in Great Britain
(by number and area in hectares)

	SCOTLAND	ENGLAND	WALES	CROSS-BORDER
European Sites				
— **Special Protection Areas**	144	78	17	3
	600,219	671,436	123,007	81,385
— **Special Areas of Conservation**	235	228	85	8
	921,207	809,144	589,871	118,030
National Nature Reserves	66	222	69	—
	137,275	92,000	25,348	—
Marine Nature Reserves	—	1	1	—
SSSIs	1455	4,120	1,019	—
	1,035,880	1,074,215	235,000	—
Ramsar Sites	50	66	7	4
	283,083	317,212	11,336	85,973
National Scenic Areas	40	—	—	—
	1,378,358			
Areas of Outstanding National Beauty	—	36	4	1
	—	2,018,400	72,700	32,600

Data from websites of Scottish Natural Heritage (*http://www.snh.org.uk*), Countryside Council for Wales (*http://www.ccw.gov.uk*), Natural England (*http://www.naturalengland.org.uk*), DEFRA (*http://www.defra.gov.uk*) and Joint Nature Conservation Committee (*http://www.jncc.gov.uk*) [All Accessed June 23, 2009), giving data as at different dates in 2008 and 2009.

European Sites

European Sites were created to give effect to the EC Birds and Habitat and **5.2.1** Species Directives. When first introduced, they marked a very significant strengthening of the protection available to any sites in Great Britain, but have now to some extent been overtaken by the new arrangements for SSSIs,[31] although the underlying need to ensure compliance with EC law provides a restraint on discretionary powers relating to those being exercised in ways that do not give priority to conservation. The sites designated under the European measures together comprise the Natura 2000 network and EC law dictates the key elements of the regime affecting them.[32] European Sites under British law are Special Protection Areas designated under the Birds Directive and Special Areas of Conservation under the Habitats and Species Directive, acquiring this status from the beginning of the prolonged designation process.[33]

A register of European Sites must be kept by the Minister and be avail- **5.2.2** able for public inspection at all reasonable hours free of charge,[34] and the Minister must notify the appropriate statutory conservation body when an entry is made or amended.[35] It is then the duty of that body to notify the owners and occupiers of land within the site, the relevant local planning authority and anyone else that the Minister directs.[36] The entry on the register is a local land charge in England and Wales, while in Scotland the planning authority has to maintain a register of European Sites of which they have been notified.[37]

In addition to the direct measures described below, European Sites are **5.2.3** also covered by the terms of the Environmental Liability Directive, described more fully below.[38] This imposes obligations to prevent or remedy the harm on those whose activities may or do cause damage to sites so as to have significant adverse effects on reaching or maintaining a favourable conservation status. These obligations are generally based on fault or negligence but apply regardless of fault in relation to the operators of certain listed activities, but inevitably there are a number of exceptions. The remedial steps required include restoration of the site or where this is not possible the provision of a suitable alternative as well as interim measures while the restoration or alternative provision is being completed.

---

[31] See section 5.5, below.

[32] See generally, C. Rodgers, "Managing Natura 2000: Priorities for Implementing European Wildlife Law" [2001] J.P.L. 265 and section 7.4, below. At the UK level issues are kept under review by the Natura 2000 and Ramsar Forum; see *http://www.defra.gov.uk/wildlife-country-side/protected-areas/natura-ramsar.htm* [Accessed May 10, 2009].

[33] CNHR 1994 reg.10, as amended; see below.

[34] CNHR 1994 reg.11, as amended by CNHASR 2004 reg.7 and CNHAR 2007 reg.5(10).

[35] CNHR 1994 reg.12.

[36] CNHR 1994 reg.13.

[37] CNHR 1994 regs 14 and 15.

[38] Directive 2004/35/EC; see section 5.12, below.

Special Protection Areas

5.2.4 Under the Directive on the Conservation of Wild Birds,[39] the Member States of the European Communities are obliged to take measures for the conservation of wild birds in their territories. In particular, states must designate the most suitable territories in number and size as Special Protection Areas (SPAs) for the conservation of the many rarer species listed in Annex I to the Directive,[40] and take "similar measures" for migratory birds not so listed.[41] The obligation once such an area has been established was originally that Member States were to take "appropriate steps to avoid pollution or deterioration of habitats or any disturbances affecting the birds",[42] but this was amended by the Habitats and Species Directive so that the obligations are now the same as for Special Areas of Conservation.[43]

5.2.5 Both the designation and treatment of Special Protection Areas have given rise to considerable litigation. In relation to designation, there is a clear obligation on states to carry out this process,[44] and to ensure that a sufficient number and size of areas are designated.[45] A series of cases have emphasised that designation is to be carried out on the basis of ornithological criteria alone, without regard for competing economic or social interests.[46] This does allow Member States an element of discretion in identifying the precise areas to be designated, but strictly limited as to the criteria to be used.

5.2.6 The most significant British contribution to the case law has been *R. v Secretary of State for the Environment, ex p. RSPB*,[47] in which the European Court of Justice confirmed that in determining whether a particular area is to be designated, economic or other factors cannot be taken into account. The case arose from the Secretary of State's exclusion of a substantial area of Lappel Bank from an SPA designated in the Medway estuary, a decision admittedly taken with regard to the economic factors arising from the potential for expanding the port of Sheerness. The European Court of Justice held that such factors should have had no place in the decision, but by the time the case was concluded, the area in question was already being

---

[39] Directive 79/409/EEC; see paras 7.4.6–7.4.17, below.
[40] Directive 79/409/EEC art.4(1).
[41] Directive 79/409/EEC art.4(2).
[42] Directive 79/409/EEC art.4(4).
[43] Directive 92/43/EEC art.7, applying art.6(2)–(4).
[44] *Commission v Italy* (C-334/89) [1991] E.C.R. I-93.
[45] *Commission v Netherlands* (C-3/96) [1998] E.C.R. I-3031; *Commission v France* (C-96/98) [1999] E.C.R. I-8351 (Marais Poitevin).
[46] *Commission v Germany* (C-57/89) [1991] E.C.R. I-883 (Leybucht Dykes); *Commission v Spain* (C-355/90) [1993] E.C.R. I-4223 (Santoña Marshes); *R. v Secretary of State for the Environment, Ex p. RSPB* (C-44/95) [1996] E.C.R. I-3805; [1997] Q.B. 206 (Lappel Bank); *Commission v Netherlands* (C-3/96) [1998] E.C.R. I-3031. See para.5.2.10, below in relation to Special Areas of Conservation.
[47] *R. v Secretary of State for the Environment, ex p. RSPB* (C-44/95) [1996] E.C.R. I-3805; [1997] Q.B. 206.

developed.[48] At a more detailed level, the issue of the boundary to be drawn was raised in *WWF-UK Ltd v Secretary of State for Scotland*.[49] The Court of Session held that deciding on a precise boundary was an integral part of the task of identifying the most suitable territories to be designated and rejected the argument that the Secretary of State had unduly fettered his discretion by using the boundaries of existing SSSIs as the starting point for this process.[50] The Directive inevitably left a degree of discretion to Member States in fixing the exact boundaries, but this discretion was to be exercised on ornithological criteria alone.

In terms of protecting an SPA once designated, the European Court of Justice's interpretation of the original provisions of the Birds Directive in the *Leybucht Dykes* case made it clear that it was only in exceptional circumstances that any action which reduced the size (and by clear implication, the quality) of an SPA could be permitted, and held that the balancing of conservation interests with economic and recreational requirements has no place in the treatment of special protection areas once they have been declared.[51] Member States were unhappy at this almost absolute priority given to conservation and the Directive was amended by the application of the provisions in the Habitats and Species Directive, which do permit conservation concerns to be sacrificed in limited circumstances where there are reasons of overriding public interest.[52] Nevertheless, there still remains a strong obligation to ensure adequate protection for designated SPAs, and even for areas that should have been included within SPAs.[53] **5.2.7**

In Great Britain, there is no formal legal procedure for designating SPAs, but as soon as classified as such by the Minister they must be added to the statutory register of European Sites.[54] Unlike Special Areas of Conservation, there is no legal status for "candidate SPAs", that is sites being considered or that might meet the criteria for designation.[55] Such areas, though, may already be subject to other designations and as a matter of policy, not law, may be treated in the same way. Indeed, the European Court of Justice has held that although the formal rules for SPAs do not apply to sites that a Member State should have designated in order to meet its obligations under the Birds Directive, in relation to these sites the state is bound by the stricter rules in the original Birds Directive (as in the *Leybucht Dykes* case) rather than the amended version under the Habitats and Species Directive which **5.2.8**

---

[48] An injunction pending the final outcome of the case was refused because the RSPB could not provide the required undertaking in damages (to compensate the port for the delays if it was finally held that there was no flaw in the initial decision), and the courts did not see EC law as providing a way of circumventing this requirement; for discussion of this point in the Court of Appeal and commentary by J. Harte see (1995) 7 J.E.L. 245, esp. at pp.276–277. In *Commission v Germany* (C-57/89) [1991] E.C.R. I-883 at 889, which is perhaps analogous, interim measures were refused by the European Court of Justice.

[49] *WWF-UK Ltd v Secretary of State for Scotland* [1999] 1 C.M.L.R. 1021; [1999] Env. L.R. 632.

[50] cf. *R(Newsum) v Welsh Assembly Government (No.2)* [2005] EWHC 538 Admin; [2006] Env. L.R. 1 where it was held reasonable to draw the boundaries of an SAC with reference to existing features and boundaries.

[51] *Commission v Germany* (C-57/89) [1991] E.C.R. I-883.

[52] See paras 5.2.25–5.2.35, below.

[53] *Commission v France* (C-96/98) [1999] E.C.R. I-8351 (Marais Poitevin).

[54] CNHR 1994 reg.11(2)(d).

[55] *Bown v Secretary of State for Transport, Local Government and the Regions* [2003] EWCA Civ 1170; [2004] Env. L.R. 26.

allow for overriding considerations.[56] It was held, though, in *Humber Sea Terminals Ltd v Secretary of State for Transport*[57] that this approach applies not to every site which is being considered as a potential SPA, but only where it is established that non-designation amounts to a breach of the Directive.

Special Areas of Conservation

5.2.9 The status of European Sites within Great Britain is also conferred on sites identified in relation to Special Areas of Conservation (SACs) under the Habitats and Species Directive.[58] This covers sites at any of four stages in the designation process. The first of these is sites that have completed the full process at national and Community level[59] and have been formally designated by the Minister as SACs.[60] The second comprises those sites which after nomination at national level have been selected by the Commission as sites of Community importance and therefore require only formal designation at national level to become a full SAC. The third category covers sites which have not been nominated at national level as candidate SACs but which the Commission proposes on the basis that they host priority habitats or species.[61] This third category are treated as European Sites only during the period that their status is being considered at EC level and they are not covered by the provisions in relation to plans and projects which play a significant part in protecting the other categories of site.[62] The fourth category (added in England in 2000, in Scotland in 2004 and in Wales in 2007) are sites which the government has submitted to the Commission as candidates for inclusion in the list of sites of Community importance.[63] Previously planning and other policy had stated that candidate sites should be treated in the same way as those which had advanced sufficiently far through the process to acquire legal protection, but they had no formal legal status.

5.2.10 The criteria for nominating or selecting an SAC are set out in Annex III of the Directive and require Member States to identify areas which represent

---

[56] *Commission v France* (C-374/98) [2001] E.C.R. I-10,799; see G. Machin, "Protecting Bird Habitat of European Importance – the view from Basses Corbières" (2004) 3 Env. L. Rev. 174 and para.7.4.14, below.

[57] *Humber Sea Terminals Ltd v Secretary of State for Transport* [2005] EWHC 1289 Admin, [2006] Env. L.R. 4.

[58] CNHR 1994 reg.10, as amended in slightly different terms by CNHASR 2004 reg.6 and CNHAR 2007 reg.5(9).

[59] Designation is governed by arts 4 and 5 of the Directive; see paras 7.4.25–7.4.28, below.

[60] CNHR 1994 reg.8; ministerial designation must be within six years of the site's acceptance at EC level.

[61] The Commission in practice has also used less formal means to encourage Member States to designate sufficient sites; see *Lafarge Redland Aggregates Ltd v Scottish Ministers*, 2000 S.L.T. 1361 at [6]–[7].

[62] CNHR 1994 reg.10(2) (disapplying regs 20(1) and (2), 24 and 48) and reg.85B(6); see below for details.

[63] CNHR 1994 reg.10(1)(e) added by the Conservation (Natural Habitats etc.) (England) (Amendment) Regulations 2000 (SI 2000/192), and substituted for England and Wales by CNHAR 2007 reg.5(9) and added for Scotland by CNHASR 2004 reg.6; the two versions are slightly differently worded, the Scottish one referring to reg.7 of the 1994 Regulations and the English and Welsh one to provisions in the Directive.

the habitats or host the species listed in the Directive as requiring protection.[64] As with SPAs, it has been held that nomination is to be based on the scientific criteria alone. In *R. v Secretary of State for the Environment, Transport and the Regions, ex p. First Corporation Shipping Ltd*,[65] the proposal to nominate the Severn Estuary as a candidate SAC was challenged by the port authority for Bristol, the argument being based on the terms of article 2(3) of the Directive which states that measures taken pursuant to the Directive should take into account economic, social and cultural requirements. The European Court of Justice rejected this argument, stating that the requirement to set up "a coherent European ecological network" of SACs under article 3 of the Directive could only be satisfied if all eligible sites were nominated at the first stage, since without detailed knowledge of the economic, social and cultural requirements in other states Member States could not judge whether omitting a particular site would jeopardise that overall objective. Only if all sites that met the technical criteria were put forward would the Commission have an exhaustive list from which to ensure that the coherent network was established. The sole focus on the scientific criteria was repeated in *R. (Newsum) v Welsh Assembly Government (No.2)*[66] where it was confirmed that no consideration should be given to which activities could lawfully be carried out on the site under planning law.

There is no legally prescribed procedure for reaching the stage of a proposal being made, but in practice there has been substantial consultation with affected parties at this stage, as demonstrated in the unsuccessful challenge to a proposal in *R. (Newsum) v Welsh Assembly Government (No.2)*.[67] That case also demonstrates the potential for judicial review to be sought, on substantive grounds as well as procedural ones. **5.2.11**

Protection

The protection of European Sites rests on a number of measures in domestic law. In order to fulfil their statutory duty to protect them from damage or deterioration, Ministers and conservation authorities can make use of management agreements, notification procedures delaying or prohibiting damaging operations, byelaws and compulsory purchase, whilst any plan or project likely to have adverse consequences on the site is to be given approval only if strict conditions are met. Several of these mechanisms control not just activities within the boundaries of a site, but also those outwith the boundaries that may have an effect on the state of the site. The whole framework is now somewhat awkward in England and Wales since it was designed to build on the legal structures for SSSIs introduced by the **5.2.12**

---

[64] Details of the selection process in the UK were given in *First report by the United Kingdom under Article 17 on implementation of the Directive from June 1994 to December 2000* (DEFRA, 2001) pp.9–20 and are in *The Habitats Directive: selection of Special Areas of Conservation in the UK* on the JNCC's website at *http://www.jncc.gov.uk/page-1457* [Accessed May 10, 2009].

[65] *R. v Secretary of State for the Environment, Transport and the Regions, ex p. First Corporation Shipping Ltd* (C-371/98) [2000] E.C.R. I-9253.

[66] *R. (Newsum) v Welsh Assembly Government (No.2)* [2005] EWHC 538 Admin; [2006] Env. L.R. 1.

[67] *R. (Newsum) v Welsh Assembly Government (No.2)* [2005] EWHC 538 Admin; [2006] Env. L.R. 1.

Wildlife and Countryside Act 1981 and to increase that level of protection for the benefit of European Sites, whereas the new provisions for SSSIs[68] establish a significantly different regime, in some respects offering greater, rather than lesser, protection than applies for European Sites.[69] Where a site is covered by both designations, there may be cases where reliance on the new SSSI provisions is preferable to the conservation authorities than utilising the measures for European Sites. In Scotland the new regime for SSSIs has been extended to apply to European Sites, replacing the earlier provisions.[70]

5.2.13   The starting point for conservation responsibilities is that Ministers and the statutory conservation bodies are under a duty to exercise their functions under the main conservation legislation so as to secure compliance with the Habitats and Species Directive,[71] which requires for European Sites that appropriate steps are taken to avoid deterioration of the habitats or disturbance of the species for which they have been designated.[72] All other "competent authorities"[73] are under the lesser duty to have regard to the requirements of the Directive.[74] The stronger duty could have been fulfilled by a willingness to make full use of the powers of compulsory purchase under that legislation to take the land into ownership which would ensure that it was managed for conservation purposes, but the approach taken was to rely primarily on the existing mechanisms used for SSSIs, strengthening them where necessary to ease the task of securing compliance with the Directive. Since almost all European Sites will already have been designated as SSSIs, and possibly as nature reserves, provision is made for existing management agreements, orders, notifications and byelaws to continue to have effect as if made under the provisions for European Sites.[75]

5.2.14   Throughout the various mechanisms described below, and in relation to various other potential threats to a European Site, there is a general requirement that applies whenever a plan or project that might affect the site is being considered for approval, in essence permitting approval to be given only if there is to be no adverse effect on the site or there is an overriding reason for giving approval. This is more fully discussed below.

---

[68] Set out for England and Wales in the 1981 Act as amended by CRWA 2000 and for Scotland in NCSA 2004; see section 5.5, below.

[69] The potential for making management notices or land management orders is one example.

[70] NCSA 2004 Part II as applied by CNHR 1994 regs 18–22 as amended by CNHASR 2004 (SSI 2004/475) reg.9.

[71] CNHR 1994 reg.3(2); the legislation covered is Pt III of NPACA 1949 (nature reserves), s.49A of the CSA 1967 (management agreements), s.15 of CA 1968 (management agreements), Pt I and ss.28–38 of WCA 1981 (species protection, SSSIs and other habitat protection), ss.131–134 of the Environmental Protection Act 1990 (nature conservation bodies and functions), ss.2, 3, 5, 6, 7 and 11 of the NHSA 1991 (duties and functions of SNH, and Natural Heritage Areas), Pt 2 of NCSA 2004 and the 1994 Regulations themselves. For the obligation in relation to marine sites see para.5.2.39, below.

[72] Directive 92/43/EEC art.6(2); see *Managing Natura 2000 Sites: The provisions of Article 6 of the 'Habitats' Directive 92/43/EEC* (European Commission, 2000).

[73] This term covers Ministers, government departments, public or statutory undertakers, public bodies and holders of public office; CNHR 1994 reg.6(1).

[74] CNHR 1994 reg.3(4).

[75] CNHR 1994 regs 17, 18, 21, 27 and 31.

In keeping with what was the dominant preference for a voluntary **5.2.15** approach to nature conservation,[76] the first mechanism provided for the protection of European Sites is the management agreement. The appropriate nature conservation body can make an agreement with the owner, lessee and occupier of land within a European Site for its management, conservation, restoration or protection.[77] The power to make agreements is extended to apply to land adjacent to such a site as well; this is one of several features where the legal regime for European Sites can have an impact outwith the boundaries of the sites themselves. These agreements may provide for the management of the land and the carrying out of specific activities or tasks and can provide for payments for the costs of work or as compensation for restrictions imposed by the agreement.[78] The agreement can thus be to secure long-term management or simply to carry out particular works, and the scope to control activities outwith the boundaries of the site may be important, particularly where water flow or drainage are significant to the state of the site. An agreement can run with the land, binding the successors to the original parties, in England and Wales as if it were a restrictive covenant that the conservation body is entitled to enforce (but without the Lands Tribunal having the power to discharge or modify it), and in Scotland by direct provision enabling the conservation body to register the agreement in the Land Register or Register of Sasines and then enforce it against anyone with an interest in the land.[79]

Further controls diverge between Scotland and England and Wales. The **5.2.16** latter maintains a structure that builds on the system for SSSIs created by the Wildlife and Countryside Act 1981, but has now been overtaken by the new regime introduced by the Countryside and Rights of Way Act 2000.[80] In Scotland, the opportunity was taken to simplify the law, making use of the fact that the sites will already be covered by the revised SSSI provisions in the Nature Conservation (Scotland) Act 2004 and making just a few adjustments.

In England and Wales the starting point is that the process for designating **5.2.17** an SSSI includes notification of a list of potentially damaging operations (PDOs) that the conservation body considers likely to damage the flora, fauna or geological or physiographical features for which the land was designated. For European Sites the basic pattern established under the 1981 Act is adjusted by permitting the conservation body at any time to amend the original notification, with regard to both the reason for designation and the list of PDOs.[81] This avoids the position where the conservation body has "only one bite at the cherry", a situation that risks either gaps in the

---

[76] The need for stronger powers to meet the obligations under EC law for European Sites itself played a major part in overcoming the political reluctance to move from a wholly voluntary approach to one where more direct regulatory powers are available; see paras 1.6.3–1.6.12, above.

[77] CNHR 1994 reg.16. The power to enter management agreements is expressly conferred on a number of limited owners of land, including tenants for life under the Settled Land Act 1925, universities and colleges under the Universities and Colleges Estates Act 1925, certain church lands, liferenters in possession and trustees (reg.86).

[78] There are further rules on the payment of farm capital grants (CNHR 1994 regs 88–89).

[79] Third parties bona fide onerously acquiring their interest prior to recording of the agreement are not bound.

[80] This regime was itself influenced by features introduced for European Sites in 1994.

[81] CNHR 1994 reg.18

notification or an excessively thorough listing of all imaginable features and operations with the consequent excessive regulatory burden on the owners.

5.2.18 The owner or occupier must give written notice before carrying out any of these operations and can proceed only if one of a number of conditions is met.[82] These are that the conservation body has given its written consent,[83] that the operation is carried out in accordance with a management agreement or that four months have passed from the date of the notification.[84] In the absence of a reasonable excuse, carrying out the operation without notice or without these conditions being met is a crime, but it expressly stated that a reasonable excuse is provided by either an emergency, provided that details are notified to the conservation body as soon as possible, or by the grant of planning permission for the operation.[85] These provisions therefore do not prohibit operations that are potentially damaging, but merely impose a four-month delay, during which time a management agreement can be reached or stronger measures imposed.

5.2.19 The stronger measures available include a special nature conservation order.[86] These orders are made by the Minister after consultation with the conservation body in relation to operations that appear likely to destroy or damage the valuable flora, fauna or features of the site. Orders take effect as soon as they are made, and can be amended, but lapse after nine months unless the Minister confirms that he has considered the order and does not propose to amend or revoke it. Notice of an order, and the means of making representations or objections (at least 28 days must be permitted for this) must be served on every owner and occupier of the land and on the local planning authority as well as advertised in the London Gazette and at least one local newspaper; the requirement to notify owners and occupiers can be replaced by notices fixed to conspicuous objects on the land. In the absence of representations or objections, the Minister is to consider the order and confirm, amend or revoke it. Where there are representations or objections within the specified period, then a local inquiry or hearing must be held before the Minister considers the order and its conformation, amendment or revocation. The confirmation order must be publicised in the same way and any legal challenge to its validity must be made within six weeks.[87] Orders are registered as local land charges and must be included in the annual reports of the conservation bodies.[88]

5.2.20 Where an order is in force, it is an offence for any person, not just the owner or occupier, to carry out a listed operation unless certain

---

[82] CNHR 1994 reg.19

[83] See paras 5.2.25–5.2.31, below on the requirements before consent can be given.

[84] The four-month period can by agreement be extended indefinitely; if notice to terminate this agreement is given, then at least one further month must pass before the operation becomes lawful (CNHR 1994 reg.87).

[85] By referring to an "operation authorised by a planning permission granted on an application under [the planning legislation]" (CNHR 1994 reg.19(4)(b)), the scope of the defence is limited to operations with the benefit of an express grant of permission, not those with deemed permission under the General Permitted Development Orders (see para.8.2.12, below). The grant of planning permission will only be lawful in circumstances where the tests for any approval for plans or projects affecting a site are met (see paras 5.2.25–5.2.33, below).

[86] CNHR 1994 reg.22.

[87] CNHR 1994 Sch.1.

[88] CNHR 1994 reg.22 (4) and (6).

requirements are met.[89] The owner or occupier is again required to give notice in advance and the operations may proceed only if the conservation body gives its written consent or if the operation is carried out in accordance with a management agreement. Where a special nature conservation order has been made, therefore, the controls on owners and occupiers are considerably strengthened, in that operations can be prohibited indefinitely, as opposed to merely delayed for four months[90] and the prohibition applies to other parties as well. The presence of a reasonable excuse provides a defence, including emergencies and operations with planning permission. The offence attracts a higher penalty than under the more general provisions, and in addition to any other penalty, the offender may be ordered to carry out operations in order to restore the land to its former condition.[91] If the effect of a special nature conservation order is to lower the value of an agricultural unit, compensation is payable by the conservation body to any applicant with an interest in the land.[92]

In Scotland, the provisions covered in the preceding four paragraphs have been repealed and replaced[93] by provisions that apply to European Sites, the revised measures that apply to SSSIs and nature conservation orders as described in the sections below.[94] The first provision makes it a criminal offence for anyone intentionally or recklessly to damage any natural feature[95] which has led to the designation of a European Site.[96] A defence is provided where the act was the incidental result of a lawful operation, where reasonable precautions were taken to avoid the harmful act or the act was not foreseen and could not reasonably have been foreseen as an incidental result of the lawful operation, and the steps that were reasonably practicable in all the circumstances were taken to minimise the damage caused. Other provisions[97] then apply to European Sites, the rules (with the necessary consequential changes) contained in the Nature Conservation (Scotland) Act 2004 dealing with nature conservation orders,[98] land management orders, offences and restoration orders, powers of entry and investigation and powers to erect and maintain signs.[99] These enable SNH to prevent damaging operations on the site and to require certain operations to be undertaken, as well as giving it the necessary powers to exercise its function, all in a way that ensures greater consistency between the law for European Sites and other designations of land. **5.2.21**

---

[89] CNHR 1994 reg.23.

[90] This is now automatically the position for SSSIs, without the need for the Minister to make any further order; see para.5.5.13, below.

[91] CNHR 1994 reg.26

[92] CNHR 1994 reg.25. The amount of compensation represents the difference between the value of the interest in the land as it is and as it would be if the order had not been made, and there are rules on assessment, payment of interest, disputes, etc. (CNHR 1994 regs 91–93).

[93] CNHASR 2004 reg.9.

[94] See paras 5.5.29–5.5.48 and section 5.6, below.

[95] For the purposes of the 1994 Regulations in Scotland, "natural feature" in relation to any land means any of its flora or fauna or any natural habitat existing on it; CNHR 1994 reg.2(1) as amended by CNHASR 2004 reg.4; this is a different definition of "natural feature" than the one in NCSA 2004 s.3(2).

[96] CNHR 1994 reg.18, as substituted by CNHASR 2004 reg.9.

[97] CNHR 1994 regs 19–22, as substituted by CNHASR 2004 reg.9.

[98] NCSA 2004 ss.23–28 and Sch.2; see section 5.6, below.

[99] NCSA 2004 ss.29–41, 43, 44, 46 and Sch.3; see section 5.5, below.

5.2.22   In both jurisdictions the nature conservation body can also make byelaws for the site under the provisions for making byelaws for nature reserves.[100] The byelaws can apply to land surrounding or adjoining the site as well as the site itself and may address a wide range of issues including entry or movement of people, animals or vehicles, killing or disturbing any creatures, taking or interfering with vegetation or soil, depositing of rubbish or the lighting of fires. The byelaws, however, cannot limit the exercise of rights of the owner, occupier or lessee of the land,[101] the exercise of public rights of way or the exercise of functions of certain statutory undertakers, drainage and fisheries bodies and telecommunication operators.[102] Compensation is payable where a person's rights are restricted by byelaws.[103]

5.2.23   The final tool available to secure that a site does not suffer deterioration or damage is compulsory purchase.[104] This is available where the statutory conservation body is satisfied that it is impossible to reach a management agreement in relation to an interest in land within the site[105] on terms that appear to it to be reasonable, or where an agreement has been reached but broken in a way that prevents or impairs the satisfactory management of the site. If the breach is capable of remedy, compulsory purchase is only possible if there has been a failure to remedy it within a reasonable time of the conservation body serving a notice requiring the remedying of the breach. Disputes over whether there has been a breach are referred to arbitration in the hands of an appointee of the Lord Chancellor or Lord President.

5.2.24   Other provisions in the 1994 Regulations provide a range of authorised officials with powers of entry to ascertain if an offence has been committed, if a special nature conservation order should be made, to assess compensation and to survey land with a view to acquiring an interest in it.[106] In England and Wales further powers to take samples and authorising the activities of wildlife inspectors have been added,[107] whereas for Scotland the purpose is served by applying the extended powers under the amended Wildlife and Countryside Act 1981.[108]

Plans and Projects

5.2.25 A major feature of the regime for protecting European Sites is the restriction on the circumstances in which approval can be given for any plan or project[109] affecting a site. The basic rules, taken directly from the Habitats and

---

[100] CNHR 1994 reg.28, applying NPACA 1949 s.20 which in turn applies ss.236–238 of the Local Government Act 1972 and ss.201–204 of the Local Government Act (Scotland) 1973, with byelaws subject to ministerial approval (reg.94); see para.5.3.5, below.

[101] Control over these parties is achieved by the restrictions on PDOs or by means of a management agreement.

[102] CNHR 1994 reg.29.

[103] CNHR 1994 regs 30, 96 and 97.

[104] CNHR 1994 reg.32; the Acquisition of Land Act 1981, Compulsory Purchase Act 1965 and the Acquisition of Land (Authorisation Procedure) (Scotland) Act 1947 apply to such purchases (CNHR 1994 reg.98).

[105] Note that whereas the power to enter management agreements extends to land adjacent to a European Site, the power of compulsory purchase is restricted to the site itself.

[106] CNHR 1994 regs 90, 95 and 99; of these only reg.95 still applies in Scotland.

[107] CNHR 1994 regs 101A–101I, added by CNHAR 2007 reg.5(58).

[108] CNHR 1994 reg.101A, added by CNHASR 2004 reg.18, applying WCA 1981 ss.19ZC and 19ZD.

[109] See paras 5.2.34 and 7.4.29, below for what qualifies as a "plan or project".

Species Directive,[110] are laid out in the 1994 Regulations, which also make specific provisions in order to incorporate these requirements into a number of specific approval mechanisms. The rules apply to any plan or project which is likely to have a significant effect on a European site and is not directly connected with or necessary to the management of the site, and not just to projects on the site itself, but to all those that may have a significant effect on it.[111] The term "plan or project" is not defined but it has been held that it should be given a broad interpretation, consistent with the purpose of the Directive,[112] although not so broad as to cover every decision which would lead to some activity on the site.[113] The body responsible for giving approval must make an "appropriate assessment" of the implications for the site, and it is provided that the proposer of the plan must provide any information that is reasonably required and that the authorising body must consult the relevant statutory conservation body, and may consult the public.

Approval can be given only if the authorising body is satisfied that there **5.2.26** will be no adverse effect on the integrity of the site[114] or, if there will be an adverse effect, that a number of very strict conditions are met. The determination of whether there are adverse effects is to be taken in the light of the Directives' objectives of avoiding any "significant" disturbance,[115] and consideration is to be given to both the effects on the survival across the natural range of the species being protected and the effects on the species on the particular site.[116] The European Court of Justice has held in the *Waddenzee* case[117] that deciding that a site will not be adversely affected requires that there be no reasonable scientific doubt that such effects would occur.[118] In many circumstances the determination of effects will take place as part of

---

[110] Directive 92/43/EEC art.6; see paras 7.4.29–7.4.30, below, for a fuller discussion of the European case-law.

[111] These requirements do not apply to sites that are European Sites only by virtue of the Commission considering that they be added to those nominated by the British authorities (CNHR 1994 regs 10(2) and 48(7)); see para.5.2.9, above.

[112] *R. (Friends of the Earth) v Environment Agency* [2003] EWHC 3193 Admin; [2004] Env. L.R. 31, at [60].

[113] In *RSPB v Secretary of State for Scotland*, 2000 S.L.T. 22 at 27–28, such a broad definition was rejected and the phrase was seen as referring to what is normally regarded as development or land use proposals, extraneous to the management of the site. Since then, European case-law, notably *Landelijke Vereniging tot Behoud van de Waddenzee, Nederlandse Vereniging tot Bescherming van Vogels v Staatssecretaris van Landbouw, Natuurbeheer en Visserij* (C-127/02) [2004] E.C.R. I-7405, has suggested that a narrow approach is not appropriate and in *Boggis v English Nature* [2008] EWHC 2954 Admin; [2009] Env. L.R. 20, it was held that, in some circumstances at least, the designation of an area as an SSSI will qualify as a "plan or project". See para.5.2.34, below.

[114] In *WWF-UK Ltd v Secretary of State for Scotland* [1999] 1 C.M.L.R. 1021; [1999] Env. L.R. 632, Lord Nimmo Smith accepted the definition given in para.2 of Appendix A to Annex D to Circular Scottish Office 6/1995: "The integrity of a site is the coherence of its ecological structure and function, across its whole area, that enables it to sustain the habitat, complex of habitats and/or the levels of populations of the species for which it was classified."

[115] Habitats and Species Directive art.6(2); see para.5.2.27, below.

[116] *RSPB v Secretary of State for Scotland*, 2000 S.L.T. 1272.

[117] *Landelijke Vereniging tot Behoud van de Waddenzee, Nederlandse Vereniging tot Bescherming van Vogels v Staatssecretaris van Landbouw, Natuurbeheer en Visserij* (C-127/02) [2004] E.C.R. I-7405.

[118] Interpreted as requiring "ascertainment with a high degree of certainty" by Jackson J. at first instance in *R(Lewis) v Redcar and Cleveland District Council* [2007] EWHC 3166 Admin at [118]; see also *Boggis v English Nature* [2008] EWHC 2954 Admin; [2009] Env. L.R. 20.

a formal environmental impact assessment of the proposal required as part of the approval process,[119] but this need not be the case, e.g. the statutory conservation bodies in deciding whether to permit a PDO will be required to assess the proposal's impact on the conservation value of the site but not to carry out a full environmental impact assessment.[120] In carrying out the assessment of whether adverse effects are likely, the authority is entitled to consider any mitigation measures that form part of the plan or project[121] and the ability to use conditions in any permission to obviate any potential adverse effects is also relevant.[122]

5.2.27　　Failure to carry out an assessment will lead to the resulting decision being held to be unlawful, even where it is likely that the result of the assessment will not affect the final outcome.[123] On the other hand, the courts have not been sympathetic to challenges that the assessment has not been adequate where the decision-making authority has sought and followed expert advice from the statutory nature conservation bodies and others.[124] Nevertheless, whereas Pill L.J. in *R. (Lewis) v Redcar and Cleveland District Council* seemed happy to rely simply on the fact that the experts were aware of the test to be applied in reaching the decision,[125] in *Skye Windfarm Action Group Ltd v Highland Council*[126] Lord Hodge initially expressed concern over how he could be sure that SNH in its advice had applied the test of "no reasonable scientific doubt" before being reassured by further documents. There is clearly an onus on those advising the decision-making authority and the authority itself in reaching its decision to make it clear that their advice and conclusions are based on a firm understanding of the relevant standards as set out in the *Waddenzee* case.[127]

5.2.28　　The main condition where there is an adverse effect is that the plan or project can be approved only if it is to be carried out for "imperative reasons of overriding public interest".[128] These reasons may include social or economic ones,[129] but in relation to some sites only a restricted category of

---

[119] See section 8.3, below.

[120] That "no particular method is required for carrying out the appropriate assessment" was the second lesson drawn from the *Waddenzee* case by Jackson J. at first instance in *R(Lewis) v Redcar and Cleveland District Council* [2007] EWHC 3166 Admin at [118].

[121] *R. (Hart District Council) v Secretary of State for Communities and Local Government* [2008] EWHC 1204 Admin; [2008] 2 P.&C.R. 16; J. Lunt and K. Lischak, "Natural England – a new dawn? Rights and responsibilities towards the natural environment and how they may change – the 'Dilly Lane' case" (2008) 20 E.L.M. 246.

[122] In *WWF-UK v Secretary of State for Scotland* [1999] 1 C.M.L.R. 1021; [1999] Env. L.R. 632, it was accepted that it may be impossible to guarantee the absence of adverse effects, but what was required was for the authority to identify potential risks so far as foreseeable and to put in place a legally enforceable framework to prevent them materialising.

[123] *Boggis v English Nature* [2008] EWHC 2954 Admin; [2009] Env. L.R. 20.

[124] See the cases mentioned in this paragraph and *R. (Hart District Council) v Secretary of State for Communities and Local Government* [2008] EWHC 1204 Admin; [2008] 2 P.&C.R. 16.

[125] *R. (Lewis) v Redcar and Cleveland District Council* [2008] EWCA Civ 746 at [85].

[126] *Skye Windfarm Action Group Ltd v Highland Council* [2008] CSOH 19 at [135].

[127] Useful guidance in relation to planning and European Sites and other designations is provided in ODPM Circular 06/2005.

[128] CNHR 1994 reg.49, following art.6(4) of the Directive.

[129] In *R. v Secretary of State for Transport, ex p. Berkshire, Buckinghamshire and Oxfordshire Naturalists Trust* [1997] Env. L.R. 80 it was held that this test would have been satisfied in relation to the Newbury bypass by virtue of the relief offered from the environmental problems caused by heavy traffic along the existing road, improved road safety and the relief of the economic burden of traffic delays; see also para.7.4.30, below.

reasons will be acceptable. Where the site hosts a priority species or habitat, then only reasons relating to human health, public safety, beneficial consequences of primary importance to the environment or reasons expressly accepted by the European Commission can be accepted.[130] The further condition to be met is that there are no alternative solutions, although it is not clear how radical the consideration of options must be.[131] It is therefore at this stage of considering particular damaging proposals, not at designation, that there is some scope for a balancing of the needs of conservation against other public interests. The hurdle to be overcome before damaging activities can be permitted is a high one, especially in relation to priority sites, but the scope for conservation to be overridden in some circumstances has made the whole scheme much more acceptable to Member States across Europe than the more absolutist approach initially adopted under the Birds Directive.

In practice the need to protect European Sites has led to the refusal of development proposals in some high-profile cases. In April 2008, plans for a windfarm of over 230 turbines in the north of Lewis, largely on one SPA and affecting others, were rejected on this basis,[132] and other renewable energy projects have also fallen foul of these rules.[133] A major port development at Dibden Bay on the Solent was refused in 2004,[134] and the impact on European Sites is a major element in debate over the Severn Barrage.[135] **5.2.29**

If a project is permitted to proceed despite its damaging effects, there is an obligation on the Minister to ensue that any necessary compensatory measures are taken to ensure that the overall coherence of Natura 2000 is protected.[136] Thus when the Cardiff Bay barrage scheme resulted in the loss of important feeding grounds for waders, a new wetlands reserve was created on the Gwent Levels east of Newport.[137] **5.2.30**

These requirements to scrutinise carefully new plans and projects extend to require a review of existing approvals when a site becomes a European Site, and their revocation or amendment if they cannot be justified according to the same criteria as for new plans.[138] Such review, however, does not affect the validity of any action already taken in pursuance of the **5.2.31**

---

[130] See L. Krämer, "The European Commission's Opinions under art.6(4) of the Habitats Directive" (2009) 21 J.E.L. 59, where it was suggested that on occasions the Commission has been too easily swayed by the arguments in favour of development.

[131] If the proposal is for a power station, do the alternatives include simply different locations or do they extend to requiring greater energy efficiency so as to avoid the need for the new station? cf. para.3.3.12, above.

[132] Decision letter available at: *http://www.scotland.gov.uk/Resource/Doc/917/0059358.doc* [Accessed May 10, 2009].

[133] See, for example A. Pillai, C. Reid and A. Black, "Reconciling Renewable Energy and the Local Impacts of Hydro-electric Development" (2005) 7 Env. L. Rev. 110.

[134] G. Machin, "Balancing Major Development Proposals against International Nature Conservation Interests: The Dibden Terminal decision" (2005) 2 *Law, Science and Policy* 285.

[135] See the material on the Severn Estuary Partnership's website at: *http://www.severnestuary.net/sep/resource.html* [Accessed May 10, 2009].

[136] CNHR 1994 reg.53.

[137] This has in turn given rise to legal disputes over the exercise of compulsory purchase powers to establish the new reserve: *Waters v Welsh Development Agency* [2004] UKHL 19; [2004] 1 W.L.R. 1304. See also M. Lawton, "Ecological Compensation within the UK Planning System: The effect of art.6(4) of the Habitats Directive on three south coast port developments" (2007) 18 *Water Law* 47.

[138] CNHR 1994 regs 50–51.

approval before the site was designated. This means that a planning permission for development on a site, or consent from the conservation body for a PDO granted when the site was simply an SSSI, would have to be reviewed if it was not yet implemented when the site was designated as a European Site, but that there are no consequences if the permission or consent has already been acted on. If revocation or modification of an approval is necessary, this should be done through the relevant statutory procedures, which may well involve the payment of compensation.[139]

5.2.32   These general requirements in relation to all forms of official approval, consent, permission or authorisation are supplemented by a number of more specific provisions which embed these requirements in the specific contexts of a number of particular approval regimes. Thus there are specific provisions in relation to roads and highways, electricity works, pipe-lines, orders under the Transport and Works Act 1992 and environmental consents in relation to integrated pollution prevention and control, waste management licensing and water pollution[140]; specific rules for water abstraction and works authorised under water legislation have been belatedly added.[141] The most thorough express incorporation relates to the grant of planning permission, where there are special rules for special development orders, simplified planning zones and enterprise zones,[142] as well as detailed rules on the grant of permission and on when and how existing permissions are to be reviewed.[143] There are also rules that prevent permitted development rights extending to authorise activities that should not be permitted under the rules designed to protect European Sites.

5.2.33   Certain activities that qualify as "development" and therefore would require planning permission are given automatic permission by means of the General Permitted Development Orders, so that there is no need to apply for an express grant of planning permission before proceeding.[144] This automatic permission is now subject to a condition that if the development is likely to have a significant effect on a European Site and is not directly concerned with the management of the site, then it can proceed only if certain further stages have been completed.[145] The developers must obtain written approval from the planning authority before the development can proceed, and this can be granted only if the authority is satisfied that there will be no adverse effect on the integrity of the site. The relevant statutory conservation body can be asked for its opinion, which is conclusive, on whether such an effect is likely.[146] If the planning authority is not satisfied that there will be no adverse effect, then the development does not enjoy

---

[139] e.g. TCPA 1990 ss.97 and 106; TCPSA 1997 ss.65 and 232.

[140] CNHR 1994 regs 69–70, 71–74, 75–78, 79–82 and 83–85 respectively.

[141] CNHR 1994 reg.84B, as added separately by CNHAR 2007 reg.5(48) and CNHASR 2007 reg.20, both as a consequence of the finding that the absence of such rules amounted to a failure to implement the Directive, despite the UK government's argument that the general provisions in the Regulations in effect ensured compliance; *Commission v UK* (C-6/04) [2005] E.C.R. I-9017.

[142] CNHR 1994 regs 64–67.

[143] CNHR 1994 regs 54–59.

[144] See para.8.2.12, below.

[145] CNHR 1994 regs 60–63.

[146] The developer may seek this opinion directly, in which case the conservation body must notify its response to both developer and planning authority, or may apply for approval from the planning authority, which must consult the conservation body.

permitted development rights and the developers must apply for planning permission in the standard way, and their application will be subject to scrutiny applying the same tests as for other plans affecting European Sites. It is asking a lot of landowners and developers, including those outwith the boundaries of a European Site, to be so vigilant when planning what is normally permitted development that they will notice when their operations may affect such a site and then to raise an issue which will at best delay their activities and at worst impose a requirement to seek express permission with the real risk of refusal.

One significant gap in the implementation of this part of the Habitats and **5.2.34** Species Directive proved to be in relation to land use plans, i.e. development plans under the town and country planning legislation.[147] In *Commission v UK*[148] it was argued successfully before the European Court of Justice that such plans fell within the definition of "plans and projects" which have to undergo an assessment and proceed only if the criteria in the Directive are met. It was accepted that development plans did not by themselves authorise any development but their impact on the final decisions was held to be significant enough to be caught by the Directive,[149] especially in view of the statutory requirement to decide applications in accordance with the plan unless material considerations indicate otherwise.[150] By not subjecting such plans to the scrutiny required by the Directive, the UK had failed to implement it properly. The same basic reasoning was applied by the English Court in *Boggis v English Nature* to decide that designation of an SSSI could qualify as a plan or project where in the particular circumstances it was clear that this was in effect determining whether the maintenance of coastal defences would be authorised.[151]

The response to the decision of the European Court of Justice has been to **5.2.35** add new rules[152] requiring that "land use plans", defined in terms of the relevant town and country planning legislation,[153] are subjected to any appropriate assessment of their impact on the conservation objectives for an European Site that may be significantly affected.[154] The plan-making authority must consult the relevant statutory conservation body and may consult with the public. The plan can only be formally adopted or approved if it will not adversely affect the integrity of the European Site,[155] or if the standard criteria for proceeding in spite of a negative assessment are satisfied, namely the absence of alternatives and an overriding public interest.[156] Where plans are being adopted by authorities other than the Minister in the face of a negative assessment, the Minister must be notified and the

---

[147] See section 8.2, below.

[148] *Commission v UK* (C-6/04) [2005] E.C.R. I-9017.

[149] The telling point was made by Advocate-General Kokott that if the Directive's provisions were restricted to the final authorisation of a proposal, then there would be no function for the word "plan" in the phrase "plan or project" in the wording of art.6(3); *Commission v UK* (C-6/04) [2005] E.C.R. I-9017 at [41] of Advocate-General's opinion.

[150] TCPSA 1997 s.25; Planning and Compulsory Purchase Act 2004 s.38(6).

[151] *Boggis v English Nature* [2008] EWHC 2954 Admin; [2009] Env. L.R. 20.

[152] CNHR 1994 regs 85A–85E, added separately by CNHAR 2007 reg.5(55) and CNHASR 2007 reg.22 and Sch.1; the two sets of rules are essentially parallel.

[153] CNHR 1994 reg.85A.

[154] CNHR 1994 reg.85B.

[155] CNHR 1994 reg.85B(4).

[156] CNHR 1994 reg.85C.

implementation of the plan delayed for 21 days, during which time the Minister may direct the authority not to put the plan into effect, indefinitely or for a specified period. The Minister must also secure that necessary compensatory measures are taken to ensure that the overall coherence of Natura 2000 is protected.[157]

Management

5.2.36 Underlying these detailed regulatory mechanisms are the fundamental management obligations required by the terms of the Habitats and Species Directive. For each SAC, Member States are required to establish the necessary conservation measures, involving management plans to meet the ecological requirements of the habitat types and species being protected, and appropriate surveillance must be carried out.[158] For both SACs and SPAs states are further required to take appropriate steps to avoid the deterioration of natural habitats and the habitats of the species for which the site was designated, as well as any disturbance of those species that could be significant to the purposes of the Directive.[159] If the overall effect of the management arrangements does not protect a site adequately, then action could be taken by the European Commission before the European Court of Justice.[160]

5.2.37 Taken together all of these measures offer a strong armoury for securing the conservation of European Sites, albeit that the measures in relation to damaging operations are based on a model that has been largely overtaken by the changes to SSSIs. To the extent that there were gaps in the more specific implementation of the Directive, the UK's attempt to point to the general obligations on authorities to secure compliance with the Directive was unsuccessful and after a number of flaws (but by no means all) were identified in *Commission v UK*[161] remedial measures were taken. Nevertheless the effectiveness of the legal armoury depends on the willingness to make use of the powerful tools that are provided, e.g. compulsory purchase to ensure the long-term management of a site, and the proper assessment of the threats to sites and weight of any overriding considerations. Moreover there can be difficulties in relation to inherently dynamic habitats, e.g. coastal lagoons, especially since any measures to preserve them artificially may in turn have an adverse effect on other protected habitats and climate change may present an insuperable obstacle to maintaining habitat in good condition. European Sites thus have the potential to offer strong protection to valuable habitats, but that result cannot be wholly guaranteed.

---

[157] CNHR 1994 reg.85E.

[158] See *First report by the United Kingdom under Article 17 on implementation of the Directive from June 1994 to December 2000* (DEFRA, 2001) and para.3.4.15, above.

[159] See paras 3.3.15 and 3.4.9, above.

[160] e.g. *Commission v France* (C-96/98) [1999] E.C.R. I-8351.

[161] *Commission v UK* (C-6/04) [2005] E.C.R. I-9017; see commentary by C.T. Reid and M. Woods at (2006) 18 J.E.L. 148 at pp.153–154.

Marine and Offshore European Sites

European Sites are not restricted to those on land, but can include areas at **5.2.38**
sea, and several marine habitats and marine species are among those given
protection by the Habitats and Species Directive.[162] This was partially
recognised in the Conservation (Natural Habitats, etc.) Regulations 1994
which make provision for European marine sites within territorial waters.
No provision, however, was made for areas further offshore. The English
courts held that this failure meant that the government had acted unlawfully
in granting oil and gas exploration licences in the Atlantic off the north-west
of Scotland since the terms of the Directive are not limited to territorial
waters but extend to all areas over which Member States exercise sovereign
rights, requiring the application of the Directive's provisions to activities
further offshore.[163] A very limited reaction to this decision followed in the
form of the Offshore Petroleum Activities (Conservation of Habitats)
Regulations 2002,[164] but these are restricted to oil and gas operations. It was
only after *Commission v UK*,[165] where the European Court of Justice held the
United Kingdom to be in breach of EC law by failing to implement the
Directive fully in relation to areas offshore that more comprehensive legislation was introduced, the Offshore Marine Conservation (Natural Habitats, etc.) Regulations 2007,[166] with further remedial legislation in early
2009.[167] The rules for European marine sites are just a variation of the
standard rules described above, but for European offshore marine sites a
separate regime is established under the 2007 Regulations, working with the
2002 Regulations which remain in force where oil and gas activities are
involved.

"European marine sites" are defined in the Conservation (Natural **5.2.39**
Habitats etc.) Regulations 1994 as "a European site which consists of, or so
far as it consists of marine areas".[168] A designated site may therefore be
wholly in the sea (up to the limits of territorial waters) or may include land
and sea, the areas below high tide being subject to the special rules for
marine sites. The starting point for the protection of marine sites is that as
well as the obligation on Ministers and conservation bodies to exercise their
conservation-related powers so as to secure compliance with the Directive,[169]
the same obligation to secure compliance is extended to a range of other
bodies in relation to their functions relevant to marine conservation. This
obligation is imposed on all "competent authorities"[170] in the exercise of
their powers under a range of specific statutory provisions covering fisheries,

---

[162] L. Warren, "Marine Protection under the EC Habitats and Species Directive" (1996) 17
ECOS 28; P. Jones, "Marine Nature Reserves in Britain: past lessons, current status and future
issues" (1999) 23 *Marine Policy* 375 at pp.388–395.

[163] *R. v Secretary of State for Trade and Industry, ex p. Greenpeace Ltd.* [2000] 2 C.M.L.R. 94;
[2000] Env. L.R. 221. See also D. Owen, "The Application of the Wild Birds Directive beyond
the Territorial Sea of European Community Member States" (2001) 13 J.E.L. 39.

[164] SI 2001/1754.

[165] *Commission v UK* (C-6/04) [2005] E.C.R. I-9017.

[166] SI 2007/1842.

[167] Offshore Marine Conservation (Natural Habitats, etc.) (Amendment) Regulations 2009
(SI 2009/7).

[168] CNHR 1994 reg.2(1); "marine area" is defined as "any land covered (continuously or
intermittently) by tidal waters" as far as the seaward limit of territorial waters (reg.2(1)).

[169] See para.5.2.13, above.

[170] See para.5.2.13, above.

pollution and harbours.[171] Compared to the position onshore, there is thus a much wider range of public authorities required to see to it that the Directive is implemented, as opposed to simply being required to have regard to its terms. Where applicable, the powers described above in relation to primarily land-based sites can be used to achieve protection (e.g. the wording of the law would appear to permit the use of management agreements to regulate activities on the shore adjacent to a marine European Site), but more specific powers are also conferred.

5.2.40　　The relevant statutory conservation body is required to install markers indicating the existence and extent of the site and to notify other public authorities of the conservation objectives for the site and of operations that may damage or disturb the features or species for which it has been designated.[172] Any of the "relevant authorities"[173] may establish a management scheme under which their functions shall be exercised so as to secure compliance with the Directive, or the Minister may direct one or more authorities to establish such a scheme.[174] This direction can include specific measures that are to be taken, the appointment of one authority to co-ordinate the scheme and instructions on reporting back to the Minister. There is also a power for the conservation bodies to make byelaws for a European Marine Site, subject to the same limitations as apply for marine nature reserves.[175] The effect of such byelaws is even further restricted by the express provision that they cannot interfere with the exercise of any functions by a relevant authority, nor with any statutory function or with the right of any person.

5.2.41　　To the extent that any plans or projects affecting a European marine site are subject to official approval, the general rules described above apply, permitting approval to be given only where there is likely to be no adverse effect, or that there are no alternative solutions and the project is required for imperative reasons of overriding public interest. Separate rules ensure that the same standards are met in relation to approvals for marine dredging.[176]

---

[171] The list covers: the Sea Fisheries Acts (as defined in s.1 of the Sea Fisheries (Wildlife Conservation) Act 1992); the Dockyard Ports Regulation Act 1865; the Military Lands Act 1900 s.2(2); the Harbours Act 1964; the Control of Pollution Act 1974 Pt II (water pollution); WCA 1981 ss.36–37 (marine nature reserves); the Civic Government (Scotland) Act 1982 ss.120–122 (control of the seashore and adjacent waters); the Water Resources Act 1991; the Land Drainage Act 1991; the Water Environment and Water Services (Scotland) Act 2003 Pt 1; the Water Environment (Controlled Activities) (Scotland) Regulations 2005; and the 1994 Regulations themselves (CNHR 1994 reg.3, as amended).

[172] CNHR 1994 reg.33.

[173] This term covers the statutory conservation bodies, local authorities, navigation and harbour authorities, the Environment Agency and the Scottish Environment Protection Agency, water and sewerage undertakers, internal drainage boards and local fisheries committees; CNHR 1994 reg.5. National Park authorities were added to this list separately by CNHAR 2007 reg.5(7) and CNHASR 2007 reg.7.

[174] CNHR 1994 regs 34–35.

[175] CNHR 1994 reg.36; see section 5.4, below.

[176] Schedule 3 to each of Environmental Impact Assessment and Natural Habitats (Extraction of Minerals by Marine Dredging) (Scotland) Regulations 2007 (SSI 2007/485); Environmental Impact Assessment and Natural Habitats (Extraction of Minerals by Marine Dredging) (England and Northern Ireland) Regulations 2007 (SI 2007/1067); Environmental Impact Assessment and Natural Habitats (Extraction of Minerals by Marine Dredging) (Wales) Regulations 2007 (SI 2007/2610).

The Offshore Marine Conservation (Natural Habitats, etc.) Regulations **5.2.42**
2007[177] follow the pattern above by beginning with a requirement on all
"competent authorities" to exercise in the offshore marine area any of their
functions relevant to marine conservation so as to secure compliance with
the Birds and Habitats and Species Directives.[178] "Competent authorities"
are defined widely to include the government, the devolved administrations
and all public and statutory undertakers, persons holding public office and
those exercising any of their functions.[179] The duty to secure compliance
with the Directives is stated to apply in particular to functions under a wide
range of statutory provisions.[180]

European offshore marine sites become so as SPAs or SACs under the **5.2.43**
Birds or Habitats and Species Directives. The designation process for SPAs
rests on the Minister declaring the site as necessary to meet the Birds
Directive's requirements[181] and for SACs applies the criteria and multi-stage
procedure set out in the Habitats and Species Directive.[182] The Regulations
repeat the Directive's condition that for aquatic species that range over wide
areas, a site is only eligible if it appears to constitute a clearly identifiable
area which is distinct in providing the physical and biological features
essential to that species for life and reproduction.[183] As with terrestrial sites,
a candidate SAC becomes a European offshore marine site when proposed
to the Commission or identified by the Commission as one which should be
included in the list.[184] In both cases the JNCC must be informed and then
notify each of the devolved administrations, competent authorities exercising functions in relation to the site and in adjacent marine areas and persons
whose activities are likely to be affected by the site being designated. An oral
or written hearing before an appointed person may be held in relation to
designation.[185] The Minister must keep a register of European offshore
marine sites.[186] Throughout the Regulations there are provisions for consultation with adjoining states[187] and for the amendment of designations,
registers, etc.

As soon as reasonably practicable after a site is designated, the JNCC **5.2.44**

---

[177] SI 2007/1842.

[178] Offshore Marine Conservation (Natural Habitats, etc.) Regulations 2007 reg.6(1).

[179] Offshore Marine Conservation (Natural Habitats, etc.) Regulations 2007 reg.5.

[180] Offshore Marine Conservation (Natural Habitats, etc.) Regulations 2007 reg.6(2); the
listed provisions are the Whaling Industry (Regulation) Act 1934, the Sea Fish (Conservation)
Act 1967, Fishery Limits Act 1976, Fisheries Act 1981, Part 2 of the Food and Environment
Protection Act 1985, s.34 of the Coast Protection Act 1949, Radioactive Substances Act 1973,
Prevention of Oil Pollution Act 1971, ss.128–129 of the Merchant Shipping Act 1995, the
Pollution Prevention and Control Act 1999, the Merchant Shipping (Prevention of Pollution)
Regulations 1996, the Merchant Shipping (Oil Pollution Preparedness, Response and Co-
operation Convention) Regulations 1998, the Offshore Installations (Emergency Pollution
Control Regulations 2002 and the 2007 Regulations themselves. Other functions are covered by
the Offshore Petroleum Activities (Conservation of Habitats) Regulations 2001 (see para.5.2.47,
below).

[181] Offshore Marine Conservation (Natural Habitats, etc.) Regulations 2007 reg.12

[182] Offshore Marine Conservation (Natural Habitats, etc.) Regulations 2007 regs 7–11.

[183] Offshore Marine Conservation (Natural Habitats, etc.) Regulations 2007 reg.7(4).

[184] Offshore Marine Conservation (Natural Habitats, etc.) Regulations 2007 reg.15; not all of
the provisions apply to those identified by the Commission, e.g. the requirement to review
existing permissions (reg.27(6)).

[185] Offshore Marine Conservation (Natural Habitats, etc.) Regulations 2007 reg.14.

[186] Offshore Marine Conservation (Natural Habitats, etc.) Regulations 2007 regs 16 and 17.

[187] e.g. Offshore Marine Conservation (Natural Habitats, etc.) Regulations 2007 reg.21.

must establish conservation objectives for the site and notify relevant competent authorities of these and of operations which may adversely affect the integrity of the site.[188] Any of the competent authorities may establish for a site a management scheme, setting out how the authority is going to exercise its functions to secure compliance with the Habitats and Species Directive. Consultations must be held with the JNCC and other competent authorities having functions in relation to the site, who must be invited to participate in establishing the scheme.[189] Schemes must be reviewed periodically and at least every five years. The scheme, however, does not have full binding force, imposing on the authorities involved in establishing it only the limited obligation to take reasonable steps to exercise their functions in accordance with it.[190]

5.2.45   A series of detailed provisions then require competent authorities to exercise their functions to give effect to the requirements of the Habitats and Species and Birds Directives, in particular to secure that protected species are not disturbed or habitats do not deteriorate, to an extent significant in relation to the objectives of the Directives.[191] These provisions include arrangements for consultation with the administration in Scotland and directions to competent authorities.

5.2.46   A series of criminal offences prohibit action within British waters (whether on ships, aircraft or offshore installations) which damages or disturbs species or habitats, but these do not apply to actions on ships not registered in a Member State.[192] In the absence of a reasonable excuse, it is a criminal offence for any person intentionally to disturb while it is in a site any of the animals for which the site has been designated as a formal or candidate SAC,[193] or any bird for which the site has been classified as an SPA. In each case this applies where the disturbance is likely significantly to affect the ability of the animal or bird to survive and reproduce or its local distribution or abundance.[194] It is also an offence without reasonable excuse intentionally or recklessly to damage or destroy a natural habitat that has led to the site being listed as an SAC or candidate SAC or which supports birds of the species for which an SPA has been declared.[195] In all cases it is a reasonable excuse that the action that caused the harm was carried out in accordance with a consent or permission granted by a competent authority.[196] Even where the actors are aware that their deliberate actions might cause the harmful result, they will not be regarded as reckless in relation to actions in the course of sea fishing if reasonable steps have been taken to ensure compliance with relevant EC law.[197]

5.2.47   Plans and projects in the offshore marine area (including the seabed, subsoil and installations) are subject to special rules if they are likely to have a significant effect on any European site (whether an offshore one or not).

---

[188] Offshore Marine Conservation (Natural Habitats, etc.) Regulations 2007 reg.18.
[189] Offshore Marine Conservation (Natural Habitats, etc.) Regulations 2007 reg.19.
[190] Offshore Marine Conservation (Natural Habitats, etc.) Regulations 2007 reg.20.
[191] Offshore Marine Conservation (Natural Habitats, etc.) Regulations 2007 regs 22–23.
[192] Offshore Marine Conservation (Natural Habitats, etc.) Regulations 2007 regs 2 and 8(3).
[193] The relevant species are listed in Annex II of the Habitats and Species Directive.
[194] Offshore Marine Conservation (Natural Habitats, etc.) Regulations 2007 reg.32(4)–(6).
[195] Offshore Marine Conservation (Natural Habitats, etc.) Regulations 2007 reg.32(7) and (8).
[196] Offshore Marine Conservation (Natural Habitats, etc.) Regulations 2007 reg.32(11).
[197] Offshore Marine Conservation (Natural Habitats, etc.) Regulations 2007 reg.32(12)–(14).

These rules are essentially the same as described above, requiring a competent authority to carry out an appropriate assessment of the likely impact on the site and to grant permission in the face of a negative assessment only if there is no alternative solution, the project is justified by imperative reasons of overriding public importance and compensatory measures are taken.[198] The detailed rules deal with consultation requirements and the devolution arrangements and require the review of existing permissions. These rules do not apply to approvals under the Petroleum Act 1998, which continue to be governed by the essentially parallel rules under the Offshore Petroleum Activities (Conservation of Habitats) Regulations 2001.[199]

5.2.48 The 2007 Regulations fill the gap identified by the European Court of Justice in relation to applying the EC Directives offshore, but do so through a detailed transposition of the relevant obligations rather than providing a more holistic approach to marine biodiversity. This is inevitable in view of the need to avoid further infraction proceedings and the fact that the whole area of marine conservation and governance is subject to imminent reshaping under the Marine Bills.[200] It is to be hoped that the eventual outcome is a properly constructed system that integrates domestic, European and international requirements into a single consolidated system.

NATURE RESERVES

5.3.1 Nature reserves are areas managed solely for a conservation purpose or for a conservation purpose and a recreational one where the conservation purpose is not compromised by the management of the land for recreation.[201] Conservation therefore takes priority, as opposed to having to be balanced with other interests or accommodated within the occupier's other objectives. A conservation purpose is defined as:

> "(a) providing, under suitable conditions and control, special opportunities for the study of, and research into, matters relating to the fauna and flora of Great Britain and the physical conditions in which they live, and for the study of geological and physiographical features of special interest in the area, or (b) preserving flora, fauna or geological or physiographical features of special interest in the area",

or both.[202]

5.3.2 The establishment, maintenance and management of nature reserves is expressly included as one of the general functions of Scottish Natural Heritage and the Countryside Council for Wales,[203] and falls within Natural

---

[198] Offshore Marine Conservation (Natural Habitats, etc.) Regulations 2007 regs 24–31.
[199] SI 2001/1754 regs 3–9.
[200] See para.1.7.6, above.
[201] NPACA 1949 s.15, as substituted by NERCA 2006 Sch.11 para.12.
[202] NPACA 1949 s.15, as substituted by NERCA 2006 Sch.11 para.12; this wording is taken from the original provision in 1949 and maintains the old terminology of "preserving" flora and fauna rather than "conserving" it. A recreational purpose is providing "opportunities for the enjoyment of nature or for open-air recreation" (NPACA s.15). *Cf.* para.2.6.6, above.
[203] EPA 1990 s.132(1), as amended by NERCA 2006 Sch.11 para.121; NHSA 1991 s.4(7).

England's general purpose of promoting nature conservation and protecting biodiversity.[204] The powers relating to nature reserves can be exercised where it appears to the conservation body expedient in the national interest that land should be managed as a nature reserve[205]; areas of the foreshore and of tidal waters can be included in a reserve.[206] A declaration by the body that land is being managed as a nature reserve is conclusive. The conservation body is under a duty to make a similar declaration if the land ceases to be managed in this way and all declarations must be publicised in the way best suited to informing those concerned.[207] The purposes of the nature reserve are achieved by the use of management agreements or by the acquisition of land, supported by byelaws.

5.3.3   A management agreement may be made with any owner, lessee or occupier of the land.[208] For the purpose of securing that the land is managed as a nature reserve, the agreement may impose restrictions on the exercise of any rights over the land by the parties, provide for the land to be managed in a particular manner and provide for work to be carried out on the land. The agreement may further provide for any management or other works to be carried out and/or paid for by the owner of the land, the conservation body or other persons, and may contain terms relating to payments by the body, in particular sums in compensation for the restriction of the parties' rights.[209] Special provision is made to allow agreements to be made with those with less than full ownership of the land, e.g. liferenters, tenants for life and trustees.[210] In Scotland agreements are to be registered in the Register of Sasines[211] and once registered can be enforced by the conservation body against the parties and those deriving title from them.[212] In England and Wales the agreement operates essentially as a restrictive covenant with the body in the position of an absolute owner of adjacent land capable of benefiting from the covenant and for whose benefit the convenant is expressed.[213] These provisions mean that the agreement runs with the land and remains in force despite any change of occupation or ownership.

5.3.4   The statutory conservation bodies may acquire any interest in the land

---

[204] NERCA 2006 s.2.

[205] NERCA 2006 s.16.

[206] NPACA 1949 s.114(1); *Burnet v Barclay*, 1955 S.L.T. 282, *Evans v Godber* [1974] 1 W.L.R. 1317.

[207] NPACA 1949 s.19.

[208] For SNH and CCW, management agreements for nature reserves can be made under NPACA 1949 s.15 and it is this specific power that is described here; for NE such agreements are made under and governed by the wider powers in NERCA 2006 s.7, but called "nature reserve agreements" by virtue of NPACA 1949 s.15A(2), as added by NERCA 2006 Sch.11 para.13, with consequential amendments to other provisions in the 1949 Act.

[209] NPACA 1949 s.16(2) and (3).

[210] NPACA 1949 s.16(4) and (5) and s.26; this is achieved by applying to management agreements the provisions for forestry dedication agreements in ss.1–4 of the Forestry Act 1947, saved for this purpose when repealed by the Forestry Act 1967 Sch.7 Pt II para.3.

[211] By virtue of the Land Registration (Scotland) Act 1979 s.29(2), all references to the Register of Sasines extend to the Land Register.

[212] NPACA 1949 s.16(5), applying Forestry Act 1947 s.3(2) (see fn.210, above); the agreement does not bind a person who bona fide onerously acquired his interest in the land prior to the registration of the agreement, nor those deriving title from such a person.

[213] NPACA 1949 s.16(4), applying Forestry Act 1947 s.1(2) and (3) (see fn.208 above); NERCA 2006 s.7.

forming a nature reserve by agreement,[214] or in some cases compulsorily. The power of compulsory purchase can be exercised, first, where the body considers it expedient in the national interest that land should be managed as a nature reserve and has been unable to obtain on what it considers to be reasonable terms an agreement relating to the interest in question securing that the land will be satisfactorily managed for this purpose.[215] The second situation in which compulsory purchase is possible is where a management agreement for a nature reserve has been breached.[216] This option is without prejudice to any of the conservation body's other legal remedies, but where the breach is one capable of remedy, it can only be invoked if the defaulting party has not put things right within a reasonable time after being served with a notice from the body requiring remedial action.[217] The approval of the Minister must be obtained before any compulsory acquisition, which proceeds under the provisions of the Acquisition of Land (Authorisation Procedure) (Scotland) Act 1947 and the Acquisition of Land Act 1981 or the Compulsory Purchase Act 1965.[218] The focus on nature conservation is perhaps most clearly shown by the fact that in order to protect a reserve, byelaws can be made excluding all visitors from the area.

Byelaws for the protection of a nature reserve can be made by a statutory **5.3.5** conservation body where land is being managed as a reserve, whether directly by the body or under a management agreement, and has been declared to be a nature reserve.[219] Such byelaws must be confirmed by the Minister and are made under the procedures for local authority byelaws, modified to refer to the conservation bodies and to require copies of proposed and confirmed byelaws to be available for inspection at local authority offices in the relevant areas as well as at the body's own head-quarters.[220] The byelaws can prohibit or restrict entry into or movement within a reserve by people or vehicles and can be made prohibiting or restricting the depositing of any rubbish or litter, the lighting of any fires or other acts likely to cause a fire, and the movement of any persons, vehicles, boats or animals into or within the reserve. Any killing, taking or disturbing of animals or plants, interference with the soil or damage to any objects in the reserve may be prohibited or restricted, as may the shooting of birds within the area surrounding or adjoining the reserve to the extent that this is required to protect the reserve itself. The byelaws may also provide for permits to be granted permitting things otherwise prohibited.[221]

There are, however, limits to the scope of the byelaws. The exercise of any **5.3.6**

---

[214] There is no express provision on the agreed acquisition of land for nature reserves, but it is covered by the general powers of the bodies; EPA 1990 s.132(3) and NHSA 1991 s.2(1).

[215] NPACA 1949 s.17.

[216] Any dispute over whether an agreement has been breached is to be determined by an arbiter appointed by the Lord President of the Court of Session or an arbitrator appointed by the Lord Chancellor.

[217] NPACA 1949 s.18.

[218] NPACA 1949 s.103 (amended by Nature Conservancy Council Act 1973 Sch.1 para.2; Acquisition of Land Act 1981 Sch.4 para.8).

[219] NPACA 1949 s.20.

[220] NPACA 1949 s.106; Nature Conservancy Council (Byelaws) Regulations 1975 (SI 1975/1970), adapting Local Government Act 1972 ss.236–238; Nature Conservancy Council (Byelaws) (Scotland) Regulations 1984 (SI 1984/918), adapting Local Government (Scotland) Act 1973 ss.202–204, amended by Civic Government (Scotland) Act 1982 s.110.

[221] NPACA 1949 s.20(2).

right vested in a person as owner, lessee or occupier of the land cannot be interfered with—any restriction on such rights must be achieved directly by means of a management agreement, not through byelaws.[222] Where the exercise of other vested rights (whether arising from an interest in the land, a licence or an agreement) is prevented or hindered by the byelaws, compensation is payable by the conservation body.[223] Also beyond the reach of byelaws is any interference with the exercise of a public right of way,[224] with the functions of statutory undertakers, drainage authorities or salmon fishery district boards, or with the running of telecommunications systems.[225]

5.3.7   The special status of nature reserves is recognised in a number of other statutory schemes. Among other points, orders can be made restricting or prohibiting vehicles on roads in a reserve[226] and any exercise in a nature reserve of the powers under the Animal Health Act 1981 to destroy wildlife requires prior notice and efforts to minimise the harm done.[227]

National Nature Reserves

5.3.8 What has been described so far are nature reserves managed by or by agreement with the statutory conservation bodies. There is, however, a potential for confusion as to their title and status. This arises because it is possible for reserves to be formally declared "National Nature Reserves" under the Wildlife and Countryside Act 1981.[228] This title can be conferred by a declaration[229] by a statutory conservation body where it considers that a nature reserve is of national importance. The risk of confusion lies in the fact that the title "National Nature Reserve" was in widespread but unofficial use for reserves managed by the Nature Conservancy Council before being given statutory recognition in 1981. A problem may occur in relation to future legislation as it could be argued that any reference to National Nature Reserves applies only to reserves which have been formally declared as such under the 1981 Act, thereby excluding any older ones that have not been subject to any such statutory declaration.[230]

5.3.9   National Nature Reserves under the 1981 Act can be on land governed by a management agreement with the statutory conservation body, held and managed as a reserve directly by the body, or managed by another body approved by the statutory conservation body.[231] This last provision is particularly significant since it means that reserves managed by organisations such as the RSPB can be brought within the statutory scheme for nature

---

[222] NPACA 1949 s.20(2).

[223] NPACA 1949 s.20(3).

[224] A right of navigation is not a public right of way for this purpose (*Evans v Godber* [1974] 1 W.L.R. 1317; cf. *Attorney General (ex rel. Yorkshire Derwent Trust Ltd) v Brotherton* [1992] 1 A.C. 425); the exercise of rights on the foreshore may be restricted (*Burnet v Barclay*, 1955 S.L.T. 282).

[225] Added by Telecommunications Act 1984 Sch.4 para.28.

[226] Road Traffic Regulation Act 1984 s.22.

[227] Animal Health Act 1981 s.22(7); see para.4.5.11, above.

[228] WCA 1981 s.35.

[229] Governed by NPACA 1949 s.19.

[230] See, e.g. the Farm Woodland Premium Scheme 1997 (SI 1997/829) para.2(1) which expressly covered both categories.

[231] WCA 1981 s.35(1).

reserves. A major consequence of this is that at the request of the organi-sation managing the reserve, the conservation body can make byelaws for such a reserve as if it were one managed through the statutory body itself.[232] This allows further legal sanctions to supplement the restrictions imposed by the managing body by virtue of its interest in the land.

Local Nature Reserves

Nature reserves can also be established by local authorities. It is within the **5.3.10** powers of planning authorities in Scotland and Wales and county, county boroughs and districts in England and National Park authorities to establish nature reserves where they consider it expedient that the land should be so managed.[233] The local authorities enjoy the same powers in this regard as the statutory conservation bodies, including powers of compulsory purchase, with references to "the interests of the locality" being substituted for those to "the national interest".[234] The authorities must consult the conservation bodies on the exercise of their functions.[235] The existence of the power to create local nature reserves allows the protection of small sites which are not of national significance, but which do offer valuable habitat, and enables authorities to provide opportunities for the study of nature as a recreational or educational facility. As always, though, there are competing demands on the resources of local authorities.[236]

MARINE NATURE RESERVES

Although nature reserves can extend to include areas covered by the sea,[237] **5.4.1** the legal machinery of land ownership and management agreements is not apt to deal with the conservation of the marine environment. Special pro-vision was made in 1981 for the creation of Marine Nature Reserves, but weaknesses in the legislation and an unwillingness to proceed in the absence of total consensus from all interested parties have meant that these reserves have had little impact in practice.[238]

Marine Nature Reserves can be created for areas of land covered by tidal **5.4.2** waters, including the foreshore, or parts of the sea which lie within the baselines for measuring the territorial sea[239] or lie seaward of the baselines or

---

[232] WCA 1981 s.35(3).

[233] NPACA 1949 s.21(1), as amended to adjust to restructuring of local government and conservation bodies.

[234] NPACA 1949 s.21(4).

[235] NPACA 1949 s.21(6).

[236] e.g. in *Giddens v Harlow District Auditor* (1972) 70 L.G.R. 485 expenditure on the purchase of a wood as a local nature reserve was challenged, unsuccessfully, by a ratepayer on the grounds that it was providing facilities which would benefit only a privileged minority.

[237] See para.5.3.2, above.

[238] See generally, J. Gibson, "Marine Nature Reserves" [1984] J.P.L. 699; J. Gibson, "Marine Nature Reserves in the United Kingdom" (1988) 3 Int. J. of Estuarine and Coastal Law 328; P. Jones, "Marine Nature Reserves in Britain: past lessons, current status and future issues" (1999) 23 *Marine Policy* 375; D. Laffoley and T. Bines, *Protection and Management of Nationally Important Marine Habitats and Species* (English Nature, 2000).

[239] Such baselines are drawn in accordance with international law and include lines drawn across the mouths of bays and firths and a line enclosing the Minch and all of the Inner and Outer Hebrides; see para.1.7.3, above.

coast to a distance of three nautical miles.[240] By Order in Council, other areas of the sea within British territorial waters (currently extending to 12 nautical miles from the shore-line or baselines) can become eligible for designation.[241] Reserves are designated by the Minister on the basis of an application made by a statutory conservation body where it appears expedient that the land and covering waters should be managed for the purposes of conserving or studying the marine flora and fauna or the geological and physiographical features of special interest in the area. Once a reserve has been designated, it is managed by the conservation body for either or both of these purposes.[242]

5.4.3   The procedure for designation requires the conservation body's application to be accompanied by a copy of the byelaws which are proposed for the protection of the reserve[243] and provides for the Minister to give wide publicity to the proposed designation and accompanying byelaws. As well as notices in the local press and at prominent positions at local authority offices within the locality, notices must be served on all those with a vested interest in or right over the land affected and on a wide range of public authorities.[244] In the event of there being objections or representations which are not withdrawn, the Minister must arrange for there to be a hearing or local inquiry before he decides whether to make an order giving effect to the designation.[245] Similar publicity is required for orders once they have been made[246] and there is a limited power to challenge the validity of an order within 42 days of its notification, after which the order is not to be questioned in any legal proceedings.[247]

5.4.4   The impact of an area being designated as a Marine Nature Reserve lies in the provisions of the byelaws which are made for it, since other than through the byelaws, the effect of designation is simply to empower the conservation body to manage a reserve and to install markers indicating its existence and extent.[248] Byelaws are made by the body for the protection of reserves[249] in accordance with the procedures for the making of local authority byelaws, as modified by regulations.[250] As well as being the confirming authority for byelaws,[251] the Minister, after consulting the conservation body, can direct it to revoke or amend any byelaws which it has made.[252]

---

[240] WCA 1981 s.36(1), amended by Territorial Sea Act 1987 Sch.1 para.6; a "nautical mile" is defined in s.1(7) of the 1987 Act as an international nautical mile of 1,852 metres.

[241] Territorial Sea Act 1987 s.3(2).

[242] WCA 1981 s.36(1).

[243] WCA 1981 s.36(2).

[244] WCA 1981 Sch.12 paras 2–3; the public authorities concerned are the "relevant authorities" (see para.5.4.6, below) and such other bodies as the Minister considers appropriate.

[245] WCA 1981 Sch.12 para.4; if the Minister decides to make the order with modifications a similar procedure must be followed if additional land is affected (WCA 1981 Sch.12 para.5).

[246] WCA 1981 Sch.12 para.7.

[247] WCA 1981 Sch.12 para.8.

[248] WCA 1981 s.36(1) and (5).

[249] WCA 1981 s.37(1).

[250] WCA 1981 s.37(5), applying the Local Government Act 1972 ss.236–238, as modified by Wildlife and Countryside (Byelaws for Marine Nature Reserves) Regulations 1986 (SI 1986/143), and the Local Government (Scotland) Act 1973 ss.202–204, amended by Civic Government (Scotland) Act 1982 s.110.

[251] WCA 1981 s.37(6).

[252] WCA 1981 s.37(7).

The byelaws may protect the reserve by prohibiting or restricting the entry **5.4.5** or movement of individuals or vessels, the killing, destruction or disturbance of animals or plants, interference with the sea bed, damage to any object in the reserve, or the deposit of rubbish in the reserve.[253] The byelaws can vary for different parts of the reserve and allow the granting of permits to do things otherwise prohibited. These apparently wide powers are, however, severely restricted in several ways. First, the byelaws cannot prohibit or restrict the exercise of any right of passage by a vessel other than a pleasure boat, nor exclude even pleasure boats from all parts of the reserve at all times of the year.[254] There is no definition of a "pleasure boat" and many doubtful cases can be imagined. Secondly, the byelaws cannot render unlawful the discharge of any substance from a vessel,[255] nor anything done more than 30 metres below the sea bed[256] or anything done for securing the safety of any vessel, preventing damage to a vessel or its cargo or saving life.[257]

The third restriction on the scope of the byelaws also extends to anything **5.4.6** else which a conservation body might do in the exercise of its powers to manage a reserve. This is that nothing which is done can interfere with the exercise of any functions conferred by an Act of Parliament (before or after the creation of the reserve and the making of byelaws), with the exercise of any right of any person or with the exercise of any function of a "relevant authority".[258] The "relevant authorities" for this purpose include all tiers of local authority, the Environment Agency and the Scottish Environment Protection Agency, water and sewerage undertakers, navigation, harbour and pilotage authorities, lighthouse authorities, salmon district fishery boards and local fisheries committees.[259]

Marine conservation is always difficult because of the wide range of **5.4.7** influences which can affect the different elements of the marine environment from the surface to the sea-bed, and because of difficulties in enforcing any restrictions.[260] The current structure does not make it easy to develop an integrated approach to conservation at the coast, considering both onshore and offshore issues. Moreover, in marine reserves the exclusion from the regulatory powers of authorities whose activities can have a major impact on the seashore and inshore waters, together with the other exclusions, severely weaken the whole mechanism of Marine Nature Reserves. This has been further weakened by slow progress towards designating reserves, with the government reluctant to proceed without full consensus from all interested parties. Only two Marine Nature Reserves have been designated, with a third (much larger) one at Strangford Lough in Northern Ireland.

The need to improve the arrangements for marine conservation is one of **5.4.8** the significant factors behind the current Marine Bills. The Marine and Coastal Access Bill before Westminster contains significant provisions for

---

[253] WCA 1981 s.37(2).
[254] WCA 1981 s.27(3).
[255] Such deposits are controlled by Part II of the Food and Environment Protection Act 1985 and other legislation on marine pollution.
[256] Detailed legal regimes exist to control the exploitation of minerals on the continental shelf.
[257] WCA 1981 s.37(4).
[258] WCA 1981 s.36(6).
[259] WCA 1981 s.36(7) (amended by Water Act 1989 Sch.25 para.66).
[260] See section 1.7, above.

Marine Conservation Zones, and the Scottish Bill also calls for the establishment of Marine Protected Areas.[261]

SITES OF SPECIAL SCIENTIFIC INTEREST

5.5.1 Whereas in nature reserves the land is primarily dedicated to the interests of nature conservation, much of the valuable habitat in Britain is provided by land which is used for other purposes, and can continue to be so used without damaging its value for wildlife. Those areas of particular value do, however, require some recognition and a degree of protection if they are not to be destroyed by their development for building, quarrying, etc. or damaged by other changes in their management. The objectives of the system of Sites of Special Scientific Interest (SSSIs) are to identify valuable sites, to notify those responsible for them of their value and to provide a mechanism which prevents some harmful actions and whereby changes to the land which might harm that value are considered by the conservation authorities before they take place, offering the opportunity for a range of controls to be agreed or imposed at that stage.

5.5.2 SSSIs were first introduced in 1949,[262] but have been transformed twice, first in 1981 and then by separate legislation for England and Wales and then Scotland earlier this decade. The original provisions were weak, merely requiring special consideration within the town and country planning system (the owners and occupiers of the land were not even informed of the designation) and a new system was introduced by the Wildlife and Countryside Act 1981.[263] This system was essentially a delaying mechanism whereby operations on the land could be delayed for a few months, but unless other stricter controls were applied, it was not possible to prevent the occupiers carrying out their wishes, however damaging to the conservation value of the site.[264] This new regime applied only to SSSIs which had been notified in accordance with the procedures in the 1981 Act, and throughout the 1980s a major task for the Nature Conservancy Council was the renotification of those SSSIs created under the previous legislation so that they could benefit from the new provisions. This task was completed in the early 1990s.

5.5.3 Although the system of SSSIs could be judged a success in tackling the main threats that the 1981 Act was designed to counter,[265] there was growing dissatisfaction at the failure of the legal mechanisms to prevent damage to protected sites.[266] Apart from the fact that the scheme did not by itself stop occupiers from carrying out damaging operations, it was noted that there

---

[261] Marine (Scotland) Bill.

[262] NPACA 1949 s.23; the legislation in the past referred to "areas which are of special interest", but the term "Sites of Special Scientific Interest" has been the universal usage, and is used in the current statutory provisions.

[263] See generally S. Ball, "Sites of Special Scientific Interest" [1985] J.P.L. 767.

[264] For details see section 5.5 in the previous edition of this book.

[265] K. Last, "Habitat Protection: Has the Wildlife and Countryside Act 1981 made a Difference?" (1999) 11 J.E.L. 15.

[266] In 2000–01, 15 per cent of SSSIs in England were said to be in decline or destroyed (HC Written Answers col.493W (December 6, 2001)).

were no restrictions on third parties, including statutory undertakers, and that the scheme was inflexible. In part inspired by the stronger measures introduced to secure compliance with the Habitats and Species Directive, proposals for reforming and strengthening the system of SSSIs were produced in 1998. There were separate consultation papers for England and Wales[267] and for Scotland.[268] These papers reflected different approaches, apparent from their very titles, for England and Wales emphasising "Better Protection" whilst in Scotland dealing with "People and Nature". The Scottish proposals paid more attention to the role of conservation in wider land use policies and the interests and concerns of the local community, an approach perhaps influenced by the much greater areas of land in Scotland covered by the designation and by the economic and social problems faced in many of the remote rural areas affected.[269]

The arrival of devolution made it even easier for the proposals to follow **5.5.4** separate legislative paths, and in England and Wales fundamental changes to the system of SSSIs were introduced by the Countryside and Rights of Way Act 2000.[270] In Scotland, reform was achieved through the Nature Conservation (Scotland) Act 2004. Although there are sufficient differences to demand the two systems being described separately, the new regimes are broadly parallel, although a further difference is being introduced by the application of the provisions of the Environmental Liability Directive to SSSIs in England and Wales but not Scotland.[271] The new regimes introduce stronger but more flexible controls on owners and occupiers within SSSIs, including provision to require positive actions to maintain a site, but also extend controls to other people whose activities can affect the site, especially by means of new criminal offences, byelaws and clear obligations on public authorities and statutory undertakers to have regard to the special features of a site. The argument that the imposition of these new controls amounted to an infringement of the landowners' right to enjoy their property that was unlawful under the European Convention on Human Rights was unsuccessful.[272]

England and Wales

The Countryside and Rights of Way Act 2000 fundamentally changed the **5.5.5** system of SSSIs in operation in England and Wales, replacing section 28 of the Wildlife and Countryside Act 1981 with new sections 28–28R.[273] The

---

[267] *Sites of Special Scientific Interest: Better Protection and Management* (DETR, 1998).

[268] *People and Nature: A New Approach to SSSI Designation in Scotland* (Scottish Office, 1998).

[269] K.Last, "Mechanisms for Environmental Regulation – A Study of Habitat Conservation" in A. Ross (ed.), *Environment and Regulation* (Hume Papers on Public Policy, Vol.8, no.1) (Edinburgh: Edinburgh University Press, 2000), at pp.57–58.

[270] Further minor changes were made by the Natural Environment and Rural Communities Act 2006.

[271] Directive 2004/35/EC; see section 5.12, esp. para.5.12.3, below.

[272] *R. (Trailer and Marina (Leven) Ltd) v Secretary of State for the Environment, Food and Rural Affairs* [2004] EWCA Civ 1580; [2005] 1 W.L.R. 1267, arguing that art.1 of Protocol 1 of the Convention had been infringed; see para.1.5.10, above.

[273] S. Payne, "From Carrots to Sticks – Natural Habitat Protection after the Countryside and Rights of Way Act 2000" (2001) 13 E.L.M. 239.

starting point remains, though, the duty on Natural England (NE) and the Countryside Council for Wales (CCW) to notify as SSSIs those areas of land which are, in its opinion, of special interest by reason of any of their flora, fauna, or geological or physiographical features.[274] All owners and occupiers of the land concerned, the relevant planning authority and the Minister must receive copies of the notification which must also be published in a local newspaper.[275] The notice must set out why the land is of special interest and specify those operations (known as "potentially damaging operations", PDOs)[276] which appear likely to damage the flora, fauna or other special features of the land and thus fall within the scope of the SSSI controls.[277] The notice must also contain a statement of the conservation body's views about the management of the land, explaining what might be appropriate for the conservation and enhancement of the site and thereby reflecting the current concern with partnership and positive management (as well as meeting the requirement for management plans under the Habitat and Species Directive where a site is doubly designated).[278] Similar statements must be produced within five years for all existing SSSIs,[279] and can be reviewed.

5.5.6   The notification takes effect at once,[280] but a period of at least three months must be allowed for representations or objections to be made.[281] These representations must be considered by the conservation body which within nine months of the original notification must notify the same people that the notification is being withdrawn, confirmed or confirmed with modifications (which cannot extend the area of the SSSI nor add to the list of potentially damaging operations).[282]

5.5.7   There is no appeal mechanism built into the designation procedure but it is subject to judicial review[283] and designations have been challenged on a number of grounds.[284] The designation must be carried out on the basis of whether or not features of special interest are present on the site,[285] and this

---

[274] WCA 1981 s.28(1); all references in this section are to the 1981 Act as amended by CRWA 2000 Sch.9 para.1.

[275] WCA 1981 s.28(1) and (2); the service of notices is governed by WCA 1981 s.70A, added by Wildlife and Countryside (Service of Notices) Act 1985 s.1, amended by Planning (Consequential Provisions) Act 1990 Sch.2 para.54, applying TCPA 1990 s.329. The notification is a local land charge (WCA 1981 s.28(9)).

[276] The word "operations" in this phrase does not bear the specialised meaning that it has been given in construing the planning legislation; *Sweet v Secretary of State for the Environment* [1989] 2 P.L.R. 14; (1989) 1 J.E.L. 245.

[277] WCA 1981 s.28(4).

[278] Directive 92/43/EEC art.6(1).

[279] CRWA 2000 Sch.11 para.6.

[280] Prior to the Wildlife and Countryside (Amendment) Act 1985 the notice took effect only once confirmed by the Nature Conservancy Council, but it was found that in the period between initial notification and confirmation some unscrupulous occupiers were taking steps which destroyed the features of the land which were of value, thereby defeating the whole system.

[281] WCA 1981 s.28(3).

[282] WCA 1981 s.28(4A)–(4C), added by Wildlife and Countryside (Amendment) Act 1985 s.2(4).

[283] See para.1.4.9 above.

[284] Some of these involve the older version of the statutory provisions but remain relevant.

[285] The fact that fossils are unexposed does not mean that the land containing them is not of current interest; *Boggis v English Nature* [2008] EWHC 2954 Admin at [74]; [2009] Env. L.R. 20.

is likewise the criterion for determining whether an appropriate size of site has been selected.[286] If those features were inevitably doomed, that might render designation unreasonable,[287] but there is no need for the survival of the features to be guaranteed before designation can be confirmed[288] and the availability of resources to protect the site is not a relevant consideration.[289] The courts have consistently refused to be drawn into making their own assessment of the scientific arguments which are to be determined by the conservation body as experts,[290] and have emphasised that the *Guidelines for Selection of Biological SSSIs*[291] produced by the Joint Nature Conservancy Council are just guidelines and do not have to be slavishly followed.[292] A site does not have to be the best example of its type before it can be designated, so long as it is an important one.[293]

In terms of procedure, the courts have emphasised the importance of the **5.5.8** stage between notification and confirmation as one requiring the conservation body to undertake investigation, consultation and the consideration and analysis of objections.[294] Confirmation is not just a rubber-stamping exercise, but one where an element of discretion remains,[295] and flaws at that stage have led to the confirmation of an SSSI being held to be invalid. This was the result in *R. v Nature Conservancy Council, ex p. Bolton Metropolitan Borough Council*,[296] where the Council had failed to correct what was clearly a mistaken belief on the part of the objectors that there was only one issue on which they were asked to respond, namely the potential of the site for restoration as an actively growing raised mire, whereas the present state of the site was also an important consideration. Where a European site may be affected, designation may be subject to the restrictions

---

[286] *R. (Fisher) v English Nature* [2004] EWCA Civ 663; [2005] 1 W.L.R. 147 at [131]. In this case arguments about the relationship between SSSIs and European designations and the impact of changes of government policy on the conservation body were seen as mere background to the fundamental question of whether the decision to notify was one legally open to the body on the information available to it (at [129]).

[287] In *Boggis v English Nature* [2008] EWHC 2954 Admin; [2009] Env. L.R. 20, it was held that "conserving" an eroding coastline could include allowing natural processes to take their course even though this involved the continuing loss of land and the fossils it contains and that it was not irrational to set the boundary on the basis of a 50-year projection of erosion, rather than at the limits of the relevant fossil-bearing sediments (225m inland from the coast as opposed to 25km).

[288] *R. v Nature Conservancy Council, ex p. London Brick Property Ltd* [1996] Env. L.R. 1; [1996] J.P.L. 227.

[289] *R. (Western Power Distribution Investments Ltd) v Countryside Council for Wales* [2007] EWHC 50 Admin; [2007] Env. L.R. 25.

[290] The approach taken by the body can legitimately change so long as there is a rational basis for such change, so that a decision not to designate at one point does not by itself create a legitimate expectation preventing future designation; *R. (Aggregate Industries UK Ltd) v English Nature* [2002] EWHC 908 Admin; [2003] Env. L.R. 3.

[291] The Guidelines are available at *http://www.jncc.gov.uk/page-2303* [Accessed May 10, 2009], as are the separate *Guidelines for the Selection of Earth Science SSSIs*.

[292] *R. (Boyd) v English Nature* [2003] EWHC 1105 Admin; *R. (Western Power Distribution Investments Ltd) v Countryside Council for Wales* [2007] EWHC 50 Admin; [2007] Env. L.R. 25.

[293] *R. (Western Power Distribution Investments Ltd) v Countryside Council for Wales* [2007] EWHC 50 Admin; [2007] Env. L.R. 25 at [38].

[294] *R. (Fisher) v English Nature* [2004] EWCA Civ 663; [2005] 1 W.L.R. 147 at [135]–[136].

[295] *R. (Fisher) v English Nature* [2004] EWCA Civ 663; [2005] 1 W.L.R. 147; *R. v Nature Conservancy Council, ex p. London Brick Property Ltd* [1996] Env. L.R. 1; [1996] J.P.L. 227.

[296] *R. v Nature Conservancy Council, ex p. Bolton Metropolitan Borough Council* [1995] Env. L.R. 237; [1996] J.P.L. 237.

on approving a "plan or project" under the Habitats and Species Directive.[297]

5.5.9   A more fundamental objection to the procedure was raised following the enactment of the Human Rights Act 1998, giving effect to the European Convention on Human Rights.[298] The confirmation process, whereby the conservation body both makes the initial notification and acts as the confirming authority, was challenged as failing to provide landowners whose civil rights were being affected with a hearing before an independent and impartial tribunal in breach of article 6 of the Convention.[299] This argument succeeded at interim injunction stage in one case[300] but was firmly rejected when fully considered in *R. (Aggregate Industries UK Ltd) v English Nature*.[301] It was held that since becoming an SSSI would restrict the way in which the land could be used, confirmation of the designation did amount to a determination of the landowners' civil rights to use and enjoy the property, so that the rights under article 6 were engaged. It was further held that there was insufficient appearance of impartiality and independence when the Council of English Nature took the decision to confirm the designation, resolving the dispute between the objecting landowners and its own officers. However, when looked at as a whole, given the nature of the decision to be taken, the procedural safeguards as the decision was taken and the possibility for judicial review, the process overall did meet the standards set by the Convention.[302] Nevertheless it has been suggested that a designation might be quashed if in an individual case it was found to impose a disproportionate burden that had not been properly taken into account.[303]

5.5.10   Whereas under the original 1981 Act designation was a one-off process, the new law allows for amendments and makes express provision for the designation of additional land. Variation notices allow the details of the original designation to be changed, but not the area of land covered, and are made and confirmed by the same procedure as for designation.[304] The power to vary the designation means that it is possible to adjust the grounds for designation to match changing physical conditions or changing appreciation of the special features on a site, whilst the potential to amend the list of PDOs removes the disadvantage of the scope of protection being frozen for ever on the basis of the original list of PDOs. This allows for action to be taken if a new danger emerges, but also should improve relationships with the landowners, since it should be possible for the initial notification to include a shorter list of PDOs, reducing the regulatory burden, safe in the

---

[297] *Boggis v English Nature* [2008] EWHC 2954 Admin; [2009] Env. L.R. 20; see para.5.2.34, above.

[298] See para.1.5.7, above.

[299] This requirement lay behind the introduction of rights of appeal against certain decisions taken by the conservation bodies once an SSSI is established; see paras 5.5.20 and 5.5.36 below.

[300] *William Sinclair Holdings Ltd v English Nature* [2001] EWHC Admin 408; [2002] Env. L.R. 4.

[301] *R. (Aggregate Industries UK Ltd) v English Nature* [2002] EWHC 908 Admin; [2003] Env. L.R. 3.

[302] This decision followed the approach and outcome in *R. (Alconbury Developments Ltd) v Secretary of State for the Environment, Transport and the Regions* [2002] UKHL 23; [2003] 2 A.C. 295 and *Runa Begum v Tower Hamlets London Borough Council* [2003] UKHL 5; [2003] 2 A.C. 430 (then at Court of Appeal stage).

[303] *R. (Fisher) v English Nature* [2004] EWCA Civ 663; [2005] 1 W.L.R. 147 at [141].

[304] WCA 1981 s.28A.

knowledge it is possible to add more extensive controls if necessary. An additional feature to deal with changing circumstances is the new obligation on owners of land in an SSSI to notify the conservation body when they dispose of any interest in the land or become aware that it is occupied by an additional or different occupier.[305]

The area of land covered by an SSSI can also be extended. There are two **5.5.11** different bases for doing this. The first is by the "notification of additional land" which applies when the conservation body is of the opinion that if land adjacent to an existing SSSI were combined with the designated land, then the combined area would meet the criterion of being of special interest.[306] The special interest in the additional land by itself may be limited, but its value as a "buffer zone" in relation to the extended site as a whole justifies designation.[307] The second is by "enlargement of an SSSI", where an area of land that includes, but extends beyond the boundaries of, an existing SSSI meets the criterion of being of special interest.[308] In both cases the procedure is the same as for initial designation, with special provisions to deal with matters arising from the status, management and control of the land originally designated. There is also provision for the denotification of an SSSI where the land is not of special interest.[309] The procedure to be followed is again essentially the same as for initial notification, except that the Minister, the Environment Agency and relevant statutory undertakers must also be informed. The denotification takes effect when the notice that the land is to be denotified is confirmed by the conservation body.

Under the original scheme of the 1981 Act, which contained powers to **5.5.12** delay but not to prevent an occupier from carrying out damaging operations, management agreements were the main way of trying to provide enduring controls on the use of the land, often providing compensation for not undertaking certain operations. Under the new provisions, management agreements still form a major element in the way in which SSSIs are protected, but financial guidelines for England have emphasised the need to secure positive management and the fact that public money is not to be used simply to prevent new damaging operations.[310] The negotiation of such agreements, however, will take place against a very different background since the formal controls on land that is designated as an SSSI are much stricter under the new rules.

The starting point is the requirement for the owner or occupier to give **5.5.13**

---

[305] WCA 1981 s.28Q.

[306] WCA 1981 s.28B.

[307] Under the original provisions a court had held that it was appropriate to consider a local environment as a whole, without distinguishing the particular places of greater or lesser importance; *Sweet v Secretary of State for the Environment* [1989] 2 P.L.R. 14; (1989) 1 J.E.L. 245, cf. *R. v Canterbury City Council, ex p. Halford* (1992) 64 P. & C.R. 513, where a similar approach was taken to conservation areas.

[308] WCA 1981 s.28C.

[309] WCA 1981 s.28D, as amended by NERCA 2006 s.56; the absence of such a provision in the 1981 Act was noted in *R. v Nature Conservancy Council, ex p. London Brick Property Ltd* [1996] Env. L.R. 1; [1996] J.P.L. 227 and the potential for denotification should better sites be identified at a later stage strengthened the conclusion that it was not only the best sites that were eligible for designation in *R. (Western Power Distribution Investments Ltd) v Countryside Council for Wales* [2007] EWHC 50 Admin; [2007] Env. L.R. 25.

[310] *Guidelines on Management Agreement Payments and Other Related Matters* (DETR, 2001), paras 1.1–1.2.

notice before carrying out any of the PDOs that have been notified (at any stage). These can lawfully be carried out only if the conservation body gives it express consent or the operation is carried out in accordance with a management agreement, management scheme or management notice (see below).[311] This transforms the effect of an SSSI from being simply a delaying device into a form of prohibition, overridden only when the conservation body gives its consent, directly or through management arrangements. Consent can be given subject to conditions or for a limited period, and a consent can subsequently be withdrawn or modified, in which case a payment must be made to any owner or occupier suffering loss as a result.[312] Reasons must be given for decision to refuse consent or grant it subject to conditions or limitations.[313]

5.5.14   In the absence of a reasonable excuse, the owner or occupier commits an offence by carrying out a PDO without giving the required notice or without the relevant authorisation being given.[314] It is stated that a reasonable excuse is provided[315] by the granting of planning permission for the operation[316] or by the granting of an authorisation by a public authority or statutory undertaker which has complied with the obligations in relation to operations affecting SSSIs included in the reforms to the 1981 Act.[317] Emergency operations also constitute a reasonable excuse, provided that the conservation body is notified as soon as practicable.

5.5.15   The maximum penalty for this offence is an unlimited fine,[318] and for all offences in relation to SSSIs the courts are directed to have regard to any financial benefit arising from the offence.[319] This is an attempt to ensure that the penalties take into account not only the damage done by the offence (which can be hard to quantify and even harder to convert to financial terms) but also what the offender has gained by not taking the requisite care of the site, whether by increased income or reduced costs, thereby avoiding the situation where a calculating offender can decide that on a strict cost-benefit analysis it is better to run the risk of prosecution and a fine than to incur the additional expenditure, or forgo the additional profit, involved in protecting the site. Whether the courts will in fact be willing to impose high fines remains to be seen.[320] A further significant sanction is provided by the power of the courts to order the restoration of the land, a power previously limited to the context of Nature Conservation Orders,[321] and this may

---

[311] WCA 1981 s.28E.
[312] WCA 1981 s.28M(1).
[313] WCA 1981 s.28E(7).
[314] WCA 1981 s.28P(1).
[315] WCA 1981 s.28P(4).
[316] As before, the provision is phrased so as to apply only where there has been an application and express grant of planning permission, not to operations which are permitted development.
[317] See paras 5.5.22–5.5.25, below.
[318] WCA 1981 s.28P(1).
[319] WCA 1981 s.28P(9).
[320] A similar provision in relation to breaches of enforcement notices in planning law does not always produce fines that match the gains of the offenders; TCPA 1990 s.179(9).
[321] WCA 1981 s.31; see section 5.6, below.

impose a substantial cost on the offender.[322] The consent of the Director of Public Prosecutions is required before anyone other than a statutory conservation body can start a prosecution for these offences[323] and in the past the number of offences actually leading to prosecutions has been low.

When the maximum effect of an SSSI was simply to delay operations for **5.5.16** at most four months, there was no need for there to be a formal appeal mechanism. Now that the impact extends to an indefinite prohibition, an appeal structure has been instituted,[324] not least to comply with the requirement of article 6 of the European Convention on Human Rights[325] that any decisions determining civil rights (in this case the extent to which landowners are free to carry out normally lawful operations on their own land) should be made by means of a fair hearing before an independent and impartial tribunal. Owners or occupiers have the right to appeal to the Minister if consent is refused, if they are aggrieved by any conditions on the consent or by the withdrawal or modification of a consent, or if there is a deemed refusal in that the conservation body has not made its decision to grant or refuse consent within four months of being notified of the intended operation. The appeal must be made within two months of the conservation body's decision (or the expiry of the four-month period) and may involve a private hearing or public inquiry. The Minister can delegate the hearing of appeals to others, e.g. planning inspectors,[326] and detailed appeal regulations can be made.[327]

A further aspect of the revised law on SSSIs is the ability to control the **5.5.17** actions of third parties, not just the owners and occupiers, closing a further weakness identified in the original provisions of the 1981 Act, and again bringing the powers in relation to SSSIs into closer alignment with those for European sites. The conservation bodies are able to make byelaws for such sites, applying the same provisions as for nature reserves.[328] This gives the conservation body the power to regulate the activities not just of the owners and occupiers, but also of visitors to the land.[329] The extension of controls to third parties is also achieved through a new criminal offence whereby it is a crime for anyone (not just the owner or occupier) intentionally or recklessly to damage the flora, fauna or features which have led to the site being designated, or intentionally or recklessly to disturb any such fauna, the maximum penalties being more severe where the person knows that his or

---

[322] e.g. restoration costs were estimated at over £500,000 in addition to a fine of £50,000 and legal costs of £237,548 following a conviction for building a track, car-park and drainage ditches in a moorland SSSI; (2008) 397 ENDS Report 61. In *Wrexham Mining Ltd v Flintshire County Council* [2003] RVR 305 land being compulsorily purchased after a company went into liquidation before restoration of a site was completed (in accordance with planning permission for development on the site, not following conviction) was valued at £40,000 but transferred for £1 to reflect the cost of the outstanding work.

[323] WCA 1981 s.28P(10); this applies to all the offences under the new provisions.

[324] WCA 1981 s.28F.

[325] Given effect through the Human Rights Act 1998; see paras 1.5.5–1.5.7, above.

[326] WCA 1981 s.28F(8)–(9) and Sch.10A.

[327] WCA 1981 s.28F(6)–(7); Wildlife and Countryside (Sites of Special Scientific Interest, Appeals) (Wales) Regulations 2002 (SI 2002/1772), Sites of Special Scientific Interest (Appeals) Regulations 2009 (SI 2009/197).

[328] WCA 1981 s.28R; see paras 5.3.5–5.3.6, above.

[329] For controls on the activities of statutory undertakers, see paras 5.5.22–5.5.25, below; for the special position where there are rights over common land, see C. Rodgers, "Environmental Management of Common Land: Towards a New Legal Framework?" (1999) 11 J.E.L. 231.

her actions are taking effect within an SSSI.[330] No offence is committed if there is a reasonable excuse for this conduct, and an express grant of planning permission or other formal authorisation[331] provides such an excuse, as does an emergency provided that details of it are notified to the conservation body as soon as reasonably practicable. The further obligations on public authorities and statutory undertakers are discussed below.

5.5.18   The law on SSSIs is not just about imposing stricter controls stopping people from doing things. It is also designed to improve the management of sites through the production of a management statement[332] and through the provision of mechanisms for securing the positive management of SSSIs by means of management schemes and notices. For all or part of an SSSI, the conservation body can make a management scheme for conserving or restoring the special features of the site.[333] Owners and occupiers must be consulted about a proposed scheme and then formally notified of it, with at least three months allowed for the making of representations about the scheme, representations which must be taken into account. The scheme is then to be confirmed (with or without modifications)[334] or withdrawn by the conservation body within nine months of its notification, and takes effect when it is notified to all owners and occupiers. The scheme can be cancelled or modified at any time through the same procedures. The scheme by itself does not directly regulate the way in which land is managed, although potentially damaging operations can proceed without express consent from the conservation body if in accordance with a scheme,[335] and management agreements can provide for any matter covered by the scheme. Payments can also be made to those covered by a management scheme.[336] The greater legal importance of a management scheme is in paving the way for a management notice if the site is suffering harm.

5.5.19   Management notices can be made by the conservation body where it appears to it that an owner or occupier is not giving effect to the provisions of a management scheme and that as a result any of the flora, fauna or other special features of the site are being inadequately conserved or restored.[337] The conservation body thus has a means of ensuring that the terms of the scheme are being carried into effect in order to achieve the protection or restoration of features on the site, emphasising the need for positive management, not simply the prevention of damaging operations, if sites are to be conserved. This extends to situations where deterioration is occurring through neglect, as well as through bad management and therefore greatly enhances the powers of the law to achieve the conservation of habitat. Management notices may only be served where the conservation body is satisfied that it cannot reach on reasonable terms an agreement for the

---

[330] WCA 1981, s.28P(6)-(7), amended by NERCA 2006, s.55; this does not apply to the authorities and undertakers covered by the new duties discussed below.

[331] Subject to the authorising body having fulfilled its obligations with respect to SSSIs; see paras.5.5.22–5.5.25, below.

[332] See para.5.5.5, above.

[333] WCA 1981, s.28J.

[334] Modifications cannot make the scheme more onerous.

[335] WCA 1981, s.28E(3); see para.5.5.13, above.

[336] WCA 1981, s.28M(2).

[337] WCA 1981, s.28K.

management of the land in accordance with the scheme and copies of the notice must be served on all the owners and occupiers of the land affected.

The effect of a management notice is to require the owner or occupier to **5.5.20** carry out work on the land or to do other things with respect to the land by the date specified. The actions specified must be reasonable in order to ensure that the land is managed in accordance with the scheme, and the notice must explain the effect of the notice and the rights of appeal. If the work specified is not carried out by the due date, the conservation body may enter the land and carry out the work itself, and recover the expenses from the defaulting owner or occupier. There is a right of appeal to the Minister against the service of a management notice, and an appeal, which can proceed by written submissions, by hearing or by local inquiry, and has the effect of suspending the operation of a notice.[338] The grounds of appeal may include that some other owner or occupier should take, or pay for, any or all of the matters specified in the notice, and in this case the appellant must serve a copy of the appeal on those others. The Minister's decision can be to vary the effect of the notice so that it imposes requirements on others or requires them to make a payment to the appellant, bearing in mind their relative interests in the land, their relative responsibility for the state of the land that prompted the notice and the relative degree of benefit they will each derive from carrying out the notice.

There is also the possibility of compulsory purchase as a means of **5.5.21** ensuring that a site is conserved.[339] This is possible only where a management agreement has not been achievable on reasonable terms, or it has been broken in such a way that the land is not being properly managed. Disputes over whether there has been a breach are to be resolved by an arbitrator appointed by the Lord Chancellor. Once the land has been acquired it can be managed by the conservation body or disposed of on terms designed to secure that it is satisfactorily managed.

A further feature of the new scheme for SSSIs is the introduction of clear **5.5.22** obligations on a range of public authorities and statutory undertakers. A duty is imposed to take reasonable steps, consistent with the authority's function, to further the conservation and enhancement of the natural features for which an SSSI has been designated. This duty is imposed on Ministers, government departments, the National Assembly for Wales, local authorities, those holding any Crown or statutory office and statutory undertakers.[340] The special nature of SSSIs must therefore be recognised in the exercise of many functions and duties. There may still be circumstances where statutory responsibilities lead an authority to act in a way adverse to the conservation of an SSSI, but the scope for claiming that the impact on

---

[338] WCA 1981 s.28L; appeal regulations may be made by the Minister (WCA 1981 s.28F(6)–(7)).

[339] WCA 1981 s.28N, applying NPACA 1949 s.103.

[340] WCA 1981 s.28G. The term "statutory undertakers" covers any person or body deemed to be such under Pt 11 of TCPA 1990 (WCA 1981 s.28G(4) as added by NERCA 2006 Sch.11 para.81). The failure of the original provisions to control damaging operations by a statutory undertaker was one of the features that led to comments on the ineffectiveness of the whole SSSI regime in *Southern Water Authority v Nature Conservancy Council* [1992] 1 W.L.R. 775. There are some exceptions for operations under the Channel Tunnel Acts 1987 and 1996 (see CRWA 2000 Sch.10 paras 6 and 11).

an SSSI is an irrelevant, and therefore unlawful, consideration when options are being examined is much reduced.

5.5.23   These public authorities and statutory undertakers are subject to more precise obligations in relation to operations that they carry out or authorise and which might damage the features of an SSSI, and these apply even if the operation will take place outside the boundaries of the SSSI itself, an important point especially when operations affecting drainage and water flow are concerned.[341] The authority or undertaker must notify the conservation body of such operations, and in relation to operations that it is to carry out itself, it may initially proceed only if the conservation body assents.[342] If assent is refused,[343] the operation can only take place if the authority or undertaker gives the conservation body further notice[344] of when it is to go ahead, if it informs the conservation body of how it has taken account of any advice from the body, if the operations are carried out in such a way as to give rise to[345] as little damage as possible to the features of the site and if, so far as is reasonably practicable, the site is restored to its former condition if any damage does occur. The operation is thus not prohibited, but its effects are mitigated and the conservation body does have a short period of time to prepare any protective measures or try further negotiations to halt the operation.

5.5.24   In relation to operations to be authorised by the authority or undertaker, it must allow at least 28 days from the notice, unless the conservation body says sooner that it can proceed, and must take into account any advice from the body as it decides whether to approve the operation and what conditions, if any, to impose.[346] If the authority or undertaker decides not to follow the conservation body's advice on any issue, it must notify the body of the permission actually granted, and must ensure that there is a period of at least 21 days between that notice and the start of the operation. Again, this means that damaging operations cannot be prevented, but does ensure that the decision to grant permission is not taken in ignorance of the damaging consequences for an SSSI.[347]

5.5.25   These obligations on public authorities and statutory undertakers are

---

[341] Recognising and raising awareness of the potential for harm is a major issue if this provision is to operate successfully. Incidents such as the harm to the special flora of the Avon Gorge from pollution by debris falling during the shot-blasting of the Clifton Suspension Bridge can only be avoided if those commissioning the work, contractors and conservation groups recognise the need for special care and communicate clearly with each other. Here the problem arose not so much from the operation itself but from the choice of materials (copper slag, with high zinc levels) and their precise composition and form (which allowed the metals to leach into the soil), neither of which may have seemed to have been particularly significant issues to some of those concerned. See F. Pearce, "Poison rains down on rare plants", *New Scientist*, February 24, 1996, 4; *The Times*, March 30, 1996.

[342] WCA 1981 s.28H.

[343] There is a deemed refusal if the conservation body does not respond in 28 days.

[344] At least 28 days' notice must be given.

[345] This somewhat unusual statutory phrase appears designed to cover more indirect consequences than the more usual "cause".

[346] WCA 1981 s.28I.

[347] In this respect these arrangements play a role similar to that of environmental impact assessments; see section 8.3, below.

enforced through the criminal law.[348] It is an offence to proceed with an operation that does cause damage without serving the initial notice that a potentially harmful operation is proposed, or notice that the operation is to go ahead, unless there is a reasonable excuse for this failure. Failing to carry out the work so as to give rise to as little damage as reasonably practicable or to restore the site is also an offence. The sanction can include an order to restore the site.[349]

The new law took effect on January 30, 2001 and there are transitional **5.5.26** measures so that designations, notices and notifications under the old provisions continue in force and in order to cover cases where procedures were under way at that date.[350] The transitional provisions include the power for the conservation body to issue a stop notice in relation to operations which the owner or occupier had notified to the conservation body before October 30, 2000[351] and which are authorised only by virtue of the passage of four months, in other words where there has been no express consent from the conservation body directly or by virtue of the terms of a management agreement.[352] The stop notice must specify the land affected, the operations to be stopped and the date when the notice takes effect.[353] The effect of the stop notice is to apply the new provisions in relation to the authorisation of operations, so that the operation is lawful only if there is express consent, either directly or through the terms of a management agreement, scheme or notice. Compensation is payable to any occupier suffering loss as a result of the notice. There is a right of appeal against stop notices, but these continue in effect pending the appeal. There are also transitional provisions to continue the effect of any existing Nature Conservation Orders.[354]

A further feature of the new provisions is giving the statutory conserva- **5.5.27** tion bodies wide powers of entry to land where necessary in relation to any stage or aspect of the SSSI regime, from whether the site merits designation to determining what if any management arrangements should be made and whether these are being followed.[355] The conservation bodies also have the power to erect and maintain on an SSSI signs or notices relating to the site, and in the absence of a reasonable excuse intentional or reckless destruction, damage or obstruction of such signs is an offence.[356]

Additional legal measures apply through the provisions of the Environ- **5.5.28** mental Liability Directive.[357] The option has been taken to extend the terms of this Directive to cover damage not only to European Sites but also to

---

[348] WCA 1981 s.28P(2)–(3), (5A) and (5B), amended by NERCA 2006 s.55; prosecutions can be brought only by the statutory conservation bodies or with the consent of the Director of Public Prosecutions (WCA 1981 s.28P(10)).

[349] WCA 1981 s.31.

[350] CRWA 2000 Sch.11.

[351] The time-scale is altered where there was an agreement to extend the standard four-month period of delay.

[352] CRWA 2000 Sch.11 paras 9–12.

[353] At least three days after the date of the notice unless special reasons demand otherwise.

[354] CRWA 2000 Sch.11 paras 15–19; see section 5.6, below.

[355] WCA 1981 s.51, as amended by CRWA 2000 s.80.

[356] WCA 1981 s.28S, added by NERCA 2000 s.58.

[357] Directive 2004/35/EC.

SSSIs in England and Wales,[358] but not for Scotland.[359] This means that those who damage sites negligently, or regardless of fault in relation to certain listed activities, or who create an imminent risk of such damage, must take steps to prevent or remedy the harm. These provisions are discussed more fully in section 5.12, below.

Scotland

5.5.29 The law on SSSIs in Scotland was reformed by the Nature Conservation (Scotland) Act 2004, which took the very welcome approach of entirely replacing all the old law rather than making amendments to existing legislation. Further simplification is provided by the application of the new SSSI rules to European Sites.[360] Since they were responding to the same problems, it is no surprise that the Scottish provisions largely mirror those in England and Wales, but there are a number of differences, most significantly in relation to the designation procedure, the existence of the Advisory Committee and the means of requiring the land to be managed in particular ways.

5.5.30 As in England and Wales there is a duty to notify land considered by SNH to be of special interest by reason of any of its natural features, namely its flora, fauna or geological or geomorphological features,[361] and in determining whether or not such special interest is present, SNH must have regard to any ministerial guidance[362] and to the extent to which the designation would contribute to the development of a series of sites representative of the diversity and geographic range of the natural features of Scotland, Great Britain and the Member States of the EU.[363] The notification must contain details of the land affected and the natural features prompting the notification and specify the acts or omissions which appear likely to damage[364] the features (known as "operations requiring consent", ORCs).[365] It must be accompanied by a site management statement, which can include information promoting understanding and enjoyment by the public of the relevant natural features, as well as guidance to owners and occupiers on how the features should be conserved or enhanced.[366] The notification takes effect as soon as it is made.[367]

5.5.31 In Scotland the notification of an SSSI must be served on a much wider range of "interested parties" than in England and Wales,[368] in keeping with the aim of ensuring that interests of the human inhabitants of the land are

---

[358] Environmental Damage (Prevention and Remediation) Regulations 2009 (SI 2009/153) reg.4; Environmental Damage (Prevention and Remediation) (Wales) Regulations 2009 (SI 2009/995).

[359] *Environmental Liability Directive: Second Consultation* (Scottish Government, May 2008).

[360] CNHR 1994 regs 18–22, amended by CNHASR 2004 reg.9.

[361] NCSA 2004 s.3(1) and (2).

[362] Issued under NCSA 2004 s.54.

[363] NCSA 2004 s.3(3).

[364] "Damage" includes causing the feature to deteriorate and disturbance or harassment of fauna to the extent that the special interest of the land has decreased significantly; NCSA 2004 s.58(2) and (3).

[365] NCSA 2004 s.3(4) and (7).

[366] NCSA 2004 s.4; the management statement can be reviewed and revised at any time, at SNH's initiative or in response to a request from any owner or occupier.

[367] NCSA 2004 ss.3(6) and 10.

[368] See para.5.5.5, above.

taken into account as well as the conservation interests. In addition to any owner and occupier, the Scottish Ministers and the local authority (and National Park authority if relevant), the notice must be served on every community council, any statutory undertaker or regulatory authority likely to be affected,[369] any community body registered under the "right-to buy" legislation[370] and any other person appearing to have an interest in the land or thought fit by the notifying body.[371] The general effect of notification must also be publicised in a local newspaper and by such other means, including the internet and other electronic means, as SNH thinks fit.[372] The notice must specify a period of up to three months during which representations can be made and after considering any such representations SNH must decide within a year of the notice[373] whether or not to confirm the notice; confirmation can be with modifications but not so as to extend the area or add to the list of operations requiring consent.[374]

The other big difference in Scotland is the role of the Advisory Committee **5.5.32** on sites of special scientific interest.[375] This committee is appointed by the Scottish Ministers from those with scientific qualifications and experience in relation to flora, fauna or the geological or geomorphological features of land but excluding any member of SNH or other committee appointed by it. Where any person with an interest in the land timeously makes and does not withdraw representations in relation to the natural features by virtue of which SNH considers the land to be of special interest, the matter must be referred to the Advisory Committee. The advice it gives must be considered by SNH which must take action as it thinks fit in consequence of the advice. This procedure therefore allows for an independent assessment of the scientific case for designation (but not of the specification of the operations requiring consent), but ultimately the Committee's role is just advisory and the test remains whether SNH considers the land to be of special interest. There is no appeal mechanism but judicial review is available. The Committee must be likewise involved in relation to any enlargement or denotification of the site, and a case must be referred to it if any owner or occupier makes representations in relation to the justification for an existing site, so long as at least 10 years have passed since the original notification or the last such representation.

As in England and Wales, the law now allows for adjustments to be made **5.5.33** after the initial designation of an SSSI. At any time SNH can vary the original notification in relation to the description of the land, the features of interest and other matters, but not so as to extend its area or adjust the list of ORCs.[376] Changes to these two aspects, and denotification, are possible but require more formal procedures, essentially the same as for the original

---

[369] See para.5.5.45, below for definitions.

[370] Part 2 of the Land Reform (Scotland) Act 2003.

[371] NCSA 2004 ss.3(1) and 48(2)

[372] NCSA 2004 Sch.1 para.2.

[373] This period can be extended to a maximum of 18 months where there has been a reference to the Advisory Committee or in the absence of objection from any owner or occupier (NCSA 2004 Sch.1 para.12).

[374] NCSA 2004 Sch.1 paras 4–8.

[375] NCSA 2004 s.21. The Public Services Reform (Scotland) Bill introduced in May 2009 proposes abolishing the Committee as a separate entity, transferring its functions to a committee within SNH's standard structure.

[376] NCSA 2004 s.8.

designation. The site can be enlarged to include land that is contiguous or otherwise associated with it where SNH considers that the combined area would be of special interest.[377] The list of ORCs, and at the same time any consents given for such operations,[378] may be reviewed at SNH's initiative and must be reviewed at the request of any owner or occupier, but in either case only after a period of six years from the original notification or last review.[379] If SNH considers that the notification should be amended, by adding, removing or modifying any of the listed ORCs, then this must be done. In urgent situations, where it appears that a person is carrying out or intending to carry out an operation that is not an ORC but which is causing or is likely to cause damage to the natural features of an SSSI, SNH can apply to the Minister for consent to add to or modify the list of ORCs, bringing the operation under their control.[380] If the Minister consents, the change must be notified to every owner and occupier and to the person whose activities sparked this measure, if not already included in the previous category. Denotification of all or part of an SSSI is permitted where SNH considers that it is no longer of special interest.[381] The process involves notification to the same people and consideration of the same factors as the original notification.

5.5.34 Control over the operations of owners and occupiers[382] remains at the heart of the SSSI system and the 2004 Act strengthens this by allowing operations to go ahead only if certain consents have been obtained. If an owner or occupier wishes to carry out an operation requiring consent, notice must be given to SNH and the operation can lawfully proceed only if SNH has given written consent or certain other conditions apply.[383] Consent can be given subject to conditions and can be modified or withdrawn, either as part of a review of the ORCs[384] or, with ministerial consent, where SNH considers that the operation will harm a natural feature in a way not foreseen at the time of giving the consent. Reasons must be given for any decisions other than full consent and in such cases SNH must consider entering a management agreement with the person proposing the operation. There is a right of appeal to the Scottish Land Court where consent is refused, granted subject to conditions, modified or withdrawn.[385]

5.5.35 An operation is lawful in the absence of SNH's consent if it is authorised[386] under permission from a relevant regulatory authority,[387] a grant of planning permission,[388] or a management agreement with the person concerned or is required under a land management order.[389] The operation is

---

[377] NCSA 2004 s.5; at this stage it is not possible to query the original notification.

[378] Consents under NCSA 2004 s.16; see para.5.5.34, below.

[379] NCSA 2004 s.6; on the initiative of SNH a review can take place after a shorter interval if every owner and occupier consents.

[380] NCSA 2004 s.7.

[381] NCSA 2004 s.9.

[382] Any change of owner or occupier must be notified to SNH; NSCA 2004 s.42.

[383] NSCA 2004 s.16.

[384] Under NCSA 2004 s.6(4); see para.5.5.33, above.

[385] NCSA 2004 s.18; see para.5.5.36, below.

[386] NCSA 2004 s.17.

[387] See para.5.5.45, below.

[388] This is expressed as "planning permission granted on an application", thereby excluding operations which are covered by the permitted development rules; see para.8.2.12, below.

[389] NCSA 2004 ss.16 and 17; for land management orders see para.5.5.39, below.

also lawful if it is an emergency operation and details are notified to SNH as soon as practicable once the necessity for it becomes apparent. If the operation causes damage and is lawful on the basis of being an emergency or authorised by a regulatory body, then the owner or occupier must consult SNH on the restoration of any natural feature and restore it as far as practicable to its former condition in accordance with the advice received. It is an offence for the owner or occupier without reasonable excuse to carry out, or to cause or permit to be carried out, an ORC unless it is lawful on one of the above grounds and it is no defence that no actual harm resulted to the natural features of the site.[390]

Since the 2004 Act introduced powers to prevent owners and occupiers **5.5.36** from carrying out certain operations an appeal mechanism was required, especially in view of the needs of article 6 of the European Convention on Human Rights. Rights of appeal are provided in relation to SNH's decisions on ORCs and on whether and on what terms to enter a management agreement[391] and the Minister's decisions in relation to land management orders.[392] Whereas in England and Wales appeals are directed to the Minister, in Scotland appeals are heard by the Scottish Land Court.[393] The Court's main task is to determine agricultural disputes, especially in relation to agricultural holdings and crofts, and although it has manifest independence of any of the parties involved and flexible procedures well-suited to such appeals (including holding hearings at or near the sites concerned), its background[394] means that it may have to make an extra effort to demonstrate that it can reach a fair balance between the interests of occupiers and of conservation. The Court is expressly instructed to consider appeals on their merits rather than by way of review and has wide powers not just to quash or approve the original decision but to add, vary or remove conditions.

Whereas the 1981 Act concentrated on controlling the operations of **5.5.37** owners and occupiers, the 2004 Act matches the provisions south of the border in controlling third parties, placing obligations on public bodies and others and providing means to secure the management of the site. In relation to third parties, SNH can make byelaws for the protection of SSSIs, following the procedure that applies for nature reserves.[395] More generally any person who intentionally or recklessly damages a natural feature specified in an SSSI notification is guilty of an offence. It is a defence to show that the act was the incidental result of a lawful operation, that reasonable precautions were taken to avoid the act or that it was not, and could not reasonably have been, foreseen that the act would have the incidental harmful

---

[390] NCSA 2004 s.19(3) and (5).
[391] NCSA 2004 s.18(1).
[392] NCSA 2004 s.34.
[393] NCSA 2004 s.18. The Court is governed by the Scottish Land Court Act 1993.
[394] The introduction to the Scottish Land Court's web-pages (*http://www.scottish-land-court. org.uk* [Accessed May 10, 2009]) say: "The Court's jurisdiction is set firmly within the context of Scottish farming", and gives very little prominence to its jurisdiction under the 2004 Act, while its non-legal members are chosen for their agricultural expertise.
[395] NCSA 2004 s.20, applying NPACA 1949 ss.106 and 107.

result and that the steps that were reasonably practicable in all the circumstances were taken to minimise the damage caused.[396]

5.5.38   In terms of the management of the site, the site management statement provided at the time of notification (and provided since the 2004 Act for existing SSSIs)[397] offers guidance and management agreements remain a key tool. There are, however, two more coercive mechanisms. The first is Nature Conservation Orders, and these are discussed in the separate section 5.6 below since their use is not restricted to SSSIs. The second is Land Management Orders, which in contrast to the management schemes and notices made by the conservation bodies in England and Wales require ministerial approval.[398] The acquisition of the land by SNH, by agreement or compulsorily, offers a further means of ensuring control over the land.[399] Compulsory purchase is possible only for securing the conservation, restoration or enhancement of the natural features of the land, which can be an SSSI, land covered by a nature conservation or land management order or contiguous or associated land. The land acquired may be disposed of by SNH, but only on terms designed to achieve the purpose noted above, so that land that has been acquired could be passed on to a body like the RSPB subject to appropriate title conditions.

5.5.39   A land management order can be sought by SNH where necessary or expedient to conserve, restore or enhance the natural features in an SSSI notification and can apply not only to land that is in SSSI but also to land contiguous or otherwise associated with it.[400] Before a proposal can be made SNH must have tried unsuccessfully[401] to enter a management agreement or there must be non-compliance with the terms of such an agreement. As well as describing the land and natural features concerned and any operations that are prohibited, the proposal must specify any operations that must be carried out to serve the purposes of the order, by whom, when and how these should be carried out and the likely costs involved and amounts SNH should pay in respect of these. The proposal must be notified and publicised in the same way as when an SSSI is designated[402] and the Minister has the power to require SNH or others to disclose relevant information.[403] At least three months must be allowed for representations to be made[404] and then within a further three months the Minister must decide to make or refuse the order as proposed or to make such other land management order thought fit.[405]

5.5.40   Like the proposal, the order must specify the land and features concerned,

---

[396] NCSA 2004 s.18(1) and (2); this sets the limits of the offence rather differently from the equivalent provision south of the border (see para.5.5.17, above).

[397] NCSA 2004 Sch.5 para.4.

[398] Both procedures aim to provide some check on the conservation bodies before coercive measures are imposed, in Scotland through ministerial involvement, and in England and Wales through using a two-stage procedure of making management schemes subject to rights of appeal before notices can be made.

[399] NCSA 2004 s.39.

[400] NCSA 2004 s.29.

[401] Whether through the owner or occupier refusing or SNH not knowing who the owner or occupier is despite placing notices on the land (as specified in NSCA 2004 s.48(10)).

[402] See para.5.5.31, above.

[403] NCSA 2004 Sch.3.

[404] NCSA 2004 Sch.3 paras 4 and 5.

[405] NCSA 2004 s.30.

the operations to be prohibited or carried out, by whom, when and how, and also the date when the order takes effect and rights of appeal. It can also provide for SNH to make payments in respect of the reasonable costs of carrying out the required operations.[406] Any aggrieved owner or occupier has 28 days within which to appeal to the Scottish Land Court against the making of the order or its terms.[407] At least every six years the Minister must review every land management order with a view to determining whether it should be amended or revoked and make an order doing so if considered appropriate.[408]

5.5.41 Enforcement of land management orders is by two routes. First the criminal law is invoked and it is an offence for any person without reasonable excuse either to fail to carry out in the required manner an operation required of them under an order, or to carry out, or cause or permit to be carried out, an operation that an order prohibits.[409] Secondly, if a required operation is not carried out by the date or in the manner specified, SNH is relieved of any obligation under the order to make any payments (and may recover any already made) and can carry out the operation itself, recovering any additional costs involved.[410]

5.5.42 Duties in relation to SSSIs are placed on a number of public bodies and separately on specific regulatory authorities. For these purposes a "public body" is any public body or office-holder including anyone exercising functions of a public nature and statutory undertakers, in turn defined by a list of specific categories.[411] A general duty is placed on these public bodies in relation to the exercise of any function on or affecting an SSSI, a duty enforceable by civil proceedings for interdict or other appropriate remedy.[412] The body must consult SNH, have regard to the advice and so far as consistent with the proper exercise of its functions exercise the function so as to further the conservation and enhancement of the natural features of the SSSI and to maintain or enhance the representative nature of the any series of sites to which the SSSI belongs.[413]

5.5.43 More specifically, a public body can only carry out operations likely to damage the features of an SSSI (whether the operation is on land within the SSSI or not) if SNH has given its written consent or certain other criteria apply.[414] Consent is not required for operations authorised by planning permission or by permission from one of the regulatory authorities as discussed below, for emergency operations notified to SNH as soon as practicable, or for those in line with a management agreement with the public body or a management plan prepared by the public body and approved in writing by SNH for this purpose.[415] Where consent is necessary, there must be an application giving the nature, dates and location of the proposed

---

[406] NCSA 2004 s.31.
[407] NCSA 2004 s.34; see para.5.5.36, above.
[408] NCSA 2004 s.33.
[409] NCSA 2004 s.36.
[410] NCSA 2004 s.37.
[411] NCSA 2004 s.58(1); the list includes airport, telecommunications, postal, gas and electricity operators, the Civil Aviation Authority, Scottish Water and statutory railway, canal, harbour and water operators.
[412] NSCA 2004 s.45(1); proceedings can be in either the sheriff court or Court of Session.
[413] NSCA 2004 s.12.
[414] NSCA 2004 s.13.
[415] NSCA 2004 s.14(1).

operation. SNH may refuse or grant consent or grant consent subject to conditions, in particular specifying the manner or period in which the operation must be carried out or limiting the area where it can take place. SNH's response must give advice on carrying out the operation, including advice on minimising any damage, and reasons must be given for any decision other than full consent. A failure to respond within 28 days is treated as a refusal.[416]

5.5.44 The refusal of consent (or the imposition of conditions) does not mean that the operation cannot go ahead as originally proposed.[417] The public body can go ahead so long as it tells SNH what (if anything) it is doing in consequence of any written advice provided by SNH in response to its application and when it is going to carry out the operation, giving at least 28 days' notice; this allows SNH time to take steps to mitigate any damage, try to agree a management agreement or to seek a nature conservation order[418] imposing further controls. The body must also carry out the operation so as to give rise to as little damage or disturbance as reasonably practicable in all the circumstances to the natural features of the SSSI and in accordance with its general duty[419] to further conservation of the site. Where damage arises as a result of an operation that goes ahead without SNH's consent on the basis of these provisions, or as a result of permission granted by a regulatory authority or as an emergency, SNH must be consulted on how the natural features should be restored to their former condition and the public body should carry out such restoration as far as reasonably practicable in accordance with the advice from SNH.[420]

5.5.45 Where operations that are likely to damage the features of an SSSI require permission from a range of "regulatory authorities", a broadly parallel procedure applies,[421] and again enforcement is by civil proceedings.[422] The regulatory authorities affected are those listed in regulations made under the 2004 Act and are: the Scottish Ministers, local authorities, the Crofters Commission, the Deer Commission for Scotland, district salmon fishery boards, the Forestry Commissioners and SEPA.[423] Before deciding whether to grant permission the authority must notify SNH and allow 28 days for a response. Any advice from SNH must be taken into account in determining whether and on what conditions to grant permission. If permission is given contrary to SNH's advice, the authority must notify SNH and the applicant of the decision, of the fact that the authority has not followed the advice and of what the authority has done in response to SNH's advice. Any permission granted in such circumstances is subject to a condition that the operation is carried out so as to give rise to as little damage or disturbance as reasonably practicable and cannot take effect until at least 28 days after the notice to SNH that the permission has been granted.

---

[416] NSCA 2004 s.12(3)–(8).
[417] NSCA 2004 s.14(2)–(5).
[418] See section 5.6, below.
[419] NSCA 2004 s.12(2)(c); see para.5.5.42, above.
[420] NSCA 2004 s.14(5) and (6).
[421] NSCA 2004 s.15.
[422] NSCA 2004 s.45(1).
[423] Nature Conservation (Designation of Relevant Regulatory Authorities) (Scotland) Order 2004 (SSI 2004/474).

The SSSI regime is supported by a number of other measures dealing with **5.5.46** information and enforcement. The Keeper of the Registers of Scotland has to keep a register of SSSI notifications and related notices, in accordance with ministerial regulation.[424] SNH may put up, maintain and remove signs to provide information to the public about land in an SSSI or covered by nature conservation or land management order; damage or destruction of such signs is an offence.[425] That offence also applies to any notices affixed to land in giving notification of matters under these provisions and detailed rules on notification are provided.[426] The police are given wide powers of entry, stop, search and seizure in relation to suspected offences in relation to SSSIs and nature conservation orders and SNH and the Minister can authorise entry onto land, other than a dwelling or lockfast premises, in order to determine whether their various powers should be exercised, assess the condition of protected natural features, and carry out operations or install signs; in some circumstances warrants are required by the police or those authorised by SNH.[427]

In terms of sanctions, SNH can seek from the Court of Session or sheriff **5.5.47** court an interdict or other order when it appears that a current or proposed operation is damaging to a protected natural feature or any other natural feature of national importance.[428] The fine following any criminal conviction is to be assessed with regard to any financial benefit accruing to the accused in consequence of the offence[429] and where someone is guilty of damaging a protected feature of an SSSI the penalty can include a restoration order.[430] Such orders require specific actions to be taken to restore the feature to its former condition so far as reasonably practicable; failure to carry these out within the specified period is a further offence and SNH is then permitted to carry them out itself and recover the costs involved. In relation to prosecutions, the time limit for bringing summary proceedings is extended and express provision allows that where an offence is committed by a body corporate or partnership, any individual director, manager, partner or the like can be individually prosecuted if the offence was committed with their consent or connivance or is attributable to their neglect.[431]

The provisions of the 2004 Act mostly took effect on November 29, 2004 **5.5.48** and transitional provisions allowed for existing notifications and orders to continue under the new scheme.[432]

---

[424] NCSA 2004 s.22. The relevant regulations are the Register of Sites of Special Scientific Interest (Scotland) Regulations 2008 (SSI 2008/221) and the register is available at *http:// www.ros.gov.uk/sssi/index.html* [Accessed May 10, 2009].

[425] NCSA 2004 s.41.

[426] NCSA 2004 s.48.

[427] NCSA 2004 s.44 and Sch.4.

[428] NCSA 2004 s.45(2).

[429] NCSA 2004 s.46(1).

[430] NCSA 2004 s.40.

[431] NSCA 2004 s.47.

[432] NSCA 2004 Sch.5.

General

5.5.49 The existence of an SSSI has effects in other legal regimes. As noted above, where an SSSI may be affected special procedures must be followed in relation to a range of statutory permits, including the grant of planning permission.[433] The fact that the land in question is an SSSI may also trigger the requirement for an environmental assessment to be carried out,[434] and SSSIs cannot be included in a Simplified Planning Zone (an area where planning controls are considerably relaxed in order to stimulate development).[435] Conserving or enhancing the area of an SSSI can be the basis for making a road traffic regulation order,[436] and in England and Wales, a ministerial order diverting a highway, including a footpath and bridleway, can be made to prevent significant damage to the features of an SSSI as a result of the public using the highway.[437]

5.5.50 As far as agricultural developments in England and Wales are concerned, special rules apply to the consideration of applications for farm capital grants for land designated as an SSSI.[438] The agriculture ministers must exercise their functions under the grant schemes so as to further the conservation of the special features of the site, so far as is consistent with the purposes of the grant provisions, and consideration must be given to any objection from the statutory conservation body that the activities in question are damaging to the flora, fauna or special geological or physiographical features of the site.[439] Where a grant has been refused as a result of objections from the conservation body, the body must within three months offer to enter a management agreement for the site.[440] Proper management of SSSIs features throughout the agricultural support schemes that now include care for the environment as an integral element.[441]

5.5.51 Although largely overtaken by the wider provisions affecting public bodies, the environmental obligations of the Environment Agency are also likely to affect SSSIs.[442] Where a conservation body considers that land is of special interest because of its flora, fauna or geological or physiographical features, and may be affected by the schemes, works or other activities carried out or authorised by the Agency, then the body must notify it of the special interest of the land.[443] The basic test for identifying land of special interest is the same as for SSSIs, but the provision is not restricted to land formally notified as an SSSI, whilst SSSIs which are safe from disturbance

---

[433] See paras 5.5.23 and 5.5.45, above.

[434] See section 8.3, below.

[435] TCPA 1990 s.87(1); TCPSA 1997 s.54.

[436] Road Traffic Regulation Act 1984 s.22 (as amended by CRWA 2000 s.66).

[437] Highways Act 1980 ss.119D and 119E, added by CRWA 2000 Sch.6 para.12, and Highways (SSSI Diversion Orders) (England) Regulations 2007 (SI 2007/1494).

[438] "Farm capital grants" are defined as those provided by schemes under s.29 of the Agriculture Act 1970 or regulations giving effect to European Community provisions; WCA 1981 s.32(3), as substituted by Agriculture Act 1986 s.20(3).

[439] WCA 1981 s.32(1), amended by Agriculture Act 1986 s.20; in England the legislation requires the Agriculture Minister to consult with the Secretary of State for the Environment, and the statutory words have not been altered to reflect the unification of ministerial roles following the creation of the Department for the Environment, Food and Rural Affairs.

[440] WCA 1981 s.32(2).

[441] See section 8.4, below.

[442] The equivalent provisions for SEPA were repealed by NCSA 2004 Sch.7 para.10.

[443] EA 1995 s.8.

by the activities of the Agency may be excluded. Before the Agency carries out or authorises any works, etc. which it considers likely to destroy or damage the special features of a site which has been notified, it must consult with the conservation body; in the case of emergency works, no prior consultation is required, but notification must be given as soon as practicable. A further provision in England and Wales is that the Minister may require that an appropriate management agreement is entered before certain land of special scientific interest held by water undertakers is sold.[444]

The system of SSSIs is the cornerstone of habitat protection in Britain, **5.5.52** but on all sides there was some dissatisfaction with the operation of the scheme created by the Wildlife and Countryside Act 1981. From the point of view of conservation interests, the system did not do enough to guarantee the protection of sites, since damaging operations could be delayed for only a short time, the protection could be overridden by a planning authority granting permission for a development and only the activities of owners and occupiers were restricted, leaving the conduct of those with lesser rights over the land, e.g. commoners, statutory undertakers and visitors, uncontrolled. Moreover the whole approach was based on preventing particular damage, not ensuring the positive management of the land, so that the value of a site could be lost by neglect, e.g. by scrub invading grassland, without any regulated operation being involved and hence no trigger for the (limited) further measures to be taken. Landowners and occupiers were often unhappy at the designation of their land on purely scientific grounds with no right of appeal or subsequent amendment or denotification and limited consideration for their ability to make a return from the land, whilst the system of notifying all potentially damaging operations presented them with what seems to be a frightening array of restrictions, apparently removing totally their right to treat their land as their own. Criticism came from both sides over the compensation scheme and the purely negative approach of the PDO system.

Some of the difficulties, from the landowners' side at least, were caused **5.5.53** not by the actual impact of the designation but by the initial impression of a much stronger set of restrictions than existed in practice. In Scotland many of these problems were considerably exacerbated by the poor handling of matters by the NCC during the 1980s when it was under great pressure to complete quickly the renotification of sites so that they could benefit from the 1981 Act. The strength of feeling on the issue was amply illustrated by the views expressed by several members of the House of Lords during the passage of the Natural Heritage (Scotland) Act 1991, when attempts were made to introduce a total reassessment of all SSSI designations.

The unhappiness with the provisions of the 1981 Act meant that during **5.5.54** the late 1990s there was clear consensus on the need for reform and this has now taken place. In both Scotland and England and Wales the position has been transformed, dealing with many of the criticisms from both sides and producing a new regulatory framework that seeks to tackle in a more positive way a wider range of threats to the future of SSSIs. The differences between the two regimes are much less important than their similarities, although it remains deeply disappointing that at the time of the reform it was only in Scotland that steps were taken to consolidate the provisions on

---

[444] Water Industry Act 1991 s.156, amended by NERCA 2006 Sch.11 para.131.

SSSIs with those for European Sites to produce a more coherent structure for habitat protection.

5.5.55   These improvements in the law have been matched by some improvement on the ground. Although the target of having 95 per cent of SSSIs in England in favourable condition may be missed, 83 per cent are now on target compared to 57 per cent in 2003.[445] However the biodiversity value of SSSIs is still being damaged by neglect and by development[446] and the whole basis of a conservation policy based on fixed sites is put into question at a time when a changing climate may radically alter the conditions in any location and hence the wildlife it can support.

NATURE CONSERVATION ORDERS

5.6.1 Nature Conservation Orders were created under the Wildlife and Countryside Act 1981 as a means of offering more protection for a site than could be provided by its designation as an SSSI.[447] The extended powers that now apply to all SSSIs exceed these additional controls and in England and Wales Nature Conservation Orders have been abolished, subject to transitional provisions.[448] In Scotland they have been retained but in a wholly different form, as provided by the Nature Conservation (Scotland) Act 2004,[449] largely as a means of imposing controls on land outwith SSSIs and European Sites and of controlling operations carried out other than by the owners and occupiers.

5.6.2   By means of a Nature Conservation Order the Minister can prohibit specified operations, wholly or in specified circumstances, from being carried out on certain land.[450] There are two grounds for making a Nature Conservation Order: the conservation of a natural feature of special interest and compliance with international obligations. The natural feature may be one by reason of which an SSSI has been designated (whether or not the designation includes the land affected by the order) or one which is otherwise considered by the Minister to be of special interest. The land affected can include land which is all or part of an SSSI or contiguous or associated land or land which the Minister considers of special interest even though not designated, so that the powers under a Nature Conservation Order offer a means of preventing damaging activities even where the relevant areas have not been made subject to any formal conservation designation. Any person who carries out, or causes or permits to be carried out, a prohibited operation is guilty of an offence and it is no defence that no harm was actually caused to the protected feature.[451]

---

[445] *Halting Biodiversity Loss*, Thirteenth Report of 2007–08 of House of Commons Environmental Audit Committee, HC Paper No.743 (Session 2007–2008), para.12.

[446] e.g. the controversial Menie Estate ("Trump") golf development north of Aberdeen given outline permission in November 2008; see *http://www.scotland.gov.uk/Topics/Built-Environment/planning/publications/foi/MenieEstate* [Accessed May 10, 2009].

[447] For the details of these "super-SSSIs" under the 1981 Act, see section 5.6 of the previous edition of this book.

[448] CRWA 2000 Sch.11 paras 15–20 and Sch.16.

[449] Existing orders are continued by virtue of NCSA 2004 Sch.5 para.11.

[450] NCSA 2004 s.23.

[451] NCSA 2004 s.27.

Orders are made by the Minister after consulting SNH and following a **5.6.3**
procedure initially the same as for designating SSSIs.[452] All "interested
parties" must be notified, the proposal must be publicised in a local newspaper and at least three months allowed for representations. In this case,
though, if there are any representations these must be considered either at a
local inquiry or at a hearing before a person appointed by the Minister. The
order takes effect immediately but must be confirmed within 12 months (or a
longer period agreed with every owner and occupier) or else it lapses;
confirmation can be with modifications but these cannot extend the area
affected.[453] Orders must be recorded in the General Register of Sasines or the
Land Register[454] and SNH must include in its annual report the details of
any new or amending order made during the year.[455] Once an order has been
made it can be amended or revoked, in full or in part,[456] and while the
Minister is free to review an order at any time, orders must be reviewed at
least every six years.[457]

These provisions have been extended to apply to European Sites, with **5.6.4**
minor adjustments so that in place of references to the special interest of the
site there is reference to its significance in relation to the objectives of the
Birds and the Habitats and Species Directives, and it is expressly stated that
the "international obligations" includes those under these Directives.[458]

Nature Conservation Orders are now restricted to Scotland and even here **5.6.5**
do not play a major part in the conservation of habitat.[459] Nevertheless, their
continuing use does suggest that there is a useful role for them as part of the
overall picture, although it would clearly be better if the necessary provisions could be integrated with other more substantial regimes rather than
having this further proliferation of legal devices.

LIMESTONE PAVEMENT ORDERS

Now applying only in England Wales,[460] special provision is made for the **5.7.1**
protection of areas of limestone pavement, i.e. areas of limestone wholly or
partly exposed on the surface of the ground and fissured by natural erosion[461]—such areas are of considerable botanical and geological value and
many are designated as SSSIs. The making of Limestone Pavement Orders is
a two-stage process. In the first place, any area of limestone pavement of

---

[452] See para.5.5.31, above.
[453] NCSA 2004 s.23(6) and (7); Sch.2 paras 5–14.
[454] NCSA 2004 Sch.2 para.15.
[455] NCSA 2004 s.28.
[456] NCSA 2004 s.24.
[457] NCSA 2004 s.26.
[458] CNHR 1994 reg.19, amended by CNHASR 2004 reg.9.
[459] At the end of March 2008, there were 18 Nature Conservation orders in force, plus five
amendment orders, and although no orders were made or amended in 2007–08 the fact that
during 2006-07 one new order was made, one amended and one revoked shows the continuing
relevance of these provisions (SNH, *Annual Reports 2007–08*, p.18, and *2006–07*, p.39).
[460] These provisions were repealed in relation to Scotland by NCSA 2004 Sch.7 para.4.
[461] WCA 1981 s.34(6). There are about 2,600 hectares of this habitat in Great Britain and
further information can be found on the web pages of the Limestone Pavement Action Group at
http://www.limestone-pavements.org.uk [Accessed May 10, 2009].

special interest by reason of its fauna, flora or geological or physiographical features is to be identified by Natural England or the Countryside Council for Wales, and notified to the local planning authority for that area.[462] The decision to make an Order then rests with the Minister or the planning authority[463]; this power is to be exercised where it appears that the character or appearance of the land is likely to be adversely affected by the removal or disturbance of the limestone.[464]

5.7.2 The procedure involves the Order taking effect at once but being reviewed by the Minister after advertisement, notification to the relevant owners, occupiers and local authority and an opportunity for objections and representations to be made. The Minister considers all Orders, whether made by himself or a planning authority. The Minister's decision to confirm, amend or revoke the Order must be advertised and notified in the same way and after six weeks, during which there is a limited right to challenge its validity, the Order cannot then be questioned in any legal proceedings.[465]

5.7.3 The effect of an Order is to designate the land affected and to prohibit the removal or disturbance of limestone on or in it.[466] It is an offence without reasonable excuse to remove or disturb limestone on or in any designated land.[467] A reasonable excuse is however provided if the action is authorised by a grant of planning permission in response to an application under the planning legislation; as with SSSIs, there must be an express grant of permission, thereby excluding operations having only deemed permission under the General Permitted Development Orders, e.g. some agricultural operations.[468] Since any significant extraction of limestone is likely to require planning permission in any case as a "mining operation",[469] the legal protection offered against disturbance is primarily in relation to activities which fall outwith the scope of planning control, or are incidental to other operations. No compensation is available to those whose land is designated under a Limestone Pavement Order.

AREAS OF SPECIAL PROTECTION

5.8.1 Sites which are of particular importance for birds can be offered additional protection through the creation of Areas of Special Protection. This designation replaced the more clearly named Bird Sanctuaries,[470] and should not be confused with Special Protection Areas under the European Community's

---

[462] WCA 1981 s.34(1).

[463] The county planning authority in non-metropolitan counties of England (WCA 1981 s.34(6)).

[464] WCA 1981 s.34(2).

[465] WCA 1981 Sch.1.

[466] WCA 1981 s.34(2).

[467] WCA 1981 s.34(4).

[468] WCA 1981 s.34(5).

[469] TCPA 1990 s.55.

[470] Bird Sanctuaries were governed by the Protection of Birds Act 1954 s.3 and, although there is no express provision, it is considered that the sanctuaries designated under that Act continue in effect as if created under the 1981 Act; *Halsbury's Statutory Instruments* (London: Butterworths, 1993 reissue), Vol.2, p.225.

Birds Directive.[471] The effect of such areas is primarily on visitors, since there are wide exemptions preserving the rights of those with any interest in the land. Orders creating Areas of Special Protection are made by the Minister, and the legislation lays down no specific criteria for when an order can be made.[472] Any proposed order must be notified to all owners and occupiers of the land affected, individually in writing or through the local press where individual notification is impracticable,[473] and three months is allowed for objections or representations to be made.[474] The order can be made by the Minister only if all the owners and occupiers consent, or at least if there are no objections or any objections are withdrawn.[475]

Orders can contain a variety of provisions, strengthening the general law **5.8.2** protecting wild birds. Within the designated area it may become an offence intentionally to kill, injure or take any wild bird, to take, damage or destroy the nest of a wild bird while it is in use or being built, to take or destroy eggs, to disturb wild birds while they are building or tending a nest or to disturb the dependent young of a wild bird; these prohibitions can apply to all wild birds or to specified species.[476] The effect of the order may thus be to apply the enhanced protection normally offered only to those species listed in Schedule 1 to the 1981 Act to all birds in the Area of Special Protection.[477] It can also be made an offence for any person to enter the designated area, or any part of it, at any time or during certain periods, e.g. protecting ground-nesting birds during the nesting season.[478]

There are, however, many exceptions to the prohibitions which can apply **5.8.3** within Areas of Special Protection. Those with rights over the land are protected from restrictions not only by the fact that designations cannot be made in the face of objections by owners or occupiers, but also by the rule that none of the prohibitions in an order can affect the exercise by any persons of rights vested in them, as owner or occupier of the land or under any licence or agreement.[479] The legislation for England and Wales also retains further rights for "authorised persons" in relation to any pest species listed in Part II of Schedule 2 to the 1981 Act.[480] The defences which apply to the general law protecting wild birds under the 1981 Act also apply to offences under the provisions of an order creating an Area of Special Protection.[481] The effect of Areas of Special Protection is thus not to offer complete protection to all birds, but rather to provide a limited sanctuary for some birds without interfering with existing rights in the land.

---

[471] Directive 79/409/EEC; see paras 5.2.3–5.2.8, above and 7.4.12–7.4.14, below. In Scotland there are 146 Special Protection Areas covering 657,456 hectares but only eight Areas of Special Protection, mostly designated in the late 1950s and early 1960s and covering 1,518 hectares; data as at October 2008 from SNHi: *http://www.snh.org.uk/snhi* [Accessed May 10, 2009].

[472] WCA 1981 s.3(1).

[473] WCA 1981 s.3(4).

[474] WCA 1981 s.3(5) and (6).

[475] WCA 1981 s.3(5).

[476] WCA 1981 s.3(1)(a).

[477] See para.3.3.6, above.

[478] WCA 1981 s.3(1)(b).

[479] WCA 1981 s.3(3).

[480] WCA 1981 s.3(2). The control of pest species is now authorised by licences rather than under that Schedule and s.3(2) has been repealed for Scotland (NCSA 2004 Sch.6 para.4).

[481] WCA 1981 s.4; see paras 3.3.3–3.3.4, above.

NATIONAL PARKS

5.9.1 National Parks have developed very differently in England and Wales and in Scotland. South of the border, the National Parks were created under the National Parks and Access to the Countryside Act 1949,[482] but at that time it was decided that there was no need for them in Scotland,[483] and it is only under the very different provisions of the National Parks (Scotland) Act 2000 that the first National Parks in Scotland were created in 2002 and 2003.

5.9.2 In both jurisdictions, the Parks are very different from the internationally accepted concept of national parks.[484] The International Union for the Conservation of Nature has recommended that the term "national park" be reserved for areas "large enough to contain one or more entire ecosystems not materially altered by current human occupation or exploitation", with the aims of protecting natural and scenic areas "for spiritual, scientific, educational, recreational or tourist purposes", perpetuating ecosystems "in as natural a state as possible", managing visitors "at a level which will maintain the area in a natural or near natural state" and "eliminat[ing] and thereafter prevent[ing] exploitation or occupation inimical to the purposes of designation." The systems of National Parks in Great Britain contravene this recommendation in many ways, a fact demonstrated that whereas National Parks are category II in the IUCN's list, Dartmoor National Park is given as an example of a category V area, Protected Landscape/ Seascape.[485]

5.9.3 The National Parks are not areas in a natural state (indeed virtually none of this country is free from significant human interference), and they are places where many people continue to live and to make a living off the land or in industrial or tourist developments. The original emphasis was firmly on recreation and the preservation of natural beauty rather than nature conservation, and indeed the Parks were better regarded as part of the town and country planning system, as areas where slightly stricter controls apply, than as a major element of the law relating to nature conservation. This is not to say that the Parks do not play a part in this latter objective, but their impact tends to be indirect and to depend on the way in which discretionary powers are exercised.[486] The changes introduced by the Environment Act 1995 give a greater role to the conservation of wildlife (and cultural heritage) while the Scottish model gives priority to conserving and enhancing the natural (and cultural) heritage of the area, but still requires regard for economic and social development.[487]

---

[482] For many purposes the Norfolk and Suffolk Broads are treated as a National Park, although subject to the individual legal regime established by the Norfolk and Suffolk Broads Act 1988; see paras 5.9.21–5.9.23, below.

[483] *National Parks and the Conservation of Nature in Scotland* (Cmd.7235, 1947).

[484] See generally A. Gillespie, *Protected Areas and International Environmental Law* (Leiden: Martinus Nijhoff, 2007).

[485] IUCN, *Guidelines for Protected Area Management Categories* (IUCN Publication Services, 1994), available at *http://www.unep-wcmc.org/protected_areas/categories/eng/index.html* [Accessed May 10, 2009].

[486] See generally, A. MacEwen and M. MacEwen, *National Parks: Conservation or Cosmetics?* (London: Allen & Unwin, 1982).

[487] See generally C. Willmore, "What's in a name? The role of 'National Park' designation" [2002] J.P.L. 1325, revised version in E. Cooke (ed.), *Modern Studies in Property Law* (Oxford: Hart, 2002), Vol.II.

England and Wales

The National Park system in England and Wales was introduced by the **5.9.4**
National Parks and Access to the Countryside Act 1949, but has been
amended many times, most notably by the Environment Act 1995 which
rewrote the purposes of the Parks and established in all cases Park
Authorities to take over functions previously left in the hands of local
authorities. The majority of Parks were created in the 1950s and after many
years without addition the process of designating new Parks this decade[488]
has both been lengthy and provoked litigation that has led to further
amendments to the law.[489]

The scheme was initially designed to further two objectives, the pre- **5.9.5**
servation and enhancement of natural beauty and the promotion of the
enjoyment of the countryside by the public.[490] These objectives were revised
by the 1995 Act and the purposes are now stated to be "conserving and
enhancing the natural beauty, wildlife and cultural heritage" of the areas
concerned and "promoting opportunities for the understanding and enjoyment" of their special qualities by the public.[491] This is a wider definition,
expressly mentioning wildlife, as opposed to this being included within the
meaning of "natural beauty", whilst emphasising the appreciation of special
qualities of the Parks, as opposed to their use as a resource for recreation.
The designation, management and legal rules for National Parks all seek to
accomplish these objectives, and it is for these purposes that the powers
given to the authorities involved can be exercised. Furthermore, all ministers, public bodies, office-holders and statutory undertakers are under an
obligation to have regard to the twin purposes of National Parks in the
exercise of their functions affecting land in a National Park.[492]

Although the preservation of the natural beauty of an area has always **5.9.6**
included the preservation of its flora, fauna and geological and physiographical features,[493] the emphasis in National Parks was on protecting
wildlife and natural features[494] as part of the beauty of the countryside to be
enjoyed and made available to the public. One of the difficulties faced by the
National Parks is that the twin objectives (in either form) which they are
created to serve are not always compatible. Increasing recreational use can
put too much pressure on a fragile environment, and even those seeking to
appreciate the peace of the countryside can destroy habitats through disturbance and erosion, to say nothing of the effect of the facilities required to
transport and cater for large numbers of visitors. The dual objectives of the
Parks must always be borne in mind and the interests of conservation must

---

[488] For the New Forest, completed in 2005, while the announcement of the South Downs
National Park was made on March 31, 2009; see *http://www.defra.gov.uk/wildlife-countryside/
protected-areas/national-parks/south-downs/index.htm* [Accessed May 10, 2009].

[489] See paras 5.9.8–5.9.10, below.

[490] NPACA 1949 s.5(1), as originally enacted.

[491] NPACA 1949 s.5A(1), as amended by EA 1995 s.61.

[492] NPACA 1949 s.11A(2), added by EA 1995 s.62.

[493] NPACA 1949 s.114(2), amended by CA 1968 s.21(7) and EA 1995 Sch.10 para.2(8); note
the older usage of "preservation" as opposed to the current "conservation", which is thought to
be more apt for living ecosystems.

[494] In 2006 it was clarified that features which are in part the product of human intervention
are not for that reason disqualified from being "natural"; NERCA 2006 s.99 (see para.5.9.10,
below).

always be tempered by those of recreation and enjoyment, although in the event of conflict greater weight must be given to the conservation and enhancement of the natural beauty, wildlife and cultural heritage[495] (although there can of course be conflicts between these as well).

5.9.7 The areas which can be chosen as National Parks are extensive tracts of country where action to further the twin objectives is particularly desirable because of their natural beauty and the opportunities they afford for open-air recreation in view of their character and location in relation to centres of population action.[496] Designation is in the hands of Natural England (in England) and the Countryside Council for Wales (in Wales),[497] subject to confirmation by the Minister after the proposal has been advertised and notified to all local authorities affected. If objections or representations are made, a local inquiry or a hearing must be held,[498] and further consultations are required if the Minister decides to confirm the proposed designation with modifications.[499] The order designating a Park can be subsequently varied by the Minister or the designating body, subject to the same procedural rules.[500]

5.9.8 The recent designation processes were disrupted by litigation when the owners of an estate challenged its inclusion within the New Forest National Park. In *Meyrick Estate Management Ltd v Secretary of State for the Environment, Food and Rural Affairs* it was held at first instance[501] first of all that the inquiry inspector had applied the wrong test in considering whether the land presented opportunities for open-air recreation. The test was not confined to current actual opportunities, but could include the potential or scope for such recreation, but it was going too far to water down the statutory test to refer to "potential scope" or "potential opportunities". The Court of Appeal agreed that the inquiry report was flawed on this issue and the designation order[502] was invalid in so far as it included the estate in question.[503]

---

[495] NPACA 1949 s.11A(2), added by EA 1995 s.62. This is known as the "Sandford Principle", following the *Report of the National Park Policies Review Committee* (1974), chaired by Lord Sandford.

[496] NPACA 1949 s.5(2).

[497] All of the powers with respect to National Parks previously exercised by the Countryside Commission for the whole of England and Wales were transferred in Wales to the Countryside Council for Wales whilst for land in England remaining in the hands of the Countryside Commission (NPACA 1949 s.4A, added by EPA 1990 Sch.8 para.2), and then subsequently transferred to the Countryside Agency (Development Commission (Transfer of Functions and Miscellaneous Provisions) Order 1999 (SI 1999/416) Sch.1) and then to Natural England (NERCA 2006 Sch.11).

[498] An inquiry must be held if there are representations from a local authority; NPACA 1949 Sch.1 para.2.

[499] NPACA 1949 s.7 and Sch.1; National Parks and Access to the Countryside Regulations 1950 (SI 1950/1066) Pt. IV.

[500] NPACA 1949 s.7(4); WCA 1981 s.45.

[501] By Sullivan J.; *Meyrick Estate Management Ltd v Secretary of State for the Environment, Food and Rural Affairs* [2005] EWHC 2618 Admin.

[502] New Forest National Park (Designation) Order 2002, subsequently confirmed with modifications by the Minister in 2005; see also the New Forest National Park Authority Establishment Order 2005 (SI 2005/421).

[503] *Meyrick Estate Management Ltd v Secretary of State for the Environment, Food and Rural Affairs* [2007] EWCA Civ 53; [2007] Env. L.R. 26.

The statutory tests have now been amended to make it clear that during **5.9.9** the designation process a more prospective approach can be adopted so that account can be taken of the extent to which it is possible to promote such opportunities for public understanding and enjoyment of the area.[504]

Of more general significance was the further decision at first instance that **5.9.10** the reference to land that was suitable because of its "natural beauty" meant that only land that had a high degree of relative naturalness could be designated. The phrase was not the same as "visual attractiveness" or "landscape quality", nor did "natural" just mean rural in contrast to urban, so that the statutory test was not met by such carefully managed areas as well-maintained parkland or well-ordered dairy farmland. This conclusion was not in line with the common understanding of the statutory criterion and before the case could be heard by the Court of Appeal the government responded by adding a provision expressly providing that for all statutory purposes an area can be one of natural beauty regardless of the fact that it comprises land used for agriculture, woodlands or as a park, or that its flora, fauna or physiographical features are partly the product of human intervention.[505] It has also been provided that in assessing natural beauty for the purposes of National Park designation, the wildlife and cultural heritage of an area can be taken into account.[506] This new legislation rendered it unnecessary for the Court of Appeal to consider the issue and should limit the scope for arguing that the rather outdated phrase "natural beauty" inhibits an approach based on wider appreciation of natural and cultural heritage.

The administrative arrangements for the National Parks were altered by **5.9.11** the Environment Act 1995 which provided for the creation of a Park Authority for each Park,[507] effected by the National Park Authorities (Wales) Order 1995 and the National Park Authorities (England) Order 1996.[508] These Authorities are constituted by the Minister and the Act lays down a detailed framework for their constitution.[509] Some of the members are appointed by the relevant local authorities, the remainder by the Minister,[510] and in England some of these must come from parish councils or meetings. Different numbers of members, between 15 and 30, have been appointed to the Authorities created. Their main task is to pursue the twin

---

[504] NPACA 1949 s.5(2A)(b), added by NERCA 2006 s.59. This new provision and the other element of s.5(2A) (added by NERCA 2006 s.59) apply to any confirmation or variation of orders after these new rules came into force (May 2006), regardless of when the order in question was made.

[505] NERCA 2006 s.99.

[506] NPACA 1949 s.5(2A)(a), added by NERCA 2006 s.59.

[507] EA 1995 s.63.

[508] SI 1995/2803, amended by the National Park Authorities (Wales) (Amendment) Order 2007 (SI 2007/3423), and SI 1996/1243, amended by the National Park Authorities (England) Order 2006 (SI 2006/3165), and supplemented by the New Forest National Park Authority Establishment Order 2005 (SI 2005/421). There were transitional measures for the existing boards and committees which had responsibility for the Parks (EA 1995 ss.63–64).

[509] EA 1995 Sch.7.

[510] The proportions of members of each class are set out in the Act: in Wales two-thirds of the members are appointed by the local authorities, in England the direct ministerial appointments are to be two less than the local authority ones and the parish members one less than half the number of direct ministerial appointments (EA 1995 Sch.7 para.1).

purposes of the National Parks, but also to seek to foster the economic and social well-being of local communities.[511]

5.9.12   The Park Authorities' most significant powers lie in relation to the planning system, where they act as the local planning authority for the area covered by the Park and therefore exercise development control.[512] As well as it being likely that different policies will be applied,[513] the normal planning controls are made more strict by means of restrictions to the range of works which qualify as "permitted development" and are thus exempt from the requirement to obtain express planning permission.[514] The authorities also enjoy a variety of other functions which had been placed in the hands of the planning authority, ranging from providing caravan sites and declaring local nature reserves to making byelaws and responsibilities in relation to ancient monuments and listed buildings.[515] There is also a general power to do anything calculated to facilitate (or conducive or incidental to) the achievement of the park purposes.[516] Funding for the Park Authorities comes from the Minister,[517] supplemented by the Authorities' power to issue levies to the local authorities within the park areas.[518]

5.9.13   Whilst executive power rests with the Park Authorities, an important advisory role is played by Natural England and the Countryside Council for Wales.[519] These bodies must be consulted before many of the powers of the Authorities are exercised, and must keep the general position in the National Parks under review. In particular, NE and the Council are to make recommendations to ministers, park and local authorities on the accomplishment of the objectives for which National Parks were created, advise on arrangements for the administration of the parks, give advice when consulted by ministers or Park Authorities on the preparation of development plans or the handling of individual applications for planning permission, and make representations when developments incompatible with the aims of a park are proposed and when their own advice is not being followed.[520] NE and the Council can also make recommendations on the payment of grants to authorities to assist in the management of the parks.[521] Only in very

---

[511] This is to be achieved through co-operation with other public bodies (NPACA 1949 s.11(A)(1), amended by NERCA 2006 s.62); cf. the higher status given to economic and social development by their inclusion in the National Park aims for Scottish Parks (see para.5.9.25, below).

[512] TCPA 1990 s.4A, added by EA 1995 s.67. The National Parks can also be given special treatment in relation to regional spatial strategies, allocating those straddling boundaries all to a single region so that they can be treated as a whole; Town and Country Planning (Regions) (New Forest National Park) (England) Order 2007 (SI 2007/3276) made under Planning and Compulsory Purchase Act 2004 s.12(2).

[513] Although these do not guarantee that what some people see as harmful major developments will not be allowed; see *R. (Council for National Parks Ltd) v Pembrokeshire Coast National Park Authority* [2005] EWCA Civ 888; [2006] J.P.L. 415.

[514] Town and Country Planning (General Permitted Development) Order 1995 (SI 1995/418) Schs 1 and 2.

[515] EA 1995 Sch.9.

[516] See para.5.9.17, below.

[517] EA 1995 s.72.

[518] EA 1995 s.71, applying Local Government Finance Act 1988 s.74 and associated regulations.

[519] As successors to the Countryside Commission that was originally created as the National Parks Commission; NPACA 1949 s.1.

[520] NPACA 1949 s.6(3) and (4).

[521] CA 1968 s.2(9).

limited circumstances, e.g. for experimental schemes,[522] can NE or the Council take direct action themselves.[523]

Each Park Authority must prepare a National Park Management Plan **5.9.14** formulating its policy for the management of the park and the exercise of its own functions, and must review and revise this plan at least every five years.[524] This plan must be drawn up in consultation with Natural England or the Countryside Council for Wales and with the local authorities affected and forms the basis on which the park will be managed with an eye to achieving the objectives of conserving and enhancing the natural beauty, wildlife and cultural heritage of the park and promoting the understanding and enjoyment of its special features. The plan covers a wider range of issues than the standard development plans under the planning system,[525] and does not enjoy the same statutory status.[526]

For each park a map must be drawn up by the Park Authority showing **5.9.15** those areas of the park whose natural beauty it is especially important to conserve.[527] The areas in question are areas of mountain, moor, heath, woodland, down, cliff and foreshore,[528] and they are to be identified in accordance with guidelines issued by Natural England and the Countryside Council for Wales.[529] Such maps, which must be revised at least every five years,[530] are to be for sale to the public, and serve as a guide identifying those areas where the authorities are likely to seek to exercise their various powers to regulate land use, etc.

While the operation of the planning system can be used to protect **5.9.16** National Parks from many forms of development, agricultural and forestry developments are largely outwith the scope of such controls. However special provisions have been introduced to protect areas of moor and heath within the parks. Where such an area has been designated, formerly by the Minister and now by the Park Authority,[531] it is an offence to plough the land, convert it into agricultural land or carry out on it other agricultural or forestry operations which have been specified as likely to affect its character or appearance.[532] These prohibitions do not apply if the land in question has been agricultural land within the last 20 years,[533] or if the owner or occupier has given written notice to the Park Authority and one of a number of other conditions is satisfied. The Authority must notify the Minister and NE or the Council.[534] Once notice has been given, the operation can go ahead as

---

[522] CA 1968 s.4, amended by WCA 1981 s.40.

[523] See paras 2.6.19 and 2.6.22, above.

[524] EA 1995 s.66.

[525] NE or the Council must be consulted in the preparation of the development plans for a National Park; NPACA 1949 s.9.

[526] See paras 8.2.7–8.2.10, below.

[527] WCA 1981 s.43(1), amended by Wildlife and Countryside (Amendment) Act 1985 s.3.

[528] WCA 1981 s.43(3), added by Wildlife and Countryside (Amendment) Act 1985 s.3.

[529] WCA 1981 s.43(1A)–(1C), added by Wildlife and Countryside (Amendment) Act 1985 s.3.

[530] WCA 1981 s.43(1), amended by Wildlife and Countryside (Amendment) Act 1985 s.3.

[531] WCA 1981 s.42(1), amended by NERCA 2006 s.63; designating orders are to be made by statutory instrument (WCA 1981 s.42(8), as amended by NERCA 2006 s.63).

[532] WCA 1981 s.42(2).

[533] WCA 1981 s.42(2); "agricultural land" does not include land used only for rough grazing (WCA 1981 s.52(1)) and any conversion in breach of this section or of its predecessor (CA 1968 s.14) is to be disregarded (WCA 1981 s.42(7)).

[534] WCA 1981 s.42(6).

soon as consent has been given by the Authority, after three months if no
decision has been made by the Authority by that time or after 12 months if
consent has been refused.[535] As with the original provisions for SSSIs, the
period of delay is intended to allow time for negotiations for management
agreements or other measures to be introduced to deal with the situation.
The importance of this procedure is now lessened by the more general rules
requiring an environmental impact assessment and consent for projects
affecting uncultivated land or semi-natural areas.[536] Where there is an
application for a farm capital grant for land in a National Park, the outcome should so far as possible be consistent with the twin objectives of the
parks, and if a grant is refused following an objection from the park
authority, an offer must be made by it to enter a management agreement.[537]

5.9.17   The Park Authorities in National Parks enjoy a range of powers to further the aims of the parks. They can arrange for the provision of facilities for
visitors, including accommodation, refreshments, litter bins, camping sites
and parking places[538] as well as study centres and other facilities for learning
about the history and natural history of the area.[539] Where there is a
shortage of such facilities, arrangements can be made to facilitate the use of
waterways for boating, bathing, fishing and other forms of recreation.[540]
Traffic on roads in National Parks can be restricted to conserve and enhance
their natural beauty and to afford better opportunities for recreation,
enjoyment of the amenities of the area and the study of nature.[541] More
generally Park Authorities are given a general competence to do anything
calculated to facilitate or conducive or incidental to the accomplishment of
the park objectives, although this does not enable them to raise money
outside their express powers to do so or to overcome any statutory
restriction on the exercise of their express powers.[542] In particular grants and
loans can be made to other bodies and individuals to further these aims.[543]

5.9.18   A further important power to assist in preserving the character of the
National Parks, is the power of the planning authority to make byelaws.
These can be made for the preservation of order, to ensure that people do
not behave so as to cause undue interference with the enjoyment of others,
and to protect from damage the land or anything thereon or therein.[544] In
particular byelaws can cover matters such as traffic controls, litter and the
lighting of fires.[545] For lakes and other stretches of open water in the parks
byelaws can be made prohibiting or restricting traffic of any description on
the water for the purposes of ensuring the safety of those using the lake,

---

[535] WCA 1981 s.42(3) and (4).
[536] Environmental Impact Assessment (Agriculture) (England) (No.2) Regulations 2006 (SI
2006/2522); Environmental Impact Assessment (Agriculture) (Wales) Regulations 2007 (SI
2007/2933).
[537] WCA 1981 s.41(3)–(5), amended by Agriculture Act 1986 s.20(4); cf. para.5.5.50, above.
[538] NPACA 1949 s.12; CA 1968 s.12(2).
[539] CA 1968 s.12(1).
[540] NPACA 1949 s.13; CA 1968 s.12(3).
[541] Road Traffic Regulation Act 1984 s.22.
[542] EA 1995 s.65(5) and (6).
[543] WCA 1981 s.44, as amended by EA 1995 s.69(4).
[544] NPACA 1949 s.90(1).
[545] NPACA 1949 s.90(3).

regulating all forms of sport or recreation which use vessels, conserving the natural beauty and amenity of the lake and surrounding area and preventing any nuisance or damage, particularly nuisance caused by excessive noise.[546] In all cases Natural England or the Countryside Council for Wales must be consulted before the byelaws are made,[547] and the byelaws must be confirmed by the Minister in accordance with the standard procedures for local authority byelaws.[548] Wardens can be appointed, to secure compliance with the byelaws, advise and assist the public, and perform other functions as directed by the authorities.[549]

Land in National Parks can be acquired by the Minister where he considers this expedient,[550] and is to be passed into the hands of others to be managed for the twin purposes of the park.[551] The terms on which land is passed on may include a financial contribution from the government for the management of the land.[552] The way in which land is dealt with by other authorities is also affected, e.g. before disposing of land in a National Park, water and sewerage undertakers must consult NE or the Council and may enter management agreements to impose other conditions before the land is transferred.[553] The water legislation also provides that, as with SSSIs, areas within the parks can be identified by the authorities as being of special value so that any body concerned with authorising or carrying out works must notify NE or the Council in advance.[554] **5.9.19**

What all of this means is that the relevant authorities in National Parks enjoy wide powers which can be used for the benefit of nature conservation as part of the general aim of conserving and enhancing the natural beauty and wildlife of these areas. The potential is there for things to be done to assist conservation through stricter planning controls, the making of byelaws and the funding or carrying out of particular projects, and to assist in educating the public through the provision of study centres. However the mere fact that an area has been designated a National Park has very little immediate and direct significance for nature conservation—even the controls on converting moor and heath apply only once introduced to an area by ministerial order and largely overlap with more general rules requiring an environmental assessment and consent before such operations. Moreover, even where action is taken to conserve nature the authority must balance this against the need to promote the enjoyment of the land.[555] **5.9.20**

---

[546] CA 1968 s.13.

[547] NPACA 1949 s.90(4); CA 1968 s.13(4).

[548] NPACA 1949 s.106; CA 1968 s.13(8); the procedure is set out in the Local Government Act 1972 ss.236–238.

[549] NPACA 1949 s.92; CA 1968 ss.13(9) and 42; WCA 1981 s.49.

[550] NPACA 1949 s.14(1); acquisition is by agreement and with the consent of the Treasury.

[551] NPACA 1949 s.14(2).

[552] NPACA 1949 s.14(3).

[553] Water Industry Act 1991 s.156; the disposal of houses in National Parks may also be restricted in the effort to avoid the spread of holiday homes at the expense of accommodation for those living in the parks (Housing Act 1985 s.37, amended by Housing Act 1988 s.125; Housing Associations Act 1985 s.11 and Sch.2 para.3).

[554] Water Industry Act 1991 s.4; Water Resources Act 1991 s.17; Land Drainage Act 1991 s.13; see para.5.5.51, above.

[555] C. Willmore, "What's in a name? The role of 'National Park' designation" [2002] J.P.L. 1325.

Norfolk and Suffolk Broads

5.9.21 Special provisions have been made for the Norfolk and Suffolk Broads, similar to those for the National Parks, but taking account of the special requirements arising from the fact that it is the waterways which are the main features of interest both for recreation and conservation.[556] A Broads Authority has been established with membership drawn from the relevant local authorities and the Secretary of State's appointees, who must include representatives of boating, farming and land-owning interests.[557] The general duty of this authority is to manage the Broads for the purposes of conserving and enhancing their natural beauty, wildlife and cultural heritage,[558] promoting opportunities for the enjoyment of the Broads by the public and protecting the interests of navigation.[559] Thus as with the National Parks, nature conservation must be balanced with and may be subordinated to the interests of recreation, and also in this case of the preservation and development of rights of navigation. Ministers, public authorities and statutory undertakers must have regard to these purposes in exercising their functions in relation to land in the Broads.[560]

5.9.22 Many of the provisions for the National Parks are repeated for the Broads. A map must be drawn up and regularly revised showing the areas whose natural beauty it is especially important to conserve,[561] and a Broads Plan must be prepared to set out the policy for managing the area.[562] Particular areas can be designated within which specified operations which might affect their character or appearance can go ahead only after the Broads Authority has been notified and has given its consent or a period of time has passed. The areas which can be designated are areas of grazing marsh, fen marsh, reed-bed or broad-leaved woodland and the time periods are three months if no response is given and 12 months if consent is refused.[563] Byelaws can be made for areas owned or occupied by the Authority or commonly used by the public.[564] The Broads Authority counts as a local authority and the Broads as a National Park for many other pieces of legislation.[565]

5.9.23 The importance of the waterways is reflected by the creation of a separate Navigation Committee with membership drawn from the Broads Authority,

---

[556] Norfolk and Suffolk Broads Act 1988 (note also the Broads Authority Bill passing through Parliament in early 2009); see generally M. Shaw, "The Broads Act 1988: A Framework for Environmental Planning and Management" [1989] J.P.L. 241.

[557] Norfolk and Suffolk Broads Act 1988 s.1, amended by EPA 1990 Sch.9 para.15; Water (Local Statutory Provisions) (Consequential Amendments) Order 1989 (SI 1989/1380) art.4; Norfolk and Suffolk Broads Act 1988 (Alteration of Constitution of the Broads Authority) Order 2005 (SI 2005/1067).

[558] This includes conserving the flora, fauna, geological and physiographical features of the area (Norfolk and Suffolk Broads Act 1988 s.25(2)); it is worth remarking that the "natural beauty" of the Broads is largely man-made, being the result of the flooding of early peat workings, see para.5.9.10, above.

[559] Norfolk and Suffolk Broads Act 1988 s.2, as amended by NERCA 2006 s.64.

[560] Norfolk and Suffolk Broads Act 1988 s.17A, added by CRWA 2000 s.97 and amended by NERCA 2006 s.64.

[561] Norfolk and Suffolk Broads Act 1988 s.4.

[562] Norfolk and Suffolk Broads Act 1988 s.3.

[563] Norfolk and Suffolk Broads Act 1988 s.5.

[564] Norfolk and Suffolk Broads Act 1988 s.6.

[565] See Norfolk and Suffolk Broads Act 1988 Sch.6.

the owners and hirers of pleasure craft and other users of the area.[566] This Committee is responsible for maintaining, improving and developing for the purposes of navigation the area specified as the "navigation area".[567] There is a power for the Committee to make byelaws for the good management of the area, the conservation of its natural beauty and amenities and the promotion of its use for recreational purposes.[568] The regulation of the navigation area in particular, as well as other aspects of the Broads Authority's powers, is subject to imminent reform under the Broads Authority Bill passing through Parliament in 2009.

Scotland

The belated introduction of National Parks in Scotland followed considerable debate[569] and consultation that spanned the period of devolution and it was the Scottish Parliament that passed the National Parks (Scotland) Act 2000. The Act sets out the framework for the parks and the procedure for their creation, but leaves many of the significant details to be determined on a case-by-case basis, as demonstrated by the differences between the first two parks, with further differences being considered for the first coastal and marine park.[570] As would be expected, half a century after the initial legislation south of the border, the Scottish provisions reflect wider environmental concerns, but a further feature is a greater concern for ensuring a strong local voice in the running of the parks. Following the introduction of National Parks, the provisions for Natural Heritage Areas were repealed without any ever having been designated.[571] **5.9.24**

The Act begins by setting out the "National Park aims", namely: **5.9.25**

"(a) to conserve and enhance the natural and cultural heritage of the area,
(b) to promote sustainable use of the natural resources of the area,
(c) to promote understanding and enjoyment (including enjoyment in the form of recreation) of the special qualities of the area by the public, and
(d) to promote sustainable economic and social development of the area's communities."[572]

It is stated that the general purpose of the Park Authorities is to ensure that these aims are collectively achieved in a co-ordinated way in relation to each

---

[566] Norfolk and Suffolk Broads Act 1988 s.9.

[567] Norfolk and Suffolk Broads Act 1988 s.10(1); the "navigation area" is defined in s.8(1).

[568] Norfolk and Suffolk Broads Act 1988 s.10(3).

[569] At times political sensitivity to the fact that Scotland was one of the few countries in the world without any areas labelled as National Parks seemed to play at least as significant a role as a clear idea of what the Parks would add to the existing catalogue of designations.

[570] The Act specifically allows modification of its provisions in relation to an area including the sea (NPSA 2000 s.31); see Scottish Executive consultation paper, *Scotland's first coastal and marine national park* (October 2006).

[571] NCSA 2004 Sch.7 para.8, repealing Natural Heritage (Scotland) Act 1991 s.6; see section 5.10 of the previous edition of this book.

[572] NPSA 2000 s.1.

park.[573] Crucially, in the event of any conflict between these aims, greater weight must be given to the first aim.[574]

5.9.26 Proposals to establish a National Park may be made by the Scottish Ministers where it appears to them that an area is of outstanding national importance on account of its natural heritage, or a combination of natural and cultural heritage, and has a distinctive character and coherent identity. The third requirement is that designation as a National Park will meet the special needs of the area and be the best means of ensuring that the National Park aims are collectively achieved in a co-ordinated way.[575] The proposal is then followed by a report from SNH (or another public body appointed for this purpose[576]) considering the desirability of the designation, the area to be designated, the functions for the Park Authority, the costs involved and any other specified matters. Preparation of this report must involve consultation with local authorities, community councils, representatives of those who live, work or carry on business in the area, and must take into account the views expressed.[577] Alternatively, the Ministers themselves can prepare a statement addressing the same issues and after similar consultation.[578] In either case, a local inquiry can then be held in relation to any matter arising in the report or statement.[579]

5.9.27 At this stage the proposal can be halted, but if it is proceeding, the final stage is for the Ministers to make a designation order, which must have regard to the report or statement. The order must be approved in draft by the Scottish Parliament, after consultation with every local authority and community council for the area concerned, local representatives and the public. The draft may be revised in the light of the responses, with the Parliament being informed of the views received during the consultation and any changes made at this stage.[580] The final designation order is then made by Statutory Instrument,[581] and copies must be sent to the local authorities affected and kept available for public inspection.[582]

5.9.28 The detailed administrative arrangements for and the precise powers of each National Park authority are to be determined on an individual basis for each park, but a framework is laid down in the Act.[583] The maximum number of members of the Park Authority is 25, some to be nominated by the Scottish Ministers, some by the relevant local authorities and some (at least a fifth of the number) directly elected by those living in the park. In the two cases so far, the full 25 have been appointed with five directly elected

[573] NPSA 2000 s.9(1).
[574] NPSA 2000 s.9(6).
[575] NPSA 2000 s.2(2).
[576] In both cases so far SNH has been chosen.
[577] NPSA 2000 s.3.
[578] NPSA 2000 s.4.
[579] NPSA 2000 s.5; the inquiry is governed by s.210 of the Local Government (Scotland) Act 1973.
[580] NPSA 2000 s.6.
[581] NPSA 2000 s.34.
[582] NPSA 2000 s.7.
[583] NPSA 2000 Sch.1. Aspects of these arrangements, especially the number of board members and their relationship with Ministers, are considered in the Scottish Government's *National Parks Strategic Review Report* (2008) and associated consultation paper.

and 10 nominated in each class.[584] A further requirement is that a proportion of the appointed members (at least a fifth) must be "local members",
that is they must have their sole or main residence in the park or must be
councillors for a local authority, ward or community council within the
park. The Ministers must consult local authorities and community councils,
local representatives and others as they think fit before making their
nominations, and the nominees must appear to the Ministers to have
knowledge or experience relevant to the park's functions, with the potential
for the designation order to specify particular interests to be covered.

The late introduction of provisions for directly-elected representatives and **5.9.29**
local members shows the general determination as the Bill went through the
Parliament that there should be a very strong local voice in the running of
the National Parks. They should not be in the hands of outside "experts".
This determination is also reflected in the roles for the local authorities and
the thorough consultation procedures which are to take place at many
stages and which make particular reference to the role of community
councils.

The maximum period of appointment for members is five years (renew- **5.9.30**
able), and there are detailed rules on removal from office in the event of
bankruptcy, incapacity or prolonged absence, the filling of vacancies and
members' interests. [585] A Convener is to be chosen from among the members
and a chief executive appointed, with the approval of the Ministers, and the
authority must appoint at least one Advisory Group. The authority can
appoint non-members to committees and has wide power to delegate to
committees and officers. It can also agree that any of its functions shall be
exercised by a local authority, or exercise functions on behalf of a local
authority[586] or the Scottish Ministers.[587]

The Ministers have the power to issue general or specific directions to a **5.9.31**
Park Authority and also guidance as to the exercise of functions by Park
Authorities. The Authorities must comply with any directions or guidance,
but these can be made only after consultation with the authorities affected
and guidance must be published and is subject to a negative resolution
procedure in the Scottish Parliament.[588] Ministers must also determine the
financial duties and procedures for Park Authorities, and the Ministers
enjoy powers to pay grants and loans, approve borrowing, offer guarantees
and require the payment of any surplus to the Ministers.[589] The park's
accounts are subject to scrutiny by the Auditor General for Scotland and
Park Authorities must prepare annual reports and accounts, to be laid
before Parliament.[590]

The Park Authority's purpose is to ensure that the National Park aims are **5.9.32**

---

[584] Loch Lomond and the Trossachs National Park Designation, Transitional and Consequential Provisions (Scotland) Order 2002 (SSI 2002/201); Cairngorms National Park Designation, Transitional and Consequential Provisions (Scotland) Order 2003 (SSI 2003/1).

[585] NPSA 2000 Sch.1.

[586] NPSA 2000 s.17.

[587] NPSA 2000 s.18; ministerial functions in relation to delegated legislation or under the 2000
Act itself cannot be delegated.

[588] NPSA 2000 s.16; the draft guidance must be laid before the Parliament for 40 days and if a
resolution is passed that the guidance should not be given, then the Ministers must comply with
that.

[589] NPSA 2000 ss.21–24.

[590] NPSA 2000 ss.25–26.

collectively achieved in a co-ordinated way.[591] Central to the management of a National Park is the National Park Plan and there is a clear statutory duty on the Scottish Ministers, the Authority, local authorities and all other public bodies and office holders to have regard to the plan in the exercise of their functions so far as they affect the park.[592] The plan is made by the Park Authority and sets out its policy for managing the park and for co-ordinating the exercise of the Authority's functions and those of other public bodies in relation to the park.[593] Production of the plan requires consultation with the relevant local authorities, community councils, representative groups and the public, and the views received must be taken into account. The plan is subject to approval by the Scottish Ministers, with or without modification, and copies must be available for public inspection.[594] In the event of a plan being rejected, a revised one must be submitted within the deadline stated at the time. Plans are to be reviewed through a similar procedure at least every five years.[595]

5.9.33 The effectiveness of the plan in securing real co-ordination and co-operation between the many authorities whose activities can help or hinder the achievement of the park's aims, and in providing a means of compromise when these aims conflict, will obviously be crucial to the smooth working and success of the parks. In particular, there is a clear need for the park plan and the development plans for the area to be consistent, which emphasises the importance of the structural arrangements for town and country planning. With respect to land within a National Park, planning authorities are under an obligation to pay "special attention" to the desirability of exercising powers consistently with the park plan.[596]

5.9.34 In relation to its own efforts to fulfil the park objectives, key mechanisms available to the Authority include planning powers and the making of byelaws, management rules and management agreements but the full range of powers is to be determined in the individual designation orders. The most important area left undetermined is the extent to which the Authority is to act as the planning authority for the Park. The Act specifies the two options of the Authority becoming the planning authority with full powers or taking over responsibility solely for development planning, but also allows for other combinations. For Loch Lomond and the Trossachs National Park, the Park Authority is the planning authority, responsible for development control and the local plan, but sharing responsibility with local authorities for the structure plan.[597] For the Cairngorms a different model has been followed, where the Park Authority has sole responsibility for the local plan, shared responsibility for enforcement and some special controls, e.g. trees, amenity notices and advertisements, the power to call in planning applications of particular significance and a role as consultee in relation to the other

[591] NPSA 2000 s.9(1).
[592] NPSA 2000 s.14.
[593] NPSA 2000 s.11.
[594] NPSA 2000 s.12.
[595] NPSA 2000 s.13.
[596] TCPSA 1997 s.264A, added by NPSA 2000 Sch.5 para.18.
[597] Loch Lomond and the Trossachs National Park Designation, Transitional and Consequential Provisions (Scotland) Order 2002 (SSI 2002/201) art.7.

planning powers that remain in the hands of the local authorities.[598] The National Park objectives are a material consideration, but not more, in determining any planning application.[599]

The Park Authority has the power to enter management agreements with **5.9.35** those holding any interest in land in order to do, or secure the doing of, whatever the parties consider necessary to achieve the park aims. This is a very broad power, and is not even formally restricted to land within the park itself. These agreements are subject to the usual terms in relation to running with the land, registration, etc. A further mechanism available is the making of management rules for land owned, occupied or managed by the Authority.[600] The Authority can also make byelaws to protect the natural and cultural heritage of the park, to prevent damage to the land or anything in, on or under it, or to secure the public's enjoyment of and safety in the National Park.[601] In particular, fires, litter, nuisances, vehicles other than on roads and the exercise of recreational activities can be controlled. Proposed byelaws must be advertised and there must be consultation with local authorities, community councils and representative groups. The byelaws must be confirmed by the Scottish Ministers.[602] The power to make byelaws has been widened[603] by the two designation orders, which also confer for Loch Lomond and the Trossachs the power to appoint rangers[604] and to exercise the local authority's powers under the Loch Lomond Registration and Navigation Byelaws 1995.[605]

The Authority also has a range of general powers to do things calculated **5.9.36** to facilitate or conducive or incidental to accomplishing the National Park functions or others conferred on it.[606] To enable it to carry out its tasks it can provide advice and assistance, carry out research, make charges and pay grants, promote or oppose private legislation, and has wide powers to enter contracts, form businesses of various sorts and invest its funds.[607] More specifically, the Authority has the power for any of its functions to acquire land by agreement or by compulsory purchase (with Ministerial approval).[608] In a number of respects, e.g. public access to meetings and documents,[609] in the exercise of some powers, such as establishing local nature reserves and acting as a consultee under a range of statutory

---

[598] Cairngorms National Park Designation, Transitional and Consequential Provisions (Scotland) Order 2003 (SSI 2003/1) art.7.

[599] *Dalfaber Action Group v Scottish Ministers* [2007] CSOH 180 at [29].

[600] NPSA 2000 Sch.2 para.10, applying ss.112–118 of Civic Government (Scotland) Act 1982.

[601] NPSA 2000 Sch.2 para.8.

[602] NPSA 2000, applying ss.202–204 of the Local Government (Scotland) Act 1973.

[603] art.8 of each Order (SSI 2002/201 and SSI 2003/1) to cover the scope of the Civic Government (Scotland) Act 1982 s.121 (seashore and inland waters).

[604] Some rangers have trained and qualified as special constables to broaden the powers at their disposal: *http://www.centralscotland.police.uk/articles/respect_the_park.php* [Accessed May 10, 2009].

[605] Loch Lomond and the Trossachs National Park Designation, Transitional and Consequential Provisions (Scotland) Order 2002 (SSI 2002/201) art.8.

[606] NPSA 2000 s.9.

[607] NPSA 2000 Sch.2.

[608] Governed by the Land (Authorisation Procedure) (Scotland) Act 1947; NPSA 2000 Sch.2 para.5.

[609] NPSA 2000 Sch.2 para.12.

procedures, including designation of SSSIs,[610] the Authority is treated as a local authority.[611]

5.9.37   Recent debates on the National Parks in Scotland have centred on the extension of the Cairngorm Park to include areas of highland Perthshire controversially excluded from the original designation[612] and the proposal for the first coastal and marine park.[613] That the debate is on extension of or the establishment of further National Parks suggests that the parks have been broadly successful, although a number of changes were proposed by the National Parks Strategic Review in 2008.[614]

LANDSCAPE AND PLANNING DESIGNATIONS

Areas of Outstanding Natural Beauty (England and Wales only)

5.10.1   Areas of Outstanding Natural Beauty (AONBs) are areas in England and Wales which are not in a National Park,[615] but are of such outstanding natural beauty that it is desirable that special provisions, primarily changes to the planning system, should apply to them.[616] The provisions for these were overhauled and considerably strengthened by the Countryside and Rights of Way Act 2000, with a duty placed on public bodies to have regard to their purposes, a new emphasis on the preparation of management plans and the potential to establish a conservation board for any individual AONB to further the purposes of the designation. Conservation of the natural beauty of an area includes conservation of its flora, fauna, and geological and physiographical features.[617]

5.10.2   The areas are selected and designated by Natural England and the Countryside Council for Wales, who must consult all the local authorities in the area and advertise the proposal. The designation must be confirmed by the Minister, who must receive any representations or objections made in response to the proposal and consult NE or the Council and local authorities if he intends to refuse to confirm the order or to confirm it with modifications.[618] Designation orders can be varied by the Minister and NE or the Council, and must be kept available for inspection by these bodies and by the local authorities in the areas affected.

5.10.3   Once an AONB has been created, all ministers, public bodies (including local authorities), statutory undertakers and public office holders are under a duty to have regard to the purpose of conserving and enhancing the natural beauty of the AONB when they exercise any functions in relation to or so as to affect land in an AONB.[619] This duty is therefore limited to land-

---

[610] WCA 1981 s.28(1)(aa), inserted for Scotland by NPSA 2000 Sch.5 para.8.

[611] NPSA 2000 s.9 and Sch.3.

[612] C.T. Reid, "Cairngorms Controversy" (2003) 95 SPEL 1.

[613] See Scottish Executive consultation paper, *Scotland's first coastal and marine national park* (October 2006).

[614] *National Parks Strategic Review Report* (Scottish Government, 2008) and associated consultation paper.

[615] Epping Forest and Burnham Beeches are also excluded; CRWA 2000 s.92(3).

[616] CRWA 2000 s.82.

[617] CWRA 2000 s.92(2).

[618] CRWA 2000 s.83.

[619] CRWA 2000 s.85.

related functions, but does apply to land outwith the boundaries of the AONB if there will be an effect inside. Natural England and the Countryside Council for Wales have roles in some ways similar to those in relation to National Parks, having the same duty to give advice and rights to be consulted on development plans and access arrangements.[620] Local authorities also enjoy a general power to take such action as appears expedient to conserve or enhance the natural beauty of the area.[621]

Some impacts of designation as an AONB apply automatically. Within an **5.10.4** AONB, Natural England or the Countryside Council for Wales must be consulted by the planning authority on the preparation of development plans and on the making of arrangements for public access to land for recreation.[622] Certain permitted development rights are withdrawn,[623] and as for National Parks there are special rules on the disposal of certain land by water and sewerage undertakers and housing bodies.[624] The planning authority is also empowered to make byelaws for its own land in an AONB[625] and to appoint wardens,[626] whilst orders can be made by the Minister restricting traffic on roads in the area.[627]

The details of further impacts depend partly on whether a conservation **5.10.5** board has been established.[628] The initiative to establish a board comes from the Minister who must consult Natural England or the Countryside Council for Wales and all the local authorities for the area and can proceed only if a majority of the local authorities consent.[629] The order creating a board is made by means of a statutory instrument which must be approved in draft by both Houses of Parliament.[630] Boards are created separately for each AONB and their composition and powers may vary. At least 40 percent of the total membership must be local authority members and the parish members in England must further comprise at least 20 percent of the total.[631] The local authority members come from the authorities in whose areas the AONB lies, and the appointing local authorities are to have regard to the desirability of appointing members with wards or electoral divisions actually within the boundaries of the AONB.[632] A parish member must be a member of a parish council lying within the AONB or the chairman of a parish meeting in such a parish that does not have a separate parish council; in the

---

[620] CRWA 2000 s.84(1), applying NPACA 1949 ss.6(4)(e), 9, 64(5), and 65(5) and (5A).

[621] CRWA 2000 s.84(4); this provision is not as sweeping as it seems, since it applies only to remove certain statutory limitations on the capacities of authorities, not to confer wholly new powers, and it does not overcome any limitations applying where express powers are given (CRWA 2000 s.84(5)–(6)).

[622] CRWA 2000 s.84, applying NPACA ss.6(4)(e), 9, 64(5), and 65(5) and (5A).

[623] Town and Country Planning (General Permitted Development) Order 1995 (SI 1995/418) Schs 1 and 2.

[624] See para.5.9.19, above.

[625] NPACA 1949 s.90.

[626] NPACA 1949 s.92.

[627] Road Traffic Regulation Act 1984 s.22.

[628] See, for example, the information about the conservation board in the Chilterns at *http://www.chilternsaonb.org/conservation_board.html* [Accessed May 10, 2009].

[629] CRWA 2000 s.86.

[630] CRWA 2000 s.88.

[631] CRWA 2000 Sch.13 para.3.

[632] CRWA 2000 Sch.13 para.4.

latter case it is the parish meeting that appoints the member.[633] The Minister's appointees shall be named after consultation with NE or CCW.

5.10.6   In its activities, the board is bound to have regard to the purposes of conserving and enhancing the natural beauty of its area and also of increasing the public's understanding and enjoyment of the special qualities of the area, giving priority to the former in the event of any conflict.[634] Its powers are to do things calculated to facilitate or conducive to the achievement of those purposes, but subject to limits, most notably the absence of any power to raise money except as specifically authorised.[635] Specific functions of local authorities can be transferred to the board, or become exercisable concurrently by the authority and board. Development control and development planning powers under the town and country planning legislation must remain wholly with the local authority, but some minor powers, e.g. in relation to tree preservation notices, can be transferred.[636] The board is also required to seek to foster the economic and social well-being of local communities in the area, but to do so by co-operation with other bodies.[637] Grants can be made to management boards by the Minister.[638]

5.10.7   Whether or not a conservation board has been created, a management plan for the AONB must be prepared, formulating the policy for managing the area and the exercise of powers in relation to it.[639] If there is a board for the area, the plan must be produced by it within two years of its establishment. If there is no board, this task is for the local authority, to be accomplished within three years of the designation of any new AONB or by May 2004[640] unless a board is established in the meantime. There are provisions for the adoption of existing plans prepared by local authorities and for the review of plans at least every five years. Natural England or the Countryside Council for Wales must be notified of the proposal to make a plan, as must every local authority affected in the case of those prepared by a conservation board, and their views must be taken into consideration.[641] These plans, however, have no statutory force[642] and there is no obligation on other bodies to pay regard to them, although they will be relevant in the context of the general obligation on all public bodies to have regard to conserving and enhancing the natural beauty of the area.[643]

5.10.8   The effect of the provisions in the Countryside and Rights of Way Act 2000 is to make AONBs much more similar to National Parks. Conservation boards may provide a focus for the management of the area, but the

---

[633] CRWA 2000 Sch.13 para.5; for both local authority and parish members there are further provisions on the termination of membership if they lose the status that rendered them eligible.

[634] CRWA 2000 s.87(1).

[635] CRWA 2000 s.87(4)–(6) and Sch.14.

[636] CRWA 2000 s.86(3)–(4); the transfer cannot include the local authorities' functions under Pts II (development plans), III (development control), VII (enforcement) and XIII (Crown land) of the TCPA 1990.

[637] CRWA 2000 s.87(2); the restriction that this was to be done "without incurring significant expenditure" was removed by NERCA 2006 Sch.12.

[638] CRWA 2000 s.91.

[639] CRWA 2000 s.89.

[640] Three years from the relevant provisions coming into force.

[641] CRWA 2000 s.90.

[642] cf. National Park Plans in Scotland; para.5.9.32, above.

[643] CRWA 2000 s.85; see para.5.10.3, above.

significant powers remain in the hands of the local authorities. Measures to conserve the natural beauty of an area may help to preserve the quality of the general habitat. The designation of an AONB will, however, have no direct effect on many agricultural or forestry developments that may significantly alter the landscape and habitat quality.

National Scenic Areas (Scotland only)

The aim of National Scenic Areas (NSAs) is to strengthen aspects of the **5.10.9** town and country planning system in order to preserve areas of high landscape value. The future of NSAs was in doubt after the Natural Heritage (Scotland) Act 1991 provided for the creation of Natural Heritage Areas[644] and prevented the creation of new NSAs,[645] but there was support for a continuing and indeed expanded role for a designation based on scenic values, operating as an accolade rather than to provide strong regulatory powers.[646] The policy changes that led to the creation of National Parks in Scotland left no room for Natural Heritage Areas but did leave a role for NSAs. After a time when they existed in a labyrinthine legislative twilight,[647] NSAs have once again been given clear recognition by virtue of the Planning etc. (Scotland) Act 2006.[648]

National Scenic Areas are areas of outstanding scenic value and beauty in **5.10.10** a national context where special protection measures are considered appropriate.[649] In deciding whether to designate an area the Ministers are to take account of whether the area is of outstanding natural beauty, its amenity (including historical, cultural or environmental importance and the nature of any buildings or structures) and also the flora, fauna and physiological features of the area, regardless of the extent to which they are the product of human intervention in the landscape.[650] The Ministers must consult with SNH and any other prescribed persons and compile and keep available a list of designations. The older NSAs were designated by the Secretary of State after consultation with the Countryside Commission for Scotland and other bodies as he thought fit and in practice were those proposed in the Commission's report, "Scotland's Scenic Heritage" in 1978.

Once an area has been designated, special attention must be paid to the **5.10.11** desirability of preserving or enhancing its character or appearance in the exercise of functions under the Town and Country Planning (Scotland) Act

---

[644] See para.5.9.24, above and section 5.10 of the previous edition of this book.

[645] NHSA 1991 s.6 and Sch.11; the relevant provisions have now been repealed (see fn.647 below).

[646] *National Scenic Areas: Scottish Natural Heritage's Advice to Government* (SNH, 1999).

[647] NSAs were first provided for by the Town and Country Planning (Scotland) Act 1972 s.262C, which was added by the Housing and Planning Act 1986 Sch.11 para.38. By virtue of NHSA 1991 s.6(8) and (9) and Sch.11, s.262C of the 1972 Act was partly repealed and the remainder amended so as to apply to Natural Heritage Areas, but its provisions continued to have effect unaltered in so far as they applied to areas which had already been designated as NSAs. When the planning legislation was consolidated, s.262C was in turn replaced by s.264 of TCPSA 1997, which referred exclusively to Natural Heritage Areas, but again the original provisions of s.262C were saved and continued to apply to existing NSAs (Planning (Consequential Provisions) (Scotland) Act 1997 Sch.3 para.11). Section 264 of the 1997 Act has now been repealed by NCSA 2004 Sch.7.

[648] Planning etc. (Scotland) Act 2006 s.50, which inserts TCPSA 1997 s.263A.

[649] TCPSA 1997 s.263A(1).

[650] TCPSA 1997 s.263A(4).

1997, and the Ministers may issue guidance to planning authorities to this end.[651] In order to assist this purpose, permitted development rights have been withdrawn from certain forms of development in NSAs, e.g. the construction of vehicle tracks.[652] For planning, SNH must be consulted on certain kinds of application and any decision contrary to its advice must be notified to the Minister.[653] Under various regimes, an environmental impact assessment will be required before approval can be given to projects within NSAs.[654] Traffic on roads can be restricted for the sake of the natural beauty of the area or to offer better opportunities for recreation or the study of nature.[655] Within NSAs therefore there is a slight strengthening of planning controls and the beauty of the landscape is to be given special attention, but there is nothing to assist directly the interests of nature conservation.

Conservation Areas

5.10.12 Planning controls and policies are also made stricter in conservation areas.[656] Local planning authorities are under an obligation to designate as conservation areas those parts of their areas which are of special architectural or historic interest, the character or appearance of which it is desirable to preserve or enhance.[657] Once a conservation area has been designated, greater publicity has to be given to certain planning applications[658] and stricter controls on demolition apply,[659] whilst further restrictions can be imposed through directions made by the planning authority.[660] Certain permitted development rights are withdrawn, as is the case for National Parks, Areas of Outstanding Natural Beauty and National Scenic Areas.[661] In all cases, any plan to cut down, lop or prune trees in a conservation area must be notified to the planning authority six weeks in

---

[651] TCPSA 1997 s.263A(2).

[652] Town and Country Planning (Restriction of Permitted Development) (National Scenic Areas) (Scotland) Direction 1987; see SDD Circular 9/1987.

[653] Town and Country Planning (Notification of Applications) (National Scenic Areas) (Scotland) Direction 1987; this has survived the substantial "thinning" of the notification requirements undertaken in 2009 (Scottish Planning Series: *Planning Circular 3 2009: Notification of Planning Applications*, para.22).

[654] National Scenic Areas (Scotland) Regulations 2008 (SSI 2008/202), amending various sets of regulations dealing with environmental impact assessments; see section 8.3, below.

[655] Road Traffic Regulation Act 1984 s.22.

[656] Planning (Listed Buildings and Conservation Areas) Act 1990 Pt II; Planning (Listed Buildings and Conservation Areas) (Scotland) Act 1997 Pt II.

[657] Planning (Listed Buildings and Conservation Areas) Act 1990 s.69; Planning (Listed Buildings and Conservation Areas) (Scotland) Act 1997 s.61. See *R. (Arndale Properties Ltd) v Worcester City Council* [2008] EWHC 678 Admin for an example of a conservation area being improperly designated for inappropriate purposes.

[658] Planning (Listed Buildings and Conservation Areas) Act 1990 s.73, amended by Planning and Compulsory Purchase Act 2004 Sch.6 para.24; Planning (Listed Buildings and Conservation Areas) (Scotland) Act 1997 s.65.

[659] Planning (Listed Buildings and Conservation Areas) Act 1990 s.74, amended by Planning and Compulsory Purchase Act 2004 (Commencement No.9 and Consequential Provisions) Order 2006 (SI 2006/1281) art.6; Planning (Listed Buildings and Conservation Areas) (Scotland) Act 1997 s.66.

[660] Town and Country Planning (General Permitted Development Order) 1995 (SI 1995/418) art.4; Town and Country Planning (General Permitted Development) (Scotland) Order 1992 (SI 1992/223) art.4.

[661] Town and Country Planning (General Permitted Development Order) 1995 Sch.1; Town and Country Planning (General Permitted Development) (Scotland) Order 1992 Schs 1 and 2.

advance, so as to allow time to consider whether a tree preservation order should be made protecting the trees.[662] Generally, the authority should develop proposals to preserve and enhance its conservation areas, acting positively as well as simply preventing degradation.[663] These provisions may serve to protect areas from intensive development and to protect small areas of trees, village greens, ponds, large gardens and other habitats of value.

INTERNATIONAL DESIGNATIONS

In addition to the measures introduced by the European Community to give **5.11.1** protection to particular sites,[664] international agreements may also call for the protection of sites of particular importance.[665] Whilst designations under international treaties may have no direct impact on the law within this country, they may be significant in terms of policy-making and the management of particular sites.[666]

In relation to international designations, these generally have no direct **5.11.2** legal consequences within Great Britain, although the international obligations have helped to shape the law here[667] and do influence the selection of sites to benefit from the application of the domestic provisions discussed above. The additional designation emphasises the importance of, and commitment to, nature conservation measures for the sites and can also be a major factor in ensuring that the policy affecting the management and protection of a site does in fact give adequate protection to the natural features in question, especially in relation to the exercise of discretionary powers. Even where there is little likelihood of meaningful action at the international level if such sites are damaged, the bad publicity generated by allowing damage to habitats which the government itself has stated to be of international importance can play a real part in securing continued protection. The two most important current designations are discussed here: Ramsar sites and World Heritage sites.

There are also many other designations under a host of international **5.11.3** schemes, with varying degrees of official recognition and support but usually lacking any legal significance, e.g. Biogenetic Reserves under the Bern Convention.[668] A further example deserving brief mention is that of Biosphere Reserves. These are areas recognised under the UNESCO Man and Biosphere programme established in 1971. During the 1970s 13 Biosphere Reserves were designated in Great Britain, but the programme developed significantly during the United Kingdom's absence from UNESCO between 1985 and 1997, with greater emphasis on sustainable development, research, education and training. The criteria for the reserves changed accordingly and after the UK rejoined UNESCO a review of the reserves was

---

[662] TCPA 1990 s.211; TCPSA 1997 s.172; see para.6.5.2, below.
[663] Planning (Listed Buildings and Conservation Areas) Act 1990 s.71; Planning (Listed Buildings and Conservation Areas) (Scotland) Act 1997 s.63.
[664] See sections 5.2, above and 7.4, below.
[665] See generally A. Gillespie, *Protected Areas and International Environmental Law* (2007).
[666] See section 7.5, below.
[667] e.g. WCA 1981; see para.1.1.15, above.
[668] See paras 7.5.15–7.5.21, below.

undertaken, leading to a reduction of the number to eight reserves which more closely fit the revised criteria.[669]

Ramsar Sites

5.11.4 The Convention of Wetlands of International Importance, especially as Waterfowl Habitat, known as the Ramsar Convention,[670] makes various provisions for the protection of wetlands, which throughout the world are disappearing as a result of drainage, land reclamation and pollution.[671] Among the measures is the establishment of a List of Wetlands of International Importance, which states undertake to protect.[672] The selection of sites for the list is the responsibility of states themselves, taking account of each site's significance in terms of ecology, botany, zoology, limnology or hydrology. More precise criteria for selection have been adopted and revised by Conferences of the Parties, suggesting, for example, that sites regularly supporting 20,000 waterbirds or one per cent of the population of a species should be designated.[673] The List is maintained by the IUCN,[674] which must also be informed of changes to the ecological character of the wetlands as a result of technological developments, pollution or human interference.[675]

5.11.5   Once a wetland has been added to the List, the state is obliged to formulate and implement its planning so as to promote the conservation of the site and the wise use of wetlands,[676] and for all wetlands states must promote the establishment of nature reserves with adequate supervision by wardens.[677] The concept of "wise use" has been the subject of further guidance developed at the Conferences of the Parties.[678] Sites which have been placed on the List can be reduced in size or deleted altogether if this is required by an "urgent national interest", but so far as possible the state concerned should compensate for such loss by the creation of additional nature reserves for birds and the protection, in the same area or elsewhere, of an adequate portion of the same habitat.[679] These obligations are far from precise and leave plenty of room for discretion on the part of each state, to say nothing of the difficulties of enforcing any such obligations in international law.

5.11.6   In Great Britain, the Convention had no recognition in the law until

---

[669] See *http://www.defra.gov.uk/wildlife-countryside/protected-areas/unesco-biosphere.htm* [Accessed May 10, 2009].

[670] After the town in northern Iran where it was signed in 1971.

[671] See paras 7.5.6–7.5.9, below. Further information can be obtained from the official Ramsar web-pages at *http://www.ramsar.org* [Accessed May 10, 2009].

[672] Ramsar Convention art.2.

[673] The Criteria are published on the Ramsar web-pages at *http://www.ramsar.org/key_criteria.htm* [Accessed May 10, 2009].

[674] International Union for the Conservation of Nature; see P. Birnie, A. Boyle and C. Redgwell, *International Law and the Environment*, 3rd edn (Oxford: OUP, 2009), pp.102–103.

[675] Ramsar Convention arts 3 and 8.

[676] Ramsar Convention art.3.

[677] Ramsar Convention art.4.1.

[678] e.g. *Handbooks for the Wise Use of Wetlands* and other material available on the Ramsar website at *http://www.ramsar.org/lib/lib_handbooks2006_e.htm* and *http://www.ramsar.org/wurc/wurc_library.htm* [Both Accessed May 10, 2009]; D. Farrier and L. Tucker, "Wise Use of Wetlands under the Ramsar Convention: A Challenge for Meaningful Implementation of International Law" (2000) 12 J.E.L. 21.

[679] Ramsar Convention art.4.2.

2000,[680] and even now the recognition takes a very restricted form. There is an obligation on the Minister to notify the conservation bodies when a site has been designated for the List and on them in turn to notify the relevant planning authority and every owner and occupier. In England and Wales those to be notified also include the Environment Agency, every relevant water undertaker and internal drainage board; in Scotland, SEPA, the National Park authority (if relevant) and every statutory undertaker and regulatory authority whose operations or functions may affect the wetland.[681] This means that those responsible for the main activities that may affect a site will at least be aware of its significance.[682]

The primary means of implementing the Convention's terms therefore **5.11.7** remains the overlap between the sites selected for Ramsar designation and those enjoying protection under domestic provisions, as European Sites, nature reserves or SSSIs.[683] As discussed above, this may not guarantee their protection, or even their protection in all but cases of "urgent national interest", but does provide mechanisms for taking action to secure their conservation, reinforced now by the fact that the key parties are formally notified of a site's Ramsar status. Planning advice and other guidance has advised on the need to promote the conservation of such sites and avoid as far as possible the loss of wetland resources, and a policy statement made for England notes the large overlap between Ramsar sites and European Sites, and in essence stated that Ramsar sites should be treated in the same way as those under the Natura 2000 programme.[684]

World Heritage Sites

The Convention Concerning the Protection of the World Cultural and **5.11.8** Natural Heritage (World Heritage Convention) was signed in 1972 to provide international recognition and assistance for the protection of monuments, buildings and sites which are the natural and man-made treasures of the world.[685] As far as nature conservation is concerned, a state can nominate any site within its territory for inclusion in the World Heritage List. The basic criterion is that the area be of "outstanding universal value" from a scientific, aesthetic or nature conservation point of view,[686] but before being added to the List each site must be approved by the World Heritage Committee which is responsible for compiling the List.[687] This Committee uses strict operational guidelines in making its decisions. Only sites which are of the utmost value and are adequately protected, both by the scale and

---

[680] In Scotland, 2004; see following note.

[681] WCA 1981 s.37A, inserted by CRWA 2000 s.77; NCSA 2004 s.38.

[682] In August 2007 the JNCC reported 146 Ramsar sites in the UK, covering almost 800,000 hectares: *http://www.jncc.gov.uk/page-1388* [Accessed May 10, 2009].

[683] Issues are considered on a UK-basis by the UK Natura 2000 and Ramsar Forum; see *http://www.defra.gov.uk/wildlife-countryside/protected-areas/natura-ramsar.htm* [Accessed May 10, 2009].

[684] *Ramsar Sites in England—A policy statement* (DEFRA, 2006); this notes that the vast majority of Ramsar sites in England coincide with or substantially overlap European Sites.

[685] See paras 7.5.10–7.5.14, below; further information is available from the World Heritage website at *http://whc.unesco.org* [Accessed May 10, 2009].

[686] World Heritage Convention art.2.

[687] World Heritage Convention art.11.

integrity of the area and by domestic law, will be accepted,[688] and there is monitoring to ensure that they continue to deserve this status.[689]

5.11.9   Each state has a duty to ensure "the protection, conservation, preservation, presentation and transmission to future generations" of the natural heritage in its territory and "to do all it can to this end, to the utmost of its own resources" and where appropriate with international assistance.[690] Effective and active measures are required, including the adoption of relevant policies, the establishment of appropriately staffed and resourced services to protect and conserve the natural heritage, the development and promotion of scientific and technical research and the adoption of the necessary legal, financial and scientific measures.[691] As with most international agreements, these provisions are broadly drafted, but the Australian High Court was prepared to hold that they did impose a duty on the state to act, although recognising that discretion was left as to precisely how this duty would be fulfilled.[692]

5.11.10   Again in Great Britain implementation of the Convention is carried out through the nomination of sites already subject to protective measures in domestic law, e.g. St Kilda which is a Special Area of Conservation and a National Nature Reserve. The nature of sites eligible for inclusion and the more specific criteria for listing combine to mean that only sites enjoying the fullest protection will be accepted, chiefly Nature Reserves. Apart from St Kilda,[693] and parts of the Dorset and East Devon coastline (and the Giant's Causeway in Northern Ireland) for their geological interest, the sites in the United Kingdom have been designated for their archaeological, architectural or historical interest.[694] Where a site has been accepted for the List, it must be protected and conserved from all threats, and entries can be deleted if this protection is not provided.[695]

ENVIRONMENTAL LIABILITY DIRECTIVE

5.12.1 In addition to the direct measures discussed above, the aim of conserving areas of importance for wildlife is also given expression through aspects of the Environmental Liability Directive.[696] The aim here is not to identify particularly sensitive areas and provide for their management. Instead it seeks to give effect to the polluter pays principle and to ensure that action is

---

[688] *Operational Guidelines for the Implementation of the World Heritage Convention* (WHC 08/01) (2008); see *http://whc.unesco.org/archive/opguide08-en.pdf* [Accessed May 10, 2009].

[689] As shown by the visit to Edinburgh to review its status in the light of major development proposals; see *http://whc.unesco.org/en/news/473* [Accessed May 10, 2009].

[690] World Heritage Convention art.4; the commitment to international co-operation and the provision of resources for poorer countries are of particular importance for the protection of the natural heritage in many parts of the world.

[691] World Heritage Convention art.5.

[692] *Commonwealth of Australia v State of Tasmania* (1983) 46 A.L.R, 625, 68 I.L.R. 266.

[693] St Kilda is listed for both its natural and cultural significance.

[694] Brief descriptions of all listed sites and the reasons for their listing are available at *http://whc.unesco.org/en/list* [Accessed May 10, 2009].

[695] The first site to be deleted was Oman's Arabian Oryx Sanctuary in 2007, when the state reduced the size of the protected area by 90%; see *http://whc.unesco.org/en/news/362* [Accessed May 10, 2009].

[696] Directive 2004/35/EC.

taken when relevant environmental damage occurs or is imminent. The Directive does this by imposing liability for taking appropriate preventive and remedial action on those responsible for activities that threaten or cause significant harm to the environment. The sorts of harm that are covered include biodiversity damage but the rules are not straightforward and there have been considerable delays in implementing this measure. The date for implementation was April 30, 2007, but it was 2008 before draft regulations were produced in Great Britain[697] and by the end of March 2009 only Regulations for England had been made, taking effect on March 1, 2009.[698]

The environmental damage that the Directive covers is of three kinds[699]: **5.12.2** water damage (significant adverse effects on the ecological, chemical or quantitative status or ecological potential of waters, as defined in the Water Framework Directive),[700] land damage (contamination which creates a significant risk of human health being adversely affected) and damage to protected species and natural habitats, namely those listed in the Birds and Habitats and Species Directives and optionally sites designated at national level.[701] For this latter kind of damage, often referred to as "biodiversity damage", the damage must have "significant adverse effects on reaching or maintaining the favourable conservation status of such habitats or species". The Directive defines "favourable conservation status" for habitats and species in terms of their long-term future and sets out criteria to be taken into account in assessing whether effects are significant; these state that any damage will not necessarily be significant if there are negative impacts within the range of natural fluctuations or of those resulting from the normal management of a site in the past, nor if it is damage from which the species or habitat will recover within a short time and without intervention.[702] The Directive therefore aims at events causing substantial harm to wildlife that has already been identified as of value, rather than at the general decline in biodiversity arising from human activities.[703] Indeed it is expressly stated that the Directive shall apply in relation to harm caused by diffuse pollution only where it is possible to establish a causal link between the damage and the activities of individual operators.[704]

---

[697] *Consultation on draft regulations and guidance implementing the Environmental Liability Directive 2004/35/EC with regard to the prevention and remedying of environmental damage* (DEFRA, February 2008)—this contained separate draft regulations for England and for Wales; *Environmental Liability Directive: Second Consultation* (Scottish Government, May 2008).

[698] Environmental Damage (Prevention and Remediation) Regulations 2009 (SI 2009/153) ("English Regulations"); these regulations also apply to certain offshore areas. The Regulations are accompanied by *The Environmental Damage (Prevention and Remediation) Regulations 2009: Guidance for England draft guidance for Wales* (DEFRA, 2009) (the guidance had to retain draft status for Wales until the implementing regulations were made). The Environmental Damage (Prevention and Remediation) (Wales) Regulations 2009 (SI 2009/995) ("Welsh Regulations") were made in April and took effect on 6 May, 2009; these are largely parallel to the English version. The Scottish regulations were made and took effect in late June 2009: Environmental Liability (Scotland) Regulations 2009 (SSI 2009/266).

[699] Directive 2004/35/EC art.2; English Regulations reg.4.

[700] Directive 2000/60/EC; see section 8.6, below.

[701] Directive 2004/35/EC art.2(3); see para.5.12.3, below.

[702] Directive 2004/35/EC art.2(4) and Annex 1; English Regulations reg.4 and Sch.1.

[703] Aquatic biodiversity is taken into account in the standards for water damage, but land damage is calculated solely on the basis of the impact on human health.

[704] Directive 2004/35/EC art.4(5); English Regulations reg.8(3).

5.12.3 The Directive allows for Member States to extend its rules on biodiversity damage beyond sites protected under European law to those designated under national provisions. The regulations for England take advantage of this by including SSSIs within the habitats where damage can trigger the obligations created under the Directive.[705] The regulations for Wales similarly extend the coverage to SSSIs,[706] but those for Scotland do not go beyond protecting the European sites that the Directive specifies. The intention not to extend the scope of the rules in Scotland was based partly on the need to wait until the new laws on SSSIs introduced by the Nature Conservation (Scotland) Act 2004 had been fully tried and tested.[707]

5.12.4 The obligations under the Directive arise in relation to two sets of circumstances where activities cause imminent or actual harm.[708] First, the operators of a number of listed activities are liable in relation to all forms of environmental damage, regardless of fault. These activities are listed in the Directive[709] and are essentially ones already subject to detailed regulation at European level, e.g. waste management, transport of hazardous substances, use or release of genetically modified organisms and activities covered by the pollution prevention and control regime.[710] Secondly, for all other "occupational activities"[711] liability arises, in relation to biodiversity damage only, where the operator has been at fault or negligent. Compared to the other forms of harm, liability for biodiversity damage is thus both wider, applying to all activities, not only those listed, but also narrower, requiring fault rather than being based on strict liability in its application beyond the listed activities.

5.12.5 Exceptions include damage arising from armed conflict, insurrection or natural phenomena of exceptional, inevitable and irresistible character or caused by activities with the main purpose of serving national defence or international security.[712] Activities covered by a number of international conventions, e.g. spillages at sea and nuclear activities, are also excluded,[713] as are events before April 30, 2007.[714] Member States also have the option of relieving operators from bearing the cost of remedial action[715] where they were not at fault or negligent and either were operating fully in compliance with a permit granted in accordance with the relevant European legislation or the activity was not thought likely to cause damage according to the state of scientific and technical knowledge at the time of the emission ("permit" and "state of the art" defences respectively).[716] These exceptions are both

---

[705] English Regulations reg.4(1).

[706] Welsh Regulations reg.4.

[707] *Environmental Liability Directive – A Consultation* (Scottish Government, 2006), paras 45–47.

[708] Directive 2004/35/EC art.3; English Regulations regs 13 and 17.

[709] Directive 2004/35/EC Annex III; English Regulations Sch.2.

[710] See section 8.5, below.

[711] A term that covers "any activity carried out in the course of an economic activity, a business or an undertaking, irrespectively of its private or public, profit or non-profit character"; Directive 2004/35/EC art.2(7) applied in slightly different form by the English Regulations reg.2(1).

[712] Directive 2004/35/EC art.4; English Regulations reg.8.

[713] Directive 2004/35/EC art.4 and Annex V; English Regulations reg.8.

[714] Directive 2004/35/EC art.17; English Regulations reg.8.

[715] This does not relieve them of their obligations to take preventive action.

[716] Directive 2004/35/EC art.8(4).

included in the English regulations.[717] They are also included in the Welsh Regulations and Scottish draft but subject to the qualification that they will not apply in relation to the release of genetically modified organisms.[718]

Where there is an imminent threat of damage occurring, the operator is **5.12.6** required to take the necessary preventive measures and to bear the cost of these. If the preventive measures do not dispel the threat the relevant national authority[719] must be informed and this authority can compel an operator to provide information or take preventive action, specifying what is to be done, and can itself take the preventive action recovering the cost from the operator.[720] Where damage has been caused, the operator must notify the authority and take steps to immediately control, remove or otherwise manage the "damage factors" to limit the harm and then undertake remedial action. The operator must submit proposals but it is the authority that must determine what remedial steps are to be taken, and it can direct such measures or undertake them itself, recovering the cost.[721] The authority can also require third parties to take the necessary preventive or remedial steps.[722] Under the English Regulations, there is power for the authority to take action itself (and where appropriate recover costs) if the operator cannot be found or does not comply with relevant notices or is not required to take remedial action.[723]

Three sorts of remedial measures are identified, with guidance as to what **5.12.7** is to be required.[724] These are "primary" remediation, which seeks to restore the environment to its previous state,[725] "complementary" remediation, which on the site or elsewhere[726] compensates for the fact that the primary remediation does not fully restore the site, and "compensatory" remediation, which makes up for the harm during the period until the primary and complementary measures take effect. Guidance is given on the choice of measures and what is appropriate for complementary or compensatory remediation where direct equivalence is not possible. The options are to be evaluated using best available technologies with regard to, among others, the effect on public health and safety, cost, likelihood of success, length of time for and extent of restoration and local social, economic and cultural factors. For conservation sites, the effect is that if a site is destroyed or cannot be wholly restored, then alternative or supplementary measures must be taken to provide the same overall conservation value, albeit not necessarily a direct equivalent to what has been lost, and before the damaged site is fully restored or a substitute provided, interim measures must be taken to

---

[717] English Regulations reg.19.

[718] Welsh Regulations reg.19(4); *Environmental Liability Directive: Second Consultation* (Scottish Government, May 2008).

[719] Under the English Regulations this can be the Environment Agency (damage to water and terrestrial aquatic habitats), Natural England (biodiversity damage), the Secretary of State (marine biodiversity) or the local authority (damage to land); reg.11.

[720] Directive 2004/35/EC art.5; English Regulations regs 13–14.

[721] arts 6–7; English Regulations regs 17–22.

[722] Directive 2004/35/EC art.11(3).

[723] English Regulations regs 15 and 23–28.

[724] Directive 2004/35/EC Annex II; English Regulations Sch.4.

[725] Measured according to "its baseline condition", its condition as it would have been had the damage not occurred, estimated on the basis of the best available information; Directive 2004/35/EC art.2(14).

[726] Where possible this should be geographically linked to the damaged site.

make up for what is temporarily lost. There are bound to be arguments over the adequacy and effectiveness of any restoration or replacement, the point at which the cost of restoration is so great that other remedial action is justified and the suitability of any alternative where direct restoration is not possible. Since in relation to damage affecting species the provisions will apply only where the damage threatens their favourable conservation status, it is highly unlikely that there are suitable habitats or nesting sites readily available to make up for a harmful incident of that scale.

5.12.8   The regime that has been created places an onus on the relevant national authority to determine what preventive or remedial action should be taken and to see that it is done, acting itself if necessary. In order to review its activities, it is provided that certain people can request the authority to take action where they consider that there is environmental damage or an imminent risk of it, submitting data and observations to support the request. If such a request is made and seems plausible, the authority must give the operator the opportunity to comment and then respond, either taking action as requested or refusing to do so, but providing reasons for this decision.[727] The procedural and substantive legality of the authority's decision can be challenged in the courts by those entitled to make a request.[728] These procedures are open to anyone affected or likely to be affected by the damage or having a "sufficient interest" in environmental decision-making relating to the damage (tests akin to the general rules on standing discussed above)[729] and also to non-governmental organisations promoting environmental protection.[730] The details of which organisations qualify are left, like so much in the Directive, to the provisions of national law.

5.12.9   The Directive adopts a new approach in nature conservation law. One criticism in the past has been that while the law through delict and tort has provided means of protecting private property from harm, the "unowned environment" has been ignored by the law. Now there is a means of requiring preventive and remedial action when the environment is threatened or harmed, and with the important difference that the remedy is not financial compensation but specific action to restore (or where that is impossible, replace) the features harmed. However, the new regime applies only to incidents that have significant consequences and is likely to affect only a few cases each year.[731] The clear preventive obligations may be more useful than the remedial measures, although where there is an imminent threat of damage it may be hard to establish that it is of damage of the scale required to invoke the Directive's provisions. Moreover, outwith the activities listed in the Directive (where strict liability occurs), the requirement of proving fault on the part of the operator may prove to be a

---

[727] Directive 2004/35/EC art.12; English Regulations reg.29.

[728] Directive 2004/35/EC art.13; no specific procedure is created or prescribed by the English Regulations, leaving this as a matter for judicial review.

[729] See paras 1.4.9–1.4.16, above.

[730] Directive 2004/35/EC art.12(1); there are no specific provisions on this in the English Regulations, but *The Environmental Damage (Prevention and Remediation) Regulations 2009: Guidance for England draft guidance for Wales* (DEFRA, 2009) at p.48 suggests that birdwatchers, fishermen and ramblers are among those who might be affected and charities whose objectives include conservation of the environment are among those with sufficient interest.

[731] *Environmental Liability Directive: Consultation on options for implementing the Environmental Liability Directive* (DEFRA et al., 2006), Annex B of Partial Regulatory Impact Assessment.

stumbling block in establishing liability, although to the extent that designated sites are involved the designation itself, any formal management plans
and other mechanisms adopted to secure the proper management of the site
may make it harder for occupiers to show that severely damaging events
were not the result of a failure to take reasonable care.

The full impact of the Directive will only be known once all the implementing regulations are in place and it has been seen how they can operate
in practice. In the meantime missing the deadline for implementation by so
much is inviting infraction proceedings before the European Court of
Justice.[732]

5.12.10

---

[732] Proceedings have been started by the European Commission; press release IP/08/1025.

6. PLANTS

The General Law

6.1.1 The legal position of plants is very different from that of wild animals. Every growing plant is the legal property of someone, and thus is subject to the ordinary laws of property, as well as to the special laws devised to deal with the conservation and regulation of plants. This might suggest that plants enjoy a greater degree of protection than other forms of wildlife, but in practice this tends not to be the case as people do not think of wild plants as being privately owned, and the owners themselves tend to value only those plants from which they gain some appreciable benefit, commercial or aesthetic. In considering the law affecting plants it is necessary to consider how plants are dealt with by the general law, examining the issues of ownership and the ways in which plants are treated by the ordinary criminal law, before turning to the specific legislation which has been enacted to deal directly with issues arising in relation to plants. The new provisions on hedgerows are then considered before the fuller provisions affecting trees in relation to forestry and town and country planning.

Ownership

6.1.2 The rule that plants belong to the owner of the soil in which they grow is of long standing[1] and is common to both Scots and English Law.[2] Indeed the proposition that plants growing in the soil belong to the owner of the soil appears to be such a basic idea that it is more or less taken for granted, and any discussion and dispute has centred on its application between those holding different interests in the land.

6.1.3   If the rule were strictly applied, problems would arise where interests in land are held by different people, e.g. in relation to agricultural tenants, as crops which they had planted would not be theirs to harvest and sell, but would belong to the landlord. In both jurisdictions the position of tenants was protected by the development of a rule that annual crops were treated as the tenant's moveable or personal property as opposed to the landlord's heritable or real property. In Scotland this exception tends to be discussed as part of the law of property in general,[3] whereas in England and Wales

---

[1] See, for example, in Roman Law D.41.1.7.13, 41.1.9.pr.

[2] See generally D.L. Carey Miller with D. Irvine, *Corporeal Moveables in Scots Law*, 2nd edn (Edinburgh: W. Green 2005), paras 3.04–3.08; W.M. Gordon, *Scottish Land Law*, 2nd edn (Edinburgh: W. Green, 1999), paras 5.38–5.40; W.S. Holdsworth, *A History of English Law*, 2nd edn (London: Methuem, 1937), Vol.7, pp.485–488.

[3] Stair, II, i, 34; Carey Miller, *Corporeal Moveables in Scots Law*, 2nd edn (2005); Gordon, *Scottish Land Law*, 2nd edn (1999).

discussion has tended to appear in the more specialised context of succession and emblements,[4] with many other points affecting the right to take growing plants being dealt with in land law by the rules on waste and *profits à prendre*.[5] In practice such matters are nowadays dealt with by the specific terms of individual leases, etc. or by statutory rules,[6] but a failure to agree on the entitlement to harvest crops growing at the time of the sale of three fields near Edinburgh has led to recent litigation resolved on the basis of general property law.[7]

The legal consequence of plants being property which is owned by **6.1.4** someone is that any unauthorised interference with a plant will amount to a civil wrong at common law. Consequently the owner could sue anyone who damages or takes his plants or obtain an interdict or injunction to prevent any harm which is threatened. Although this is an area lacking in reported authority, any damage to plants being usually only an incidental part of a wider claim,[8] it would appear that any deliberate or negligent harm caused to wild plants certainly could give rise to liability, with the possibility of wider liability if the claim can be framed in trespass, whether to land or (in England) to property. It would follow that anyone picking wild flowers or even causing damage by walking on vegetation could face a civil action at the instance of the owner of the plants affected.

However, although wild plants may be part of their owner's property, **6.1.5** they are not generally recognised as having any monetary value, so that the pursuer may be unable to demonstrate that any loss has been suffered by the harm done. This will pose a major practical problem in assessing the value of damage done, and may even lead the courts to say that in fact no actionable wrong has occurred.[9] The aesthetic or spiritual value placed on the wild plants is unlikely to affect this position, although a trust established for the purposes of nature conservation may have a stronger case if the achievement of its aims is being affected by damage to its plants, especially if it is seeking an interdict rather than damages.

Criminal Law

Since plants are private property, they are protected by the general criminal **6.1.6** law. This is very much the case in Scotland, although in England and Wales statutory exceptions have been created to limit considerably the application

---

[4] Modern texts tend not to offer any detailed discussion of these "vegetable chattels", but they are discussed in older books on personal property, e.g. J. Williams, T.C. Williams and W.J. Byrne, *Principles of the Law of Personal Property*, 18th edn (London: Sweet & Maxwell, 1926), pp.161–162.

[5] C. Harpum, S. Bridge and M.Dixon, *Megarry & Wade: The Law of Real Property*, 7th edn (London: Sweet & Maxwell, 2008), pp.81–84 and 1303–1306.

[6] Agricultural Holdings Act 1986; Agricultural Holdings (Scotland) Acts 1991 and 2003.

[7] *Boskabelle Ltd v Laird*, 2006 S.L.T. 1079.

[8] In the well-known nuisance case of *St Helens Smelting Co v Tipping* (1865) 11 HLC 642 the primary damage alleged related to "hedges, trees, shrubs, fruit and herbage", while an example of a reported action based solely on plants is *Mills v Brooker* [1919] 1 K.B. 555, where a neighbour was successfully sued in conversion for taking apples from trees overhanging his boundary.

[9] e.g. in *Winans v Macrae* (1885) 12 R. 1051 one of the grounds for refusing interdict to prevent a cottar's pet lamb straying onto a 200,000-acre shooting estate where it might indeed have taken "a blade of grass", was that no appreciable wrong had been suffered so as to justify the court's intervention (Lord Young at 1063–64).

of the law to wild plants. In Scotland there is nothing to restrict the application to plants growing wild of the ordinary law of theft, malicious mischief, vandalism and fire-raising[10] so that anyone taking or damaging a plant without the permission of the owner or other lawful excuse is guilty of a crime. The few reported cases have dealt with plants that were being to some extent cultivated, e.g. in *Rigg v Trotter*[11] the accused were convicted of malicious mischief after treading down plants in a nursery and destroying turf prepared for and partially laid for a bowling green, while *James Miln*[12] involved the shearing and taking of grass and the pulling up of growing pease, and *John Young*[13] the digging of potatoes. Likewise in *HM Advocate v Alexander Robertson*[14] the plants concerned in a charge of theft were turnips, although here the court reserved its opinion on whether this was an appropriate charge where the alleged theft was achieved by pasturing sheep in a field.

6.1.7   Exactly the same should apply to wild plants, which are as much the landowner's property as the most carefully nurtured crops or garden plants, although in such circumstances it may be more difficult to establish the necessary mens rea. In *Ward v Robertson*[15] the court was not prepared to say that a person was guilty of malicious mischief simply by reason of damage done by walking across a field of cultivated grass where the accused had not deliberately sought to do harm and indeed had thought that no harm was being done. It was suggested, though, that a conviction might have been possible had there been evidence of a deliberate trampling down of grass, or if the field had contained other crops in which case knowledge that harm was being done might have been inferred. In the case of picking wild flowers, it may be obvious that damage is being done, but belief that the owner would not object might again raise difficulties in establishing mens rea.

6.1.8   In England and Wales the position is different, as wild plants are expressly excluded from the law of theft and criminal damage. For theft, it is provided that a person who picks flowers, fruit or foliage from a plant growing wild, or who picks any fungus growing wild, does not steal them, unless he does so for reward or for sale or for some other commercial purpose.[16] A theft charge is therefore possible only if there is a commercial motive or if an entire plant is uprooted and taken, as opposed to merely parts of the plant being removed.[17] For criminal damage, no offence is committed if the only property affected is any fungus growing wild or the flowers, fruit or foliage of a plant growing wild. Again, therefore the uprooting of a plant or its total destruction may give rise to prosecution, but lesser damage cannot.[18]

---

[10] For muirburn see para.8.4.14, below.
[11] *Rigg v Trotter* (1714) Hume, i, 123.
[12] *James Miln* (1758) Hume, i, 79.
[13] *John Young* (1800) Hume, i, 79.
[14] *HM Advocate v Alexander Robertson* (1867) 5 Irv. 480.
[15] *Ward v Robertson*, 1938 J.C. 32.
[16] Theft Act 1968 s.4(3).
[17] Every year or so there are press reports of convictions based on the digging up of large numbers of snowdrop or bluebell bulbs.
[18] Criminal Damage Act 1971 s.10(1).

STATUTORY PROVISIONS

Statutory measures relating to wild plants largely mirror those for wild **6.2.1**
animals, with the establishment of a general level of protection which is
enhanced for certain species, while legislation also allows for pest control
and measures against the spread of disease. Aside from the enforcement
difficulties resulting from the fact that few people can identify the rare
species entitled to special protection (especially as there are often similar
cultivated or more common species) two particular problems afflict legislation relating to plants.

First, the naming of plants in legislation can be problematic, as common **6.2.2**
names frequently apply to more than one species, or vary throughout the
country, while plant taxonomists are continually reassessing the classification of plants, so that the scientific names,[19] and indeed the recognition of
plants as distinct species, may be liable to change. Secondly, plants hybridise
much more easily than animals, so that particularly in relation to weed
species, one can be faced in the field with hybrids which do not fall exactly
within the terms of the legislation but which may be as vigorous as the
named species. Both of these issues affect the Japanese knotweed, an invasive alien which it is illegal to spread in the wild.[20] In the legislation it is
referred to as *Polygonum cuspidatum*, but it is generally known to botanists
today as *Fallopia japonica*, whilst previously called other names, including
Reynoutria japonica.[21] In the wild in Britain, hybrids have been found
between this plant and *Fallopia sachalinensis*,[22] and these show a wide
diversity, calling into question the adequacy of the current taxonomy. The
first problem is one of untidiness rather than substance, as the alternative
names are well recorded and the relevant plant can be identified, but the
second is potentially more serious, since on a strict interpretation (arguably
appropriate where criminal liability can be imposed) legal provisions based
on listed species will apply only to the named, pure-bred, species, not to
hybrids. To avoid such problems some Scottish legislation, but not that in
England and Wales, now expressly applies to hybrids of the species listed.[23]

Protection

Wild plants are given general legal protection under the Wildlife and **6.2.3**
Countryside Act 1981, with additional protection for some species under
both that Act and the Habitats and Species Directive. Under section 13 of

---

[19] In any event the legislation rarely gives the full scientific name, almost invariably omitting
the reference to the author who described the plant, a reference which forms an integral part of
the proper scientific name.

[20] See para.6.2.11, below; for the history of this plant see J. Bailey and A. Connolly, "Prize-
winners to Pariahs – A History of Japanese Knotweed *s.l.* (Polygonaceae) in the British Isles"
Watsonia 23: 93 (2000).

[21] Full names, *Polygonum cuspidatum* Siebold & Zucc., *Fallopia japonica* (Houtt.) Ronse
Decraene, *Reynoutria japonica* Houtt.; a closely related species is *Fallopia sachalinensis* (F.
Schmidt ex Maxim.) Ronse Decraene.

[22] The hybrids are known as *Fallopia x bohemica*, and the genetic complexity of this species
(or cluster of species) is discussed by M. Hollingsworth and J Bailey, "Hybridisation and clonal
diversity in some introduced *Fallopia* species (Polygonaceae)" Watsonia 23: 111 (2000).

[23] e.g. WCA 1981 s.14(2) as amended by NCSA 2004 Sch.6 para.12, dealing with invasive
non-native species; cf. the Scottish deer legislation where express reference is also made to
hybrids; Deer (Scotland) Act 1996 s.45(1).

the 1981 Act, it is an offence for anyone other than an authorised person[24] intentionally, or in Scotland intentionally or recklessly, to uproot any wild plant. It is a defence to show that the uprooting was the incidental result of a lawful act, provided that in England and Wales this result could not reasonably have been avoided, or in Scotland that reasonable precautions had been taken, that the result was not and could not reasonably have been foreseen as a result of the lawful activity and that the person concerned took the reasonably practicable steps to minimise the harm as soon as the consequences became apparent.[25] In Scotland a person who knowingly causes or permits such unlawful acts is also guilty of a crime.[26] Throughout Great Britain a "wild plant" is one which is growing wild and is of a kind which ordinarily grows in Great Britain in a wild state,[27] a definition which may leave uncertain the status of certain plants which have escaped from gardens and which are not part of the indigenous British flora but are now widespread in a wild state, e.g. giant hogweed.[28] Licences may be granted by the appropriate bodies to authorise conduct otherwise unlawful under the provisions discussed here in and in the next paragraph.[29]

6.2.4   Further protection is offered to the many plants (including mosses and lichens) listed in Schedule 8 to the 1981 Act. In England and Wales, it is an offence for anyone (even an authorised person) intentionally to pick, uproot or destroy any wild plant listed in that Schedule.[30] In Scotland this offence extends to reckless conduct as well as intentional and to the picking or destruction of any seed or spore attached to the plant.[31] The same defences apply covering some incidental results of lawful operations.[32] It is also an offence to sell or offer for sale any live or dead plant listed in Schedule 8 (or any part or derivative of such a plant), or to possess or transport such items for the purpose of sale[33]; for the purpose of this provision any plant is presumed to be wild unless the contrary is shown.[34] An offence is also committed if a person publishes or causes to be published an advertisement indicating that he does or intends to buy or sell such plants or their derivatives.[35]

6.2.5   A small group of plants enjoys protection as European protected species[36] under the terms of the Habitats and Species Directive as implemented by the

---

[24] "Authorised persons" include the owner and occupier of the land and those authorised by the local authority (WCA 1981 s.26(1)); see para.3.2.15, above.

[25] WCA 1981 s.13(3), as amended for Scotland by NCSA 2004 Sch.6 para.11.

[26] WCA 1981 s.13(3A), as added by NCSA 2004 Sch.6 para.11; this provision applies likewise to the offences involving plants in Sch.8 in the Act (see para.6.2.4, below).

[27] WCA 1981 s.27(1).

[28] See para.6.2.11, below.

[29] WCA 1981 s.16; CNHR 1994 regs 44–45; see Appendix C.

[30] WCA 1981 s.13(1)(a); see Appendix A.

[31] WCA 1981 s.13(1)(a)(ii), as amended by NCSA 2004 Sch.6 para.11.

[32] WCA 1981 s.13(3), in Scotland as amended by NCSA 2004 Sch.6 para.11.

[33] WCA 1981 s.13(2)(a).

[34] WCA 1981 s.13(4).

[35] WCA 1981 s.13(2)(b).

[36] CNHR 1994 Sch.4; see Appendix A. These are the species in Annex IV(b)) to the Habitats and Species Directive whose natural range includes any area of Great Britain (CNHR 1994 reg.42).

Conservation (Natural Habitats, etc.) Regulations 1994.[37] As is the case with animals, the relevant provisions have been substituted following the decision in *Commission v United Kingdom* with differences between Scotland and England and Wales[38] The plants enjoy protection at all stages of their bio-logical cycle, so that seeds and bulbs are covered by the law as much as whole plants,[39] and a plant is presumed to be wild or to have been taken from the wild unless the contrary is shown.[40] In Scotland it is a crime deliberately or recklessly to pick, collect, cut, uproot or destroy any such wild plant.[41] It is also a crime to possess, control, transport,[42] sell or exchange a plant or any part of or thing derived from such a plant taken in the wild and belonging to species listed in Annex II(b) or IV(b) to the Habitats and Species Directive, other than a bryophyte listed in Annex II(b).[43] A defence is available if it can be shown that the specimen was lawfully taken from the wild,[44] except in the case of European protected species that are being sold or exchanged or kept or transported for that reason.[45] A person who knowingly causes or permits the above offences is also guilty.[46] In England and Wales to pick, collect, cut, uproot, or destroy a wild plant of a European protected species is an offence only if done deliberately,[47] but the same offences in relation to possession and sale apply as in Scotland.[48] The same defences apply,[49] with additional provisions expressly allowing action for the enforcement of this and related legislation.[50]

These provisions offer plants some protection from intentional direct **6.2.6** harm, but obviously the conservation of plants will rely heavily on the various mechanisms to safeguard habitats as a whole.[51] It is only by ensuring broader action under specific habitat protection measures and those affecting the wider countryside that the conditions necessary for plants to survive and propagate can be ensured and that the non-listed plants can be safeguarded against the actions of the owner or occupier of the land. A further practical problem faced by those concerned with botanical

---

[37] As with animals, the confusing overlap between the enhanced protection under the 1981 Act and the provisions in the 1994 Regulations has been resolved by the species being deleted from the Schedule to the Act (for most purposes); CNHAR 2007 reg.7(8), CNHASR 2007 reg.29.

[38] See para.3.4.8, above. The relevant provision of the 1994 Regulations—reg.43—has been substituted for Scotland by CNHASR 2007 reg.14 and for England and Wales by CNHAR 2007 reg.5(17).

[39] CNHR 1994 reg.43(4) as substituted.

[40] In both jurisdictions; CNHR 1994, in Scotland reg.43(9), in England and Wales reg.43(10) and (11).

[41] CNHR 1994 reg.43(1).

[42] The offences in this form apply only to possession, control and transport after May 1, 2007; CNHR 1994 reg.43(2)(a) and (b).

[43] CNHR 1994 reg.43(2) and (3).

[44] This is defined as being in accordance with the Habitats and Species Directive at times when it has applied to a Member State or with the relevant local law at the time; CNHR 1994 reg.43(7).

[45] CNHR 1994 reg.43(5) and (6).

[46] CNHR 1994 reg.43(8).

[47] CNHR 1994 reg.43(1).

[48] CNHR 1994 reg.43(2) and (3).

[49] CNHR 1994 reg.43(7)–(9).

[50] CNHR 1994 reg.43(5) and (6).

[51] See C. de Klemm, *Wild Plant Conservation and the Law* (Bonn: IUCN, 1990).

conservation (as by those concerned with invertebrates) is that although there is widespread public support for protecting birds and other high-profile animals, the public generally shows little regard for the native flora, apart from, perhaps, a few dramatic orchids.

6.2.7   Very different forms of statutory protection are offered to certain plants through provisions on hedgerows and the system of tree preservation orders, discussed in sections 6.3 and 6.5, below.

Weeds

6.2.8   In the days before modern herbicides, the control of weeds was a major problem for agriculture. Nostalgic appreciation of the beauty of a wheatfield sprinkled with the bright flowers of poppies and cornflowers overlooks the fact that to farmers these weeds posed a serious threat to the yield and value of their crop. The law did not ignore this threat, and in mediaeval Scotland legislation stated that not only did the tenant have to cleanse his land of *maneleta*, or guld (the corn marigold), but he was liable to a fine of one sheep for each plant found.[52]

6.2.9   The current legislation is to be found in the Weeds Act 1959, under which the Minister can require the occupier of any land to take such action as may be necessary to prevent the spread of certain "injurious weeds".[53] The weeds affected are spear thistle, creeping or field thistle, curled dock, broad-leaved dock, and ragwort[54]; further weeds can be added to this list by the Minister. If occupiers unreasonably fail to comply with a notice requiring them to take action against injurious weeds, an offence is committed, and a failure to take the required action within 14 days of conviction is a further offence.[55] If an occupier does not take the necessary steps, action can be taken by the Minister himself,[56] the costs being recovered from the occupier.[57] The owner of the land is involved only where the Minister has had to take direct action and it is not practicable to trace the occupier; in these circumstances the cost of the intervention can be recovered from the owner, but the owner has the right to recover from the missing occupier.[58] A further provision added for England and Wales allows the Minister to make a code of practice providing guidance on how to prevent the spread of ragwort; this code is admissible in evidence and can be taken into account by a court in any relevant legal proceedings.[59]

6.2.10   More generally, it would appear that as weeds are not being deliberately cultivated, they fall within the definition of "wild plants" for the purpose of section 13 of the Wildlife and Countryside Act 1981, and therefore it is an offence for anyone other than an "authorised person" intentionally (or in

---

[52] Frag. Coll. 11, 12 (*A.P.S.* i, 750).

[53] Weeds Act 1959 s.1.

[54] *Cirsium vulgare* (Savi) Ten., *Cirsium arvense* L. Scop., *Rumex crispus* L., *Rumex obtusifolius* L., *Senecio jacobaea* L.; for once the statute includes the authors' names, but omits the conventional capital letter for the generic name.

[55] Weeds Act 1959 s.2.

[56] The standard legal phrasing conjures a lovely image of a team of Her Majesty's Ministers, in their best attire, slowly digging weeds out of an unkempt field in some rural wilderness!

[57] Weeds Act 1959 s.3(1).

[58] Weeds Act 1959 s.3(2) and (4).

[59] Weeds Act 1959 s.1A, added by Ragwort Control Act 2003 s.1.

Scotland recklessly) to uproot such a plant.[60] However, it may be expected that permission from the owner or occupier of the land will readily be given and may easily be inferred. The question of whether the spread of weeds could constitute an actionable nuisance at common law is discussed later.[61]

Invasive Non-native Species

In order to protect the native flora, and the country in general, from invasive alien species, the law prohibits the release into the wild of a number of plants which aggressively take over any habitat where they become established. It is an offence to plant or otherwise cause to grow[62] in the wild any plant listed in Part II of Schedule 9 to the Wildlife and Countryside Act 1981.[63] The plants listed include giant hogweed, Japanese knotweed[64] and several species of seaweed,[65] and in Scotland the prohibition extends to hybrids of the listed species.[66] It is a defence that the accused took all reasonable steps and exercised all due diligence to avoid committing the offence, but where this defence involves an allegation that another person's act or default was responsible for the commission of the offence, prior notice identifying that person must be given to the prosecutor.[67] Those authorised by the Minister enjoy a power of entry to land (other than a dwelling) to ascertain whether an offence has been committed, and obstruction of such an investigation is an offence.[68] As with non-native animals, there is power for the Minister to ban the sale of certain species and to issue guidance or codes of practice that offer advice in relation to certain species.[69]

6.2.11

Plant Health

Although designed to control pests and diseases injurious to trees and bushes and to agricultural and horticultural crops,[70] the legislation on plant health is broad enough in its scope to encompass all plants growing wild, necessarily so as wild plants may harbour threats to their cultivated relatives. The Plant Health Act 1967 and the Orders made under it confer on the "competent authorities" wide powers to take action to prevent or control pests, defined as including all forms of harmful insects, bacteria, fungi, plant

6.2.12

---

[60] See para.6.2.3, above.

[61] See section 8.8, below.

[62] The precise scope of this phrase remains to be tested, e.g. in what circumstances, if any, would failing to prevent the spread of a plant from a garden to the wild be regarded as having "caused it grow" there?

[63] WCA 1981 s.14(2); as usual, licences may be granted to authorise such conduct (WCA 1981 s.16(4); see Appendix C).

[64] On the problems caused by Japanese knotweed, including the legal problems of disposing of contaminated soil see G. Crowhurst, "Managing Japanese Knotweed on Development Sites" (2006) 18 E.L.M. 296.

[65] See Appendix A.

[66] WCA 1981 s.14(2), as amended by NCSA 2004 Sch.6 para.12.

[67] WCA 1981 s.14(3) and (4).

[68] WCA 1981 s.14(5) and (6) in Scotland; in England and Wales superseded by the wider enforcement powers of wildlife inspectors (WCA 1981 s.19ZA, added by CRWA 2000 Sch.12 para.8).

[69] In Scotland WCA 1981 ss.14A and 14B as added by NCSA 2004 Sch.12 para.13; in England and Wales WCA 1981 ss.14ZA and 14ZB as added by NERCA 2000 ss.50–51. See para.7.2.6, below.

[70] Plant Health Act 1967 s.1(1).

and animal organisms, and all other agents causative of transmissible disease.[71] The "competent authorities" are Ministers, and the Forestry Commission for matters relating to forest trees and timber.[72] Orders made under the Act can require local authorities (counties and metropolitan districts in England) to take the necessary steps to carry the measures into effect.[73]

6.2.13 The 1967 Act itself is an enabling provision, allowing for orders to be made to deal with specific problems and to comply with European Community requirements.[74] The powers available include the removal, treatment or destruction of any crops, plant or seed found to be infected, the prohibition of the sale or keeping of any living specimens of a pest, the prohibition of the entry into this country of any pests or infected items, as well as powers of entry and inspection and powers to take direct action in default of compliance with official requirements. The detailed provisions are to be found in the orders made under the 1967 Act, of which the most general are the Plant Health (England), Plant Health (Wales) and Plant Health (Scotland) Orders[75] and Plant Health (Forestry) Order 2005,[76] all subject to frequent amendment. These specify a number of pests, and in relation to these impose import restrictions in relation to any plants, soil or other growing medium and machinery which might be infected, prohibit the keeping of living specimens of the pests and establish a regime of phytosanitary certificates to ensure the health of material being imported and exported. Further restrictions are imposed in relation to specific problems such as the Colorado beetle and progressive wilt disease of hops.

6.2.14 Only in a few cases are these provisions likely to have much effect on nature conservation, but the potential is there and has been demonstrated by the provisions made under the 1967 Act in relation to Dutch Elm Disease. In order to prevent the spread of the disease, the Dutch Elm Disease (Local Authorities) Order 1984[77] and its predecessors gave powers to local authorities in the specified areas to serve notices requiring particular elm trees to be cut down, destroyed by fire or subjected to specified treatments. The ravages of the disease itself and of such preventive action during the height of the outbreak around 1980 wrought significant changes to the landscape and local habitats in many of the affected areas. An outbreak of some other pest or disease which affects both cultivated and wild plants could similarly lead to widespread action which could have major consequences for the flora of particular areas, and consequently for the habitat as a whole.

---

[71] Plant Health Act 1967 s.1(1).

[72] Plant Health Act 1967 s.1(2).

[73] Plant Health Act 1967 s.5 (amended for England and Wales by Local Government Act 1972 Sch.29 Pt II para.34; for Scotland by Local Government etc. (Scotland) Act 1994 Sch.13 para.68; and for Wales by Local Government (Wales) Act 1994 Sch.16 para.28).

[74] Primarily Directive 2000/29/EC.

[75] Plant Health (England) Order 2005 (SI 2005/2530); Plant Health (Wales) Order 2006 (SI 2006/1643) and Plant Health (Scotland) Order 2005 (SSI 2005/613).

[76] SI 2005/2517.

[77] SI 1984/687.

HEDGEROWS

The conservation value of hedgerows has long been recognised, both as a **6.3.1** habitat in their own right and for their role as "corridors" linking other fragmented habitats.[78] They are also valued for their contribution to the landscape.[79] The loss of hedgerows has long been identified as a significant matter,[80] but a specific legal response was introduced only in 1997. Prior to that, uncertainty over whether the mix of "tree" and "shrub" species in a hedgerow permitted the use of Tree Preservation Orders had constrained the use of that mechanism to provide some legal protection,[81] and the absence of other provisions had stimulated the investigation of innovative legal approaches. Thus in *Seymour and Yorkshire Wildlife Trust v Flamborough Parish Council*[82] campaigners convinced the county court that an Inclosure Act of 1765 imposed a continuing obligation on the Parish Council to maintain a living hedge at a particular location. Apart from the fact that this success depended on the specific wording of the Act in question, subsequent cases have suggested that difficulties over establishing locus standi[83] and the interaction with more modern legislation, such as the planning system,[84] may limit the effectiveness of this approach, although in some cases reliance on Inclosure Acts may still offer a way to protect hedges that fall outwith the new statutory scheme. Agricultural stewardship schemes nowadays may also provide support for hedgerow conservation.[85]

Specific statutory protection for hedgerows is provided by the Hedgerows **6.3.2** Regulations 1997,[86] but extends to England and Wales only.[87] Protection is provided for "important" hedgerows and much of the Regulations is taken up with attempting to define this concept, although there is no definition of "hedgerow" itself. The Regulations apply only to hedgerows in or adjacent

---

[78] Hedgerows are a prime example of the features which Member States must endeavour to have managed with a view to their wildlife importance under art.10 of the Habitats and Species Directive: "features ... which by virtue of their linear and continuous structure (such as ... traditional systems for marking field boundaries) are essential for the migration, dispersal and genetic exchange of wild species"; see para.7.4.32, below.

[79] See generally: House of Commons Environment, Transport and Regional Affairs Committee, *Protection of Field Boundaries*, 13th Report of 1997–98, HC Paper No.969 (Session 1997-1998); J. Holder, "Law and Landscape: the legal construction and protection of hedgerows" (1999) 62 MLR 100; C. Mynors, "Hedgerows: Biodiversity or Rupert Bear" in N. Herbert-Young (ed.), *Law, Policy and Development in the Rural Environment* (Cardiff: University of Wales Press, 1999); J. Holder, "Hedgerows, Laws and Cultural Landscape" in J. Holder and D. McGillivray, *Locality and Identity: Environmental Issues in Law and Society* (Aldershot: Ashgate Dartmouth, 1999).

[80] See, e.g. *Biodiversity: the UK Action Plan* (Cm.2428, 1994) pp.94–98.

[81] See para.6.5.6, below.

[82] *Seymour and Yorkshire Wildlife Trust v Flamborough Parish Council* Unreported 1997, discussed in House of Commons Environment, Transport and Regional Affairs Committee, *Protection of Field Boundaries*, 13th Report of 1997–98, HC Paper No.969 (Session 1997-1998) at paras 106–119 and Mynors, "Hedgerows: Biodiversity or Rupert Bear" in N. Herbert-Young (ed.), *Law, Policy and Development in the Rural Environment* (1999), at pp.153–157.

[83] *Marlton v Turner* [1998] 3 E.G.L.R. 185.

[84] *R v Solihull Borough Council, ex p. Berkswell Parish Council* (1998) 77 P. & C.R. 312.

[85] See section 8.4, below.

[86] SI 1997/1160, made under the Environment Act 1995 s.97.

[87] See generally *The Hedgerow Regulations 1997: A Guide to the Law and Good Practice* (DETR/Welsh Office, 1997) which both helps to explain the scheme and provides practical advice.

to common land, land used for agriculture, forestry or grazing horses or land designated as a National Nature Reserve or SSSI, and exclude those within the curtilage or marking the boundary of a dwelling-house. The hedgerow must be at least 20 metres long, with additional provisions to deal with gaps in the length and where a shorter stretch meets another hedgerow.

6.3.3 The basic scheme is that for such hedgerows the owners of the land, or utility operators[88] if they are to be responsible for the work, must give the local planning authority notice of their intention to remove or destroy the hedgerow. The authority then has 42 days in which to consult the local parish or community council and decide whether to permit the work to proceed. A hedgerow retention notice preventing the removal can be served only if the hedgerow meets the criteria for being "important", but the authority is under a duty to serve a retention notice for important hedgerows unless satisfied that the circumstances justify their removal, having particular regard to the reasons for removal. There are rights of entry to assist the authority in its function and a right of appeal to the Minister (in practice the Planning Inspectorate) against a hedgerow retention notice.

6.3.4 Where the Regulations apply, it is an offence intentionally or recklessly to remove[89] a hedgerow, or to cause or permit its removal, without giving notice, without acting in accordance with the terms of the notice given or without either having approval from the authority or waiting 42 days from the date of the notice before starting the work. An unchallenged hedgerow removal notice authorises work during the next two years only. Defences apply where the work is authorised by an express grant of planning permission,[90] where the removal is for reasons of national defence or to give access to land in an emergency in circumstances where any other means of access would entail disproportionate cost, where the work is required for flood defence or land drainage, where the removal is to prevent the spread of plant or tree pests, or where the work is undertaken in order to prevent obstruction or danger in relation to electricity lines or as part of the Minister's functions as highway authority. A further defence applies where the removal of the hedgerow is to provide a new access to land in substitution for an existing one, provided that the old gap is filled within eight months by planting a hedge. Finally, no offence is committed by work which is required for the proper management of the hedgerow.

6.3.5 These provisions were considered in *R. (Conwy County Borough Council) v Lloyd*[91] where it was noted that since failure to give notice is not in itself an offence and there is no requirement to have the work inspected at any stage, there may be difficulties in determining after the event whether or not a hedgerow that has been removed was "important" or its removal fell within some of these defences. More significantly it was held that the

---

[88] Essentially electricity, gas, telecommunications, water or sewerage undertakers; Hedgerows Regulations 1997 reg.2.

[89] "Remove" means to uproot or otherwise destroy (EA 1995 s.97(8)) so that the Regulations do nothing to protect a hedgerow from gradual deterioration (see para.6.3.7, below); cf. the meaning of "destroy" in relation to tree preservation orders (para.6.5.12, below).

[90] Works granted permission through the operation of the General Permitted Development Order therefore do not qualify.

[91] *R. (Conwy County Borough Council) v Lloyd* [2003] EWHC 264 (Admin); [2003] Env. L.R. 27.

wording of the regulations[92] unavoidably meant that the exception for the proper management of hedgerows could cover their complete removal, even in the case of a hedgerow 100 metres in length. These two features risk undermining the impact of the regulations in the face of some unscrupulous landowners.

The definition of "important hedgerows" is crucial to the Regulations and **6.3.6** is provided in great detail. In order to be important, the hedgerow must be at least 30 years old and satisfy at least one of the eight criteria in Schedule 1 to the Regulations. The criteria are divided into two broad groups. The first group relates to archaeology and history, including the fact that the hedgerow marks the historic boundary of a parish or township since before 1850, the boundary of an estate or manor from before 1600, is part of a field system pre-dating the Inclosure Acts or is within a scheduled ancient monument. The second group relates to wildlife and landscape and depends on the presence of rare or specially protected species of birds, plants and animals, or the presence of certain numbers and mixes of species of woody, woodland and other plants, the number and mix varying depending on the setting of the hedgerow and between the north and south of England. Further provisions specify exactly which species qualify (e.g. listing the 56 woody species and 57 woodland species to be looked for), how hybrids and multi-stemmed trees are to be counted and the sources and dates to be used in the process. The overall effect is overwhelming.

The Hedgerows Regulations 1997 thus create an astonishingly detailed **6.3.7** scheme for protecting some hedgerows in the countryside. The scheme has been criticised for its reliance on a centrally determined and technical definition of importance, its virtual uniformity across the whole of England and Wales, its lack of emphasis on the contribution of hedgerows to landscape, and the rigidity of the permitted sources which prevent new information being taken into account. Further points include the failure to protect hedgerows against gradual deterioration (as a result of which a valuable hedgerow may decline so that it is no longer important) or to protect young or damaged hedgerows which may mature or recover to meet the criteria for importance, and the extent to which the decision in *R. (Conwy CBC) v Lloyd* may handicap those trying to enforce the law in the face of occupiers willing to remove hedgerows without notice. There is also the question of whether hedgerows in urban and suburban settings should benefit from similar specific protection, as opposed to relying on the fact that the most likely causes of removal in such settings will lead to some scrutiny as planning permission will be required. The Regulations were introduced in March 1997, and a review was announced in May 1997,[93] before they even took effect, but no changes have been made despite the apparent legislative opportunities presented by the Countryside and Rights of Way and Natural Environment and Rural Communities Bills. In practice, the fact that good management of hedgerows now features as an element in the various

---

[92] Hedgerows Regulations 1997 reg.6(1)(j).

[93] *Review of the Hedgerows Regulation 1997* (DETR, 1998); see also the Government Response to the House of Commons Environment, Transport and Regional Affairs Committee Report on *The Protection of Field Boundaries* (Cm.4200, 1999). The need for rapid reconsideration was at least partly due to the haste to get some Regulations, albeit not perfect, in place before the General Election in 1997.

agricultural support schemes may well be more significant than these specific legal provisions.[94]

6.3.8   The separate issue of high hedges causing disputes between neighbours has been the subject of legislation in England and Wales and of official consultation and legislative proposals from private members in Scotland.[95] For England and Wales, the Anti-Social Behaviour Act 2003[96] makes the matter a responsibility of local authorities and establishes a complaints system and a mechanism for requiring remedial action to be taken, with the focus exclusively on the adverse effect on the reasonable enjoyment of domestic property.[97] There is no mention in the legislation of regard for nature conservation but the general biodiversity duty imposed on public authorities means that this is an issue that the local authority should take into account in deciding what should happen.[98]

TREES: FORESTRY

6.4.1 Trees are the subject of a variety of special legal and administrative provisions. Almost all of the woodland in Great Britain has been managed or exploited at some time in the past, and even those which do not reveal signs of recent human intervention are referred to as "ancient" or "semi-natural" woodland, rather than as being truly natural, reflecting the likelihood of past human interference. Throughout the centuries trees have been planted to provide shelter, for their wood and other products, and as a decorative feature of the landscape.

6.4.2   The area of woodland in Britain had been constantly reduced for centuries as timber was harvested and land was cleared for other purposes, but during the twentieth century the conscious policy of reducing the country's dependence on imported timber, initially for strategic but then for commercial reasons, has led to considerable new planting and a significant increase in the area supporting trees.[99] In the last three decades environmental considerations have been taken into account in the preservation of ancient woodlands and the design of new plantations, whilst forestry strategy has embraced multiple objectives, not just timber production, aiming "to protect and expand Britain's forests and woodlands and increase their value to society and the environment."[100] The potential for forestry to

---

[94] See section 8.4, below.

[95] *Consultation Paper on High Hedges, the Extent of Problems and Possible Solutions in Scotland* (Scottish Executive Justice Department, 2000); J. Watchman, *High Hedges* (2006) 117 SPEL 101.

[96] Anti-Social Behaviour Act 2003 ss.65–84.

[97] Anti-Social Behaviour Act 2003 s.65.

[98] NERCA 2006 s.40; see para.1.2.9, above.

[99] From a level of about 5% at the start of the twentieth century, woodlands now account for 17.1% of Scotland, 13.8% of Wales and 8.6% of England (*Scottish Forestry Strategy 2006*, p.15; *Woodlands for Wales Progress Report 2001–05*, p.21; *Draft National Delivery Plan 08-12 for England's Trees, Woods and Forests*, p.4; all published by the relevant national Forestry Commission bodies).

[100] The "mission" of the Forestry Commission; see *http://www.forestry.gov.uk/forestry/infd-6val65* [Accessed May 14, 2009].

contribute to the reduction in net greenhouse gas emissions is now emerging as a further consideration.[101]

Woodlands of various sorts are important for biodiversity and are well **6.4.3** represented in the habitats selected for protection under the measures already discussed in Chapter 5, e.g. Caledonian forest is a priority habitat type under the Habitats and Species Directive.[102] The hedgerow provisions will also protect some trees, but there are two areas of law which deal directly with trees, and although neither is primarily directed at nature conservation, the exercise of the relevant powers may lead to considerable benefits or harm to conservation interests. First, there is forestry, where the planting, maintenance and felling of trees are regulated by some direct legal controls, but even more by the effects of the grant schemes operated by the Forestry Commission. Secondly, the town and country planning system makes a number of special provisions, recognising the value of trees to the character and amenity of particular localities.

The regulation of forestry lies primarily in the hand of the Forestry **6.4.4** Commission,[103] which now operates largely on a devolved basis which has led to some divergence of policy and the means to implement it between Scotland, England and Wales. This fragmentation of policy and administration has been balanced by a greater integration of forestry with other land uses and wider sustainable development policies, shown most clearly in Scotland where the specific forestry grant schemes have been replaced by relevant Options as part of the Rural Development Contracts—Rural Priorities within the wider Scottish Rural Development Programme.[104]

Greater awareness of environmental concerns has been a feature of for- **6.4.5** estry policy in recent decades and the imposition in 1985 of a duty on the Commission to seek a balance between timber production and conservation[105] reflected a change of approach which was already becoming evident. The design of plantations nowadays takes account of the interests of landscape and nature conservation,[106] and the grant schemes no longer limit their support to woodland grown exclusively for timber production.[107] The extent to which such policies really effect major changes in British forestry will become apparent in future years as the older plantations are felled and the recent ones grow to maturity.

The regulatory mechanisms have been transformed by amended **6.4.6** requirements for environmental assessment, which for the first time demand express approval before planting is undertaken in some circumstances.[108] The development of forestry is also shaped by the nature of the grant schemes, which replaced taxation measures as the main economic instrument influencing forestry in this country. The tax system still contains a

---

[101] Climate Change (Scotland) Bill s.47 (as introduced in December 2008); *Climate Change (Scotland) Bill: Forestry Provisions* (SPICe Briefing, SB 09-09).

[102] See para.7.4.23, below.

[103] See paras 2.7.5–2.7.10, above.

[104] See *http://www.scotland.gov.uk/Topics/Rural/SRDP* [Accessed May 14, 2009].

[105] Forestry Act 1967 s.1(3A), added by Wildlife and Countryside (Amendment) Act 1985 s.4; see para.2.2.8, above.

[106] See the Standard Notes in *The UK Forestry Standard: The Government's Approach to Sustainable Forestry* (Forestry Commission, 2004).

[107] See para.6.4.9, below.

[108] See paras 6.4.19–6.4.23, below.

number of special provisions for commercial forestry,[109] but these are not so influential as in the past. Prior to 1988, the income tax system allowed a means of gaining considerable tax relief when a taxpayer was involved in the expensive stage of establishing a new plantation, but of escaping tax on the income when the timber came to be harvested. This led to claims that for short-term financial gain large plantations unsuitable and unsympathetic to local conditions were being established, and in the 1988 Budget the tax system was changed. The current position is that commercial forestry falls outwith the income tax system, so that the expenses of establishing a plantation cannot be set off against other income, but there is no tax to pay on the income when the trees are harvested.[110] For the purposes of capital gains tax, the value of growing timber is not included in any valuations,[111] and for inheritance tax, the payment of tax can be deferred until the woodland is harvested or disposed of, with no further tax due in the event of another death during the intervening period.[112]

Planting

6.4.7 Until 1999, the planting of trees was not subject to any direct legal controls, and today formal approval is required only in the circumstances covered by the environmental assessment regulations discussed below. In other circumstances it remains the case that no form of official permission is required to plant trees, however large an area is affected. Furthermore, it is expressly declared that the afforestation of land is not "development" for the purposes of the town and country planning system,[113] and consequently no permission is required for changing the use of land to forestry, while most forestry operations are likewise exempted from planning control.[114] However, planning authorities were encouraged to prepare indicative forestry strategies as part of the structure plans for their areas. These are intended to indicate the preferred, potential and sensitive areas for forestry, identifying areas where the physical and other conditions are suitable for commercial projects, where the ground is suitable but there are some constraining interests and other areas where there are serious or multiple constraints on forestry development.[115] The role of these strategies is now largely being fulfilled by other elements in the process of regional planning.

6.4.8   In most circumstances, instead of direct legal controls, the regulation of new planting is achieved through the grant schemes operated by the

[109] The growing of Christmas trees does not qualify (*Jaggers (trading as Shide Trees) v Ellis* [1997] STC 1417), whilst growing "short-rotation coppice" (defined as involving perennial tree species harvested above the ground at intervals of less than 10 years) is treated as an agricultural activity for tax purposes (Finance Act 1995 s.154).

[110] Income Tax (Trading and Other Income) Act 2005 ss.11 and 254; Corporation Tax Act 2009 ss.37, 134 and 980.

[111] Taxation of Chargeable Gains Act 1992 s.250.

[112] Inheritance Tax Act (née Capital Transfer Tax Act) 1984 ss.125–130.

[113] TCPSA 1997 s.19(2)(e); TCPA 1990 s.55(2)(e).

[114] Town and Country Planning (General Permitted Development) (Scotland) Order 1992 (SI 1992/223) art.3 and Sch.1 Pt 7 (class 22); Town and Country Planning General Development Order 1995 (SI 1995/418) art.3 and Sch.2 Pt 7.

[115] SODD Circular 9/99, DoE Circular 29/92; for a critical view N. Marshall, *Forestry Plan Scan '96: A review of Indicative Forestry Strategies* (RSPB, 1996).

Forestry Commission and discussed below; in Scotland these are now integrated into the wider rural development schemes. Small-scale planting and planting purely for amenity may receive financial support from other public bodies, such as Natural England, Scottish Natural Heritage and the Countryside Council for Wales in their countryside role, and accordingly come under some form of scrutiny. However unless the environmental assessment regulations apply, if no financial support is sought, there is nothing to prevent landowners planting as much of their land with whatever sort of trees in whatever form they choose, regardless of environmental and amenity considerations. The replanting of areas following harvesting will usually be controlled through conditions attached to the felling licence authorising the felling.[116]

Apart from the provision giving basic authority to pay grants,[117] the **6.4.9** Forestry Commission's grant schemes and the procedural arrangements for them are not in statutory form, although it has been held that the Commission's decisions may be subject to judicial review.[118] The best source of information on the schemes is the material produced by the Commission itself and the information on its web pages.[119] There are now quite separate schemes for each part of Great Britain and new grants in Scotland are now mainly dealt with as part of the Rural Development Contracts scheme.[120] All the schemes reflect the contributions that forestry can make to sustainable development Whereas earlier schemes stressed that "timber production must be the primary objective",[121] recent schemes have had multiple purposes. For example the Woodland Grant Scheme that applied throughout the UK until the early 2000s aimed:

"— to encourage people to create new woodlands and forests to

- increase the production of wood,
- improve the landscape,
- provide new habitats for wildlife, and
- offer opportunities for recreation and sport;

— to encourage good management of forests and woodlands,
— including their well timed regeneration, particularly looking
— after the needs of ancient and semi-natural woodlands;
— to provide jobs and improve the economy of rural areas and
— other areas with few other sources of economic activity; and
— to provide a use for land instead of agriculture."[122]

---

[116] See paras 6.4.11–6.4.18, below.
[117] Forestry Act 1979 s.1.
[118] *Kincardine & Deeside District Council v Forestry Commissioners*, 1992 S.L.T. 1180.
[119] See *http://www.forestry.gov.uk* [Accessed May 14, 2009].
[120] Currently in England, the English Woodland Grant Scheme and Farm Woodland Payments; in Wales, the Better Woodlands for Wales scheme, and in Scotland mainly as Rural Development Contracts within the Scottish Rural Development Programme (see *http://www.scotland.gov.uk/Topics/Rural/SRDP* [Accessed May 14, 2009]), although there are two separate Forestry Challenge Funds authorised by the Forestry Challenge Funds (Scotland) Regulations 2008 (SSI 2008/135).
[121] Forestry Commission leaflet, *Forestry Grant Scheme* (1987), p.1.
[122] *A Guide to the Woodland Grant Scheme* (2000), p.3.

More recently, renewable energy has also featured in some schemes.[123]

6.4.10   The range of grants cover both the establishment and management of woodland, and the rates payable vary depending on the species involved and the nature of the planting and related operations. Payments are usually made in stages dependent on the successful establishment of new planting, etc. Applications may be subject to environmental impact assessment[124] and in all cases the procedures involve consultation with various public bodies and applications must live up to the Forestry Standards which incorporate nature conservation concerns.[125] Public registers of applications are maintained.

Felling

6.4.11   Whereas the regulation of afforestation is largely carried out indirectly through the grant schemes, the felling of trees is controlled by a legal licensing regime. Subject to many exceptions, it is a criminal offence to fell any growing trees without first having obtained a licence from the Forestry Commission.[126] The maximum penalty is a fine of level 4 on the standard scale, or twice the value of the trees which were felled, whichever is the higher.[127] In some circumstances an environmental assessment must be carried out, as discussed below.[128] The relationship between felling licences and tree preservation orders is also considered below.[129]

6.4.12   Topping and lopping of trees fall outwith this provision, as do the trimming and laying of hedges, the felling of trees in a garden,[130] orchard, churchyard or public open space, and the felling of trees no more than 8 centimetres in diameter[131] (or 15 centimetres in the case of underwood or coppice).[132] The occupier of land is allowed to fell up to 5 cubic metres in any calendar quarter without a licence, provided that no more than 2 cubic

---

[123] See the information for Scotland on Rural Development Contracts—Rural Priorities at *http://www.forestry.gov.uk/forestry/infd-6wxjmk* [Accessed May 14, 2009].

[124] See paras 6.4.19–6.4.23, below.

[125] *The UK Forestry Standard: The Government's Approach to Sustainable Forestry* (Forestry Commission, 2004).

[126] Forestry Act 1967 ss.9 and 17 (the provisions on tree felling do not apply in Inner London (Forestry Act 1967 s.36)); *Forestry Commission v Grace* (1992) 4 L.M.E.L.R. 127.

[127] Forestry Act 1967 s.17 (amended by Criminal Procedure (Scotland) Act 1975 ss.289F and 289G (added by Criminal Justice Act 1982 s.54); Criminal Justice Act 1982 s.46); *Campbell v Webster*, 1992 S.C.C.R. 167.

[128] See para.6.4.20, below.

[129] See paras 6.5.21–6.5.24, below.

[130] A garden that had been neglected for two-and-a-half years and had become overgrown was held no longer to be a garden for this purpose in the absence of any evidence that it was to continue in such use; *McInerney v Portland Port Ltd* [2001] J.P.L. 1295. But in *Rockall v Department of Environment, Food and Rural Affairs* [2008] EWHC 2408 Admin *McInerney* was distinguished and felling to restore what had previously been a garden was held not to require a licence, it being emphasised that each case depended on its own facts and circumstances and that the owner's mere assertion that the land and work were for a garden would not by itself be enough. In planning law a different test for the abandonment of a use is utilised (*Hughes v Secretary of State for the Environment, Transport and the Regions* [2000] 1 P.L.R. 76).

[131] Measured over the bark at 1.3 metres above ground level (Forestry Act 1967 s.9(6)); all of the measurements in these provisions were rendered metric by the Forestry Act 1979 s.2 and Sch.1.

[132] Forestry Act 1967 s.9(2).

metres are sold, and to fell trees of no more than 10 centimetres in diameter as thinnings.[133] Also exempt from the licensing requirement is felling in the following circumstances: in order to prevent danger or to prevent or abate a nuisance[134]; in compliance with a statutory obligation[135]; at the request of an electricity operator where the trees are close to electric lines or plant[136]; or when immediately required for development authorised under the town and country planning system.[137] Further exemptions apply to felling by statutory undertakers, felling required by water and drainage authorities, the felling of elms badly affected by Dutch Elm disease[138] and most significantly, felling in accordance with a plan of operations agreed with the Forestry Commission as part of one of its grant or dedication schemes.[139] The onus lies on the accused to show that any unlicensed felling falls within one of these exceptions.[140]

It is the landowner, or a tenant who is entitled to fell the trees, who must **6.4.13** apply to the Forestry Commission for a licence.[141] The trees will usually be inspected, consultations similar to those for grant applications will be held and the application will appear on the public register. Where it appears to the Commission expedient in the interests of good forestry, agriculture, the amenities of the district or the maintenance of an adequate supply of growing timber, conditions may be imposed on the grant of a licence,[142] requiring that after the felling has taken place the land (or other land agreed by the applicant and the Commission) be restocked with trees.[143] Such restocking conditions are usually imposed. In Scotland, the reasons for imposing conditions additionally include the purposes of conserving or enhancing the flora, fauna, geographical or physiographical features or the natural beauty or amenity of any land.[144]

If a licence is refused, the applicant is entitled to compensation.[145] The **6.4.14** sum available is the depreciation in the value of the trees which is attributable to the deterioration in the quality of their timber as a result of felling

---

[133] Forestry Act 1967 s.9(3), amended by the Forestry (Modification of Felling Restrictions) Regulations 1985 (SI 1985/1958).

[134] Forestry Act 1967 s.9(4).

[135] Forestry Act 1967 s.9(4).

[136] Forestry Act 1967 s.9(4), amended by Electricity Act 1989 Sch.16 para.13.

[137] Forestry Act 1967 s.9(4), amended by Planning (Consequential Provisions) (Scotland) Act 1997 Sch.2 para.13; Planning (Consequential Provisions) Act 1990 Sch.2 para.14.

[138] Forestry (Exceptions from Restriction of Felling) Regulations 1979 (SI 1979/792) reg.4, amended by Forestry (Exceptions from Restriction of Felling) (Amendment) Regulations 1988 and 1998 (SI 1988/970 and SI 1998/603).

[139] Forestry (Exceptions from Restriction of Felling) Regulations 1979 (SI 1979/792) reg.4, amended by Forestry (Exceptions from Restriction of Felling) (Amendment) Regulations 1988 and 1998 (SI 1988/970 and SI 1998/603).

[140] *R. (Grundy & Co Excavations Ltd) v Halton Division Magistrates Court* [2003] EWHC 272 (Admin); [2003] 1 P.L.R. 89; N. Parpworth, "Unlicensed Tree Felling: A further example of a Regulatory Offence?" [2003] J.P.L. 1234.

[141] Forestry Act 1967 s.10; the time-limits and other procedural aspects of the licensing scheme and related matters are largely governed by the Forestry (Felling of Trees) Regulations 1979 (SI 1979/791), amended by the Forestry (Felling of Trees) (Amendment) Regulations 1987 (SI 1987/632) and the Forestry (Felling of Trees) (England and Wales) (Amendment) Regulations 2002 (SI 2002/226).

[142] Forestry Act 1967 s.10(2).

[143] Forestry Act 1967 s.12.

[144] Forestry Act 1967 s.10(2)(c), added by NCSA 2004 Sch.7 para.2.

[145] Forestry Act 1967 s.11.

being refused. However, as the Commission is unlikely to refuse permission to fell trees which are so far past their prime that their value is diminishing, this appears to be a redundant provision in practice.

6.4.15 An applicant aggrieved by the conditions imposed on a licence may request the Minister to refer the case to a special reference committee, and the Minister must do so unless he considers the grounds for the request to be frivolous.[146] The reference committee will give the applicant a hearing and consider the matter before reporting to the Minister who may confirm, overturn or modify the Commission's decision. The committee is appointed by the Minister and comprises a chairman, and two members drawn from panels selected after consultations with the relevant Regional Advisory Committee[147] and organisations representing the interests of the owners of woodland and timber merchants, and organisations involved in the study and promotion of forestry.[148] A similar procedure is followed where an applicant is aggrieved by the refusal of a licence, but only if a licence for the same land has been refused more than three years previously.[149]

6.4.16 If a restocking condition is not complied with, the owner of the land can be served with a notice requiring him to make good the default within a set time.[150] If the recipient considers that the specified steps have already been taken or that they are not required in order to fulfil the condition, he can request the Minister to refer the matter to a special reference committee as described above, and the notice is suspended pending its review.[151] In the absence of a reasonable excuse, failure to carry out the steps required is a criminal offence,[152] and the Forestry Commission has the power to enter the land and carry out the necessary work itself,[153] recovering expenses from the landowner.[154]

6.4.17 If a person in Scotland has been convicted of felling trees without a licence, or in England and Wales if it appears to the Forestry Commission that a person has committed such an offence, the Commission can serve a notice requiring that the land concerned, or other land as agreed, be restocked with trees. The notice can include a requirement to maintain the trees for up to 10 years in accordance with the rules and practice of good forestry. Such a notice can be enforced in the same way as a restocking condition in a licence.[155]

6.4.18 The Forestry Commission also has the power to direct the felling of trees in order to prevent the deterioration in the quality of the timber in the trees or to improve the growth of other trees.[156] The recipient of a felling direction can ask for it to be reviewed in the same way as a condition in a felling

---

[146] Forestry Act 1967 s.16.
[147] See para.2.7.9, above.
[148] Forestry Act 1967 s.27.
[149] Forestry Act 1967 s.16(4).
[150] Forestry Act 1967 s.24(2).
[151] Forestry Act 1967 s.25.
[152] Forestry Act 1967 s.24(4).
[153] Forestry Act 1967 s.24(3).
[154] Forestry Act 1967 s.26.
[155] Forestry Act 1967 ss.17A–17C, added by Forestry Act 1986 s.1, amended by Regulatory Reform (Forestry) Order 2006 (SI 2006/780) reg.4.
[156] Forestry Act 1967 s.18; this section includes a number of exceptions and factors which must be taken into account before the power is exercised—in practice the power is not used.

licence,[157] and can require the Commission to buy the trees for immediate felling or the Minister to acquire his interest in the land where that interest does not entitle the recipient to sell the trees in this way.[158] A felling direction is enforced in the same way as a restocking condition in a licence.[159]

Environmental Impact Assessment

Where there is a requirement for an environmental assessment, very dif- **6.4.19** ferent procedures apply, for both felling and planting, including a requirement for express permission before trees can be planted. Initially the EC Directive[160] on environmental assessment was implemented simply by adding the assessment to the consideration of grant applications, but this meant that projects not seeking grant support fell outwith the procedure,[161] and however unlikely this was in practice, such an arrangement was clearly inadequate to ensure that the terms of the Directive were observed. Although the amendments to the Directive led to new Regulations in 1998,[162] these took the same flawed approach.[163] Now, though, Regulations approved in 1999 do impose a clear requirement for express approval before relevant projects can go ahead.

The 1999 Regulations[164] apply to initial afforestation, to deforestation for **6.4.20** the purpose of converting the land to another use and to forest road and quarry works, where the project is likely to have significant effects of the environment,[165] but not where the work is already covered by the need for express planning permission or the more general environmental impact assessment provisions.[166] A project is to be taken as not likely to have such effects if its area falls below certain specified thresholds, ranging from five hectares for planting (one hectare for deforestation) in land free from environmental designations, through two hectares (half a hectare) in a National Scenic Area or Area of Outstanding Natural Beauty, to zero where

---

[157] Forestry Act 1967 s.20.

[158] Forestry Act 1967 s.21.

[159] Forestry Act 1967 s.24.

[160] See section 8.3, below for a discussion of the Directive and its requirements.

[161] Environmental Assessment (Afforestation) Regulations 1988 (SI 1988/1207). The fact that even this imperfect implementation was late led to litigation; *Kincardine & Deeside District Council v Forestry Commissioners*, 1992 S.L.T. 1180.

[162] Environmental Assessment (Forestry) Regulations 1998 (SI 1998/1713).

[163] The adequacy of the 1988 and 1998 Regulations was challenged in *Swan v Secretary of State for Scotland*, 1998 S.C. 479, but as the 1999 Regulations were in place before the final resolution of that case, this issue was not considered when the substantive issues were finally dealt with by the court; *Swan v Secretary of State for Scotland (No.2)* [2000] Env. L.R. 60.

[164] Environmental Impact Assessment (Forestry) (Scotland) Regulations 1999 (SSI 1999/43), amended by Pt V of the Environmental Impact Assessment (Scotland) Amendment Regulations 2006 (SSI 2006/614); Environmental Impact Assessment (Forestry) (England and Wales) Regulations 1999 (SI 1999/2228), amended by the Environmental Impact Assessment (Forestry) (England and Wales) (Amendment) Regulations 2006 (SI 2006/3106). The two sets of Regulations were almost identical and the 2006 amendments did not alter the fundamental scheme.

[165] In assessing this, the impact of the proposed new use must also be considered; *R. (Trees and Wildlife Action Committee Ltd) v Forestry Commissioners* [2007] EWHC 1623 Admin; *The Times*, July 17, 2007.

[166] Environmental Impact Assessment (Forestry) (Scotland) Regulations 1999 reg.3; Environmental Impact Assessment (Forestry) (England and Wales) Regulations 1999 reg.3.

an SSSI or European Site is concerned.[167] A formal opinion on the need for an assessment can be requested from the Forestry Commission, with further reference to the Minister.[168] Individual projects can be exempted by the Commission but they must consider whether alternative forms of assessment and publicity are appropriate.[169]

6.4.21 Where the Regulations apply, consent from the Commission must be sought before any work begins, and the work must be carried out in compliance with any conditions imposed on the consent.[170] The application must be presented with an environmental statement and the standard requirements for consultation, publicity and co-operation from other bodies apply, and the Commission is specifically directed to consider the environmental factors listed in Schedule 4 to the Regulations.[171] All consents are subject to a condition that the work must be begun and completed within the periods specified by the Commission (not more than 5 and 10 years, respectively), but the Commission is free to add further conditions.[172] There is a right of appeal to the Minister against a refusal of consent or the imposition of conditions (other than specifying the maximum periods just noted), and any person aggrieved has the right to apply to the courts on the grounds that he or she has been substantially prejudiced by a failure to take account of representations or other material considerations.[173] A public register is maintained of all applications, environmental statements and decisions.[174]

6.4.22 The Forestry Commission has the power to serve an enforcement notice in the event of work proceeding other than in full accordance with a consent. Again there is a right of appeal to the Minister, which has the effect of suspending the notice. Failure to comply with an enforcement notice is a criminal offence, punishable with a fine of up to level 5 on the standard scale, and if any remedial work specified in the notice is not carried out, the Commission enjoys a power to enter the land and carry out the work itself, recovering the costs from the defaulter. There are also powers of entry to

[167] Environmental Impact Assessment (Forestry) (Scotland) Regulations 1999 reg.3 and Sch.2; Environmental Impact Assessment (Forestry) (England and Wales) Regulations 1999 reg.3 and Sch.2. For National Parks the thresholds in England and Wales are the same as for Areas of Outstanding Natural Beauty, but zero in Scotland.

[168] Environmental Impact Assessment (Forestry) (Scotland) Regulations 1999 regs 5–8; Environmental Impact Assessment (Forestry) (England and Wales) Regulations 1999 regs 5–8.

[169] Environmental Impact Assessment (Forestry) (Scotland) Regulations 1999 reg.4(2) and (5), added by the Environmental Impact Assessment (Scotland) Amendment Regulations 2006 (SSI 2006/614) reg.11(2) and Environmental Impact Assessment (Forestry) (England and Wales) Regulations 1999 reg.4(2) and (5), added by the Environmental Impact Assessment (Forestry) (England and Wales) (Amendment) Regulations 2006 (SI 2006/3106) reg.2(3).

[170] Environmental Impact Assessment (Forestry) (Scotland) Regulations 1999 reg.4; Environmental Impact Assessment (Forestry) (England and Wales) Regulations 1999 reg.4.

[171] Environmental Impact Assessment (Forestry) (Scotland) Regulations 1999 regs 9–16; Environmental Impact Assessment (Forestry) (England and Wales) Regulations 1999 regs 9–16.

[172] Environmental Impact Assessment (Forestry) (Scotland) Regulations 1999 regs 15 and 18; Environmental Impact Assessment (Forestry) (England and Wales) Regulations 1999 regs 15 and 18.

[173] Environmental Impact Assessment (Forestry) (Scotland) Regulations 1999 regs 17 and 19; Environmental Impact Assessment (Forestry) (England and Wales) Regulations 1999 regs 17 and 19. In Scotland it is provided that a "non-governmental organisation promoting environmental protection" may meet this criterion; reg.19(1A), added by Environmental Impact Assessment (Scotland) Amendment Regulations 2006 (SSI 2006/614) reg.11(6).

[174] Environmental Impact Assessment (Forestry) (Scotland) Regulations 1999 reg.24; Environmental Impact Assessment (Forestry) (England and Wales) Regulations 1999 reg.24.

land where it is reasonably suspected that unauthorised work is being carried out.[175]

These provisions may seem unremarkable when compared with the town **6.4.23** and country planning system, and indeed aspects of the system of felling licences, but they marked a major change in the regulation of countryside activities. Agriculture and forestry in the past operated essentially outwith the planning and many other formal regulatory systems, and changes in rural land use were generally not subject to any such direct control. For most projects it will still be the indirect control exercised through grant schemes that matters, but the imposition of such a formal consent procedure was a significant departure from the reliance on the voluntary principle which had been so dominant in the regulation of the countryside.

TREES: PLANNING

The importance of trees for the appearance and amenity of an area is **6.5.1** recognised by the town and country planning system in several ways.[176] Most important is the scheme for tree preservation orders (TPOs), but other provisions are also worthy of note. The most general is the requirement that planning authorities ensure where appropriate that conditions in a grant of planning permission should be used to ensure the preservation or planting of trees.[177] There is also in England and Wales a general power for local authorities to plant trees on land in their area for the purposes of preserving or enhancing natural beauty.[178]

Special rules exist for trees within conservation areas. Although the aim of **6.5.2** such areas is to protect and enhance areas of special architectural and historical interest,[179] natural features will often play a major part in the overall appearance of the area. It is an offence in most circumstances to cut down, top, lop, uproot, or wilfully damage or destroy a tree in a conservation area unless notice has been given in advance to the planning authority, and either the authority has given its consent or six weeks have elapsed.[180] The aim of this provision is to allow time for the authority to decide whether a TPO should be made to protect the trees in question, and for this reason the provision does not apply to trees which are already subject to such an order.[181] The planning authority is not, however, prevented from making an order after the six weeks have elapsed.[182] If the operations have not been

---

[175] Environmental Impact Assessment (Forestry) (Scotland) Regulations 1999 regs 20–23; Environmental Impact Assessment (Forestry) (England and Wales) Regulations 1999 regs 20–23.

[176] Note that while the changes made by the Town and Country Planning (Trees) (Amendment) (England) Regulations 2008 (SI 2008/2260) came into force in October 2008, not all of the changes introduced by the Planning etc. (Scotland) Act 2006 were in force by the end of March 2009.

[177] TCPSA 1997 s.159; TCPA 1990 s.197.

[178] NPACA 1949 s.89(1).

[179] Planning (Listed Buildings and Conservation Areas) (Scotland) Act 1997 s.61; Planning (Listed Buildings and Conservation Areas) Act 1990 s.69; see para.5.10.12, above.

[180] TCPSA 1997 s.172; TCPA 1990 s.211. These provisions have been extended so as to apply, with adjustments, to the Crown: Planning and Compensation Act 2004 ss.86 and 96.

[181] TCPSA 1997 s.172(2); TCPA 1990 s.211(2).

[182] *R. v North Hertfordshire District Council, ex p. Hyde* (1990) 88 L.G.R. 426.

carried out within two years of the notice, a new notice must be served before the operations are lawful.[183] The planning authority must keep a register of the notices which it receives under these provisions.[184]

6.5.3   The criminal offence, which is subject to the same penalties as a breach of a TPO,[185] is committed by the person who carries out the unlawful felling, etc. but the owner of the land also becomes liable to plant another tree of appropriate size and species at the same place as the one unlawfully felled, uprooted or destroyed.[186] Replanting may also be required where the removal of the tree was not unlawful, but only because it fell within certain of the exceptions discussed below. It is made clear that this obligation is owed by the owner of the land from time to time, regardless of his involvement in the offence, although the owner can apply to the planning authority to dispense with this requirement. The obligation can be enforced in the same way as the replacement provisions relating to TPOs.[187]

6.5.4   Where a tree is already covered by a TPO, this more general offence does not apply, and several further categories of trees and operations are excluded from the provisions, in line with the exceptions which apply in relation to TPOs themselves.[188] Trees which are no bigger than 75 millimetres in diameter are exempt (100 millimetres if the tree is in woodland and is uprooted or felled to improve the growth of others).[189] Felling on land managed by or in accordance with a plan of operations agreed with or a felling licence granted by the Forestry Commission is exempt, as are actions by a planning authority and a range of statutory undertakers on land which they occupy. More generally no offence is committed if the uprooting, felling or lopping is in the interests of safety, or necessary for the prevention or abatement of nuisance.[190] Steps taken in compliance with an obligation imposed by an Act of Parliament are exempt, together with ministerially approved action taken to avoid danger or hindrance to air navigation.

---

[183] TCPSA 1997 s.172(3); TCPA 1990 s.211(3).

[184] TCPSA 1997 s.175; TCPA 1990 s.214.

[185] TCPSA 1997 s.172(4); TCPA 1990 s.211(4); see para.6.5.13, below.

[186] TCPSA 1997 s.174; TCPA 1990 s.213.

[187] See para.6.5.18, below.

[188] Town and Country Planning (Tree Preservation Order and Trees in Conservation Areas) (Scotland) Regulations 1975 (SI 1975/1204) reg.11, amended by the Town and Country Planning (Application of Subordinate Legislation to the Crown) (Scotland) Order 2006 (SSI 2006/270) art.4; Town and Country Planning (Trees) Regulations 1999 (SI 1999/1892) reg.10, amended by Town and Country Planning (Application of Subordinate Legislation to the Crown) Order 2006 (SI 2006/1282) art.23(2). The wording of the English legislation differs slightly from the Scottish, and the differences may be significant in some cases; this is discussed more fully at paras 6.5.14–6.5.16, below.

[189] The measurement is to be taken 1.5m above the ground as opposed to at 1.3m for felling licences; does this mean that planning officers are taller than foresters?

[190] The precise exceptions here are the same as relate to TPOs; see paras 6.5.14–6.5.16, below.

Tree Preservation Orders

Tree Preservation Orders offer the strongest protection to trees under the **6.5.5**
planning legislation, but also the most complex,[191] with the rules in England
and Wales subject to impending change.[192] The issue is often a controversial
one, not only because mature trees are a very conspicuous feature of the
landscape, but also because the protection of even a single tree may thwart
any plans for developing a particular site. In any event, the whole idea of
tree "preservation" is somewhat odd, as trees are living organisms which
grow old and die, and perhaps only fossilisation can truly "preserve" a tree
effectively. Many of the most striking trees in the landscape are already
mature, if not past their prime, and rather than trying to protect a tree in its
declining years it may often be better in the long-term for efforts to be made
to secure the planting and tending of young trees to ensure the regeneration
and sustainability of attractive features. This is particularly the case in parks
and avenues where all the trees may well have been planted together at the
same time; unless thought is given to their replacement decades before the
trees reach the end of their natural life, the result will be many years of
barren landscape as the trees die and young replacements grow slowly.

The legislation offers no definition of "tree", and this basic issue can cause **6.5.6**
difficulties, particularly in relation to hedgerows, where there may well be
plants of differing sizes and species, some normally viewed as trees, others as
shrubs. In one case Lord Denning expressed the view that, in a woodland at
least, only something over seven or eight inches in diameter should count as
a tree,[193] but there seems to be no basis for such a requirement[194] and his
view has been firmly rejected by later courts.[195] The test appears to be left to
common sense, and in *Bullock v Secretary of State for the Environment*[196]
Phillips J. said that an order could refer to anything which one would
ordinarily call a tree, as opposed to bushes, shrub and scrub; accordingly
coppice fell within the meaning of "trees" and could be made the subject of a
TPO. Similarly in *Palm Developments Ltd v Secretary of State for*

---

[191] The legislation in Scotland is TCPSA 1997 ss.160–171, amended by Planning etc. (Scotland) Act 2006, and the Town and Country Planning (Tree Preservation Order and Trees in Conservation Areas) (Scotland) Regulations 1975 (SI 1975/1204), significantly amended by the Town and Country Planning (Tree Preservation Order and Trees in Conservation Areas) (Scotland) Amendment Regulations 1981 and 1984 (SI 1981/1385 and SI 1984/329)—hereafter the 1975 Regulations; in England and Wales, TCPA 1990 ss.198–214D, significantly amended by the Planning and Compensation Act 1991 s.23, and the Town and Country Planning (Trees) Regulations 1999 (SI 1999/1892), amended by Town and Country Planning (Trees) (Amendment) (England) Regulations 2008 (SI 2008/2260)—hereafter the 1999 Regulations.

[192] Planning Act 2008 s.192, amending Pt 8 of TCPA 1990 and in particular adding ss.202A–202G which confer power to make further regulations on this subject.

[193] *Kent County Council v Batchelor* (1976) 33 P. & C.R. 185 at 189.

[194] e.g. the express exemption for trees below certain sizes in conservation areas clearly suggests that the legislation contemplates smaller plants counting as trees; see *Palm Developments Ltd v Secretary of State for Communities and Local Government* [2009] EWHC 220 Admin at [40].

[195] *Bullock v Secretary of State for the Environment* (1980) 40 P. & C.R. 246 at 251; see also *Brown v Michael B. Cooper Ltd*, 1990 S.C.C.R. 675 at 678. For a somewhat whimsical discussion of the issue see [1977] J.P.L. 5.

[196] *Bullock v Secretary of State for the Environment* (1980) 40 P. & C.R. 246.

Communities and Local Government,[197] it has been held that saplings are trees, with the suggestion that prosecutorial discretion is the appropriate way to resolve problems arising when someone harms a protected tree in the form of a shoot emerging from an acorn. Hedgerows in England and Wales are now subject to the protective measures described above.[198]

6.5.7   Subject to the default powers of the Minister,[199] it is the planning authority which has the power to make a TPO, the test being that it is "expedient in the interest of amenity" to make provision for the preservation of trees or woodland.[200] An alternative further test of the trees or woodland being of cultural or historical significance will also apply in Scotland once the relevant provisions of the Planning etc. (Scotland) Act 2006 come into force.[201] The trees may be specified individually, as trees in a specified area, or as a woodland.[202] The way in which the trees are described may be significant, as there are minor differences in the legislation for each form of order. The description will also affect the extent to which the order applies to trees established on the site after the order has been made. In *Brown v Michael B. Cooper Ltd*[203] it was held that an order referring to trees in a specified area applied only to trees in existence at the time when the order was made, so that young trees in the area, which could not be proven to have been in existence at that date, were not protected.[204] By contrast, in *Palm Developments Ltd v Secretary of State for Communities and Local Government*[205] it has been held that an order that refers to an area of woodland covers the undifferentiated mass of trees in the area, including those that grow or are planted after the order is made.[206]

6.5.8   Before an order can come into effect it must be advertised, notified to those with an interest in the land, made available for inspection and in Scotland notified to the Forestry Commission[207] and to the Keeper of the Registers of Scotland.[208] Objections and representations may be made within 28 days and a local inquiry may be held. The planning authority must then decide whether or not to confirm the order (with or without

---

[197] *Palm Developments Ltd v Secretary of State for Communities and Local Government* [2009] EWHC 220 Admin; J. Lowther, "Seeing the Wood for the Trees: some clarification on tree preservation orders" (2009) 21 E.L.M. 22.

[198] See section 6.3, above.

[199] TCPSA 1997 s.164; TCPA 1990 s.202.

[200] TCPSA 1997 s.160(1); TCPA 1990 s.198(1).

[201] Planning etc. (Scotland) Act 2006 s.28(2), amending TPSA 1997 s.160(1)–(1A).

[202] 1975 Regulations, First Schedule to Model Order; 1999 Regulations, Schedule 1 to Model Order.

[203] *Brown v Michael B. Cooper Ltd*, 1990 S.C.C.R. 675.

[204] It should be remembered that in any case a TPO will only protect trees, not any of the other vegetation which is vital to the ecological and amenity value of woodland.

[205] *Palm Developments Ltd v Secretary of State for Communities and Local Government* [2009] EWHC 220 Admin.

[206] See also *R. (Plimsoll Shaw Brewer) v Three Rivers District Council* [2007] EWHC 1290 Admin, where a land-owner was content with an order applying to specific mature trees but opposed to a "woodland order" which would affect grazing in an area where there had been some natural regeneration of trees but which it was argued (unsuccessfully) could not be regarded as woodland.

[207] This requirement can be waived

[208] 1975 Regulations regs 5–10; 1999 Regulations reg.3.

modifications),[209] and if confirmed, the same parties must be notified,[210] and the confirmed order advertised and deposited for public inspection.[211] In Scotland the order must be recorded in the Register of Sasines or Land Register of Scotland[212]; in England and Wales the order is registrable as a local land charge.[213] It is only when an order has been confirmed that it takes effect, unless the authority directs that it should take effect immediately without confirmation.[214] Such provisional orders lapse after the passage of six months unless they are confirmed. All orders may subsequently be revoked or modified.[215]

The precise extent and effect of the order will depend on its terms, but **6.5.9** essentially a TPO renders it a criminal offence for any person to cut down, uproot, fell, lop, or wilfully damage or destroy the protected trees without the consent of the planning authority. Such consent is applied for in broadly the same way as an application for planning permission, and consent may be given subject to conditions.[216] If the applicant is aggrieved by a refusal of consent or the conditions imposed, there is a right of appeal to the Minister.[217] There is, however, no right of appeal against the making of the order itself. In relation to woodland, it is stated that consent shall be given so far as it accords with the principles of good forestry, except where in the planning authority's opinion refusal is necessary in the interest of amenity in order to maintain the special character of the woodland or the woodland character of the area.[218]

If consent is refused, or granted subject to conditions, there is generally a **6.5.10** right to compensation for any loss or damage suffered in consequence of such refusal, an issue where the 1999 Regulations have significantly changed the law in England and Wales for orders made after that date. Under the old

---

[209] The modifications cannot change the area specified so as to include additional woodland beyond the boundaries of the original order; *Evans v Waverley Borough Council, The Times*, July 18, 1995.

[210] This notification need not include a copy of the order if it is confirmed without modification; *R. (Brennon) v Bromsgrove District Council* [2003] EWHC 752 Admin; [2003] 2 P. & C.R. 33.

[211] If no copy is available for inspection the order is invalid; *Vale of Glamorgan Borough Council v Palmer and Bowles* (1983) 81 L.G.R. 678.

[212] TCPSA 1997 s.161(2).

[213] Local Land Charges Act 1975 s.1.

[214] TCPSA 1997 s.163; TCPA 1990 s.201; such directions are usual in order to avoid the trees being removed or damaged during the interval between notification and confirmation. Amendments to the Scottish legislation, not yet in force, will change the position so that orders will always take effect when made but expire after six months if not confirmed (Planning etc. (Scotland) Act 2006 s.28(3), amending TCPSA 1997 s.161).

[215] In Scotland a duty on planning authorities to review orders and consider whether they should be varied or revoked will be introduced; Planning etc. (Scotland) Act 2006 s.28(1), amending TCPSA 1997 s.159.

[216] TCPSA 1997 s.160(3) and 1975 Regulations, Model Order paras 3–7; TCPA 1990 s.198(1) and 1999 Regulations reg.9A (England only) and Model Order arts 6–7, as amended for England by Town and Country Planning (Trees) (Amendment) (England) Regulations 2008 (SI 2008/2260) reg.3.

[217] 1975 Regulations, Third Schedule to Model Order paras 33–34; 1999 Regulations regs 11–17 (as amended for England by Town and Country Planning (Trees) (Amendment) (England) Regulations 2008 reg.5 and Town and Country Planning (Trees) (Amendment No.2) (England) Regulations 2008 (SI 2008/3202)) and Model Order art.7 (Wales).

[218] 1975 Regulations, Model Order para.5; 1999 Regulations Sch.2 to Model Order, adapting TCPA 1990 s.70

law, and still the case in Scotland,[219] the most significant form of loss may be a diminution in the value of the land since its potential uses are restricted, as in *Bell v Canterbury City Council*,[220] where the refusal of consent to fell trees meant that the landowner was not able to convert his land from woodland to agricultural use. The court there held that this was a form of loss for which compensation was due, and that it was properly attributable to the refusal of consent, not to the initial making of the order as the council had argued. Other forms of loss may include the unrealisable timber value of the trees, the cost of an expert's report on the possible threat being caused to nearby buildings[221] and the additional costs of felling a tree in accordance with conditions attached to a consent.[222] However, no compensation will be paid if the planning authority has certified that the refusal of consent or the conditions attached to it are in the interests of good forestry or, in the case of trees other than those in woodlands, that the trees have an outstanding or special amenity value.[223] There is a right of appeal to the Minister against the making of such a certificate.

6.5.11   Under the new rules in England, the right to compensation is more limited.[224] There is no right to compensation for loss of development value or any other diminution in the value of the land, for any loss not reasonably foreseeable when consent was refused or granted subject to conditions, or for any loss that was reasonably foreseeable and can be attributed to the claimant's failure to take reasonable steps to mitigate or avert the loss. The costs of an appeal against the decision on consent are no longer recoverable,[225] nor is compensation for any loss under £500. The only time when losses under £500 can be recovered is where consent is refused for felling in the course of forestry operations in a woodland area, and in these circumstances recovery is limited to the amount by which the timber has depreciated in value as a result of the refusal.

6.5.12   It is a criminal offence for any person in contravention of a TPO to cut down, top, lop, uproot, wilfully damage or wilfully destroy[226] a tree, or to cause or permit such action.[227] The offence is committed by the person who

---

[219] TCPSA 1997 ss.165–166 and 1975 Regulations, Model Order paras 9–12.

[220] *Bell v Canterbury City Council* (1988) 56 P. & C.R. 211; see also *Duncan v Epping Forest District Council* [2004] RVR 275.

[221] *Fletcher v Chelmsford Borough Council* [1992] J.P.L. 279; *Duncan v Epping Forest District Council* [2004] RVR 275.

[222] *Deane v Bromley Borough Council* [1992] J.P.L. 279.

[223] 1975 Regulations, Model Order paras 6 and 9; the certificate must be issued at the time that the decision is taken on the application for permission to fell the trees; *Beyers v Secretary of State for the Environment, Transport and the Regions* (2001) 82 P. & C.R. 5.

[224] 1999 Regulations, Model Order art.9.

[225] Under the old rules (and presumably those that still apply in Scotland), appeal costs were recoverable; *Buckle v Holderness Borough Council* (1996) 71 P. & C.R. 428.

[226] For a tree to be "destroyed" it is sufficient that so radical an injury is inflicted on it that any reasonably competent forester would decide that it ought to be felled, taking into account all the circumstances, e.g. a tree by a highway requires greater vigour and stability than one in a field; *Barnet London Borough Council v Eastern Electricity Board* [1973] 1 W.L.R. 430 (where the severing of between a half and one-third of the root systems of trees was held to have destroyed them, even though the trees might have survived for some years).

[227] TCPSA 1997 s.171; 1975 Regulations, Model Order para.2; TCPA 1990 s.210, 1999 Regulations, Model Order art.4

actually carries out the act, and is an offence of strict liability, committed regardless of whether the offender knows of the order and its terms.[228] Employers may be vicariously liable for the acts of their employees,[229] but the occupier will not be liable if a contractor acts in defiance of instructions not to damage a tree.[230] Contractors hired to cut down trees should always check the legal position first as they will still be liable for breaching the TPO even though they have been assured by the occupier that the felling is lawful, although the penalty imposed in such circumstances should reflect the lack of culpability.[231] It has been suggested that there may be problems in ensuring that the person truly at fault in such circumstances can be prosecuted,[232] although there seems to be no reason why recourse should not be had to the general rules of art and part guilt and of incitement, aiding and abetting. In Scotland a power is being introduced to allow the planning authority to enter land and fix a copy of the TPO conspicuously on trees considered to be in imminent danger of being felled, lopped, etc.[233]

The penalties for breaching a TPO can be substantial, with no limit to the **6.5.13** fines following conviction on indictment and in summary proceedings there can be fines of up to £20,000 or twice the value of the trees.[234] In assessing the fine the courts are expressly instructed to take into account any financial benefit which appears likely to accrue to the offender as a result of the offence.[235] Deliberate flouting of a TPO is likely to incur a fairly large penalty,[236] and in *R. v Razzell*[237] a developer who stood to gain £50,000 if he had been able to develop land free of trees was fined £10,000 on each of two charges of breaching a TPO, together with £12,000 in costs. The planning authority can seek to support a TPO with an interdict or injunction,[238] although this is likely to be apt only where there is some aggravating feature such as a deliberate and flagrant flouting of the law.[239]

A number of exceptions are provided where the felling, etc. of a tree will **6.5.14** not be unlawful, despite the existence of a TPO. The wording of some of the main exceptions differs in the two sets of legislation. In Scotland an order cannot prohibit the uprooting, felling or lopping of any tree if such action is urgently necessary in the interests of safety, or is necessary for the prevention or abatement of a nuisance, provided that notice is given to the planning authority as soon as possible after the necessity has arisen.[240]

---

[228] *Maidstone Borough Council v Mortimer* [1980] 3 All E.R. 552, where it was said that the preservation of trees was "of the utmost importance" (Park J. at 554).

[229] *Bath City Council v Pratt (t/a Crescent Investments)* Unreported, see [1988] C.L.Y. 3422.

[230] *Groveside Homes Ltd v Elmbridge Borough Council* (1987) 55 P. & C.R. 214.

[231] *Maidstone Borough Council v Mortimer* [1980] 3 All E.R. 552.

[232] C. Crawford and P. Schofield, "A Weak Branch in the Law of Trees?" [1981] J.P.L. 316.

[233] Planning etc. (Scotland) Act 2006 s.28(4), adding TCPSA 1997 s.161A.

[234] TCPSA 1997 s.171(1); TCPA 1990 s.210(2), amended by Planning and Compensation Act 1991 s.23. A lesser penalty is set for topping and lopping which is not likely to destroy the tree; TCPSA 1997 s.171(4); TCPA 1990 s.210(3).

[235] TCPSA 1997 s.171(3); TCPA 1990 s.210(4).

[236] e.g. a £1,000 fine in *White v Hamilton*, 1987 S.C.C.R. 12.

[237] *R. v Razzell* (1990) 12 Cr. App. R. (S) 142.

[238] TCPSA 1997 s.146; TCPA 1990 s.214A, added by Planning and Compensation Act 1991 s.23.

[239] *Newport Borough Council v Khan (Sabz Ali)* [1990] 1 W.L.R. 1185 (although this was decided before express provision for the use of injunctions was made in the Planning and Compensation Act 1991).

[240] TCPSA 1997 s.160(6)

6.5.15 In England and Wales the equivalent provision exempts actions affecting trees which are dying, dead or have become dangerous, or so far as may be necessary for the prevention or abatement of nuisance.[241] The test of necessity has been held not to be satisfied if the proposed felling would remove the nuisance but other solutions less damaging to the tree itself were available to cure the situation,[242] whereas it has also been held that the wording used means that once a tree has "become dangerous", any felling or lopping is exempt, even though it does nothing to remove or reduce the danger.[243] Whether a tree is dangerous is a matter of fact, the onus of proving which lies on the person claiming the exception,[244] and a tree may be dangerous as a result of its size and location (e.g. by damaging a building's foundations) even though it is perfectly healthy and safe in itself.[245] In one case it has been said that a developer cannot lawfully fell the tree as one which has become dangerous when it was his own actions as part of the continuing development which made it dangerous, nor can he argue that a tree is a nuisance when he owns and occupies the land on which the nuisance is said to occur.[246]

6.5.16 Other exceptions apply in both jurisdictions. Felling required by any Act of Parliament is exempt,[247] as is felling by or on behalf of the Forestry Commission on land that it manages or in accordance with a plan of operations or working plan approved by the Commission.[248] Felling immediately required for a development which has been authorised by a grant of planning permission is exempt, as is felling which is necessary in order to carry out works on or for the safety of operational land held by a range of statutory undertakers and equivalents, or necessary for the safety of air navigation.[249] In England and Wales, further exceptions apply to fruit trees cultivated for fruit production or in an orchard or garden[250] and in some circumstances where the trees are interfering with the functions of water and drainage authorities in relation to the maintenance, improvement or construction of water courses or drainage works. Express consent under the TPO may not be required for felling authorised by a felling licence from the Forestry Commission[251] or authorised for opencast coal works.[252]

6.5.17 In addition to the penalty, steps can be taken to ensure the replacement of

---

[241] TCPA 1990 s.198(6).

[242] *Perrin v Northampton Borough Council* [2007] EWCA Civ 1353; [2008] Env. L.R. 17; J. Findlay, R. Kohli and C. Ricciardello, "When does a Tree Preservation Order protect?" [2008] J.P.L. 615.

[243] *Smith v Oliver* [1989] 2 P.L.R. 1.

[244] *R. v Alath Construction Ltd* [1990] 1 W.L.R. 1255.

[245] *Smith v Oliver* [1989] 2 P.L.R. 1.

[246] *Bath City Council v Pratt (t/a Crescent Investments)* Unreported, see [1988] C.L.Y. 3422; on the issue of whether a nuisance must be an "actionable nuisance" before the exemption can apply see *Perrin v Northampton Borough Council* [2007] EWCA Civ 1353; [2008] Env. L.R. 17.

[247] TCPSA 1997 s.160(6); TCPA 1990 s.198(6).

[248] TCPSA 1997 s.162; TCPA 1990 s.200, both as substituted by Planning and Compulsory Purchase Act 2004 s.95 and s.85.

[249] 1975 Regulations, Second Schedule to Model Order, as amended by the Electricity Act 1989 (Consequential Modifications of Subordinate Legislation) Order 1990 (SI 1990/526); 1999 Regulations, Model Order art.5.

[250] Whether fruit trees meet this test is a matter of fact; *R. v Clearbrook Group Plc* [2001] EWCA Crim 1654; [2002] J.P.L. 567.

[251] See paras 6.5.21–6.5.24, below.

[252] TCPSA 1997 s.160(7); TCPA 1990 s.198(7).

the trees. The replacement provisions apply if a tree is unlawfully removed, uprooted or destroyed in contravention of a TPO, or (except in relation to woodland) is removed, uprooted or destroyed or dies at a time when its removal, etc. is lawful only in the interest of safety. In such circumstances there is a duty on the owner of the land to plant another tree of appropriate size and species at the same place as soon as he reasonably can, or in the case of trees in woodland, to replace the trees by planting the same number of trees on or near the affected land, or on other land as agreed with the planning authority.[253] It is made clear that this obligation rests with the owner of the land for the time being, but the planning authority can waive the replanting requirement. The relevant TPO applies to any replacement trees as it applied to the original ones. In Scotland, a replanting or replacement condition can also be imposed when the authority gives consent for trees to be felled, and must be imposed in relation to any felling of woodland (other than silvicultural thinning) unless the consent was for development which has been granted planning permission or the Minister approves the planning authority's waiver of this requirement.[254] In England and Wales replanting directions can be made following consent for felling in woodland areas in the course of forestry operations.[255]

A replanting requirement (whether following a breach of an order or **6.5.18** imposed as a condition to felling consent) can be enforced by the planning authority, in Scotland within two years of becoming aware of the failure to comply,[256] in England and Wales within four years of the date of the alleged failure.[257] A notice requiring compliance and specifying the necessary steps is served on the landowner, who has a right of appeal to the Minister on the grounds that he has complied with the requirement, that the requirement is not applicable or should be dispensed with, that the specified timescale or species for the replacement are unreasonable, that the planting is not required in the interest of amenity or would be contrary to good forestry practice, or that the place specified is unsuitable for the purpose.[258] If the notice is not complied with, the authority has the power to enter the land and carry out the required steps itself, the costs being recoverable from the landowner who has in turn a right to recover from the person responsible for the removal of the original trees.[259]

In order to assist in the operation of all of the provisions relating to TPOs, **6.5.19** the planning authority enjoys a power of entry to land in order to ascertain whether its powers should be exercised, whether any order is being complied with and in order to take any necessary enforcement action. In the absence of co-operation, warrants can be obtained to ensure that the powers can be

---

[253] TCPSA 1997 s.167; TCPA 1990 s.206.

[254] 1975 Regulations, Model Order paras 5 and 7.

[255] 1999 Regulations, Model Order art.8.

[256] TCPSA 1997 s.168. The provision that the original TPO applies to replacement trees is to be extended to trees planted as a result of this power as well as those under s.167; PSA 2006 s.28(5) adding TCPSA 1997 s.168(3A).

[257] TCPA 1990 s.207, amended by Planning and Compensation Act 1991 s.23.

[258] TCPSA 1997 s.169; TCPA 1990 s.208, amended by Planning and Compensation Act 1991 s.23.

[259] TCPSA 1997 s.170; TCPA 1990 s.209, amended by Planning and Compensation Act 1991 s.23.

exercised, and wilful obstruction of anyone exercising the powers is a criminal offence.[260]

6.5.20   The Planning Act 2008 makes new provisions for TPOs for England and Wales,[261] but does so by conferring wide powers to make regulations on this issue rather than setting out the details of the law itself. When the new rules are made, existing TPOs will take effect on that basis rather than continuing under the old rules described above.[262]

6.5.21   There is obviously an overlap between the provisions in the planning and in the forestry legislation relating to the felling of trees. The arrangements changed with the ending of Crown immunity (which extended to the Forestry Commission) throughout the planning system and the legislation now simply exempts from the application of TPOs and the rules on conservation areas any land managed by the Commission and felling by others in accordance with approved plans.[263]

6.5.22   Where both a felling licence[264] and consent under a TPO are necessary for the felling of trees, the legal starting point is that the matter should be dealt with under the forestry legislation and no application for consent from the planning authority should be made.[265] If the Forestry Commission refuses a licence, that is the end of the matter. However, the Commission may decide to refer the matter to the planning authority for decision under the Planning Acts, and in any event, if it proposes to grant a licence, then the planning authority must be notified.[266] If the authority objects to the proposed grant of a felling licence and the objections cannot be resolved, the Commission must refer the case to the Minister for final determination and the matter is dealt with under the planning legislation.[267] Only if the matter has been referred in either of these ways will it be determined under the planning legislation; in all other cases the grant or refusal of the felling licence decides the issue.

6.5.23   The practice in such cases is slightly different, as set out in the Forestry Commission's booklet *Tree Felling: Getting Permission*.[268] In Scotland, applications for felling licences relating to trees covered by a TPO are sent with the Commission's comments to the planning authority which then takes the decision. In England and Wales, the position is closer to that envisaged in the statute. It is the Commission, after consulting the planning authority who decides whether to grant the felling licence, but if the planning authority objects the case is referred to the Minister.

6.5.24   At one stage all cases were simply passed over to the planning authorities, but the differing schemes for compensation meant that the legal basis of any refusal of permission to fell could have considerable significance. If the case is dealt with under the forestry legislation, the obligation to pay

[260] TCPSA 1997 ss.176–178; TCPA 1990 ss.214B–214D, added by Planning and Compensation Act 1991 s.23.

[261] TCPA 1990 ss.202A–202G, added by Planning Act 2008 s.192 but not yet in force.

[262] Planning Act 2008 s.193.

[263] TCPSA 1997 s.162; TCPA 1990 s.200, both as substituted by Planning and Compulsory Purchase Act 2004 s.95 and s.85; see para.6.5.4, above in relation to conservation areas.

[264] See paras 6.4.11–6.4.17, above.

[265] Forestry Act 1967 s.15(5).

[266] Forestry Act 1967 s.15(1).

[267] Forestry Act 1967 s.15(2).

[268] *Tree Felling: Getting Permission* (Forestry Commission, 2007).

compensation rests with the Forestry Commission, but the sum is limited to the loss (if any) in the value of the trees as timber.[269] On the other hand, if the matter is dealt with by the refusal of consent under the tree preservation provisions, it is the planning authority which is responsible, and the measure of compensation was, and remains for Scotland and older orders, all of the loss suffered in consequence of the refusal.[270] Following *Bell v Canterbury City Council*[271] it was realised that dealing with all cases under the planning system might result in planning authorities being liable to pay very large sums in compensation for the loss of development value, or being influenced to grant consent reluctantly in order to avoid such payments. The practice was therefore changed so that more responsibility was taken by the Forestry Commission.[272]

Miscellaneous

Trees also feature in other legislation which provides means of ensuring that **6.5.25** trees do not interfere with other activities. Thus trees or shrubs which cause a danger or obstruction to road-users or obstruct their view, a public lamp or a traffic sign (or additionally in Scotland increase the likelihood of a road being obstructed by drifting snow) may be removed by the roads or high-ways authority, initially by requiring action from the occupier, but with the possibility of direct action.[273] On the other hand, the roads legislation also grants express powers to plant trees.[274] Similarly action can be taken against trees which are overhanging a street in such a way as to obstruct any electronic communications apparatus used as part of an operator's net-work,[275] or trees that interfere with electrical lines or plant or pose a danger in connection with these.[276] Trees in danger of falling on a railway so as to obstruct traffic may be removed on the authority of the local magistrates,[277] and an even more formal procedure allows the Minister to make for the purpose of securing the safe and efficient use of land for civil aviation an order restricting the height of any trees in the area or requiring the pruning or felling of any trees.[278]

---

[269] See para.6.4.14, above.
[270] See paras 6.5.10–6.5.11, above.
[271] *Bell v Canterbury City Council* (1988) 56 P. & C.R. 211; see para.6.5.10, above.
[272] See [1988] J.P.L. 531.
[273] Roads (Scotland) Act 1984 s.91 (see also s.92); Highways Act 1980 ss.79 and 154.
[274] Roads (Scotland) Act 1984 ss.50–52; Highways Act 1980 ss.141–142 and 282.
[275] Telecommunications Act 1984 Sch.2 para.19.
[276] Electricity Act 1989 Sch.4 para.9.
[277] Regulation of Railways Act 1868 s.24.
[278] Civil Aviation Act 1982 s.46.

7. EUROPEAN AND INTERNATIONAL ASPECTS

7.1.1 Nature conservation law must obviously be tailored to meet the needs of each particular country—there is little point in a law protecting wild giraffes in Britain—but it should also take account of the fact that no ecosystem is wholly isolated. As far as natural connections are concerned, many birds, marine creatures and, in the case of continental states, land creatures are merely visitors to any particular country, living in or passing through several national jurisdictions as their annual or life cycles progress. Species in one country may depend on water or other resources flowing from the territory of another, and the viability of many populations may depend on contacts with individuals on the other side of international frontiers.

7.1.2   When human activities are also considered, the potential for international repercussions becomes even greater. Non-native species introduced, deliberately or accidentally, by man may threaten the native flora and fauna, as predators or as competitors for the same limited resources. Pests and diseases can be spread across the world and wreak havoc with populations never previously exposed to such threats. Human exploitation of animals can reach across the globe so that plants and animals in one country are destroyed in order to meet a demand in another country thousands of miles away. For all of these reasons, it is essential that nature conservation law should not only look to what is happening in the national environment, but also consider the issue on an international scale. The challenges are all the more pressing as a result of increasing international trade and travel and the impact of climate change, which may alter the climatic conditions that have previously restricted the spread of many species, especially those arriving in Britain from warmer areas.

7.1.3   In Britain, the law addresses these issues in several ways. First, there are national laws regulating the introduction of non-native species to the natural environment. Secondly, commerce in wild plants and animals is controlled by measures at the national, European and international levels. Thirdly, the European Community has taken steps to protect natural habitats and wildlife throughout the Community. Fourthly, there is a growing series of international agreements under which states throughout the world have agreed to take steps to further the interests of nature conservation. Each of these must be considered.

NON-NATIVE SPECIES AND REINTRODUCTIONS

7.2.1 Throughout history, as humans have travelled from one land to another, they have taken with them plants and animals to establish in their new home, in order to provide food or other resources, either as a commercial enterprise or merely for pleasure. In countries such as New Zealand the capacity of introductions to devastate the indigenous wildlife can be clearly seen as the introductions and their effects have been recorded over a comparatively short period. In a country such as Britain, with a long history of settlers from beyond these shores, it can be almost impossible to determine whether some species which are firmly established here are truly indigenous or are rather introductions of long standing, and many species generally regarded as part of the natural scene are in fact introductions within historical times, e.g. the rabbit. Other species such as the mink[1] and Japanese knotweed[2] have made an impact in much more recent times.

Some introductions into the wild have been deliberate, but in other cases **7.2.2** plants and animals have escaped from the gardens, parks or farms where they were being tended and have been able to establish themselves away from human care. In recent years, major problems have been discovered in aquatic environments as a result of organisms travelling the globe in ballast water, taken on board (often at larval stage) off one continent and discharged off another.[3] Many introductions have been beneficial to humans and caused little interference to the indigenous flora and fauna, but others have had serious and undesirable consequences.[4]

The introduction of new animal species[5] is controlled indirectly by some **7.2.3** of the import restrictions which extend to cover the keeping and release of the affected species,[6] but more directly by section 14 of the Wildlife and Countryside Act 1981, which has been extended for Scotland in two ways. Under the original provision, as still applies in England and Wales, it is an offence to release or to allow to escape into the wild any animal which is not ordinarily resident in or is not a regular visitor to Great Britain in a wild state.[7] In order to prevent the reinforcement of alien species which have managed to establish a foothold here as a result of past releases and escapes (and may thus qualify as being "ordinarily resident in a wild state") the prohibition is extended to cover the specific species listed in Schedule 9, which are not native but may already be found in the wild somewhere in Great Britain.[8] This list ranges from well-known species which are now widespread (such as the grey squirrel) to the more exotic (such as the ring-necked parakeet and the red-necked wallaby) and unloved (such as New Zealand flatworms). As far as plants are concerned, it is an offence to plant or otherwise cause to grow in the wild any of the species of plant listed in Part II of Schedule 9 to the 1981 Act.[9] In Scotland the offences are extended

---

[1] Mink pose a significant threat to ground-nesting birds and other species and between 2001 and 2006 £1.65 million was spent on the Hebridean Mink Project to eradicate mink in North and South Uist and Benbecula; see *http://www.snh.org.uk/scottish/wisles/intro.asp* [Accessed May 15, 2009].

[2] J. Bailey and A. Connolly, "Prize-winners to Pariahs – A History of Japanese Knotweed *s.l.* (Polygonaceae) in the British Isles" *Watsonia* 23: 93 (2000).

[3] To deal with this problem the International Convention for the Control and Management of Ships' Ballast Water and Sediments was agreed in 2004 under the auspices of the International Maritime Organisation but as yet it is well short of the number of ratifications necessary for it to enter into force; see *http://www.imo.org/conventions/mainframe.asp?topic_id=867* [Accessed May 15, 2009].

[4] See generally, C. Shine, N. Williams and L. Gündling, *A Guide to Designing Legal and Institutional Frameworks on Alien Invasive Species* (IUCN—Environmental Law Centre: Environmental Policy and Law Paper No.40) (2000).

[5] The equivalent provisions for plants are discussed at para.6.2.11, above.

[6] See paras 7.3.1–7.3.5, below.

[7] WCA 1981 s.14(1)(a).

[8] WCA 1981 s.14(1)(b) and Sch. 9 Pt I; see Appendix A.

[9] WCA 1981 s.14(2) and Sch.9 Pt II, amended by NCSA 2004 Sch.6 para.12; see para.6.2.11, above and Appendix A.

to apply to hybrids as well as pure-bred specimens of the species covered and in relation to the species listed in Schedule 9 and their hybrids a further offence has been created of releasing them or allowing their escape from captivity.[10]

7.2.4   In relation to these charges it is a defence for the accused to prove that all reasonable steps were taken and that all due diligence was used in order to avoid committing the offence.[11] Prior notice must be given to the prosecution if this defence involves an allegation that the release or escape was due to the act or omission of another person.[12] In England and Wales wildlife inspectors can exercise their powers in relation to these offences,[13] while in Scotland, those investigating whether an offence has been committed and authorised by the Scottish Ministers enjoy a power of entry to land,[14] and obstruction of those involved in the exercise of this power is itself a criminal offence.[15]

7.2.5   Licences to authorise releases of non-native species may be granted by the Minister,[16] and in England and Wales a general licence permits the release of wild-bred barn owls and sea eagles that have recovered after being tended while disabled.[17] The willingness to grant licences for the release of grey squirrels that have been trapped has generated some controversy.[18]

7.2.6   To support these main provisions supplementary measures have been introduced. The sale and activities related to sale, including advertising and possession for sale, of non-native species specified in a ministerial order is an offence. In England and Wales the species that can be specified are any animal or plant covered by the above provisions as they apply in those jurisdictions and the defence of due diligence applies.[19] In Scotland as well as hybrids being included in any specification, the Minister can additionally specify any plant which does not ordinarily grow in Great Britain in a wild state.[20] In both jurisdictions the Minister may issue or approve guidance[21] in relation to non-native species. Breach of the guidance will not by itself give rise to criminal or civil liability but may be taken into account by any court, e.g. in establishing whether or not due diligence was exercised.[22] The EC Birds Directive also requires that any introductions of non-native birds should not be prejudicial to the native flora and fauna[23] and the Habitats

---

[10] WCA 1981 s.14(1) and (1A), as amended by NCSA 2004 Sch.6 para.12.

[11] WCA 1981 s.14(3).

[12] WCA 1981 s.14(4).

[13] WCA 1981 s.18A–18F, as added by NERCA 2006 Sch.5 para.1; see para.3.2.8, above.

[14] WCA 1981 s.14(5).

[15] WCA 1981 s.14(6).

[16] WCA 1981 s.16(4) and (9).

[17] Licence WML Gen-L20 (12/08).

[18] See *The Times*, February 16, 2008. This contrasts with the robust measures against grey squirrels in the Saving Scotland's Red Squirrels project launched in early 2009.

[19] WCA 1981 s.14ZA, added by NERCA 2006 s.50.

[20] WCA 1981 s.14A, added by NCSA 2004 Sch.6 para.13.

[21] A "code of practice" in England and Wales.

[22] WCA 1981 s.14B, added by NCSA 2004 Sch.6 para.13; WCA 1981 s.14ZB, added by NERCA 2006 s.50.

[23] Directive 79/409/EEC art.11; see para.7.4.7, below.

and Species Directive requires that any deliberate introductions are regulated so as not to prejudice natural habitats and wild flora and fauna.[24]

At sea around the UK,[25] it is an offence deliberately to introduce any live **7.2.7** animal or plant of a kind whose natural range does not include these waters. The offence can be committed by those on offshore marine installations and in or on board a ship, but in the latter case no offence is committed in relation to the discharge of ballast water when necessary for safety reasons and reasonable care is taken to avoid or minimise the risk of prejudice to natural habitats and native species.[26] The Minister can grant licences authorising such introductions, provided that he is satisfied that the action authorised will not prejudice natural habitats within their natural range or wild native fauna and flora, and general advice has been provided by the Joint Nature Conservation Committee.[27] Within territorial waters around England and Wales,[28] a broadly similar offence and licensing power have been created,[29] whereas in Scotland the view is that the matter is adequately covered by the provisions of section 14 of the Wildlife and Countryside Act 1981.[30]

The impact of introduced species on more local biodiversity is also **7.2.8** gaining increasing attention. Ecosystems can be severely affected by the introduction of species that may occur naturally in the area but are absent from particular locations, most notably in the case of islands and lochs. The impact of the introduction of hedgehogs on ground-nesting birds in the Uists and the controversy over their removal is a clear example of this,[31] as is the impact of introducing fish to lochs where their absence has previously allowed other, rarer species to flourish, e.g. the damage to powan in Loch Lomond following the release of ruffe used as live bait by fishermen. It is in relation to fish that the first legal controls have been imposed. In Scotland it is an offence to introduce any live fish or spawn to inland waters (other than a fish farm) without the written consent of the district salmon fishery board (for salmon) or the Minister.[32] At EC level a Regulation imposing controls on the introduction of alien species for aquaculture extends to those which are locally absent from an area within their natural distribution range.[33] Proposals to prohibit the release on offshore islands of many species of

---

[24] Directive 92/43/EEC art.22; see para.7.2.12, below. The Convention on Biological Diversity also requires states to "prevent the introduction of, control or eradicate those alien species which threaten ecosystems, habitats or species" (art.8(h)); see para.7.5.23, below.

[25] Technically the areas designated under the Continental Shelf Act 1964 s.1(7), which includes waters up to 200 nautical miles or the agreed boundaries with neighbouring states.

[26] Offshore Marine Conservation (Natural Habitats, etc.) Regulations 2007 (SI 2007/1842) reg.48.

[27] Offshore Marine Conservation (Natural Habitats, etc.) Regulations 2007 reg.49(11)–(13).

[28] Although the general provisions in WCA 1981 s.14 will apply within this area.

[29] CNHR 1994 regs 37C–37E, as added by CNHAR 2007 reg.5(12).

[30] Letter to author from Scottish Government Marine Directorate.

[31] See the Uist Wader Project and Uist Hedgehog Rescue web-pages at *http://www.snh.org.uk/scottish/wisles/waders* and *http://www.uhr.org.uk* [Both Accessed May 15, 2009].

[32] Salmon and Freshwater Fisheries (Consolidation) (Scotland) Act 2003 s.33A, added by Aquaculture and Fisheries (Scotland) Act 2007 s.35; this is another offence where conviction is possible on the evidence of a single witness (s.33A(6); see para.3.2.11, above).

[33] Reg. (EC) 708/2007, supplemented by Reg. (EC) 535/2008.

mammals that are native but locally absent were included in a Scottish consultation paper late in 2006.[34]

7.2.9   The adequacy of these measures has been questioned as an increasing number of species, especially aquatic ones, are found in British territory, and steps are being taken towards a more coherent effort to tackle the issue and towards the law adopting a more precautionary approach. *The Invasive Non-Native Species Framework Strategy for Great Britain* was published in 2008 and concluded that "there is still a need to create a better sense of cohesion across existing powers and a need for further improvements".[35]

7.2.10   The restrictions on the import of animals and plants provide a further means of preventing damaging releases. In addition to the general provisions, the import of some animals is further restricted by measures specifically designed to prevent the introduction of harmful pests. The Destructive Imported Animals Act 1932[36] and the orders made under it impose controls on the importation and keeping of a number of species: musk rats,[37] grey squirrels,[38] non-indigenous rabbits,[39] mink[40] and coypus.[41] The ban on fur farming removes a potential source of further escapes[42] and the legislation on zoos[43] and on keeping dangerous wild animals[44] also serves to ensure that alien species are unlikely to escape to the wild.

---

[34] *Consultation on proposals to amend Schedule 9 and the use of an order made under Section 14A of the Wildlife and Countryside Act 1981* (SEERAD, Nov. 2006).

[35] *The Invasive Non-Native Species Framework Strategy for Great Britain* (Welsh Assembly Government, Scottish Government and DEFRA, 2008), p.23. Proposals for substantial changes in the law in Scotland are contained in the consultation paper on a Wildlife and Natural Environment Bill published in June 2009.

[36] As amended to exclude imports from within the European Community (as part of the achievement of the Single Market) by the Destructive Imported Animals Act 1932 (Amendment) Regulations 1992 (SI 1992/3302).

[37] Musk Rats (Prohibition of Importation and Keeping) Order 1933 (S.R. & O. 1933 No.106).

[38] Grey Squirrels (Prohibition of Importation and Keeping) Order 1937 (S.R. & O. 1937 No.478).

[39] Non-indigenous Rabbits (Prohibition of Importation and Keeping) Order 1954 (SI 1954/927); strictly speaking, it is unlikely that any rabbits in this country are truly indigenous, and the order refers to rabbits "other than those of the species Oryctolagus Cuniculus [sic.] (commonly known as the European rabbit)."

[40] Mink (Keeping) Regulations 1975 (SI 1975/2223); Mink Keeping (Scotland) Order 2003 (SSI 2003/528); Mink Keeping (Prohibition) (England) Order 2004 (SI 2004/100). The relevant order in Wales (Mink (Keeping) (Wales) Order 2000 (SI 2000/3340)) expired at the end of 2003 and has not been replaced.

[41] Coypus (Prohibition on Keeping) Order 1987 (SI 1987/2195); the populations that had established themselves in the wild in England have now been eradicated.

[42] Fur Farming (Prohibition) Act 2000; Fur Farming (Prohibition) (Scotland) Act 2002.

[43] Zoo Licensing Act 1981; a licence will only be granted on conditions that include preventing the escape of animals (ss.1A(d) and 5(2A); added by Zoo Licensing Act 1981 (Amendment) (England and Wales) Regulations 2002 (SI 2002/3080) regs 5 and 8 and Zoo Licensing Act 1981 (Amendment) (Scotland) Regulations 2003 (SSI 2003/74) regs 5 and 8). See also art.3 of Directive 1999/22/EC, requiring states to take measures to prevent animals escaping from zoos and presenting possible ecological threats to indigenous species.

[44] Dangerous Wild Animals Act 1976; see, e.g. s.1(3) which states that a licence will only be granted if the animal is held in accommodation which secures that it will not escape. The Schedule, which lists the animals subject to controls, has been substituted and amended over the years, most recently by the Dangerous Wild Animals Act 1976 (Modification) (No.2) Order 2007 (SI 2007/2465) and the Dangerous Wild Animals Act 1976 (Modification) (Scotland) Order 2008 (SSI 2008/302).

Reintroductions

The legal controls on non-native species also control schemes to reintroduce **7.2.11**
species to parts of their natural range from which they have disappeared,
with the release of individuals being authorised by licences under the provisions discussed above. Such schemes have been successful in some cases,
e.g. the sea eagle, but remain very controversial in others, as shown by the
lengthy debates over the introduction of beavers to Scotland,[45] with much
more heated discussions to be expected if serious plans are put forward for
species such as the lynx or wolf.

A specific legal obligation in relation to reintroductions appears in the **7.2.12**
Habitats and Species Directive where states are obliged to study the desirability of re-introducing the species listed in Annex IV, where this will
contribute to re-establishing the species at a favourable conservation status
and provided that the public concerned are properly consulted before any
reintroduction takes place.[46] This provision is implemented for offshore
areas by the Offshore Marine Conservation (Natural Habitats, etc.) Regulations 2007.[47] The Birds Directive more directly requires the re-establishment of destroyed biotopes and of habitats[48] and less directly the
obligation to "adapt the population" of bird species to "a level which corresponds ... to ecological, scientific and cultural requirements" would seem
to call for the reintroduction of species to areas where the population that
might be supported is missing.[49] Similarly the ecological criteria that must be
fulfilled to meet the obligation to restore waters to good water status mean
that the Water Framework Directive requires states to restore habitats
which in some cases will require the reintroduction of species that have
locally disappeared.[50]

Plans for reintroductions can create interesting legal problems when dif- **7.2.13**
ferent areas of law converge, as faced by the ambitious plans for restoring
the flora and fauna of a large area of "wilderness" at Alladale in Sutherland.[51] Without approval for releasing predators such as the wolf and the
lynx into the wild, the area must be securely fenced, but this denies public
access to large areas of countryside, contrary to the spirit (at least) of the
access rights enshrined in the Land Reform (Scotland) Act 2003. At the
same time, the enclosed area must be regarded as a zoo where there is a
conflict between the required participation in conservation measures, which
include reintroductions into the wild,[52] and the Standards of Modern Zoo
Practice which restrict the feeding of live vertebrate prey and require that
animals that may interact in an excessively stressful way must not be kept
together, [53] which run against the creation of a natural predator-prey relationship within even very extensive enclosures.

---

[45] See *http://www.scottishbeavers.org.uk/* [Accessed June 22, 2009].
[46] Directive 92/43/EEC art.22.
[47] SI 2007/1842 reg.69.
[48] Directive 79/409/EEC art.3.
[49] Directive 79/409/EEC art.2.
[50] Directive 2000/60/EC art.4 and Annex V(1.2).
[51] See *http://www.alladale.com/wilderness-reserve/* [Accessed May 15, 2009].
[52] Zoo Licensing Act 1981 s.1A; see para.7.2.10, above.
[53] Standards 1.6 and 5.4; available at *http://www.defra.gov.uk/wildlife-countryside/protection/zoo/standards.htm* [Accessed May 15, 2009].

TRADE

7.3.1 The import and export of animals and plants is heavily regulated, primarily in order to ensure that no pests or diseases are allowed to enter the country. British law in this area has been strict, in order to continue the natural advantage enjoyed by an island nation, as most publicly shown by the anti-rabies measures that in the past prevented the landing of dogs without a long quarantine period.[54] The law has become more complex following Britain's membership of the European Community, as the need to ensure the free movement of goods and to establish the Single Market[55] has required both common standards and the establishment of schemes for mutual recognition of licences, certificates, etc.[56] Most of the law is primarily directed at domesticated animals and cultivated plants,[57] and will not be discussed in detail here, although wild species will also be covered by its terms. However, there are important measures designed specifically to protect wild species from over-exploitation, and these will be looked at more thoroughly.

7.3.2 As far as animals are concerned, the main provisions affecting their import and export rest on the Animal Health Act 1981 and its predecessors. Under section 10 of the 1981 Act, the agriculture ministers may make orders as they think fit to prevent the introduction to or spread within Britain of disease through the import of animals, carcases, eggs, or any other animate or inanimate thing by which disease can be transmitted.[58] For the purpose of this provision, "animal" and "disease" are not restricted in their definition as they are for many other aspects of the Act, so that although directed at domesticated species, any import of wild animals is likely also to be affected.[59] Under this power, and equivalent powers under earlier legislation, a large volume of delegated legislation has been made. The orders detail the various licences, certificates, quarantine and other arrangements required for the lawful import of animals from abroad.

7.3.3 Exports are also subject to restrictions in order to prevent the spread of diseases to other members of the European Community. The relevant enabling provision is section 11 of the Animal Health Act 1981,[60] and again

---

[54] Now subject to the Community-wide pet travel scheme. The UK's specific rules on cats, dogs and ferrets are continuing in force until June 2010 pending the finalisation of the Community-wide arrangements: Regulations (EC) 998/2003 and 454/2008; Non Commercial Movement of Pet Animals (England) Regulations 2004 (SI 2004/2363); Pet Travel Scheme (Scotland) Order 2003 (SSI 2003/229); Rabies (Importation of Dogs, Cats and Other Mammals (Amendment) Wales) Order 2002 (SI 2002/882). The UK rules extend to precautions against ticks and tapeworm.

[55] The main EC measures are Directives 90/425/EEC and 91/496/EEC (as amended).

[56] These extend to special rules on the movement of circus animals: Reg. (EC) No.1739/2005.

[57] A "plant passport" scheme operates: Plant Health (England) Order 2005 (SI 2005/2530); Plant Health (Scotland) Order 2005 (SI 2005/613); Plant Health (Wales) Order 2006 (SI 2006/1643).

[58] Animal Health Act 1981 s.10(1). Under s.10A (added by Animal Health Act 2002) there is a duty in England and Wales annually to review the position and the effectiveness of orders made under s.10.

[59] Animal Health Act 1981 s.10(4); e.g. the Importation of Birds, Poultry and Hatching Eggs Order 1979 (SI 1979/1702) expressly defines "poultry" as meaning live birds of every species (art.2).

[60] Extended by Animal Health and Welfare Act 1984 s.3.

there is delegated legislation making provision for licences, certificates, etc. and compliance with EC rules.

Whilst fish and shellfish can be dealt with under the Animal Health Act **7.3.4** 1981,[61] more specific provision has also been made. Under the Import of Live Fish (Scotland) Act 1978 and the Import of Live Fish (England and Wales) Act 1980,[62] the Minister can make orders prohibiting or requiring a licence for the import, keeping or release of live fish or live eggs of fish of species which are not native and which it is thought might compete with, displace, prey on or harm the habitat of any freshwater fish, shellfish or salmon.[63] There are the usual provisions creating offences, granting powers of search, etc. to give effect to the basic provision. The Diseases of Fish Act 1937 likewise confers powers to regulate imports.[64]

Plant health within Great Britain is similarly protected by restrictions on **7.3.5** imports. Again the main statute is an enabling Act, the Plant Health Act 1967, under which some general and other more specific measures have been introduced, with the usual requirements for licences, etc.[65]

Endangered Species

Of greater significance for nature conservation are the measures designed to **7.3.6** restrict trade in endangered species. Since ancient times the ownership of wild animals, their skins, plumage or other products, has frequently been strongly desired in some quarters, primarily as a luxury item or as a component in perfumes or medicinal products. Inevitably considerable efforts have been made to meet this demand, and since at least Roman times, it has been apparent that the efforts of hunters supplying this market can devastate and ultimately destroy populations of certain animals. Tragically, the value of the animal may increase as it becomes rarer, encouraging even greater efforts on the part of hunters and collectors, and increasing the risk that such exploitation will eventually lead to extinction. The continuing battles against elephant and rhinoceros poachers in parts of Africa and the threat which they pose to the survival of the species demonstrate both the effects of such exploitation and the strength of the incentive to continue the hunting even once a species becomes rare.

A similar fate can befall species of plant. At present orchids, cacti and **7.3.7** Mediterranean bulbs are probably most at risk, but in the past the fashion was for other species, particularly ferns, and great damage was done to many populations and whole species. In the case of both plants and animals the effect of the trade is exacerbated by the fact that the demand is usually in

---

[61] See, e.g. the Shellfish and Specified Fish (Third Country Imports) Order 1992 (SI 1992/3301).

[62] A rare but most welcome example of non-Scottish legislation prior to devolution the title of which properly indicated its limited application.

[63] Whereas previously orders were narrowly targeted, e.g. Import of Live Fish (Coho Salmon) (Prohibition) (Scotland) Order 1980 (SI 1980/376), over 50 species are listed in the Prohibition of Keeping or Release of Live Fish (Specified Species) (Scotland) Order 2003 (SSI 2003/560) and its equivalent: Prohibition of Keeping or Release of Live Fish (Specified Species) Order 1998 (SI 1998/2409), as amended by Prohibition of Keeping or Release of Live Fish (Specified Species) (Amendment) (England) Order 2003 (SI 2003/25) and Prohibition of Keeping or Release of Live Fish (Specified Species) (Amendment) (Wales) Order 2003 (SI 2003/416).

[64] e.g. Importation of Live Fish of the Salmon Family Order 1986 (SI 1986/283).

[65] See paras 6.2.12–6.2.13, above.

a part of the world distant from the supply (that, after all, is part of the attraction) and the difficulties of transporting live specimens mean that in order to supply a particular number of individual specimens in good condition, many, many more are collected from the wild and perish en route.

7.3.8   It should be recognised, however, that if properly regulated, trade in a species can actually be beneficial to its survival. The fact that a plant or animal has a commercial value can encourage measures to ensure its survival at a level permitting its long-term and sustainable exploitation. Thus its habitat may be preserved and those with an interest in its lawful trade may endeavour to protect it from accidental harm or destructive poaching. The strength of this argument and its validity in individual circumstances is, however, a point of heated debate among conservationists.

7.3.9   If destructive trade is to be controlled, the law can obviously try to control the hunters and collectors in the countries where the specimens are to be found, but it has also been realised that there is a need to approach the problem from the other end, regulating the market for such goods so as to stifle the demand which fuels the trade. In Great Britain, this approach was first taken at a time when the fashion for colourful feathers in ladies' hats was threatening a number of tropical bird species. With the exceptions of ostrich feathers and eider down, the Importation of Plumage (Prohibition) Act 1921 prohibited the import of any plumage from wild birds unless a special licence had been obtained.[66] More recently, the problem has been tackled on a global scale.

7.3.10   The basis for the current law at a British and European level is the Convention on International Trade in Endangered Species of Wild Fauna and Flora (CITES), concluded in Washington in 1973.[67] Many states around the world have become parties to this treaty which endeavours to regulate international trade by requiring licences to be granted before specimens of plants and animals, or items derived from them, can be imported or exported. In some cases commercial trade is essentially prohibited, in others controlled exploitation remains possible, and the needs of individual countries are taken into account both by the separate treatment of distinct populations of certain species and the potential for a state to use the CITES machinery to further its own conservation plans.

7.3.11   The animals and plants covered by the Convention are divided into three categories.[68] Those listed in Appendix I, e.g. tigers, are those "threatened with extinction which are or may be affected by trade", and trade in these must be permitted only in exceptional circumstances. Appendix II is for species which "may become [threatened with extinction] unless trade in specimens of such species is subject to strict regulation in order to avoid utilisation incompatible with their survival", e.g. all species of southern fur seals. Also covered by Appendix II are species whose listing is necessary to

---

[66] This Act contains many of the features of the modern legislation, most notably the use of a variable Schedule to list the species covered by or excepted from the main rules and the appointment of a specialist body to advise on what should be included in the Schedule.

[67] For a fuller account and references to more detailed works, see P. Birnie, A. Boyle and C. Redgwell, *International Law and the Environment*, 3rd edn (Oxford: OUP, 2009), pp.685–692; see also the CITES Secretariat website at *http://www.cites.org* and the CITES websites of the UK government and the EU at *http://www.defra.gov.uk/animalhealth/CITES/* and *http://ec.europa.eu/environment/cites/reports_en.htm* [All Accessed May 15, 2009].

[68] CITES art.2.

ensure the effectiveness of the controls on the other Appendix II species—this allows for "look-alike" species to be listed, preventing the enforcement of the treaty being undermined by the difficulties of distinguishing between similar species, only some of which are listed. Appendix III is an optional one which allows individual states to invoke the provisions of CITES for particular species which they wish to protect but which have not been listed in the main Appendices; these are protected only in relation to trade with the states which added the species to the list. The listing applies to living and dead specimens and to "any readily recognizable part or derivative thereof".[69]

The contents of the Appendices can be amended at the regular Con- **7.3.12** ferences of the Parties which are a feature of CITES,[70] and many changes have been made since the Convention was first agreed. The meetings attract considerable publicity, e.g. the continuing debates over the status of the African elephant, concerning whether its long-term conservation is best served by a ban on the trade in ivory or the continuation of limited and controlled trade. Geographically separate populations of a species can be treated independently when it comes to listing,[71] so that it is possible for a plant or animal which is severely threatened in one part of its range to be fully protected there whilst allowing limited commercial trade from other parts where there is no risk of extinction.

The basic structure of the CITES provisions is that for species in **7.3.13** Appendix I, any trade requires both an export permit from the supplying state and an import permit from the destination state. Export permits should be granted only where the trade will not be detrimental to the survival of the species, where the specimen has been lawfully obtained and an import permit has been granted by the receiving state, and where there are appropriate facilities to ensure that any living specimen is protected during transit. An import permit should only be granted if the import is for purposes not detrimental to the survival of the species, if there are appropriate facilities to house the specimen once it arrives, and the trade is not for primarily commercial purposes.[72] In essence therefore, there can be no lawful commercial trade in such species and only in exceptional cases can specimens be transferred from one country to another.

For species in Appendix II, it is merely an export permit which is **7.3.14** required, the granting of such permits being subject to the same restrictions as for Appendix I, apart from the requirement for an import permit to have been issued. Imports do not require specific approval, but are subject to the prior presentation of an export permit.[73] For Appendix III, again it is merely an export permit which is required, to be issued if the specimen was lawfully taken and appropriate transit requirements are made.[74]

These essentials of CITES are supported by a number of other provisions **7.3.15** dealing with exemptions,[75] the confiscation and subsequent dealing with

---

[69] CITES art.l(b); *The Times* on December 10, 1996 reported a postgraduate ecology student having to seek a licence in order to take rhinoceros dung into the UK for detailed analysis.

[70] CITES art.15.

[71] CITES art.1(a).

[72] CITES art.3.

[73] CITES art.4.

[74] CITES art.5.

[75] CITES art.7.

specimens unlawfully traded,[76] formalities for permits and certificates,[77] re-exports and the handling of goods in transit through a state,[78] the restriction of the ports, etc. through which such trade can be carried out,[79] and the landing of listed species taken on the high seas.[80] More significantly the treaty requires each party to identify a scientific authority and a management authority within the state which are to have responsibility for advising on and overseeing the operation of the treaty.[81] The treaty also requires that detailed records (open for public inspection) are kept of all trade authorised under CITES and that regular reports are made to the Secretariat.[82] This recording system ensures that the treaty does not become a dead-letter, although the experience has been that even where apparently full returns have been made, the records of imports and exports between countries rarely tally exactly. The reports also serve to demonstrate the scale and complexity of international trade in wild plants and animals.[83]

7.3.16   The vitality of CITES is also maintained by the biennial Conferences of the Parties, at which amendments to the treaty, and in particular the Appendices, are discussed.[84] These meetings are open to international agencies and approved non-governmental bodies, which can participate in discussions but not vote. In this way publicity is guaranteed and states may have to contend with open criticism from conservation bodies which are not affected by the broader considerations of international relations which can mute inter-governmental criticism.

7.3.17   As a result of these measures, CITES has in some ways proved to be a comparatively successful treaty, although there are conflicting assessments of its true impact.[85] Moreover, because it allows both strict conservation and regulated trade it has attracted a large number of parties, both suppliers and recipients of animals, plants and their products. Its provisions apply directly only to trade between parties, but the parties must impose some similar requirements on trade with other states, and the treaty expressly allows the parties to maintain stricter domestic rules on any international or internal trade.[86] Nevertheless, there remains a massive problem of illegal trade in wildlife and wildlife products, a trade that, perhaps in part because of the successes of CITES, can be very profitable. The demand for some products in certain parts of the world continues to pose a very real threat to the survival of some species.

7.3.18   Both the United Kingdom, as a party to CITES, and the European

---

[76] CITES art.8(1)–(4).

[77] CITES art.6.

[78] CITES arts 3(4), 4(5) and 5(4).

[79] CITES art.8(3).

[80] CITES arts 3(5) and 4(6).

[81] CITES art.9.

[82] CITES art.8(6)–(8); the Secretariat was established through the United Nations Environment Programme (CITES art.12).

[83] In the latest EC report, *Convention on International Trade in Endangered Species of Wild Fauna and Flora: EC Annual Report 2005* (2007) there are 370 pages listing the import, export and re-export of specimens involving Member States.

[84] CITES art.11; full details are on the CITES Secretariat website at *http://www.cites.org* [Accessed May 15, 2009].

[85] See Birnie, Boyle and Redgwell, *International Law and the Environment*, 3rd edn (2009), pp.689–692.

[86] CITES arts 10 and 14(1).

Community, not formally a party but accepting its terms,[87] have taken steps to implement its provisions. At the European level, the main provision is Regulation (EC) 338/97 which requires Member States to comply with the provisions of the treaty. The Regulation goes beyond the Convention's provisions by requiring both import and export permits[88] for species listed in Appendices I and II.[89] It also provides for a number of additional species to be treated as if contained in Appendix I of CITES, and for import permits to be required in relation to others.[90] The protected species are listed in the Annexes to the Regulation which are regularly updated in accordance with amendments to the CITES Appendices.[91] This measure is supported by a Regulation laying down standard requirements for the forms, certificates and labels necessary for the operation of the controls.[92]

Information on the scientific and management authorities within each of **7.3.19** the Member States responsible for the operation of CITES and on the ports through which trade is permitted is collected and published at a European level,[93] and the Commission produces an annual report recording all the trade carried out by Member States under the CITES arrangements.[94]

In the United Kingdom,[95] the implementation of CITES has been rather **7.3.20** complex as legislation to give effect to the European Community's adoption of CITES existed alongside the more general Endangered Species (Import and Export) Act 1976, enacted to give effect to the UK's individual accession to CITES. The position has now been simplified, removing the duplication, so that import and export controls are essentially achieved through the EC regulations.[96] These are supported by the Control of Trade

---

[87] The "Gaborone Amendment" to the Convention to allow a "regional economic integration organisation" such as the EC to become a full party was agreed in 1983, but has not yet been ratified by enough states to come into force.

[88] In *R. (Greenpeace Ltd) v Secretary of State for the Environment, Food and Rural Affairs* [2002] EWCA Civ 1036; [2002] 1 W.L.R. 3304 the majority in the Court of Appeal held that in the absence of fraud the national authorities should accept an export permit at face value and not investigate whether its issue was justified, although Laws L.J. dissented strongly, arguing that considerations of ecology and protection of the environment should be given weight in interpreting the relevant statutory provisions.

[89] Only export permits are required for Appendix II species under CITES. On the differences between CITES and the EC Regulation and other aspects of EC implementation and enforcement see *http://ec.europa.eu/environment/cites/home_en.htm* [Accessed May 15, 2009].

[90] Member States can go further by prohibiting in their own territories the commercial use of Annex A species (equivalent to Appendix I) but can do so for Annex B species (equivalent to Appendix II) only if this is shown to be a proportionate measure to achieve the conservation objectives that cannot be achieved by less restrictive means: *Criminal Proceedings against Xavier Tridon* (C-510/99) [2001] E.C.R. I-7777.

[91] A restructured and consolidated version of the Annexes is given in Regulation (EC) 318/ 2008.

[92] Regulation (EC) 865/2006.

[93] See *http://ec.europa.eu/environment/cites/info_en.htm* [Accessed May 15, 2009].

[94] *Convention on International Trade in Endangered Species of Wild Fauna and Flora: EC Annual Report 2005* (2007).

[95] For more details and practical guidance see the UK CITES website at *http://www.ukcites.gov.uk* [Accessed May 15, 2009].

[96] A match between the UK and EC restrictions was achieved by the Endangered Species (Import and Export) Act 1976 (Amendment) Order 1996 (SI 1996/2677), and then the UK restrictions in effect removed by the Endangered Species (Import and Export) Act 1976 (Amendment) Regulations 1996 (SI 1996/2684).

in Endangered Species (Enforcement) Regulations 1997[97] which provide for offences in relation to breaches of the Community Regulations implementing CITES[98] and contain provisions on powers of search and entry to assist in its enforcement. In the operation of the Act, the Department of the Environment, Food and Rural Affairs has been designated as the "Management Authority" required by CITES, with the Joint Nature Conservation Committee serving as the "Scientific Authority" for animals and the Royal Botanic Gardens, Kew for plants.[99] The Control of Trade in Endangered Species (Designation of Ports of Entry) Regulations 1985[100] further assist the enforcement of CITES by designating particular groups of ports and airports as the only ones through which live animals of different categories may be imported.

7.3.21 In addition to the direct controls on imports[101] and exports, it is an offence for anyone to purchase, sell, offer to purchase or sell, possess or transport with a view to sale or use for commercial gain any plant or animal listed in Annex A of the EC Regulation, or unlawfully imported or acquired specimens of species listed in Annex B.[102] Similar offences apply in relation to the further species of animal listed in Schedule 4 or plant in Schedule 5 of the 1976 Act, or anything made of these species, unless the import was prior to the end of October 1981.[103] The offences do not apply to imports authorised by a licence,[104] and it is a defence for the person charged to show that at the time of the offence he had no reason to believe that the item was restricted under these provisions, and that when it first came into his possession he made reasonable enquiries to ascertain whether it was restricted.[105] The requirement for reasonable enquiries will be satisfied if the item was acquired with a signed certificate from the supplier stating that enquiries have been made and that there is no reason to believe that the item was restricted at the time the supplier passed it on.[106] Further provisions in the

---

[97] SI 1997/1372 (known as CoTES), amended by Control of Trade in Endangered Species (Enforcement) (Amendment) Regulations 2005 and 2007 (SI 2005/1674 and SI 2007/2952). These regulations were made under the European Communities Act 1972, not the slightly more restricted delegated powers under the Endangered Species (Import and Export) Act 1976, and by virtue of the Criminal Justice Act 2003 s.307 regulations implementing EC rules on this topic can impose penalties greater than those normally allowed under the 1972 Act.

[98] Regulation (EC) 865/2006; see para.7.3.18, above.

[99] See para.7.3.15, above; the JNCC handled over 20,000 applications for CITES permits in 2007–2008 (JNCC, *Annual Report 2007/2008*, p.14).

[100] SI 1985/1154.

[101] The direct effect of the EC Regulations means that the UK courts can deal with cases even where the entry to the EC was not though the UK itself: *R. v Sissen* [2001] 1 W.L.R. 902.

[102] Control of Trade in Endangered Species (Enforcement) Regulations 1997 (SI 1997/1372) reg.8, as substituted by Control of Trade in Endangered Species (Enforcement) (Amendment) Regulations 2005 (SI 2005/1674) reg.3.

[103] Endangered Species (Import and Export) Act 1976 s.4(2); these Schedules are now restricted to some species that are not covered by the EC's CITES Regulations (Endangered Species (Import and Export) Act 1976 (Amendment) Regulations 1996 (SI 1996/2684) Schs 1 and 2).

[104] Endangered Species (Import and Export) Act 1976 s.4(1B), added by WCA 1981 Sch.10 para.5(2).

[105] Endangered Species (Import and Export) Act 1976 s.4(2).

[106] Endangered Species (Import and Export) Act 1976 s.4(3).

1976 Act allow the Minister to make orders restricting the airports and ports through which live animals can be imported to the United Kingdom.[107]

As well as the specific offences created by the relevant provisions, any **7.3.22** attempt to evade the restrictions on the import and export of wild animals and plants will constitute an offence under the general law relating to customs and excise.[108] This may allow for more severe penalties, including custodial sentences, than are prescribed in the more specific legislation.[109]

The European Community has also introduced a handful of other mea- **7.3.23** sures specifically directed at the trade in wildlife products (in addition to the general laws on plant and animal health), although these have largely been overtaken by the implementation of CITES. The commercial importation of whale products is banned by the requirement for a licence for any import of any meat, oil or other products derived from cetaceans, or of goods treated with such products, coupled with a provision that no such licence is to be granted for commercial purposes.[110]

Concerns over cruelty, as well as potential over-exploitation, contributed **7.3.24** to further measures, and the commercial importation of the skins of whitecoat pups of harp seals and of the pups of hooded seals (blue-backs) is prohibited.[111] Plans to ban the import of pelts from animals caught in leg-hold traps[112] ran into difficulties on the basis that they represented a unilateral restriction of international trade, and were suspended,[113] although agreements have been made with the major producers on standards for humane trapping.[114]

Trade and Environment

Concern for wildlife has featured prominently in the wider debates over the **7.3.25** relationship between international trade and the environment.[115] To what extent is a state entitled to impose environmental controls that act as a restriction on free trade? At both EC and global levels it is accepted that environmental concerns can be a legitimate ground for measures that do

---

[107] Endangered Species (Import and Export) Act 1976 s.5; in practice the designation has been carried out by regulations made to give effect to the European Community's accession to CITES; see para.7.3.20, above.

[108] Customs and Excise Management Act 1979 s.170.

[109] *R. v Sperr* (1992) 13 Cr. App. Rep. (S.) 8; *R. v Humphrey* [2003] EWCA Crim 1915; [2003] 1 Cr. App. Rep. (S.) 39. The penalty can include forfeiture of the specimens illegally imported and others with which they have become mixed; *R. (Sissen) v Newcastle-upon-Tyne Crown Court* [2004] EWHC 1905 Admin; [2005] Env. L.R. 17.

[110] Regulation (EEC) 348/81.

[111] Directive 83/129/EEC, implemented in the UK by the Import of Seal Skins Regulations 1996 (SI 1996/2686); see also the Seal Fisheries (North Pacific) Act 1912 (Amendment) Regulations 1996 (SI 1996/2685).

[112] Regulation (EEC) 3254/91.

[113] Regulation (EEC) 1771/94.

[114] Agreements on International Humane Trapping Standards with Canada and the Russian Federation (Council Decision 98/142/EC), and with the USA (Council Decision 98/487/EC). See generally A. Nollkaemper, "The Legality of Moral Crusades Disguised in Trade Laws: An Analysis of the EC 'Ban' on Furs from Animals taken by Leghold Traps" (1996) 8 J.E.L. 237; S. Harrop, "The International Regulation of Animal Welfare and Conservation Issues through Standards dealing with the Trapping of Wild Mammals" (2000) 12 J.E.L. 334.

[115] A convenient source for a fuller account of the issue and for references to the primary materials and extensive literature is P. Birnie, A. Boyle and C. Redgwell, *International Law and the Environment*, 3rd edn (2009), Ch.14.

stand in the way of international trade, but how far this extends remains unclear and at times controversial. The perceived danger is that environmental concerns are used to dress up restrictions which are really adopted for other, protectionist or discriminatory, reasons, or that restrictions have a disproportionate effect when their legitimate aims could be met in a less disruptive way. What follows is a very brief indication of the fundamental issue in a very complex subject.

7.3.26   Within the European Community, the Treaty provisions prohibit any quantitative restrictions on imports and exports between Member States and any measures that have an equivalent effect.[116] This is qualified, though, to permit restrictions to be imposed where they are necessary and proportionate for a number of reasons, including for "the protection of health and life of humans, animals or plants".[117] Moreover the law here must be formulated and interpreted in the light of the obligation to integrate environmental protection requirements into the definition and implementation of Community policies.[118] The difficulty in practice comes in determining whether a particular measure is a legitimate means of environmental protection or an unjustified restriction on the free movement of goods. If there are any common or harmonised rules on the issue adopted at Community level, those will determine the issue of where the balance is to be struck, but in the absence of such a common position disputes can arise over the legitimacy of particular measures.

7.3.27   Two contrasting cases can illustrate this point. In *Commission v Germany*,[119] Germany imposed a total ban on imports of live crayfish in the attempt to stop the spread of disease affecting wild populations. In *Ditlev Bluhme*,[120] Denmark permitted only bees of the local variety to be kept on a certain island in order to ensure the survival of that strain. In both cases it was held that the measures did amount to a restriction on free trade, but also that the reasons for which they were imposed did fall within the permitted exceptions.[121] Therefore, since there were no EC norms dealing with the specific matters, the question in both cases was whether the national measures were necessary and proportionate in the circumstances. The Danish restrictions were upheld, but the European Court of Justice held that the German import ban could not be justified since other measures that had less effect on trade within the Community, such as health checks on all imports, could be equally effective in achieving the desired aim.

7.3.28   Essentially the same pattern applies at the global level.[122] The General Agreement on Tariffs and Trade (GATT) contains prohibitions on discriminatory trade measures,[123] but permits exceptions "necessary to protect human, animal or plant life or health" and "relating to the conservation of exhaustible natural resources if such measures are made effective in

---

[116] EC Treaty arts 28–29.
[117] EC Treaty art.30.
[118] EC Treaty art.6; see para.2.9.3, above.
[119] *Commission v Germany* (C-131/93) [1994] E.C.R. I-3303.
[120] *Ditlev Bluhme* (C-67/97) [1998] E.C.R. I-8033.
[121] *Ditlev Bluhme* (C-67/97) [1998] E.C.R. I-8033 at [33], where the contribution to biodiversity is expressly mentioned.
[122] A useful overview is O. Perez, "International Trade Law and the Environment" in B. Richardson and S. Wood (eds), *Environmental Law for Sustainability* (Oxford: Hart, 2006).
[123] GATT arts I, III and XI.

conjunction with restrictions on domestic production or consumption", provided that there is no unjustifiable discrimination between states and the measures are not in fact a disguised restriction on trade.[124] In the *Tuna-Dolphin* and *Shrimp-Turtle* cases[125] national prohibitions on imports of seafood caught in ways that threatened other vulnerable species were held not to be justified under the terms of GATT.[126] The World Trade Organisation has had a Committee on Trade and Environment since 1994[127] and finding means of reconciling environmental concerns with the structures for free trade is a problem that is recognised as requiring attention,[128] but so far with limited progress. Issues include how environmental concerns fit into the GATT structure, when national measures claimed to be based on environmental concerns can be justified, and the relationship between multilateral environmental agreements and the trade structures.

EUROPEAN COMMUNITY WILDLIFE INITIATIVES

The measures to implement CITES discussed in the preceding section and **7.4.1** other restrictions on the trade in wildlife fall naturally within the European Community's concern for creating a single market between Member States, but the Community has also adopted two measures aimed to provide more direct protection for wild plants and animals within its territory.[129] Even before there was an express power in the Treaty to take action on environmental matters, the Directive on the Conservation of Wild Birds[130] was made in 1979[131] and subsequently the Directive on the Conservation of Natural Habitats and of Wild Fauna and Flora[132] was made in 1992[133] although it has still not reached full implementation. Both of these require the Member States to introduce laws to secure that the species and sites

---

[124] GATT art.XX(b) and (g). There are equivalent provisions in the related treaties, e.g. General Agreement on Trade in Services (GATS) art.XIV.

[125] *US - Restrictions on Imports of Tuna* (1991) 30 I.L.M. 1598 (*Tuna-Dolphin I*); *US - Restrictions on Import of Tuna* (1994) 33 I.L.M. 839 (*Tuna-Dolphin II*); *US - Import Prohibition of Certain Shrimp and Shrimp Products* (1998) 37 I.L.M. 832 (*Shrimp-Turtle* case).

[126] For a more thorough account of disputes before the WTO involving environmental matters see N. Bernasconi-Osterwalder et al., *Environment and Trade: A Guide to WTO Jurisprudence* (London: Earthscan, 2005)

[127] Further information on the World Trade Organisation and its activities are available at *http://www.wto.org* [Accessed May 15, 2009].

[128] e.g. paras 30–32 of the Ministerial Declaration from the Sixth WTO Ministerial Conference (Hong Kong, December 2005).

[129] The Birds Directive (by art.1(1)) and the Habitats and Species Directive (by art.2(1)) are limited to the European territory of the Member States, thereby excluding the French overseas territories, but including the Azores and Canary Islands. On their application beyond the territorial seas of Member States see *Commission v United Kingdom* (C-6/04) [2005] E.C.R. I-9017, [115]–[120]; D. Owen, "The Application of the Wild Birds Directive beyond the Territorial Seas of European Community Member States" (2001) 13 J.E.L. 39.

[130] Directive 79/409/EEC.

[131] Under the rather loose authority of what was art.235 of the EEC Treaty; see para.2.9.2, above.

[132] Directive 92/43/EEC.

[133] Under the much clearer authority of art.130s (now art.175) of the Treaty; see para.2.9.4, above.

identified are given protection.[134] Their requirements have been discussed at the relevant places in the previous Chapters, but it is also worth looking at them in a less fragmented way.

7.4.2   Any overall picture must also include the Environmental Liability Directive[135] which expressly imposes obligations to take preventive or remedial steps in the face of environmental damage, supporting the protection given to species and habitats designated under the two main provisions, as discussed in section 5.12, above. In addition, the Water Framework Directive,[136] through its use of ecological criteria to set standards for water resources, can also be seen as a wildlife measure to some extent, and is discussed in section 8.6 below. The same can be said for the Marine Strategy Framework Directive which aims to achieve or maintain good environmental status in the marine environment by the year 2020.[137]

7.4.3   As Directives, the main way in which their provisions take effect should be through the presence in the national law of each Member State of appropriate measures implementing their terms, and both Directives have been important in shaping the British legislation in this field. However, if the national law does not fully meet the requirements of the Directive, it should be remembered that under general Community law the courts (at national and Community level) should always interpret and apply any national provisions in the light of the Directive, and should give direct effect to any provision in the Directive which is clear, precise and unconditional. Where necessary, the terms of a Directive which are capable of having direct effect override any national law.[138] Disputes can be referred to the European Court of Justice and the European Commission can take proceedings before that court, ultimately leading to the imposition of fines, if a Member State does not properly meet the requirements imposed by a Directive.[139]

7.4.4   The European Court of Justice has been kept busy with these Directives, through both infringement actions brought by the Commission[140] and references from national courts called on to interpret and apply their provisions. Their implementation by states has been slow and incomplete,[141]

---

[134] A. Nollkaemper, "Habitat Protection in European Community Law: Evolving Conceptions of a Balance of Interests" (1997) 9 J.E.L. 271.

[135] Directive 2004/35/EC.

[136] Directive 2000/60/EC.

[137] Directive 2008/56/EC; the aims of the marine strategies that this requires are to "protect and preserve the marine environment, prevent its deterioration or, where practicable, restore marine ecosystems in areas where they have been adversely affected" and to "prevent and reduce inputs in the marine environment, with a view to phasing out pollution ... so as to ensure that there are no significant impacts on or risks to marine biodiversity, marine ecosystems, human health or legitimate uses of the sea." (art.1(2)).

[138] See paras 2.9.5–2.9.8, above.

[139] See generally M. Hedemann-Robinson, *Enforcement of European Union Environmental Law: Legal Issues and Challenges* (London: Routledge-Cavendish, 2007).

[140] The Environment has consistently been the area with the highest number of infringement actions taken by the Commission (in 2007, 739 open files plus 461 new files opened), accounting for over a fifth of the infringement cases being pursued, with nature accounting for a high proportion of these (Commission Staff Working Document accompanying the 25th Annual Report on Monitoring the Application of Community Law (2007) (SEC (2008) 2854), pp.104–110, Situation In The Different Sectors).

[141] The Natura 2000 Barometer records that at the end of 2007 the process of designating sites was "largely complete" for only six states in relation to the Birds Directive and five states for the Habitats and Species Directive; *http://ec.europa.eu/environment/nature/natura2000/barometer/index_en.htm* [Accessed May 15, 2009].

with many instances of states conceding before the Court that they have not properly transposed the Directives' provisions, although so far no state has reached the stage of being fined for continued non-compliance.[142] As can be seen from the cases discussed below, the Court has consistently taken a firm line in expecting Member States to deliver the high level of protection provided by the Directives, emphasising that "faithful transposition is particularly important in the case of the Directive where management of the common heritage is entrusted to the Member States in their respective territories".[143] In line with the general jurisprudence of the Court on transposition, it also requires that the requirements of the Directives be fully transposed into clear and specific provisions with legal force.[144] Thus neither administrative practices,[145] the appointment of relevant officials,[146] broad constitutional duties[147] nor general duties on authorities to secure compliance[148] will by themselves be sufficient.

The terms of these two Directives must be borne in mind whenever the **7.4.5** British legislation on these matters is being considered, since any failure to live up to their requirements may lead to claims that UK authorities are acting unlawfully,[149] as well as to action against the state leading to changes in the law.[150] In this regard it is worth noting the different structures of the EC and domestic law in this area. As described in preceding Chapters, the domestic provisions provide protection for nature through a series of control mechanisms, specifying detailed procedures designed to prevent damaging activities and creating related criminal offences. The EC legislation, however, is structured around the objectives to be achieved, e.g. requiring that states "take appropriate steps to avoid . . . the deterioration of natural habitats and the habitats of species as well as disturbance of the species",[151] rather than specifying the controls to be imposed. These different legislative styles, and the greater specificity of the British style, can be one element in a mismatch between the domestic and EC law.[152]

---

[142] Under art.228 of the EC Treaty.

[143] *Commission v Austria* (C-507/04) [2007] E.C.R. I-5939 at [92].

[144] *Commission v Belgium* (C-324/01) [2002] E.C.R. I-11,197; *Commission v Belgium* (C-415/01) [2003] E.C.R. I-2081; *Commission v Austria* (C-507/04) [2007] E.C.R. I-5939; *Commission v Greece* (C-293/07) December 11, 2008.

[145] *Commission v Luxembourg* (C-75/01) [2003] E.C.R. I-1585.

[146] *Commission v Ireland* (C-183/05) [2007] E.C.R. I-137.

[147] *Commission v Greece* (C-103/00) [2002] E.C.R. I-1147.

[148] *Commission v United Kingdom* (C-6/04) [2005] E.C.R. I-9017; *Commission v Austria* (C-507/04) [2007] E.C.R. I-5939.

[149] As successfully argued in *R. v Secretary of State for the Environment, ex p. RSPB* (C-44/95) [1996] E.C.R. I-3805.

[150] As in relation to the multiple points of non-compliance with the Habitats and Species Directive found in *Commission v United Kingdom* (C-6/04) [2005] E.C.R. I-9017 which have led to the Conservation (Natural Habitats, etc.) Amendment (Scotland) Regulations 2007 (SSI 2007/80), the Conservation (Natural Habitats, etc.) Amendment (No.2) (Scotland) Regulations 2007 (SSI 2007/349), the Conservation (Natural Habitats, etc.) (Amendment) Regulations 2007 (SI 2007/1843) and Offshore Marine Conservation (Natural Habitats, etc.) Regulations 2007 (SI 2007/1842) and then further legislation in response to the Commission's view that these remedial steps were not sufficient: Conservation (Natural Habitats, etc.) Amendment (No.2) (Scotland) Regulations 2008 (SSI 2008/425); Conservation (Natural Habitats, etc.) (Amendment) (England and Wales) Regulations 2009 (SI 2009/6); Offshore Marine Conservation (Natural Habitats, etc.) (Amendment) Regulations 2009 (SI 2009/7).

[151] Habitats and Species Directive art.6(2).

[152] C.T. Reid and M. Woods, "Implementing EC Conservation Law" (2006) 18 J.E.L. 135.

Birds Directive

7.4.6 The Directive on the Conservation of Wild Birds[153] begins by imposing a
very general obligation on the Member States to take the requisite measures
to maintain the population of all species of bird naturally occurring in their
territory[154] at a level which corresponds to ecological, scientific and cultural
requirements, while taking account of economic and recreational requirements, or to adapt the populations to that level.[155] Not surprisingly, it has
been held that this provision is too vague to have direct effect,[156] and it
already embodies what has been a key issue in relation to the Directive, the
impact of economic factors which might conflict with conservation
requirements. To achieve the stated objective, Member States are to take the
requisite measures to preserve, maintain or re-establish a sufficient diversity
and area of habitats for all the naturally occurring species, primarily by the
creation of protected areas, the management of habitats in accordance with
ecological needs, and the re-establishment or creation of habitats.[157] Again,
this provision is too vague to have direct effect and is to some extent an
exhortatory measure. The Directive applies to wild birds, not those raised in
captivity, and Member States must take the necessary steps to protect all
such birds that occur in the Community, even though they are not naturally
present in that state's territory.[158] Where there are several sub-species of a
bird, all of these are covered, even though only some occur within the
Community.[159]

7.4.7 For all species, subject to certain exceptions, a general system of protection is to be established. In particular there is a prohibition on any
deliberate[160] killing or taking of birds, deliberate destruction of nests and
eggs, deliberate disturbance of birds during the breeding season where this
will be significant for the general aims of the Directive, and the taking and
keeping of eggs; the keeping of birds other than those species which may be
hunted should also be prohibited.[161] Even where hunting is permitted,[162] any
methods used for the large-scale or non-selective capture or killing of birds
is to be prohibited, especially those expressly listed in Annex IV(a), which
includes limes, explosives, nets, artificial lights, mirrors, and semi-automatic
and automatic weapons; also prohibited is hunting by the means described
in Annex IV(b), namely from aircraft, motor vehicles and boats moving at
above five kilometres per hour.[163] If any species of bird which does not

---

[153] Directive 79/409/EEC. For a thorough analysis of the Directive see W. Wils, "The Birds
Directive 15 Years Later: A survey of the case law and a comparison with the Habitats
Directive" (1994) 6 J.E.L. 219.

[154] Birds Directive (by art.1(1)) is limited to the European territory of the Member States,
thereby excluding the French overseas territories, but including the Azores and Canary Islands.

[155] Birds Directive art.2.

[156] *Kincardine and Deeside District Council v Forestry Commission*, 1992 S.L.T. 1180; it was
suggested that some other provisions, e.g. those requiring controls on the sale and hunting of
birds, may be sufficiently precise to have direct effect.

[157] The Birds Directive art.3.

[158] *Ministère Public v Didier Vergy* (C-149/94) [1996] E.C.R. I-299; *Commission v Austria* (C-
507/04) [2007] E.C.R. I-5939.

[159] *van der Feesten v Openbaar Ministerie* (C-202/94) [1996] E.C.R. I-355.

[160] On the meaning of "deliberate" see para.7.4.35, below.

[161] The Birds Directive art.5.

[162] See para.7.4.9, below.

[163] Birds Directive art.8 Annex IV.

naturally occur in the European territory of the Community is introduced, Member States must see to it that this does not prejudice the local flora and fauna.[164]

Whereas for most species there is a prohibition on the sale of birds, alive **7.4.8** or dead, and of readily recognisable parts or derivatives, as well as on the transport and keeping for sale,[165] this ban is relaxed in some cases. For the species listed in Annex III/1 the ban is lifted throughout the Community provided that the birds have been lawfully killed or captured or otherwise acquired.[166] For those listed in Annex III/2, Member States have a discretion whether to make exceptions to the general rule, again provided that the birds have been lawfully taken, but subject to restrictions and an examination to ensure that the marketing will not lead to the species being endangered; this examination is to be carried out jointly by the State and the Commission.[167]

The hunting of birds may be allowed by national legislation, but only for **7.4.9** those species in Annex II and always subject to a requirement that the hunting does not jeopardise conservation efforts in the hunting area.[168] The species listed in Annex II/1 may be hunted throughout the Community,[169] whereas those in Annex II/2 may be hunted only in the Member States specified.[170] The Commission must be informed of the relevant hunting laws, which should ensure the wise use and ecologically balanced control of the species and protect them during the breeding season.[171]

Member States are allowed to derogate from the specific prohibitions and **7.4.10** restrictions on the killing, taking, hunting and sale of birds, but only on a limited number of grounds and where there is no other satisfactory solution.[172] Such derogations may be justified in the interests of public health and safety or of air safety, to prevent serious damage to crops, livestock, forests, fisheries and water, and for the protection of flora and fauna. Also permitted are action for teaching and education, action taken to allow for repopulation or reintroduction (including captive breeding) and other strictly supervised and selective keeping or other "judicious use" of small numbers of birds.[173] The derogations must be detailed and specific and must be notified to the Commission together with information on the authority

---

[164] Birds Directive art.11.

[165] Birds Directive art.6(1).

[166] Birds Directive art.6(2).

[167] Birds Directive art.6(3).

[168] Birds Directive art.7(1).

[169] Birds Directive (by art.1(1)) is limited to the European territory of the Member States, thereby excluding the French overseas territories, but including the Azores and Canary Islands.

[170] Birds Directive art.7(2) and (3).

[171] Birds Directive art.7(4); see *Association pour la Protection des Animaux Sauvages v Préfet de Maine et Loire* (C-435/92) [1994] E.C.R. I-67; *Commission v Austria* (C-507/04) [2007] E.C.R. I-5939.

[172] See Appendix C. It must be shown that another solution is not available, as opposed not convenient (*Ligue Royale Belge pour la Protection des Oiseaux v Région Wallonne* (C-10-96) [1996] E.C.R. I-6775) and the Scottish courts have held that a satisfactory solution must be one that deals with the actual harm in question (*RSPB v Secretary of State for Scotland*, 2000 S.L.T. 1272), so that a scheme to compensate farmers for the loss resulting from grazing by geese could not count as an alternative solution; see para.3.3.12, above.

[173] Birds Directive art.9.

which is empowered to declare that the criteria for the derogation have been met.[174] By initially granting in Great Britain a legislative exemption of indefinite duration to all "authorised persons" in relation to a number of pest species, the Wildlife and Countryside Act 1981 was considered to fall foul of this requirement for specific derogations, and the control of pests is now authorised under a scheme of more precise annual licences granted by government departments.[175]

7.4.11   There has been considerable litigation on the scope of permissible derogations. The list of grounds for derogations stated in the Directive is an exhaustive one,[176] and the restrictive parameters that are set must be complied with. Hunting can be a "judicious use" of birds,[177] but national laws that permit hunting during the breeding season, a period when birds are entitled to special protection,[178] will not satisfy the Court that there is no other satisfactory solution if the birds are available to be hunted at other times of the year.[179] The methods of hunting used must be selective and based on the grounds justifying the action against birds.[180] There must be controls to ensure that only "small numbers"[181] of birds are taken,[182] the reference point for "small numbers" being less than one per cent of the total annual mortality of the relevant population.[183]

7.4.12   As usual with such legislation, particular categories of birds are picked out for special treatment, in some cases by additional protection, and in others, less.[184] Special conservation measures are to be taken for the species (over 170 in number[185]) listed in Annex I of the Directive, the listing taking account of species in danger of extinction, vulnerable to specific changes in their habitat, with small populations or restricted local distribution or requiring specific habitat.[186] For these species the most suitable areas are to be classified as Special Protection Areas,[187] where appropriate steps are to be taken to avoid pollution or deterioration of habitats or disturbance of the

---

[174] *Associazione Italiana per il WWF v Regione Veneto* (C-118/94) [1996] E.C.R. I-1223; *Commission v Italy* (C-159/99) [2001] E.C.R. I-4007; *Commission v Austria* (C-507/04) [2007] E.C.R. I-5939.

[175] Under WCA 1981 s.16; see paras 3.3.10–3.3.15, above.

[176] *Commission v Spain* (C-79/03) [2004] E.C.R. I-11,619; *Commission v Austria* (C-507/04) [2007] E.C.R. I-5939.

[177] Birds Directive art.9(1)(c); *Ligue pour la protection des oiseaux v Premier ministre* (C-182/02) [2003] E.C.R. I-12,105.

[178] By virtue of the Birds Directive art.7(4).

[179] *Ligue pour la protection des oiseaux v Premier ministre* (C-182/02) [2003] E.C.R. I-12,105; *Commission v Finland* (C-344/03) [2005] E.C.R. I-11,033.

[180] *Commission v Spain* (C-79/03) [2004] E.C.R. I-11,619.

[181] Birds Directive art.9(1)(c).

[182] This will require national co-ordination if permits can be granted by different local or regional authorities; *WWF Italia v Regione Lombardia* (C-60/05) [2006] E.C.R. I-5083.

[183] This figure is based on the work of the ORNIS Committee established under the Birds Directive art.16; the figure is not legally binding but in the absence of contrary scientific evidence is used on the basis of the acknowledged scientific value of the committee's findings. See *Commission v Spain* (C-79/03) [2004] E.C.R. I-11,619; *Commission v Finland* (C-344/03) [2005] E.C.R. I-11,033.

[184] The various Annexes have been replaced and amended at various times.

[185] As they list the birds by their names in all of the Community's official languages, as well as by their scientific names, the Annexes provide a useful phrase book for any birdwatcher travelling in Europe.

[186] Birds Directive art.4(1).

[187] Birds Directive art.4(1); see paras 5.2.4–5.2.8, above.

birds. In other areas states are to strive to avoid pollution or deterioration of habitats.[188] Similar steps are to be taken for regularly occurring migratory species not listed in Annex I, paying particular attention to wetlands.[189] The Commission is to be kept informed of the steps taken with a view to co-ordinating such action to secure that the protective measures form a coherent whole.[190] These sites now form part of the Natura 2000 programme with the Special Areas of Conservation under the Habitats and Species Directive.[191]

It is the habitat protection provisions which have proved the most con- **7.4.13** troversial. At the core of the early arguments was the extent to and stage at which competing economic and social interests could be taken into account in determining whether areas are to be designated and how they are to be protected. The original text of the Directive was essentially silent on this point, and in a series of major cases, the European Court of Justice held that designation of sites was to be determined by ornithological criteria alone, and that only in the most exceptional circumstances could activities that damage or lessen the quality of the site be permitted.[192] This approach was considered by some to be giving too much priority to conservation, and the Habitats and Species Directive amended the Birds Directive so as to apply to Special Protection Areas the same obligations as were being introduced for Special Areas of Conservation, permitting an overriding public interest to take priority over the protective requirements.[193] Providing protection may require positive measures to preserve and improve a site as well as avoiding harmful human effects,[194] and the more general obligation under the Directive to strive to avoid pollution or the deterioration of habitats outside the designated areas remains in force.[195]

It has been consistently emphasised, though, that the designation stage is **7.4.14** determined by ornithological criteria alone. Member States have some dis-cretion in applying the relevant criteria, but cannot decide that for any other reason it is not appropriate to designate a site.[196] In the absence of contrary evidence provided by a state, the *Inventory of Important Bird Areas in the*

---

[188] Birds Directive art.4(4); this provision was not affected when the rest of art.4(4) was replaced by the Habitats and Species Directive (see below).

[189] Birds Directive art.4(2).

[190] Birds Directive art.4(3).

[191] See para.7.4.24, below.

[192] *Commission v Germany* (C-57/89) [1991] E.C.R. I-883 (Leybucht Dykes); *Commission v Spain* (C-355/90) [1993] E.C.R. I-4223 (Santoña Marshes); *R. v Secretary of State for the Environment, ex p. RSPB* (C-44/95) [1996] E.C.R. I-3805; [1997] Q.B. 206 (Lappel Bank).

[193] Habitats and Species Directive art.7, applying art.6 of that Directive in place of art.4(4) of the Birds Directive, with effect from 1994; A. Nollkaemper, "Habitat Protection in European Community Law: Evolving Conceptions of a Balance of Interests" (1997) 9 J.E.L. 271, at pp.273–278. Several of the cases discussed below on the application of art.6 of the Habitats and Species Directive relate to sites designated as Special Protection Areas. A. Dodd, "EU nature directives: rights, responsibilities and results – are we striking the right balance?" (2008) 20 E.L.M. 237.

[194] *Commission v Ireland* (C-418/04) [2007] E.C.R. I-10,947 at [154].

[195] The last sentence of art.4(4), unaffected by the amendments made by the Habitats and Species Directive.

[196] *Commission v Austria* (C-209/02) [2004] E.C.R. I-1211. The ornithological criteria used must be sound and based on natural boundaries, not artificially isolated areas; *Commission v Ireland* (C-418/04) [2007] E.C.R. I-10,947 at [142].

European Community (IBA 89)[197] and its successor (IBA 2000), although not legally binding, can be used as a reference for assessing whether a sufficient number and size of areas have been designated.[198] The state is bound to keep the position under review itself to ensure that it has designated all the appropriate sites.[199] Only on the production of scientific evidence that an area is no longer among the most suitable for the conservation of any birds covered by the Directive may the declassification of a site be considered.[200] States can be held accountable before the Court if their designations cover a number and total area of sites manifestly less than that justified on scientific grounds,[201] and are required to take steps to prevent the deterioration not just of designated sites but also of areas that should have been designated as Special Protection Areas.[202] It has been held that these "constructive SPAs" that have not been formally designated as such are still governed by the original terms of the Directive, not those of the Habitats and Species Directive that replaced them,[203] but this still requires that disturbances are avoided, a requirement that cannot be overridden by economic and social requirements.[204]

7.4.15 As well as the specific measures to protect birds, the Directive requires Member States to report to the Commission every three years on its implementation and to encourage research on the protection, management and use of birds.[205] It is expressly stated that Member States may introduce stricter measures than those provided for by the Directive.[206]

7.4.16 As noted above, the Member States have been far from perfect in their implementation of the Directive, with the Commission taking enforcement action against many states which have failed to transpose the laws properly or ensure that they are implemented in practice.[207]

7.4.17 As far as Great Britain is concerned, the provisions in the Wildlife and Countryside Act 1981, introduced partly to secure such implementation, did achieve broad compliance with the Directive. Further refinements in the law, e.g. the changes relating to pest species, those introduced by the Conservation (Natural Habitats, etc.) Regulations 1994 for all European Sites

---

[197] Prepared for the Commission by the Eurogroup for the Conservation of Birds and Habitats and the International Council of Bird Protection in 1989.

[198] e.g. *Commission v Spain* (C-235/04) [2007] E.C.R. I-5415 at [26]; *Commission v Greece* (C-334/04) [2007] E.C.R. I-9215 at [33].

[199] *Commission v Greece* (C-334/04) [2007] E.C.R. I-9215.

[200] *Commission v Portugal* (C-191/05) [2006] E.C.R. I-6853.

[201] *Commission v Netherlands* (C-3/96) [1998] E.C.R. I-3031; *Commission v France* (C-166/97) [1999] E.C.R. I-1719.

[202] *Commission v France* (C-96/98) [1999] E.C.R. I-8531; this approach, established in cases with proceedings that began before the amendments in the Habitats and Species Directive took effect, remains the correct approach as confirmed in *R. v Seceraty of State for the Environment, Transport and the Regions, ex p. First Corporation Shipping Ltd* (C-371-98) [2000] E.C.R. I-9253 (see para.7.4.25, below).

[203] *Commission v France* (C-374/98) [2001] E.C.R. I-10,799; see G. Machin, "Protecting Bird Habitat of European Importance – the view from Basses Corbières" (2004) 3 Env. L. Rev. 174.

[204] *Commission v Spain* (C-186/06) [2007] E.C.R. I-12,093.

[205] Birds Directive art.12; *Commission v Portugal* (C-72/02) [2003] E.C.R. I-6597.

[206] Birds Directive art.14.

[207] There are now too many cases to continue the practice in previous editions of giving a comprehensive list of infraction proceedings arising from the Directive, and in any event the non-compliance is conceded in many instances depriving the cases of wider interest. A single press release in 2007 announced action against 11 states for failing to designate sufficient Special Protection Areas (IP/07/938).

and the first steps towards the extension to some offshore activities,[208] brought our law closer into line with the Directive's requirements before the decision in *Commission v UK* revealed the extent to which it was still falling short of the requirements of the Birds and Habitat and Species Directives, prompting significant remedial measures.[209]

Habitats and Species Directive

The Directive on the Conservation of Natural Habitats and of Wild Fauna **7.4.18** and Flora[210] is more far-reaching and in some respects takes over from the Birds Directive. It is based on the Bern Convention[211] and aims to establish a network of protection for habitats which are of ecological value (in themselves or as the host to threatened species) and to protect rare or vulnerable species of plants and animals from harm. A novel feature of the Directive is the potential for the Community to propose for special protection sites which have not been suggested by the Member State concerned.

The overall objective is to "contribute towards ensuring bio-diversity **7.4.19** through the conservation of natural habitats and wild flora and fauna",[212] based on the network of protected sites known as Natura 2000. However, in the preamble it is stated that the aim is to:

"[P]romote the maintenance of biodiversity, taking account of economic, social, cultural and regional requirements, [making] a contribution to the general objective of sustainable development",

and one of the significant differences from the Birds Directive is the inclusion of express provisions to determine how competing conservation and other interests are to be resolved. As with the Birds Directive, the scope of this new measure is limited to the European territory of the Member States.[213] Member States should have had the appropriate legislative and administrative machinery in place by May 1994, with separate timetables for the designation of special areas, but many states have failed to meet these obligations.[214]

The targets of the Directive are species and habitats "of Community **7.4.20** interest", a concept defined in article 1. As far as species are concerned, this term covers those within the Community which are endangered, vulnerable, rare or endemic and in need of particular attention.[215] Species which are

---

[208] The Offshore Petroleum Activities (Conservation of Habitats) Regulations 2001 (SI 2001/1754).

[209] *Commission v United Kingdom* (C-6/04) [2005] E.C.R. I-9017.

[210] Directive 92/43/EEC.

[211] Convention on the Conservation of European Wildlife and Natural Habitats; see paras 7.5.15–7.5.21, below.

[212] Habitats and Species Directive art.2(1).

[213] Habitats and Species Directive art.2(1); it extends beyond territorial waters to all seas under the Member States' jurisdiction (*R. v Secretary of State for Trade & Industry, ex p. Greenpeace Ltd (No.2)* [2000] 2 C.M.L.R. 94; [2000] Env. L.R. 221; *Commission v United Kingdom* (C-6/04) [2005] E.C.R. I-9017).

[214] Habitats and Species Directive art.23(1).

[215] Habitats and Species Directive art.1(g).

endangered within the Community may be excluded if their presence in the Community is marginal to their natural range and they are not endangered or vulnerable in the broader western palaearctic region.[216] Vulnerable species are those believed likely to move into the endangered category in the near future "if the causal factors continue operating", presumably a reference to whatever causal factors are producing a decline in the species. Rare species are ones which are not at present endangered or vulnerable, but are at risk through being found in restricted geographical areas or being thinly scattered over a more extensive range. Species in all four of these categories can be listed for direct protection and to ensure protection for their habitat.

7.4.21   The habitat provisions are directed both at particular habitat types and at the habitat necessary for species of Community interest. Habitat types of Community interest which can qualify for listing are those which are in danger of disappearance in their natural state, have a small natural range by reason of their intrinsically restricted area or as a result of their regression, or present outstanding examples of one or more of the five listed biogeographical regions: Alpine, Atlantic, Continental, Macaronesian (i.e. the Azores) and Mediterranean.[217] The other category of habitats which can be listed is that which stipulates the homes of the listed species of Community interest.[218]

7.4.22   The Annexes of the Directive contain lists of the habitats and species which meet these criteria. Annex I lists almost 200 habitat types of Community interest, varying from fairly general descriptions such as estuaries and large shallow inlets or bays, through more specific instances, e.g. Caledonian forest, to very detailed examples, e.g. *Tetraclinis articulata* forests in Andalucia. Annex II lists the many species of animals and plants whose habitats are to be protected, with a separate list of plants for the Azores.[219] Annex IV lists the animals and plants which are to be given direct protection. The lists of animals and plants contain only a few species found in the United Kingdom, the emphasis being more on Mediterranean species. Generally the animal lists cover a broad range of animals, including not only mammals which have in the past tended to dominate such lists, but many reptiles, amphibians, fish, insects, molluscs and other invertebrates. All of the lists are, however, somewhat difficult to use, requiring considerable knowledge of the ecological classification of habitats,[220] and giving only the

---

[216] Especially before the accession of Sweden and Finland in 1995, this qualification was potentially significant for the United Kingdom, since for a few species their presence within the limits of the Community was limited to small numbers in Britain, suggesting that they should qualify as endangered, whereas they were in fact plentiful in other northern lands.

[217] Habitats and Species Directive art.1(c).

[218] Habitats and Species Directive art.4(1).

[219] Within the UK there were reckoned to be 76 Annex I habitats (including 22 priority types) and 51 Annex II species have been recorded in the UK (although 10 of these are extinct or have been recorded only as vagrants); *First report by the United Kingdom under Article 17 on implementation of the Directive from June 1994 to December 2000* (DEFRA, 2001) (hereafter "*First Implementation Report*"), p.8.

[220] The classification used is that produced through the Community's Corine programme, established under Council Decision 85/338, but was described as having "inherent weaknesses" (*First Implementation Report*, p.8). The European Commission has produced an *Interpretation Manual of European Union Habitats* (version 2, 1999).

Latin names of individual species.[221] As usual, there is provision for the lists to be amended.[222]

For the habitat provisions, there are marked in Annexes I and II the **7.4.23** "priority natural habitat types" and the "priority species" identified in accordance with the definitions in article 1. In both cases the crucial points are that either the habitat or species is in danger of disappearing and that there is a particular responsibility on the Community for their conservation in view of the proportion of their natural range which falls within its territory.[223]

The aim of the habitat provisions is to establish a coherent network of **7.4.24** Special Areas of Conservation under the title "Natura 2000", enabling the conservation and restoration of the natural habitat types listed in Annex I and of the habitats necessary for the species listed in Annex II.[224] Each Member State is required to contribute to the creation of this network in proportion to the representation within its territory of the habitats concerned, primarily through the recognition of Special Areas of Conservation.

The designation of such areas is a two-stage process. In the first place, **7.4.25** each Member State has to propose to the Commission a list of sites identified by the application of the criteria set out in Annex III (Stage I)[225]; these criteria cover such factors as the degree of conservation and potential for restoration of the habitat, the extent to which the habitat is representative of the habitat type, the proportion of the habitat or of the local population of the particular species present in relation to their presence in the state as a whole, and a global assessment of the value of the site for conserving the habitat type or species. The grounds for proposing each site must be fully stated, and any priority habitat types or habitats for priority species must be identified in the proposal. The European Court of Justice has confirmed that the designation process is to be based purely on the scientific criteria, without any place for arguments based on economic or social concerns.[226] At this first stage of being proposed by the national authorities, sites are not covered by the specific protective rules set out in the Directive and discussed below, but states must take appropriate protective measures to safeguard the ecological interest that has led to the sites being nominated.[227] No Member State had provided what was regarded as a complete list by the initial date for completing this stage in May 1995 and as with Special Protection Areas under the Birds Directive, the Commission has successfully

---

[221] From frustrating experience immediately after the Directive was made, it took several days of consulting a wide range of books and experts to discover what some of the listed species are, far less whether they are likely to occur in the UK.

[222] Habitats and Species Directive art.19.

[223] Habitats and Species Directive art.1(d) and (h).

[224] Habitats and Species Directive art.3(1).

[225] Habitats and Species Directive art.4(1).

[226] *R. v Secretary of State for the Environment, ex p. RSPB* (C-44/95) [1996] E.C.R. I-3805; *R. v Secretary of State for the Environment, Transport and the Regions, ex p. First Corporation Shipping Ltd* (C-371/98) [2000] E.C.R. I-9253.

[227] *Società Italiana Dragaggi SpA v Ministero delle Infrastrutture e dei Trasporti, Regione Autonoma del Friuli Venezia Giulia* (C-117/03) [2005] E.C.R. I-167, *Bund Naturschutz in Bayern eV v Freistaat Bayern* (C-244/05) [2006] E.C.R. I-8445.

taken infringement proceedings against several states over their failure to propose sufficient sites.[228]

7.4.26   The second stage involves the Commission preparing, from the individual lists and in agreement with each Member State, a draft list of sites of Community importance.[229] This selection is carried out in accordance with the criteria set out in Annex III (Stage II), which require the selection of all sites containing priority habitats or species, and consideration of the relative value of the site at national level, the situation of the site on migration routes or as part of a continuous ecosystem straddling national frontiers, the total area of the site, the number of habitat types or species present and its global ecological value. However, where the sites containing one or more priority habitat type or species amount to more than five per cent of the national territory of a state, that state can request the flexible application of these criteria.[230] The final list of sites selected as of Community importance was due to be adopted by May 1998[231] by the Council of Ministers following consideration by a committee chaired by a member of the Commission and comprising representatives of the Member States.[232] The Committee and the Council can act on the basis of qualified majority votes. This timetable, however, slipped and progress was patchy and slow, but there is now a considerable area of land fully designated and enjoying the protection of the Directive.[233]

7.4.27   This designation procedure obviously leaves the prime initiative in the hands of the Member State, and the interests of individual states are further protected by the potential for the rules to be relaxed if more than five per cent of a state is likely to be designated.[234] However, in a novel feature of this Directive, the Commission has "in exceptional cases" the power to initiate the designation of a site containing priority habitat or species and which the Member State has failed to mention.[235] Consultations are to take place (for up to six months), but ultimately (within three further months) the Council, acting unanimously, can take the final decision on including the site. The requirement for unanimity in effect preserves the Member State's veto over the designation of sites in its territory, but the potential for an outside body to intervene in the selection of such sites is a major innovation.

7.4.28   Once a site has been fully recognised at Community level, the Member State must designate it as a Special Area of Conservation as soon as possible and within six years at most,[236] giving priority according to the importance

---

[228] e.g. *Commission v Ireland* (C-67/99) [2001] E.C.R. I-5757; *Commission v Germany* (C-71/99) [2001] E.C.R. I-5811; *Commission v France* (C-220/99) [2001] E.C.R. I-5831.

[229] Habitats and Species Directive art.4(2).

[230] For those wishing to have economic, social and cultural criteria taken into account when designation is being determined, the acceptance at this stage of departures from the strict scientific criteria may open the door for renewing the arguments that were unsuccessful in relation to the first, national stage in *R. v Secretary of State for the Environment, Transport and the Regions, ex p. First Corporation Shipping Ltd* (C-371/98) [2000] E.C.R. I-9253.

[231] Habitats and Species Directive art.4(3).

[232] Habitats and Species Directive arts 20 and 21.

[233] See the Natura Barometer at *http://ec.europa.eu/environment/nature/natura2000/barometer/index_en.htm* [Accessed May 15, 2009].

[234] Habitats and Species Directive art.4(2).

[235] Habitats and Species Directive art.5.

[236] With Member States being slow to live up to their obligations and the accession of further states, it is likely to be many years before the designation process is complete.

of the site for the listed habitat and species and for the coherence of Natura 2000 and to any threats to which the site is exposed.[237] The consequences of such designation are that the state shall establish the necessary conservation measures, including management plans and appropriate statutory, administrative or contractual measures to meet the ecological needs of the site. In particular steps are to be taken to avoid the deterioration of the habitat and the disturbance of the species for whose benefit the habitat has been designated.[238] This requires not only the presence of suitable legal protection but also its effective implementation,[239] and may require positive management to prevent deterioration, not just protection from damaging activities. These provisions for the protection of sites replace the provisions relating to Special Protection Areas under the Birds Directive.[240]

Where a site may be affected by human activity, the protection given to Natura sites is a two-stage process.[241] Where any plan or project other than one directly connected with the management of the site is likely to have a significant effect on the site,[242] it must be subject to an appropriate assessment[243] of its implications for the conservation objectives of the site.[244] As a general rule only if it will not affect the integrity of the site can approval for the project be given.[245] The European Court of Justice has held that these provisions set a very high threshold before projects can be approved. In the *Waddenzee* case[246] it was held that approval could be given only where the authorities were certain that the integrity of the site would not be adversely affected, a stage reached only where no reasonable scientific doubt remains that such effects would occur. Given our limited knowledge of complex and dynamic ecosystems, especially at a time when climate change may add a further layer of complexity, dynamism and uncertainty, this is a hard test to

7.4.29

---

[237] Habitats and Species Directive art.4(4).

[238] Habitats and Species Directive art.6(1) and (2); see *Managing Natura 2000 Sites: The provisions of Article 6 of the 'Habitats' Directive 92/43/EEC* (European Commission, 2000).

[239] *Commission v Ireland* (C-117/00) [2002] E.C.R. I-5335.

[240] Habitats and Species Directive art.7.

[241] *Commission v Netherlands* (C-441/03) [2005] E.C.R. I-3043.

[242] Note that there is no requirement for the project to be on the site or even neighbouring it; what counts is that the site will be affected.

[243] European Commission, *Assessment of plans and projects significantly affecting Natura 2000 sites: Methodological guidance on the provisions of Article 6(3) and (4) of the Habitats Directive 92/43/EEC* (Official Publications of the European Communities, 2002). The assessment need not be part of a complete environmental impact assessment such as required under Community or national law; see section 8.3, below.

[244] In *Commission v Italy* (C-179/06) [2007] E.C.R. I-8131 a complaint failed because the Commission did present the Court with sufficient evidence to establish that development proposals would do harm in the context of the specific conservation objectives of a site.

[245] Habitats and Species Directive art.6(3); it is further stated that the authorities should give approval "if appropriate, after having obtained the opinion of the general public", an unclear provision which should, however, be satisfied by the degree of advertisement, etc. which applies to projects undergoing a standard environmental assessment (see section 8.3, below). For a simple example of permission being given unlawfully in the face of a negative assessment see *Commission v Austria* (C-209/02) [2004] E.C.R. I-1211.

[246] *Landelijke Vereniging tot Behoud van de Waddenzee, Nederlandse Vereniging tot Bescherming van Vogels v Staatssecretaris van Landbouw, Natuurbeheer en Visserij* (C-127/02) [2004] E.C.R. I-7405 (see commentary by J. Verschuuren at (2005) 17 J.E.L. 265); see also *Commission v Ireland* (C-418/04) [2007] E.C.R. I-10,947.

satisfy.[247] The issue of what counts as a "plan or project" has also given rise to disputes, with the term being held to extend to each annual renewal of cockle dredging licences[248] and to development plans which do not themselves authorise specific future projects but do have a "considerable influence" on development decisions.[249]

7.4.30 The second stage does allow a Member State to approve a project that may have adverse effects on a site, but only if strict criteria are met.[250] These are that there are no alternative solutions,[251] that the plan or project is justified by imperative reasons of overriding public interest (which includes social and economic ones)[252] and that appropriate compensatory measures are to be taken by the state to ensure that the overall coherence of Natura 2000 is not harmed.[253] Where a site contains a priority habitat or species, the only overriding factors which are acceptable without seeking an opinion from the Commission are those relating to human health or public safety, or to environmental benefits of primary importance.[254] In this way the Special Areas of Conservation and Special Protection Areas are given very considerable protection from development which might damage them, and it is made clear that it is at this stage, not initial designation, that competing factors are to be taken into account.[255]

7.4.31 Member States are to be assisted in fulfilling their obligations to conserve the Special Areas of Conservation by the availability of Community funds.[256] Each state is to submit to the Commission estimates of the co-financing considered necessary to allow it to meet its obligations, and after full discussions, a "prioritized action framework of measures" is to be taken when the sites in question are designated. Final decisions in the light of the funds available rest with the Council acting after consideration of the issues by the Committee referred to above.[257]

7.4.32 Apart from their obligations with regard to Special Areas of Conservation and Special Protection Areas, Member States are required generally to endeavour to improve the ecological coherence of Natura 2000 by

---

[247] The issue is to be judged at the time the project is considered and it is immaterial that expected adverse effects do not in fact materialise; *Commission v Portugal* (C-239/04) [2006] E.C.R. I-10,183.

[248] *Landelijke Vereniging tot Behoud van de Waddenzee, Nederlandse Vereniging tot Bescherming van Vogels v Staatssecretaris van Landbouw, Natuurbeheer en Visserij* (C-127/02) [2004] E.C.R. I-7405.

[249] *Commission v United Kingdom* (C-6/04) [2005] E.C.R. I-9017; see also *Boggis v English Nature* [2008] EWHC 2954 Admin; [2009] Env. L.R. 20.

[250] Habitats and Species Directive art.6(4); European Commission, *Guidance Document on Article 6(4) of the "Habitats Directive" 92/43/EEC* (2007).

[251] In *Commission v Portugal* (C-239/04) [2006] E.C.R. I-10,183 the decision to build a motorway through a SPA was held unlawful since it was not shown that alternative routes avoiding the SPA had been considered.

[252] A. Nollkaemper, "Habitat Protection in European Community Law: Evolving Conceptions of a Balance of Interests" (1997) 9 J.E.L. 271, at pp.279–284.

[253] See M. Lawton, "Ecological Compensation within the UK Planning System: The effect of art.6(4) of the Habitats Directive on three south coast port developments" (2007) 18 *Water Law* 47.

[254] See L. Krämer, "The European Commission's Opinions under art.6(4) of the Habitats Directive" (2009) 21 J.E.L. 59, where it is suggested that on occasions the Commission has been too easily swayed by the arguments in favour of development.

[255] See paras 5.2.25–5.2.31, above.

[256] Habitats and Species Directive art.8; *Financing Natura 2000* COM (2004) 431 final.

[257] See para.7.4.26, above.

maintaining and developing features of the landscape of major importance for wild fauna and flora.[258] Where they consider it necessary, land use planning and development policies should encourage the management of features of value to wildlife, as being essential for the migration, dispersal and genetic exchange of wild species.[259] The features identified are those whose linear or continuous structure offers corridors or pathways for wild species (e.g. rivers and their banks, traditional forms of field boundary) or which act as stepping stones (e.g. ponds or small woods). The obligation here is not strong and leaves ample discretion to the Member States, but has at least been reflected in the United Kingdom by inclusion in the development planning process under the town and country planning legislation.[260]

7.4.33 The Commission, in conjunction with the Committee established under the Directive, is to review periodically the contribution of Natura 2000 towards the achievements of the general objectives of the Directives.[261] Such reviews may consider the declassification of Special Areas of Conservation where warranted by natural developments. To inform such reviews and other decision-making, e.g. in relation to the measures necessary for the species given direct protection as discussed below, Member States are required to undertake surveillance of the conservation status of the habitats and species covered by the Directive.[262]

7.4.34 The measures designed to protect particular species of plant follow a standard pattern. For the species listed in Annex IV(b), Member States are to take the requisite steps to prohibit their deliberate picking, collecting, cutting, uprooting or destruction in their natural range in the wild.[263] Also to be prohibited are the keeping, transport, sale, offer for sale or exchange of specimens taken in the wild, except those legally taken before the Directive is implemented.[264]

7.4.35 The measures relating to animals are more complex.[265] The main provision requires the protection of the species listed in Annex IV(a).[266] This requires the prohibition of all forms of deliberate capture or killing in the wild,[267] or deliberate disturbance of these species especially during periods of breeding, rearing, hibernation or migration, and of deliberate destruction or taking of eggs in the wild,[268] as well as the banning of the keeping, transport, sale and offer for sale or exchange of specimens taken from the wild, except for those taken lawfully before the Directive is implemented. The meaning

---

[258] Habitats and Species Directive art.3(3).

[259] Habitats and Species Directive art.10.

[260] CNHR 1994 reg.37.

[261] Habitats and Species Directive arts 9 and 21.

[262] Habitats and Species Directive art.11; this duty to carry out surveillance must be transposed into a specific duty in domestic law (*Commission v United Kingdom* (C6/04) [2005] E.C.R. I-9107).

[263] Habitats and Species Directive art.13.

[264] The temporal provision here and under art.12(2) must be fully implemented in domestic law; *Commission v United Kingdom* (C-6/04) [2005] E.C.R. I-9017.

[265] European Commission, *Guidance document on the strict protection of animal species of Community interest under the Habitats Directive 92/43/EEC* (2007).

[266] Habitats and Species Directive art.12.

[267] This includes the taking of a protected species in snares set for other animals; *Commission v Spain* (C-221/04) [2006] E.C.R. I-4515.

[268] Birds are not included in the Annex, remaining subject to the separate Birds Directive, but virtually all of the non-mammalian species listed are oviparous.

of "deliberate" has given rise to some discussion, and it has been held that this extends beyond cases where the intention was to kill or capture the animal to include those where the purpose may be different but the perpetrator accepted the possibility of this occurring.[269]

7.4.36   These measures follow the standard pattern for such protective legislation, but there are two further requirements. First, Member States should prohibit the deterioration or destruction of breeding sites or resting places of these species.[270] Although some derogations may be allowed,[271] this is a potentially significant provision, especially as the prohibition is not restricted to deliberate deterioration or destruction,[272] and reflects both the focus in the Directive in the outcomes to be achieved rather than the intentions of any parties and the general awareness throughout the Directive of the importance of directing the law at the conservation of habitat if nature conservation measures are to be effective. Secondly, states are required to establish a system to monitor the incidental capture and killing of the listed species, and to undertake research or conservation measures to ensure that the incidental capture and killing does not have a significant negative impact on the species.[273]

7.4.37   Annex V contains a list of animals and plants which are not automatically entitled to protection. However, if a Member State deems it necessary in the light of its general surveillance of conservation matters, it is to take measures to ensure that any taking in the wild or exploitation of a species is compatible with its being maintained at a favourable conservation status.[274] The protective measures may include regulations regarding access to property, temporary or local prohibitions of the taking of specimens in the wild or of exploiting particular populations, regulation of the periods and methods permitted for taking specimens, the establishment of licensing or quota systems, regulation of the purchase, sale, offering for sale and keeping of specimens, and the application of hunting and fishing rules which take account of conservation. The measures may also include strictly controlled captive breeding and artificial propagation schemes with a view to reducing the taking of specimens in the wild, and should include an assessment of the effect of the measures adopted.

7.4.38   Member States may claim exceptions from the provisions offering direct protection to the species in Annexes IV and V. Such derogations are admissible only where they meet three tests that have been strictly applied by the European Court of Justice[275]: that the action is not detrimental to the maintenance of the affected population at a favourable conservation status, that no satisfactory alternative exists, and that the harmful action is justified

---

[269] *Commission v Spain* (C-221/04) [2006] E.C.R. I-4515 at [71] and see the discussion in the opinion of Advocate-General Kokott at [37]–[54].

[270] Habitats and Species Directive art.12(2); e.g. *Commission v Greece* (C-103/00) [2002] E.C.R. I-1147 (disturbance of beaches used for turtle nests).

[271] See paras 7.4.38–7.4.39, below.

[272] *Commission v United Kingdom* (C-6/04) [2005] E.C.R. I-9017; *Commission v Germany* (C-98/03) [2006] E.C.R. I-53; *Commission v Ireland* (C-183/05) E.C.J. January 11, 2007.

[273] Habitats and Species Directive art.12(4); again these are duties that must be given legal status in domestic law (*Commission v United Kingdom* (C-6/04) [2005] E.C.R. I-9017).

[274] Habitats and Species Directive art.14; "favourable conservation status" is defined in art.1(e).

[275] *Commission v Germany* (C-98/03) [2006] E.C.R. I-53; *Commission v Finland* (C-342/05) [2007] E.C.R. I-4713.

on one of the specified grounds.[276] These permit derogations: in the interests of protecting wild fauna and flora and in conserving natural habitats; to prevent serious damage, in particular to crops, livestock, forests, fisheries and water; in the interests of public health and public safety; for other imperative reasons of overriding public interest, including those of a social or economic nature and the achievement of beneficial consequences of primary importance to the environment. Also covered is action taken for research and education, and for repopulating an area or reintroducing species (including any breeding and artificial propagation which may be necessary). Apart from these specific grounds, Member States are permitted to allow under strictly supervised conditions, on a selective basis and to a limited extent, the taking of Annex IV species in the limited numbers determined by the appropriate national authorities.

Every two years the Member States must submit to the Commission a **7.4.39** report on the derogations applied, giving details of the species affected, the reasons for the derogation, including where appropriate a reference to the alternatives considered and scientific data employed, the means of capturing or killing any animal which are permitted, the authority empowered to regulate and supervise the exceptions and the results of their supervision.[277] Within 12 months the Commission must give its opinion on the report and enforcement action may follow if the Commission considers that a state is in breach of its obligations under the Directive. The wide scope of some of the grounds for permitting exceptions, together with the general statement that social, economic, cultural and local factors are to be taken into account,[278] means that despite the apparently rigid rules laid down in the Directive, Member States will in fact enjoy a considerable discretion when it comes to carrying these provisions into practice.

In any case where the killing or capture of an animal listed in Annexes IV **7.4.40** or V is permitted, Member States are to prohibit the use of all indiscriminate means capable of causing the local disappearance of, or serious disturbance to, populations of the animals.[279] In particular Annex VI lists a number of methods to be banned, including explosives, electric devices, tape recorders, blind or maimed decoys, artificial lights and mirrors, night sights, non-selective nets and traps, poisons, gases and automatic and semi-automatic weapons, as well as any killing from aircraft or moving motor vehicles. Derogations are possible in relation to the specific methods listed, but not from the general obligation to prohibit the use of destructively indiscriminate methods.[280]

The Directive contains further provisions relating to information and **7.4.41** research. Member States are required to prepare a report on the implementation of the Directive every six years, containing information on the impact of the measures and the results of their surveillance[281] of the species and habitats affected.[282] On the basis of these reports, which are to be

---

[276] Habitats and Species Directive art.16(1); see Appendix C.
[277] Habitats and Species Directive art.16(2) and (3).
[278] Habitats and Species Directive art.2(3).
[279] Habitats and Species Directive art.15.
[280] Habitats and Species Directive art.16(1); *Commission v United Kingdom* (C-6/04) [2005] E.C.R. I-9017.
[281] See para.7.4.33, above and Habitats and Species Directive art.11.
[282] Habitats and Species Directive art.17(1).

accessible to the public, the Commission is to prepare a composite report for presentation to the Member States, the European Parliament, the Council and the Economic and Social Committee.[283] More generally, the Member States and Commission should encourage research and scientific work related to the objectives of the Directive, ensuring the exchange of information and coordination of work.[284] Particular attention should be paid to transboundary cooperation and scientific work relating to the conservation of Special Areas of Conservation and other features of landscape valuable to wildlife. States should also consider the reintroduction of species and promote education and general information on the need to protect wildlife and conserve habitats.[285]

7.4.42   Meeting the requirements of the Directive in Great Britain required clear legislative changes which were achieved by the Conservation (Natural Habitats, etc.) Regulations 1994.[286] These went a considerable way towards meeting the key elements of the Directive, but even before they were brought in to force it was noted that they did not fully cover all aspects of the Directive.[287] Both the domestic courts[288] and the European Court of Justice[289] have confirmed gaps in the implementation, including the failure to extend the provisions beyond territorial seas, inadequate surveillance to monitor the health of habitats and species and their incidental capture, failure to assess the impact of land use development plans on sites, gaps in the provisions on possessing and selling protected species and the existence of defences allowing non-deliberate but harmful conduct to be lawful. The formal identification of these failings has led to remedial legislation,[290] followed by further amending legislation when the Commission threatened further action over the inadequacy of aspects of that first response.[291] It should be noted, though, that the United Kingdom is far from alone in being found to have fallen short of full implementation on several points,[292] and has embarked on what seems to be the usual iterative process of moving

---

[283] Habitats and Species Directive art.17(2).

[284] Habitats and Species Directive art.18.

[285] Habitats and Species Directive art.22.

[286] SI 1994/2716.

[287] C.T. Reid and M. Woods, "Implementing EC Conservation Law" (2006) 18 J.E.L. 135 at 148.

[288] *R. v Secretary of State for Trade & Industry, ex p. Greenpeace Ltd. (No.2)* [2000] 2 C.M.L.R. 94; [2000] Env. L.R. 221.

[289] *Commission v United Kingdom* (C-6/04) [2005] E.C.R. I-9017; *Commission v United Kingdom* (C-131/05) E.C.J. November 17, 2005.

[290] Offshore Petroleum Activities (Conservation of Habitats) Regulations 2001 (SI 2001/1754); Conservation (Natural Habitats, etc.) Amendment (Scotland) Regulations 2007 (SSI 2007/80); Conservation (Natural Habitats, etc.) Amendment (No.2) (Scotland) Regulations 2007 (SSI 2007/349); Conservation (Natural Habitats, etc.) (Amendment) Regulations 2007 (SI 2007/1843) and Offshore Marine Conservation (Natural Habitats, etc.) Regulations 2007 (SI 2007/1842).

[291] Conservation (Natural Habitats, etc.) Amendment (No.2) (Scotland) Regulations 2008 (SSI 2008/425); Conservation (Natural Habitats, etc.) (Amendment) (England and Wales) Regulations 2009 (SI 2009/6); Offshore Marine Conservation (Natural Habitats, etc.) (Amendment) Regulations 2009 (SI 2009/7).

[292] e.g. *Commission v Luxembourg* (C-75/01) [2003] E.C.R. I-1585; *Commission v Belgium* (C-324/01) [2002] E.C.R. I-11,197; *Commission v Italy* (C-143/02) [2003] E.C.R. I-2877; in many of the cases on this issue the Member State has conceded at least some of its failings.

ever closer to a perfect match between the Directive and national law,[293] a process in which the government, official and non-official conservation bodies, the Commission, courts and individual complainants and litigants all have a role to play.

INTERNATIONAL OBLIGATIONS

As a party to a number of treaties, the United Kingdom has accepted **7.5.1** obligations in international law with respect to nature conservation. Unlike the provisions of European Community law, the terms of these treaties are not part of the law which can be relied on in the British courts. It is only if an Act of Parliament has been passed to incorporate such terms into domestic law, as has happened with the Antarctic Act 1994, that the treaties have any legal effect within the United Kingdom. Nevertheless, the fact that the government is bound by these obligations at the international level should have a significant impact on the policy and legislation which are adopted here.[294]

At the international level, there is no strict monitoring or enforcement **7.5.2** mechanism to ensure that states are fully complying with their treaty obligations.[295] Moreover, because of states' reluctance to be bound by concrete obligations that others may try to enforce, many of the international agreements in the environmental field take the form of provisions which are very general in their phrasing and exhortatory in their tone, setting out broad aims and intentions rather than creating precise rules and obligations, or there is reliance on "soft law", in the form of declarations and guidelines which it is not intended should be directly enforceable.[296] Critics can therefore argue that many of these measures are not "law" at all in the sense understood in a national context and are essentially worthless.

Although the weaknesses of the international law must be acknowledged, **7.5.3** the treaties which exist do play an important role. They provide the framework for international co-operation[297] in the field of nature conservation, co-operation which is essential if long-term conservation measures are to be taken on a regional or global scale. This co-operation can take many forms, from providing protection to migratory species throughout their range, to ensuring practical support for developing countries to ensure that the demands of economic development do not always override conservation interests.[298] At the very least treaties serve as public declarations of intent on the part of the states concerned, setting a standard

---

[293] The same process of initial implementing measures followed by amendments, often prompted by actual or threatened litigation has occurred in relation to the Birds and Environmental Impact Assessment Directives see para.7.4.17, above and para.8.3.7, below.

[294] See generally P. Birnie, A. Boyle and C. Redgwell, *International Law and the Environment*, 3rd edn (Oxford: OUP, 2009); M. Bowman and C. Redgwell (eds), *International Law and the Conservation of Biodiversity* (London: Kluwer, 1996).

[295] See generally S. Lyster, *International Wildlife Law* (Cambridge: Grotius, 1985), Chs 1 and 14, Birnie, Boyle and Redgwell, *International Law and the Environment*, 3rd edn (2009), Ch.4.

[296] Birnie, Boyle and Redgwell, *International Law and the Environment*, 3rd edn (2009), at pp.34–37.

[297] Birnie, Boyle and Redgwell, *International Law and the Environment*, 3rd edn (2009), Chs 1–5.

[298] Birnie, Boyle and Redgwell, *International Law and the Environment*, 3rd edn (2009), Ch.11.

against which their conduct can be judged. Some treaties, such as CITES, themselves provide some continuing mechanism, such as a central Secretariat or regular meetings of the parties, to ensure that states cannot simply forget about their terms, and in the modern world pressure groups can be relied on to draw attention to governmental failings. All governments are sensitive to criticism that they are in breach of their international obligations.

7.5.4 Perhaps more in the political than in the legal world, treaties do play a significant role in shaping the conduct of states, and provide strong bargaining counters when one state is trying to influence or seek co-operation from others. In a similar way, although the United Kingdom's treaty obligations lack legal force within this country, they have helped to shape domestic law and the need to comply with international obligations can be a strong argument in persuading the government to act in a particular way, even though there may be no realistic fear of any sanction being imposed if the obligation is broken.

7.5.5 The following conventions are discussed as examples of the main conservation treaties to which the United Kingdom is a party. There are many more agreements.[299] Some are of largely historical interest, e.g. the late nineteenth-century agreements on sealing in the northern Pacific,[300] whereas others are very much the subject of heated current debate, e.g. the International Convention for the Regulation of Whaling.[301] The impact during the past decades of the resolutions of the International Whaling Commission established by that treaty illustrate the power which such international agreements and organisations can have, as well as the ultimate weakness arising from the absence of direct, formal sanctions to ensure that decisions are observed. A number of other treaties deal directly with nature conservation, e.g. the Bonn Convention,[302] whilst many more, e.g. those relating to marine fishing and pollution of the seas and climate change, will also have an effect on the conservation of wild flora and fauna.[303]

---

[299] See, e.g. J. Beer-Gabel and B. Labat, *La protection internationale de la faune et de la flore suavages* (Brussels: Bruylant, 1999); M. Austen and T. Richards, *Basic Legal Documents on International Animal Welfare and Wildlife Conservation* (London: Kluwer, 2000); E. Louka, *International Environmental Law: Fairness, Effectiveness and World Order* (Cambridge: CUP, 2006), Ch.7; M. Bowman, "International Treaties and the Global Protection of Birds" (1999) 11 J.E.L. 87 and 281.

[300] See, e.g. the Behring Sea Award Act 1894 and the Seal Fisheries (North Pacific) Acts 1895 and 1912. This legislation is not wholly without current relevance; see the Seal Fisheries (North Pacific) Act 1912 (Amendment) Regulations 1996 (SI 1996/2685) (para.7.3.24, above).

[301] Agreed in 1946; see Lyster, *International Wildlife Law* (1985), Ch.2; Austen and Richards, *Basic Legal Documents on International Animal Welfare and Wildlife Conservation* (2000), p.121; Birnie, Boyle and Redgwell, *International Law and the Environment*, 3rd edn (2009), pp.724–727; and the International Whaling Commission's web pages at *http://www.iwcoffice.org* [Accessed May 15, 2009].

[302] Convention on the Conservation of Migratory Species of Wild Animals; see Lyster, *International Wildlife Law* (1985), Ch.13; Austen and Richards, *Basic Legal Documents on International Animal Welfare and Wildlife Conservation* (2000), p.30; Birnie, Boyle and Redgwell, *International Law and the Environment*, 3rd edn (2009), p.659; Bowman, "International Treaties and the Global Protection of Birds" (1999) 11 J.E.L. 87 and 281, at pp.282–293. See web pages at *http://www.cms.int* [Accessed May 15, 2009].

[303] See Birnie, Boyle and Redgwell, *International Law and the Environment*, 3rd edn (2009), Chs 11–13.

Ramsar

The Convention on Wetlands of International Importance Especially as **7.5.6**
Waterfowl Habitat was signed in 1971 in the town of Ramsar in northern
Iran, whence it takes its common name. The loss of wetlands through
drainage, development and pollution was identified as being a major and
widespread occurrence, threatening many species of plants and animals. The
impact of such loss of habitat may be felt far distant from the wetlands
themselves, as such habitat may provide breeding, feeding and resting
grounds for animals, fish and birds which travel far from a particular site in
their life cycles or annual migrations. The Convention imposes fairly general
obligations, centred on the identification of particular sites to be designated
by the parties as Wetlands of International Importance.[304]

For the purposes of Ramsar, "wetlands" is given a broad definition **7.5.7**
covering areas of marsh, fen, peatland or water, natural or artificial, permanent or temporary, with water that is static or flowing. The water may be
fresh, salt or brackish and the definition includes marine areas where the
depth of water at low tide does not exceed six metres.[305] In relation to all
wetlands in their territory, parties should formulate and implement their
planning to promote as far as possible the wise use of wetlands,[306] and
should promote the conservation of wetlands and waterfowl[307] by establishing nature reserves and providing for their wardening.[308] Parties must
also encourage research and the exchange of data and publications relating
to wetlands and their flora and fauna,[309] promote the training of personnel
competent in relevant research, management and wardening,[310] and should
endeavour through management to increase the waterfowl populations on
appropriate wetlands.[311] International consultation and co-operation are
required, especially where parties share a water system.[312]

Each party is also bound to designate suitable wetlands for inclusion in **7.5.8**
the List of Wetlands of International Importance, as discussed in
section 5.11 above.[313] The conservation of these wetlands should be promoted and their condition monitored,[314] and compensatory measures should
be taken if a party in its "urgent national interest" deletes any wetland from
the List or restricts it.[315] The List is to be maintained by a bureau operated

---

[304] See generally, Lyster, *International Wildlife Law* (1985), Ch.10; Austen and Richards, *Basic Legal Documents on Basic Animal Welfare and Wildlife Conservation* (2000), p.9; Birnie, Boyle and Redgwell, *International Law and the Environment*, 3rd edn (2009), pp.672–677; Bowman, "International Treaties and the Global Protection of Birds" (1999) 11 J.E.L. 87, at pp.94–100; and web pages at *http://www.ramsar.org* [Accessed May 15, 2009].

[305] Ramsar Convention art.1(1).

[306] Ramsar Convention art.3(1); D. Farrier and L. Tucker, "Wise Use of Wetlands under the Ramsar Convention: A Challenge for Meaningful Implementation of International Law" (2000) 12 J.E.L. 21.

[307] Defined as "birds ecologically dependent on wetlands"; Ramsar Convention art.1(2).

[308] Ramsar Convention art.4(1).

[309] Ramsar Convention art.4(3).

[310] Ramsar Convention art.4(5).

[311] Ramsar Convention art.4(4).

[312] Ramsar Convention art.5.

[313] Ramsar Convention art.2; the law in Great Britain now requires that these sites are notified to various authorities (WCA 1981 s.37A, inserted by CRWA 2000 s.77; NCSA 2004 s.38); see paras 5.11.4–5.11.7, above.

[314] Ramsar Convention art.3.

[315] Ramsar Convention art.4(2).

by the IUCN,[316] and conferences of the parties can be called to discuss the implementation of and amendments to the Convention, and other related matters.[317]

7.5.9   The obligations imposed by Ramsar are not particularly strong, requiring the promotion and encouragement of and endeavour towards the stated aims, rather than demanding more specific action. Although its terms may not provide any strict legal protection, nevertheless, by focusing attention on the plight of wetlands and establishing the List conferring international status on particular sites, the Convention should ensure that the parties cannot ignore the fate of wetlands and should pay some heed to their conservation in their policy and legislation. The extent to which this will be reflected in practice will obviously depend on the importance of nature conservation in the political battles within each state.

World Heritage Convention

7.5.10 The Convention Concerning the Protection of the World Cultural and Natural Heritage was agreed in 1972 under the auspices of UNESCO.[318] The Convention is based on the idea that certain great treasures of the world, such as the Taj Mahal and the Grand Canyon, constitute part of the heritage not merely of one state but of mankind as a whole. Accordingly, such treasures should be given international recognition and protection, and the international community should provide positive and practical assistance to ensure their conservation. The aim is to ensure the long-term conservation of the outstanding natural and man-made features of the world.

7.5.11   The Convention imposes a general obligation on parties to ensure the identification, protection, conservation and transmission to future generations of the cultural and natural heritage situated in their territory.[319] The natural heritage is defined as: natural features consisting of physical or biological formations of outstanding universal value from the aesthetic or scientific point of view; geological and physiographical formations and precise areas which constitute the habitat of threatened species of animals and plants of outstanding value from the point of view of science or conservation; natural sites or precise areas which are of outstanding universal value from the point of view of science, conservation or natural beauty.[320] The definition thus covers aesthetic merits as well as scientific ones.

7.5.12   In relation to this heritage, the parties are to ensure that effective and active measures are taken for the protection, conservation and presentation of the heritage in their territory.[321] As far as possible, each party should adopt a general policy integrating the protection of the heritage into its comprehensive planning programmes, establish services for the protection,

---

[316] Ramsar Convention arts 2(1) and 8.

[317] Ramsar Convention art.6; it is expressly provided that the parties' representatives should include experts on wetlands and waterfowl (art.7(1)).

[318] See Lyster, *International Wildlife Law* (1985), Ch.11; Birnie, Boyle and Redgwell, *International Law and the Environment*, 3rd edn (2009), pp.677–680; and web pages at *http://whc.unesco.org* [Accessed May 15, 2009].

[319] World Heritage Convention art.4; the words used require states to "do all [they] can to this end, to the utmost of [their] resources".

[320] World Heritage Convention art.2; the Operational Guidelines for identifying such sites is available at the website noted above.

[321] World Heritage Convention art.5.

etc. of the heritage, undertake research and develop operating methods to counteract dangers to the heritage, take legal, administrative, financial and scientific measures to ensure the identification, protection and rehabilitation of the heritage and foster the establishment of training for the protection, etc. of the heritage. Parties should also endeavour, particularly through education and information, to strengthen appreciation and respect by their peoples of the cultural and natural heritage and to keep the public broadly informed of the dangers threatening the heritage and the activities carried out under the Convention.[322]

In practice these obligations are focused on the sites which have been **7.5.13** accepted for the World Heritage List, as discussed earlier,[323] but they do apply more generally and do require measures to identify the outstanding features within each state and to conserve them pending consideration for the List. With regard to other states, the parties are required to offer assistance when requested in the identification, protection, etc. of the heritage of other states, and to refrain from any deliberate measures which might damage that heritage directly or indirectly.[324] The obligation to offer assistance is given more tangible form through the World Heritage Fund,[325] to be used for financial or other assistance to states undertaking appropriate measures for the benefit of their heritage.[326] Parties may also take an active role in furthering the aims of the Convention by participating in the World Heritage Committee which is responsible for deciding on which sites are to be listed and on the use of the Fund and other forms of international assistance.[327]

Through the World Heritage Convention, the fate of the natural and **7.5.14** man-made treasures of the world legitimately become the concern of the international community as a whole, not merely an internal matter for the state where each lies. For developing countries this concern can take the tangible form of financial and technical support to ensure the conservation of those treasures. For the developed world, the international attention should ensure that states live up to their declared intentions of ensuring proper protection for the sites identified. Any detailed conservation measures will remain a matter for the particular state, but the obligations in the Convention present a standard against which they can be judged by the public and by other states and the delisting of a site will be a considerable embarrassment to any state claiming to be supportive of the Convention's objectives.

---

[322] World Heritage Convention art.27.
[323] See paras 5.11.8–5.11.10, above.
[324] World Heritage Convention art.6.
[325] World Heritage Convention arts 15–18.
[326] World Heritage Convention arts 19–26.
[327] World Heritage Convention arts 8–14.

Bern Convention

7.5.15 The Convention on the Conservation of European Wildlife and Natural Habitats was agreed in Bern in 1979,[328] under the auspices of the Council of Europe.[329] It aims to conserve wild flora and fauna and their habitats, especially where this will require the co-operation of several states and particularly with regard to endangered and vulnerable species.[330] The Convention has played a major role in inspiring and providing the formulation for the European Community Directives on Wild Birds and on Habitats and Species.[331]

7.5.16 The Convention begins by imposing very general obligations on the parties to maintain the population of wild flora and fauna at, or to adapt it to, a level which corresponds to ecological, scientific and cultural requirements, taking account of economic and recreational requirements.[332] Steps are to be taken to promote national policies for the conservation of wild flora, wild fauna and natural habitats, while regard is to be paid to the requirements of such conservation in each party's planning and development policies and in measures to control pollution. Each party should also promote education and disseminate general information on the need to conserve species of wild flora and fauna and their habitats.[333] The parties undertake to co-ordinate their efforts under the Convention in relation to migratory species,[334] and to encourage and co-ordinate research related to the purposes of the Convention.[335] Also to be encouraged is the reintroduction of native species where this would contribute to the conservation of endangered species, while the introduction of non-native species is to be strictly controlled.[336]

7.5.17 As far as habitat is concerned, the parties are obliged to take appropriate and necessary legislative and administrative measures to ensure the conservation of the habitats of wild flora and fauna, especially those listed in Appendices I and II. As far as possible the deterioration of such habitat should be minimised by conservation requirements being taken into account in planning and development policies. Special attention should be paid to sites used by migratory species, and states should co-ordinate their efforts in relation to habitats in frontier areas.[337] Such provisions, whilst ensuring that regard should be had to the needs of conservation, do allow very considerable discretion to each party and avoid any identification of particular sites at an international level.

---

[328] See Lyster, *International Wildlife Law* (1985), Ch. 8; Austen and Richards, *Basic Legal Documents on International Animal Welfare and Wildlife Conservation* (2000), p.171; Bowman, "International Treaties and the Global Protection of Birds" (1999) 11 J.E.L. 87, at pp.106–119; and the Council of Europe's relevant web-pages at *http://www.coe.int/t/dg4/cultureheritage/Conventions/Bern/* [Accessed May 15, 2009].

[329] The Convention is open to signature by non-members of the Council and indeed by non-European states, as its provisions affect species which travel beyond Europe (Burkino Faso, Morocco, Senegal and Tunisia have become parties); Bern Convention art. 20.

[330] Bern Convention art.1.

[331] See section 7.4, above.

[332] Bern Convention art.2; cf. Birds Directive art.2 (para.7.4.6, above).

[333] Bern Convention art.3.

[334] Bern Convention art.10.

[335] Bern Convention art.11(1).

[336] Bern Convention art.11(2).

[337] Bern Convention art.4.

The particular species of plants in Appendix I and animals in Appendix II **7.5.18** are to be given special protection by appropriate legislative and administrative measures. For the plants listed in Appendix I, the deliberate picking, collecting, cutting or uprooting is to be prohibited, as is their possession and sale.[338] For the animals in Appendix II, the measures should include the prohibition of all forms of deliberate capture, keeping and killing, deliberate damage to or destruction of breeding or resting sites, deliberate disturbance which is significant in relation to the aims of the Convention, deliberate destruction, taking or keeping of eggs, and the possession and trading in the animals, alive or dead.[339]

For a further category of animals, listed in Appendix III, measures are to **7.5.19** be taken to ensure their protection.[340] The exploitation of such animals is permitted, but must be controlled by measures such as close seasons, temporary or local prohibitions on exploitation to allow populations to recover, and regulation of their sale and related activities.[341] Where capture and killing is permitted, either of Appendix III animals or those of Appendix II under special exceptions, all indiscriminate methods are to be prohibited, as are those capable of causing serious disturbance to the local population and those methods specified in Appendix IV.[342]

Exceptions to the protective measures discussed above are permitted **7.5.20** where there is no other satisfactory solution, the exception will not be detrimental to the survival of the population concerned, and is required on one of the following grounds:

(a) the protection of flora and fauna;
(b) the prevention of serious damage to crops, livestock, forests, fisheries, water and other forms of property;
(c) in the interests of public health and safety, air safety or other overriding public interests;
(d) research, education, repopulation and reintroduction; or
(e) judicious and selective exploitation of certain species under strictly supervised conditions.[343]

These exceptions must be notified in reports made every two years to the Standing Committee established under the Convention.

As mentioned earlier, these provisions lie behind much that is in the **7.5.21** European Community's Birds and Habitats and Species Directives. Since these Directives have legal force within the United Kingdom and impose more detailed obligations, especially in relation to particular sites and the scrutiny of any exceptions to the protection provided, it is the Directives rather than the Convention that will have a practical impact. However, in extending beyond the Member States the commitment to and co-operation on nature conservation, and in providing a further layer of legal recognition

---

[338] Bern Convention art.5.
[339] Bern Convention art.6.
[340] As opposed to the "special protection" for Appendix II animals.
[341] Bern Convention art.7.
[342] Bern Convention art.8.
[343] Bern Convention art.9; cf. Habitats and Species Directive art.16 (see para.7.4.38, above).

for the needs of certain endangered species, the Convention does still play a role in the conservation of Europe's natural heritage.

Convention on Biological Diversity

7.5.22 The Convention on Biological Diversity was signed at the Earth Summit in Rio de Janeiro in June 1992.[344] The aims of the Convention are the conservation of biological diversity, the sustainable use of its components ("genetic resources, organisms ... or any other biotic component of ecosystems with actual or potential use or value for humanity"), and the fair and equitable sharing of the benefits of such use, including access to biological resources and the transfer of technology.[345] Much of the Convention, and most of the controversy surrounding its adoption, concerns the provisions on access to biological resources, the exploitation of which is clearly stated to be a sovereign right of the state where they are found.[346] Other states should have access to a nation's resources on an agreed basis, which should include arrangements for sharing the benefits of their use and the transfer of the technology to exploit them.[347] In particular the developed countries should provide technical and financial assistance to the developing countries to further the aims of the Convention.[348]

7.5.23 As far as conservation is concerned, there are broadly phrased obligations on all of the signatories, obligations qualified by phrases such as "as far as possible and appropriate". National strategies for the conservation and sustainable use of biological resources should be developed and integrated into the other policies of the state.[349] Protected areas should be established, and in the areas surrounding these environmentally sound and sustainable development should be promoted to further their protection. Degraded ecosystems should be rehabilitated, threatened species should be protected and the introduction of damaging aliens should be prohibited or controlled.[350] Away from the habitats in question, but preferably within the state of origin, steps should be taken to further such *in situ* measures,[351] and to promote research and training and public education and awareness.[352] Economically and socially sound measures that act as incentives for the conservation and sustainable use of biological resources should be adopted.[353] Environmental impact assessment should be employed where proposed projects are likely to have significant adverse effects on biological diversity, such effects should be minimised, and responses prepared to

---

[344] See Birnie, Boyle and Redgwell, *International Law and the Environment*, 3rd edn (2009), pp.612–649; website at *http://www.cbd.int*, especially *Handbook of the Convention on Biological Diversity* at *http://www.cbd.int/convention/refrhandbook.shtml* [Both Accessed May 15, 2009].

[345] Convention on Biological Diversity art.1.

[346] Convention on Biological Diversity art.3.

[347] Convention on Biological Diversity arts 15–19.

[348] Convention on Biological Diversity art.20; it is expressly stated that the extent to which the developing world will effectively implement its obligations will depend on the extent to which the developed world effectively implements its commitments in relation to finance and the transfer of technology (art.20(4)).

[349] Convention on Biological Diversity arts 6 and 10; see para.1.2.4, above.

[350] Convention on Biological Diversity art.8.

[351] Convention on Biological Diversity art.9.

[352] Convention on Biological Diversity arts 12 and 13.

[353] Convention on Biological Diversity art.11.

emergencies, natural or man-made, presenting grave and imminent danger to biological diversity.[354]

All of these measures, and the general exhortation to international co- **7.5.24** operation,[355] are too vague to have any direct legal significance here. The Convention is primarily a political statement, but does try to ensure continuing attention and action through the Conferences of the Parties and the requirements on parties to report on their progress,[356] as well as through the operation of financial mechanisms to assist developing countries. The Conference has already led to one further agreement in 2000, adding to the Convention a Protocol on Biosafety, dealing with transit, handling and use of genetically modified organisms.[357] The immediate practical results of the Convention may be very limited, but it serves to place issues of conservation and sustainable use firmly on the international negotiating table.

Antarctic Treaties

Although unlikely to be of practical relevance to many readers of this book, **7.5.25** the various treaties designed to protect the Antarctic environment merit a brief mention since certain key provisions have been incorporated into domestic law. The parties to the Antarctic Treaty of 1959[358] have agreed further measures to protect that region, most notably the Protocol on Environmental Protection agreed in 1991, which designates Antarctica as a "natural reserve, devoted to peace and science" and recognises protection of its environment as fundamental to all activities in the area.[359] This was in part a reaction to the abortive Convention on the Regulation of Antarctic Mineral Resource Activities (1988) and supports or supersedes the earlier conservation measures, under the Agreed Measures for the Conservation of Antarctic Fauna and Flora (1964), the Convention for the Conservation of Antarctic Seals (1972), and the Convention on the Conservation of Antarctic Marine Living Resources (1980).[360]

The Antarctic Act 1994 has given effect to these provisions so that there **7.5.26** are severe restrictions enforceable under British law.[361] For the purposes of this legislation, Antarctica is defined as the whole area south of the sixtieth parallel of south latitude,[362] and restrictions also apply to certain areas north of that latitude designated as protected places under the 1980 Convention.[363]

---

[354] Convention on Biological Diversity art.14.

[355] Convention on Biological Diversity art.5.

[356] See para.1.2.4, above.

[357] Known as the Cartagena Protocol; see *http://www.cbd.int/biosafety/* [Accessed May 15, 2009].

[358] Relevant provisions of the Treaty were incorporated into UK law by the Antarctic Treaty Act 1967.

[359] Protocol on Environmental Protection to the Antarctic Treaty (1991) arts 2 and 3(1).

[360] See Lyster, *International Wildlife Law* (1985), Ch.9; further information is available on the web pages of the British Antarctic Survey, at *http://www.antarctica.ac.uk/* [Accessed May 15, 2009], in the "About Antarctica" section, and on those of the Commission for the Conservation of Antarctic Marine Living Resources (CCAMLR) at *http://www.ccamlr.org/pu/e/gen-intro.htm* [Accessed May 15, 2009].

[361] Also the Antarctic Regulations 1995 (SI 1995/490) and a series of Antarctic (Amendment) Regulations (SI 1998/1007, SI 2000/2147, SI 2002/2054, SI 2003/323, SI 2004/2782 and SI 2008/3066).

[362] Antarctic Act 1994 s.1.

[363] Antarctic Act 1994 s.11.

Unless a permit has been obtained, UK nationals[364] commit a crime under the 1994 Act if they do any of the following in Antarctica: intentionally kill, capture, handle or molest any native mammal or bird; intentionally disturb breeding or moulting birds or concentrations of mammals or birds; use vehicles, vessels or explosives to disturb such concentrations; significantly damage concentrations of native plants or remove or damage plants so that their local abundance or distribution is affected; or do anything likely to cause significant damage to habitat.[365] The introduction of any non-native animal or plant is also an offence, unless they are kept on board a vessel.[366]

7.5.27   Permits are required for any person to enter or remain in Antarctica on a British expedition (i.e. one organised in or taking its final departure from the UK), for any person to stay at a British Antarctic station, or for any British vessel or aircraft to enter Antarctica, except in transit or for commercial fishing (which is separately regulated).[367] Without a specific permit it is an offence for any UK national to engage in any mineral-related activities (including surveying)[368] and separate permits are needed to enter designated protected areas.[369] In granting permits the Minister is to have regard to the terms and objectives of the 1980 Protocol.[370] No damage is to be done to Antarctic Historic Sites or Monuments. Defences exist in emergency situations and where the events were beyond the control of an accused who had taken all reasonable precautions.[371]

Other Treaties

7.5.28   Amongst other treaties, a number relate to the conservation of particular species. These include:

- the Convention for the Conservation of Salmon in the North Atlantic Ocean[372]: This restricts fishing for salmon in the North Atlantic, within and beyond national fisheries jurisdiction, and establishes the North Atlantic Salmon Conservation Organisation, with regional Commissions. These act to gather information and assist co-operation in relation to the conservation, enhancement and rational management of salmon stocks, with limited powers to introduce regulatory measures;
- the Agreement on the Conservation of Bats in Europe (EURO-BATS)[373]: under this agreement, states are required to prohibit, except under specific permit, the deliberate capture, keeping or

---

[364] Defined in Antarctic Act 1994 s.31(1) and including British companies.
[365] Antarctic Act 1994 s.7.
[366] Antarctic Act 1994 s.8.
[367] Antarctic Act 1994 ss.3–5.
[368] Antarctic Act 1994 s.6.
[369] Antarctic Act 1994 s.10.
[370] Antarctic Act 1994 s.15.
[371] Antarctic Act 1994 s.18.
[372] Convention for the Conservation of Salmon in the North Atlantic Ocean 1982; Austen and Richards, *Basic Legal Documents on International Animal Welfare and Wildlife Conservation* (2000), p.283; see *http://www.nasco.int/* [Accessed May 15, 2009].
[373] Agreement on the Conservation of Bats in Europe (EUROBATS) 1991; Austen and Richards, *Basic Legal Documents on International Animal Welfare and Wildlife Conservation* (2000), p.296; see *http://www.eurobats.org/* [Accessed May 15, 2009] and para.3.4.21 above.

killing of all species of bats within their territory. They should also identify and protect sites that are important for the conservation status of bats and endeavour to protect important feeding areas; and

- the Agreement on the Conservation of Small Cetaceans of the Baltic and North Seas (ASCOBANS)[374]: building on the Bonn and Bern Conventions,[375] this calls on states to co-operate closely in order to improve the conservation status of all toothed whales in the seas that are covered by the agreement, in particular introducing legislation to prevent the taking and killing of these animals, working towards the prevention of pollution, disturbance, fishing practices and other activities that threaten the species, carrying out joint research and establishing systems for reporting and retrieving by-catches and stranded specimens. The area covered by the Convention was significantly extended in 2008 to cover areas west of the United Kingdom, Ireland, France, Spain and Portugal.[376]

These and the other measures listed in this Chapter are just examples of a large body of international law affecting nature conservation in many direct and indirect ways.

---

[374] Agreed in 1992 and now formally the Agreement on the Conservation of Small Cetaceans of the Baltic, North East Atlantic, Irish and North Seas following amendments that came into force in 2008; Austen and Richards, *Basic Legal Documents on International Animal Welfare and Wildlife Conservation* (2000), p.300; see *http://www.ascobans.org/index0401.html* [Accessed May 15, 2009] and paras 3.4.38–3.4.40 above.

[375] See paras 7.5.5 and 7.5.15–7.5.21, above.

[376] Agreement on the Conservation of Small Cetaceans of the Baltic, North East Atlantic, Irish and North Seas.

8. MISCELLANEOUS

8.1.1 The previous Chapters have covered the law which is most directly concerned with nature conservation, but many other areas of the law can also have a considerable impact on conservation and on the fate of wild plants and animals and their habitat. This Chapter aims to draw attention to some of these further areas of law. As almost all human activities do or could have some effect on the environment many more areas of legal regulation could be included. Indeed one of the challenges today is to ensure that the political rhetoric on sustainability and environmental concern, and the legal duties in relation to biodiversity, are matched by an awareness of the ways in which so many areas of policy and law have environmental consequences, albeit unintentionally and indirectly.

8.1.2 Town and country planning is an obvious candidate for a brief treatment here, followed by the linked topic of environmental assessment. As its effect on the countryside is so great, agriculture must be considered, and pollution control is important both for the general health of the environment and to protect sites from particular threats. The control of water resources is crucial to many habitats, while the development of genetic modification has added a new dimension to concerns about contamination of the natural world. Finally the extent to which wildlife can be a legal liability to a landowner is considered.

Town and Country Planning

8.2.1 The system of town and country planning is the most important means by which land use is regulated in this country and is therefore of great importance to nature conservation. We have already seen in Chapter 5 how in many cases provisions designed to conserve habitats operate in conjunction with the planning legislation. This section offers a very brief and vague account of the planning system, followed by an indication of the opportunities at various stages in the planning process for nature conservation to be taken into account.

8.2.2 The brevity and vagueness are the product of two factors. The first is that the subject is thoroughly covered by other books and journals where an understanding of the detailed operation of the system can be obtained.[1] The

---

[1] In Scotland, J. Rowan Robinson et al., *Scottish Planning Law and Procedure* (Edinburgh: W. Green, 2001), N. Collar, *Planning*, 2nd edn (Edinburgh: W. Green, 1999), A. McAllister and R. McMaster, *Scottish Planning Law*, 2nd edn (Edinburgh: Butterworths, 1999), B. Gill and M. Thomson (eds), *Scottish Planning Encyclopaedia* (looseleaf) (Edinburgh: W. Green), and the journal *Scottish Planning and Environmental Law*. In England there is a very wide choice of books—the recent general texts include J. Cameron Blackhall, *Planning Law and Practice*, 3rd edn (Abingdon: Routledge-Cavendish, 2005); R. Duxbury, *Telling & Duxbury's Planning Law and Procedure*, 14th edn (Oxford: OUP, 2009), V. Moore, *A Practical Approach to Planning Law*, 10th edn (Oxford: OUP, 2007); there are also a number of looseleaf works and the leading periodical is the *Journal of Environmental and Planning Law*. New editions and books can be expected as the recent legislation comes into force.

second is that both in Scotland and in England and Wales the system is undergoing significant transformation.[2] In Scotland, the Planning etc. (Scotland) Act 2006 introduces changes at many levels of the process, but it is coming into force incrementally, with much depending on detailed regulations which have not yet all emerged.[3] In England and Wales the Planning and Compulsory Purchase Act 2004 introduced a new framework for development planning. This has been followed by the Planning Act 2008 which was passed only at the end of that year after much debate, heated at times, which led to considerable alterations during the parliamentary process; implementing the new Act will, as in Scotland, be a prolonged operation.

Despite the recent legislative activity, the fundamentals of the modern **8.2.3** planning system remain unchanged since its introduction in 1947.[4] There are two main elements. The first is development planning, the establishment of broad plans, setting out general policies for development and providing, together with national policy statements, the framework within which individual decisions are taken. The second element is development control or management,[5] which requires that permission from the planning authority must be obtained before it is lawful to proceed with certain operations on land or changes in the use of land. Unlike systems in other countries which rely on rigid zoning, the outcome of each application is at the discretion of the authority, guided, but not dictated, by the relevant policy. The system is operated by a partnership (not always harmonious) of central and local government.[6] The detailed procedures involved have varied over the decades, as have the balance between Ministers and planning authorities, the opportunities for public participation and the weight given to development plans and national policies, but for all the talk at various times of fundamental reform, this basic structure remains unaltered.

In terms of who takes decisions, general policy is set by the Minister, **8.2.4** expressed primarily through national policy statements and the many more detailed policy guidance notes and circulars that are of major importance in determining how the system operates in practice. The Minister (acting through reporters or inspectors[7] who decide most cases independently) also decides appeals against the individual decisions taken by local planning authorities and can "call in" particular cases for initial determination. At local level, planning functions are divided between the tiers of local government where there is not a unitary system, with some matters being dealt with on a joint basis. Special rules do or may apply for many specially

---

[2] With the unfortunate consequence that the works noted above are, or are becoming, out of date.

[3] Whereas the Scottish Executive's *Planning etc. (Scotland) Act 2006 Implementation Timetable* produced in March 2007 set "Autumn 2008" for the final stage in the implementation process, the version in March 2009 extends to November 2010.

[4] Town and Country Planning Act 1947 and Town and Country Planning (Scotland) Act 1947.

[5] The new name "development management" is introduced by the Planning etc. (Scotland) Act 2006.

[6] With the addition of the Infrastructure Planning Commission in England and Wales; see para.8.2.14, below.

[7] "Reporters" in Scotland and "inspectors" in England and Wales.

designated areas, e.g. National Parks[8] or conservation areas.[9] In England and Wales an innovation being introduced is the ministerially appointed Infrastructure Planning Commission which will determine applications in relation to specified nationally significant infrastructure projects.[10]

8.2.5   The planning procedures offer several opportunities for nature conservation to be taken into account, and this forms the subject of substantial ministerial guidance.[11] As planning is undoubtedly a statutory function relating to land, all the authorities in the exercise of their powers are under a duty to have regard to conserving the natural heritage of Scotland (Scotland) or to the desirability of conserving the natural beauty and amenity of the countryside (England and Wales).[12] Authorities are also bound by their general obligations to exercise functions so as to further biodiversity.[13] In addition, various functions are expressly stated as ones to be fulfilled with the objective of contributing to sustainable development.[14] Where European sites or other designated areas are affected, more direct obligations will apply, as described in Chapter 5, and in some cases an environmental impact assessment will be necessary.[15] Arguments based on nature conservation are thus very relevant to the planning process.

8.2.6   If attention is going to be paid to nature conservation, it is important that it should be considered at an early stage in proceedings. Conservation should not be seen as something to be added on at the last minute once all the important points of a plan or a proposal have been finalised. Instead, nature conservation should be one of the fundamental factors considered right from the start, along with, for example, basic infrastructure provision. If conservation is considered at this stage, it will often be possible to choose an option which can at least go a long way towards meeting the concerns of the environment without unduly compromising the ambitions of the developer. Nature conservation should help to shape the final decision, and not be seen as something fighting against it. These issues are as significant in urban areas as in rural ones. The value of urban areas in conservation is slowly being appreciated, both as refuges from the pressures of intensive agriculture and as the place where most people first come into contact with wildlife, and in the urban areas it is the planning system that will be the dominant means of regulating land use and development.

---

[8] See section 5.9, above.

[9] See section 5.10, above.

[10] Planning Act 2008 Pts 1–8; see para.8.2.14, below.

[11] In Scotland, NPPG 14: *Natural Heritage* (1999) and PAN 60: *Planning for Natural Heritage* (2000 and updates) (in April 2009 consultation began on a draft Scottish Planning Policy which proposes replacing NPPG 14 and integrating a shorter version of the guidance on this and many other issues into a single document); in England PPS 9: *Biodiversity and Geological Conservation* (2005) and accompanying Circular (06/05) and *Guide to Good Practice*; in Wales TAN 5, *Nature Conservation and Planning* (1996).

[12] CSA 1967 s.66, amended by NHSA Sch.10; CA 1968 s.11; the references to the natural heritage and the natural beauty of the countryside are expressly stated to include the flora and fauna and geological and physiographical features of the land; see para.2.2.6, above.

[13] NHSA 2004 s.1; NERCA 2006 s.40; see paras 1.2.8–1.2.10, above.

[14] e.g. the National Planning Framework and development planning in Scotland (TCPSA 1997 ss.3D–3E, added by Planning etc. (Scotland) Act 2006 ss.1–2); national policy statements in England and Wales (Planning Act 2008 s.10).

[15] See section 8.3, below.

Development Planning

Development planning requires planning authorities to establish plans set- **8.2.7**
ting out their policies for their areas. It is provided that "unless material
considerations indicate otherwise", individual planning decisions are to be
made in accordance with these development plans.[16] As these plans will
obviously be of great significance for individual decisions, those with an
interest in land use issues must ensure that they take the opportunity to
become involved in the making of the plans, as by the time that a specific
application comes to be considered it may be too late to raise questions of
general policy. Public participation takes the form of consultation and on
occasions an "examination in public", a form of public inquiry into aspects
of the plan.

The pattern until recently has generally been for the development plan to **8.2.8**
be a combination of two tiers, the structure and the local plans, although
unitary development plans exist for some areas. The structure plan, prepared at the regional or county level, is designed to provide "a long-term
vision, looking forward at least 10 years, as part of an overview of an area's
development requirements",[17] setting out major policies and proposals and
providing strategic development control policies, covering both development and protection of the built and natural heritage, and which will in turn
guide the preparation of local plans. Local plans are more specific, including
a map of the area affected, and should provide clear guidance to potential
developers and a clear statement of the planning authority's development
control policies. A recurring problem has been the difficulty of keeping plans
up to date, especially where the holding of lengthy inquiries slows progress.

This pattern is now changing. In Scotland the National Planning Fra- **8.2.9**
mework which sets out general policy has been put on a statutory footing
(but does not count as part of "the development plan" for an area)[18] and also
identifies certain "national developments" which will be subject to different
approval procedures in which the need for the development will not be
reopened. In addition to the National Planning Framework, most of the
country will in the future be covered by single local development plans. For
the four main city regions[19] the relevant planning authorities must also
combine to produce a strategic development plan. Local development plans
must be consistent with the National Framework and where relevant the
strategic plan, which must also be consistent with the National Framework.[20]

---

[16] TCPSA 1997 s.25, as substituted by Planning etc. (Scotland) Act 2006 s.2; Planning and
Compulsory Purchase Act 2004 s.38(6).

[17] NPPG 1: *The Planning System* (SEDD, 2000), para.29.

[18] Planning etc. (Scotland) Act 2006 Pt 1. The Framework must be laid before, but does not
need approval from, the Parliament.

[19] Glasgow, Edinburgh, Aberdeen and Dundee; Strategic Planning Development Authority
Designation (Nos 1–4) Orders 2008 (SSIs 2008/195–198). The requirement for Fife Council to
participate in both the Edinburgh and Dundee plans is an interesting echo of the soundly
argued proposal in the Report of the Wheatley Commission that Fife should be split between
these two areas when local government was restructured on the basis of regions and districts, a
proposal defeated by a vociferous local campaign to keep Fife as a region in its own right
(Royal Commission on Local Government in Scotland 1966–69 (1969) Cmnd.4150).

[20] Planning etc. (Scotland) Act 2006 Pt 2; Town and Country Planning (Development
Planning) (Scotland) Regulations 2008 (SSI 2008/426); Planning etc. (Scotland) Act 2006
(Development Planning) (Saving, Transitional and Consequential Provisions) Order 2008 (SSI
2008/427).

In England and Wales, the pattern of development policy is to be the National Policy Statements (prepared by the Minister and laid before Parliament),[21] the Regional Spatial Strategies (prepared by the Regional Planning Board)[22] and local development plan documents (prepared by the local authority).[23] Throughout the country policy and decisions will also be affected by National Park Plans[24] and River Basin Management Plans.[25]

8.2.10   Development planning functions must be exercised so as to contribute to sustainable development,[26] and plans can only be approved where they have been assessed and found to meet the requirements of the Habitats and Species Directive, either because they do not envisage adverse impacts on protected features or such impacts are justified according to the standards set there.[27] In particular the plans must include policies encouraging the management of features of the landscape which are of particular importance for wild flora and fauna. For this purpose these are specified as those features which by their linear or continuous structure (e.g. rivers, traditional field boundaries) or through their role as "stepping-stones" (e.g. ponds or small woodlands) are essential for the migration, dispersal or genetic exchange of wild species.[28] There is thus a direct statutory requirement to give assistance to nature conservation through the preservation of "green corridors", i.e. corridors of undeveloped land which link areas of park and countryside. Such corridors are very valuable in providing pathways for wildlife between different areas, enabling plants and animals to colonise new habitats and to recover from any local setbacks, thereby safeguarding the longer term conservation value of parks, etc. and are also likely to be of amenity value as walks, cycle tracks or simply breaks in otherwise built-up areas. Plans can also include policies to protect the most valuable sites, to discourage development likely to be harmful and to preserve the variety of habitats in the relevant area, and to encourage the enhancement of biodiversity, especially when derelict land or old mineral sites are being restored. Such action should be seen as making a worthwhile contribution to the general amenity of an area, not simply as a matter of nature conservation.

Development Control and Management

8.2.11   The other main aspect of the planning system is development control,[29] the grant or refusal of planning permission for particular proposals.[30] The most important concept here is "development", as whether or not permission is required for a proposal depends on whether or not it qualifies as "development". In this context "development" is defined as "the carrying out of building, engineering, mining or other operations in, on, over or under land

---

[21] Planning Act 2008 Pt 2.
[22] Planning and Compulsory Purchase Act 2004 Pt 1.
[23] Planning and Compulsory Purchase Act 2004 Pt 2.
[24] See section 5.9, above.
[25] See section 8.6, below.
[26] TCPSA 1997 s.3E, added by Planning etc. (Scotland) Act 2006 s.2; Planning and Compulsory Purchase Act 2004 s.39.
[27] CNHR 1994 regs 85A–85E, added separately by CNHAR 2007 reg.5(55) and CNHASR 2007 reg.22 and Sch.1; see para.5.2.34, above.
[28] CNHR 1994 reg.37, implementing art.10 of the Habitats and Species Directive.
[29] Renamed "development management" by the Planning etc. (Scotland) Act 2006.
[30] TCPSA 1997 Pt III; TCPA 1990 Pt III.

or the making of any material change in the use of any buildings or other land."[31] This definition has given rise to a wealth of case-law, individual cases being complicated by the problems of multiple and ancillary uses and the difficulty of ascertaining the correct area of ground ("planning unit") in relation to which the activity in question should be considered. Only through a study of the case-law can the full meaning of this evolving term be understood.[32]

The scope of "development" is qualified by a number of other provisions. **8.2.12** Some things are expressly declared not to amount to development, e.g. the use of land for agriculture or forestry, while others are expressly declared to be development, e.g. the deposit of waste material (however authorised) to a height above that of the surrounding land.[33] Further qualifications exist through the Use Classes Orders,[34] which provide that a change of use within a particular class, e.g. from one kind of shop to another, or between particular categories of industrial uses, is to be taken as not involving development. The General Permitted Development Orders[35] grant deemed permission to certain operations and uses, e.g. minor alterations to houses, agricultural and forestry operations, and land drainage works; these do still count as development but within the prescribed limits they are automatically authorised by the deemed permission, without any need to apply for express planning permission for the individual project. There are thus several sources to be considered before it can be said with certainty whether a particular proposal does involve development and requires an application to be made for planning permission.

From the point of view of nature conservation, several of the activities **8.2.13** falling outwith the meaning of "development", and hence outwith the planning system, are of considerable significance, particularly in relation to agriculture and forestry. It does not amount to a material change of use, and hence is not development, if what is involved is:

> "[T]he use of land for the purposes of agriculture or forestry (including afforestation)[36] and the use for any of those purposes of any building occupied together with land so used."[37]

---

[31] TCPSA 1997 s.26(1); TCPA 1990 s.55(1).

[32] "'Development' is a key word in the planners' vocabulary but it is one whose meaning has evolved and is still evolving. It is impossible to ascribe to it any certain dictionary meaning, and difficult to analyse it accurately from the statutory definition." Lord Wilberforce in *Coleshill and District Investment Co v Minister of Housing and Local Government* [1969] 1 W.L.R. 746 at 763.

[33] TCPSA 1997 s.26(2) and (3); TCPA 1990 s.55(2) and (3).

[34] Town and Country Planning (Use Classes) (Scotland) Order 1997 (SI 1997/3061); Town and Country Planning (Use Classes) Order 1987 (SI 1987/764).

[35] Town and Country Planning (General Permitted Development) (Scotland) Order 1992 (SI 1992/223); Town and Country Planning (General Permitted Development) Order 1995 (SI 1995/418); these are subject to frequent minor amendments.

[36] This definition is not restricted to the land where the trees, crops, etc. are being grown, and can even include land some distance from the primary site; *Farleyer Estate v Secretary of State for Scotland*, 1992 S.L.T. 476.

[37] TCPSA 1997 s.26(2)(e); TCPA 1990 s.55(2)(e).

This means that no permission is required for converting land to such uses, a change which can radically transform the nature of the land and the habitats provided.[38] Equally, the General Permitted Development Orders grant deemed permission, subject to some limitations, to agricultural buildings and operations (including mineral workings reasonably necessary for agricultural purposes on that unit)[39] and to forestry operations and buildings.[40] Thus there is no need to seek planning permission before carrying out such operations, even though they fundamentally alter the land affected, although in some cases planning or equivalent controls have been imposed in order to ensure that an environmental impact assessment is carried out as required by EC law.[41] Also of potentially major significance are deemed permissions (again subject to various limitations) for land drainage works,[42] operations carried out by statutory undertakers,[43] operations relating to mineral exploration and ancillary to mineral workings,[44] and in Scotland the taking of peat for individual domestic requirements.[45]

8.2.14   If planning permission is required, an application must be made to the relevant planning authority. Controversially, in England and Wales the Planning Act 2008 transfers responsibility for approving "nationally significant infrastructure projects" to the Infrastructure Planning Commission[46]; in Scotland responsibility for national developments identified by the National Planning Framework remains with the local authority but since the need for the project is established by the Framework the discretion of the authority is constrained.[47] Full permission may be sought, or outline

---

[38] Although consent may be required under the Regulations requiring environmental assessment for some forestry operations (see paras 6.4.19–6.4.23, above) and for activities "involving the use of uncultivated land or semi-natural areas for intensive agricultural purposes or restructuring of rural land holdings on agricultural land" (see para.8.3.8, below).

[39] Town and Country Planning (General Permitted Development) (Scotland) Order 1992 (SI 1992/223) Sch.1 Pt 6; Town and Country Planning (General Permitted Development) Order 1995 (SI 1995/418) Sch.2 Pt 6.

[40] Town and Country Planning (General Permitted Development) (Scotland) Order 1992 Sch.1 Pt 7; Town and Country Planning (General Permitted Development) Order 1995 Sch.2 Pt 7.

[41] See section 8.3, below.

[42] Town and Country Planning (General Permitted Development) (Scotland) Order 1992 (SI 1992/223) Sch.1 Pt 6; Town and Country Planning (General Permitted Development) Order 1995 (SI 1995/418) Sch.2 Pt 14.

[43] Town and Country Planning (General Permitted Development) (Scotland) Order 1992 Sch.1 Pt 13; Town and Country Planning (General Permitted Development) Order 1995 Sch.2 Pt 17.

[44] Town and Country Planning (General Permitted Development) (Scotland) Order 1992 Sch.1 Pts 15–19; Town and Country Planning (General Permitted Development) Order 1995 Sch.2 Pts 19–23.

[45] Town and Country Planning (General Permitted Development) (Scotland) Order 1992 Sch.1 Pt 6, class 21.

[46] Planning Act 2008 Pts 3–7. This can have some impact in Scotland since this new procedure applies to cross-border oil and gas pipelines (Planning Act 2008 s.240(4)).

[47] In both cases these measures are a reaction to a perception that the planning system causes damaging delays in carrying out important infrastructure projects and have focused concerns on the adequacy of the public participation arrangements when such projects are being identified and approved.

permission,[48] which approves the general principle of a particular development but leaves detailed aspects for approval at a later stage, allowing developers to test the acceptability of a proposal without the effort (and cost) of preparing fully detailed plans and enabling the final development to be shaped in accordance with the planning authority's concerns as expressed in the grant of outline permission. Applications are available for inspection and must generally be notified to neighbours and in some cases advertised in the press. Members of the public have the opportunity to make representations to the planning authority before it decides whether or not to grant permission. In some instances an environmental impact assessment may be necessary.[49]

The authority may grant or refuse permission, or grant permission subject **8.2.15** to conditions. It may also seek to agree with the developer planning obligations to cover related matters which cannot be dealt with by means of conditions.[50] If a development goes ahead without planning permission or in breach of conditions, the authority can take enforcement action, leading ultimately to criminal prosecution if the developer fails to comply with the various forms of enforcement notice which can be served.

If permission is refused, or if the developer is unhappy with any condi- **8.2.16** tions imposed, the developer can appeal to the Minister.[51] Although the Minister may become personally involved in major cases, appeals are usually decided by the reporters (inspectors in England and Wales) appointed to hear them, most commonly on the basis of written representations but sometimes after a public inquiry at which the developer, the authority and any objectors or others who have become involved in the process have the opportunity to present evidence and arguments before the reporter. If permission is granted, there is no right of appeal to objectors, although they may seek to challenge the decision by means of judicial review, a course also open to developers who consider that appeal proceedings in which they were unsuccessful were flawed.[52]

In addition to the general pattern of development control described **8.2.17** above, special rules apply to regulate particular aspects of development.[53] As already noted in Chapter 5, there are special rules for National Parks, conservation areas and other areas designated for landscape or similar purposes.[54] Buildings of special architectural or historical interest can be

---

[48] To become "planning permission in principle" in Scotland (TCPSA 1997 s.59 as substituted by Planning etc. Scotland Act 2006 s.21); for some categories of development pre-application consultation will be required (TCPSA 1997 ss.35A–35C as added by Planning etc. Scotland Act 2006 s.11.).

[49] See section 8.3, below.

[50] TCPSA 1997 s.75, substituted by Planning etc. (Scotland) Act 2006 s.23; TCPA 1990 ss.106–106B, as amended by s.12(1) of the Planning and Compensation Act 1991, SI to be further amended by the Planning Act 2008 s.174.

[51] These appeal mechanisms survived a challenge based on the argument that the Minister's involvement meant that there was not an "independent and impartial tribunal" as guaranteed under the Human Rights Act 1998; see para.1.5.6, above.

[52] Several statutory procedures are provided for referring matters to the courts, rather than the general judicial review procedures being used; TCPSA 1997 Pt XI, TCPA 1990 Pt XII.

[53] TCPSA 1997 Pt VII, Planning (Listed Buildings and Conservation Areas) (Scotland) Act 1997; TCPA 1990 Pt VIII, Planning (Listed Buildings and Conservation Areas) Act 1990.

[54] See sections 5.9 and 5.10, above.

listed by the Minister, becoming subject to special rules designed to conserve them,[55] while trees can become subject to Tree Preservation Orders.[56] Advertisements and mineral workings are also governed by special rules, as are the storage and use of hazardous substances.[57]

8.2.18   Where a European Site may be affected, the stringent tests set out in the Habitats and Species Directive must be met before permission can be given.[58] More generally, nature conservation is a material consideration in the determination of individual applications for planning permission. Conservation arguments may help to bolster the case for or against a particular development, and may be particularly relevant where the possibility of alternative sites is considered. If a proposal will cause serious damage to the natural environment, permission could be refused. Frequently, though, a concern for nature can be accommodated by fairly minor changes to the proposed development or by the imposition of conditions, e.g. ensuring that watercourses are protected, that areas of a site are left undisturbed and that appropriate restoration work is carried out after construction is completed. Indeed the planning legislation includes an express provision that where appropriate, conditions should be used to ensure the preservation or planting of trees.[59] More generally, it may be possible to take account of the needs of flora and fauna, not merely aesthetics, in considering the landscaping, etc. of the final development, e.g. providing for the creation of wildlife ponds and an appropriate mix of vegetation, and even the timing of particular operations to avoid breeding seasons. Again, such requirements can be seen as a positive factor for a developer and future occupiers; they offer good publicity, and should be no more onerous than the sort of landscaping more commonly carried out.

Planning Obligations

8.2.19 Planning obligations under section 75 of the Town and Country Planning (Scotland) Act 1997 and section 106 of the Town and Country Planning Act 1990[60] may be made "for the purpose of restricting or regulating the development or use of the land" affected. Clearly it is possible to use this device for the purposes of nature conservation, e.g. to ensure appropriate protection or enhancement of a local habitat, or to secure the long-term management of a site or cooperation and assistance in the conservation work being carried out by others. There is a further possibility in the power of a planning authority at any time to enter an agreement with a landowner to do whatever is thought necessary to preserve and enhance the natural beauty of the countryside.[61]

---

[55] Planning (Listed Buildings and Conservation Areas) (Scotland) Act 1997; Planning (Listed Buildings and Conservation Areas) Act 1990.

[56] See section 6.5, above.

[57] Planning (Hazardous Substances) (Scotland) Act 1997; Planning (Hazardous Substances) Act 1990.

[58] See paras 5.2.25–5.2.33, above.

[59] TCPSA 1997 s.159; TCPA 1990 s.197.

[60] TCPSA 1997 s.75, substituted by Planning etc. (Scotland) Act 2006 s.23; TCPA 1990 ss.106–106B, as amended by s.12(1) of the Planning and Compensation Act 1991, and to be further amended by the Planning Act 2008 s.174.

[61] CSA 1967 s.49A(2), added by Countryside (Scotland) Act 1981 s.9 and amended by NHSA 1991 Sch.10; WCA 1981 s.39.

Conservation Areas[62]

Although the aim of conservation areas is to protect and enhance areas of **8.2.20** special architectural and historic interest, not the natural heritage,[63] the natural environment will often be a significant element in their special features. Large gardens, open spaces and mature trees may all contribute to the character and appearance of the areas which are to be preserved and enhanced, and all can make a contribution to nature conservation. Action taken to achieve the objectives of a conservation area can also be useful for nature conservation, and this aspect should be taken into account when considering how to deal with such areas.

Tree Preservation Orders

Tree preservation orders are also part of the town and country planning **8.2.21** system and, as discussed in section 6.5, above, can be used for the benefit of nature conservation, to protect individual trees or, more usefully, groups of trees or small areas of woodland.

ENVIRONMENTAL IMPACT ASSESSMENT

The modern planning system has always offered an opportunity for the **8.3.1** environmental impact of proposed development to be considered, but special emphasis is placed on assessing the environmental consequences of proposals as a result of European Community initiatives.[64] These lay down formal procedures through which the likely impact of proposals must be identified and taken into account before the proposal can be officially approved. There is no obligation on the decision-makers to avoid decisions that have harmful environmental consequences,[65] but any such decision should be the result of a conscious weighing of the various costs and benefits involved.[66]

The first step was a Directive made in 1985, and amended in 1997[67] ("the **8.3.2** EIA Directive"), imposing a requirement that before certain types of major project are given official approval there should be carried out a thorough assessment of the impact of the project on the environment. This Directive has been implemented in Britain mainly by adding the requirement for an environmental impact assessment to existing procedures for approval. In most cases the mechanism involved is the planning system, as the projects in question already required planning permission before they could proceed, but for some projects the environmental assessment has had to be grafted on

---

[62] See para.5.10.12, above.

[63] Planning (Listed Buildings and Conservation Areas) (Scotland) Act 1997 s.61; Planning (Listed Buildings and Conservation Areas) Act 1990 s.69.

[64] See also the Espoo Convention on Environmental Impact Assessment in a Transboundary Context (1991); information available on the UN Economic Commission for Europe web-pages at *http://www.unece.org/env/eia* [Accessed May 16, 2009].

[65] But see para.8.3.19, below.

[66] See generally J. Holder, *Environmental Assessment: The Regulation of Decision-making* (Oxford: OUP, 2004); J. Holder and D. McGillivray (eds), *Taking Stock of Environmental assessment: Law, Policy and Practice* (Abingdon: Routledge-Cavendish, 2007).

[67] Directive 85/337/EEC as amended by 97/11/EC and further amended by art.3 of Directive 2003/35/EC on public participation.

to other procedures, or new procedures established. A further step has been the extension of environmental assessment to cover not just individual projects but the plans and programmes that provide the background for the projects themselves. Such strategic environmental assessment is provided for in a Directive made in 2001[68] ("the SEA Directive") and implemented separately and with significant differences for Scotland and for England and Wales.

8.3.3 The EIA Directive requires that before consent is given, projects likely to have a significant effect on the environment by virtue inter alia of their nature, size or location are subjected to an assessment of their effects.[69] The assessment must deal with the direct and indirect effects of the project on human beings, flora and fauna, soil, water, air, climate, the landscape, material assets and cultural heritage.[70] The proposer of the project must supply an environmental statement with information on the project and its environmental effects, with any public authorities holding relevant information making that available to him,[71] and the statement should be the subject of consultation with environmental bodies and the public.[72] All of the information gathered through this process must be taken into consideration in the development consent procedure, and the main reasons for the final decision made available to the public, as well as the main measures to avoid, reduce or offset the major adverse effects.[73] There must be a means for the decision to be reviewed before a court or other independent body.[74]

8.3.4 This measure therefore does not attempt to guarantee that certain environmental consequences will be avoided. Rather it aims to ensure that those taking the decision on whether or not to approve a project are fully aware of its likely environmental effects so that these can be put in the balance with the other factors—economic, social and perhaps aesthetic—to be considered before the final determination is made. The requirement for public consultation, strengthened by the Directive on public participation in 2003,[75] is a significant feature of the process[76] and offers an opportunity for pressure groups and concerned individuals to ensure that environmental considerations are truly taken into account. In order to ensure that this consultation is meaningful, it is expressly stated that the information provided must include a non-technical summary[77] thereby preventing the developer from stifling public comment by providing a statement which may be technically excellent but is incomprehensible to all but experts in the various scientific fields involved.

8.3.5 The Directive states when an environmental impact assessment is required. It specifies the projects affected, dividing them into two categories.

---

[68] Directive 2001/42/EC.

[69] Directive 85/337/EEC art.2(1).

[70] Directive 85/337/EEC art.3.

[71] Directive 85/337/EEC art.5.

[72] Directive 85/337/EEC art.6; if significant effects are likely to be felt in another Member State, then cross-boundary consultation should also take place (art.7).

[73] Directive 85/337/EEC art.9.

[74] Directive 85/337/EEC art.10a.

[75] Directive 2003/35/EC, following the Aarhus Convention—see *http://www.unece.org/env/pp/welcome.html* [Accessed May 16, 2009].

[76] See *Berkeley v Secretary of State for the Environment, Transport and the Regions (No.1)* [2001] 2 A.C. 603 (para.8.3.13, below).

[77] Directive 85/337/EEC Annex IV para.6.

For projects listed in Annex I, an environmental assessment will always be necessary; for those in Annex II, it is only when a particular project in its individual circumstances is likely to have significant effects on the environment that the assessment must be carried out.[78] The requirement does not, however, apply to projects approved by a specific act of national legislation,[79] and there is a power for Member States in exceptional cases to exempt specific projects.[80]

Annex I includes major projects with obvious environmental effects such **8.3.6** as oil refineries, power stations, radioactive waste sites, integrated chemical works, motorways, airports, trading ports, waste disposal installations for the incineration, treatment or landfill of toxic and dangerous wastes, and some large intensive poultry or pig rearing installations. The list of projects in Annex II is longer and much more varied, and only some of the projects in each category will actually require an environmental assessment as being "likely to have significant effects on the environment by virtue inter alia of their nature, size or location."[81] More than 80 kinds of project are listed under 13 headings: Agriculture (e.g. intensive livestock or fish farming projects), Extractive Industry (e.g. mining and quarrying), Energy Industry (e.g. generating stations and overhead electricity transmission lines), Production and Processing of Metals (e.g. iron and steelworks, manufacture and assembly of motor vehicles), Mineral Industry (e.g. glass, cement or brick manufacture), Chemical Industry, Food Industry (e.g. packing and canning, slaughter of animals), Textile, Leather, Wood and Paper Industries, Rubber Industry, Infrastructure Projects (e.g. industrial estates, urban developments and transport works), Other Projects (e.g. waste disposal installations, waste water treatment plants and storage of scrap iron), Tourism and Leisure (e.g. ski-runs, marinas and holiday villages) and changes or extensions to previously authorised Annex I projects.

Implementing the requirements of the Directive in Great Britain has been **8.3.7** a slow and complex process. The various regulations initially made to implement the original Directive were both late and incomplete, and there was a steady trickle of further regulations to fill gaps in the implementation before the amendments to the Directive in 1997 required a further tide of regulations (again late in many cases) in the effort to ensure that the procedures here do provide full implementation. Further gaps were identified and led to the Commission taking successful infraction proceedings before the European Court of Justice,[82] leading to further amendments to the regulations in Britain. The regulations have generally been made under the

---

[78] The decision whether an assessment is required for an Annex II project can be made by reference to national thresholds or criteria, provided that these do not exclude whole categories of project and that the projects excluded by the thresholds cannot collectively have significant effects on the environment; *World Wildlife Fund v Autonome Provinz Bozen* (C-435/97) [1999] E.C.R. I-5613; *Commission v Ireland* (C-392/96) [1999] E.C.R. I-5901.

[79] Directive 85/337/EEC art.1(5), subject to the proviso that the information equivalent to that required from the environmental statement is considered as part of the legislative process; *Luxembourg v Linster* (C-287/98) [2000] E.C.R. I-6917.

[80] Directive 85/337/EEC art.2(3).

[81] Directive 85/337/EEC art.4(2); Annex III provides a list of the criteria to be used in determining whether this test is met.

[82] *Commission v UK* (C-508/03) [2006] E.C.R. I-3969 in relation to the absence of an assessment on reserved matters after a grant of outline planning permission and *Commission v UK* (C-37/05) [2006] E.C.R. I-6 in relation to Crown development.

authority of the European Communities Act 1972,[83] but since this power is limited to the making of legislation necessary to implement Community law, direct statutory powers have been granted to make it possible to extend the requirement for an assessment beyond the strict limits of the categories listed in the Directive.[84]

8.3.8   In most cases the projects listed in the Annexes of the Directive were already subject to formal approval through the planning system, so that the environmental assessment procedure has been added to the existing planning process.[85] Special provision has however been necessary for a number of projects which are subject to approval under different statutory procedures or for which there was no formal approval mechanism in place. Thus a requirement for environmental assessment has been added to the special rules for roads,[86] electricity projects,[87] land drainage works,[88] pipelines,[89] some harbour and coastal protection works, [90] and other infrastructure projects.[91] Further significant areas not covered by existing approval mechanisms were forestry and agriculture. Since both afforestation and deforestation can fall within the terms of the Directive, a new procedure, incorporating the assessment, has been introduced requiring projects to obtain formal consent from the Forestry Commission,[92] whilst ministerial consent is now needed for activities "involving the use of uncultivated land or semi-natural areas for intensive agricultural purposes or restructuring of

---

[83] European Communities Act 1972 s.2(2).

[84] TCPA 1990 s.71A, added by Planning and Compensation Act 1991 s.15; TCPSA 1997 s.40.

[85] Environmental Impact Assessment (Scotland) Regulations 1999 (SSI 1999/1) Pt II (this was the very first Scottish Statutory Instrument made by the Scottish Executive when devolution took effect); Town and Country Planning (Environmental Impact Assessment) (England and Wales) Regulations 1999 (SI 1999/293). Both of these regulations and virtually all of the other provisions mentioned in this and succeeding paragraphs have been subject to amendment, many on multiple occasions.

[86] Roads (Scotland) Act 1984 ss.20A, 20B, 55A and 55B, added by Environmental Impact Assessment (Scotland) Regulations 1999 (SSI 1999/1) Pt III; Highways Act 1980 Pt VA (as substituted by Highways (Assessment of Environmental Effects) Regulations 1999 (SI 1999/369)).

[87] Electricity Works (Environmental Impact Assessment) (Scotland) Regulations 2000 (SSI 2000/320); Electricity Works (Environmental Impact Assessment) (England and Wales) Regulations 2000 (SI 2000/1927).

[88] Environmental Impact Assessment (Scotland) Regulations 1999 (SSI 1999/1) Pt IV; Environmental Impact Assessment (Land Drainage Improvement Works) Regulations 1999 (SI 1999/1783).

[89] Public Gas Transporter Pipe-line Works (Environmental Impact Assessment) Regulations 1999 (SI 1999/1672); Pipe-line Works (Environmental Impact Assessment) Regulations 2000 (SI 2000/1928); Offshore Petroleum Production and Pipe-lines (Assessment of Environmental Effects) Regulations 1999 (SI 1999/360).

[90] Marine Works (Environmental Impact Assessment) Regulations 2007 (SI 2007/1518).

[91] Transport and Works (Assessment of Environmental Effects) Regulations 1998 (SI 1998/2226); Transport and Works (Applications and Objections Procedure) (England and Wales) Rules 2006 (SI 2006/1466); Transport and Works (Scotland) Act 2007 (Applications and Objections Procedure) Rules 2007 (SSI 2007/570).

[92] Environmental Impact Assessment (Forestry) (Scotland) Regulations 1999 (SSI 1999/43); Environmental Impact Assessment (Forestry) (England and Wales) Regulations 1999 (SI 1999/2228); see paras 6.4.19–6.4.23, above.

rural land holdings on agricultural land".[93] For fish farming in the sea, where there was no existing statutory procedure, the environmental impact assessment (where necessary) has been made a prerequisite of the consent required from the Crown Estate Commissioners[94]; in Scotland some marine fish farming is now covered by the standard planning system.[95] An approval mechanism has also been introduced for marine dredging.[96]

The exemption in the Directive for projects specifically authorised by the legislature creates a potential gap in the system in view of the actual and potential use of private legislation procedure to approve major and controversial projects. This gap has been filled by changes to the detailed rules of procedure so that an environmental assessment can now be held as part of the legislative process,[97] and by the Transport and Works Act 1992 and Transport and Works (Scotland) Act 2007 which establish new procedures for authorising many projects which would previously have been the subject of private legislation. The procedural rules made under the Acts make provision for environmental assessments.[98] **8.3.9**

The various sets of regulations all follow the same pattern, giving effect to the main provisions of the Directive as described above. Thus the regulations state the test to be applied in deciding whether an assessment is necessary, namely, is the project one for which an assessment is mandatory in accordance with Annex I of the Directive or if it falls within Annex II, is it likely to have significant effects on the environment? The regulations then specify in varying degrees of detail the information and issues to be contained in the environmental statement provided by the proposer, the obligations on the statutory conservation and other bodies to supply information useful in preparing the statement, the requirements for publicity and consultation[99] and the obligation on the determining authority to take the results of the statement and consultation into account. **8.3.10**

A difficulty in many instances is in deciding whether a particular project which falls within Annex II of the Directive meets the test of being "likely to **8.3.11**

---

[93] Environmental Impact Assessment (Agriculture) (Scotland) Regulations 2006 (SSI 2006/582); Environmental Impact Assessment (Agriculture) (England) (No.2) Regulations 2006 (SI 2006/2362); Environmental Impact Assessment (Agriculture) (Wales) Regulations 2007 (SI 2007/2933).

[94] Environmental Impact Assessment (Fish Farming in Marine Waters) Regulations 1999 (SI 1999/367).

[95] TCPSA 1997 ss.26(1), 26AA and 31A, as added by Planning etc. (Scotland) Act 2006 s.4, and Town and Country Planning (Marine Fish Farming) (Scotland) Order 2007 (SSI 2007/1).

[96] Environmental Impact Assessment and Natural Habitats (Extraction of Minerals by Marine Dredging) (Scotland) Regulations 2007 (SSI 2007/485); Environmental Impact Assessment and Natural Habitats (Extraction of Minerals by Marine Dredging) (England and Northern Ireland) Regulations 2007 (SI 2007/1067); Environmental Impact Assessment and Natural Habitats (Extraction of Minerals by Marine Dredging) (Wales) Regulations 2007 (SI 2007/2610).

[97] See B. Winetrobe, "Environmental Assessment and Private Legislation" (1992) 35 S.P.L.P. 7; J. Rowan-Robinson and B. Winetrobe, "Environmental Assessment and Private Legislation Procedures" (1992) 36 S.P.L.P. 51.

[98] Transport and Works (Assessment of Environmental Effects) Regulations 1998 (SI 1998/2226); Transport and Works (Applications and Objections Procedure) (England and Wales) Rules 2006 (SI 2006/1466); Transport and Works (Scotland) Act 2007 (Applications and Objections Procedure) Rules 2007 (SSI 2007/570)..

[99] The significance of the views of the statutory conservation body is shown in *R. (Buglife: The Invertebrate Conservation Trust) v Thurrock Thames Gateway Development Corp* [2009] EWCA Civ 29.

have significant effects on the environment by virtue inter alia of its nature, size or location." In some cases the opportunity has been taken to specify thresholds below which a project will be viewed not to have significant effects,[100] but beyond that there remains considerable scope for argument. Large-scale projects and those on sites where there is an SSSI or other conservation or landscape designation are the most likely to meet the test. It is usually possible for a developer to seek a "screening" opinion from the relevant authority on whether an environmental assessment will be required for a particular application, sometimes subject to an application to the Minister for a final direction on the matter. Similarly a "scoping" opinion may be available, setting out the information to be included in the environmental statement.

8.3.12   Environmental impact assessment has generated considerable litigation. Disputes have ranged from general issues such as the legal position in relation to projects that fall under the Directive but where there is no domestic implementing legislation,[101] to matters specific to the individual proposal such as the adequacy of aspects of the detailed information supplied.[102] It has been held that measures mitigating the impact of a project can be taken into account in determining whether a formal assessment is necessary[103] and that the future use of land being cleared of woodland must be considered to determine the significance of this change.[104]

8.3.13   The importance of the process was emphasised in *Berkeley v Secretary of State for the Environment (No.1)*[105] where it was argued that although the formal procedural requirements had not been complied with, the outcome of a planning decision could be upheld since all of the relevant information had in fact been available in one form or another to those involved in the decision-making process. In rejecting that view and quashing the grant of planning permission, the House of Lords stressed that the "cornerstone of the regime"[106] is the provision of an environmental statement, "a single and accessible compilation, produced by the applicant at the very start of the application process",[107] and that this could not be replaced by a "paper

---

[100] Such thresholds cannot exclude whole categories of project unless it is clear that none of them can have significant effects; *Aannemersbedrijf PK Kraaijeveld BV v Gedeputeerde Staten van Zuid-Holland* (C-72/95) [1996] E.C.R. I-5430. The thresholds must take into account more than just the size of the project and must take account of the cumulative effect of projects that may individually fall below the threshold; *Commission v Ireland* (C-392/96) [1999] E.C.R. I-5901; *Commission v Spain* (C-227/01) [2004] E.C.R. I-8253.

[101] e.g. in relation to mineral permissions: *R. v North Yorkshire CC, ex p. Brown* [2000] 1 A.C. 397; *R. v Oldham Metropolitan Borough Council, ex p. Foster* [2000] Env. L.R. 395; *R. v Durham County Council, ex p. Huddlestone* [2000] 1 W.L.R. 1484.

[102] e.g. *Atkinson v Secretary of State for Transport* [2006] EWHC 995 Admin, *Skye Windfarm Action Group Ltd v Highland Council* [2008] CSOH 19.

[103] *R. (Catt) v Brighton and Hove City Council* [2007] EWCA Civ 298; [2007] Env. L.R. 32.

[104] *R. (Tree and Wildlife Action Committee Ltd) v Forestry Commissioners* [2007] EWHC 1623 (Admin); [2008] Env. L.R. 5.

[105] *Berkeley v Secretary of State for the Environment (No.1)* [2001] 2 A.C. 603.

[106] *Berkeley v Secretary of State for the Environment (No.1)* [2001] 2 A.C. 603, Lord Bingham at 608.

[107] *Berkeley v Secretary of State for the Environment (No.1)* [2001] 2 A.C. 603, Lord Hoffmann at 617.

chase"[108] through other documents provided at different stages throughout the process.[109]

Environmental impact assessment is now a firmly established element in the approval of many different sorts of project. It must always be remembered, though, that it regulates the process by which decisions are reached, not the substantive outcomes. The value of the process in relation to protecting the natural heritage therefore depends both on the quality of the information and analysis that is provided in the environmental statement (and in contributions from other parties), and the willingness of the decision-makers to give environmental considerations weight as they reach their conclusions.[110] One weakness of the whole system is that too often there are inadequate procedures for revisiting the issues considered in the assessment, so that if the impact of a project turns out to be different from that predicted, there may be no straightforward way of revising the original permission, whether to tighten or relax the controls imposed at the time.[111] **8.3.14**

A further weakness of the process was that it applied only in the context of individual projects, whereas often these are simply the manifestations of wider policy decisions that had been reached without the same rigour in the consideration of environmental impacts. This flaw has been tackled by a further Directive on strategic environmental assessment.[112] Under this Directive, certain draft plans or programmes produced by government at all levels must be accompanied by an environmental report setting out their likely effects on the environment and before they can be adopted there must be consultation with environmental bodies[113] and if necessary other Member States and an opportunity for public participation.[114] All of this information and the opinions and representations received must be taken into account in reaching the final decision whether or not to adopt the plan or programme.[115] The Directive also addresses another flaw in the project-based assessment procedure by requiring the state to: **8.3.15**

---

[108] *Berkeley v Secretary of State for the Environment (No.1)* [2001] 2 A.C. 603, Lord Hoffmann at 617.

[109] cf. *Younger Homes (Northern Ltd) v First Secretary of State* [2004] EWCA Civ 1060; [2005] Env. L.R. 12.

[110] There are areas where the introduction of environmental assessment clearly has made a difference to the decisions being made, e.g. C.T. Reid, A.L. Pillai and A.R. Black, "The Emergence of Environmental Concerns: Hydroelectric Schemes in Scotland" (2005) 17 J.E.L. 361, esp. pp.378–379.

[111] CT. Reid, "Regulation in a Changing World: Review and Revision of Environmental Permits" (2008) 67 C.L.J. 126.

[112] Directive 2001/42/EC. See also the Kiev (SEA) Protocol to the Espoo Convention; further information on the UN Economic Commission for Europe web-pages at *http://www.unece.org/env/eia/sea_protocol.htm* [Accessed May 16, 2009].

[113] This was at issue in the first UK case involving strategic environmental assessment, where it was held that the consultation within different divisions of the Northern Ireland Department of the Environment did not meet the requirement for consultation with external environmental bodies; *Re Application for Judicial Review by Seaport Investments Ltd* [2007] NIQB 62; [2008] Env. L.R. 23.

[114] Directive 2001/42/EC arts 5–7.

[115] Directive 2001/42/EC art.8.

"[M]onitor the significant environmental effects of the implementation of plans and programmes in order, inter alia, to identify at an early stage unforeseen adverse effects, and to be able to undertake appropriate remedial action."[116]

8.3.16 In England and Wales and for UK matters, implementation of the Directive has involved fairly direct transposition.[117] The assessment requirement therefore applies to plans and programmes of the sort specified in the Directive, namely those prepared for a number of purposes (agriculture, forestry, fisheries, energy, industry, transport, waste management, water management, telecommunications, tourism, town and country planning or land use) and setting the framework for future development consent for projects covered by the EIA Directive or which require an assessment under the Habitats and Species Directive in view of the likely effect on designated sites. The regulations follow the scheme of the Directive closely.

8.3.17 In Scotland, a more ambitious policy has been adopted. Regulations along the same lines as those in England were adopted to ensure timeous implementation of the Directive,[118] but these were a temporary measure pending legislation to give effect to the decision to apply strategic environmental assessment more broadly. The Environmental Assessment (Scotland) Act 2005 renders all plans, programmes and strategies prepared by Scottish public bodies and office-holders subject to an environmental assessment, not just those in the categories listed in the Directive.[119] Financial and budgetary plans and those relating to national defence or civil emergency are excluded,[120] as are those that relate to individual schools or are likely to have no or minimal effect on the environment.[121] Where plans are exempted on the latter ground there may still be a need to contact the statutory consultees and to notify Ministers of the decision and to publicise it.[122]

8.3.18 Given the fact that many important matters (e.g. energy) have both devolved and reserved aspects and the extent to which plans and strategies developed outside Scotland undergo some form of environmental assessment on a voluntary basis, the differences in the legal position may not produce such obvious differences as might be imagined. Nevertheless, the law does provide a stronger commitment to strategic environmental assessment in Scotland, and an emphasis on keeping it distinct from the wider concept of sustainability appraisal,[123] ensuring a separate recognition of environmental matters as opposed to these being masked by being balanced against the other elements that are part of the notion of sustainable development.[124] At this stage it is too early to tell whether strategic

---

[116] Directive 2001/42/EC art.10.
[117] Environmental Assessment of Plans and Programmes Regulations 2004 (SI 2004/1633); Environmental Assessment of Plans and Programmes (Wales) Regulations 2004 (SI 2004/1656).
[118] Environmental Assessment of Plans and Programmes (Scotland) Regulations 2004 (SSI 2004/258).
[119] Environmental Assessment (Scotland) Act 2005 ss.4–5.
[120] Environmental Assessment (Scotland) Act 2005 s.4.
[121] Environmental Assessment (Scotland) Act 2005 ss.6–7.
[122] Environmental Assessment (Scotland) Act 2005 ss.8–10.
[123] A. Ross, "Sustainable Development in Scotland Post Devolution" (2006) 8 Env. L. Rev. 6, esp. at pp.18–19.
[124] See paras 2.2.2–2.2.5, above.

environmental assessment will make much difference, but nature conservation matters should at least be given some thought as important policies are
developed, and as with project-based assessments, the requirements to
consult with the statutory conservation bodies and the public do provide an
opportunity to raise concerns and suggest ways of avoiding or minimising
the harm that may result. A key test will come when it is seen how thorough
the monitoring is of the effects of implementing the plans and policies, and
the willingness "to undertake appropriate remedial action".[125]

Assessment of likely effects is also a fundamental element in the operation **8.3.19**
of the Habitats and Species Directive, being a necessary step before
approval can be given for activities that may adversely affect a designated
site.[126] The process here differs from that under the EIA Directive in that
there are no detailed rules on the procedure or content of the "appropriate
assessment" that is required (and no explicit public participation requirements). More significantly the purpose is different, not just informing the
decision-makers but constraining their discretion. In standard environmental assessment cases, the aim is to ensure that the decision-makers have
and take into account all the relevant information, leaving them to balance
environmental and other considerations as they think fit. By contrast, in
relation to European Sites if the assessment reveals negative impacts then
approval must not be given unless certain strict criteria are met. Only in
those defined circumstances is the decision-maker free to favour other
considerations over the harm to biodiversity.[127]

AGRICULTURE

As so much of Britain is actively farmed, changes in agricultural practices **8.4.1**
have a great impact on nature conservation. Agriculture in turn is greatly
affected by the range of subsidies and other aids by means of which governments give effect to their agricultural policies, and by the laws which
regulate the rights of agricultural tenants and others involved in the
industry. Indeed, changing agricultural practices during the second half of
the twentieth century have almost certainly had a greater effect on nature
conservation than any other factor. Therefore, any thorough examination of
the law affecting nature conservation must at least mention the law relating
to agriculture.[128]

---

[125] Directive 2001/42/EC art.10, implemented be Environmental Assessment (Scotland) Act
2005 s.19 and equivalents in the UK and Welsh Regulations; see para.8.3.15, above.

[126] See paras 5.2.25–5.2.27 and 7.4.29, above.

[127] Similar comments can be made in relation to strategic environmental assessment and the
Water Framework Directive; W. Howarth, "Substance and procedure under the strategic
environmental assessment directive and the water framework directive" in J. Holder and D.
McGillivray, *Taking Stock of Environmental Assessment: Law, Policy, and Practice* (Abingdon:
Routledge-Cavendish, 2007).

[128] See generally, W. Howarth and C.P. Rodgers (eds.), *Agriculture, Conservation and Land
Use* (Cardiff: University of Wales Press, 1992); N. Hawke and N. Kovaleva, *Agri-Environmental
Law and Policy* (London: Cavendish, 1998); I. Hodge, "Agri-environmental Policy: A UK
Perspective" in D. Helm (ed.), *Environmental Policy: Objectives, Instruments and Implementa-
tion* (Oxford: OUP, 2000).

8.4.2   The agricultural policy adopted by the British government and by the European Community through the Common Agricultural Policy (CAP)[129] used to have the simple goal of stimulating production. This led in Britain to highly mechanised and highly specialised agricultural units which produce high yields but require large fields for intensive crop growing or industrial buildings for intensive livestock rearing, in all cases calling for the substantial use of fertilisers, pesticides and herbicides. Such developments were encouraged by a range of grants and other aids available to farmers wishing to "improve" their land through the construction of new buildings, drainage, or the cultivation of rough grassland or heath. These changes have been harmful to the "traditional" countryside and to the flora and fauna which it supports.

8.4.3   It was realised that this policy had been too successful and the Community was faced with twin problems. The first was the overproduction of many agricultural products, which could not be sold on the open market but which were still paid for in order to prevent agricultural collapse leading to the depopulation of large areas of rural Europe. The second has been the realisation of the unsustainable nature of certain agriculture practices and the risk to the environment created by incentives to greater intensity and further production.[130] At the same time, there was tension between the structure of subsidies and the free trade rules at an international level. Agricultural policies have changed to address these issues in a series of reforms outlined below, although the disruption to agriculture prices during 2008 has brought renewed concern over the medium-term affordability of agricultural products and security of supply,[131] shifting attention back to the importance of food production.

8.4.4   One aspect of the reforms has been the view that the farmers' role in protecting the rural environment and managing the landscape should be recognised more fully and remunerated accordingly.[132] The change of attitude to include environmental concern is reflected in several specific schemes and in broader measures, such as the obligation on the agriculture ministers to seek a balance between the promotion of agriculture and the conservation and enjoyment of the countryside.[133] The new approach is emphasised by the division of the CAP into two "pillars" under the Agenda 2000 Programme—direct aid and market measures ("first pillar") and rural development measures ("second pillar")—and by bringing various agriculture (and forestry and conservation) schemes under the umbrella of the respective Rural Development Programmes for 2007–2013.[134]

8.4.5   The detailed schemes are constantly being revised and replaced and the

---

[129] See generally, J.A. Usher, *EC Agricultural Law*, 2nd edn (Oxford: OUP, 2002), J. McMahon, *EU Agricultural Law* (Oxford: OUP, 2007).

[130] B. Jack, "Protecting the European environment from the Community: the case of agriculture" (2001) 3 Env. L. Rev. 44.

[131] With some further concerns over the impact of climate change on global agriculture.

[132] "The integration of environmental goals into the CAP and the development of the role farmers can and should play in terms of management of natural resources and landscape conservation are another increasingly important objective for the CAP." Agenda 2000, COM (97) 2000 vol.I at p.27.

[133] Agriculture Act 1986 s.17; see para.2.2.8, above.

[134] Regulation (EC) 1698/2005, amended by Regulation (EC) 74/2009; see, for example the Scotland Rural Development Programme at *http://www.scotland.gov.uk/Topics/Rural/SRDP* [Accessed May 16, 2009].

position is complicated by the fact that many involve commitments over several years so that land continues to be affected by arrangements under schemes that are no longer available to new applicants. In the long term, though, of greater significance will be whether the totality of agricultural reforms affecting policy, subsidies and markets will lead to general changes in practice as thorough as those produced in past decades by the drive for maximum production.

At Community level there have been three main stages in the introduction **8.4.6** of environmental concerns into agricultural policy, although some measures were introduced earlier.[135] The first came with the launch of the "agri-environment" programme in 1992 which made provision for schemes to encourage agricultural methods compatible with the requirements for the protection of the environment and the maintenance of the countryside.[136] By authorising the use of state funds in this way, the agri-environment programme enabled Member States to develop their own schemes to support environmentally beneficial activities.[137]

The second stage came as part of the Agenda 2000 programme, which as **8.4.7** well as addressing the challenges of possible enlargement of the Community endeavoured to respond to the higher priority for environmental considerations embedded into the Treaty provisions by the Amsterdam Treaty.[138] This led to a greater integration of environmental issues into new agricultural measures, and to a closer link between agricultural and rural development policy, recognising what has been referred to as the "multi-functionality of agriculture", i.e. the many roles of the farming community over and above the production of food, encompassing its wider contribution to the overall social, environmental and economic health and sustainability of rural areas.

The 2003 Cap Reform marked a further significant stage in the integra- **8.4.8** tion of environmental concerns into agricultural policy,[139] with further revisions being introduced following the CAP "Health Check" in late 2008.[140] A key innovation was the introduction of the Single Farm Payment Scheme which is now the principal agricultural subsidy scheme in the Community.[141] The scheme decouples payment of subsidies from production and funding is instead linked to the area of land. The intended effect is that farm management decisions should be based on the market and the

---

[135] e.g. the provisions that led to the creation of Environmentally Sensitive Areas discussed in section 5.9 of the previous edition of this book. This scheme closed to new applications at the end of 2000 but similar features are now incorporated into the Rural Development Programmes.

[136] Regulation (EEC) 2078/92.

[137] N. Hawke and N. Kovaleva, *Agri-Environmental Law and Policy* (London: Cavendish, 1998), Ch.5.

[138] EC Treaty art.6; see para.2.9.3, above.

[139] Regulation (EC) 1782/2003 sets out the general framework of the 2003 reform.

[140] See *http://ec.europa.eu/agriculture/healthcheck/index_en.htm* [Accesed May 16, 2009].

[141] See Factsheet: *Single Payment Scheme – The Concept*, available at *http://ec.europa.eu/agriculture/capreform/infosheets/pay_en.pdf* [Accesed May 16, 2009] and the DEFRA web-pages with explanations and links to the legislation at EU and devolved levels at *http://www.defra.gov.uk/farm/singlepay/index.htm* [Accesed May 16, 2009]. The legitimacy of there being different rules within the UK as a result of devolution is the subject of litigation that has been referred to the European Court of Justice; *R. (Horvath) v Secretary of State for the Environment, Food and Rural Affairs* (C-428/07) following [2007] EWCA Civ 620.

incentive for overproduction removed. A key element is that payments under this and all other CAP direct payment schemes are subject to cross compliance requirements.[142] These comprise statutory management requirements established at Community level in the areas of public, animal and plant health, the environment and animal welfare; and the requirement to keep land in Good Agricultural and Environmental Condition (GAEC) in line with minimum standards set by Member States. GAEC standards set requirements for farmers relating to soils and the preservation of certain habitats and landscape features.[143] The consequence of non-compliance is a reduction or even cancellation of direct payments.[144]

8.4.9　A further development has been what is known as "modulation",[145] a term now used to refer to the transfer of funds from Pillar 1 to Pillar 2 of the CAP. After initially being introduced as an optional measure for Member States, this is now a mandatory scheme, with the "Health Check" agreements increasing the sums involved to 10 per cent of certain payments by 2012.[146]

8.4.10　It is not just the grand thrust of Community policy that is important, but also the precise terms. Similarly, care must be taken that what appear to be simple administrative rules do not inadvertently stand in the way of beneficial practices, as shown by the negotiations over the rules on how areas of arable land are to be measured, which threatened to penalise significantly farmers who left wide field margins for their cultivated fields, despite the considerable benefits of this practice for wildlife of many kinds.[147]

8.4.11　Scotland provides an example of the consolidation of agri-environment and rural development measures (including schemes formerly run by SNH and the Forestry Commission) under the Rural Development Programme.[148] This delivers measures through seven different funding mechanisms, including the Less Favoured Areas Support Scheme and Crofting Counties Agricultural Grants Scheme. Rural Development Contracts are the largest funding mechanism, delivering 41 per cent of the overall RDP budget of £1.6 billion.[149] There are two levels of such contracts, the first being the Land Manager's Options scheme.[150] Land managers can apply for funding to

---

[142] Regulation (EC) 73/2009 arts 4–6 and Annex II.

[143] Introduced by Common Agricultural Policy Schemes (Cross-Compliance) Scotland Regulations 2004 (SSI 2004/518) Sch.1; Common Agricultural Policy Single Payment and Support Schemes (Cross-Compliance) (Wales) Regulations 2004 (SI 2004/3280) Sch.1; Common Agricultural Policy Single Payment and Support Schemes (Cross-Compliance) (England) Regulations 2005 (SI 2005/3458) Sch.1. The management requirements include compliance with key elements of the Birds and Habitats and Species Directives.

[144] See para.1.6.35, above.

[145] "We are appalled by the term 'modulation' but unfortunately, for the purposes of this report, we are unable to find a way around using it"; House of Commons Environment, Transport and Regional Affairs Committee, *Rural White Paper*, 7th report of 1999–2000, HC Paper No.32 (Session 1999–2000), para.50.

[146] Regulation (EC) 74/2009, amending Regulation (EC) 1698/2005; see *http://ec.europa.eu/ agriculture/healthcheck/index_en.htm* [Accesed May 16, 2009].

[147] House of Commons Environment, Transport and Regional Affairs Committee, *UK Biodiversity*, 20th report of 1999–2000, HC Paper No.441 (Session 1999–2000), para.83.

[148] See *http://www.scotland.gov.uk/Topics/Rural/SRDP* [Accessed May 16, 2009].

[149] See SRDP public meetings presentation at *http://www.scotland.gov.uk/Resource/Doc/931/ 0056608.pdf* [Accessed May 16, 2009].

[150] Rural Development Contracts (Land Managers Options) (Scotland) Regulations 2008 (SSI 2008/159).

carry out a range of economic, social and environmental improvements that go beyond the requirements of cross-compliance, including for example, the improvement of rush pasture for wildlife and small scale woodland creation.[151] The second level is a competitive funding mechanism under the Rural Priorities scheme.[152] Contracts are awarded for proposals which best meet the agreed rural priorities options, which include specialist agri-environment plans, management of mown grassland for wildlife and sustainable management of forests and woodlands.[153] The main schemes in England and Wales follow a similar two-tier approach. [154]

The agricultural set-aside scheme that was so prominent in the 1990s also **8.4.12** incorporated environmental concerns to some extent.[155] Although the primary aim was a reduction in the quantity of crops being produced, the details of the scheme were shaped with some regard for conservation. Thus within the scheme there were specific management options for the land that were expressly directed at conservation targets, e.g. wild bird cover, whilst the general conditions insisted that the land be managed in a way that preserves features of conservation value, such as hedges, trees, ponds and streams.[156] Set-aside was reduced in 2007 and then abolished by the CAP "Health Check",[157] leading to a significant reduction in the area of uncultivated land and losing the marked environmental benefits of the scheme.[158] Attempts are being made to recapture these benefits by other routes, working within the new structure of support mechanisms.[159]

Particular aspects of agricultural activity which might have implications **8.4.13** for nature conservation are also regulated. Some regulatory schemes allow action to be taken which might be prejudicial to the wild flora and fauna, but often limitations are imposed which should reduce the harm resulting. There are detailed legal schemes on animal and plant health which include powers to destroy diseased or suspect animals and plants, including those in the wild.[160] A range of pest control measures allows action to be taken against particular species, primarily rodents, but at the same time places

---

[151] Rural Development Contracts (Land Managers Options) (Scotland) Regulations 2008 Sch.2.

[152] Rural Development Contracts (Rural Priorities) (Scotland) Regulations 2008 (SSI 2008/100), amended by the Rural Development Contracts (Rural Priorities) (Scotland) Amendment Regulations 2008 and 2009 (SSI 2008/233 and and SSI 2009/1).

[153] Rural Development Contracts (Rural Priorities) (Scotland) Regulations 2008 Sch.2.

[154] In England, the main scheme is Environmental Stewardship, which is divided into Entry Level and Higher Level schemes: Environmental Stewardship (England) Regulations 2005 (SI 2005/261) (as amended by Environmental Stewardship (England) and Countryside Stewardship (Amendment) Regulations 2006 (SI 2006/991)). Tir Cynnal is the agri-environment entry-level scheme in Wales, with more demanding requirements made under the Tir Gofal scheme; Rural Development Programme (Wales) Regulations 2006 (SI 2006/3343).

[155] N. Hawke and N. Kovaleva, *Agri-Environmental Law and Policy* (London: Cavendish, 1998), Ch.4.

[156] Arable Area Payment Regulations 1996 (SI 1996/3142).

[157] See *http://ec.europa.eu/agriculture/healthcheck/index_en.htm* [Accesed May 16, 2009]. At the same time the increase in agricultural prices has also led to more land being taken into active production.

[158] *Farming and the Environment: Final Report of Sir Don Curry's High Level Set-Aside Group* (DEFRA, 2008).

[159] *Consultation on proposed changes to standards in cross compliance, Good Agricultural and Environmental Condition (GAEC) and related measures in England* (DEFRA, 2009), pp.6–29.

[160] Animal Health Act, 1981, see para.4.5.11, above; Plant Health Act 1967, see paras 6.2.12–6.2.14, above.

restrictions on the use of indiscriminate measures.[161] The use of pesticides is controlled by Part III of the Food and Environment Protection Act 1985 and associated regulations. Under these provisions pesticides must gain ministerial approval before they can be advertised, sold or used, and the conditions in any approval will include a duty to take all reasonable precautions to safeguard the environment.[162]

8.4.14   Fire has long been used as an agricultural tool, but can be particularly destructive to natural habitats. Legal controls affect both muirburn and the burning of crop residues. As far as muirburn is concerned in Scotland, the basic rule is that it is an offence to make muirburn except before April 16 or after September 30 in any year, although for the proprietor of land (or tenant with the proprietor's approval) the permitted period is extended to April 30, or May 15 for land over 450 metres. A direction from the Minister can extend the generally permitted period until a specified date not later than May 1, or May 16 in the case of land over 450 metres.[163] It is an offence to make muirburn between one hour after sunset and one hour before sunrise, and in all cases the person responsible must notify neighbours and provide sufficient staff and equipment to control the burning operations so as to prevent damage to woodlands and all neighbouring land and property.[164] Making muirburn without due care so as to cause damage to adjoining lands is a criminal offence[165] as well as giving rise to civil liability.[166]

8.4.15   In England and Wales the burning of heather, bracken, grass and vaccinium is controlled by regulations made by the Minister.[167] These prohibit burning between March 31 and November 1, or between April 15 and October 1 in upland areas,[168] although a special licence from the Secretary of State can authorise burning at other times.[169] No burning is allowed between sunset and sunrise, neighbours must be notified, sufficient staff and equipment must be provided to control the fires and all reasonable precautions must be taken to prevent injury or damage to adjoining property.[170] The prohibitions do not apply to pleasure grounds, private gardens and allotments,[171] and special rules apply for railway land.

---

[161] See section 4.5, above.

[162] See para.4.4.2, above.

[163] Hill Farming Act 1946 s.23, amended by Agriculture (Adaptation of Enactments) (Scotland) Regulations 1977 (SI 1977/2007); WCA 1981 s.72. The Climate Change (Scotland) Bill introduced in late 2008 includes provisions to allow the dates to be varied where necessary or expedient in relation to climate change (s.46 of Bill as introduced) and further changes are discussed in the consultation paper on a Wildlife and Natural Environment Bill published in June 2009.

[164] Hill Farming Act 1946 s.25.

[165] Hill Farming Act 1946 ss.25 and 27.

[166] *Mackintosh v Mackintosh* (1864) 2 M. 1357; *Lord Advocate v Rodger*, 1978 S.L.T. (Sh. Ct) 31.

[167] Heather and Grass, Etc. (Burning) Regulations 1986 (SI 1986/428), amended by Heather and Grass, Etc. (Burning) (Amendment) Regulations 1987 (SI 1987/1208), made under the Hill Farming Act 1946 s.20, amended by Hill Farming (Amendment) Act 1985.

[168] As defined on maps kept for this purpose; Heather and Grass, Etc. (Burning) Regulations 1986 reg.2(1).

[169] Heather and Grass, Etc. (Burning) Regulations 1986 reg.6; the provisions governing licences are in reg.7.

[170] Heather and Grass, Etc. (Burning) Regulations 1986 reg.5.

[171] Heather and Grass, Etc. (Burning) Regulations 1986 reg.3.

The burning of crop residues is now also subject to strict legal control, as **8.4.16** much to prevent nuisance, air pollution and the dangers from smoke obstructing visibility on roads, as to avoid the dangers of fires getting out of control. The Minister has the power to make regulations to prohibit or restrict the burning of crop residues on agricultural land by persons engaged in agriculture,[172] but so far this power has only been exercised in relation to England and Wales.

Under the Crop Residues (Burning) Regulations 1993[173] it is an offence to **8.4.17** burn on agricultural land any of the specified crop residues[174] except for the purposes of education or research, or for disease control under statutory notices.[175] Where burning of these residues is permitted, or where linseed residues are burnt, very detailed requirements must be complied with. These extend to such matters as the times and dates of burning (not at weekends or on bank holidays), the precautions to prevent fire or smoke affecting buildings, trees, hedges, nature reserves, ancient monuments, roads and railway lines, the notice to be given to various authorities, and the fire-fighting equipment and personnel to be available, as well as imposing an obligation to incorporate the ash into the soil within 24 hours.[176] Burning is permitted for the disposal of straw stack remains or broken bales.

Special measures have also been taken to prevent water pollution arising **8.4.18** from agricultural activities, particularly in an attempt to control the build-up of nitrates in lochs, rivers and groundwater. As well as its potential to harm human health, the presence of nitrates in water can radically affect the fauna and especially the flora which it supports. The eutrophication of water previously low in nutrients destroys the habitat of many species which have evolved to take advantage of poor conditions and can lead to huge "blooms" of algae, which can stifle all other life in the water and can in themselves be poisonous to animals and humans. This phenomenon is largely attributable to years of intensive cultivation, as both inorganic fertilisers and natural processes working on the much increased volumes of vegetable matter have led to nitrates entering and accumulating in the water system. Any measures taken now can at most prevent the accelerated deterioration of the situation; there are decades of accumulated damage to be dealt with, and the slow leaching of nitrates currently in the soil will continue to affect the water system for years to come.

Action against nitrate pollution has been led by developments within the **8.4.19** European Community. The Directive on protecting waters against pollution caused by nitrates from agricultural sources[177] requires Member States to identify waters which contain more than 50mg per litre of nitrates, fall foul of the limits set in Community legislation on drinking water, are found to be subject to eutrophication, or may fall into any of these categories if steps are not taken. The areas draining into such waters are to be designated as vulnerable zones, and within these action programmes are to be

---

[172] EPA 1990 s.152.

[173] SI 1993/1366.

[174] Cereal straw or stubble, and residues of oil-seed rape or of field beans or peas harvested dry; Crop Residues (Burning) Regulations 1993 Sch.1.

[175] Referring to the now revoked Plant Health (Great Britain) Order 1993 (SI 1993/1320) art.22.

[176] Crop Residues (Burning) Regulations 1993 Sch.2.

[177] Directive 91/676/EEC.

implemented in the endeavour to reduce water pollution caused or induced by nitrates from agricultural sources and to prevent further such pollution. These programmes, and supporting voluntary codes of practice, deal with issues such as the periods during which the application of fertilisers[178] is inappropriate, the methods of application, the ground conditions in which application is inappropriate (e.g. saturated or frozen ground, or steeply sloping ground), and the storage of livestock manure to prevent run-off. Other matters such as crop rotation, the maintenance of vegetation cover on the soil, the prevention of run-off and individual fertiliser limits for farms may also be included.

8.4.20   British farmers challenged the validity and implementation of the Directive on the grounds that it was wrong for nitrate vulnerable zones to be declared where agriculture was not the only source of the nitrates and that the action programmes by imposing restrictions on farmers alone, even though there might be other sources of nitrates, constituted a disproportionate response to the problem and offended against the principles of polluter pays and rectifying pollution at source,[179] as well as infringing the farmers' rights to deal with their own property as they wished. This challenge was rejected by the European Court of Justice on both grounds; the Directive did not require agriculture sources to be the sole source of nitrate pollution, provided that they made a significant contribution to the pollution, whilst the Directive's provisions were sufficiently flexible to allow Member States to avoid offending against any of the general principles relied on by the farmers.[180]

8.4.21   The implementation of this Directive in Great Britain has not been straightforward, and the United Kingdom has been held to be in breach of its duty to implement it, as a result of the initial failure to take any action in Northern Ireland and of considering only waters from which drinking water is extracted when identifying the waters at risk of nitrate pollution.[181] The position was not fully rectified immediately, leading to threats of further infraction proceedings and various amendments to the law both at the start of this century and again during 2008.

8.4.22   Initially the approach in Britain was based on Nitrate Sensitive Areas, where although there was the potential for stronger measures, the emphasis was on voluntary agreements under which farmers accepted obligations in respect to the management of their land designed to prevent pollution by nitrates in exchange for payments.[182] Now implementation rests on the stronger provisions for Nitrate Vulnerable Zones. In such Zones (which

---

[178] All forms of fertiliser containing nitrogen compounds are included, including animal manure and sewage sludge.

[179] These principles are embedded in the environmental provisions of the EC Treaty at art.174; see para.2.9.4, above.

[180] *R. v Secretary of State for the Environment, ex p. Standley* (C-293/97) [1999] E.C.R. I-2603; [1999] Q.B. 1279.

[181] *Commission v United Kingdom* (C-69/99) [2000] E.C.R. I-10,979.

[182] Control of Pollution Act 1974 ss.31B–31D, added by Water Act 1989 Sch.23; Water Resources Act 1991 ss.94–96; Nitrate Sensitive Areas (Designation) Order 1990 (SI 1990/1013); Nitrate Sensitive Areas Regulations 1994 (SI 1994/1729); Hawke and Kovaleva, *Agri-Environmental Law and Policy* (1998), pp.170–174.

cover the majority of England but less of Scotland and Wales)[183] the action programme imposes (without compensation) mandatory restrictions on agricultural activity in order to prevent the accumulation of nitrates.[184] These deal with the quantity, timing and method of applying nitrogen, chemical and organic fertilisers (including manure and slurry), and the treatment of unharvested residues of certain crops, as well as specifying the data to be kept for monitoring purposes. Failure to observe the requirements of the programme is a criminal offence, although in Scotland an enforcement notice may be served as the initial step when failure to comply is detected.[185] To assist compliance with the law some specific grants were available to assist in paying for improved facilities for storing or treating manure, slurry and silage effluent.[186]

Agricultural activity is also considerably affected by further measures **8.4.23** introduced to limit water pollution. In Scotland, for example, the Water Environment (Diffuse Pollution) (Scotland) Regulations 2008[187] control many activities by setting restrictions which must be complied with to avoid the need for express authorisation under the water pollution legislation,[188] whilst the construction and siting of tanks for the making of silage and the storage of silage and slurry are also controlled in order to prevent water pollution, including the leaching of nitrates into the soil.[189] There is also provision for Codes of Practice to be issued giving practical advice and promoting good practice with a view to preventing or minimising water

[183] For Scotland, designation is by the Designation of Nitrate Vulnerable Zones (Scotland) Regulations 2000 (SSI 2000/26) and the Designation of Nitrate Vulnerable Zones (No.2) (Scotland) Regulations 2002 (SSI 2002/546) which cover much of the eastern lowlands and Nithsdale; for England the Nitrate Pollution Prevention Regulations 2008 (SI 2008/2349), cover 70% of the country, and small areas in Wales (4% of the area) are designated under the Nitrate Pollution Prevention (Wales) Regulations (SI 2008/3143). The 2008 regulations prescribe the procedures for designation and obligations to review the situation; for Scotland see the Protection of Water Against Agricultural Nitrate Pollution (Scotland) Regulations 1996 (SI 1996/ 1564) reg.6A, added by Nitrate (Public Participation etc.) (Scotland) Regulations 2005 (SSI 2005/305) reg.2.

[184] Nitrate Pollution Prevention Regulations 2008 (SI 2008/2349); Nitrate Pollution Prevention (Wales) Regulations 2008 (SI 2008/3143); Action Programme for Nitrate Vulnerable Zones (Scotland) Regulations 2008 (SSI 2008/298), amended by Action Programme for Nitrate Vulnerable Zones (Scotland) Amendment Regulations 2008 (SSI 2008/394).

[185] Action Programme for Nitrate Vulnerable Zones (Scotland) Regulations 2008 (SI 2008/ 298) reg.28.

[186] Nitrate Vulnerable Zones (Grants) (Scotland) Scheme 2003 (SSI 2003/52), as amended by Nitrate Vulnerable Zones (Grants) (Scotland) Amendment Scheme 2003 (SSI 2003/518); Farm Waste Grant (Nitrate Vulnerable Zones) (Wales) Scheme 2004 (SI 2004/1606).

[187] SSI 2008/54. For developments in England see *Government response on way forward following consultation on diffuse sources in England for the protection of waters against pollution from agriculture* (DEFRA, 2008).

[188] Water Environment (Controlled Activities) (Scotland) Regulations 2005 (SSI 2005/348); see para.8.6.7, below.

[189] Control of Pollution (Silage, Slurry and Agricultural Fuel Oil) (Scotland) Regulations 2003 (SSI 2003/531) (the requirements in relation to oil storage now appear in the Water Environment (Oil Storage) (Scotland) Regulations 2006 (SSI 2006/133)); in England and Wales, Control of Pollution (Silage, Slurry and Agricultural Fuel Oil) Regulations 1991 (SI 1991/324), amended by Control of Pollution (Silage, Slurry and Agricultural Fuel Oil) (Amendment) Regulations 1996 and 1997 (SI 1996/2044 and SI 1997/547).

pollution arising from agricultural activities.[190] A breach of such codes does not give rise to any civil or criminal liability but is a factor to be taken into account when the environment agencies consider whether to exercise their other powers.

8.4.24   A final point to note in relation to agriculture is the potential significance of the law on land tenure in restricting the extent to which the occupier of agricultural land can give priority to nature conservation. Much of the countryside is held under the terms of agricultural tenancies, which impose obligations on the tenant to farm the land in an efficient manner. The rights of the landowner to trees,[191] minerals, game and other aspects of the land may also affect the ability or willingness of tenants to manage their land in particular ways. Notice to quit can be served on tenants who are failing to farm the land in accordance with the rules of good husbandry.[192] A landlord can apply to the Land Court (Scotland) or the Agricultural Land Tribunal (England and Wales) for a certificate to this effect,[193] and once this has been granted a notice to quit on that basis is not subject to further scrutiny.[194] Similarly one of the statutory conditions applied to crofts is that the crofter shall cultivate the croft.[195]

8.4.25   The rules of good husbandry require that the tenant maintains a reasonable standard of efficient production,[196] and in Scotland specify such matters as the proper stocking of livestock units, regular muirburn on hill farms, and systematic control of vermin, bracken, whins, broom and injurious weeds.[197] The rules now allow for the acceptance of conservation practice adopted in England and Wales in pursuance of any term of the tenancy or other agreement between tenant and landlord which has as its objective the conservation of flora, fauna or geological or physiographical features, or the protection of buildings or sites of archaeological, architectural or historic interest, or the conservation and enhancement of the natural beauty and amenity of the countryside.[198] In Scotland the equivalent refers to practice in accordance with any statutory agreement or public funding.[199] The inclusion of such practice is welcome but may not cover

---

[190] Control of Pollution Act 1974 s.51, substituted by Water Act 1989 Sch.23 para.5; Water Resources Act 1991 s.97. Codes have been approved by the Water (Prevention of Pollution) (Code of Practice) Order 1998 (SI 1998/3084), the Water (Prevention of Pollution) (Code of Practice) (Scotland) Order 2005 (SI 2005/63) and the Water (Prevention of Pollution) (Code of Good Agricultural Practice) (England) Order 2009 (SI 2009/46).

[191] For example, special legislation was necessary to enable crofters to use common grazings for forestry purposes; Crofter Forestry (Scotland) Act 1991(see now Crofters (Scotland) Act 1993 s.50).

[192] See para.8.4.25, below.

[193] Agricultural Holdings (Scotland) Act 1991 s.26; Agricultural Holdings Act 1986 Sch.3 Pt I Case C and Pt II para.9.

[194] Agricultural Holdings (Scotland) Act 1991 s.22; Agricultural Holdings Act 1986 s.26.

[195] Crofters (Scotland) Act 1993 s.5 and Sch.2 paras 3 and 13. The Scottish Government's consultation paper on the draft Crofting Reform (Scotland) Bill (May 2009) proposes that managed action to conserve flora, fauna or natural beauty would also be acceptable (para.6.2.4.4).

[196] Agriculture Act 1947 s.11, applied by Agricultural Holdings Act 1986 s.96(3).

[197] Agriculture (Scotland) Act 1948 Sch.6, applied by Agricultural Holdings (Scotland) Act 1991 s.85(2).

[198] Agricultural Holdings Act 1986 Sch.3 Pt II para.9(2), amended by Water Consolidation (Consequential Provisions) Act 1991 Sch.1 para.43.

[199] Agricultural Holdings (Scotland) Act 1991 s.85(2A), added by Agricultural Holdings (Scotland) Act 2003 s.69; Agricultural Holdings (Scotland) Act 2003 s.18.

tenants acting on their own, without formal support, if they pursue conservation activities which do not result in efficient agricultural production.
Moreover it has been held that the Land Court has no discretion to refuse a
certificate of bad husbandry once it has concluded that the rules are being
broken, regardless of mitigating circumstances.[200] The extent to which
occupiers may dedicate their land to nature conservation may thus be
restricted by their status as agricultural tenants.[201]

CONTROL OF POLLUTION

The environment is now protected by a large number of measures designed **8.5.1**
to prevent or restrict pollution. Most of these have been introduced with a
view to human health and comfort, but obviously they will also serve to
benefit wild flora and fauna. Such measures are found in European legislation, Acts of Parliament and detailed statutory regulations and operate in
a number of ways: imposing emission controls, setting quality standards for
air and water, and providing product standards so that only goods meeting
certain anti-pollution requirements can enter the market. The volume of
legislation involved is daunting.[202] Any attempt here to sketch even the
outline of the law on pollution would be hopelessly inadequate, not least
because the coming of devolution is producing increasing divergence, often
in detail but sometimes in substance, across Great Britain.[203] Moreover, with
a steady flow of new legislation, as well as the gradual coming into force of
provisions once they have been made, any account is likely to be either out
of date or premature. This section will therefore limit itself to making three
points of fairly general application.

The first is the ever-widening scope of anti-pollution legislation to have a **8.5.2**
greater impact within the countryside. In the same way as agriculture was
largely exempt from planning controls, most agricultural activities fell
outwith the scope of the earlier anti-pollution laws but are now increasingly
subject to control. A clear example was the inclusion of some food-
processing and intensive agricultural activities within the pollution prevention and control scheme,[204] showing that the reach of the anti-pollution

---

[200] *Cambusmore Estate Trustees v Little*, 1991 S.L.T. (Land Ct) 33.

[201] See M. Cardwell, "Set-aside Schemes and Alternative Land Uses: Some Problems for the
Tenant Farmer" [1992] Conv. 180. See also *Williams v Schellenberg*, 1988 G.W.D. 29-1254
where one pro-indiviso owner of land argued that her interest had been damaged by the
proprietor in occupation encouraging the designation of the land as an SSSI, thereby restricting
its management and reducing its value.

[202] For general surveys see: S. Bell and D. McGillivray, *Environmental Law*, 7th edn (Oxford:
OUP, 2008); the Environmental Permitting (England and Wales) Regulations 2007 (SI 2007/
3538), alone run to 130 pages whilst the sheer bulk of the multi-volume looseleaf encyclopaedias
on the topic demonstrates the amount of legislation and official guidance in this area: *Encyclopaedia of Environmental Law* (London: Sweet & Maxwell, 1993–), *Garner's Environmental
Law* (London: LexisNexis, 1991–).

[203] e.g. in England and Wales several regimes have been brought together under the Environmental Permitting (England and Wales) Regulations 2007 (SI 2007/3538), whilst remaining
separate in Scotland.

[204] Pollution Prevention and Control (England and Wales) Regulations 2000 (SI 2000/1973)
(now the Environmental Permitting (England and Wales) Regulations 2007); Pollution Prevention and Control (Scotland) Regulations 2000 (SSI 2000/323), both made under the Pollution Prevention and Control Act 1999 to implement Directive 96/61/EC.

legislation extends well beyond the stereotype of a dirty factory belching out dark fumes and foaming effluent. Over 30 topics are covered in the guidance to the agricultural industry provided by the environment agencies through NetRegs,[205] demonstrating how many aspects of countryside management are now affected by such measures.

8.5.3   Secondly, there is concern that as the problems caused by major "point-source" pollution come under control, the overall health of the environment is at greater risk from diffuse pollution. The factories, refineries and treatment works that were the obvious and major sources of pollution are now subject to restrictions, and the greater contribution to environmental degradation comes from the cumulative effects of the many small-scale emissions which inevitably fall below the threshold for significant direct regulation.[206] Some diffuse sources are now the subject of regulatory measures, notably in agriculture,[207] but for others reliance has so far been placed largely on codes of practice and other forms of encouraging good practice. Inevitably, though, as the major direct sources of pollution are cleaned up, and diffuse pollution becomes a more significant element in poor environmental quality,[208] stronger measures will be required.

8.5.4   The final point to note is the extent to which the broader environment, including the health of flora and fauna, is a legitimate concern in the aims of the anti-pollution measures. As will be seen in the next section, ecological quality is fundamental to the Water Framework Directive which now dominates the regime for water resources, but some concern for nature appears throughout pollution law. The general duties of the Environment Agency and the Scottish Environment Protection Agency include duties to have regard to the conservation of the natural heritage[209] and to promote the conservation of flora and fauna dependent on an aquatic environment.[210] The Pollution Prevention and Control Act 1999 authorises measures designed to prevent environmental pollution that may give rise to any harm, and such terms are defined in a way which protects other species in addition to man; "harm" includes "impairment of, or interference with, the ecological systems of which any living organisms form part".[211] Similar broad definitions are used in other areas, e.g. the provisions on waste management define "harm" as including "harm to the health of living organisms or other interference with the ecological systems of which they form part",[212] whilst specific powers can be exercised in the interests of wildlife, e.g. one of the grounds on which the Minister can direct the revocation or modification of a consent to discharge into waters in England and Wales is for "the protection of ... flora and fauna dependent on an aquatic environment".[213] Designated sites are also given recognition by means of additional consultation

---

[205] NetRegs offers environmental guidance for small and medium-sized businesses and is available at *http://www.netregs.gov.uk/* [Accessed May 16, 2009].

[206] See SEPA's Diffuse Pollution Website at *http://www.sepa.org.uk/water/diffuse_pollution.aspx* [Accessed May 16, 2009].

[207] e.g. Water Environment (Diffuse Pollution) (Scotland) Regulations 2008 (SSI 2008/54).

[208] e.g. SEPA, *Significant water management issues in the Scotland river basin district* (2007), pp.24–35.

[209] EA 1995 ss.7 and 32.

[210] EA 1995 ss.6 and 34.

[211] Pollution Prevention and Control Act 1999 s.1(3).

[212] EPA 1990 s.29(5).

[213] Water Resources Act 1991 Sch.10 para.7(4), substituted by EA 1995 Sch.22 para.183.

requirements when they may be affected, both as a general obligation[214] and as a specific part of particular procedures, e.g. in relation to waste management proposals in Scotland.[215] The powers to control pollution are therefore to be exercised for the benefit of plants and animals as well as man.

WATER RESOURCES

Many communities and species of plants and animals depend directly on an aquatic environment, from otters and kingfishers to the less appreciated midges whose larval stages are aquatic. Moreover the maintenance of the underlying water table at particular levels is crucial to the existence of many kinds of habitat, including water meadows, marshes and fens. The conservation of water resources is thus of great significance. Threats to a healthy aquatic environment come from drainage, pollution and the overuse of water taken from rivers, lochs and underground strata. All of these are to some extent regulated by law. **8.6.1**

The law in this field is complex and four main elements in its make-up can be identified.[216] The background is a mixture of common law and older statutes that balanced the rights of landowners to do as they wish on their land both with the protection of the rights of neighbours and of downstream owners and with the public interest, in preventing abuses of water resources and in ensuring that individual landowners cannot prevent or hinder schemes which offer a wider benefit. Secondly, since the 1970s there has then been a flood of legislation at domestic and EC levels introducing stricter measures to control water resources and set quality standards for waters used for different purposes.[217] Statutory controls exist over discharges into water[218] (including dumping at sea),[219] land drainage[220] and the abstraction of water,[221] with further powers in relation to flood control[222] and drought[223] **8.6.2**

---

[214] EA 1995 ss.8 and 35.

[215] EPA 1990 s.36(7).

[216] See generally, F. Lyall, "Water and Water Rights" in *The Laws of Scotland: Stair Memorial Encyclopaedia*, Vol.25 (Edinburgh: LexisNexis / Law Society of Scotland, 1989), M. Poustie, "Environment" paras 352–511 in *Stair Memorial Encyclopaedia Reissue* (Edinburgh: LexisNexis / Law Society of Scotland, 2009), S.Hendry, "Water Resources and Water Pollution", Title 6 in F. McManus (ed.), *Environmental Law in Scotland* (Edinburgh: W. Green, 2007); W. Howarth, *Wisdom's Law of Watercourses*, 5th edn (Crayford: Shaw & Sons, 1992); W. Howarth and D. McGillivray, *Water Pollution and Water Quality Law* (Crayford: Shaw & Sons, 2001); W. Howarth, *Legal Aspects of Flooding and Land Drainage* (Crayford: Shaw & Sons, 2002).

[217] The 1,200 pages of W. Howarth and D. McGillivray, *Water Pollution and Water Quality Law* (Crayford: Shaw & Sons, 2001) themselves testify to the volume and complexity of the law here.

[218] Water Resources Act 1991 Pt III; Water Environment (Controlled Activities) (Scotland) Regulations 2005 (SSI 2005/348) (known as "CAR" for Controlled Activities Regulations).

[219] Food and Environment Protection Act 1985 Pt II.

[220] Land Drainage (Scotland) Acts 1930 and 1958, Flood Prevention and Land Drainage (Scotland) Act 1997; Land Drainage Acts 1976, 1991 and 1994.

[221] Water Resources Act 1991 Pt II c.II; Water Environment (Controlled Activities) (Scotland) Regulations 2005 (SSI 2005/348).

[222] Flood Prevention (Scotland) Act 1961; Water Resources Act 1991 Pt IV. Changes in the law can be expected as a result of the Directive on the assessment and management of flood risks, Directive 2007/60/EC, and the Flood Risk Management (Scotland) Act 2009.

[223] Natural Heritage (Scotland) Act 1991 Pt III; Water Resources Act 1991 Pt II c.III.

and measures to protect the quality of water used for bathing[224] and certain fisheries[225] as well as laws directed at particular threats such as discharges of dangerous substances[226] and inadequate treatment of waste water from urban areas.[227]

8.6.3   The third element has been the restructuring of the water industry and water regulation since the late 1980s. In England and Wales the substantial changes involved in privatisation of the industry provided the opportunity for a wider overhaul of the legislation.[228] In Scotland the industry was left in public hands[229] and there were simply adjustments to, rather than a rewriting of, the environmental controls, leaving a complicated patchwork of legislative provisions.[230] Finally, the dominant feature is the Water Framework Directive, adopted in 2000.[231] The need to implement this and to meet its requirements has led to new approaches to river basin management planning and in Scotland to a complete restructuring of the main regulatory controls. The detailed working of all these arrangements can obviously have a major impact on water quantity and quality and thus on conservation.

8.6.4   In England and Wales, one feature of the structural reforms and statutory consolidation that took place has been the inclusion in the relevant statutory provisions of express duties on the various authorities to have regard to and to further the interests of nature conservation. Thus the Environment Agency is under a general duty, so far as it considers desirable, to promote the conservation of flora and fauna which are dependent on an aquatic environment,[232] in addition to the general duty on the Agency and Ministers to further the conservation of flora and fauna.[233] There is also provision for the preparation of Codes of Practice giving practical guidance and promoting good practice on such matters.[234] Similar obligations are present in the other legislation, applying to Ministers, water and sewerage undertakers and regulators.[235]

8.6.5   In Scotland, the restructuring of the water industry, culminating in the creation of Scottish Water in 2002, also gave the opportunity for a recasting of the environmental obligations of the various authorities. The Ministers and Scottish Water are under a duty to exercise their functions so as to further the conservation and enhancement of natural beauty, the conservation of flora and fauna and the conservation of geological and

---

[224] Bathing Waters Directive, Directive 2006/7/EC.

[225] e.g. Shellfish Water Directive 2006, Directive 2006/113/EC.

[226] Dangerous Substances Directive, now consolidated as Directive 2006/11/EC.

[227] Urban Waste Water Directive, Directive 91/271/EEC; meeting the requirements of this Directive has entailed very substantial investment in new and improved infrastructure.

[228] Howarth and McGillivray, *Water Pollution and Water Quality Law* (2001), pp.97–108.

[229] See now the Water Industry (Scotland) Act 2002 and Water Services etc. (Scotland) Act 2005.

[230] F. Lyall, "Water Pollution", Ch.3 in C.T. Reid (ed.), *Environmental Law in Scotland*, 2nd edn (Edinburgh: W. Green 1997) pp.54–55 and 63–64.

[231] Directive 2000/60/EC.

[232] EA 1995 s.6.

[233] EA 1995 s.7.

[234] Water Industry Act 1991 s.5; EA 1995 s.9; Water and Sewerage (Conservation, Access and Recreation) (Code of Practice) Order 2000 (SI 2000/477).

[235] e.g. Water Industry Act 1991 s.3; Land Drainage Act 1991 ss.61A–61C, added by Land Drainage Act 1994 s.1; Food and Environment Protection Act 1985 s.8; see paras 2.2.10 and 2.7.19, above.

physiographical features of special interest.[236] Additional consultation requirements apply before starting any work or schemes adversely affecting European Sites or National Parks.[237]

The law and its application are now in the process of fundamental change **8.6.6** to meet the requirements of the EC Water Framework Directive.[238] This requires water resources (surface water, groundwater and coastal waters) to be managed on the basis of river basin districts,[239] with controls on point source and diffuse pollution, abstraction, impoundment and engineering works such as land drainage and flood and coastal protection that affect the water systems.[240] The aim of these measures is to meet the environmental objectives, or quality targets, established for each body of water under the management plan for each river basin district,[241] and significantly these objectives are based primarily on ecological criteria.[242] Subject to some qualifications, the overall aim is that there should be no deterioration in any waters and that all should attain good status (as exhaustively defined) by 2015, or for heavily modified waters that they attain good ecological potential and good chemical status.[243] Nature conservation issues inevitably play a significant part as these plans and objectives are put into practice.

Implementation of the Directive has involved general obligations on the **8.6.7** Ministers and environment agencies to secure compliance with its requirements[244] and in Scotland all Scottish Ministers and every public body and office-holder must have regard to the desirability of protecting the water environment in the exercise of their functions.[245] This means that as well as the formal planning mechanisms arising from the Directive, the various powers to control discharges, abstractions, etc. must be exercised in line with its objectives. In Scotland this is simplified by the creation of a single regulatory framework for controls on pollution, abstraction and impoundment and building or engineering works in or by surface waters.[246] The river basin district planning process is well under way, involving the definition of "basins", an initial characterisation of these (covering their physical characteristics, the impact of human activity and an economic analysis of water use) and then the development of management plans to include environmental objectives designed to ensure compliance with the overall objectives

---

[236] Water Industry (Scotland) Act 2002 s.53.

[237] Water Industry (Scotland) Act 2002 s.54.

[238] Directive 2000/60/EC.

[239] Directive 2000/60/EC art.3.

[240] Directive 2000/60/EC art.11.

[241] Directive 2000/60/EC art.4

[242] Directive 2000/60/EC Annex V.

[243] Directive 2000/60/EC art.4.

[244] Water Environment and Water Services (Scotland) Act 2003 s.2; Water Environment (Water Framework Directive) (England and Wales) Regulations 2003 (SI 2003 No.3242) reg.3.

[245] Water Environment and Water Services (Scotland) Act 2003 s.2(5). The 2003 Act states that its purpose is to "make provision for protection of the water environment", which is defined as including "preventing further deterioration of, and protecting and enhancing, the status of aquatic ecosystems and, with regard to their water needs, terrestrial ecosystems and wetlands directly depending on those aquatic ecosystems" (s.1).

[246] Water Environment (Controlled Activities) (Scotland) Regulations 2005 (SSI 2005/348).

of the Directive.[247] All public authorities are under a duty to have regard to the plans and any sub-basin or supplementary plans once these are in place.[248] The process also includes the identification and inclusion in a public register of protected areas, which include areas designated under Community measures for the protection of habitats or species where the maintenance or improvement of the status of water is an important factor in such protection.[249] The process therefore incorporates concern for designated sites as well as having overriding ecological objectives.

8.6.8 It will be some time before the real impact of the measures to comply with the Directive is seen, but its requirements are already shaping regulatory decisions. In meeting its general objectives, particular difficulties are caused by diffuse pollution which is becoming the dominant threat to water quality.[250] Measures to deal with pollution by nitrates have already been discussed [251] and in Scotland regulations have also been introduced to tackle other rural sources of pollution.[252] Other measures, such as the development of Sustainable (Urban) Drainage Schemes (SUDS), offer ways of limiting diffuse pollution and creating new habitats as ponds, ditches and swales are created.[253]

Genetically Modified Organisms

8.7.1 A new threat to the conservation of flora and fauna is posed by the creation of genetically modified organisms. For thousands of years man has been involved in genetic manipulation through the selective breeding of crops and domesticated animals, but now much more rapid and much more far-reaching changes to plants and animals are possible. The long-term effects of such modified organisms being released and coming into contact with wild plants and animals are largely unknown. Many interactions with wildlife and domesticated plants and animals are possible—as competitors, as predators or grazers, as food-plants or prey that alter nutritional intake or introduce toxins, or as breeding partners that spread new genes and create new hybrids. The experience of releases of natural but geographically alien species such as mink or Japanese knotweed has shown the damage which can be caused. Moreover, there is concern about indirect effects arising from changes in agricultural practices that might follow the introduction of genetically modified crops. In the late 1990s this issue became one of great public controversy in Britain, initially in relation to the presence of genetically-modified ingredients in food and then focused on the programme of field-scale trials of genetically modified crops. Attention has therefore been

---

[247] Water Environment and Water Services (Scotland) Act 2003 ss.4–19; Water Environment (Water Framework Directive) (England and Wales) Regulations 2003 (SI 2003/3242) regs 4–20.
[248] Water Environment and Water Services (Scotland) Act 2003 s.16; Water Environment (Water Framework Directive) (England and Wales) Regulations 2003 reg.17.
[249] Water Environment and Water Services (Scotland) Act 2003 s.7; Water Environment (Water Framework Directive) (England and Wales) Regulations 2003 reg.8.
[250] SEPA, *Significant water management issues in the Scotland river basin district* (2007), pp.24–35.
[251] See paras 8.4.19–8.4.22, above.
[252] Water Environment (Diffuse Pollution) (Scotland) Regulations 2008 (SSI 2008/54).
[253] e.g. SEPA, *Ponds, Pools and Lochans* (2000), Ch.7 and the material on SUDS at *http://www.sepa.org.uk/water/water_publications/suds.aspx* [Accessed May 16, 2009].

drawn to the legal measures controlling the circumstances and conditions under which genetically modified organisms can be released into the environment. This has led to developments at domestic, European and international levels.[254]

In Great Britain the issue is primarily governed by Part VI of the **8.7.2** Environmental Protection Act 1990[255] and detailed Regulations that implement European Community measures on the topic. The relevant provisions in the Act have effect:

> "[F]or the purpose of ensuring that all appropriate measures are taken to avoid damage to the environment which may arise from the escape or release from human control of genetically modified organisms".[256]

The Act gives a broad definition of "genetically modified organisms", allowing the term to cover all forms of genetic manipulation other than those such as selective breeding that involve merely assistance to naturally occurring reproductive processes[257] and more precise and technical definitions are provided in the Regulations. Broad definitions are also given to phrases such as "damage to the environment" and "harm", which ensure that effects on flora and fauna are to be fully considered, and organisms are "released" or "escape" when they are no longer contained by measures designed to limit their contact with humans and the environment and to prevent or minimise the risk of harm.[258] Field-trials of genetically modified crops therefore count as a release to the environment.

Under the Act, risk assessments are required from anyone intending to **8.7.3** import, acquire, release or market genetically modified organisms, and notification to the Minister may be required.[259] If there is a risk of damage to the environment despite the precautions which are to be taken, the organism should not be imported, kept, etc. and at all times the best available techniques not entailing excessive costs shall be used to prevent damage to the environment.[260] The Minister can prohibit any dealings with organisms[261] or require that consents be obtained before organisms are imported, kept, released, etc. the conditions of such consents including continuing obligations on the person authorised to keep informed of any risks involved or damage being caused to the environment and to inform the Minister if the risks appear more serious than at the time the consent was given.[262] As usual, there are a number of powers granted to assist the enforcement of these controls, and the Minister has the power to act immediately in the case

---

[254] See generally G.Little, "The Regulation of Genetically Modified Organisms as an Environmental Risk" in F. McManus (ed.), *Environmental Law in Scotland* (2007).

[255] Most of the provisions of the Act discussed below have been amended by the Genetically Modified Organisms (Deliberate Release) Regulations 2002 (SI 2002/2443), the Genetically Modified Organisms (Deliberate Release) (Wales) Regulations 2002 (SI 2002/3188) and the Genetically Modified Organisms (Deliberate Release) (Scotland) Regulations 2002 (SSI 2002/541).

[256] EPA 1990 s.106(1).

[257] EPA 1990 s.106(4)–(4D).

[258] EPA 1990 s.107.

[259] EPA 1990 s.108.

[260] EPA 1990 s.109.

[261] EPA 1990 s.110.

[262] EPA 1990 s.112.

of imminent danger to the environment in order to render any genetically modified organism harmless.[263] In all cases there are registers of notifications, applications and consents, so that the public can be informed of the nature of the organisms and where they are being released.

8.7.4   The detailed Regulations[264] on the deliberate release to the environment of genetically modified organisms follow the terms of EC legislation.[265] The Regulations distinguish between consent to put products on the market and other forms of release, e.g. for research and development. In the latter case ("Part B consents"), applicants must provide information in response to the long list of issues to be addressed as part of the risk assessment; the list for higher plants[266] contains over 40 items, that for other organisms almost 90 and both include the proximity of the intended site to officially recognised biotopes or protected areas. Applications are placed on the public register, a range of statutory authorities is consulted and all applications are carefully examined by the UK Advisory Committee on Releases to the Environment (ACRE), which advises the Minister taking the decision. Consents include monitoring requirements both during and after the experimental period.

8.7.5   In the case of applications to market genetically modified products ("Part C consents"), e.g. to sell modified seed, consent must be given at EC level, involving consultation with all Member States. Decision-making lies initially in the hands of the state that receives the application for consent, but it can decide the matter only if there are no objections from the Commission or Member States. Where there are objections, the effective decision is taken by the Commission.[267] Applications must be advertised, the statutory conservation bodies (and many other bodies) must be consulted and full information on the proposed release and its effects provided, additional to the data for other forms of release.

8.7.6   Separate Regulations,[268] again following EC measures,[269] deal with the contained use of genetically modified organisms, including requirements to notify the Health and Safety Executive of the intention to use premises for this purpose and to carry out a risk assessment (submitted to the Executive) for each particular operation, while in some cases ministerial consent is required. Exposure of humans and the environment to genetically modified micro-organisms is to be reduced to the lowest level that is reasonably practicable and emergency plans for dealing with any escape may also be required. In addition to the controls mentioned here, further legislative

---

[263] EPA 1990 s.117.

[264] Genetically Modified Organisms (Deliberate Release) Regulations 2002 (SI 2002/2443), the Genetically Modified Organisms (Deliberate Release) (Wales) Regulations 2002 (SI 2002/3188) and the Genetically Modified Organisms (Deliberate Release) (Scotland) Regulations 2002 (SSI 2002/541); these have been subject to amendment.

[265] Directive 2001/18/EC, amended by Directive 2008/27/EC.

[266] *Gymnospermae* and *Angiospermae*.

[267] While the Scottish Regulations expressly say that consent must be given where the application has been approved by the Commission (reg.24), the equivalent provisions for England (reg.24) and Wales (reg.25) simply list such approval as prerequisite for national consent.

[268] Genetically Modified Organisms (Contained Use) Regulations 2000 (SI 2000/2831), amended by Genetically Modified Organisms (Contained Use) (Amendment) Regulations 2002 and 2005 (SI 2002/63 and SI 2005/2466).

[269] Directive 90/219/EEC, now replaced by Directive 2009/41/EC.

measures[270] deal with genetically modified food and feed,[271] the traceability of food and feed products[272] and transboundary movement of genetically modified organisms,[273] the latter implementing the Cartagena Protocol on Biosafety.[274] In the face of this battery of controls at EC level, the scope for individual Member States or regions to adopt a different approach to the use of genetically modified organisms is tightly constrained.[275]

The legislation aims to ensure that genetically modified organisms are **8.7.7** used only after a thorough assessment of the known risks involved, but it is the unknown risks that perhaps lie at the core of present debate. Many issues are raised about the state of scientific knowledge, the understanding of risk and uncertainty, the application of the precautionary principle and the role of public attitudes.[276] Moreover to the mix of arguments over potential impacts (good or bad) on health and biodiversity must be added to social and economic impacts of the availability of new crops, their supply and marketing chains and their effect on farming practices, changes in which may by themselves have a big impact on the countryside even if the organisms themselves do not. Differences of approach between the administrations within Great Britain are revealed by the differences in how the release of genetically modified organisms is being treated in implementing the Environmental Liability Directive.[277] The debate will continue.

LIABILITY FOR WILDLIFE

The encouragement of wild plants and animals on a piece of land may cause **8.8.1** problems if the result is an increase in what others regard as weeds and pests which then spread to neighbouring land. There are a number of statutory measures under which a landowner can be forced to take action to control "injurious weeds"[278] or pests[279] on his land. Moreover, in England and Wales the law on statutory nuisance has been extended to apply to "insects emanating from relevant industrial, trade or business premises and being

---

[270] European measures supported by implementing legislation within Great Britain.

[271] Regulation (EC) 1829/2003.

[272] Regulation (EC) 1830/2003.

[273] Regulation (EC) 1946/2003.

[274] A protocol to the Convention on Biological Diversity which has been signed and ratified by almost 150 states, including the UK, and by the European Community; see *http://www.cbd.int/biosafety* [Accessed May 16, 2009].

[275] *Land Oberösterreich and Republic of Austria v Commission* (T-366/03 and 235/04) [2005] E.C.R. II-4005, unsuccessful appeal at (C-439/05 P and C-454/05 P) [2007] E.C.R. I-7141; but see "EU Environmental Ministers back national GM bans" (2009) 410 ENDS Report 57.

[276] See G. Little, "The Regulation of Genetically Modified Organisms as an Environmental Risk" in F. McManus (ed.), *Environmental Law in Scotland* (Edinburgh: W. Green 2007) and the literature referred to there and H. Somsen, "Some Reflections on EU Biotechnology Regulation" in R. Macrory (ed.), *Reflections on 30 Years of EU Environmental Law: A High Level of Protection?* (Groningen: Europa, 2006).

[277] See para.5.12.5, above. For a separate aspect of liability issues see C. Rodgers, "Liability for the release of GMOs into the environment: exploring the boundaries of nuisance" (2003) 62 C.L.J. 371–402.

[278] See paras 6.2.8–6.2.10, above.

[279] See section 4.5, above.

prejudicial to health or a nuisance",[280] although the exemptions mean that this is extremely unlikely to apply in a wildlife context. The nuisance provisions do not apply to insects that are protected species under Schedule 5 to the Wildlife and Countryside Act 1981[281] nor to land used for agriculture, to land forming part of an SSSI, to any lake, pond, river or watercourse (other than a sewer or drain),[282] nor to land benefitting from many agriculture, forestry and country stewardship support schemes.[283] Similar provisions, but with fewer qualifications, apply in Scotland as well.[284]

8.8.2   There remains, though, the question of whether at common law the neighbour who claims that his property is being damaged by wildlife from a neighbour's land is entitled to compensation.[285] This issue is currently one of some difficulty as it is not wholly clear how far the law has moved from its once definite position that no compensation was available in such circumstances. In practice, anyone seeking compensation may also face difficulties in establishing that the defenders' land is indeed the source of the problem, that the problem has been worsened by their action, and that the level of damage caused by the weeds or pests is greater than could normally be expected.

8.8.3   A convenient starting point for both Scots and English law is *Giles v Walker*,[286] where a farmer sought to sue his neighbour for the damage caused by thistles spreading from the latter's land after it had been cleared of trees and brought into cultivation. This claim was rejected by the court which asserted that there could be "no duty as between adjoining occupiers to cut the thistles, which are the natural growth of the soil."[287] This approach was followed in both jurisdictions in relation to rats in *Steam v Prentice Bros Ltd*,[288] pheasants in *Seligman v Docker*,[289] and rabbits in *Marshall v Moncrieffe*,[290] *Gordon v Huntly Lodge Estates Co Ltd*,[291] and *Forrest v Irvine*.[292] In these cases though, the courts noted that the defender had not been taking any active or unusual steps to encourage the offending wildlife and left open the possibility of the position being different if such

---

[280] Environmental Protection Act 1990 s.79(1)(fa), as amended by Clean Neighbourhoods and Environment Act 2005 s.101.

[281] Unless they are listed in Schedule 5 in relation only to s.9(5) of the Act (sale); Environmental Protection Act 1990 s.79(5A).

[282] Environmental Protection Act 1990 s.79(7C).

[283] Statutory Nuisances (Insects) Regulations 2006 (SI 2006/770).

[284] Environmental Protection Act 1990 s.79(1)(faa) and (5AA)–(5AD), added by Public Health etc. (Scotland) Act 2008 s.109.

[285] Even more difficult issues, involving the interaction between various areas of statutory and common law, may also arise if it is claimed that land management practices designed to favour wildlife, especially in relation to wetlands, have caused or contributed to flooding or erosion; see generally W. Howarth, *Flood Defence Law* (Crayford: Shaw & Sons, 2002), esp. Ch.2.

[286] *Giles v Walker* (1890) 24 Q.B.D. 656.

[287] *Giles v Walker* (1890) 24 Q.B.D. 656 at 657, Lord Coleridge C.J.

[288] *Steam v Prentice Bros Ltd* [1919] 1 K.B. 394.

[289] *Seligman v Docker* [1949] Ch. 53.

[290] *Marshall v Moncrieffe* (1912) 28 Sh. Ct Rep. 343.

[291] *Gordon v Huntly Lodge Estates Co Ltd* (1940) 56 Sh. Ct Rep. 112.

[292] *Forrest v Irvine* (1953) 69 Sh. Ct Rep. 203; also *McDonald v British Railways Board* Unreported November 5, 1986, Aberdeen Sheriff Court; and *Hall v Dart Valley Light Railway Plc* [1998] CLY 3933.

steps had been taken.[293] Unless the measures taken were specifically designed for the multiplication of the damaging species, it seems unlikely that nature conservation measures would fall into that category.

More recent developments in England and related jurisdictions have **8.8.4** overturned this general rule that a landowner cannot be liable for the spread of naturally occurring items from his land. In an Australian case, *Goldman v Hargrave*[294] the Privy Council imposed liability for the spread of a naturally occurring fire, while the New Zealand courts have allowed compensation for the harm caused by the spread of thistles to grazing land.[295] Finally, *Giles v Walker* was formally overruled[296] by the English courts in *Leakey v National Trust for Places of Historic Interest and Scenic Beauty*,[297] where it was held that a landowner was liable for the fall of earth due to natural causes from a steep bank overlooking another's house.

It follows that in these jurisdictions the law may allow compensation for **8.8.5** harm caused by the spread of naturally occurring things from one piece of land to another. However, liability does not rest on the fact of harm alone. Strict liability exists under the rule in *Rylands v Fletcher*[298] only in cases of non-natural use of the land (which appears to rule out liability arising as a result of all but the most eccentric nature conservation measures), so that in the absence of deliberate harm, one is left with a claim based directly on negligence or on the arguments in *Leakey*.[299] There, although the claim was held to be appropriately framed in nuisance,[300] liability rested on a failure of the landowner to take such steps as were reasonable to prevent or minimise the risk of harm which the landowner knew or ought to have known would be caused to his neighbour. Therefore, whether the claim is framed in nuisance or negligence, there must be shown some failure to take reasonable care on the part of the landowner from whose land the danger has spread.

In *Goldman v Hargrave*[301] and *Leakey*[302] the harm was caused by a one-off **8.8.6** occurrence against which specific preventive action might have been taken, but assessing whether reasonable steps have been taken will be much harder where the injury is in the form of more diffuse harm, such as that caused by weeds or rabbits or other pests. In *French v Auckland City Corporation*,[303] where liability was imposed for damage caused by thistles growing from seed blown from neighbouring land, the court emphasised that everything depended on the surrounding circumstances, such as the extent of the spread of weeds, the damage likely to ensue, the cost and practicality of preventing

---

[293] In *Pole v Peake*, *The Times*, July 22, 1998 it was held that the holder of sporting rights including the right to rear game was not liable to the owner of the land for damage caused by the pheasants introduced or reared in the reasonable exercise of those rights.

[294] *Goldman v Hargrave* [1967] 1 A.C. 645.

[295] *French v Auckland City Corporation* [1974] 1 N.Z.L.R. 340.

[296] The fact that *Giles v Walker* has been overruled did not stop it being relied on in *Hall v Dart Valley Light Railway Plc* [1998] CLY 3933, but the outcome there can be supported by other authorities.

[297] *Leakey v National Trust for Places of Historic Interest and Scenic Beauty* [1980] Q.B. 485.

[298] *Rylands v Fletcher* (1868) L.R. 3 H.L. 330.

[299] *Leakey v National Trust for Places of Historic Interest and Scenic Beauty* [1980] Q.B. 485.

[300] Megaw L.J., *Leakey v National Trust for Places of Historic Interest and Scenic Beauty* , at 514; cf. McMullin J. in *French v Auckland City Corporation* [1974] 1 N.Z.L.R. 340 at 350.

[301] *Goldman v Hargrave* [1967] 1 A.C. 645.

[302] *Leakey v National Trust for Places of Historic Interest and Scenic Beauty* [1980] Q.B. 485.

[303] *French v Auckland City Corporation* [1974] 1 N.Z.L.R. 340.

the spread and the location of the properties. It was suggested in *French* and in *Goldman* that the individual circumstances of the parties may be relevant in assessing this, i.e. a poor defendant may not be required to do what might be expected of a rich one, and the duty may in some circumstances be satisfied simply by the defendant enabling the claimant to enter the land to take remedial steps as he thinks fit. It may therefore be difficult to predict whether liability will exist in any particular case, but it is clear that the courts will be looking for something much more than mere annoyance arising from generally acceptable land management practices employed by a neighbour.[304]

8.8.7   The latest significant case, *Wandsworth London Borough Council v Railtrack Plc*[305] confirms the trend toward potential liability, but relates to rather special circumstances. The action was brought in public nuisance, based on the extent to which the droppings from pigeons roosting under a railway bridge owned by the defendant were causing a nuisance to pedestrians passing under the bridge and additional costs to the council which had responsibility for cleaning the road. Railtrack was found liable, on the basis that once it was aware of the problem it had failed to take reasonable steps to remedy the nuisance. It did not matter that the nuisance was not the result of its own actions.[306] Since the argument on public nuisance was successful, issues of private nuisance or negligence were not considered. At first instance,[307] though, doubts were expressed whether the council would have a claim on those grounds in the absence of physical damage to its property. The thorough examination of the law by Gibbs J. at first instance shows the potential for liability, confirmed on appeal, but also shows the wide range of issues to be considered in deciding on the existence and extent of liability, including the potential for earlier mitigating action.

8.8.8   As yet, the Scottish courts have not given any indication of whether they would be prepared to follow the English movement away from the position stated in *Giles v Walker*, a position expressly approved in the Scottish cases noted above.[308] In any event, it has been made abundantly clear in *R.H.M. Bakeries (Scotland) Ltd v Strathclyde Regional Council*[309] that the basis of liability in nuisance is *culpa*,[310] so that some fault on the part of the landowner would have to be established. As discussed above, this raises issues as to the extent to which the management of land in a way which causes unintentional but foreseeable harm to others can be classed as culpable when the harm arises not from any specific danger but from an allegedly

---

[304] Several of the same issues arise in relation to the potential for the common law to impose liability for harm arising from the release of genetically modified organisms; see C. Rodgers, "Liability for the Release of GMOs into the Environment: Exploring the Boundaries of Nuisance" (2003) 62 C.L.J. 371, esp. at 387–392.

[305] *Wandsworth London Borough Council v Railtrack Plc* [2001] EWCA Civ 1236; [2002] Q.B. 756.

[306] *Attorney General v Tod Heatley* [1897] 1 Ch. 560; see also Rowlatt J. in *Noble v Harrison* [1976] 2 Q.B. 332 at 338.

[307] *Wandsworth London Borough Council v Railtrack Plc* [2001] 1 W.L.R. 368.

[308] See W.M. Gordon, "Is Moving Land a Nuisance?" (1980) 25 J.L.S.S. 323. Scots law does not have the category of public nuisance.

[309] *R.H.M. Bakeries (Scotland) Ltd v Strathclyde Regional Council*, 1985 S.L.T. 214.

[310] See generally G. Cameron, "Common Law of Nuisance" in Ch.14 of J.M. Thomson (ed.), *Delict* (Edinburgh: W. Green 2007).

greater incidence of a sort of naturally occurring harm which everyone must accept as part of the everyday risks of owning land.

Although it cannot be wholly ruled out, it therefore seems unlikely that a **8.8.9** landowner taking measures on his own land to further nature conservation will be liable to a neighbour who claims to have suffered damage as a result of wild plants or animals being encouraged.

APPENDIX A

SCHEDULES TO THE WILDLIFE AND COUNTRYSIDE ACT 1981

Each Schedule is accompanied by a note in the following terms:
   The common name or names given in the first column of this Schedule are included by way of guidance only; in the event of any dispute or proceedings, the common name or names shall not be taken into account.

SCHEDULE ZA1 (England & Wales only)[1]

BIRDS WHICH RE-USE THEIR NESTS

Common name	Scientific name
Eagle, Golden	Aquila chrysaetos
Eagle, White-tailed	Haliaetus albicilla
Osprey	Pandion haliaetus

SCHEDULE A1 (Scotland only)[2]

PROTECTED NESTS AND NEST SITES: BIRDS

Common name	Scientific name
Eagle, White-tailed	Haliaetus albicilla

SCHEDULE 1

BIRDS WHICH ARE PROTECTED BY SPECIAL PENALTIES

PART I
AT ALL TIMES

Common name	Scientific name
Avocet	Recurvirostra avosetta
Bee-eater	Merops apiaster
Bittern	Botaurus stellaris
Bittern, Little	Ixobrychus minutus
Bluethroat	Luscinia svecica

---

[1] Schedule ZA1 was inserted in relation to England and Wales by the Natural Environment and Rural Communities Act 2006.
   [2] Schedule A1 was inserted in relation to Scotland by the Nature Conservation (Scotland) Act 2004.

Brambling	Fringilla montifringilla
Bunting, Cirl	Emberiza cirlus
Bunting, Lapland	Calcarius lapponicus
Bunting, Snow	Plectrophenax nivalis
Buzzard, Honey	Pernis apivorus
Capercaillie (Scotland only)	Tetrao urogallus
Chough	Pyrrhocorax pyrrhocorax
Corncrake	Crex crex
Crake, Spotted	Porzana porzana
Crossbills (all species)	Loxia
Curlew, Stone	Burhinus oedicnemus
Divers (all species)	Gavia
Dotterel	Charadrius morinellus
Duck, Long-tailed	Clangula hyemalis
Eagle, Golden	Aquila chrysaetos
Eagle, White-tailed	Haliaetus albicilla
Falcon, Gyr	Falco rusticolus
Fieldfare	Turdus pilaris
Firecrest	Regulus ignicapillus
Garganey	Anas querquedula
Godwit, Black-tailed	Limosa limosa
Goshawk	Accipiter gentilis
Grebe, Black-necked	Podiceps nigricollis
Grebe, Slavonian	Podiceps auritus
Greenshank	Tringa nebularia
Gull, Little	Larus minutus
Gull, Mediterranean	Larus melanocephalus
Harriers (all species)	Circus
Heron, Purple	Ardea purpurea
Hobby	Falco subbuteo
Hoopoe	Upupa epops
Kingfisher	Alcedo atthis
Kite, Red	Milvus milvus
Merlin	Falco columbarius
Oriole, Golden	Oriolus oriolus
Osprey	Pandion haliaetus
Owl, Barn	Tyto alba
Owl, Snowy	Nyctea scandiaca
Peregrine	Falco peregrinus
Petrel, Leach's	Oceanodroma leucorhoa
Phalarope, Red-necked	Phalaropus lobatus
Plover, Kentish	Charadrius alexandrinus
Plover, Little Ringed	Charadrius dubius
Quail, Common	Coturnix coturnix
Redstart, Black	Phoenicurus ochruros
Redwing	Turdus iliacus
Rosefinch, Scarlet	Carpodacus erythrinus
Ruff	Philomachus pugnax
Sandpiper, Green	Tringa ochropus
Sandpiper, Purple	Calidris maritima
Sandpiper, Wood	Tringa glareola

Scaup	Aythya marila
Scoter, Common	Melanitta nigra
Scoter, Velvet	Melanitta fusca
Serin	Serinus serinus
Shorelark	Eremophila alpestris
Shrike, Red-backed	Lanius collurio
Spoonbill	Platalea leucorodia
Stilt, Black-winged	Himantopus himantopus
Stint, Temminck's	Calidris temminckii
Swan, Bewick's	Cygnus bewickii
Swan, Whooper	Cygnus cygnus
Tern, Black	Chlidonias niger
Tern, Little	Sterna albifrons
Tern, Roseate	Sterna dougallii
Tit, Bearded	Panurus biarmicus
Tit, Crested	Parus cristatus
Treecreeper, Short-toed	Certhia brachydactyla
Warbler, Cetti's	Cettia cetti
Warbler, Dartford	Sylvia undata
Warbler, Marsh	Acrocephalus palustris
Warbler, Savi's	Locustella luscinioides
Whimbrel	Numenius phaeopus
Woodlark	Lullula arborea
Wryneck	Jynx torquilla

PART II
DURING THE CLOSE SEASON

Common name	*Scientific name*
Goldeneye	Bucephala clangula
Goose, Greylag (in Outer Hebrides, Caithness, Sutherland and Wester Ross only)	Anser anser
Pintail	Anas acuta

SCHEDULE 1A (Scotland only)[3]

BIRDS WHICH ARE PROTECTED FROM HARASSMENT

Common name	*Scientific name*
Eagle, White-tailed	Haliaetus albicilla

---

[3] Schedule 1A was inserted in relation to Scotland by the Nature Conservation (Scotland) Act 2004 (asp 6).

SCHEDULE 2

BIRDS WHICH MAY BE KILLED OR TAKEN

PART I
OUTSIDE THE CLOSE SEASON

Common name	**Scientific name**
Capercaillie (in England and Wales only)	Tetrao urogallus
Coot	Fulica atra
Duck, Tufted	Aythya fuligula
Gadwall	Anas strepera
Goldeneye	Bucephala clangula
Goose, Canada	Branta canadensis
Goose, Greylag	Anser anser
Goose, Pink-footed	Anser brachyrhynchus
Goose, White-fronted (in England and Wales only)	Anser albifrons
Mallard	Anas platyrhynchos
Moorhen	Gallinula chloropus
Pintail	Anas acuta
Plover, Golden	Pluvialis apricaria
Pochard	Aythya ferina
Shoveler	Anas clypeata
Snipe, Common	Gallinago gallinago
Teal	Anas crecca
Wigeon	Anas penelope
Woodcock	Scolopax rusticola

PART II
BY AUTHORISED PERSONS AT ALL TIMES

[All the birds previously listed in this Part of the Schedule were removed by the Wildlife and Countryside Act 1981 (Variation of Schedules 2 and 3) Order 1992 (SI 1992/3010)]

SCHEDULE 3

BIRDS WHICH MAY BE SOLD

PART I
ALIVE AT ALL TIMES IF RINGED AND BRED IN CAPTIVITY

Common name	*Scientific name*
Blackbird	Turdus merula
Brambling	Fringilla montifringilla
Bullfinch	Pyrrhula pyrrhula
Bunting, Reed	Emberiza schoeniclus
Chaffinch	Fringilla coelebs
Dunnock	Prunella modularis
Goldfinch	Carduelis carduelis
Greenfinch	Carduelis chloris
Jackdaw	Corvus monedula
Jay	Garrulus glandarius
Linnet	Carduelis cannabina
Magpie	Pica pica
Owl, Barn	Tyto alba
Redpoll	Carduelis flammea
Siskin	Carduelis spinus
Starling	Sturnus vulgaris
Thrush, Song	Turdus philomelos
Twite	Carduelis flavirostris
Yellowhammer	Emberiza citrinella

PART II
DEAD AT ALL TIMES

Common name	*Scientific name*
Woodpigeon	Columba palumbus

PART III
DEAD FROM 1ST SEPTEMBER TO 28TH FEBRUARY

Common name	*Scientific name*
Capercaillie (in England and Wales only)	Tetrao urogallus
Coot	Fulica atra
Duck, Tufted	Aythya fuligula
Mallard	Anas platyrhynchos
Pintail	Anas acuta
Plover, Golden	Pluvialis apricaria
Pochard	Aythya ferina
Shoveler	Anas clypeata
Snipe, Common	Gallinago gallinago
Teal	Anas crecca
Wigeon	Anas penelope
Woodcock	Scolopax rusticola

SCHEDULE 4

BIRDS WHICH MUST BE REGISTERED AND RINGED IF KEPT IN CAPTIVITY (ENGLAND AND WALES)[4]

Common name	*Scientific name*
Buzzard, Honey	Pernis apivorus
Eagle, Golden	Aquila chrysaetos
Eagle, White-tailed	Haliaeetus albicilla
Falcon, Peregrine	Falco peregrinus
Goshawk	Accipiter gentilis
Harrier, Marsh	Circus aeruginosus
Harrier, Montagu's	Circus pygargus
Merlin	Falco columbarius
Osprey	Pandion haliaetus

Any bird one of whose parents or other lineal ancestor was a bird of a kind specified in the foregoing provisions of this Schedule.

BIRDS WHICH MUST BE REGISTERED AND RINGED IF KEPT IN CAPTIVITY (SCOTLAND)

Common name	*Scientific name*
Bunting, Cirl	Emberiza cirlus
Bunting, Lapland	Calcarius lapponicus
Bunting, Snow	Plectrophenax nivalis
Buzzard, Honey	Pernis apivorus
Chough	Pyrrhocorax pyrrhocorax
Crossbills (all species)	Loxia
Eagle, Adalbert's	Aquila adalberti
Eagle, Golden	Aquila chrysaetos
Eagle, Great Philippine	Pithecophaga jefferyi
Eagle, Imperial	Aquila heliaca
Eagle, New Guinea	Harpyopsis novaeguineae
Eagle, White-tailed	Haliaeetus albicilla
Falcon, Barbary	Falco pelegrinoides
Falcon, Gyr	Falco rusticolus
Falcon, Peregrine	Falco peregrinus
Fieldfare	Turdus pilaris
Firecrest	Regulus ignicapillus
Fish-Eagle, Madagascar	Haliaeetus vociferoides
Forest-Falcon, Plumbeous	Micrastur plumbeus
Goshawk	Accipiter gentilis
Harrier, Hen	Circus cyaneus
Harrier, Marsh	Circus aeruginosus
Harrier, Montagu's	Circus pygargus
Hawk, Galapagos	Buteo galapagoensis

---

[4] Schedule 4 amended in relation to England by the Wildlife and Countryside Act 1981 (Variation of Schedule 4) (England) Order 2008 (SI 2008/2356) and Wales by Wildlife and Countryside Act 1981 (Variation of Schedule 4) (Wales) Order 2009 (SI 2009/780).

Hawk, Grey-backed	Leucopternis occidentalis
Hawk, Hawaiian	Buteo solitarius
Hawk, Ridgway's	Buteo ridgwayi
Hawk, White-necked	Leucopternis lacernulata
Hawk-Eagle, Wallace's	Spizaetus nanus
Hobby	Falco subbuteo
Honey-Buzzard, Black	Henicopernis infuscatus
Kestrel, Lesser	Falco naumanni
Kestrel, Mauritius	Falco punctatus
Kite, Red	Milvus milvus
Merlin	Falco columbarius
Oriole, Golden	Oriolus oriolus
Osprey	Pandion haliaetus
Redstart, Black	Phoenicurus ochruros
Redwing	Turdus iliacus
Sea-Eagle, Pallas'	Haliaeetus leucoryphus
Sea-Eagle, Steller's	Haliaeetus pelagicus
Serin	Serinus serinus
Serpent-Eagle, Andaman	Spilornis elgini
Serpent-Eagle, Madagascar	Eutriorchis astur
Serpent-Eagle, Mountain	Spilornis kinabaluensis
Shorelark	Eremophila alpestris
Shrike, Red-backed	Lanius collurio
Sparrowhawk, New Britain	Accipiter brachyurus
Sparrowhawk, Gundlach's	Accipiter gundlachi
Sparrowhawk, Imitator	Accipiter imitator
Sparrowhawk, Small	Accipiter nanus
Tit, Bearded	Panurus biarmicus
Tit, Crested	Parus cristatus
Warbler, Cetti's	Cettia cetti
Warbler, Dartford	Sylvia undata
Warbler, Marsh	Acrocephalus palustris
Warbler, Savi's	Locustella liuscinioides
Woodlark	Lullula arborea
Wryneck	Jynx torquilla

Any bird one of whose parents or other lineal ancestor was a bird of a kind specified in the foregoing provisions of this Schedule.

SCHEDULE 5

ANIMALS WHICH ARE PROTECTED

Those that are marked with an asterisk are also European Protected Species under the Conservation (Natural Habitats, etc.) Regulations 1994 Schedule 2 (see below). For Scotland they have been wholly removed from this Schedule, but for England and Wales they remain for some purposes.[5]

---

[5] Conservation (Natural Habitats, etc.) Amendment (Scotland) Regulations 2007 (SSI 2007/ 80) and Conservation (Natural Habitats, etc.) (Amendment) Regulations 2007 (SI 2007/1843).

Common name	Scientific name
Adder (in respect of s.9(1) so far as it relates to killing and injuring and s.9(5) only)	Vipera berus
Allis Shad (in respect of s.9(1) and 9(4)(a) only)	Alosa alosa
Anemone, Ivell's Sea	Edwardsia ivelli
Anemone, Startlet Sea	Nematosella vectensis
Apus	Triops cancriformis
Atlantic Stream Crayfish (in relation to s.9(1) so far as it relates to taking and s.9(5) only)	Austropotamobius pallipes
*Bats, Horseshoe (all species, but in respect of s.9(4)(b) and (c) and (5) only) (England & Wales only)	Rhinolophidae
*Bats, Typical (all species, but in respect of s.9(4)(b) and (c) and (5) only) (England & Wales only)	Vespertilionidae
Beetle	Graphoderus zonatus
Beetle	Hypebaeus flavipes
Beetle	Paracymus aeneus
Beetle, Lesser Silver Water	Hydrochara caraboides
Beetle, Mire Pill (in respect of s.9(4)(a) only)	Curimopsis nigrita
Beetle, Rainbow Leaf	Chrysolina cerealis
Beetle, Stag (in respect of s.9(5) only)	Lucanus cervus
Beetle, Violet Click	Limoniscus violaceus
Burbot	Lota lota
Butterfly, Heath Fritillary	Mellicta athalia (otherwise known as Melitaea athalia)
*Butterfly, Large Blue (but in respect of s.9(4)(b) and (c) and (5) only) (England & Wales only)	Maculinea arion
Butterfly, Swallowtail	Papilio machaon
Butterfly, Northern Brown Argus (in respect of s.9(5) only)	Aricia artaxerxes
Butterfly, Adonis Blue (in respect of s.9(5) only)	Lysandra bellargus
Butterfly, Chalkhill Blue (in respect of s.9(5) only)	Lysandra coridon
Butterfly, Silver-studded Blue (in respect of s.9(5) only)	Plebejus argus
Butterfly, Small Blue (in respect of s.9(5) only)	Cupido minimus
Butterfly, Large Copper	Lycaena dispar
Butterfly, Purple Emperor (in respect of s.9(5) only)	Apatura iris
Butterfly, Duke of Burgundy Fritillary (in respect of s.9(5) only)	Hamearis lucina

Butterfly, Glanville Fritillary (in respect of s.9(5) only)	Melitaea cinxia
Butterfly, High Brown Fritillary	Argynnis adippe
Butterfly, Marsh Fritillary	Eurodryas aurinia
Butterfly, Pearl-bordered Fritillary (in respect of s.9(5) only)	Boloria euphrosyne
Butterfly, Black Hairstreak (in respect of s.9(5) only)	Strymonidia pruni
Butterfly, Brown Hairstreak (in respect of s.9(5) only)	Thecla betulae
Butterfly, White Letter Hairstreak (in respect of s.9(5) only)	Stymonida w-album
Butterfly, Large Heath (in respect of s.9(5) only)	Coenonympha tullia
Butterfly, Mountain Ringlet (in respect of s.9(5) only)	Erebia epiphron
Butterfly, Chequered Skipper (in respect of s.9(5) only)	Carterocephalus palaemon
Butterfly, Lulworth Skipper (in respect of s.9(5) only)	Thymelicus acteon
Butterfly, Silver Spotted Skipper (in respect of s.9(5) only)	Hesperia comma
Butterfly, Large Tortoiseshell (in respect of s.9(5) only)	Nymphalis polychloros
Butterfly, Wood White (in respect of s.9(5) only)	Leptidea sinapis
*Cat, Wild (but in respect of s.9(4)(b) and (c) and (5) only) (England & Wales only)	Felis silvestris
Cicada, New Forest	Cicadetta montana
Cricket, Field	Gryllus campestris
Cricket, Mole	Gryllotalpa gryllotalpa
Damselfly, Southern	Coenagrion mercuriale
*Dolphins (all species but in respect of s.9(4A) and (5) only) (England & Wales only)	Cetacea
*Dormouse (in respect of s.9(4)(b) and (c) and (5) only) (England & Wales only)	Muscardinus avellanarius
Dragonfly, Norfolk Aeshna	Aeshna isosceles
Frog, Common (in respect of s.9(5) only)	Rana temporaria
Goby, Couch's	Gobius couchii
Goby, Giant	Gobius cobitis
Grasshopper, Wart-biter	Decticus verrucivorus
Hatchet Shell, Northern	Thyasira gouldi
Hydroid, Marine	Clavopsella navis
Lagoon Snail	Paludinella littorina
Lagoon Snail, De Folin's	Caecum armoricum
Lagoon Worm, Tentacled	Alkmaria romijni
Leech, Medicinal	Hirudo medicinalis

*Lizard, Sand (in respect of s.9(4)(b) and (c) and (5) only) (England & Wales only)	Lacerta agilis
Lizard, Viviparous (in respect of s.9(1) so far as it relates to killing and injuring and s.9(5) only)	Lacerta vivipara
Marten, Pine	Martes martes
Mat, Trembling Sea	Victorella pavida
Moth, Barberry Carpet	Pareulype berberata
Moth, Black-veined	Siona lineata (otherwise known as Idaea lineata)
Moth, Essex Emerald	Thetidia smaragdaria
Moth, Fiery Clearwing	Bembecia chrysidiformis
*Moth, Fisher's Estuarine (in England & Wales, in respect of s.9(4)(b) and (c) and (5) only)	Gortyna borelii
Moth, New Forest Burnet	Zygaena viciae
Moth, Reddish Buff	Acosmetia caliginosa
Moth, Sussex Emerald	Thalera fimbrialis
Mussel, Fan (in respect of s.9(1), 9(2) and 9(5) only)	Atrina fragilis
Mussel, Freshwater Pearl	Margaritifera margaritifera
*Newt, Great Crested or Warty (in respect of s.9(4)(b) and (c) and (5) only) (England & Wales only)	Triturus cristatus
Newt, Palmate (in respect of s.9(5) only)	Triturus helveticus
Newt, Smooth (in respect of s.9(5) only)	Triturus vulgaris
*Otter, Common (in respect of s.9(4)(b) and (c) and (5) only) (England & Wales only)	Lutra lutra
*Porpoises (all species, but in respect of s.9(5) only) (England & Wales only)	Cetacea
Sandworm, Lagoon	Armandia cirrhosa
Sea Fan, Pink (in respect of s.9(1), 9(2) and 9(5) only)	Eunicella verrucosa
Seahorse, Short Snouted (with respect to England and Wales only)	Hippocampus hippocampus
Seahorse, Spiny (with respect to England and Wales only)	Hippocampus guttulatus
Sea Slug, Lagoon	Tenellia adspersa
Shad, Twaite (in respect of s.9(4)(a) only)	Alosa fallax

Shark, Angel (in respect of s.9(1) only and only in England and Wales and within the first 6 nautical miles from their territorial sea baselines)[6]	Squatina squatina
Shark, Basking	Cetorhinus maximus
Shrimp, Fairy	Chirocephalus diaphanus
Shrimp, Lagoon Sand	Gammarus insensibilis
Slow-worm (in respect of s.9(1) so far as it relates to killing and injuring and s.9(5) only)	Anguis fragilis
Snail, Glutinous	Myxas glutinosa
Snail, Roman (in respect of s.9(1), (2) and (5) only and with respect to England and Wales)	Helix pomatia
Snail, Sandbowl	Catinella arenaria
Snake, Grass (in respect of s. 9(1) so far as it relates to killing and injuring and s.9(5) only)	Natrix helvetica
*Snake, Smooth (in respect of s.9(4)(b) and (c) and (5) only) (England & Wales only)	Coronella austriaca
Spider, Fen Raft	Dolomedes plantarius
Spider, Ladybird	Eresus niger
Squirrel, Red	Sciurus vulgaris
*Sturgeon (in respect of s.9(4)(b) and (c) and (5) only) (England & Wales only)	Acipenser sturio
Toad, Common (in respect of s.9(5) only)	Bufo bufo
*Toad, Natterjack (in respect of s.9(4)(b) and (c) and (5) only) (England & Wales only)	Bufo calamita
Turtle, Flatback (England & Wales only)	Natator depressus
*Turtle, Green Sea (in respect of s.9(4)(b) and (c) and (5) only) (England & Wales only)	Chelonia mydas
*Turtle, Hawksbill (in respect of s.9(4)(b) and (c) and (5) only) (England & Wales only)	Eretmochelys imbricata
*Turtle, Kemp's Ridley Sea (in respect of s.9(4)(b) and (c) and (5) only) (England & Wales only)	Lepidochelys kempii
*Turtle, Leatherback Sea (in respect of s.9(4)(b) and (c) and (5) only) (England & Wales only)	Dermochelys coriacea

---

[6] Note inserted by the Wildlife and Countryside Act 1981 (Variation of Schedule 5) (England) Order 2008 (SI 2008/431) and subsequently amended by the Wildlife and Countryside Act 1981 (Variation of Schedule 5) (Wales) Order 2008 (SI 2008/1927).

*Turtle, Loggerhead Sea (in respect of s.9(4)(b) and (c) and (5) only) (England & Wales only)	Caretta caretta
Turtle, Olive Ridley (England & Wales only).	Lepidochelys olivacea
Vendace	Coregonus albula
Vole, Water (in Scotland, only in respect of s.9(4))	Arvicola terrestris
Walrus	Odobenus rosmarus
*Whale (all species, but in respect of s.9(4A) and (5) only) (England & Wales only)	Cetacea
Whitefish	Coregonus lavaretus

SCHEDULE 6

ANIMALS WHICH MAY NOT BE KILLED OR TAKEN BY CERTAIN METHODS

Common name	*Scientific name*
Badger	Meles meles
Bats, Horseshoe (all species)	Rhinolophidae
Bats, Typical (all species)	Vespertilionidae
Cat, Wild	Felis silvestris
Dolphin, Bottle-nosed	Tursiops truncatus (otherwise known as Tursiops tursio)
Dolphin, Common	Delphinis delphis
Dormice (all species)	Gliridae
Hedgehog	Erinaceus europaeus
Marten, Pine	Martes martes
Otter, Common	Lutra lutra
Polecat	Mustela putorius
Porpoise, Harbour (otherwise known as Common porpoise)	Phocaena phocaena
Shrews (all species)	Soricidae
Squirrel, Red	Sciurus vulgaris

[Schedule 7 is not reproduced]

SCHEDULE 8

PLANTS WHICH ARE PROTECTED

Those that are marked with an asterisk are also European Protected Species under the Conservation (Natural Habitats, etc.) Regulations 1994 Schedule 4 (see below). For Scotland they have been wholly removed from this Schedule, but for England and Wales they remain for some purposes.[7]

Common name	*Scientific name*
Adder's-tongue, Least	Ophioglossum lusitanicum
Alison, Small	Alyssum alyssoides
Anomodon, Long-leaved	Anomodon longifolius
Beech-lichen, New Forest	Enterographa elaborata
Blackwort	Southbya nigrella
Bluebell (in respect of s.13(2) only)	Hyacinthoides non-scripta
Bolete, Royal	Boletus regius
Broomrape, Bedstraw	Orobanche caryophyllacea
Broomrape, Oxtongue	Orobanche loricata
Broomrape, Thistle	Orobanche reticulata
Cabbage, Lundy	Rhynchosinapis wrightii
Calamint, Wood	Calamintha sylvatica
Caloplaca, Snow	Caloplaca nivalis
Catapyrenium, Tree	Catapyrenium psoromoides
Catchfly, Alpine	Lychnis alpina
Catillaria, Laurer's	Catellaria laureri
Centaury, Slender	Centaurium tenuiflorum
Cinquefoil, Rock	Potentilla rupestris
Cladonia, Convoluted	Cladonia convoluta
Cladonia, Upright Mountain	Cladonia stricta
Clary, Meadow	Salvia pratensis
Club-rush, Triangular	Scirpus triquetrus
Colt's-foot, Purple	Homogyne alpina
Cotoneaster, Wild	Cotoneaster integerrimus
Cottongrass, Slender	Eriophorum gracile
Cow-wheat, Field	Melampyrum arvense
Crocus, Sand	Romulea columnae
Crystalwort, Lizard	Riccia bifurca
Cudweed, Broad-leaved	Filago pyramidata
Cudweed, Jersey	Gnaphalium luteoalbum
Cudweed, Red-tipped	Filago lutescens
Cut-grass	Leersia oryzoides
Deptford Pink (in respect of England and Wales only)	Dianthus armeria
Diapensia	Diapensia lapponica
*Dock, Shore (in respect of s.13(2) only) (England and Wales only)	Rumex rupestris
Earwort, Marsh	Jamesoniella undulifolia

[7] Conservation (Natural Habitats, etc.) Amendment (Scotland) Regulations 2007 (SSI 2007/80) and Conservation (Natural Habitats, etc.) (Amendment) Regulations 2007 (SI 2007/1843).

Eryngo, Field	Eryngium campestre
Feather-moss, Polar	Hygrohypnum polare
Fern, Dickie's Bladder	Cystopteris dickieana
*Fern, Killarney (in respect of s.13(2) only) (England and Wales only)	Trichomanes speciosum
Flapwort, Norfolk	Leiocolea rutheana
Fleabane, Alpine	Erigeron borealis
Fleabane, Small	Pulicaria vulgaris
Galingale, Brown	Cyperus fuscus
Frostwort, Pointed	Gymnomitrion apiculatum
Fungus, Hedgehog	Hericium erinaceum
Gentian, Alpine	Gentiana nivalis
Gentian, Dune	Gentianella uliginosa
*Gentian, Early (in respect of s.13(2) only) (England and Wales only)	Gentianella anglica
Gentian, Fringed	Gentianella ciliata
Gentian, Spring	Gentiana verna
Germander, Cut-leaved	Teucrium botrys
Germander, Water	Teucrium scordium
Gladiolus, Wild	Gladiolus illyricus
Goblin Lights	Catolechia wahlenbergii
Goosefoot, Stinking	Chenopodium vulvaria
Grass-poly	Lythrum hyssopifolia
Grimmia, Blunt-leaved	Grimmia unicolor
Gyalecta, Elm	Gyalecta ulmi
Hare's-ear, Sickle-leaved	Bupleurum falcatum
Hare's-ear, Small	Bupleurum baldense
Hawk's-beard, Stinking	Crepis foetida
Hawkweed, Northroe	Hieracium northroense
Hawkweed, Shetland	Hieracium zetlandicum
Hawkweed, Weak-leaved	Hieracium attenuatifolium
Heath, Blue	Phyllodoce caerulea
Helleborine, Red	Cephalanthera rubra
Helleborine, Young's	Epipactis youngiana
Horsetail, Branched	Equisetum ramosissimum
Hound's-tongue, Green	Cynoglossum germanicum
Knawel, Perennial	Scleranthus perennis
Knotgrass, Sea	Polygonum maritimum
*Lady's-slipper (in respect of s.13(2) only) (England and Wales only)	Cypripedium calceolus
Lecanactis, Churchyard	Lecanactis hemisphaerica
Lecanora, Tarn	Lecanora archariana
Lecidea, Copper	Lecidea inops
Leek, Round-headed	Allium sphaerocephalon
Lettuce, Least	Lactuca saligna
Lichen, Arctic Kidney	Nephroma arcticum
Lichen, Ciliate Strap	Heterodermia leucomelos
Lichen, Coralloid Rosette	Heterodermia propagulifera
Lichen, Ear-lobed Dog	Peltigera lepidophora
Lichen, Forked Hair	Bryoria furcellata

Lichen, Golden Hair	Teloschistes flavicans
Lichen, Orange Fruited Elm	Caloplaca luteoalba
Lichen, River Jelly	Collema dichotomum
Lichen, Scaly Breck	Squamarina lentigera
Lichen, Stary Breck	Buellia asterella
Lily, Snowdon	Lloydia serotina
Liverwort	Petallophyllum ralfsi
Liverwort, Lindenberg's Leafy	Adelanthus lindenbergianus
Marsh-mallow, Rough	Althaea hirsuta
*Marshwort, Creeping (in respect of s.13(2) only) (England and Wales only)	Apium repens
Milk-parsley, Cambridge	Selinum carvifolia
Moss	Drepanocladius vernicosus
Moss, Alpine Copper	Mielichoferia mielichoferi
Moss, Baltic Bog	Sphagnum balticum
Moss, Blue Dew	Saelania glaucescens
Moss, Blunt-leaved Bristle	Orthotrichum obtusifolium
Moss, Bright Green Cave	Cyclodictyon laetevirens
Moss, Cordate Beard	Barbula cordata
Moss, Cornish Path	Ditrichum cornubicum
Moss, Derbyshire Feather	Thamnobryum angustifolium
Moss, Dune Thread	Bryum mamillatum
Moss, Flamingo	Desmatodon cernuus
Moss, Glaucous Beard	Barbula glauca
Moss, Green Shield	Buxbaumia viridis
Moss, Hair Silk	Plagiothecium piliferum
Moss, Knothole	Zygodon forsteri
Moss, Large Yellow Feather	Scorpidium turgescens
Moss, Millimetre	Micromitrium tenerum
Moss, Multifruited River	Cryphaea lamyana
Moss, Nowell's Limestone	Zygodon gracilis
Moss, Rigid Apple	Bartramia stricta
Moss, Round-leaved Feather	Rhyncostegium rotundifolium
Moss, Schleicher's Thread	Bryum schleicheri
Moss, Triangular Pygmy	Acaulon triquetrum
Moss, Vaucher's Feather	Hypnum vaucheri
Mudwort, Welsh	Limosella australis
Naiad, Holly-leaved	Najas marina
*Naiad, Slender (in respect of s.13(2) only) (England and Wales only)	Najas flexilis
Orache, Stalked	Halimione pedunculata
Orchid, Early Spider	Ophrys sphegodes
*Orchid, Fen (in respect of s.13(2) only) (England and Wales only)	Liparis loeselii
Orchid, Ghost	Epipogium aphyllum
Orchid, Lapland Marsh	Dactylorhiza lapponica
Orchid, Late Spider	Ophrys fuciflora
Orchid, Lizard	Himantoglossum hircinum
Orchid, Military	Orchis militaris

Orchid, Monkey	Orchis simia
Pannaria, Caledonia	Pannaria ignobilis
Parmelia, New Forest	Parmelia minarum
Parmentaria, Oil Stain	Parmentaria chilensis
Pear, Plymouth	Pyrus cordata
Penny-cress, Perfoliate	Thlaspi perfoliatum
Pennyroyal	Mentha pulegium
Pertusaria, Alpine Moss	Pertusaria bryontha
Physcia, Southern Grey	Physcia tribacioides
Pigmyweed	Crassula aquatica
Pine, Ground	Ajuga chamaepitys
Pink, Cheddar	Dianthus gratianopolitanus
Pink, Childling	Petroraghia nanteuilii
*Plantain, Floating Water (in respect of s.13(2) only) (England and Wales only)[8]	Luronium natans
Polypore, Oak	Buglossoporus pulvinus
Pseudocyphellaria, Ragged	Pseudocyphellaria lacerata
Psora, Rusty Alpine	Psora rubiformis
Puffball, Sandy Stilt	Battarraea phalloides
Ragwort, Fen	Senecio paludosus
Ramping-fumitory, Martin's	Fumaria martinii
Rampion, Spiked	Phyteuma spicatum
Restharrow, Small	Ononis reclinata
Rock-cress, Alpine	Arabis alpina
Rock-cress, Bristol	Arabis stricta
Rustworth, Western	Marsupella profunda
Sandwort, Norwegian	Arenaria norvegica
Sandwort, Teesdale	Minuartia stricta
Saxifrage, Drooping	Saxifraga cernua
*Saxifrage, Marsh (in respect of s.13(2) only) (England and Wales only)	Saxifrage hirulus
Saxifrage, Tufted	Saxifraga cespitosa
Solomon's-seal, Whorled	Polygonatum verticillatum
Solenopsora, Serpentine	Solenopsora liparina
Sow-thistle, Alpine	Cicerbita alpina
Spearwort, Adder's-tongue	Ranunculus ophioglossifolius
Speedwell, Fingered	Veronica triphyllos
Speedwell, Spiked	Veronica spicata
Spike-rush, Dwarf	Eleocharis parvula
Stack Fleawort, South	Tephroseris integrifolia (ssp maritima)
Star-of-Bethlehem, Early	Gagea bohemica
Starfruit	Damasonium alisma
Stonewort, Bearded	Chara canescens
Stonewort, Foxtail	Lamprothamnium papulosum
Strapwort	Corrigiola litoralis

---

[8] Entry referred to as Plantain, Floating-leaved Water (Luronium natans) in Conservation (Natural Habitats, etc.) Regulations 1994 (SI 1994/2716).

Sulphur-tresses, Alpine	Alectoria ochroleuca
Threadmoss, Long-leaved	Bryum neodamense
Turpswort	Geocalyx graveolens
Viper's-grass	Scorzonera humilis
Violet, Fen	Viola persicifolia
Water-plantain, Ribbon-leaved	Alisma gramineum
Wood-sedge, Starved	Carex depauperata
Woodsia, Alpine	Woodsia alpina
Woodsia, Oblong	Woodsia ilvensis
Wormwood, Field	Artemisia campestris
Woundwort, Downy	Stachys germanica
Woundwort, Limestone	Stachys alpina
Yellow-rattle, Greater	Rhinanthus serotinus

SCHEDULE 9

ANIMALS AND PLANTS TO WHICH SECTION 14 APPLIES

PART I
ANIMALS WHICH ARE ESTABLISHED IN THE WILD

Common name	*Scientific name*
Bass, Large-mouthed Black	Micropterus salmoides
Bass, Rock	Ambloplites rupestris
Bitterling	Rhodeus sericeus
Budgerigar	Melopsittacus undulatus
Capercaillie	Tetrao urogallus
Coypu	Myocastor coypus
Crayfish, Noble	Astacus astacus
Crayfish, Signal	Pacifastacus leniusculus
Crayfish, Turkish	Astacus leptodactylus
Deer, any hybrid one of whose parents or other lineal ancestor was a Sika deer	Any hybrid of Cervus nippon
With respect to the Outer Hebrides and the islands of Arran, Islay, Jura and Rum—	
(a) Deer, Cervus (all species)	Cervus
(b) Deer, any hybrid one of whose parents or other lineal ancestor was a species of Cervus Deer	Any hybrid of the genus Cervus
Deer, Muntjac	Muntiacus reevesi
Deer, Sika	Cervus nippon
Dormouse, Fat	Glis glis
Duck, Carolina Wood	Aix sponsa
Duck, Mandarin	Aix galericulata
Duck, Ruddy	Oxyura jamaicensis
Eagle, White-tailed	Haliaetus albicilla
Flat-worm, New Zealand	Artiposthia triangulata
Frog, Edible	Rana esculenta

Frog, European Tree (otherwise known as Common tree frog)	Hyla arborea
Frog, Marsh	Rana ridibunda
Gerbil, Mongolian	Meriones unguiculatus
Goose, Canada	Branta canadensis
Goose, Egyptian	Alopochen aegyptiacus
Heron, Night	Nycticorax nycticorax
Lizard, Common Wall	Podarcis muralis
Marmot, Prairie (otherwise known as Prairie dog)	Cynomys
Mink, American	Mustela vison
Newt, Alpine	Triturus alpestris
Newt, Italian Crested	Triturus carnifex
Owl, Barn	Tyto alba
Parakeet, Ring-necked	Psittacula krameri
Partridge, Chukar	Alectoris chukar
Partridge, Rock	Alectoris graeca
Pheasant, Golden	Chrysolophus pictus
Pheasant, Lady Amherst's	Chrysolophus amherstiae
Pheasant, Reeves'	Syrmaticus reevesii
Pheasant, Silver	Lophura nycthemera
Porcupine, Crested	Hystrix cristata
Porcupine, Himalayan	Hystrix hodgsonii
Pumpkinseed (otherwise known as Sun-fish or Pond-perch)	Lepomis gibbosus
Quail, Bobwhite	Colinus virginianus
Rat, Black	Rattus rattus
Snake, Aesculapian	Elaphe longissima
Squirrel, Grey	Sciurus carolinensis
Terrapin, European Pond	Emys orbicularis
Toad, African Clawed	Xenopus laevis
Toad, Midwife	Alytes obstetricans
Toad, Yellow-bellied	Bombina variegata
Wallaby, Red-necked,	Macropus rufogriseus
Wels (otherwise known as European catfish)	Silurus glanis
Zander	Stizostedion lucioperca

PART II

PLANTS

ENGLAND & WALES

Common name	Scientific name
Hogweed, Giant	Heracleum mantegazzianum
Kelp, Giant	Macrocystis pyrifera
Kelp, Giant	Macrocystis angustifolia
Kelp, Giant	Macrocystis integrifolia
Kelp, Giant	Macrocystis laevis
Kelp, Japanese	Laminaria japonica
Knotweed, Japanese	Polygonum cuspidatum
Seafingers, Green	Codium fragile tomentosoides
Seaweed, Californian Red	Pikea californica
Seaweed, Hooked Asparagus	Asparagopis armata
Seaweed, Japanese	Sargassum muticum
Seaweeds, Laver (except native species)	Porphyra spp except —
	p. amethystea
	p. leucosticta
	p. linearis
	p. miniata
	p. purpurea
	p. umbilicalis
Wakame	Undaria pinnatifida

SCOTLAND

Common name	Scientific name
False-acacia	Robinia pseudoacacia
Fanwort	Cabomba caroliniana
Fern, Water	Azolla filiculoides
Fig, Hottentot	Carpobrotus edulis
Hyacinth, water	Eichhornia crassipes
Hogweed, Giant	Heracleum mantegazzianum
Kelp, Giant	Macrocystis angustifolia
Kelp, Giant	Macrocystis integrifolia
Kelp, Giant	Macrocystis laevis
Kelp, Japanese	Laminaria japonica
Kelp, Giant	Macrocystis pyrifera
Knotweed, Japanese	Polygonum cuspidatum
Leek, Few-flowered	Allium paradoxum
Lettuce, water	Pistia stratiotes
Parrot's-feather	Myriophyllum aquaticum
Pennywort, Floating	Hydrocotyle ranunculoides
Salvinia, Giant	Salvinia molesta
Seafingers, Green	Codium fragile tomentosoides
Seaweed, Californian Red	Pikea californica
Seaweed, Hooked Asparagus	Asparagopis armata

Seaweeds, Laver (except native species)	Porphyra spp except- p. amethystea p. leucosticta p. linearis p. miniata p. purpurea p. umbilicalis
Seaweed, Japanese	Sargassum muticum
Shallon	Gaultheria shallon
Stonecrop, Australian swamp	Crassula helmsii
Wakame	Undaria pinnatifida.
Waterweed, Curly	Lagarosiphon major

SCHEDULES TO THE CONSERVATION (NATURAL HABITATS, ETC.) REGULATIONS 1994

Each Schedule is accompanied by a note in the following terms:

"The common name or names given in the first column of this Schedule are included by way of guidance only; in the event of any dispute or proceedings, the common name or names shall not be taken into account."

SCHEDULE 2

EUROPEAN PROTECTED SPECIES OF ANIMAL

In England and Wales these are also included for some purposes in Schedule 5 to the Wildlife and Countryside Act 1981 (above) and are marked by an asterisk there.

Common name	*Scientific name*
Bats, Horseshoe (all species)	Rhinolophidae
Bats, Typical (all species)	Vespertilionidae
Butterfly, Large Blue	Maculinea arion
Cat, Wild	Felis silvestris
Dolphins, porpoises and whales (all species)	Cetacea
Dormouse	Muscardinus avellanarius
Frog, Pool (England and Wales only)[9]	Rana lessonae
Lizard, Sand	Lacerta agilis
Moth, Fisher's Estuarine(England and Wales only)[9]	Gortyna borelii lunata
Newt, Great Crested (or Warty)	Triturus cristatus
Otter, Common	Lutra lutra

---

[9] Added in relation to England and Wales only by Conservation (Natural Habitats, etc.) (Amendment) (England and Wales) Regulations 2008 (SI 2008/2172).

Snail, Lesser Whirlpool Ram's-horn (England and Wales only)[9]	Anisus vorticulus
Snake, Smooth	Coronella austriaca
Sturgeon	Acipenser sturio
Toad, Natterjack	Bufo calamita
Turtles, Marine	Caretta caretta
	Chelonia mydas
	Lepidochelys kempii
	Eretmochelys imbricata
	Dermochelys coriacea

SCHEDULE 2A[10]

EXCLUDED POPULATIONS OF CERTAIN SPECIES

Common Name	Scientific Name	Excluded countries and areas
Beaver, Eurasian	Castor fiber	Estonia, Finland, Latvia, Lithuania, Poland, and Sweden
Hamster, Common (or Black bellied)	Cricetus cricetus	Hungary
Wolf, Grey	Canis lupus	Bulgaria, Estonia, Greece north of the 39th parallel, Latvia, Lithuania, Poland, Slovakia, Spain north of the [River] Duero, and the reindeer management area in Finland as defined in paragraph 2 of Finnish Act No 848/90 of 14 September 1990 on reindeer management 3
Lynx, Eurasian	Lynx lynx	Estonia
Viper, Seoane's	Vipera seoanni	Spain

SCHEDULE 3

ANIMALS WHICH MAY NOT BE TAKEN OR KILLED IN CERTAIN WAYS

Common name	Scientific name
Barbel	Barbus barbus
Grayling	Thymallus thymallus

---

[10] Inserted in relation to Scotland by Conservation (Natural Habitats, etc.) Amendment (Scotland) Regulations 2007 (SSI 2007/80), and amended by Conservation (Natural Habitats, etc.) Amendment (Scotland) Regulations 2008 (SSI 2008/17). Inserted in relation to England and Wales by Conservation (Natural Habitats, etc.) (Amendment) Regulations 2007 (SI 2007/1843).

Hare, Mountain	Lepus timidus
Lamprey, River	Lampetra fluviatilis
Marten, Pine	Martes martes
Polecat	Mustela putorius (otherwise known as Putorius putorius)
Salmon, Atlantic	Salmo salar (only in fresh water)
Seal, Bearded	Erignathus barbatus
Seal, Common	Phoca vitulina
Seal, Grey	Halichoerus grypus
Seal, Harp	Phoca groenlandica (otherwise known as Pagophilus groenlandicus)
Seal, Hooded	Cystophora cristata
Seal, Ringed	Phoca hispida (otherwise known as Pusa hispida)
Shad, Allis	Alosa alosa
Shad, Twaite	Alosa fallax
Vendace	Coregonus albula
Whitefish	Coregonus lavaretus

SCHEDULE 4

EUROPEAN PROTECTED SPECIES OF PLANTS

In England and Wales these are included for some purposes in Schedule 8 to the Wildlife and Countryside Act 1981 (above) and are marked by an asterisk there.

Common name	Scientific name
Dock, Shore	Rumex rupestris
Fern, Killarney	Trichomanes speciosum
Gentian, Early	Gentianella anglica
Lady's-slipper	Cypripedium calceolus
Marshwort, Creeping	Apium repens
Naiad, slender	Najas flexilis
Orchid, Fen	Liparis loeselii
Plantain, Floating-leaved water	Luronium natans
Saxifrage, Yellow Marsh	Saxifraga hirculus

APPENDIX B

OPEN SEASONS

Birds

	Scotland	England & Wales	Authority
Red grouse	Aug 12–Dec 10	Aug 12–Dec 10	1772/1831[1]
Ptarmigan	Aug 12–Dec 10	—	1772/1831
Black grouse	Aug 20–Dec 10	Aug 20–Dec 10	1772/1831
Pheasant	Oct 1–Feb 1	Oct 1–Feb 1	1772/1831
Partridge	Sep 1–Feb 1	Sep 1–Feb 1	1772/1831
Common snipe	Aug 12–Jan 31	Aug 12–Jan 31	WCA[2]
Woodcock	Sep 1–Jan 31	Oct 1–Jan.31	WCA
Wild duck and geese (below high-water mark)	Sep 1–Feb 20	Sep 1–Feb 20	WCA
All other cases	Sep 1–Jan 31	Sep 1–Jan 31	WCA

NOTES
1. Game (Scotland) Act 1772 s.1; Game Act 1831 s.3.
2. Wildlife and Countryside Act 1981 s.2(4).

Deer

		Scotland[1]	England & Wales[2]	
Red Deer[3]	stags	July 1–Oct 20	Aug 1–Apr 30	
	hinds	Oct 21–Feb 15	Nov 1–Feb 28/29	
Sika Deer[3]	stags	July 1–Oct 20	Aug 1–Apr 30	
	hinds	Oct 21–Feb 15	Nov 1–Feb 28/29	
Fallow Deer	bucks	Aug 1–Apr 30	Aug 1–Apr 30	
	does	Oct 21–Feb 15	Nov 1–Feb 28/29	
Roe Deer	bucks	Apr 1–Oct 20	Apr 1–Oct 31	
	does	Oct 21–Mar 31	Nov 1–Feb 28/29	

NOTES
1. Deer (Scotland) Act 1996 s.5; Deer (Close Seasons) (Scotland) Order 1984 (SI 1984/76).
2. Deer Act 1991 Sch.1.
3. In Scotland, expressly including hybrids.

Permitted Firearms

Scotland[1]

All deer	Rifle	Bullet of expanding type not less than 100 grains; muzzle velocity not less than 2,450 feet per second; muzzle energy not less than 1,750 foot pounds.
	Shotgun[2]	Not less than 12 bore; rifled slug not less than 380 grains or cartridge of not less than 450 grains of shot not smaller than 0.268 inches in diameter (size SSG).
Roe Deer	Rifle	Bullet of expanding type of not less than 50 grains; muzzle velocity not less than 2,450 feet per second; muzzle energy not less than 1,000 foot pounds.
	Shotgun[2]	Not less than 12 bore; cartridge of not less than 450 grains of shot not smaller than 0.203 inches in diameter (size AAA).

England and Wales[3]

All deer	Rifle	Calibre not less than 0.240 inches or muzzle energy of 1,700 foot pounds; bullet soft or hollow-nosed.
All deer	Shotgun[2]	Not less than 12 bore; slug not less than 350 grains or cartridge of shot not smaller than 0.203 inches in diameter (size AAA).

NOTES
1. Deer (Firearms) (Scotland) Order 1985 (SI 1985/1168).
2. The use of shotguns is permitted only in preventing serious damage on cultivated or enclosed land.
3. Deer Act 1991 s.7(2) and Sch.2.

APPENDIX C

PURPOSES FOR LICENCES AND DEROGATIONS

UK LEGISLATION

Licences under the Wildlife and Countryside Act 1981 s.16

Birds

(a) scientific, research or educational purposes;
(b) ringing or marking, or examining any ring or mark on, wild birds;
(c) conserving wild birds;
(ca) the re-population of an area with, or the re-introduction into an area of, wild birds, including any breeding necessary for those purposes;
(cb) conserving flora or fauna;
(d) protecting any collection of wild birds;
(e) falconry or aviculture;
(f) any public exhibition or competition;
(g) taxidermy;
(h) photography;
(i) preserving public health or public or air safety;
(j) preventing the spread of disease; or
(k) preventing serious damage to livestock, foodstuffs for livestock, crops, vegetables, fruit, growing timber, fisheries or inland waters.

Licences can also be granted for: (a) a gannet on the island of Sula Sgeir; or (b) a gull's egg or, in England and Wales only, at any time before April 15 in any year, a lapwing's egg.

Animals and Plants

The words in square brackets apply in Scotland only.

(a) scientific [, research] or educational purposes;
(b) ringing or marking, or examining any ring or mark on, wild animals;
(c) conserving [wild birds,] wild animals or wild plants or introducing them to particular areas;
[(ca) conserving any area of natural habitat;]
(d) protecting any zoological or botanical collection;
(e) photography;
(f) preserving public health or public safety;
(g) preventing the spread of disease; or
(h) preventing serious damage to livestock, foodstuffs for livestock, crops, vegetables, fruit, growing timber or any other form of property or to fisheries.

EUROPEAN LEGISLATION

Purposes for which derogations can be made under EC legislation.

Derogations under the Birds Directive art.9

Where there is no other satisfactory solution:

(a) — in the interests of public health and safety,
— in the interests of air safety,
— to prevent serious damage to crops, livestock, forests, fisheries and water,
— for the protection of flora and fauna;

(b) for the purposes of research and teaching, of re-population, of re-introduction and for the breeding necessary for these purposes;

(c) to permit, under strictly supervised conditions and on a selective basis, the capture, keeping or other judicious use of certain birds in small numbers.

Derogations under the Habitats and Species Directive art.16

Provided that there is no satisfactory alternative and the derogation is not detrimental to the maintenance of the populations of the species at a favourable conservation status in their natural range:

(a) in the interest of protecting wild fauna and flora and conserving natural habitats;

(b) to prevent serious damage, in particular to crops, livestock, forests, fisheries and water and other types of property;

(c) in the interests of public health and public safety, or for other imperative reasons of overriding public interest, including those of a social or economic nature and beneficial consequences of primary importance for the environment;

(d) for the purpose of research and education, of repopulating and re-introducing these species and for the breeding operations necessary for these purposes, including the artificial propagation of plants;

(e) to allow, under strictly supervised conditions, on a selective basis and to a limited extent, the taking or keeping of certain specimens of the species listed in Annex IV in limited numbers specified by the competent national authorities.

INDEX